Services Marketing

SECOND EDITION

Services Marketing

SECOND EDITION

WILLIAM CHITTY
STEVEN D'ALESSANDRO
DAVID GRAY
ANDREW HUGHES

OXFORD
UNIVERSITY PRESS
AUSTRALIA & NEW ZEALAND

Oxford University Press is a department of the University of Oxford.

It furthers the University's objective of excellence in research, scholarship, and education by publishing worldwide. Oxford is a registered trademark of Oxford University Press in the UK and in certain other countries.

Published in Australia by
Oxford University Press
8/737 Bourke Street, Docklands, Victoria 3008, Australia

A catalogue record for this book is available from the National Library of Australia

Edited by Mary-Jo O'Rourke and Anne Mulvaney
Typeset by Newgen KnowledgeWorks Pvt. Ltd., Chennai, India
Proofread by Susan Keogh of Apostrophes, Etc.
Indexed by Mei Yen Chua
Printed in China by Leo Paper Products Ltd.

Part 1 Service Organisations and Their Customers 1

PART 1 CASE STUDIES

Part 2 Marketing Strategies for Services....................151

Brief Contents

OXFORD UNIVERSITY PRESS

Expanded Contents

Part 1   Service Organisations and Their Customers 1

Expanded Contents

CHAPTER 6   THE SERVICE-DELIVERY PROCESS AND SELF-SERVICE
TECHNOLOGY 189

Steven D'Alessandro

Expanded Contents

OXFORD UNIVERSITY PRESS

CHAPTER 13   CUSTOMER RELATIONSHIP MANAGEMENT 445
William Chitty

PART 3 CASE STUDIES

Figures

OXFORD UNIVERSITY PRESS

Figures

OXFORD UNIVERSITY PRESS

Tables

Case Studies

OXFORD UNIVERSITY PRESS

The grid below identifies the chapter in which each case sits (*) and also shows other chapters for which the cases apply due to integration of ideas (✔).

Cases	CH 1	CH 2	CH 3	CH 4	CH 5	CH 6	CH 7	CH 8	CH 9	CH 10	CH 11	CH 12	CH 13	CH 14
Nomads: A new banking customer segment		✔		*	✔						✔			
Tourism adds $120 billion to the Australian economy	✔			*						✔				✔
Take a break		✔							*					
Trick or treat: Cyber security in Australia					✔	✔		✔	*					✔
Google Home: The smart-home service									✔				*	
Unruly passengers								✔				✔	*	✔

William Chitty is a retired lecturer in marketing, formerly at the Murdoch Business School, Murdoch University. He taught Marketing Communications and Services Marketing, and retains a research interest in AI for Marketing. He has co-authored two other textbooks—three editions of *Marketing*, and four editions of *Integrated Marketing Communications*—as well as research papers that have been published in the *Journal of Marketing Communication*, the *Journal of Internet Business Studies*, *Marketing Intelligence and Planning*, and *Psychology and Marketing* together with several refereed conference papers that have been presented at various academic conferences in Australia and overseas. Before joining Murdoch University in 1992, Bill was a marketing manager in the telecommunications industry, responsible for the market development of network products.

Dr **Steven D'Alessandro** is a professor in the School of Management and Marketing at Charles Sturt University. Steve has published books, conference papers and 108 refereed papers in leading international journals (including *The European Journal of Marketing*, *Journal of Business Research*, *International Marketing Review*, *Psychology and Marketing*, *Marketing Letters*, *Journal of Services Marketing*, *Journal of Macromarketing*, *International Journal of Consumer Studies*, *Food Quality and Preference*, *Journal of Retailing and Consumer Services*, *Accounting and Finance*, *Journal of Environmental Management and Applied Economics*). Steve has also worked as a market research consultant for blue-chip companies such as Pacific-Dunlop, ANZ, Challenge Bank, BHP, Telstra and Ford. He has published some market-leading textbooks on Market Research, Consumer Behaviour and Services Marketing. In 2012 he was awarded the ANZMAC Distinguished Marketing Educator of the Year Award, in recognition of his sustained excellence and innovation in marketing education. Steve is also a member of the CRC in Cybersecurity and is also part of a grant team with Macquarie University researching responsible drinking. He is currently co-editor of *The Journal of Consumer Behaviour*. Steve would again like to dedicate this book to Shirley Thorton, a real trouper and rock for her family.

Dr **David Gray** is an Adjunct Associate Professor at Charles Sturt University and an Honorary Fellow at Macquarie University. He currently teaches Postgraduate Marketing Communications and Customer Behaviour at Charles Sturt University. David's current research interests are business to business marketing, relationship marketing and branding. Dr Gray's most recent full-time posting was as a Senior Lecturer in Marketing at Macquarie University for nearly 11 years. David has published over 50 academic papers, many in leading academic marketing journals including the *Journal of Brand Management*, *Marketing Letters*, *Journal of Advertising Research*, *Journal of Nonprofit & Public Sector Marketing*, *Journal of Retailing and Consumer Services*, *The Journal of Applied Business Research*, *Services Marketing Quarterly*, *International Journal of Business and Management*, *Australasian Marketing Journal*, *The Marketing Review*, and the *International Journal*

OXFORD UNIVERSITY PRESS

of Learning and Change. David has over 30 years' experience in a wide range of educational, management and marketing consulting roles including corporate trainer, university lecturer, instructional course designer and coach. He has extensive experience in teaching both undergraduate and post-graduate teaching in Marketing and Entrepreneurship.

Andrew Hughes is a lecturer in marketing in the Research School of Management at ANU, where he teaches at undergraduate and postgraduate levels. He is considered one of the leading researchers in political marketing in Australia, with his thesis, 'The relationship between advertisement content and pacing on emotional responses and memory for televised political advertisements' nominated for ANU's prestigious thesis prize, the J.G. Crawford Award in 2015.

In 2017 he won an ANU Vice-Chancellor's award for Public Policy Impact for his analysis during the 2016 Federal Election, his research into political advertising and his role in the ANU political vodcast, 'Off the Hill'. Since 2014 he has won four ANU Vice Chancellor media awards for his analysis and impact in the media. He currently has five regular radio segments in three states and the ACT.

In 2017, Andrew was awarded a competitive grant to research how political engagement varies in different cultures and systems domestically and globally. His research into roadside signs in election campaigns has already been used to change campaign laws in the ACT.

His areas of research span strategy, the role of stakeholders in strategy, emotions in advertising and marketing, consumer culture, public policy, political leadership, and sports marketing. Connect with him on Twitter @marketingandrew.

Preface

This second edition, full-colour services marketing text has been written for senior marketing students with the aim of helping those students understand the role that services marketing plays in creating customer value, and the increasing contributions that the services sector makes to national economies. We believe that it is imperative that service marketers understand the practical implications associated with the definitive characteristics of services because that knowledge will enable them to recognise, and effectively manage, the marketing opportunities that arise from global service-based economies.

Content features

The authors' primary objective was to create a services marketing text that engages and encourages our students to develop an understanding of the service processes that create value for identified target markets. An analytical learning approach, based on applying established and evolving marketing concepts for service organisations, is the rationale of the pedagogy that has been adopted. That approach is warranted for two reasons:

→ Australian and New Zealand service organisations are developing closer economic ties with the growing markets of their South-East Asian counterparts.

→ By understanding Australasian service organisations, students will be able to adopt an international perspective on services marketing.

The pedagogy of this text will therefore provide students with the necessary skills to analyse those successful service strategies that create customer value, achieve customer satisfaction and foster customer lifetime brand loyalty for a broad range of services.

The text sequentially examines various services marketing concepts, enabling students to develop the conceptual foundations for critical evaluation of the marketing activities of selected Australasian service organisations, and develop the skills needed to apply those service concepts. The written content of each chapter is supported by full-colour tables, models and illustrations.

Structure of the text

This text contains 13 chapters, to align with most Australian universities' semester teaching timetables. The pedagogy of the text is based on problem-based learning, supported by practical in-chapter *Service in Action*, and *Industry Insight* feature boxes, together with comprehensive case studies at the end of each part of the text.

There are three main parts. Part 1: Service Organisations and Their Customers consists of four chapters that consider the marketing fundamentals of market segmentation and positioning, customer decision-making, and the service encounter, and how those core concepts apply to the unique characteristics of services and their influence on consumer behaviour.

Part 2: Marketing Strategies for Services contains five chapters that discuss developing service products and the service-delivery process (including self-service technology, cost and pricing strategies, and marketing communications for services)—the essential elements for successfully marketing service products.

OXFORD UNIVERSITY PRESS

The third part, Delivering Service Value, includes four chapters that discuss the service experience, customer satisfaction and service quality, service recovery, and customer relationship management. It also discusses how these elements of a service deliver customer value.

Each chapter follows a consistent framework, beginning with an opening vignette that broadly aligns with the chapter's core content, followed by an introduction and learning objectives. In addition, throughout each chapter, *Service in Action* and *Industry Insight* feature boxes highlight contemporary examples of recent services marketing theory and practice. Each chapter concludes with review questions and lists of URLs, journal articles and texts for further analysis of the chapter topic. There are two case studies at the end of the chapters in each part. A glossary of important terms that have been used in the text is included at the end of the book, preceding the index.

We would like to thank the various academics who reviewed and contributed to the chapters of the second edition of *Services Marketing*, and we are grateful for the assistance we received from the team at Oxford University Press (Australia and New Zealand), especially Karen Hildebrandt, Emily Wu and Alex Chambers who melded all of our ideas and queries into this textbook. We would also like to thank Michelle D'Alessandro for writing the Lecturer Test Bank for this edition.

Acknowledgments

The author and the publisher wish to thank the following copyright holders for reproduction of their material.

123RF, Figure 11.3; ABC for 'United Airlines: What can we learn from company's "breathtakingly bad" crisis management?' by Emily Sakzewski, ABC News 13 April 2017, on p. 431; ACCC © Commonwealth of Australia, Figure1.3; Choice Hotels Group, Case Study C, Figure 2; Courtesy InterContinental Hotels Group, Figure 3.8; Eurostar, Figure 11.2; Federal Group, Figure 9.3; geoTribes, Figure 2.1; Getty Images/Bettmann, p. 126; Getty Images/Andrew Harrer/Bloomberg, p. 431; Getty Images/Bettmann, Figure 3.4; istockphoto/Christine Gonsalves, Figure 6.6; iStockphoto/Elena Elisseeva, Figure 6.5; Jim's Group, Figure 6.1; Courtesy Maria Island Walk and designed by Ron Mather, Figure 2.10; New Zealand Tourism, p. 292; Qantas Figures 9.6 &13.3; Quit Victoria, Figure 1.1; Roy Morgan, Figure 2.4; Shutterstock; cover image, chapter opening images 1–10, 12–13, Figures 2.11, 2.5, 2.6, 2.7, 2.8, 3.2, 3.5, 3.9, 4.6, 6.2, 6.3, 6.4, 7.7, 9.2, 9.8, pp. 173, 233, 237, 246, 352, 452, 454, Case Study B, Figure 1, Case Study E, Figure 1; Singapore Airlines, Figure 9.1, TAC, p. 323, Telstra, Case Study E, Figure 2, Terri Scheer, Figure 3.6, United States Library of Congress, p. 127, Warehouse Fitness, Figure 11.7, WestPix/Dean Alston, Case Study F, p. 485, www.siemens.com/press, chapter opener 11 & Figure 11.1.

Every effort has been made to trace the original source of copyright material contained in this book. The publisher will be pleased to hear from copyright holders to rectify any errors or omissions.

Introductory Vignette: Each chapter opens with a short vignette about a contemporary topic to engage the reader and introduce the subject through a concrete example.

Tourism New Zealand is encouraging Aussies to take a road trip to the South Island

The latest evolution of the successful South Island Road Trip campaign 'Every day a different journey' was launched in 2015 by Tourism New Zealand with the primary target market being the eastern seaboard of Australia. The campaign highlights the diversity of the naturally hidden gems and experiences of the south island of New Zealand and encourages Australians to visit the island. The three-year partnership between Tourism New Zealand and the Regional Tourism Organisations (RTOs) will cost $3 million dollars, and offers Australians a road trip around the South Island. In addition to the direct spend, there will be a wide range of media and travel agent activity that will see the value delivered by the campaign reach as much as NZ$4–6 million.[1]

Learning Objectives: A bulleted list of learning objectives is included at the beginning of each chapter to help you focus on the key points of the chapter, and highlights the abilities and skills you should be able to demonstrate after reading the chapter.

Learning objectives

After reading this chapter you should be able to:

↘ understand the definition of services

↘ explain the importance of the service industries to the Australian economy

↘ discuss the four defining characteristics of a service product

↘ explain the differences between goods and services

↘ outline the differences between a service product, service interactions and a customer experience

↘ discuss the challenges of marketing a service product.

Key Terms: To aid your understanding of important concepts, key terms are defined in the margin notes, as well as collated in a complete glossary at the back of the book for easy reference.

> ⬊
> **core service**
> The main service that provides customers with a solution to their needs, such as transport or financial security

> ⬊
> **peripheral services**
> Supplementary services that facilitate the core service and are often the factors that differentiate and position the core service

Services in Action: Each chapter includes Services in Action boxes to reinforce the key themes in that chapter. These put the theory into action, providing practical and contemporary examples of these key themes from a range of sources.

Services in Action

Promising the luxury of a timeless escape

The Saffire Freycinet luxury lodge, as shown in Figure 9.3, is situated at Coles Bay on the east coast of Tasmania and

Figure 9.3 Tasmania's Saffire Freycinet combines customers' desire for luxury with their environmental concerns

Source: Saffire Freycinet.

caters for guests in 20 pavilion suites that fan out from the stingray-shaped main communal Sanctuary lodge.[6]

In conjunction with Wildcare, an environmental volunteer group in Tasmania, the Menzies Institute for Medical Research and the Tasmanian Parks and Wildlife Service rangers, the Sanctuary lodge provides a rehabilitation centre for endangered Tasmanian devils. The rangers conduct information sessions for guests staying at the lodge to raise funds that are being used to develop a vaccine that will combat the contagious facial tumours that are threatening the survival of the local Tasmanian devils.[7]

OXFORD UNIVERSITY PRESS

Industry Insights: Industry Insights highlight the application of services marketing in business.

BY EMILY SAKZEWSKI, ABC NEWS

A public relations (PR) expert says United Airline's problems could have been avoided with an immediate, earnest apology. So, how did it get this

that was to apologise,' Ms Muir said. Instead, Mr Munoz issued a poorly executed statement a full day after the video went viral.

'This is an upsetting event to all of us here at United. I apologize for having to re-accommodate these customers. Our team is moving with a sense of urgency to work with the authorities and conduct our own detailed review of what happened. We are also reaching out to this passenger to talk directly to him and further and resolve this situation'. Source: Twitter, Oscar Munoz, CEO United Airlines' United

⬊
INDUSTRY INSIGHT

United Airlines: What can we learn from company's 'breathtakingly bad' crisis management?

Chapter Summary: A short summary of key points is included at the end of each chapter, to reinforce comprehension of the learning objectives and the central themes of the chapter.

This chapter discusses two important and related topics: segmenting and targeting service customers; and positioning a service brand. First, the chapter examines consumer groups with specific demographics, values and lifestyles, and/or purchasing behaviour variables, which are the variables of a service brand's segmentation strategy and are complementary to its positioning strategy.

The major variables in segmenting a market that are reviewed include the demographic structure of the Australian population, namely ages, life cycles and incomes; the values and lifestyles of the Australian population, using the Roy Morgan Values Segments model; and elements of behavioural segmentation, that is, consumers' purchase behaviour.

Review Questions: Carefully designed review questions have been provided at the end of every chapter. These can be used to check your understanding of the key topics before moving on to the next chapter.

Review questions

1   What is a critical incident? Why is it important for service providers? List three possible critical incidents in the provision of higher education for international students.
2   What is customer delight? How can a service provider continue to delight its customers?
3   Why is benchmarking used in service delivery? What are the advantages and disadvantages of this approach?
4   What can be done when customers become angry and enraged?
5   What is the role of blueprinting in service delivery?
6   Why do consumers use online forums and social media to co-create value?

Further Reading, Weblinks and Endnotes: Further reading, weblinks and endnotes are placed at the end of each chapter to help broaden your understanding of the topics covered in each chapter.

Further reading

Frei, F.X. (2008). The four things a service business must get right. *Harvard Business Review*, 86(4), 70.

Grönroos, C. (1990). Relationship approach to marketing in service contexts: The marketing and organizational behavior interface. *Journal of Business Research*, 20(1), 3–11.

Grönroos, C. (2006). Adopting a service logic for marketing. *Marketing Theory*, 6(3), 317–33.

Scartz, T.A. & Iacobucci, D. (eds) (2000). *Handbook of Services Marketing and Management*. Thousand Oaks, CA: Sage Publications.

Vargo, S.L. & Lusch, R.F. (2008). Service-dominant logic: Continuing the evolution. *Journal of the Academy of Marketing Science*, 36(1), 1–10.

Vargo, S.L., Maglio, P.P. & Akaka, M.A. (2008). On value and value co-creation: A service systems and service logic perspective. *European Management Journal*, 26(3), 145–52.

Weblinks

Australian Consumer Law. <www.consumerlaw.gov.au>

Australian Customer Service Awards. <www.serviceexcellence.com.au>

Customer Service Institute of Australia. <www.csia.com.au>

Vodafail. <www.vodafail.com>

Endnotes

1   Based on B. Ice (2015). Customer-centric strategy boosts revenue performance—study. *Marketing*, 6 October. <www.marketingmag.com.au/news-c/customer-centric-strategy-boosts-revenue-performance-study/?inf_contact_key=ae92d6f19b26624d5688884ddaaeec85d199746e3c542189c07ad72bbbc343dc>.

Case Studies: The Case Studies in the book apply the theory being discussed in each part to real-life situations.

Case

Case study E

Google Home: The smart-home service

In the second half of 2017, Google launched a digital service in Australia that gave local customers the opportunity to create a smart home that had a list of expected benefits ranging from connecting internet devices in their homes to asking the Google Assistant to engage with local services.[1] Google Home, as shown in Figure 1, is powered by Google's voice-controlled Google Assistant. It is a device which, when connected via wi-fi to a home internet system, can control lights, appliances and smart power switches, and answer trivia questions, set calendar reminders and provide weather forecasts.

Figure 1   Google Home connects via wi-fi to access the internet

Part

1

Service Organisations
and Their Customers

Identifying the triggers of smoking

In terms of marketing, a service—because of its fundamental characteristic of intangibility—is an intangible product, unlike a physical good that has tangible dimensions. A service, regardless of its nature or how it is provided, offers customers a form of value. Consider, for example, public health services—such as a campaign that encourages smokers to quit smoking. Public health services are intangible products delivered by government agencies and have similar characteristics to the services provided by commercial organisations such as banks or insurance companies that offer some form of benefit to their customers. Smokers who quit enjoy the positive benefits of a healthy and satisfying lifestyle.

Public health service agencies provide benefits to various segments of the population by raising awareness of the dangers associated with risky behaviour such as smoking or drink-driving. Many of the most successful public health campaigns, such as previous quit campaigns, have relied as much on legislation—such as the *Tobacco Plain Packaging Act* for tobacco products—as on education programs to raise public awareness of the dangers of smoking. In 2014 Quit Victoria, a division of the Cancer Council Victoria, launched a public awareness campaign to encourage smokers to quit by helping them identify the triggers that raise their desire to smoke. The campaign was designed to empower smokers to have the confidence and ability to recognise those triggers so they could resist the urge to smoke.

'Triggers changes the idea of quitting from something you "just do", to something that you consider and have prepared for,' said Tim Holmes, Creative Director, the JWT agency in Melbourne.[1]

As part of the public awareness campaign, a television commercial (shown in Figure 1.1)—was launched with a six-week, high-frequency schedule across all free-to-air television channels and supported by digital displays and out-of-home promotions such as large-format outdoor posters, venue ads and coasters. The television commercial was Quit Victoria's first animated communication aimed at smokers who are trying

» *continued over page*

Chapter 1

An Overview of Services Marketing

William Chitty

Figure 1.1   Television commercial for Quit Victoria

Source: Quit Victoria. <www.campaignbrief.com/2014/09/quit-victoria-highlights-smoki.html>.

to quit smoking and was very different from the usually graphic anti-smoking messages. Exposure to mass media, like free-to-air television in this case, usually occurs during routine media contact rather than being explicitly sought, and so it provided a means of reaching those individuals who were already thinking about quitting, as well as those who had not yet made a decision to quit. Campaign messages that are transmitted by mass media can directly influence individual decision-making about quitting, because as smokers view and hear those messages, they gain new insights and can reflect on the implications for their own lives.[2] Unlike previous behaviour-change messages, the triggers campaign offered supportive advice and encouragement to smokers, who often struggle to quit when facing common smoking triggers such as stress or socialising with friends.

The public health campaign was a new communications program for Quit Victoria that used a point of difference to 'cut through' and highlight a public health issue. The campaign specifically targeted 30- to 49-year-old smokers to help them recognise the triggers that activate their desire to smoke—such as stress or alcohol—and develop ways to deal with their tobacco cravings in advance.

Data from the Cancer Council Victoria indicates that:

↘ Women are more likely than men to nominate stress (83% versus 74%) and phone calls (30% versus 18%) as smoking triggers.

↘ Men are significantly more likely than women to report that work breaks trigger their desire to smoke (66% versus 52%).

↘ Smokers planning to quit in the next month (87%) are significantly more likely to identify stress as a trigger compared to smokers not planning to quit in the next month (77%).

↘ Smokers who have made two or three attempts (79%) or more than four attempts (79%) to quit are also significantly more likely to state that parties and nights out trigger their desire to smoke compared to smokers who have made no previous attempts to quit (65%).[3]

The ad asked people to identify those situations that triggered their urge to smoke and, when they recognised those triggers, to use strategies, like changing their routines, to avoid and overcome them.

A list of the most common triggers (shown in Table 1.1)—was included in a mobile app, so that people trying to quit smoking could get tips on how to beat their triggers from other ex-smokers or submit their own trigger tips.[4]

Table 1.1 indicates the percentage of current smokers and recent quitters—both male and female—who identified the following activities as smoking triggers.

Table 1.1   The top smoking triggers

Being around friends who smoke	80%
Stress	78%
Parties/nights out	76%
After eating a meal	69%
Work breaks	60%
Coffee	45%
Driving	41%
Telephone calls	23%

Source: Quit Victoria.

Quit Victoria's Acting Director, Craig Sinclair, said, 'Research has shown that most smokers don't want to smoke but lack the confidence, self-awareness and skills to quit smoking successfully'. Previous research shows that the majority (84%) of Victorian smokers have tried to quit at least once, while over half (52.7%) have tried to quit multiple times. Quit Victoria used the triggers campaign to encourage smokers who had made some unsuccessful attempts to quit to prepare for the next time by thinking about what triggered their smoking urges and developing strategies to successfully deal with them.[5]

About the research: Data collected as part of 2014 Victorian Social Marketing Tracking Survey conducted by Behavioural Science Division at Cancer Council Victoria.

Introduction

Services are products that have distinctive and defining characteristics that set them apart from physical goods. Service products may be delivered by the employees of large commercial organisations, such as tellers in banks, technicians with telecommunications companies and the cabin staff of airlines, through to smaller service providers such as accountants, dentists and solicitors, who are often the owners of their businesses.

Both Commonwealth and state governments provide community services like education, transport and public health, while welfare services are provided by both governments and not-for-profit organisations such the Brotherhood of St Laurence and St Vincent de Paul. The quit campaign discussed at the beginning of this chapter is an example of a public health initiative by a state government, to make members of the population who smoke tobacco—rather than the total population—aware of the health risks associated with smoking.

Services influence the everyday activities of everybody, so it is important for marketers to recognise the distinctions that exist between services, such as core service products, the peripheral services that support those core service products and customer service. Understanding the differences between the various types of goods and services requires identifying the characteristics of the two broad categories of products, and then learning how consumers evaluate those differences. Customer service is not a product *per se*, but an essential element of both goods and services that provides an evaluative criterion for customers to determine their level of satisfaction with the performance of a product. Services consist of a broad and diverse range of activities that are intangible, and that can often be difficult for customers to evaluate. Services do have some similar attributes to those of physical products; they have a brand, and they consist of features and desired benefits, all of which offer varying levels of value to customers.

A *feature* is a function that a service performs. For example, the price comparisons of rooms from several hotels using a single search command that a hotel booking service provides are a feature of that service; the functionality of the price comparisons is a feature of the hotel booking service. *Benefits*, however, are the outcomes or results that a customer experiences from using a service. For example, the hotel booking service that provides price comparisons of hotel rooms offers the benefit of saving time for consumers and may be the reason consumers become potential long-term customers; customers tend to purchase only services that have features that offer them a form of benefit. In other words, like the traditional concept of marketing, a service product is delivered to an identified group of customers by a service organisation—using either employees or technology—to satisfy those customers' needs, wants and expectations, and must do so more efficiently and effectively than competing service organisations. For some specialised types of services, such as orthopaedic surgery, the surgeon is the specialist service provider, while for other more standardised services—such as everyday banking—the service is delivered using digital technology via an ATM.

OXFORD UNIVERSITY PRESS

The learning objectives of this text are premised on understanding the various processes associated with marketing a service as a product; that is, how service organisations manage their services as a total marketing program from developing a service and making prospective customers aware of the service to managing long-term customer relationships. Chapter 1 begins by discussing the evolution of the service industry in Australia and the various macro environmental forces—the political, economic, social and technological (PEST) forces—that have transformed the Australian service economy. That is followed by discussion of the defining characteristics of a service, then evaluation of the practical issues associated with marketing service products by examining the differences between physical goods and intangible services. The last section of the chapter discusses how service interactions influence customer perceptions of value, and it concludes by presenting a broad outline of the challenges of marketing services.

Learning objectives

After reading this chapter you should be able to:

↘ understand the definition of services

↘ explain the importance of the service industries to the Australian economy

↘ discuss the four defining characteristics of a service product

↘ explain the differences between goods and services

↘ outline the differences between a service product, service interactions and a customer experience

↘ discuss the challenges of marketing a service product.

Understanding services

A service can be considered from two perspectives. A service (I) is an act, performance or experience that provides some form of value in the production and delivery of the service; customers do not, however, generally take anything tangible from that service experience. For example, when fans go to a football match, they are entertained by the experience of watching two teams trying to gain possession of the ball to kick a goal and, ultimately, by their team winning the game. Fans barrack for their team and are involved with its victory, but at the end of the game they will not take anything physical away from it—only elation or disappointment.

A service (II) can also be considered an economic process that provides time, place and form value in solving customers' problems. For example, the value of those solutions may be derived from saving time by catching a taxi instead of public transport to an airport or using BPAY as a convenient distribution channel to pay a phone account, while form value is created when customers have their hair styled by a hairdresser. These economic

↘
service (I)
An act, performance or experience that provides some form of value in the production and delivery of the service

↘
service (II)
An economic process that provides time, place and form value in solving customers' problems

processes deliver value to customers, but do not transfer the ownership of anything tangible from the service encounter.

Services, as products, are often confused with customer service. Customer service is a universal marketing requirement to satisfy customers—whether the product is as tangible as a motor vehicle, or as intangible as a university education. To gain a competitive advantage, a car manufacturer may offer a 100 000-kilometre warranty for its vehicles, with roadside assistance. The core product that is purchased, however, is not an act or performance; it's a tangible motor vehicle. The warranty is a peripheral, intangible element of the core product. Conversely, universities offer tertiary education programs that are intangible core service products, supported by some equally intangible peripheral services, such as those offered by a university library that enables students to achieve the research objectives of the various academic courses. Tertiary education is the core service product offered by a university; the library is a peripheral student service.

The customer service process, then, is an organisational function—similar to marketing and sales—that manages the interactions that take place between organisations and their customers. For service organisations, customer service involves 'a moment of truth' for customers. Customer service is an element of *customer experience*, which is the culmination of a series of interactions that service organisations undertake across all touch points with their customers. Customer experience is discussed in detail in Chapter 10.

The importance of Australia's service industries

As shown in Figure 1.2, the principal macro environmental forces that have influenced the transformation of the services industries in Australia are political/regulatory forces; economic trends; social changes; and developments in technology. Together these forces are changing the competitive environment and reshaping consumers' buying and consuming behaviour.

Figure 1.2   The major environmental forces that influence Australia's service industries

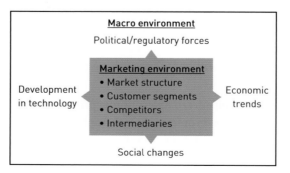

The effects that those major environmental forces have on Australia's service industries are discussed next.

Political/regulatory forces

The pre-eminent legislation to enforce competition in Australia, and provide protection for consumers, is the *Competition and Consumer Act 2010*. For the purposes of consumer protection, the relevant provisions are now found in Schedule 2 to the *Trade Practices Amendment (Australian Consumer Law) Act (No. 2) 2010*—which is now known as the Australian Consumer Law (ACL). For example, the important sections—ss 52 and 53 of the former *Trade Practices Act 1974*—became ss 18 and 29 respectively of the ACL.

The Australian Competition and Consumer Commission (ACCC) is an independent Commonwealth statutory authority that administers the *Competition and Consumer Act 2010* and a range of additional legislation that promotes competition and fair trading. The role of the ACCC—in addition to enforcing competition in Australia—is to protect the rights and obligations of businesses and consumers. As such, it ensures compliance with the Commonwealth laws of competition, fair trading and consumer protection. There are, however, occasions when social issues arise that do not fall within the ambit of the law. In these cases, a comprehensive review of the market can help both policy-makers and consumers better understand the social landscape and determine whether policy changes are needed. Such is the case outlined in the following Industry insight feature.

↘
INDUSTRY INSIGHT

Australians lose over $229 million to scams in 2015

The ACCC's *Targeting Scams Report* reveals that 105 200 scam complaints—worth $85 million—were reported to its Scamwatch reporting system in 2015. In 2014, the ACCC received 91 600 scam complaints, with almost $82 million reported lost. For the first time, the ACCC has also reviewed data from other jurisdictions that receive reports or detect scams, to get a clearer view of the losses caused by scam activity in Australia. After removing those scams already reported to the ACCC, reports to the Australian Cybercrime Online Reporting Network (ACORN) revealed losses of over $127 million from 25 600 complaints in 2015.

Various scam-disruption programs have also detected Australians sending funds to high-risk jurisdictions and a combined estimate of losses to this unreported scam activity is $17.1 million. The 2015 *Targeting Scams Report* indicates that investment scams and dating/romance scams resulted in the largest financial losses—these two types of scams accounted for half of the money reported lost by over-55s in 2015.[6]

William Chitty

Figure 1.3 Scam activities in 2015

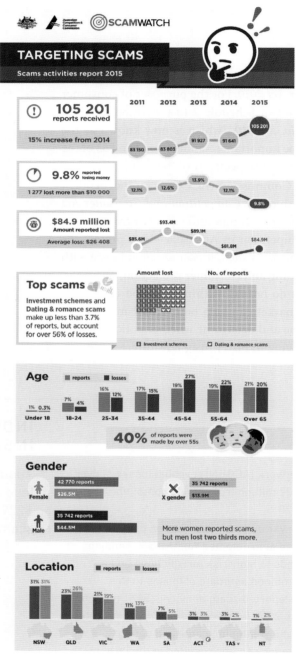

Source: Scamwatch. <www.scamwatch.gov.au/news/
australians-lose-over-229-million-to-scams-in-2015>.

Scamwatch reports for fraudulent investment schemes across all age groups in 2015 doubled to over $24 million from 1262 complaints. When that $24 million is added to the investment scams reported to ACORN, the total amount reported totals more than $41 million. Of those reported scams, almost $6.3 million was lost by victims aged over 55, with 213 complaints from this age group. Scams pose a significant risk to Australians looking for investment opportunities, especially those people looking to grow their retirement funds. They come in many guises, including business ventures, superannuation schemes, managed funds, and the sale or purchase of shares and property. Scammers dress up so-called 'opportunities' with professional-looking brochures and websites to mask their fraudulent operations and trick unsuspecting Australians.

In 2015, Scamwatch reports for dating and romance scams decreased slightly, but were still significant with just under $23 million in reported losses from 2620 complaints. Of these, $5.6 million was lost by victims aged over 55, with 464 complaints. ACORN reports for romance scams totalled $15 million. When those losses are added to those from the disruption work ($17 million), the total losses for relationship scams are more than $54 million.

Dating/romance scams take advantage of people looking for romantic partners, often via dating websites, apps and social media. Scammers spend months and even years establishing relationship with their victims before making up a reason as to why they need to 'borrow' money, such as for medical emergencies or travel expenses. Figure 1.3 provides demographic data associated with the various types of scams.

OXFORD UNIVERSITY PRESS

Economic trends

Australia is a world-class provider of a range of services such as education, telecommunications, tourism, banking and insurance. The services sector is a significant part of the Australian economy and in 2014–15 the economy produced services worth about $970 billion, which represents about 60 per cent of national GDP. Within the services sector, growth was strongest in information technology, media and telecommunications, accommodation and food services, financial and insurance services, and healthcare and social assistance.[7]

Only about a third of services produced are sold to households, while the majority of services—classified as *enabling services*—are used to support other businesses in the production of their final products. Those enabling services are a vital part of the economy because they are a key input to businesses in getting their final products to market. It is essential, therefore, that the services sector remains both competitive and productive.

Whereas conventional methods of industry analysis typically focus on *what* is being produced, analysis of the services sector focuses on *who* purchases the services. Shifting the focus to *who* provides an alternative approach to examining the services sector, because it indicates how enabling services are used by a range of other industries and how they help those industries create their final products.

That approach has identified four types of enabling services:

→ professional and support services

→ information and communications technology (ICT) and the digital economy

→ trade, transport and logistics

→ utilities services.

In 2014–15, these enabling services produced approximately $465 billion of output (29% of GDP) and employed approximately 3.1 million workers (27% of the total employed).

Professional and support services are the largest of the four types of enabling services, employing the most people and making up around 20 per cent of GDP in 2014–15. The other three types are much smaller, collectively producing around 9 per cent of GDP. The enabling services are a vital part of the economy, a key requirement for businesses in getting their products to market.[8]

Employment in services sector

Recent Reserve Bank of Australia (RBA) analysis of the trends in business and household services found that, between them, these account for almost 80 per cent of employment in Australia. Business services employ highly skilled people in highly paid positions, while household services mainly employ low-skilled people in low-paid jobs.[9] The RBA analysis classified 300 service occupations into high-, average- and low-paying employment positions. In business services there has been a steady increase in the number of highly

William Chitty

Figure 1.4 Industry gross value

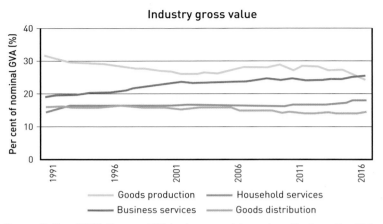

Source: D. Uren (2017). Treasury, RBA bank on growth in services. *The Australian*, 11 September, p. 17.

paid positions, with about 850 000 jobs created since 2000, compared with slightly less than 300,000 average-paying jobs and about 150 000 low-paying jobs over the same period. In household services, since 2000 there have been 700 000 low-paying jobs, 350 000 high-paying jobs and 300 000 jobs on average wages created.[10] The industry gross value of goods and services is depicted in Figure 1.4.

Australia's services exports

Travel is the largest component of services exports, contributing $37 billion to the Australian economy in 2014–15. Export growth across key services industries is shown in Figure 1.5. Business and personal travel and education travel are the largest contributors to services exports. Service provision to people travelling for personal and educational reasons is a globally contested industry, as countries compete to attract tourists and students from critical markets such as China. Recent falls in the exchange rate have allowed the Australian tourism and education industries to capitalise on rising global demand, with the number of short-term arrivals into Australia increasing by 6.6 per cent in 2014–15.[11]

Export income earned from international education in 2016–17

Export income earned from international students studying and living in Australia was $28 billion during the financial year 2016–17, an increase of 16 per cent from the earnings of international education activity in 2015–16 ($24.1 billion). Education activity contributes 34 per cent of total service export earnings to the Australian economy, exceeding personal travel services ($21.6 billion) and professional and management consulting services

Figure 1.5 Key components of service exports 2013–14 and 2014–15

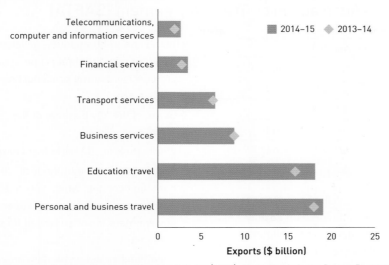

Source: Department of Industry, Innovation and Science (2015). *Australian Industry Report*. December. Canberra.

($4.8 billion). Education export earnings from education activity are the economic value of everything international students spend during their time in Australia, and include money spent on food, rent, utilities, transport, recreation and domestic holidays.[12]

During the 2016–17 financial year, the higher education sector generated $19.1 billion in export income followed by vocational education and training (VET), which generated $4.8 billion; English language intensive courses for overseas students (ELICOS) generated $1.4 billion, and schools earned $1.2 billion. The top five export markets for Australian education activity in 2016–17 are shown in Figure 1.6.

Figure 1.6 The top five export markets for Australian education in 2016–17

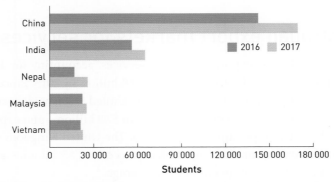

Source: ICEF Monitor. Australian education exports approaching AUS$ 25 October 2017. <http://monitor.icef.com/2017/10/australian-education-exports-approaching-aus29-billion>.

William Chitty

Singapore–Australia Free Trade Agreement (SAFTA)

Singapore market snapshot	
GDP	US$295.7 billion (2013)
GDP per capita	US$54 775 (2013)
GDP growth	3.5% (2013)
Population	5.4 million (2013)
Trade with Australia	AU$29.0 billion (2012–13)

The Singapore–Australia Free Trade Agreement came into force on 28 July 2003 and was Australia's first bilateral free trade agreement since the Closer Economic Relations Trade Agreement with New Zealand came into force in 1983. The SAFTA is the central pillar of the economic relationship with Singapore—Australia's largest trade and investment partner in South-East Asia. In addition to tariff elimination, the SAFTA provides increased market access for Australian exporters of services, particularly education, environmental, telecommunications and professional services. It also provides a more open and predictable business environment across a range of areas,

including competition policy, government procurement, intellectual property, e-commerce, customs procedures and business travel.

Some of the key benefits of the SAFTA are:

↘ elimination of all tariffs from entry

↘ restrictions on the number of wholesale banking licences, which will reduce over time, and an enhanced operating environment for providers of financial services

↘ conditions eased on establishment of joint ventures involving Australian law firms and the number of Australian law degrees recognised in Singapore doubled from four to eight

↘ removal/easing of residency requirements for Australian professionals and short-term entry for Australian businesspeople extended from one month to three months

↘ agreement to facilitate paperless trading in order to reduce business transaction costs.[13]

Major Australian export markets for services

China was Australia's largest export market for services, accounting for 14.9 per cent of total services exports—a rise of 19.8 per cent to $9.8 billion in 2015. Since 2010, exports have risen 10.7 per cent per annum on average. The United States was Australia's second-largest services export market—up by 18.7 per cent to $7.9 billion—and exports have risen by an average of 8.8 per cent per annum since 2010. The United Kingdom was Australia's third-largest services export market—up by 8.8 per cent to $5 billion—and since 2010, exports have risen by 5.4 per cent per annum on average.[14]

Social changes

From a services marketing perspective, a major social change that is occurring in Australia is the growing but ageing population. The implications of the ageing population are that older Australians will need more specialised healthcare and retirement facilities, and that these services will need more trained service employees. The Australian population is ageing because of increased life expectancy and a sustained low level of fertility that has resulted in proportionally fewer children in the population. A decline in the number of births—together with an increase in the number of women aged 15 to 49 years—is contributing to Australia's overall fertility rate falling from 1.93 births per woman in 2012 to 1.78 in 2020. The natural replacement level for growth in the population is considered to be a fertility rate of 2.1 births per woman.[15]

Population of Australia 2006–20

Figure 1.7 shows the growth in Australia's population from 2006 to 2015. The population of Australia was expected to be 24.28 million by the end of 2016, according to Trading Economics global macro models and projections. By 2020, the Australian population is projected to be about 25.62 million.[16]

Figure 1.7   Growth in Australian population 2006–15

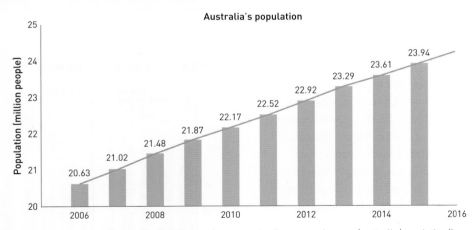

Source: Trading Economics. <www.tradingeconomics.com/australia/population/forecast>.

A distinctive feature in the age distribution of the Australian population as at June 2014 was the high representation of people aged 20 to 39 years. People in this age group represented 31 per cent of the combined capital city population, compared to 24 per cent of the population in the rest of Australia. This reflects the attraction of younger adults to education, employment and other social opportunities in capital cities. In contrast, older adults aged 40 years and over made up a smaller proportion of the population in capital cities, at 44 per cent, than in the rest of Australia, at 50 per cent.[17]

William Chitty

Developments in technology

Easier access to technology and greater reliance on it by customers have given service organisations new direct communication channels that allow them to focus on developing closer relationships with their customers. Growth in the speed of the internet and access to broadband is changing the nature of services marketing. The technology that provides consumer accessibility, convenience and efficiency is now a general consumer expectation and taken for granted. Technology has also transformed industries. Typically, music and entertainment companies offer search facilities on the internet that enable their consumers to find the prices and availability of their services. Those organisations also use the internet to provide basic customer service and product information, and as a direct distribution channel for online retailing.

Technology has influenced the service diffusion process and facilitated widespread adoption of new digital service-delivery systems. New markets and new product categories, such as online newspapers and personal global positioning systems (GPS), have been more readily adopted because of the availability of technology. Technology also enables customers and service organisations to be effective in receiving and providing services.[18] The major banks, for example, offer online banking services that allow their customers to serve themselves more effectively when they want to check their balances, pay bills or transfer funds between their accounts.

Australia leads the world in adopting mobile banking

Recent research by consultants Bain and Company suggests that mobile banking in Australia is now more common than online banking, with Australian bank customers among the world's fastest adopters of mobile banking. Survey results from Bain (see Figure 1.8) indicate that 38 per cent of Australian customers' interactions with their banks occurred via a smartphone or tablet in 2014, up from 22 per cent a year earlier, making mobile banking now preferred to online banking, which fell from 42 per cent to 35 per cent of customer interactions.

These findings are based on surveys of 83 000 consumers from 22 countries, including 2700 people in Australia. Although the trend is global, Australian consumers are leading the world in their use of mobile banking and the

Figure 1.8   How we do our banking

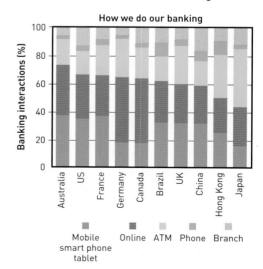

Source: C. Yeates (2015). Australia leads the world in mobile banking. *Sydney Morning Herald*, 15 June. <www.smh.com. au/business/banking-and-finance/australia-leads-the-world-in-mobile-banking-20150614-ghngd5.html.

rate of change over the previous 12 months was increasing. Bain's research suggests that, at the same time, Australian consumers are less likely to visit a branch than customers in other countries, thereby taking their unnecessary interactions out of the branches. While it is convenient for customers, their embrace of mobile technology could be seen as a potential threat to Commonwealth Bank, Westpac, ANZ Bank and National Australia Bank. The high rate of adoption of mobile banking—along with the lucrative profits earned by the big four—could make these banks a target for the growing number of technology-based businesses competing with them in payments and lending.

In contrast to Bain's view, other analysts believe the local banks are less vulnerable to 'digital disruption' because they have invested heavily in digital technology. Citibank analysts report that the impact of digital disruption on Australian lenders is likely to be minimal, citing the banks' already high level of capital investment in technology coupled with the role of regulation in deterring new entrants to the market.[19]

According to Telsyte research, Australian households are in an Internet of Things (IoT) home revolution, with more than 40 per cent of Australian households in 2017 having at least one IoT@Home device—an increase from 29 per cent in 2016. IoT devices are smart internet-connected devices that allow consumers to typically control, monitor and enhance their lifestyles by using mobile apps. Telsyte estimates that the average Australian household in 2017 has 13.7 internet-connected devices, but that number is expected is grow to almost 31 by 2021, with 14 being IoT@Home devices. By 2021, Australian households are expected to have a total of 311 million connected devices, nearly half of which are expected to be new IoT@Home devices. Telsyte estimates that the collective value of the IoT@Home market in Australia by 2021 will be worth $4.7 billion—a significant increase from $377 million in 2016.[20]

As a result of the widespread adoption of information technology, there is a greater degree of competition, in both the number and the structure of online service organisations, with more entertainment services being offered to customers based on their propensity to adopt new technology. The internet, for example, is not restricted by international boundaries, and the global reach of Australian service organisations is rapidly increasing. Service interactions that used to require personal contact can now be performed anywhere in the world using the internet and video-conferencing. Advances in technology have also led to an exodus of services skills from countries that have high labour costs, like Australia, to low-labour-cost countries like India and Pakistan. That migration of service employment covers a range of employment, from call centre operations to IT development and financial analysis.

The challenges of marketing a service

The well-known marketing mix variables for the marketing of tangible products are the four Ps: *products*, *price*, *promotion* (marketing communications) and *place* (distribution and logistics). To understand the challenges of marketing services, however, requires understanding three additional variables: *people*, *processes* and *physical facilities*.

William Chitty

The marketing mix for services

The following sub-sections describe the seven Ps.

Products

Service *products* are the foundation of a service organisation's marketing strategies and are based on the service's benefits, attributes and brand. Product planning for a service begins with developing a service concept that represents a value proposition for the organisation's identified target market. That service product consists of core, supplementary and experiential attributes that together satisfy the target market's needs, wants and expectations. Services are produced and consumed simultaneously, and often require some form of interaction between an organisation and its customers. The development of new services should therefore take into account employees' actions, because in many cases they deliver or provide the service.

Price

The *price* of a service must satisfy two requirements: the target market must be willing and able to pay the asking price because it facilitates an exchange based on customer perceived value; and the price of the service must generate income and future profits. Pricing strategies for services are developed based on the relationships that exist between the different segments of the market, the time and place of delivery, customer demand and available operating capacity. Customers, on the other hand, often see prices as the costs, and time and effort, they must expend to receive the benefits they want. Airlines, for example, have price structures that take into account the seasonality of demand for air travel.

Promotion

For simplicity, *promotion* has traditionally been used as a generic label for marketing communications because it fits with the other Ps of the marketing mix. A more up-to-date definition of integrated marketing communications (IMC) brings together two essential organisational activities: marketing and communication. *Marketing* is the set of strategies that organisations develop to deliver value, through service interactions, to their identified target consumers, while *communication* is a process that conveys shared meaning between individuals, or between organisations and individuals.

Marketing communications represent all the elements of an organisation's marketing mix that facilitate exchanges by communicating the service's benefits, attributes and brand, positioning the brand as distinctively different from competitive brands, and sharing the brand's meaning and differences with identified target consumers.[21]

Place

When services are delivered to customers, there are several elements of the distribution process (*place*) that must be considered. The first is decisions about *where* and *when*, as well as *what* distribution channels will be used and *how*. Service-delivery systems are dependent on the type of service being offered. A delivery system may use physical channels, which include the where and when of interpersonal activities with service providers for customised services, or it may use the what and how of electronic channels for more routine or standardised services, such as using internet banking to pay bills. The second important element associated with the effective and efficient delivery of services is convenience, in terms of both location and time. Many customers value convenience because they believe it saves their time and reduces the effort needed to purchase the service.

People

People are the interactive variable in many service interactions; there are services, such as medical procedures, that can only be delivered by direct interaction between patients and medical practitioners, while other interactions, such as hotel accommodation, may be delivered indirectly to groups of customers. The intensity of the interactions associated with many services often influences customers' perceptions of how the service was delivered rather than what was delivered, which will determine the degree of satisfaction that they derive from the customer experience. Customers also play a part in service interactions and may cause other customers to experience a less than satisfactory service outcome. For example, in crowded or noisy service environments, the actions of a few rowdy customers can cause the dissatisfaction of many others with the service and its providers.

↘
satisfaction
A transaction-specific evaluation of how well each service encounter fulfilled the customer's needs, wants and expectations

Processes

Service *processes* are closely aligned with delivery procedures and specify how an organisation's marketing activities deliver value to customers. Some service processes are similar to face-to-face, interactive service-delivery activities, while other activities that are part of the service process take place away from, and out of sight of, the customers. Those two different types of process activities are separated by what has been called a 'line of visibility'.[22] Those service activities are discussed in later chapters.

Processes can be examined in terms of complexity and divergence. *Complexity* consists of the number and depth of operational activities that are required to deliver a service, while *divergence* is the degree of variability or situational latitude allowed to each provider in the service process.[23] For many service organisations, complexity and divergence are inverse elements in delivering a service. For example, if a service organisation aims to simplify the service-delivery process, it can design a system with a limited number of standardised steps. The divergence of the delivery process is thereby reduced, but the complexity is likely to increase.

Service organisations that offer a standardised service—such as government agencies like Centrelink, Medicare and public utilities—often reduce divergence in order to lower service production costs and to provide a uniform quality of service; such approaches, however, reduce process flexibility. From a customer's perspective, reducing divergence reduces customisation. Technology can reduce the 'apparent' complexity of delivering a service because in many cases the technology can increase process flexibility, allowing each service provider to tailor the service experience to the needs of each customer.

Physical facilities

The *physical facilities* of a service organisation are all of those tangible cues that communicate the value of the service and help consumers to evaluate the quality of that service. The physical facilities associated with a service, including an organisation's buildings, signage, interior furnishings, staff uniforms, printed materials and even its business cards, all shape consumers' perceptions of the organisation's image and its competitive position. The physical facilities also help consumers to evaluate a service that is performed beyond their line of visibility. This is why professional service providers such as accountants, surgeons and financial analysts prominently display their degree certificates and professional accreditations—their tangible cues of quality—so as to engender trust in their prospective customers.

The characteristics of services

The characteristics that define the nature of services had their origins in Berry's research,[24] which argued that services are different from physical goods because they have four defining characteristics: services are intangible, inseparable, variable and perishable.

The four defining characteristics of services

The following sub-sections describe these four characteristics.

Intangibility

The *intangible* elements of a service mean that it may be difficult for customers to evaluate the quality of a service, because often they cannot touch, taste or smell, or even see and hear, a service. The intangibility of a service can make it difficult to evaluate the service before purchase and therefore introduces an element of perceived risk that is associated with the purchase. Customers cannot, for example, take a service for a test drive, and that means they may have trouble determining the value of a service. There are, however, some

OXFORD UNIVERSITY PRESS

tangible elements of a service, such as the desks and seats in tutorial rooms, or the engine oil that is changed when a customer's car is serviced—both of which are, of course, tangible elements of the service process.

It is often useful to consider the intangibility of services as a continuum, by comparing services with physical goods, rather than considering them separate categories. As shown in Figure 1.9, at one end of the continuum are the 'intangible-dominant' services, such as teaching, while at the other end of the continuum there are 'tangible-dominant' products, such as salt.[25]

Figure 1.9 Physical versus intangible elements of goods and services

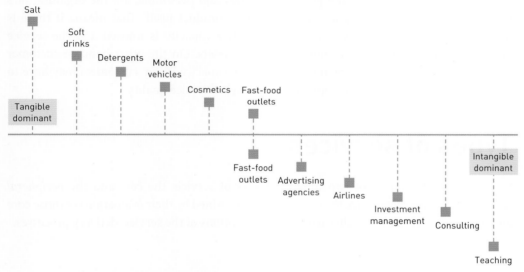

Source: G.L. Shostack (1977). Breaking free from product marketing. *Journal of Marketing*, 41(April), 73–80.

Inseparability

When a manufacturer produces physical products, the production process is usually *separated* from the end consumer. Unlike the production of physical goods, however, it is difficult to separate a service performance from the service employee (who is the provider) and the end consumer because both co-produce the service product—the what of the service. The service also consists of the service interaction—the how of the service—that takes place between the service provider and the consumer. Both the what and the how dimensions influence the consumer's perceptions of the service and, overall, determine their satisfaction with it.

Variability

The *variability* of a service relates to the difficulty of maintaining a uniform standard of service quality. Variability occurs in service interactions because, while different service providers may perform the same service, not all perform it in the same way and not all service providers are the same. Service organisations often attempt to eliminate the variability of their services by substituting technology in delivering the service, thereby removing the variable human responses of the providers. Banks, for example, use widespread ATM networks to offer non-variable, simple banking services using technology, rather than employing tellers for those standardised services.

Perishability

Services are performances or experiences, which means that they cannot be stored after production to be used later to satisfy customer demand. *Perishability* has the greatest influence on demand and yield management. The inputs that are required to produce the service product, such as the physical facilities and personnel, are the organisation's productive capacity, but they are not the service product itself. That means if there is no customer demand for a service, the productive capacity is unused and the service organisation does not create income from those assets. On the other hand, if customer demand is greater than the organisation's service capacity, many customers may have to wait longer for the service or accept a reduced level of service quality.

Types of services

Service products consist of two different layers of service: the *core* and the *peripheral* services. The value of a service to customers is determined by their evaluations of those core and peripheral services, together with their perceptions of the service-delivery processes.

Core services

The core service is the reason that customers are willing to purchase the product—because it provides a solution to their needs. Successful completion of a university marketing degree, for example, provides graduates with the skills and expertise to develop a well-paid and satisfying career in marketing.

Peripheral services

Peripheral services, as the name suggests, facilitate the consumption of the core service, and they are often the factors that differentiate and position the core service. For example, the core service of Telstra and Optus is mobile communications; their peripheral services, such as the call centre staff, provision of mobile phones and telephone network performance, are the service activities that differentiate these two telcos and allow them to charge differential product prices for a similar service. Examples of core service products and their supporting services are shown in Table 1.2.

Table 1.2 Examples of core and peripheral services

Core services	Peripheral services
Airlines (core service is air transport)	Ground services (online bookings, baggage handling) Flight services (food and beverage service, in-flight entertainment)
Banks (core service is security of customers' funds)	ATM network (convenience, 24/7 access) Credit cards (reliability, security)
Hospitals (core service is health care and facilities)	Radiology services Pathology services
Telecommunications (core service is personal communication)	Mobile communications Broadband data services
Five-star hotels (core service is accommodation)	Comfortable rooms and facilities Room service
Sporting events (core service is entertainment)	Sports teams Sporting venues
Accounting and tax services (core service is management of clients' funds)	Accounting Tax returns Financial advice

Source: C. Lovelock & J. Wirtz (2007). *Services Marketing: People, Technology, Strategy* (6th edn). Upper Saddle River, NJ: Pearson Education, p. 17.

Differences between goods and services

Service organisations face different marketing challenges from those of organisations that manufacture tangible products. As shown earlier in Figure 1.9, most products have varying degrees of tangibility; some, like a laptop, are tangible-dominant, while others are a combination of physical facilities and intangible services, like staying in a holiday resort. It is important to note that the following differences between goods and services are not common to all service categories.

Services cannot be stored

Most service products are performance acts or experiences that exist in the present, which makes it next to impossible to store them for later sale or consumption. As in most marketing assertions, there are exceptions to the rule; some service activities can be stored in electronic form for later use, while other service products, such as a music concert or speech, can be recorded.

William Chitty

In general, however, when hotel rooms are unoccupied or aircraft seats are not sold, it is difficult to make up for the lost opportunity of having no customer demand—the inseparability of service and consumer does not allow the service to be rented. Although the staff and physical facilities may be available to create the service, these staff and facilities represent the service organisation's productive capacity, not accommodation or air travel themselves. Perishability is therefore a consequence of inseparability.[26] Similarly, a service cannot be returned after it has been purchased. For example, after customers have used a service such as making a mobile phone call, the service cannot be returned to the vendor in the same way that a physical product can be returned to the retailer.

Intangible elements create the value proposition

The core element of most services is produced by the interaction between customers and service organisations' physical facilities, such as hotel rooms, aircraft seats and mobile phones. It is the intangible elements associated with how the service is provided, such as the process of checking into a hotel, the online booking system for a flight or the expertise of the technical staff of a mobile phone company, that put value into the service experience and in turn create customer satisfaction. The intangibility of those elements makes it difficult for customers to assess the quality of the service, and to evaluate competing service organisations, prior to the service interaction. That means that there may be risk in purchasing a high-involvement service because it cannot be returned or replaced if the customer is not satisfied.

Services are more difficult to evaluate

Compared to products, services are more difficult to evaluate because service organisations generally provide few tangible product cues. The ease of evaluating goods and services depends to a large extent on three product characteristics: the search, experience and credence dimensions.[27]

The search dimensions of a product are the tangible attributes that allow consumers to try, taste or assess the product before purchase. Services tend to have few search dimensions. Most physical goods can be physically evaluated on the basis of their search characteristics, which helps to reduce any risk associated with their purchase. But search dimensions are not automatically excluded from services. Consumers can assess some service attributes in terms of price, while other services, such as health clubs, can be evaluated by a brief trial of the facilities.

The experience dimensions are those product characteristics that can only be evaluated during and after performance of the service processes. Consumers must experience a concert, tennis match or holiday resort before they can judge the excellence or otherwise of those services. Marketing communications can describe a holiday resort, but consumers need to experience the joy of sailing a catamaran or dining on exotic meals in order to

↘
search dimensions
The tangible attributes that allow consumers to try, taste or assess a product before purchase

↘
experience dimensions
The product characteristics that can only be evaluated during and after performance of the service processes

feel the effects of those activities. Even friends may not be able to describe their holiday experiences accurately, because different people do not respond to a similar event in the same way.

In some cases, even after the purchase and consumption of a service, consumers are unable to evaluate the service experience because the nature of the service requires that they trust the service provider to perform certain expected tasks. When the consumers cannot evaluate the outcome, they must rely on the service provider to provide the expected benefits and these form the credence dimensions of a service. Successful service organisations that provide high-credence services rely on developing trusting relationships to engender consumer confidence in their skills. For example, if a customer has a problem with their motor vehicle but they have limited mechanical knowledge, it is not easy for them to determine whether the motor mechanic has fixed the problem; they must trust the mechanic to fix the problem.

↘
credence dimensions
The product characteristics that require consumers to trust the service provider to perform certain expected tasks or provide expected benefits

A traditional view of service value

The key to understanding services is to compare the similarities that service organisations share with manufacturers, and to contrast the manufacturing differences that services have with other forms of production.[28] The traditional approach to determining value for customers grew from a manufacturing perspective that viewed value as an integral part of the organisation's production process; that is, customer value was seen as the result of an exchange between customers and the organisation. An alternative approach to understanding customer value has evolved from the idea that value is co-created by customers when they interact with an organisation's value-generating processes to satisfy their needs, wants and expectations, rather than merely receiving a standardised value from the service process.[29]

The service-dominant logic view of value

Service-dominant logic (S-D logic) was first proposed by Vargo and Lusch (2004) and is a relatively new approach to understanding how customers determine the value of a service. The fundamental proposition of S-D logic is that consumers are primarily concerned with the competencies (knowledge and skills) of the marketing organisation in providing the promised form of value to the customer.[30] To better understand the principles of S-D logic, its fundamental proposition can be contrasted with the business systems that traditionally existed in industrial firms. Vargo and Lusch (2004) refer to those systems as G-D (goods-dominant) and suggest that G-D logic is built on the expectation that economic value is added by industrial processes that produce goods that create some form of value-in-exchange.[31]

The S-D logic approach proposes that a knowledge-based interaction between a customer and a supplier is the provision of a service. According to S-D logic, organisations provide services and customers assess the value of the interactions with suppliers as well as the interactions with the services they purchase. A distinction is made between *operand resources*, which are usually tangible, static resources that require some action to make them valuable, and *operant resources*, which are usually intangible and are the dynamic resources that are capable of creating value (have four defining characteristics: services are intangible, inseparable, variable and perishable). Whereas the emphasis is on operand resources under G-D logic, from an S-D logic perspective operant resources are necessary for competitive advantage.[32]

These approaches to understanding customer-generated value are not mutually exclusive; effectively marketing a service requires knowing both the what and how of a service. The what refers to the production process that is the end result, while the how is a customer's evaluation of the service interaction that has created value. Value then is created throughout the service interaction where the focus is on value in use, rather than on the production process.[33]

Customers usually co-produce the service product

A list of the common differences between goods and services is shown in Table 1.3. The service characteristic of inseparability, by definition, requires customers to at least be present during a service interaction. In fact, some services require customers to be involved in the service process to co-produce the desired outcome. For example, to achieve desirable education results, students must interact with their tutors and the subject learning materials to co-create the desired level of knowledge. The same is true of many service providers, such as hairdressers and dentists, even taxi drivers taking customers to their destinations. Advances in computer-based service applications have to a large extent increased customers' acceptance of self-service technology. That technology has made it easier for customers to co-produce the service they want; they use ATMs to conduct simple banking transactions rather than going into a bank branch, they use self-service kiosks in airports to check in for their flights and they download apps from the internet for their mobile phones.

In terms of efficiency, self-service technology offers service organisations the benefits of being able to offer their service 24/7, often at lower operating costs, and customers gain the benefits of saving time on routine tasks and at convenient locations.

Maintaining service quality can be a problem

The variability and inseparability of services, coupled with the effects of other customers in the service process, influence the quality of the overall service experience. Each interaction has a different level of quality compared to previous performances because of the differing levels of customer involvement. It is difficult to apply consistent quality standards to each

Table 1.3   Common differences between goods and services

Difference	Marketing implications	Marketing tasks
Most service products cannot be stored.	Customers may not be served or may have to wait.	Balance supply with demand using pricing, queues or reservations.
Intangible elements of the service dominate value creation.	Intangible elements are hard to evaluate; it is more difficult to distinguish service providers from competitors.	Emphasise tangible elements and use concrete images in marketing communications.
Services can be difficult to visualise and understand.	Customers may be more uncertain and perceive greater risk in purchasing a service.	Explain the benefits of the service; offer service guarantees.
Customers may be involved in co-production.	Customers interact with processes and providers in producing the service.	Design user-friendly processes and physical facilities; provide customer support services.
Other people may be part of the service interaction.	Service providers and other customers shape the service experience and the customer's satisfaction.	Shape customers' behaviour.
Operational processes tend to vary between service organisations.	It is harder to maintain service consistency and reliability; service recovery strategies are important in maintaining customer satisfaction.	Design service processes to maintain quality; design service recovery procedures.
Temporal factors are often important to customers.	Customers dislike having to wait— they believe time spent in queues is a waste.	Develop processes that minimise waiting times; offer extended service hours.
Distribution often occurs through non-physical channels.	Information-based services can be delivered through electronic channels.	Offer safe and reliable electronic channels.

Source: C. Lovelock & J. Wirtz (2007). *Services Marketing: People, Technology, Strategy* (6th edn). Upper Saddle River, NJ: Pearson Education, p. 17.

service interaction because customer expectations vary, and the appearance, actions and personality of employees can also influence customers' perceptions of the service performance. Delivering a high-quality service is an important corporate objective because improvements in customers' perceptions of service quality have been shown to increase the likelihood of repeat purchase behaviour, consumer willingness to pay a price premium for a quality service, and lower marketing and administrative costs.[34]

Delivering service quality for hospital patients

Services in Action

Delivering service quality is a basic requirement for any business, but it is essential for the viability of service industries such as banking and finance that have built their reputations on the delivery of outstanding customer experience. Traditionally, however, that service philosophy has not applied to hospitals or health systems. While the core service of a hospital—its medical and surgical

William Chitty

expertise—is usually satisfactory, it is the peripheral hospital service interactions that are often below patients' expectations. Managing customers' expectations plays a critical role in understanding their evaluations of service quality. Hospital 'customers' are very different from those in any other service industry for one important reason—they don't want to be there. From their previous experience of a hospital service interaction, hospital patients develop an expectation that, because healthcare is a necessity, they will not receive a superior patient experience.[35]

A focus on patients should be the most important aspect in delivering healthcare services because a patient's hospital experience can be an easily understood service-differentiator for hospitals. Customers in other service industries can vote with their wallets; if they don't like a bank's service, they can transfer their business to another bank. For many hospitals, however, the quality of a patient's service experience is about keeping their patients satisfied.

What does quality customer service provided by a hospital actually look like? The answer is really not that different from that for any other service industry because it hinges on two concepts— attention and communication—both of which can be enhanced by the use of ICT. The new Fiona Stanley Hospital (FSH) in Perth (see Figure 1.10) is one of the most technologically advanced hospitals in Australia and uses the latest ICT systems to deliver new levels of patient care and convenience—from streamlining admission, discharge, bookings and record-keeping to providing video links

Figure 1.10 Fiona Stanley Hospital in Perth, WA

Source: Magellan Power. <http://magellanpower.com. au/Projects/Fiona-Stanley-Hospital>.

for doctors and patients, and the bedside entertainment systems.

For the FSH healthcare providers, that means everything they need to know about a patient can be accessed at the patient's bedside on a single screen—patient records, x-rays, scans, medication management and other vital medical information—while for patients, that screen delivers television, movies and the internet to their bed—as well as giving them the ability to make video-calls to family and friends outside the hospital. Both those service functions provide greater convenience for patients and staff, and help to deliver higher levels of a quality hospital service.[36]

Although data for customer satisfaction with FSH is limited, a report commissioned by the Australian Government in 2012 found that most public and some private hospitals are using a combination of patient experience and satisfaction questions to survey patients' satisfaction with their services.[37]

Patient satisfaction

Patient satisfaction surveys are different from other sources of hospital quality data, because they provide information on hospital services from the patient's perspective. Such surveys can be useful for obtaining information on patient views of both clinical and non-clinical hospital care (such as whether patients feel they were treated with respect and provided with appropriate information regarding their treatment).

A report on government services found that, on average, the satisfaction ratings of patients who were treated in public hospitals in 2015–16 were above 80 per cent, with satisfaction generally higher in relation to nurses than doctors/specialists.[38] Table 1.4 indicates the levels of patient satisfaction with public hospitals in Western Australia and Australia, and these can be used surrogate indicators for the satisfaction of the patients of FSH, which began operation in 2014.

Table 1.4   Patient satisfaction in public hospitals 2015–16

	Western Australia	Australia
Emergency department patients		
Proportion of people who went to an emergency department in the last 12 months reporting the emergency department doctors, specialists or nurses always or often listened carefully to them.		
Doctors or specialists	90.0	87.0
Nurses	91.2	90.3
Proportion of people who went to an emergency department in the last 12 months reporting the emergency department doctors, specialists or nurses always or often showed respect to them.		
Doctors or specialists	88.7	88.3
Nurses	91.4	91.5
Proportion of people who went to an emergency department in the last 12 months reporting the emergency department doctors, specialists or nurses always or often spent enough time with them.		
Doctors or specialists	86.7	83.6
Nurses	90.4	87.1
Admitted hospital patients		
Proportion of people who were admitted to hospital in the last 12 months reporting the hospital doctors, specialists or nurses always or often listened carefully to them.		
Doctors or specialists	93.2	92.2
Nurses	94.3	92.0
Proportion of people who were admitted to hospital in the last 12 months reporting the hospital doctors, specialists or nurses always or often showed respect to them.		
Doctors or specialists	94.1	92.5
Nurses	94.3	92.6
Proportion of people who were admitted to hospital in the last 12 months reporting the hospital doctors, specialists or nurses always or often spent enough time with them.		
Doctors or specialists	89.3	88.9
Nurses	91.0	90.2

Source: ABS *Patient experience survey 2015–16* (unpublished).

Time influences customers' perceptions of value

Many services can only be performed when customers are physically involved in the service interaction, and that process takes time to deliver the service. There is a general perception among consumers that they should not have time to waste on non-productive tasks and that wasted time is a cost they should avoid. Consumers have been promised that services will be available to them when they want them, rather than when the service organisation can provide them, which has had a ratchet effect on their expectations. For example, when one organisation can offer its services 24/7, competitors will usually follow.

Customers' perceptions of value may also be influenced by their service experiences. If they have used the service previously, they will already have formed expectations about the length of time the service should take. Successful service organisations tend to adopt strategies that minimise customer waiting time by using self-service technology or queuing systems, or simply by taking reservations. There are, of course, some very simple things that organisations can do to minimise customers' perceptions of waiting times—for example, distracting them with televisions tuned to sporting events or placing large mirrors in areas where customers congregate, such as lift lobbies.

Distributing a service product tends to use non-physical channels

Tangible goods manufacturers need physical distribution channels to move their products through intermediaries from the factory to the retailer's store. Distributing a service, however, can be achieved using electronic channels such as the internet. The internet is changing the distribution systems of different types of information-based services.

There are core services that satisfy customers' primary needs, and there are supplementary services that facilitate the purchase of physical products.[39] Core services, for example, include the online external study programs offered by universities, while airlines such as Qantas use online supplementary services to enable their customers to access flight schedules and fares, and book flights on their websites.

Customers and the service experience

A service experience is the culmination of a series of interactions undertaken by both the service provider and the customer, and includes the interactions associated with producing and using both the core and supplementary services. Customer service is, however, not only offered by service organisations. The role of customer service is to directly support an organisation's core product, which may be a tangible good or a service. Computer manufacturers offer online customer service but their core product is a physical good and, while long-distance railways provide customer service, their core product is rail transport.

Service interactions, together with the outcomes from a service transaction, form the customer experience, which should satisfy customers' needs, wants and expectations. Service interactions can take different forms according to their duration and complexity.

Types of service interactions

Service interactions cover a range of interactions between customers and various service organisations. The four types of service interactions are based on their *duration* and *complexity* and range from straightforward single activities, such as using a mobile phone service, to more complex, continuous activities such as managing financial contracts. The four types of service interactions are shown in Figure 1.11.

Figure 1.11   Four types of service interactions

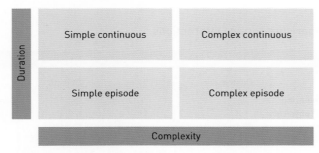

Source: J.R. McColl-Kennedy (2003). *Services Marketing: A Managerial Approach*. Milton, Qld: John Wiley & Sons Australia, p. 5.

Categorising service interactions

Identifying the core service is the most difficult part of categorising a service interaction. In many cases, because customers can touch and see the physical facilities that deliver the service, they assume that those tangible elements of the service interactions are the service.

The physical elements associated with a service facilitate those core activities that satisfy customers' needs. For example, when customers use their mobile phones to call a friend, they generally do not consider the processes and equipment that are involved in transmitting their phone call—they select the required number in their handsets and, when their friend answers, they begin a conversation. The core service in this case is their ability to access the mobile telecommunications network in most locations when they want, wherever they are using the handset—which is a tangible element of the service. After the conversation, they will have experienced the core service, which was an intangible service activity that satisfied their need to contact their friend.

William Chitty

There are several aspects of service activities that should be considered when categorising services, because the service providers, processes and physical facilities that form the delivery system are what create the service experience and transfer value to customers. The types of service processes that create a service experience depend to a large extent on the nature of the service and on where, and to whom, that service is directed.

From the customer's perspective, the form of a service interaction is dependent on two principal factors:

1 the degree of involvement—the personal relevance—of the service interaction, the importance of which is determined by whether customers, or their possessions, are the recipient of the service

2 the extent to which the service interaction is influenced by the tangible elements of the service, including any service employees of the organisational provider.

Figure 1.12 shows the four primary categories of interactive service interactions: services requiring customers' physical presence; services performed on customers' possessions; services involving customers' minds; and services performed on customers' intangible assets.[40]

Figure 1.12 Categorising service interactions

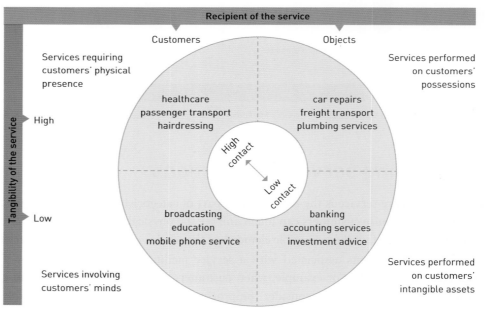

Source: A. Palmer (1994). *Principles of Services Marketing* (6th edn). Berkshire, UK: McGraw-Hill, pp. 150–2.

Services requiring customers' physical presence

Service interactions that require the physical presence of customers, where the customers are the direct recipients of the service, are high-contact interactions with a high degree of tangibility. For example, healthcare, passenger transport and hairdressing services require customers to be physically present to co-produce the service products, because the customers are an integral part of service. Customers must actively participate in the service production process. If a customer wants to have their hair cut and styled, they must cooperate with the hairdresser by saying what they want done and then sitting in a chair while their hair is cut and styled.

Close physical contact between customers and service employees has a number of implications for the type of service interaction. Quality control—which is an integral part of a customer's service experience—is an important factor for high-contact services because the service performance can be variable and the customer is a co-producer of the end result. A one-on-one type of service interaction often makes it difficult for customers to evaluate service quality before consuming the service. The location of the service provider is also important, because consumers may not be prepared to travel a great distance merely to have their hair cut.

From the service provider's perspective, that kind of interaction can present problems in managing the service processes, because any delays in the process can adversely influence the outcome and have an unfavourable impact on customer satisfaction.

Services performed on customers' possessions

In this type of service interaction, the service is performed on customers' possessions rather than on the customers themselves. Many of these activities are production-type services that involve simultaneous production and consumption. When a customer's possession requires servicing, the customer does not become directly involved in the process because the procedure does not require the customer's presence. In most situations where the service is performed on customers' possessions, the customer's involvement is, as in the example just cited, limited to dropping their car off at the motor mechanic's workshop, explaining the problems and returning later to pick up the vehicle and pay the bill.

The process of fixing the car, which is the core service, may be of little concern to the customer as long as they are satisfied with the result. The interpersonal skills of the mechanic may, however, be more important than their technical skills. If the mechanic treats customers in an offhand or condescending manner, it is very likely that they will not return to that mechanic when they need to have their cars serviced again.

Services involving customers' minds

The type of service interaction that involves customers' minds, like those that are performed on customers' possessions, does not need the customers to be physically present during the interaction. Services that involve customers' minds provide intangible benefits, which means the service process can be spatially separated from the customer. These types of services, however, have the power to change attitudes and influence consumers' behaviour. For example, marketing communications that are transmitted via traditional broadcast media such as television do not require the viewers to physically engage with the message, but the marketing messages can persuade them to purchase the service in question.

William Chitty

The core element in this type of service interaction is information, which can be stored, packaged and then marketed in much the same way as a tangible good. In this way, services that are directed at consumers' minds can be stored for later use, rather than being produced and consumed simultaneously. The extent of customer involvement in the production of information services has traditionally been based on face-to-face interactions. The widespread use of ICT to distribute some services, like distance education for example, has removed the need for regular face-to-face interactions with service providers.

Services performed on customers' intangible assets

Services that are performed on customers' intangible assets are similar to services that involve the customer's mind: both are dependent on the effective collection and storage of information. For such interactions, there are few tangible elements in the production and consumption process, and that means the customer does not need to be present for the service process to take place. A major part of the service process for customers does not require any direct contact with the service provider.

Marketing the four types of service interactions

Marketing of services is about providing service products that satisfy customers' needs, wants and expectations more effectively and efficiently than those of other service organisations. The marketing strategies for services encompass the seven elements of the marketing mix that are used to build long-term relationships between the service organisation and its customers.

An examination of the different categories of service interactions, which included both how the service is produced and the end product, has highlighted some of the similarities between the four categories. The extent of customers' involvement in co-producing a service depends on the type of service, and varies according to whether customers want to be served face to face or prefer to use self-service facilities. Customer behaviour also changes according to where and when customers interact with a service provider, and whether or not they need to be present and actively participate in the service process.

The widely accepted use of ICT for many services has removed the need for customers to be involved in the production of those services, which has increased the value of those services by providing time-saving benefits and convenience.

OXFORD UNIVERSITY PRESS

A service product is an activity or a performance that has four general characteristics. It is intangible, which makes it difficult for consumers to readily evaluate the product before purchase. It is inseparable, which means that the customer and the provider both produce the service together. It is variable in that, since no two persons are identical, customers and service personnel are not the same, which means customers' perceptions of value and satisfaction will vary from one service interaction to another. It is perishable because it cannot be stored for later consumption.

Service transactions consist of tangible and intangible actions. When customers have their cars serviced by a motor mechanic, it is the tangible actions of the mechanic that are directed at their cars. Intangible actions associated with service transactions can be directed towards consumers' minds, which is the case with marketing communication messages, or those actions can be directed towards intangible things, such as accounting and financial services.

When service organisations consider how they can deliver their services to customers, they need to resolve whether their customers should come to the organisation's premises, or the service should go to the customers. Sometimes service transactions can be conducted at some distance using electronic channels such as the internet, which provides added value to customers by offering convenience and saving time.

Professional services, such as medical care, are provided to meet individual customer's needs, while other services, such as taxation advice from an accountant, is standardised as per Australian taxation law and is very similar for every customer.

An important marketing consideration is whether to offer all customers the same service, or whether the service organisation should adapt the service attributes and service-delivery processes to individual needs and wants. Those decisions involve understanding the nature of the service, customer expectations and preferences, and the costs associated with customising the service.

The duration of the service relationship can be either discrete—involving a single interaction—or continuous—based on multiple interactions between a customer and a service provider. The customer experience provided by the service process will, to a large degree, be the result of the interactions between people, service processes and physical facilities. The inseparability of service interactions suggests that different types of processes will produce different levels of customer involvement and result in the processes being perceived as either high-contact or low-contact services.

Customer service is a critical element of a service product that involves interactions with customers; it is not, however, sold by an organisation. Customer service is not limited to service products; car manufacturers, for example, offer customer service in the form of guarantees and roadside assistance. Whatever its application, a service should be designed, performed and communicated with two goals in mind: customer satisfaction and operational efficiency.

Australia's service markets have developed under the influence of political/regulatory, economic, social and technological changes. Those macro environmental forces are changing the way that service organisations compete and reshaping consumers' buying behaviour. The telecommunications, airline and banking service markets, for example, have been deregulated and opened to competition, requiring them to offer services that satisfy their customers. Long-term socio-demographic changes are being driven by an ageing population needing a greater number of services, limited by the decreasing proportion of working-age people.

The challenges of marketing services are tied to understanding the differences between goods and services. In addition, service marketers must be aware of the two important elements of service processes: complexity and divergence. Complexity is the number and intricacy of steps, or activities, that are required to deliver a service, while divergence relates to the degree of variability that is allowed in each step of the process. While the various categories of services suggest that they often share many common characteristics, it is important to understand that not all services fit standard industry classifications.

Review questions

1 After re-reading the anti-smoking vignette at the beginning of the chapter, outline the reasons that you think that the approach taken by Quit Victoria will, or will not, encourage smokers to quit.
2 What are the most influential factors that have an impact on the success, or otherwise, of Australian service industries?
3 Re-read the Industry Insight, 'Australia leads the world in adopting mobile banking', and suggest the reasons that more Australian customers have adopted online technology to satisfy their online banking needs, wants and expectations than bank customers in other developed economies.
4 Which of the four defining characteristics of a service product plays the greatest role in consumers' decision-making when they are considering the purchase of a service?
5 Explain the differences between goods and services by comparing a physical product, such as hair shampoo, with a service, like an airline ticket offered by a low-cost carrier such as Jetstar.
6 Using examples, explain the differences between service products, service interactions and customer service.
7 Explain the differences between the search, experience and credence dimensions of three different services.
8 Consider a service process that you have recently experienced. Explain how the service provider applied each of the seven Ps in the marketing mix for services to your service interaction.

Further reading

In addition to the specific references in the notes at the end of this chapter, the following references are included to enable you to increase your understanding of services marketing.

Bitner M. J. (1992). 'Servicescapes: The impact of physical surroundings on customers and employees'. *Journal of Marketing*, 56(April), 57–71.

Butcher, K., Sparks B. & O'Callaghan, F. (2003). 'Beyond core service'. *Psychology and Marketing*, 20(3), 187–208.

Heinonen, K., Strandvik T., Mickelsson K.-J., Edvardsson B., Sundström E. & Andersson, P. (2010). 'A customer-dominant logic of service'. *Journal of Service Management*, 21(4), 531–48.

McDougall, G. & Snetsinger, D. (1990). 'The intangibility of services: Measurement and competitive perspectives'. *Journal of Services Marketing*, 4(4), 27–40.

Mitra, K., Reiss M. & Capella, L. (1999). 'An examination of perceived risk, information search and behavioural intentions in search, experience and credence services'. *Journal of Services Marketing*, 13(3), 208–28.

Swan, J., Bowers M. & Grover R. (2002). 'Customer involvement in the selection of service specifications'. *Journal of Services Marketing*, 16(1), 88–103.

Vargo, S. L. & Lusch, R. F. (2006). Service-dominant logic: What it is, what it is not, what it might be. In R.F. Lusch & S.L. Vargo (eds), *The Service-Dominant Logic of Marketing: Dialog, Debate, and Directions* (pp. 43–56). Armonk, NY: M.E. Shape.

Vargo, S. L. & Lusch, R. F. (2008). 'Service-dominant logic: Continuing the evolution'. *Journal of the Academy of Marketing Science*, 36(1), 1–10.

Endnotes

1 R. Tilley (2014). Campaign: Identifying smoking triggers. 10 September. <www.bandt.com.au/marketing/campaign-identifying-smoking-triggers?utm_source=*|LIST_LIST_LIST_NAME|*&utm_campaign=93089ce43b-Newsletter_September_10_09_14&utm_medium=email>.

2 M.M. Scollo & M.H. Winstanley (2016). *Tobacco in Australia: Facts and Issues*. Chapter 14.4, Examining the effectiveness of public education campaigns. Melbourne: Cancer Council Victoria. <www.tobaccoinaustralia.org.au/chapter-14-social-marketing>.

3 Quit Victoria (2014). Top smoking triggers revealed as Quit launches new animated campaign. <www.cancervic.org.au/about/media-releases/2014-media-releases/august-2014/top-smoking-triggers-revealed.html>.

4 Quit Victoria (2014). Recognising your triggers. <www.quit.org.au/staying-quit/triggers>.

5 ibid.

6 Based on Australian Competition and Consumer Commission (2016). Australians lose over $229 million to scams in 2015. Scamwatch, 16 May. <www.scamwatch.gov.au/news/australians-lose-over-229-million-to-scams-in-2015>.

7 Department of Industry, Innovation and Science (2015). *Australian Industry Report*. December. Canberra, p. 3.

8 ibid.

9 D. Uren (2017). Treasury, RBA bank on growth in services. *The Australian*, 11 September, pp. 17, 23.

10 ibid.

11 Austrade (2015). *Why Australia? Benchmark Report 2015*. 12 January. Canberra: Australian Trade and Investment Commission. <http://apo.org.au/node/58787>.

12 Department of Education and Training (2017). Export income to Australia from international education activity in 2016–17. Research snapshot, December. Canberra, ACT: DET. <https://internationaleducation.gov.au/research/Research-Snapshots/Documents/Export%20Income%20FY2016%E2%80%9317.pdf>.

13 Department of Foreign Affairs and Trade (2017). Singapore–Australia Free Trade Agreement. <www.dfat.gov.au/fta/safta>.

14 Department of Foreign Affairs and Trade (2016). *Trade in Services 2015*. August. p. 7. Data based on ABS catalogue 5368.0.

15 Australian Bureau of Statistics (2014). Australia's birth rate falls, but older mothers buck the trend. Media release 148/2014.

16 Trading Economics (2017). Australia population forecast. <www.tradingeconomics.com/australia/population/forecast>.

17 ibid.

18 M.J. Bitner, S.W. Brown & M.L. Meuter (2000). Technology infusion in service encounters. *Journal of the Academy of Marketing Science*, 28(Winter), 10–11.

19 Based on C. Yeates (2015). Australia leads the world in mobile banking. *Sydney Morning Herald*, 15 June. <www.smh.com.au/business/banking-and-finance/australia-leads-the-world-in-mobile-banking-20150614-ghngd5.html>.

20 Telsyte (2017). IoT@Home market set to soar with more than 300 million devices in Australian homes by 2021. 9 May.

21 W. Chitty, E. Luck, N. Barker, M. Valos & T. Shimp (2015). *Integrated Marketing Communications* (5th edn). Melbourne, Vic.: Cengage Learning Australia.

22 G.L. Shostack (1987). Service positioning through structural change. *Journal of Marketing*, 51(January), 34–43.

23 ibid.

24 L.L. Berry (1980). Services marketing is different. *Business*, 30(May–June), 24–9.

25 G.L. Shostack (1977). Breaking free from product marketing. *Journal of Marketing*, 41(April), 73–80.

26 L. McGuire (1999). *Australian Services Marketing and Management*. Melbourne, Vic.: Macmillan Education Australia, p. 61.

27 V.A. Zeithaml (1981). How consumer valuation processes differ between goods and services. In J.H. Donnelly & W.R. George (eds), *Marketing of Services*. Chicago, IL: AMA, pp.186–90.

28 J. Howells (2004). Innovation consumption and services: Encapsulation and the combinational role of services. *Services Industry Journal*, 24(1), 19–36.

29 C. Grönroos (2008). Service logic revisited: Who creates value? And who co-creates? *European Business Review*, 20(4), 298–314.

30 S.L. Vargo & R.F. Lusch (2004). Evolving to a new dominant logic for marketing. *Journal of Marketing*, 68, 1–17.

31 ibid.

32 C. Kowalkowski (2010). What does a service-dominant logic really mean for manufacturing firms? *CIRP Journal of Manufacturing Science and Technology*, 3(4), 285–92.

33 C. Grönroos (2007). *Service Management and Marketing: Customer Management in Service Competition*. West Sussex, UK: John Wiley & Sons, p. 27.

34 V.A. Zeithaml (2000). Service quality, profitability, and the economic worth of customers: What we know and what we need to learn. *Journal of the Academy of Marketing Science*, 28(1), 67–85.

35 J. Merlino (2013). Why customer service matters in the healthcare industry. 7 August. <http://finance.yahoo.com/blogs/the-exchange/why-customer-matters-healthcare-industry-214727535.html>.

36 Government of Western Australia, South Metropolitan Health Service, Fiona Stanley Hospital. <www.fsh.health.wa.gov.au>.

37 Australian Commission on Safety and Quality in Health Care (2012). *Review of Patient Experience and Satisfaction Surveys Conducted within Public and Private Hospitals in Australia*. 5 May Sydney, NSW. <www.safetyandquality.gov.au/wp-content/uploads/2012/03/Review-of-Hospital-Patient-Experience-Surveys-conducted-by-Australian-Hospitals-30-March-2012-FINAL.pdf>.

38 Productivity Commission (2017). *Report on Government Services 2017.* Volume E, Chapter 12, Public hospitals.

39 C. Lovelock, P. Patterson & R. Walker (2007). *Services Marketing: An Asia–Pacific and Australian Perspective* (4th edn). Frenchs Forest, NSW: Pearson Education Australia, p. 19.

40 A. Palmer (1994). *Principles of Services Marketing* (6th edn). Berkshire, UK: McGraw-Hill, pp. 150–2.

Chapter 1 An Overview of Services Marketing

Market segmentation using geo-demographic variables

geoTribes[R] segmentation is a recently developed method of segmenting consumer behaviour using a segmentation system that is based on the various stages of consumers' life cycles and socio-economic status to define their differing needs and behaviours.[1] geoTribes[R] segmentation is a spatial modelling and database tagging process that combines the various stages of consumer lifecycles with socioeconomic status by modelling demographic data from the Australian Census and survey microdata sourced from the Australian Bureau of Statistics (ABS). The results of this segmentation process are shown in Figure 2.1.

Unlike the typical household-level segmentation process, geoTribes[R] uses consumers' addresses and their actual ages to create archetypes that define market segments according to their socio-economic status as one of 15 life-cycle stages. That means the methodology can be used to segment markets regardless of neighbourhood differences.

The 15 archetypes of geoTribes[R] segmentation are defined as follows:

T1 Rockafellas—affluent, mature families who want exclusivity, genuine status and quality

T2 Achievers—ambitious younger and middle-aged families who want accessible status and memorable experiences that show they are successful

T3 Fortunats—financially secure retirees and pre-retirees who want comfortable lives while enjoying sophisticated, quality experiences

T4 Crusaders—career-oriented professional singles and couples who want fashionably branded products and experiences

T5 Preppies—the mature children of affluent parents who want great lives, to be high in the popularity stakes and to experience safe rebellion

» continued over page

Chapter

2

Market Segmentation and Service Positioning

William Chitty

Figure 2.1   The archetypes of geoTribes[R] segmentation

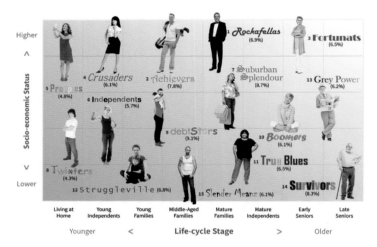

Source: RDA Research. <https://rdaresearch.com/geotribes>.

T6 Independents—young singles and couples who like having fun and work to get ahead; they want affordable products and experiences

T7 Suburban Splendour—middle-class, mature families who want to fit into suburban lifestyles and participate in local events like sports and hobbies

T8 Twixters—mature children still living at home who enjoy life with their friends and want affordable experiences

T9 Debt Stars—financially extended younger families who are coming to grips with family responsibilities; they purchase affordable, mass-status products

T10 Boomers—white-collar post-family pre-retirees who are conserving the best things in life; they are more than a little cynical

T11 True Blues—blue-collar mature families and pre-retiree singles who are realistic accepters of life; they want traditional values in a genuine community

T12 Struggleville—struggling young and middle-aged families who push ahead with life—often on government assistance; they want low-cost products and experiences

T13 Grey Power—better-off retirees who are ageing comfortably; they want the familiar basics together with financial security

T14 Survivors—retirees living on minimal incomes; they are holding onto what they can and want traditional basic products

T15 Slender Meanz—those people living in underprivileged circumstances; they are living on the edge and live for now

The clustering assigns a single segment code to each neighbourhood representing a highly condensed summary of its defining population characteristics, capturing the essential differences in lifestyles, purchasing motivations and household expenditure.

Introduction

To successfully market their services, service organisations must develop marketing strategies that reach the actual—and potential—buyers of those services. Based on market analysis, service marketers must, however, also consider how they can successfully compete against many competitors, rather than trying to control the total market. That requires each service provider to identify those groups of consumers that it can serve best: by satisfying the unique needs, wants and expectations of broadly defined groups of buyers who may differ in their buying behaviour.

The first section of this chapter examines the segmentation, targeting and positioning (STP) model, as shown in Figure 2.2. The STP model is a strategic approach that prioritises service-value propositions, which are then used to develop effective marketing communications to target the different needs, wants and expectations of the identified customer segments.

Figure 2.2 The segmentation, targeting and positioning model

The STP approach also builds commercial effectiveness by selecting the most valuable segments for a service organisation and then developing a marketing mix and service positioning strategy for each segment. Market segmentation is the first step and covers why marketers, when segmenting a service market, must identify the characteristics of the various consumer groups that form the market segments for a service organisation's products.

When the characteristics of those market segments have been identified, then consumer profiles can be developed based on their comparable common variables, such as the consumers' demographics, their values and lifestyles, and their buying behaviours. These resultant market segments will also have relatively homogeneous service needs, wants and expectations, which will allow service organisations to develop marketing programs to satisfy their customers' specific service requirements.

The second section of this chapter discusses how market segmentation provides the basis for establishing and communicating a distinctive service brand, and the attributes and benefits of the organisation's service product; that is, the service elements—the attributes and benefits—that consumers use to position a service. Positioning relates to how the target market customers perceive the elements of a service brand, and how they

market segmentation
A marketing approach for evaluating a market; it is typically based on demographics, values and lifestyles, and behavioural variables, so that service marketing strategies can effectively target one or more groups of consumers who form a market segment for a service organisation's products

positioning
The key idea that relates to a customer's unique perceptions about the brand, attributes and benefits of a service, and how these service elements are evaluated and compared with those of competing service organisations

then evaluate and distinguish those service elements against competing service products. The challenge for service organisations is to identify the service elements that their target market consumers value, and then to align those service elements with the organisation's other marketing strengths.

Learning objectives

After reading this chapter you should be able to:

↘ profile the target market for a service by identifying the relevant consumer variables

↘ evaluate the market segments for a service product

↘ select the different targeting strategies for various segments

↘ describe the role of positioning in service marketing and explain how different positioning strategies can be used to position service brands.

Market segmentation stage 1: Profile the target market

The first stage in segmenting a market is to identify those consumer variables that can best segment the market for a particular service product. An important point to remember is that there is no one way that will guarantee the best results when segmenting a market. The relevant consumer variables that can used to profile and segment the target market into relatively homogeneous consumer groups, based on their needs, wants and expectations, are the consumers' *demographics*, their *values and lifestyles*, their *buying behaviour* and sometimes their *geographical location*.

Demographic segmentation

Demographic segmentation divides consumers into homogeneous groups based on variables such as age, gender, income, family life cycle, income, occupation, education, religion and nationality.

The Australian population numbers, age structure and gender split are shown in Table 2.1.

The age structure of a population affects a nation's key socio-economic issues. Countries with young populations—with a high percentage under age 15—need to invest more resources in schools, while countries with older populations—with a high percentage of people aged 65 and over—need to invest more in the health sector. The age structure can also be used to help predict potential political issues. For example, the rapid growth of a young adult population unable to find employment can lead to social unrest.[2]

↘ **demographics**
Objective variables such as age, gender, income and family structure, as distinct from values and lifestyles, used to segment consumers

OXFORD UNIVERSITY PRESS

Table 2.1 Demographic segmentation of the Australian population

	Percentage of population	Male (millions)	Female (millions)
0–14 years	17.84	2.105	1.997
15–24 years	12.96	1.528	1.451
25–54 years	41.55	4.862	4.691
55–64 years	11.82	1.347	1.369
65+ years	15.1	1.569	1.829

Source: Index Mundi. Australia age structure. Sourced from *CIA World Factbook*. <www.indexmundi.com/australia/age_structure.html>.

Population pyramid

As shown in Figure 2.3, a population pyramid depicts the age structure, numbers and gender split of the population of a country, and may provide insight into its economic development. The shape of the population pyramid gradually evolves over time based on national fertility, mortality and international immigration trends.

Between 1996 and 2016, the proportion of Australia's population aged 15–64 years remained fairly stable, decreasing only from 66.6 per cent to 65.9 per cent of the total population. During the same period, the proportion of people aged 65 years and over increased from 12 per cent to 15.3 per cent, and the proportion of people aged 85 years and over almost doubled, from 1.1 per cent of the total population in 1996 to 2 per cent in 2016. Conversely, the proportion aged less than 15 years decreased from 21.4 per cent to 18.8 per cent.[3]

Figure 2.3 Australian population, age and gender, 1996–2016

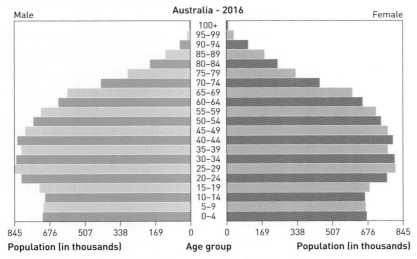

Source: Index Mundi. Population pyramid. Sourced from *CIA World Factbook*. Last updated 9 July 2017. <www.indexmundi.com/australia/age_structure.html>.

William Chitty

For an example of how the demographic variables associated with segmentation can be applied, the Australian banking industry can be considered. Traditionally, the retail banks did not actively differentiate the market for their services, because all the banks' services were regulated by government legislation and consumers were less concerned with the costs of the banks' services. There was very little incentive for the banks to be competitive, because the regulatory barriers that were imposed by government effectively maintained prices and the competitive status quo.

The wide-ranging deregulation of the financial industry that began in the early 1970s changed the retail banks' consumer complacency. Competition from the entry of new banks—and restructured financial institutions—forced the established banks to adopt a customer focus in marketing their services, including segmenting and profiling their target markets. The banks traditionally segmented their markets according to customers' family life cycles. Those life cycles are:

→ *Primary school students:* Although there is very little profit in servicing this segment, there are long-term benefits in establishing banking relationships at an early age. It is difficult to promote this service because it largely depends on parents' motivation to encourage their children to save. The Commonwealth Bank was the dominant bank for this segment.

→ *Teenagers:* This segment is seen as an effective base from which to reach the more profitable adult segments. Convenience is very important to this segment, as are brand names and logos.

→ *Young professionals:* Young (mid–late twenties) urban professionals with high levels of disposable income and a propensity for conspicuous consumption are a profitable segment, but they are difficult to attract. Familiarity with new financial services often leads them to the newer banks, which, because they are smaller, offer higher levels of professional relationship marketing.

→ *DINKS:* These are 'double-income families with no kids'. This segment is similar to the young professionals in having higher levels of disposable income than families. But they are more likely to have traditional views of bank services and see them as being functional; this segment also desires excellence in customer service, together with convenience, access and value.

→ *Families:* The family segment evolves according to the age of the children and stage of home ownership. Five sub-segments have been identified:
  - *Newly married, no kids*: This group has low discretionary income; they are saving for or buying their first home; they are more family-oriented than the DINKS and have a less sophisticated lifestyle.
  - *Families with young children*: This group has low disposable incomes with high levels of household debt and is likely to use consumer credit cards for day-to-day transactions; this group will test the strength of a bank–client relationship.

- *Families with older children*: This group is better off financially because many mothers have returned to the workforce and these families are better able to service their debts; they tend to have modest savings.
- *Families with independent children*: This group has higher levels of discretionary income; their home loans are close to being finalised, and they have saving, superannuation and life assurance accounts with good balances.
- *Pre-retirement families:* At this stage, couples own their homes and have enough money to take regular overseas holidays.

→ *Retirement:* Australia's ageing population is increasing this segment, in both size and buying power. They often have substantial superannuation accounts to invest and are attracted to investment accounts that provide a regular income.

Values and lifestyle segmentation

Consumers' values and lifestyles include their activities, interests and opinions, which have a greater influence on their buying behaviour than demographics; consumer demographics do not tell marketers *why* consumers buy one service product rather than another. Traditional market segmentation used various types of demographic variables but, as markets have become more dynamic, marketers now realise that relying on demographic data generally provides insufficient information to highlight the significant differences in consumer behaviour. To effectively segment a market now requires a combination of segmentation variables. For example, Jetstar markets its domestic flights to holiday destinations aimed primarily at younger, more price-sensitive consumers (age and income are *demographic* variables) who take short breaks from work, rather than extended holidays (a *lifestyle* factor).

By using a combination of consumers' *activities, interests and opinions* (AIO), service marketers can customise their marketing messages for their service categories to encourage specific types of behaviour from particular consumer segments. For example, a service organisation that offers camping holidays in remote inland locations could examine the particular AIO that best characterise the buyers of its holidays and also those of its competition. This lifestyle information could then be used to design marketing communications and to select the most appropriate media vehicles. Table 2.2 lists examples of various AIO components of services.

Numerous market research firms conduct research for individual service organisations. That research is usually customised to the client's specific service category and includes AIO items selected on the basis of the unique characteristics of the consumers who buy and use those services. For example, a chain of hotels that caters to holidaymakers may conduct a market research study to investigate the buying behaviour of its customers using the AIO items in Table 2.2. The research would include questions on consumers' work, hobbies,

↘
values and lifestyles
Psychosocial personal variables, such as lifestyles, personality types and psychological traits, as distinct from demographics, that can be used to segment consumers

Table 2.2 AIO components of services

Activities	Interests	Opinions
Work	Family	About themselves
Hobbies	Home	Social issues
Social events	Job	Politics
Holidays	Community	Business
Entertainment	Recreation	Economics
Club membership	Fashion	Education
Community	Art	Consumer protection
Visiting museums	Media	Future
Sports	Achievement	Culture

Source: Adapted from D.I. Hawkins, R.J. Best & K.A. Coney (1995). *Consumer Behavior: Implications for Marketing Strategy* (6th edn). Chicago, IL: Irwin, p. 329. Reprinted by permission from McGraw-Hill, a division of the McGraw-Hill Companies.

entertainment and sporting activities, together with items that tap into family structures, recreation and community activities that are linked with their social, political and cultural opinions. It is likely that the findings of this research would show hotel customers have similar demographic profiles—that is, it is likely that they are approximately the same in terms of age, income and maybe gender—but they are very likely to have different values and lifestyles.

In addition to AIO research, there are other services that develop consumer profiles that are independent of any particular product or service. In Australia, the best known of these is the Roy Morgan Values Segments classification model. While demographic segmentation can often answer *who* is buying particular services, information about AIO can suggest reasons *why* consumers buy a service product, by considering their attitudes and interests.

Roy Morgan Values Segments

The Roy Morgan Values Segments model, as shown in Figure 2.4, consists of 10 values segments arranged in a two-dimensional perceptual map. The horizontal axis represents consumers' *Price Expectations, Attraction to Innovation* and *Perceived Progressiveness*, while the vertical axis represents consumers' perceptions of *Life Satisfaction, Individualism* and *Quality Expectations*.

The 10 values segments that are shown in Figure 2.4 can be summarised as follows:[4]

1   *Basic Needs* refers to respondents who are focused on getting by each day. They are often retirees, pensioners and people on welfare, and are generally content with what they have and enjoy watching the world go by. This segment has a strong sense of community and is often involved with community services such as Safety House and Neighbourhood Watch, as part of their desire for order and security in their environment.

OXFORD UNIVERSITY PRESS

2   *A Fairer Deal* represents people who feel they get a raw deal out of life. Pessimistic, cynical and often struggling financially, they think everybody else gets all the fun and they are missing out. This segment often sees escape, either with their friends and a drink or by watching television, as the only way to deal with their frustration and anger. Within this segment, there is an emphasis on physical objects and things they can do with their hands, perhaps as this is all they feel they can control.

3   *Real Conservatism* refers to the segment of consumers who are cautious about new things and ideas, and have a central concern about maintaining a disciplined, predictable and safe society. They hold very conservative social, moral and ethical values, and generally feel that things are not as good as they used to be. This segment is willing to pay more for services that they perceive to offer consistent value and quality, and are particularly attracted to familiar, well-established brands.

4   *Look At Me* refers to a group of people who are associated with rebellion against the family or household and are looking for fun, freedom and being a part of 'their generation', the in-crowd of their peers. This segment is fashion and trend-conscious, wishing to stand out from their parents' generation but very desirous of conforming to their peer group norms. Being active socially, they prefer socialising with their peers and taking part in 'cool' activities, rather than staying at home.

5   *Conventional Family Life* refers to consumers who represent the core of 'middle Australia', with values centred on the significant events in their personal and family lives. This segment tends to include people seeking greater financial security,

Figure 2.4   Roy Morgan Values Segments

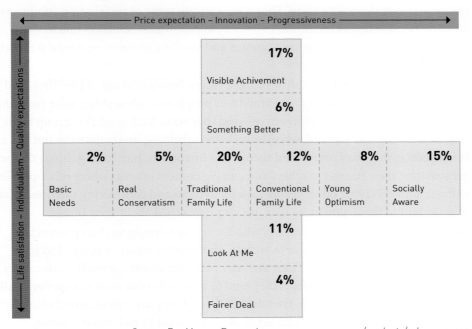

Source: Roy Morgan Research. <www.roymorgan.com/products/values-segments>.

William Chitty

struggling to improve their basic living standards and giving their families better opportunities than they had in their own childhood. Good, solid and reliable services are important to this group and they generally look for value for money in their purchases.

6   *Traditional Family Life* refers to a group of consumers who are the older counterparts of the *Conventional Family Life* segment and share similar activities, interests and opinions. This segment is motivated by similar values in terms of security, reliability and providing better opportunities for their families. However, they are generally empty-nesters or part of extended families. With their children grown, their focus is on rebuilding their relationships with one another and finding time to do all the things they never could while their children were growing up.

7   *Visible Achievement* applies to consumers who are visible success stories. They have made it in whatever field they are involved in, and are confident in their own abilities and position. Despite being successful, they retain traditional values about home, work and society, and they place great emphasis on providing their families with a high-quality environment. They work for financial reward and job stimulation. While they can afford to buy the best of everything, they look for quality and value for money, not necessarily items that are expensive.

8   *Socially Aware* refers to a segment of people who are community minded and socially active. Information collectors, this segment is always searching for something new and different. They strongly believe in the concept of learning and actively look for new training, education and knowledge opportunities. Given a choice between services, they will seek more information and consider the consequences of each choice before making a decision. They have a strong sense of social responsibility and an attraction to convincing others of their opinions, which results in much of this segment being involved in pressure groups and working as public servants, politicians and researchers.

9   *Something Better* refers to people wanting a bigger, better deal out of life. They tend to be competitive, individualistic and ambitious people who are seeking more from their lives; they want more than others have—and they want it all now! This group tends to be found among 'the Joneses', who always have something better than the rest. As a consequence, they may overextend themselves financially, purchasing things that will demonstrate their success to others and cutting corners in areas where other people will not notice. Having other people look up to them and considering them successful is important to this segment, so they are very concerned about their image.

10   *Young Optimism* refers to consumers who are trying to improve their prospects in life and gain a respected place in society, and who are aware of image and style rather than fads and fashions. They are busy planning careers, attending university and thinking about their futures. They tend to be people who want to experience all life has to offer: travel, a career, friends, family, and they are still idealistic enough to believe they can have it all. This segment is interested in technology, surfing

the internet and developing an international perspective on the world; eating international food; watching the ABC and SBS; and dreaming of working in New York or London for a few years to further their career prospects.

Although the Roy Morgan Values Segments model provides useful marketing information for values and lifestyle segmentation purposes, as compared to demographic variables these characteristics are more difficult to identify and measure. Secondary research on published data can tell a service marketer how many female consumers aged 25 to 34 have their hair cut by a well-known hairdresser; that secondary research, however, cannot tell the service marketer how many female *Visible Achievement* consumers aged 25 to 34 have their hair cut by that well-known hairdresser. Consumer values and lifestyle variables must therefore be used in conjunction with consumer demographic variables, to develop profiles of each market segment.

Behavioural segmentation

Behavioural segmentation classifies consumers into segments based on their knowledge of, attitude towards or perhaps their uses for or responses to a service offer. Consumers may use a service for different reasons and in different amounts, so their buying behaviour can be used for behavioural segmentation. Behavioural segments include:

→ benefits sought

→ user status

→ usage rate

→ user occasion

→ brand loyalty.

If a service organisation adopts a 'benefits sought' approach to developing a behavioural segmentation strategy, those benefits sought provide reasons *why* customers purchase a particular service, while the 'user/usage/occasion' segmentation suggests *how* consumers use the service.

For example, if customer demographics—such as age, gender and income—were the only variables used to segment the market for mobile phones, it would be difficult to develop an effective service marketing strategy. The age, gender and income of mobile phone users does not provide a clear distinction between the various customer segments, because mobile phones are used universally by customers of all ages and genders to communicate with each other; age and gender are, therefore, unlikely be significant indicators of *why* mobile phones are used. One approach to segmenting the market for a mobile phone service would be to apply the *average revenue earned per user* (ARPU) to the earnings of a telecommunications company. The mobile phone market could then be segmented by arbitrarily defining low, medium and high revenue-earning divisions based on the average usage rates by customers. But usage rates still do not provide a strong reason as to *why* customers purchase a particular mobile phone service.

↘
behavioural segmentation
The various ways that consumers buy and use service products, which are measured by answering questions such as: How much is purchased? How often is the service purchased? Where is it purchased from?

William Chitty

Brand loyalty as a behavioural segmentation variable derives from consumers having a positive brand attitude towards a service organisation that, over time, develops into brand preference and ultimately long-term brand loyalty for the service product. If brand loyalty is simply based on habit, it does not translate into a useful segmentation variable because the service will be seen by customers as merely fulfilling a habitual functional role, rather than being the result of a service decision that is based on value. In effect this situation applies to many non-personal services such as mobile phones, as they have become universally available and accepted by consumers. The number of times a smartphone service is used—*how often*—can then be linked with *why* and *how* customers use a particular service, to produce useful behavioural segmentation data.

↘ INDUSTRY INSIGHT

Understanding the behaviour of Asia's digital banking customers

Across Asia it is estimated that more than 700 million consumers use digital banking regularly, a significant proportion of them living in the fast-growing market economies of China and India. Consumers are using computers, smartphones and tablets more often to do business with their banks, at the same time visiting branches and calling service lines less frequently. In a recent survey, 92 per cent of respondents in developed Asian economies reported that they used internet banking, compared with 58 per cent from a survey conducted in 2011. And 61 per cent also accessed banking services using smartphones, more than three times higher than in 2011. Internet banking in emerging Asian economies showed an even faster shift, although from a much smaller base, rising from 10 per cent to 28 per cent between 2011 and 2014, while smartphone access increased from 5 per cent to 26 per cent over the same period.

Increases in internet access and smartphone adoption have contributed to the growing use of digital banking and, notably, have helped demand for digital banking

move from early adopters to a wider range of customers. For established banks, this significant increase in the use of digital banking channels may not, however, prevent customers changing banks. More than 80 per cent of consumers in developed Asian markets said they would be willing to transfer some of their holdings to a bank that offers a compelling digital service, while more than 50 per cent of consumers in emerging Asian markets indicated such willingness to change their bank. For the various types of accounts, respondents indicated that they might shift 35 to 45 per cent of savings account deposits, 40 to 50 per cent of credit card balances, and 40 to 45 per cent of investment balances, such as those held in mutual funds.

Risks and opportunities for Asian banks

This research suggests that, in developed Asian economies, consumers value the quality of basic services, the strength of financial products, a bank's brand reputation, and the quality of customer service and experience. Among these factors, they are typically least satisfied with the financial products offered and with their service experience. Survey results from emerging Asia were less conclusive, indicating these markets are in the early stages of digital banking.

The results also indicate that simplicity and security are crucial aspects of online offerings. Of those who had not used any online banking products, 47 per cent in developed Asian markets and 35 per cent in emerging Asian markets reported that a primary obstacle to using these services was that they were so complicated that they needed a person to explain them. Security concerns also stopped about 56 per cent of the respondents in emerging Asian markets and 44 per cent of those in developed Asian markets from purchasing products online.[5]

Market segmentation stage 2: Evaluate each segment

The second stage is to evaluate market segments using three key variables:

1   segment size and growth
2   segment structure
3   business objectives and resources.

To evaluate the market segments that have been identified by one or a combination of those three key variables, a service organisation must consider the following factors.

The first is *measurability*, which is the size and purchasing power of the market segments that can be measured. Some variables, such as lifestyle, brand loyalty and attitude, are difficult to measure, so service organisations must collect and analyse sales data, growth rates and profit margins for each service segment to detect any identifiable trends. Market analysis, including any service capacity constraints, should then be considered to determine the most suitable market segment.

The second factor is *accessibility*, which is the degree to which segments can be effectively reached, and served, by a service organisation's marketing communications messages and media. If the marketing costs exceed the sales revenue of serving some segments, it is not in the organisation's financial interests to continue marketing its services to those segments. The organisation must then consider its resources, even if a particular segment shows positive growth and is structurally sound. The issue to be considered is whether that market segment will develop the organisation's core business and, if so, in which time frame.

The final factor is *substantiality*, the degree to which the identified segments are substantial enough to be profitable. A segment should be the largest homogeneous group of consumers to which a service organisation can market a tailored service. The organisation must appraise the impact that current and potential competitors may have on the segment's profitability, and consider such things as:

→ Are there any substitute services?

→ What are the barriers to market entry facing competitors?

→ What is the bargaining power of those competitors relative to the current service provider?

Services in Action

Segment profiles of visitors to Victoria

For the year ending December 2014, Victoria experienced a year-on-year increase of 14.1 per cent in revenue to $11.5 billion for the overnight tourism market, compared to a 5.7 per cent increase nationally. Victoria also received a total of 20.3 million international and domestic visitors in the same period, which represented an increase of 16.2 per cent.

The number of day-trip visitors to Victoria increased by 4.2 per cent in the same period, while spending by day-trip visitors to Victoria increased by 8.3 per cent to $4.7 billion. Regional Victoria experienced an increase in expenditure of 12.4 per cent to $5.0 billion, the number of visitors increased by 11.4 per cent to 13.1 million and the number of visitor night stays rose to 40.3 million. Melbourne experienced strong growth in interstate overnight visitors of 13.9 per cent to 5 million, with interstate overnight expenditure growing by 25 per cent to $3.9 billion.

Tourism Victoria's research unit has developed visitor profiles for each of the key and niche market segments of Victoria's $19.1 billion tourism industry using visitor demographics and behaviour. The key market segments are adventure tourism, caravan and camping tourism, events tourism, shopping tourism, and snow and ski tourism, while the niche market segments are food and wine tourism, arts and cultural heritage tourism, nature-based tourism, Aboriginal tourism, backpacker tourism, spa and wellbeing tourism, and golf tourism.

Three examples of visitor profiles for adventure tourism, events tourism, and snow and ski tourism are now discussed in terms of visitors' age, purpose of visit, length of visit, travel groups, seasonality and accommodation.

Adventure tourism

For the year ending June 2014, Victoria hosted 3.4 million domestic overnight adventure visitors, who stayed for an estimated 12.8 million visitor nights with an average length of stay of 3.8 nights.

Profile of domestic adventure visitors

Intrastate visitors were the key market for the adventure segment, accounting for 85 per cent of total domestic overnight visitors within Victoria. The number of interstate overnight adventure visitors was primarily driven by visitors from New South Wales, who accounted for 50 per cent of all interstate adventure visitors, followed by those from South Australia, with 21 per cent of the total number of adventure visitors.

Age segmentation

Domestic overnight adventure visitors to and within Victoria were most likely to be aged 25–44 years (39%) or 45–64 years (33%). These domestic visitors tended to be younger than domestic overnight travellers in general.

Age (years)	Adventure visitors to Victoria (%)	Adventure visitors to Australia (%)	Total domestic travellers (%)
15–24	17	18	15
25–44	39	40	36
45–64	33	32	34
65+	11	10	14

Purpose of visit

Of domestic overnight adventure visitors to and within the state, 76 per cent were holiday visitors and 18 per cent were visiting friends and relatives. Domestic overnight adventure visitors were more likely to be travelling on holiday, and less likely to be visiting friends and relatives or travelling on business, than domestic travellers in general.

Length of visit

Of domestic overnight adventure visitors to and within Victoria, 61 per cent were on a short visit of one to three nights. A further 28 per cent stayed four to seven nights, while the remaining 11 per cent stayed eight or more nights. Domestic overnight adventure visitors were more likely to stay four to seven nights, and less likely to stay one to three nights, when compared with domestic overnight travellers overall.

Travel groups

The majority of domestic overnight adventure visitors to and within Victoria

Figure 2.5 Misty mountains of Gariwerd (Grampians National Park) in western Victoria

travelled with friends or relatives (32%), as an adult couple (27%) or as a family group (26%). Domestic overnight adventure visitors were more likely to travel with friends or relatives or in a family group, and less likely to travel alone, than domestic overnight travellers overall.

Seasonality

Domestic overnight adventure visitation to and within Victoria peaked during summer, attracting the highest proportion of adventure visitors (35%), and stayed strong through autumn (27%). In comparison, visitation during winter was relatively low, attracting only 15 per cent of visitors.

Accommodation

Of all domestic adventure visitor nights in the state, 31 per cent were spent in caravan parks or camping (compared to 15 per cent of domestic visitor nights overall), while 27 per cent were spent at the homes of friends or relatives (compared to 39 per cent of domestic visitor nights overall). Domestic overnight

William Chitty

Chapter 2 Market Segmentation and Service Positioning

adventure visitors to and within Victoria tended to spend fewer nights at hotels, resorts, motels or motor inns (9%) than domestic overnight travellers in general (25%).

Adventure activities

Of Victorian domestic overnight adventure visitors, 56 per cent had been on a bush or rainforest walk and 28 per cent went fishing while on their trip.

Events tourism

Events tourism visitors are those who attended festivals, fairs, cultural events and/or organised sporting events while on their trip to Victoria.

Profile of events tourism visitors

During the year ending June 2014, Victoria hosted an estimated 1.8 million domestic overnight events visitors, who accounted for approximately 5.7 million visitor nights. The average length of stay for events visitors to Victoria was 3.1 nights. There were 2.2 million day trips undertaken by domestic events visitors, with the segment accounting for 5.1 per cent of all domestic day trips in Victoria.

The domestic events tourism segment in Victoria was relatively evenly split between intrastate and interstate overnight visitors (52% and 48%, respectively). Interstate overnight events visitors were primarily driven by the New South Wales market—contributing about 37 per cent of all events interstate overnight visitors. South Australia accounted for 20 per cent of domestic overnight events visitors to Victoria, while Western Australia and Queensland

Figure 2.6 The Melbourne Cricket Ground under lights

accounted for 15 per cent and 14 per cent, respectively.

Age segmentation

Domestic overnight events visitors to and within Victoria were most likely to be aged 45–64 years (36%) or 25–44 years (34%).

Age (years)	Events visitors to Victoria (%)	Events visitors to Australia (%)	Total domestic travellers (%)
15–24	18	15	15
25–44	34	33	36
45–64	36	37	34
65+	13	15	14

Purpose of visit

Of domestic overnight events visitors to and within the state, 69 per cent were holiday visitors and 24 per cent were visiting friends or relatives. Domestic overnight events visitors were more likely to travel for leisure, and less likely to be visiting friends or relatives or travelling for business, than domestic travellers in general.

Purpose of visit	Events visitors to Victoria (%)	Events visitors to Australia (%)	Total travellers (%)
Holiday or leisure	69	68	42
VFR	24	27	36
Business	5	6	19
Other	2	4	6

Length of visit

Of domestic overnight events visitors to and within Victoria, 69 per cent were on a short visit of one to three nights. A further 25 per cent stayed four to seven nights, while the remaining 6 per cent stayed at least eight nights.

Travel groups

The majority of domestic overnight events visitors to and within the state travelled as a couple (29%), with friends or relatives (25%) or as a family group (23%).

Seasonality

Domestic overnight events visitation to and within Victoria peaked during autumn, attracting the highest proportion of domestic overnight events visitors (32%). In comparison, domestic overnight events visitation during spring was the lowest of the seasons (19%).

Accommodation

Of all domestic events visitor nights in the state, 36 per cent were spent at a hotel, resort, motel or motor inn, and 34 per cent were spent with friends or relatives.

Events activities

Of domestic overnight events visitors to and within Victoria, 64 per cent went to an organised sporting event such as the

Australian Open tennis, while 39 per cent went to a festival, fair or cultural event such as an exhibition of artworks at the National Gallery of Victoria in Melbourne.

Snow and ski tourism

Profile of domestic snow/ski tourism visitors

The majority of domestic overnight snow/ski visitors within Australia for the three years ending December 2013 came from New South Wales (46%) and Victoria (32%).

Age segmentation

Domestic overnight snow/ski visitors to and within Victoria were most likely to be aged 25–44 years (46%) or 15–24 years (34%).

Age (years)	Snow and ski visitors to/within Victoria (%)	Snow and ski visitors within Australia (%)	Total Australia (%)
15–24	34	33	15
25–44	46	42	36
45–64	18	21	35
65+	2	3	14

Figure 2.7   Falls Creek Alpine Resort

William Chitty

Market segmentation stage 3: Select the targeting strategies for a particular segment

The third stage in segmenting a market is to identify the distinctive segment strategy that will satisfy the segment criteria of size, growth potential and structure. A *target market* is a group of buyers in an identified market segment who have common needs, wants and expectations that can be satisfied by a service organisation's products. An organisation can adopt one or more of four market-coverage strategies:

1   *Mass (undifferentiated) marketing:* In adopting this strategy, an organisation ignores any segment differences and offers one service to the total market. While mass marketing is an efficient means of providing a service, a service provider that offers only one service at a fixed price may suffer losses if competitors can cherry-pick those segments that together are more profitable than the overall market.

    For example, all local telephone calls offered by Telstra—regardless of the locality within Australia—consist of a four-number exchange code plus four numbers that identify the local telephone service. Each local call is charged at a uniform price to both residential and business customers, and does not reflect the costs associated with the length of time of a local call.

2   *Differentiated marketing:* This is a market strategy that allows an organisation to target several segments and design a separate service for each. By satisfying the needs and wants of several segments, a service organisation that uses a differentiated strategy can generate greater sales than if it adopted an undifferentiated strategy. Some travel agencies, for example, have adopted differentiated marketing strategies to reach segments with specialised travel requirements.

3   *Niche (concentrated) marketing:* This is a market strategy in which an organisation aims for a large share of the sub-market and concentrates on one segment. This

Figure 2.8 Telstra's local-call services are marketed using mass or undifferentiated marketing

approach can be used by smaller service organisations that lack the financial leverage of their larger competitors, and by service organisations that offer specialised services. For example, telephone companies often offer a slower download speed for data services, at a cheaper rate, for use in homes and small businesses, than the faster speed that is offered, at a higher price, to major corporate customers.[7]

4   *Micro-marketing:* This more recent marketing strategy has become popular with some service organisations that hold personal data about their individual customers. The internet has allowed organisations to promote lower prices or new service features directly to individual customers based on their personal preferences and previous behaviour. Qantas, for example, communicates directly with its frequent flyers via the internet.

↘
INDUSTRY INSIGHT

Market coverage strategies for airlines

Budget airlines—known as low-cost carriers (LCCs)—emerged as a result of airline deregulation in the United States, which led to air travel becoming more affordable. Southwest Airlines was instrumental in revolutionising the industry with a differentiated marketing strategy. The point-to-point operational model adopted by Southwest, JetBlue and other LCCs focuses on short-distance, regional, non-stop routes between origin and destination, rather than having connecting flights at hubs—as in the hub-and-spoke model adopted by full-service US airlines like Delta, American and United.

Southwest's point-to-point structure has facilitated more direct non-stop routes—72 per cent of US customers now fly on non-stop routes. Direct flights are used for routes with shorter stage lengths—the average aircraft trip-stage length in the United States is 693 miles (about 1110 km) with an average duration of 1.9 hours. Although the hub-and-spoke model provides broad network coverage for airlines with large and diversified fleets, it adds to operational

William Chitty

Figure 2.9 The characteristics of airline business models

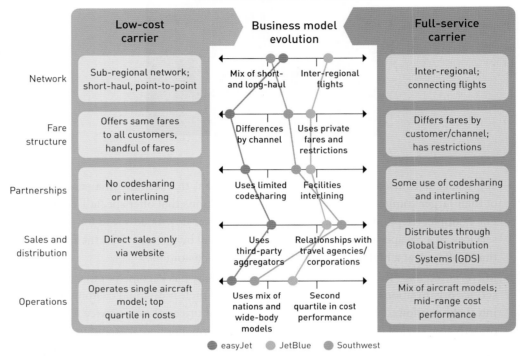

Characteristics of airline business models:
network carriers vs low-cost carriers

	Low-cost carrier	Business model evolution		Full-service carrier
Network	Sub-regional network; short-haul, point-to-point	Mix of short- and long-haul	Inter-regional flights	Inter-regional; connecting flights
Fare structure	Offers same fares to all customers, handful of fares	Differences by channel	Uses private fares and restrictions	Differs fares by customer/channel; has restrictions
Partnerships	No codesharing or interlining	Uses limited codesharing	Facilities interlining	Some use of codesharing and interlining
Sales and distribution	Direct sales only via website	Uses third-party aggregators	Relationships with travel agencies/ corporations	Distributes through Global Distribution Systems (GDS)
Operations	Operates single aircraft model; top quartile in costs	Uses mix of nations and wide-body models	Second quartile in cost performance	Mix of aircraft models; mid-range cost performance

● easyJet ● JetBlue ● Southwest

Source: T. Cederholm (2014). Must-know: Airline business models. *Market Realist*, 21 July. <http://marketrealist.com/2014/07/must-know-airline-business-models>.

complexity and costs. The characteristics of airline business models for network carriers versus LLCs are shown in Figure 2.9.

In an industry characterised by intense competition, with customers expecting wider network coverage at competitive prices, many airlines have been forced to adopt competitive hybrid business models. These hybrid models combine the cost-effectiveness of LCCs with the diversified and broader range of services and routes offered by network carriers.

Many full-service airlines, such as Qantas, operate a point-to-point service for certain routes but also fly their own LCC brands on regional routes to gain passenger traffic and increase market share for the overall airline brand. Jetstar, which is an independent subsidiary of Qantas, has transitioned from being solely a domestic carrier in the Qantas network to an international medium-haul LCC. In addition to its domestic Australian operations, Jetstar operates between Australia and the Asia–Pacific region, and has established partnerships with local airlines within Asia.[8]

Regardless of the service organisation's particular competitive strategy, a framework for relating its operations to its service performance is needed to analyse the key elements that must be addressed in service development processes. The purpose of the framework is to position the firm's service product, relative to its competitors. It is a road map of where the organisation is going. Questions like 'Where are we now?' and 'Where do we want to be?' are more easily communicated to all members of the organisation if they can see how these questions relate to the company's positioning strategies.

Market segmentation stage 4: Position a service organisation's brand

The final stage in segmenting a market is to develop brand-positioning strategies for each market segment. The service brand is positioned by consumers on the basis of what they perceive as the important service attributes. An effective brand-positioning strategy develops an intended image of a particular service in customers' minds in relation to competitors' brands. Positioning is used to differentiate competing brands in a mass market, or to position a firm's brand in relation to its market niches. Typically, the service brand becomes the focal point of a positioning strategy to differentiate the product from a competitor's offering. Conceptually, the term *positioning* suggests two interrelated ideas. First, the service marketer must create a specific meaning for the service brand and clearly establish that meaning in consumers' minds, so that the service is *positioned in the consumers' minds*. Second, a brand's specific meaning in consumers' minds is compared to what they know and what they feel emotionally about competitive brands in the same service category; the service in this instance is *positioned against the competitors' brands*.

Strategically, positioning is a word or short statement that represents the message that the marketer wants to 'imprint in the minds of customers and prospects'.[9] This statement tells consumers how the service brand differs from, and is superior to, competitive brands. It gives consumers a reason they should buy a particular service rather than a competitor's and promises a solution to the customer's needs, wants or expectations. An effective positioning statement for a service should satisfy two requirements:

1 It should reflect a service brand's competitive advantage.
2 It should motivate customers' buying behaviour.[10]

A *positioning statement* for a service represents how marketers want consumers and prospects to think and feel about their particular brand. These thoughts and feelings should be prominent when comparing the particular service brand with competitive offerings, and motivate the customer or prospective consumer to buy the communicated brand.

↘
competitive advantage
The part or parts of a service that an organisation can do better than all of its competitors; this may be based on a unique service proposition, but does not necessarily have to be

Positioning is the process of establishing and maintaining a distinctive place in the minds of the target market for an organisation's brand. In a competitive market, the particular position reflects consumers' perceptions of a service brand's performance based on specific attributes, relative to one or more competitors. Establishing a position in the minds of a target market is critical to the success of a service organisation's brand because intangibility can distort a consumer's ability to differentiate one attribute of a service from others offered by competitors. Positioning involves managing the seven internal elements of the marketing mix (the seven Ps—see Chapter 1) to counteract the uncontrollable variables of the external environment: that is, the political, economic, social and technological plus competitive variables (PEST + C). Positioning links the strengths and weaknesses of the internal environment of a service organisation to the opportunities and threats (from a Strengths, Weaknesses, Opportunities and Threats analysis) of its external environment.

Every service-delivery system embodies a unique set of choices that relate to service quality, customer expectations and operational capacity. What determines an organisation's competitive position is the degree to which the critical factors that influence its core service are clearly superior to those of its rivals.

Developing a brand-positioning strategy

There are three basic types of analysis required to develop a market-positioning strategy:

1 *Market analysis* is required so that market characteristics—such as potential demand, the seasonality of demand and geographical location—can be determined and an appraisal made of customers' preferences in each of the different segments.

2 *Corporate analysis* in its basic form identifies the strengths and weaknesses of the organisation's resources—its expertise and any limitations of its management. Information obtained from that analysis enables the organisation to best select the number of market segments that it can supply with its services.

3 *Competitive analysis* provides an approach to gauging competitors' strengths and weaknesses, and in turn may suggest opportunities for the organisation to differentiate its services and offer those benefits that are suited to the selected target market segments.

The result of integrating these three analyses is a positioning strategy that defines the desired position of the organisation in its selected market. Before any service organisation begins to develop its services, it must conduct consumer research to identify what attributes of its proposed service are considered important by prospective customers, and how those prospective customers perceive the service offerings of competing firms.

As a general rule, consumers set differing criteria for service attributes according to:

→ the consumer's purpose in using the service

→ who makes the decision to use the service

OXFORD UNIVERSITY PRESS

→ the timing of use—time of day, week or perhaps season

→ whether the service is for an individual or a group

→ the composition of that group.

What a service brand represents depends on what consumers know about the service benefits. A service organisation's brand owns a certain position in the market because it is perceived to provide different benefits to those of other segments. Optus, Virgin Australia and Westpac, for example, ensure that their brand names are on every service they market so that customers can identify those different service products. Positioning can help consumers evaluate a service.

Services, like physical products, have three quality dimensions that help consumers evaluate them: search, experience and credence dimensions.[11]

1 *Search dimensions* are those attributes, such as price, that can be evaluated before purchasing a service.

2 *Experience dimensions* are those attributes, such as quality, that can only be evaluated over time because, at the time of purchase, only promises can be made about the quality of the service encounter.

3 *Credence qualities* are those attributes that may never be evaluated because the consumer does not possess the expertise to determine, or may not be able to physically judge, what service was performed or how it was performed.

Generally, services have few search qualities, some experience qualities and relatively numerous credence qualities, which partly explains why consumers often rely on personal sources of information, such as word of mouth from family and friends, when selecting a service.

A service-positioning strategy must encapsulate a brand's meaning and its distinctiveness, and that requires understanding the points of difference and the points of parity when comparing a service brand with competitive brands in the same service category.

Points of difference

Point-of-difference (POD) associations are strong, favourable and perhaps unique brand associations for a service. PODs are those service attributes or benefits that consumers strongly associate with a brand and believe that no other competitive brand can offer to the same level.[12]

Determinant attributes are those that determine customer choice and are often not the top service characteristics that are considered important by consumers.[13] They are, however, the attributes that a consumer may use to decide between competing services— for example, airlines. The task for an airline, then, is to identify which service attributes are determinant—that is, those service characteristics that strongly influence consumers'

↘
determinant attributes
Service attributes that determine customers' choice between competing service organisations; those attributes that offer customers compelling reasons to purchase

William Chitty

decision-making processes—and to analyse how well the competitors' services perform on those determinant attributes.

Some service attributes are very easy to quantify; for example, price is expressed in a currency, and punctuality can be measured as the number of flights departing and arriving within the scheduled time period. Both those criteria are objective measures and can therefore be generalised for a range of airline operators. Other attributes are more qualitative and are therefore subject to individual interpretation—how can a service marketer measure which airline provides the best first-class service? The unique attributes of a service brand are what set it apart from competitors and attract customers. Just being different, however, is not enough to develop a successful positioning strategy, because a brand should offer both attraction and distinction. Attraction provides attributes and benefits that consumers need or want, while distinction provides attributes and benefits that consumers can receive only when they buy a particular service brand.

Points of parity

Point-of-parity (POP) associations are brand associations that are not necessarily unique to one brand but may be shared with several other service brands. POPs can exist in two basic forms—category and competitive. *Category POPs* are those associations that consumers believe a brand must have to be considered a credible service within a particular service category. Operational safety, for example, represents a necessary attribute for an airline, but it may not be a strong or unique enough reason to influence brand choice in a customer's purchase decisions, because the safety of an airline is a generic association expected of all airlines.

Competitive POPs are those associations that are developed to negate the points of difference of competitive brands. If a brand can equalise a competitive brand's benefits and create a unique brand attribute, it should be able to achieve a strong competitive position in the minds of its target market.[14] For example, in 1962 Avis launched a new advertising campaign that highlighted that it was a challenger brand to market leader Hertz. The tagline was 'When you're only No. 2, you try harder', which emphasised the second-place status of Avis as a means to make consumers aware of the company's customer service. This was a POP positioning strategy that said Avis tried harder to satisfy every customer and could not afford to offer anything less than great customer service; that marketing strategy closed the gap in market share with Hertz, and was retained by Avis for the next fifty years.[15]

Positioning of a service brand is determined more by the intangible characteristics of a service, because it is often as much about achieving a point of difference as it is about achieving a competitive point of parity.

OXFORD UNIVERSITY PRESS

Telstra repositions for digital disruption

Telstra is a well-known brand and competes in every telecommunications market throughout Australia. Prior to the introduction of the National Broadband Network (NBN) optic-fibre network, Telstra provided 9.2 million fixed-line services (phone and broadband) and 9.7 million active mobile plans. The company had a reputation for reliable coverage—coupled with a quality telecommunications service—across Australia, although it fell behind its customers' expectations of customer support. Telstra's positioning strategy was premised on it being a premium service provider with very reliable broadband internet connectivity. Its marketing approach, however, has recently shifted from being a premium service provider to a more affordable and competitive Internet Service Provider (ISP) that is aiming for a larger share of the broadband market. That shift is being undertaken because the NBN will become the owner of a new optic-fibre national network, and Telstra and other ISPs will have equal and homogenous access to resell the NBN internet services using their brands.[16]

The senior management of Telstra is moving to reposition the organisation to make it capable of dealing with digital disruption by allocating up to $3 billion over a three-year period starting in the 2017–18 financial year. When announcing the company's financial results for 2016–17, Telstra CEO Andrew Penn said that digital

disruption was continuing to accelerate and the telecommunications market was being transformed by the rollout of the NBN. For the first time in its history, Telstra is having to compete without owning the fixed-line telecommunications infrastructure, and that means it has to compete by offering the best customer experiences on the new network, creating Telstra-branded services that satisfy its customers and deliver segmented products to the market.[17]

At the presentation of Telstra's operating results for 2016–17, Mr Penn announced that its connections to the NBN grew by 676 000 to 1 176 000 customers, taking the organisation's market share (excluding satellite) to 52 per cent.[18] As part of its repositioning strategy, Telstra is planning to improve its customers' experiences by offering the NBN Wi-Fi Gateway service, which has higher download and upload speeds, to home users on its entry-level plans.

One of the strategies that will be used to deliver segmented services is offering the low-cost mobile services to price-sensitive customers. In April 2017, TPG announced that it would spend $1.9 billion to build Australia's fourth mobile network, which will be rolled out over a three-year period from 2018. That competitive action by TPG is one of the reasons Telstra entered the low-cost mobile market.[19]

Belong Mobile will target the mobile market by offering a discount, to compete against other mobile virtual network operators (MVNOs) such as amaysim, Kogan, Aldi and Woolworths that sell the Optus and Vodafone networks rebadged as their own cheap brands. Belong is part of the broadband market with a separate brand image to Telstra's premium brand positioning, and already has 150 000 customers, representing 5 per cent of Telstra's fixed-line broadband business.[20]

Belong Mobile now puts Telstra in the same market as Optus, which operates Virgin Mobile as a low-cost brand on its own mobile network.

Positioning via service attributes

Service *attributes* can be distinguished as being either service-related or non-service-related features. For example, the location of a five-star hotel (in a central business district) and its business facilities (conference services and meeting rooms) represent service-related attributes. Non-service-related attributes may include consumer perceptions of the type of people who stay at five-star hotels (user imagery) and the occasions when such a hotel would be used (usage imagery). A service brand can be positioned on the basis of its features or attributes, provided that the specific service attributes represent a competitive advantage and can motivate customers to purchase that service rather than a competitive offering.

Service-related features

Innovative service delivery, superior physical facilities and knowledgeable staff are just a few of the long list of attributes that can provide the foundation for positioning a service brand. The benefits of a service brand should be highlighted, especially if the benefit is something that consumers truly desire in the particular service category.

Usage and user imagery

Service brands can be positioned in terms of their unique usage symbolism or with respect to the kinds of people who use them. A service positioned according to the image associated with how it is used displays the brand in terms of the specific and unique usage that becomes associated with it (*usage imagery*).

User imagery associates the service brand with representations of the kinds of people who are portrayed in advertisements as being the typical users of the service brand. The service being advertised is positioned *not* in terms of its features (the benefits that it satisfies), but in terms of the types of people who use the brand—that is, user imagery. Health clubs, for example, often promote their services by showing their members using exercise equipment to achieve their desired level of fitness.

OXFORD UNIVERSITY PRESS

Positioning via service benefits

Service *benefits* are the ways that a brand can satisfy customers' needs, wants and expectations. Positioning with respect to a service brand's benefits can be achieved by appealing to the three categories of consumer needs and wants: functional, symbolic and experiential.[21] A service brand's benefits are generally expected to satisfy customers' needs, while the brand's attributes or features are expected to satisfy their wants.

A service that is positioned on the basis of its service benefits, in terms of satisfying functional needs, attempts to provide solutions to consumers' current consumption-related problems, or potential problems, by communicating the specific service benefits of the brand. The ad for the Maria Island Walk shown in Figure 2.10 appeals to consumers' functional needs by promising a four-day break from work to relax and recharge.

↘
functional needs
Consumer needs that include current consumption-related problems

Figure 2.10   Maria Island in Tasmania offers a functional benefit: staying on the island helps customers unwind and relax

Source: The Maria Island Walk. <www.youtube.com/watch?v=2b9YJMo73zE>.

In general, appeals to functional needs are the most prevalent form of a service brand's benefit positioning. In B2B (business-to-business) marketing, for example, service organisations typically appeal to their customers' functional needs for fast delivery times or better customer service in their call centres. Services are regularly pitched to consumers' needs for convenience, safety and pleasant surroundings, which are the functional needs that can be satisfied by the benefits of the service experience.

Marketing communication that appeals to symbolic needs includes those messages directed at consumers' desire for self-enhancement, group membership, affiliation and belonging. Service brand positioning, in terms of symbolic needs, attempts to associate brand use with a desired group, role or self-image. Marketers of luxury service brands, such as luxury hotels, frequently appeal to symbolic needs.

Consumers' experiential needs represent their desires for services that provide sensory pleasure, variety and sometimes cognitive stimulation. Positioning directed at experiential

↘
B2B services
Services delivered from business to business

↘
symbolic needs
Consumer needs that are related to desired self-image, role position or group affiliation

↘
experiential needs
Consumer needs for services that provide sensory pleasure, variety and/or cognitive stimulation

William Chitty

needs promotes service brands as being out of the ordinary and high in sensory value—looking elegant, feeling wonderful or smelling great.

It is important to recognise that brands frequently offer a mixture of functional, symbolic and experiential benefits. In Figure 2.11, Virgin Australia promises low prices—a functional benefit—to holiday destinations that offer pleasurable experiences—an experiential benefit.

Figure 2.11   Virgin Australia promises both functional and experiential benefits when customers fly to its holiday destinations

Perceptual maps

Brand mapping, which uses multidimensional perceptual maps to represent consumers' perceptions of service performance, is a useful tool that service organisations can use to understand the relationship between a service category and its target markets. A *perceptual map* typically consists of a diagram with two axes that represent two specific service attributes of an organisation's service that can be compared with those of other services in the category. Perceptual maps provide an indication of a service's performance in a particular market segment over time, as well as allowing an organisation to anticipate consumer responses to new competitors.

Positioning maps, as shown in Figure 2.12, are a convenient way of visually representing consumers' preferences regarding alternative service products, and are derived from market research data. Information about a service brand's position can generally be obtained from

Figure 2.12 Positioning map for cruise line industry

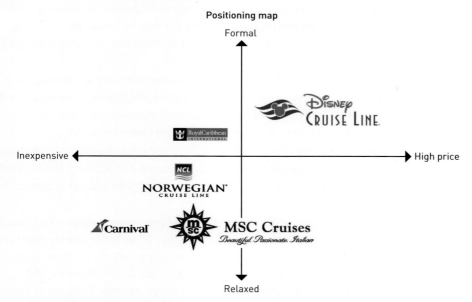

Source: <https://faculty.cit.cornell.edu/jl2545/4160/presentation/2012presentations/Cruise%20Line%20Industry%20Presentation.ppt>.

the three basic types of research for developing market-positioning strategies: *market analysis*, *corporate analysis* and *competitive analysis*. These analyses provide a service organisation with the diagnostic data to gauge its competitors' strengths and weaknesses, and to develop service strategies that will differentiate its services and achieve a position of competitive advantage.

This chapter discusses two important and related topics: segmenting and targeting service customers; and positioning a service brand. First, the chapter examines consumer groups with specific demographics, values and lifestyles, and/or purchasing behaviour variables, which are the variables of a service brand's segmentation strategy and are complementary to its positioning strategy.

The major variables in segmenting a market that are reviewed include the demographic structure of the Australian population, namely ages, life cycles and incomes; the values and lifestyles of the Australian population, using the Roy Morgan Values Segments model; and elements of behavioural segmentation, that is, consumers' purchase behaviour.

As a practical example, segmentation of holiday visitors to Victoria based on the domestic tourism market's needs, wants and expectations has been considered in terms of what each group wants, how they travel around the state, their social interactions with other visitors and their length of stay.

The chapter concludes by examining the nature and role of positioning services. The issues of differentiation and consumer evaluation are discussed as they relate to the search, experience and credence dimensions of a service. Positioning involves using marketing communications to develop an image in the target audience's minds of what a service brand stands for and what it means to that target market in comparison with competitive brands. The basis of brand positioning is establishing a value proposition in the minds of the target market.

As a practical example of positioning, Telstra's BigPond broadband service positioning is considered as a part of its marketing strategy. The positioning strategies that can be applied to a service brand are examined using a service brand's attributes and benefits, and the functional, symbolic and/or experiential needs that it satisfies. A brief discussion of positioning maps, which can be used to visually depict the brand image that customers hold about a service company, concludes the section on positioning services.

Review questions

1   Reread the Services in Action feature 'Segment profiles of visitors to Victoria'. As a services marketing analyst, develop a segmentation strategy (including a brand name) for a specific holiday destination in your home state using the variables of what each segment looks for in an ideal holiday destination. Your analysis should include two positioning statements for the new brand—one based on *user imagery* and the other based on *usage imagery*—for 'typical' visitors to the chosen holiday destination.

2   Traditionally, family life cycles have been used to segment the markets for trading banks. Assume that you are the marketing analyst for one of the four major banks and explain why family life cycles are not a valid criterion for segmenting the banks' non-business customers.

3   Australians aged 25 to 39 represent a much smaller percentage of the population than they did 30 years ago. In view of this demographic change, what actions would you take if you were the marketer for a service firm that offers service products to families with primary school–aged children?

4　Identify a service that appeals to at least four of the 10 Roy Morgan Values Segments groups. Explain why that service appeals to the selected groups of consumers.

5　Using the three key variables—segment size and growth, segment structure, and business objectives and resources—evaluate the consumer market segments of one of the four major trading banks in Australia.

6　Develop three positioning statements for an Australian holiday destination that satisfy the functional, symbolic and experiential needs of families with teenage children.

7　*Customers do not always distinguish competing service providers on the service attributes that they rate as being important.* Fully explain what this statement means, using a service industry example.

8　Select a particular service category of interest and describe the positioning of the major competitors in that category, including the variables that differentiate the brand of each organisation. Then draw a positioning map—based on those variables—of the major competitors and explain how different positioning strategies can be used to reposition service brands.

Further reading

Blankson, C. & Kalafatis, S. (2007). Positioning strategies of international and multicultural-oriented service brands. *Journal of Services Marketing*, 21(6), 435–50.

de Chernatony, L. & Segal-Horn, S. (2003). The criteria for successful services brands. *European Journal of Marketing*, 37(7/8), 1095–118.

Elliott, G. & Glynn, W. (1998). Segmenting financial services markets for customer relationships: A portfolio-based approach. *Service Industries Journal*, 18(3), 38–54.

Keller, K.L. (2003). *Strategic Brand Management: Building, Measuring, and Managing Brand Equity*. Upper Saddle River, NJ: Prentice Hall.

Long, M. & Schiffman, L.G. (2000). Consumption values and relationships: Segmenting the market for frequency programs. *Journal of Consumer Marketing*, 17(3), 214–32.

Endnotes

1　RDA Research. geoTribes: It's all about people. <https://rdaresearch.com/geotribes>.

2　Index Mundi. Australia age structure. Sourced from CIA World Factbook. <www.indexmundi.com/australia/age_structure.html>.

3　Index Mundi. Population pyramid. Sourced from CIA World Facebook. Last updated 9 July 2017. <www.indexmundi.com/australia/age_structure.html>.

4　Roy Morgan Single Source October 2006–September 2007. Roy Morgan Values Segments developed in conjunction with Colin Benjamin of the Horizon Network.

5　Based on S. Barquin & H.V. Vinayak (2015). Capitalizing on Asia's digital-banking boom. McKinsey & Company Financial Services, March. <www.mckinsey.com/insights/financial_services/capitalizing_on_asias_digital-banking_boom>.

6　Source of segment profiles for visitors to Victoria: Tourism Victoria . <www.tourism.vic.gov.au/research/domestic-and-regional-research/product-segment-market-profiles.html>.

7   O.C. Ferrell & M.D. Hartline (2008). *Marketing Strategy* (4th edn). Mason, OH: Thomson South Western, pp. 164–6.

8   T. Cederholm (2014). Must-know: Airline business models. Market Realist, 21 July. <http://marketrealist.com/2014/07/must-know-airline-business-models>.

9   C.H. Lovelock, P.G. Patterson & R.H. Walker (2007). *Services Marketing: An Asia–Pacific and Australian Perspective* (4th edn). Sydney, NSW: Pearson Education Australia, pp. 150–2.

10 K.J. Clancy & P.C. Kreig (2000). *Counterintuitive Marketing: Achieve Great Results Using Uncommon Sense.* New York, NY: Free Press, p. 110.

11 C.H. Lovelock, P.G. Patterson & R.H. Walker (2007). *Services Marketing: An Asia–Pacific and Australian Perspective* (4th edn). Sydney, NSW: Pearson Education Australia.

12 K.L. Keller (2003). *Strategic Brand Management: Building, Measuring, and Managing Brand Equity* (2nd edn). Upper Saddle River, NJ: Prentice Hall, p. 131.

13 C.H. Lovelock, P.G. Patterson & R.H. Walker (2007). *Services Marketing: An Asia–Pacific and Australian Perspective* (4th edn). Sydney, NSW: Pearson Education Australia.

14 K.L. Keller (2003). *Strategic Brand Management: Building, Measuring, and Managing Brand Equity* (2nd edn). Upper Saddle River, NJ: Prentice Hall, p. 135.

15 S. Stevenson (n.d.). We're no. 2! We're no. 2! How a *Mad Men*–era ad firm discovered the perks of being an underdog. <www.slate.com/articles/business/rivalries/2013/08/hertz_vs_avis_advertising_wars_how_an_ad_firm_made_a_virtue_out_of_second.html>.

16 R. Pearce (2015). Telstra's three-pronged strategy for the NBN. *Computerworld*, 29 October. <www.computerworld.com.au/article/587769/telstra-three-pronged-strategy-nbn>.

17 Telstra (2017). Telstra announces financial results for FY 17. Market release, 17 August. <www.telstra.com.au/content/dam/tcom/about-us/investors/pdf-e/170817-MR-Full-Year-Stat-Accounts-2017.pdf>.

18 ibid.

19 T. Yoo (2017). Telstra is entering the low-cost mobile market with its budget brand Belong. *Business Insider Australia*, 17 August. <www.businessinsider.com.au/Telstra-is-entering-the-low-cost-mobile-market-with-its-budget-brand-belong-2017-8>.

20 ibid.

21 C.W. Park, B.J. Jaworski & D.J. MacInnes (1986). Strategic brand concept-image management. *Journal of Marketing*, 50(October), pp. 135–45. The discussion of functional, symbolic and experiential needs is based on Park et al.'s conceptualisations.

Ignoring the human touch in services: Costing Australian firms around $122 billion a year

Poor customer service in Australia is costing businesses $122 billion per year according to new research from Accenture.[1] This cost is the lost business as customers switch to alternative providers. A major reason for people's frustration with many service organisations, as noted in Accenture's report, is being forced into online channels, with 81 per cent expressing dissatisfaction with this approach and preferring to have human contact. Nearly half of those surveyed also said they were willing to pay more for better customer service.

According to Luca Martini, Managing Director for Accenture Strategy in Australia and New Zealand, 'Companies have lost sight of the importance of human interaction and often make it too difficult for consumers to get the right level of help and service that they need. The beauty of the possibilities offered by today's technology is that the human touch can be blended into the digital experience (and vice versa) allowing companies to deliver amazing customer service across all channels, whilst removing the usual pain points.'

Accenture's consultants argue there are four ways companies should look to rebalance service channels:

1   Put the human and physical elements back into customer services.

2   Make it easy for customers to switch channels to get the experiences they want.

3   Root out toxicity: define and address the most toxic customer experiences across all channels.

4   Guarantee personal data security: 88 per cent of consumers say it is extremely important that companies protect the privacy of their personal information.

» continued over page

Chapter 3

Customer Decision-making

Steven D'Alessandro

Since Australia can now be considered a service economy, with around 85 per cent of people employed in service industries, we may wonder why so many Australian companies seem to be mistaken in thinking that providing services in a non-personal and perhaps cost-effective manner is the optimum strategy. An understanding of consumer behaviour in relation to services is useful because continued trust in government and the patronage of many companies that supply services are fundamental elements in the functioning of an effective economy and society. This chapter discusses the nature of consumer behaviour with respect to services and includes examples to show how some companies and governments provide services that meet customer expectations and others do not.

Introduction

In order to consider consumer behaviour in relation to services, it is necessary to follow the various stages of consumer decision-making. These are shown in Figure 3.1. It may appear from this diagram that the consumption or use of services is a linear and planned process. However, many services are purchased or used without much planning or thought at all. As with products, we can think of various types of decision-making that occur with services. This is first discussed, then each part of the consumer decision-making model in Figure 3.1 is examined in detail.

Learning objectives

After reading this chapter you should be able to:

↘ understand the different types of purchases that occur with services

↘ examine the six-stage model of consumer decision-making: pre-purchase stage; information search; evaluation of alternatives; purchase of a service; service encounter post-purchase evaluation

Figure 3.1 The consumer decision-making process

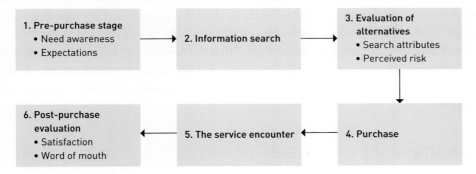

The types of purchase decisions

Routine purchase of services

In many instances, consumers purchase or use services routinely without much thought or deliberation. Examples include catching a taxi, paying bills, writing an email or using a telephone. These types of activities are characterised by little or no search or evaluation of alternatives. Services are often chosen by reference to well-known brand names (e.g. Telstra, Singapore Airlines and Westpac) on the basis of convenience and habit. As long as services meet consumer expectations, consumers are unlikely to change providers. Routine purchases of services may also occur where there is no choice of providers, such as using Australia Post and other government or semi-government agencies.

Unwanted purchases of services

There are many services that we are occasionally forced to acquire and use. We can consider legal services as one example and health services as another. With regard to some government services, such as the Child Support Agency and the Australian Taxation Office, some payees would rather not use their services! In these cases, consumers or clients of such services have already formed unfavourable expectations. In the case of many government services there is no choice of provider, and consumers may instead be more concerned about the nature of service encounters (e.g. have they been treated equally and justly by the Australian Taxation Office?).

There may be other cases, such as health and legal services, where limited choices are available to the consumer, but the consumer may be without some kind of savings or insurance; these are generally an unplanned type of expenditure. Questions of pricing and the value received from such providers, especially in legal and medical services, may therefore be important to consumers. They will also require assistance and rely on sources of trusted information (e.g. professional accreditation and training, or recommendations from others) when choosing providers of these specialised services. They will seek redress from government and professional bodies should services not be delivered at a satisfactory standard. It is not surprising, therefore, to find that the Australian Medical Association and other medical colleges have accredited training, and dispute and complaint procedures in place. The legal professions in all states of Australia also have legal boards and grievance procedures.

Emergency purchases of services

This is when the consumer, without any choice of provider, needs to purchase or use a service immediately. Examples include ambulance services, emergency hospital visits, and fire, police and rescue services. These services are usually provided by government. Consumer expectations are about access to the service and waiting times for delivery, hence the concern that many state governments have about hospital waiting lists and call-out times for police and ambulance services.

Other emergency services may be commercially provided and include emergency vehicle towing, vehicle breakdown services, plumbing and dental suppliers. Consumers may be willing to pay a premium to access a service of a satisfactory standard at short notice, as long as waiting times can be minimised. Research suggests that the provision of services to disaster survivors, such as those in the 2004 Pacific Rim tsunami, is invaluable in helping people cope with and readjust to the normality of life.[2]

OXFORD UNIVERSITY PRESS

Limited problem-solving in the purchases of services

In these cases, the consumer has prior knowledge and understanding of a number of providers to select from and is not obliged to make a choice. Examples include choosing a mobile phone provider, a restaurant or a new computer game. Decisions of this kind are characterised by some search for information. Given the difficulty of trialling many services, the recommendations of others are likely to be important, as is the reputation of the company or brand of provider.

Extensive problem-solving in the purchase of services

This occurs when the consumer has little or no experience regarding the service, the service is considered important to them and it is quite complex, meaning that there are many factors to be considered before a decision is made. Examples include enrolling in a university course for the first time, moving interstate or overseas for the first time and investing in a retirement plan. To some consumers, new or novel methods of payment can also be considered extensive problem-solving. When purchasing products online, many consumers may need additional information and assistance with the new form of transaction. Today many organisations provide assistance with password recovery, delivery options and additional online chat services to help with customers unfamiliar with purchasing services and products in this way.

It is important to remember that, with extensive problem-solving, consumers actively seek information regarding services and outcomes. They also rely on the reputation of the provider or brand to reduce perceived risk (discussed later in this chapter). The reputation of companies providing services that are complex (e.g. financial services) may be enhanced by co-branding with more trusted sources of information or by the recommendations of others. Online sales sites like eBay use feedback from buyers and sellers to rate each party in future exchanges and display this information on buyers' and sellers' accounts. Many such sites also use PayPal, a more secure means of protecting the sensitive payment details of buyers.

Customer decision-making: The six-stage model of consumer behaviour of services

While it is recognised that various different types of consumer decision-making occur with respect to services, all types of decision-making follow the six-stage model. The only difference lies in the nature of the deliberation and length of each stage of the decision process.

Pre-purchase stage

Need awareness

The first stage of the decision-making process for a service is need awareness; that is, the customer is aware of a need or problem to be solved. A consumer becomes aware of a need when they see that their actual state does not match their desired state. Table 3.1 shows factors that influence people in Australia to change mobile phone providers. As can be seen, it is important to classify consumer behaviour here into which services people buy, why they buy, where they buy and when they buy. Note that the top three reasons for switching a mobile phone provider are poor coverage (39%), poor customer service (30%) and wanting a new handset (30%).

Table 3.1 Factors influencing the selection of a mobile phone provider in Australia

What they buy	85% on contract (40% 24-month cap plan); Telstra 47%, Optus 28%, Vodafone 19%
Why they buy/switched	Poor coverage (39%)
	Poor customer service (30%)
	They wanted a new handset (30%)
	They used their mobile phone more than anticipated and needed a new plan (22%)
	Friends and family on a different network (17%)
	Their mobile was being used less than anticipated (17%)
Where they buy	Nearly half (i.e. 48.8%) preferred to buy their phone and plan from their local telecommunications carrier store
	15% preferred to buy their mobile phone and plan over the phone
	14.75% preferred to buy their mobile phone and plan online
	10% preferred to buy their phone and plan through a reseller
When they buy	68% switched providers in less than a week
How often they buy	16% switched in the last 12 months

Note: respondents could nominate more than one influence.

Source: MQ State of the Mobile Nation, based on a national survey of 1600 mobile phone consumers.

The consumer decision-making action example opposite shows how a New Zealand provider, Farmside, targeted a specific segment, rural users, by offering cheaper services that provide greater coverage with good customer service.

New market segments for mobile and broadband users in New Zealand

Services in Action

Even in a small country like New Zealand, with a population of 4.8 million, opportunities exist for mobile and broadband providers to provide specialised services to market niches at a profitable margin. In Wellington, Run the Red, a mobile marketing company, expected to deliver more than 100 million text messages through its services in 2012, up from 20 million the previous year. These mobile services give clients' own customers choice about how they communicate—through text messaging, a smartphone application or a mobile site—and cut the costs of customer contact. Businesses can also measure engagement and the effectiveness of their campaigns. Run the Red's (now part of Modicagroup) customer list includes Kiwibank, PSIS, BP, ANZ Bank,

Microsoft and the NZ Department of Internal Affairs, which uses Run the Red technology to allow people to report spam via text message. The 15-person, $3 million-revenue company manages Facebook and Twitter messaging on the Vodafone network.

Another example is Farmside, a broadband and mobile phone provider that serves some 25000 rural customers. Customers sign up to one of several monthly plans and there are also monthly extras available for those who need more call minutes or texts to any New Zealand landline or mobile. Features of the plans include free calls to other Farmside mobiles, and options to combine broadband, phone line and mobile services in a single package that can be charged through rural supply accounts.[3]

Marketers therefore need to ascertain what consumers' needs are when designing services. Needs of consumers can be identified by survey research or by more in-depth, qualitative research. Some major industry tips for identifying new consumer service needs are:

→ identify key trends that might affect consumption patterns; this may be done through content media analysis and online research

→ for each trend, provide a subjective probability estimate of its likelihood of occurrence and impact on the organisation

→ create different market scenarios based on each of the key trends and design service offerings that meet each of the needs in each scenario.[4]

Service expectations

What consumers expect from a service will determine the nature of their search, choice and evaluation. Table 3.2 lists service expectations of US consumers regarding fast-food standards. These service expectations have been grouped according to accepted categories

⬊
service expectations
What consumers expect from a service; can be a minimum standard or what consumers expect from an excellent service

of expectations from SERVQUAL, a model for the evaluation of service quality, which compares expectations with performance.[5] It is important to note that expectations can be of a minimum standard, as presented in Table 3.2, or as what consumers would regard as excellent service quality.[6] This is often the reason that expectations by themselves do not accurately predict a consumer's satisfaction with service performance, but do predict service quality.[7] (Service expectations are discussed in greater detail in Chapter 10.)

Table 3.2 List of service expectations in the fast-food industry

Tangibles
The organisation's physical facilities should be visually appealing.
The organisation's employees should appear neat.
The appearance of the facilities should be in keeping with the type of food served.
The organisation's facilities should be kept clean.
The bathrooms at the organisation should be kept clean.
Reliability
The organisation's employees should take orders with speed and accuracy.
It is reasonable to expect the organisation's employees to take orders accurately in the drive-through service.
Responsiveness
The organisation should be able to tell customers exactly when their food will be ready.
It is realistic for customers to expect prompt service from this organisation.
The organisation's employees should be willing to help customers.
The organisation should respond to a customer's request promptly.
The organisation should have prompt drive-through service.
Assurance
The organisation should take measures to resolve customer complaints.
The organisation should have a toll-free telephone number for customer complaints.
Empathy
The organisation should provide a self-service atmosphere.
The organisation should offer convenient operating hours.

Source: R. Yelkur & S. Chakrabarty (2006). Gender differences in service quality expectations in the fast food industry. *Services Marketing Quarterly*, 27(4), 141–51.

Figure 3.2 shows how consumer expectations often guide decision-making. An important expectation in selecting a mobile phone plan in Australia is the provision of a new handset.

We might see a similar sort of difference in expectations between economy and first-class airline passengers. First-class passengers will want a higher level of service (more legroom, perhaps a bed, better food and drink, and more in-flight entertainment choices)

Figure 3.2   A new handset is expected when selecting a new mobile phone provider

than will economy-class passengers. Major differences have also been found between Western and Chinese consumers. Research in Hong Kong found that Chinese supermarket consumers, unlike Western ones, rated expectations about the ease of service transactions (convenience of use, dependability and speed of checkout) higher than what they expected in terms of product displays and shopping environment.[8]

Nevertheless, expectations for services are important for marketers to consider, as they guide future search and evaluation. It is also important to note that standards of service or expectations will differ among consumers. This is shown in Table 3.3, which reports on research that shows Gen Y consumers (born 1980–94) preferred mobile phone plans with a set of included data/internet access (60% of mentions), followed closely by a new smartphone (56%) and a set of included value of phone calls (52%). Gen X (born 1965–79) had similar expectations to those of Gen Y, except that the included value of phone calls (64% of mentions) was seen as the most important, followed by included value of data/internet access (57%) and then a new smartphone (53%). For baby boomers (born 1945–64), the included value of phone calls was the most important expectation (57% of mentions), then free calls to peer and family networks (43%), closely

Table 3.3 Selected Gen Y, Gen X, baby boomer and senior differences in expectations of mobile phone plans in Australia

Expectation of a new mobile plan—percentage mentioned	Gen Y	Gen X	Baby boomers	Seniors
Free access to social media	56	40	25	12
A set of included value in phone calls	52	64	57	50
A set of included value of data/internet access	60	57	41	20
A smartphone or new handset	57	53	27	27
Free calls to people on the same network	43	45	43	40

Note: Respondents could nominate more than one expectation.

Source: MQ State of the Mobile Nation, based on a national survey of 1600 mobile phone consumers.

followed by included data/internet access (41%). A similar pattern occurred for seniors (born before 1945).

Information search

Consumers, when making a selection from competing service alternatives, often engage in *information search*.[9] There are two types of search: *internal*, or relying on expertise, experience and memory; and *external*, where consumers consult a number of sources and actively search for information. As many services are difficult to trial and evaluate without first consuming them, the opinions and recommendations of others are considered more important for services than for products. Information search is also likely to take place if the service is infrequently purchased, complex and/or important to the consumer. It is also likely if consumers are highly involved, and the service is expensive and carries considerable risk. Table 3.4 shows the importance of family, relatives and referrals by mature consumers (over 55 years of age) for services such as home services (such as hiring tradespeople), medical and financial services.[10] Note that these consumers overall use few sources of information (generally from one to two) and rely less on using the internet to search for information about services.

Some organisations produce credible publications and guides that help consumers to select complex or expensive services. One such guide is shown in Figure 3.3.

Interestingly, when a consumer considers highly complex services that are difficult to evaluate, such as higher education in another country, few information sources are consulted. This is illustrated in Table 3.5, which shows that across Taiwan, India, China and Indonesia the recommendations of parents and relatives are among the most important sources of information regarding the choice of country in which to study, although it

OXFORD UNIVERSITY PRESS

Table 3.4 Sources for an information search for different types of services

Source	Home services (%)	Medical services (%)	Financial services (%)
Friends	64	36.4	46.2
Spouse	13.5	16.9	21.5
Family	18	23.4	12.3
Referral from other professional	30.3	48.2	27.7
Advertisements	18	16.9	7.7
Yellow Pages	18	2.6	0
Internet	1.1	1.3	4.6
Overall average number of sources used	**1.76**	**1.56**	**1.25**

Note: Respondents could nominate more than one source.

Source: S. Altobello Nasco & D. Hale (2009). Information search for home, medical, and financial services by mature consumers. *Journal of services Marketing*, 23(4), 231.

Figure 3.3 *Good Universities Guide 2018* is a publication that aids consumer search

Source: *Good Universities Guide 2018*. Good Education Group. <https://ebook.gooduniversitiesguide.com.au/#folio=1>.

Steven D'Alessandro

Table 3.5 Importance of recommendations used by higher education international students when selecting a country of study

Influence on choice (%)	Taiwan (n=361)	India (n=152)	China (n=689)	Indonesia (n=404)
Parents/relatives	67	60	52	80
Agents recommend	47	30	35	62
Reputation of institution	83	94	77	93

Note: Respondents could nominate more than one recommendation.

Source: T. Mazzarol & G. Soutar (2002). Push–pull factors influencing international student destination choice. *International Journal of Educational Management*, 16(2), 82–90.

appears that in Indonesia the recommendations of recruitment agents are also important. To simplify the search for what is potentially a risky choice, international students also consider the reputations of the institutions in that country.

Figure 3.4 John D. Hertz

Source: Wikipedia. John D. Hertz. <http://en.wikipedia.org/wiki/John_D._Hertz>.

MARKETING PROFILE: JOHN D. HERTZ
Founder of the affordable rent-a-car business

Born Schandor Herz in a small village in modern-day Martin, Slovakia, John D. Hertz (1879–1961) emigrated with his family to Chicago in the United States when he was five.

Hertz was the founder of the rental car industry and an early developer of the taxi industry. He could not drive, but in 1904 began selling cars and came up with the idea of creating a cab company with low prices so ordinary people could afford them. In 1907, he had a fleet of seven used cars that he used as cabs. He founded the Yellow Cab Company in Chicago in 1915. The distinctive yellow cabs became popular and were soon franchised throughout the United States. In 1924, he acquired a rental car business, renaming it Hertz Drive-Ur-Self Corporation.

In 1926, he sold a majority share in the Yellow Cab Manufacturing Company together with its subsidiaries, the Yellow Coach Manufacturing Company and Hertz Drive-Ur-Self, to General Motors and became a board director of GM. Using the Omnibus Corporation he repurchased the car rental business from GM in 1953. The Omnibus Corporation then divested itself of its public transport interests, changed its name to the Hertz Corporation and was floated on the New York Stock Exchange the following year.[11]

Evaluation of alternatives

The next stage of the decision-making stage is selection among competing alternatives. A good model to consider when evaluating alternatives is Fishbein and Ajzen's attitude model of attributes and the evaluation of consequences of those actions.[12] This model of choice is compensatory in nature: what is lacking in one aspect can be made up by other attributes if they are considered important enough to the consumer. According to this model, the attitude towards an object (in this case, as shown in Table 3.6, a service: internet service provision) is the sum of the strength of beliefs given evaluation of the consequences or the importance of each belief. The results in Table 3.6 suggest that a consumer would be more likely to purchase the service provided by Telco B, as the attribute evaluations are weighted (multiplied) by evaluation. The theory is that consumers will be drawn more to objects that are evaluated positively and are more likely to purchase services towards which they have established a positive attitude.[13]

↘
attitude model of attributes
A model of the attitude towards an object, consisting of the sum of the strength of beliefs given evaluation of the consequences or importance of each belief

Table 3.6   The evaluation of alternatives according to attitude theory

Evaluation of attribute (unlikely 1 2 3 4 5 likely)					
Attribute	Telco A	Telco B	Evaluation of consequences	Overall attitude Telco A	Overall attitude Telco B
1 Connection will be established successfully every time.	3	5	+3	9	15
2 The connection will be established speedily.	4	3	+2	8	6
3 The connection will be dropped in the middle of the session.	4	3	−3	−12	−9
4 The price (monthly fee) will be high.	2	5	−1	−2	−5
Overall attitude to provider	$A_B = \sum_{i=1}^{6} b_i e_i$			+3	+7

Note: Very bad −3 −2 0 +2 +3.

For Telco A, the overall attitude can be represented as follows:

1   Connection will be established every time $(3 \times 3) = 9$
2   The connection will be established speedily $(4 \times 2) = 8$
3   The connection will be dropped in the middle of the session $(4 \times -3) = -12$
4   The price (monthly fee) will be very high $(2 \times -1) = -2$

giving a total attitude score of 3 for Telco A as an internet service provider (ISP).

For Telco B, the results are:

1 Connection will be established every time (5 × 3) = 15
2 The connection will be established speedily (3 × 2) = 6
3 The connection will be dropped in the middle of the session (3 × –3) = –9
4 The price (monthly fee) will be very high (5 × –1) = –5

giving a total attitude score for Telco B of 7.

Therefore a consumer is likely to select this company as their ISP based on these evaluation and consequences outcomes. It is clear in this hypothetical example that, in order to be competitive for the business of this type of consumer, Telco A needs to consider its reliability of service rather than price.

Decisions about service choices can also be influenced by the opinions and views of others. This is especially so given the importance of recommendations for complex and more important services. Fishbein and Ajzen developed another choice model that considers more the individual behaviour of consumers. This model includes the subjective norms of others and the motives to comply with those norms. An example of this type of decision-making is in the choice of an overseas holiday. As shown in Table 3.7, the model predicts that the consumer will slightly favour a trip to England (+8) rather than Japan (+7) based on the possible evaluation of possible positive and negative beliefs about visiting each country.

However, for important decisions we often consult the views of others. Table 3.8 illustrates the effect of others' opinions (their normative beliefs about the suitability of

Table 3.7 Attitude towards the behaviour: different holiday destinations

Salient beliefs about consequences	Belief strengths		Evaluation score (e_i)	Service ($b_i e_i$)	
Taking the trip in December will ...	England trip	Japan trip		England trip	Japan trip
Increase my social contacts	+2	–2	+3	+6	–6
Provide a restful holiday	+2	+1	+1	+2	+1
Improve my mental attitude	+1	+3	+2	+2	+6
Be expensive	+2	+3	–2	–4	–6
Make me an interesting person	+1	+3	+2	+2	+6
Overall attitude to purchase	$A_B = \sum_{i=1}^{6} b_i e_i$			+8	+1

Table 3.8 The effect of subjective norms on the purchase of different holiday destinations

Salient referents	Normative belief strength (b_i)			Product $(b_i m_i)$	
	England trip	Japan trip	Motivation to comply (m_i)	England trip	Japan trip
Brother	2	1	1	2	1
Special friend	−1	2	3	−3	6
Boss	1	2	2	2	4
Subjective norm $= \displaystyle\sum_{i=1}^{1} b_i m_i$				1	11

each decision). This, multiplied by the motive to comply (note that there is little motivation to comply with the views of a brother, but more from a special friend), provides a measure of the impact of opinions of others in choosing each destination. The measures shown in Table 3.8 are added to the outcome to show the most likely decision. For the England trip this is: Overall attitude to purchase (+8) + Subjective norm (+1) = 9. For the Japan trip this is: Overall attitude to purchase (+1) + Subjective norm (+11) = 12. Therefore it seems the trip to Japan is preferred, mainly because of the views of others.

Search attributes

Decisions regarding the purchase of services can be made not on the basis of a series of considerations of a number of factors (often called compensatory decision-making) but according to a few more important search attributes (features or benefits of a service). As shown in Table 3.9, the motivations of adolescents and parents in selecting holiday destinations in New Zealand differ somewhat. They would all like a relaxing holiday, but adolescents would prefer to be with friends and relatives (ranked 2), while parents would like to see new things (their second-ranked motivation).

Marketers of services must therefore realise that different attributes or factors can influence service choices.

Different consumer needs or goals also influence search attributes and therefore the selection of a particular service. This is illustrated in Table 3.10, which shows different financial goals by asset level. As can be seen, those with higher net wealth have quite different financial goals and therefore will be interested in different financial services. There is of course some commonality across asset levels, as shown by the concern for planning for retirement, which is the most important financial goal for those with assets up to $1 million. For some segments there are unique financial goals. Reducing taxes seems to be an issue for those with assets between $500 000 and $999 999 (30), while for those with assets over $1 million the particular issue is estate planning (32).

↘
search attributes
Features or benefits of a service that influence consumer evaluation, e.g. price, location, friendliness of staff

Table 3.9   Top 10 holiday motivations of adolescents and parents in travelling to New Zealand

Adolescents			Parents	
Motivation	Average	Rank	Motivation	Average
To relax	1.62	1	To relax	1.44
To be with friends and relatives	2.03	2	To see new things	2.19
To get away from responsibilities	2.52	3	To get away from responsibilities	2.52
To see new things/places	2.62	4	To be with friends and relatives	2.85
To visit friends and relatives	2.80	5	To experience nature	3.09
To make new friends	3.55	6	To visit friends and relatives	3.25
To shop	3.91	7	To enrich your education	3.37
To party and dance	3.97	8	To visit heritage and historical sites	3.77
To engage in sport or exercise	4.03	9	To engage in sport or exercise	3.96
To experience nature	4.05	10	To experience different cultures	4.00

Note: 1 = very important, 7= not important at all.

Source: N. Carr (2005). A comparison of adolescents' and parents' holiday motivations and desires. *Tourism and Hospitality Research*, 6(2), 134.

Figure 3.5   Families often choose holidays based on the mix of motivations of their members

Table 3.10 Primary financial goals by asset level (top 3 shown)

Income level	<$100 000	$100 000–$499 999	$500 000–$999 999	>$1 000 000
Top financial goal	Planning for retirement (65)	Planning for retirement (62)	Planning for retirement (59)	Saving money/ accumulation of wealth (62)
Second financial goal	Saving money/ accumulation of wealth (56)	Saving money/ accumulation of wealth (57)	Saving money/ accumulation of wealth (57)	Planning for retirement (51)
Third financial goal	Credit/debt management (35)	Credit/debt management (34)	Reducing taxes (30)	Estate planning (32)

Note: respondents could nominate more than one financial goal.

Perceived risk

An important factor that influences the choice of a service provider is perceived risk,[14] which is defined as the negative consequences that may occur as part of a transaction. These negative consequences include:[15]

→ functional risk (the service will not be performed as expected; e.g. poor legal representation in the courts)

→ physical risk (risk to the self and others that the service may pose; e.g. travelling on an unsafe airline)

→ financial risk (the service will not be worth the cost; e.g. the investment does not meet expected returns or cover the cost)

→ social risk (the use of the service may lead to social embarrassment; e.g. a bad haircut or hair colouring)

→ psychological risk (the choice of the service may hurt the consumer's ego; e.g. finding out that one has been conned by a dubious real estate agent)

→ time risk (the time spent in experiencing the service may have been wasted, e.g. a holiday or honeymoon does not live up to expectations).

Because of the difficulties in prior observation of services—it is hard to trial and evaluate them before purchase—buyers of services seek to minimise perceived risk.[16] Risk reduction strategies include using a reputable provider; relying on personal recommendations; looking for tangible evidence for the intangible nature of the service; and spending more money in the hope that this provides a price–service quality effect, resulting in getting what you paid for. The high perceived risk for many services (e.g. education and tourism) means that consumers tend to search less and rely on risk-reduction strategies more.[17] For example, when selecting a hotel this can include the hotel's physical appearance, its reputation and the anticipated behaviour of its staff.[18]

↘
perceived risk
The negative consequences that may occur as part of a transaction

Steven D'Alessandro

Chapter 3 Customer Decision-making

Figure 3.6   A service that reduces perceived risk

Source: Terri Scheer

Figure 3.6 shows an advertisement for landlord insurance, a service that helps to reduce the consequences of perceived risk in renting holiday houses. As mentioned in the advertisement, this can include 'commonly occurring risks including loss of rent [financial risk, etc.], and accidental and malicious loss or damage to the building and contents [functional risk, etc.]; risks your standard home and contents insurance may not cover'. The Jekyll-and-Hyde image of the tenant in the advertisement also alludes to the psychological and social risk inherent in this situation.

The purchase of a service

Services can be purchased before consumption (e.g. in the case of a holiday), paid after delivery of an outcome (e.g. a dentist's bill) or paid in instalments, as is usually the case with private education and university fees. The different nature of payments means that services are evaluated differently in terms of value. Expectations of service standards may well be higher if the consumer has paid a lot of money before receiving the service. There is also a risk that the promised service may not be delivered, in which case guarantees and the reputation of the service provider are extremely important. For services where payment is made after the service is received, some prior evaluation of service may be possible through examination of the physical cues of the service provider. These may include the provider's website and the premises where the service will be delivered.

It is also possible for consumers to make the wrong choice of service, as is the case with financial services, since they may have poor understanding and inability to evaluate the involved risks. Therefore, for some marketers such as banks, financial institutions and government, consumer education services may need to be provided so that poor purchase outcomes can be avoided.[19]

The service encounter

In service encounters, the provider and the consumer together co-produce the service. As discussed, the provision of appropriate financial services relies on the consumer's understanding and knowledge. In other words, consumer actions and understanding both influence the standard of service received. This is clearly also the case with specialist services such as legal and medical services, where the information provided to the professional is crucial to the outcome of the service received, as is following the advice of professionals such as doctors and lawyers. The evaluation of less complex and demanding services also takes place during the service encounter.

Figure 3.7 shows how the evaluation of a service occurs during a stay at a backpacker hostel. This evaluation is based on the European Customer Satisfaction Index (ECSI).[20] These hostels offer low-cost accommodation in convenient locations throughout Australia. The service product of those hostels can be characterised as a series of intangible activities that are co-produced by the customers, who become part of the service consumption process. As shown in Figure 3.7, the image or reputation of the hostel plays an important part in the evaluation of perceived value, satisfaction and loyalty towards the hostel.

Figure 3.7   The evaluation of service for backpacker hostels

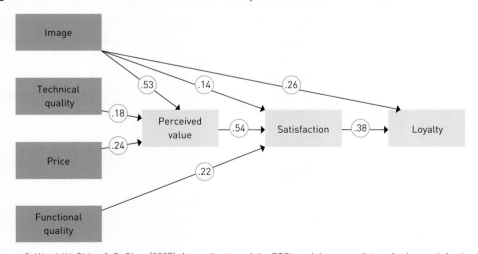

Source: S. Ward, W. Chitty & C. Chua (2007). An application of the ECSI model as a predictor of value, satisfaction and loyalty for backpacker hostels. *Marketing Intelligence and Planning*, 25(6), 563–80.

Technical qualities such as the standard of the room and the availability of facilities have been found to influence the perceived value of the service, while functional qualities such as the helpfulness and customer service of the staff influenced satisfaction. This research, based on 281 respondents, is unique as all were interviewed while experiencing the service at the backpacker hostels.

The importance of the servicescape

↘
servicescape
The effect of the physical surroundings on the quality of a service encounter

Many important service interactions take place in a physical location and the environment that accompanies it. In services marketing, this is termed the *servicescape*, defined as the effect of the physical surroundings on the quality of the service encounter.[21] The physical environment affects not only consumer judgments, evaluation and moods, but also the behaviours and attitudes of the staff who serve them.[22] This is even the case for components of the physical environment not related to the performance of a service.[23] Importantly, customers have been found to base their evaluation of front-line staff on aspects of the physical environment where the service encounter takes place.[24]

Servicescapes are particularly important in leisure services such as hotels,[25] resorts[26] and casinos.[27] They have also been found to be important in the evaluation of services, as they often represent a tangible element that is used as a cue for quality.[28] Important aspects of servicescapes include cleanliness,[29] music,[30] the design of physical facilities[31] and the perceived level of crowding.[32] Ethnic and other subcultural groups can symbolically interpret servicescapes as indicating that they are welcome at a particular establishment. This has been found to be the case, for example, for Jewish and homosexual consumers in the United States,[33] who interpreted layouts in hotels in deciding whether or not they felt welcome.

It is claimed that some servicescapes present restorative environments for consumers, as places of rest or excitement.[34] Servicescapes employed by chains like Starbucks have created memorable experiences for many consumers in global markets.[35] One of the key aspects of the servicescape may be to encourage approach behaviour or, sometimes, avoidance behaviour. This is particularly so for cleanliness, which seems to be the most important factor in encouraging approach behaviour.[36] The layout of consulting rooms and the physical appearance of physicians have also been found to be important in the evaluation of medical services.[37] Online retailers[38] can develop a servicescape by focusing on ambient conditions, spatial layout, functionality, signs, symbols and artefacts.

Services in Action

A 'sound strategy' for InterContinental Hotels

The InterContinental Hotels Group (IHG) is the world's largest hotel operator in respect of number of rooms. In 2008, it was reported that the chain operated 585094 rooms in 3949 hotels. The company estimated that this resulted in more than 160 million guest stays every year. IHG has seven hotel brands—InterContinental,

Crowne Plaza, Hotel Indigo, Holiday Inn, Holiday Inn Express, Staybridge Suites and Candlewood Suites. The largest part of the business is franchised, with over 3500 hotels under franchise agreements.

The company was interested in making the stay for the customer as memorable as possible. A central theme was thought to be background music. But what kind of music was suitable? As the IHG's CEO, Andy Coslett, asked, 'Why do we play "The girl from Ipanema" when no one in the bar is over 40?' IHG approached a company called Sound Strategy to develop music that would position IHG in terms of the Unique Emotional Proposition (UEP) of the brand. A four-stage strategy was agreed on:

1 Identify the InterContinental values.
2 Position the sound strategy.
3 Review and select suppliers.
4 Involve managers in acoustic workshops.

The outcome was the InterContinental Music brand. At each of the IHG hotels, playlists including international brand artists, local artists and emerging artists were used.

Given the design of many hotels, where for example high ceilings, glass and marble tend to make sounds bounce, so that music that has a lot of high-end percussion can easily become distorted, the company tended to select music lower in pitch (alto, baritone) with a shorter dynamic range (smaller musical arrangements: chamber music instead of full orchestras), which helps to keep the 'bounce' to a minimum and creates a more relaxed, intimate and pleasing sound quality. The heritage of the hotel and age of the property were also considered in the music selection.

Figure 3.8 InterContinental Hotel club bar in Sydney

Source: Courtesy InterContinental Hotels Group

The selected music also reflected the natural biorhythms of customers. For instance:

↘ softer selection in the morning, building to a mid-tempo during lunch
↘ from 3 pm to 6 pm, the pace of the music slowed
↘ in the early evening, the tempo picked up, perhaps with a jazz selection, as people met for drinks before an evening out
↘ later in the evening, the music was more up-tempo and perhaps more adventuresome, tapering off into a mellower mood very late in the evening and throughout the early morning

There was also an emphasis on acoustic music, because it cultivates a feeling of refined elegance and acoustic artists tend to make a more personal statement. Acoustic music was also seen as more relaxing and created an interesting environment where it did not dominate the acoustic space and so allowed for conversations and hotel interactivity. Most importantly, the acoustic model was found to be very adaptable to various parts of the world.[39]

Language and culture in service interactions

As most services involve consumer interactions with the possibilities of different ethnic backgrounds, language and in particular linguistic servicescapes are an important element that requires planning. Services marketers need to consider not only the use of language as critical, but also how language is represented symbolically during a service encounter. The nature of services means that language, as the medium of communication, can significantly impact on how the customer perceives the service provider and even the whole service encounter.[40] Research shows that using the same language as the customer is not enough; there needs to be cultural understanding of specific rituals and customs, which may not be directly related to the service encounter.[41] Not surprisingly, people prefer to be served by those from their own cultural or national group, especially for medical services.[42]

Services in Action

Universal Theme Park, Osaka, Japan: Language and servicescape

The billion-dollar-plus Universal Studios Japan theme park, set on 57 hectares in the coastal industrial hub of Osaka, has altered its service offering and design of the servicescape for Japanese consumers as the result of market research.[43] For example, in some shows and attractions such as the Wild West stunt show, where there was a lot of dialogue, this is now performed in the Japanese language. Food portions were adjusted down to traditional Japanese serving sizes, which are smaller. But some things, such as hot dogs and pizzas, were adjusted up in size to create an American image. Pies were made less sweet and barbecue sauce more sweet.

Japanese people buy a lot more souvenirs for friends and work acquaintances than do park patrons in other countries. This is called *omiyagi*. Sweets and household and stationery products are popular. There is also a great dominance in the marketplace of teenage girls, who love cartoon character items. Clothing is not as important as in other countries.[44]

Figure 3.9 Visitors pose outside the Wizarding World of Harry Potter at Universal Studios Japan

The customer as a co-producer of value

For any service exchange to be successful, there must be a degree of cooperation between the provider and the consumer. Consumers may in fact be part of the production of the service, as co-producers. The level of service between a doctor and a patient depends as much on the information provided to the doctor and the following of medical recommendations as on the expertise of the physician.[45] Important aspects of co-production of a service are the level of customer participation and the psychological factors at work.

At a low level of customer participation, the employee and company systems do most of the work. The only level of participation may be payment for the service. Examples of this are catching a train and attending a concert. At a moderate level of participation, some input from the customer is required as part of the service-delivery process. Generally, customers must outline the type of service required and give some information so that the service can be provided for them; examples are tax returns and haircuts. At a high level of participation, the level of customer interest and information shown to the service provider are crucial; examples are medical, legal, counselling, rehabilitation and weight-loss services. Many specialised B2B (business-to-business) services such as consulting, engineering and construction services rely on the service provider and customer working closely as partners. Leading scholars in marketing also suggest that the co-creation of value occurs now in the service components of many products, as well as services, suggesting that in this digital age co-creation of value always requires the presence and interaction of the consumer.[46]

Service failure and recovery

Things do not always go according to plan in the delivery of a service. Mistakes may occur, requests may be misunderstood and equipment used to supply the service may fail or be unavailable. Services by their very nature are hard to standardise and rely on the quality of interaction between client and provider for effective delivery. It is not surprising, then, that recovery from a service failure has become an important area of consideration for both policy-makers and researchers.[47] We discuss this very important issue in greater detail in Chapter 12.

Post-purchase evaluation

Satisfaction

Consumers judge the adequacy of a service by comparing their expectations of it with the performance of the service. If performance is equal to or above that expected, then consumers are likely to be satisfied with the transaction. The quality of a service emerges over time as the result of a series of service transactions. Some researchers believe that consumers can also be 'delighted' with a service when there is a high level of performance, leading to arousal (surprise, excitement) and positive affect (joy, happiness and pleasure).[48] However, research suggests that continually seeking to exceed customer expectations may not produce long-term financial objectives for the organisation (it also costs the organisation money to continually improve service performance levels, without much noticeable return).[49] Therefore, at least meeting customer expectations seems to be the more realistic outcome for many organisations. See Chapter 11 for more on customer satisfaction and satisfaction models.

Word-of-mouth recommendations

↘
word-of-mouth (WOM)
recommendations
Positive or negative
discussion with and
comments to others
about one's own
experience with a
service provider

Consumers who have experienced a service often discuss their experiences with others. Table 3.11 shows some reasons for people providing positive word-of-mouth (WOM) recommendations. Note that some of the strongest motives for positive WOM are 'I wanted them to experience good service in the future' and 'I wanted to help them make a choice', which suggest the importance of recommendations from others in the search for a service by consumers. Consumers are also likely to be asked for their opinion, which is shown in Table 3.11 as another reason for providing WOM.

Table 3.11   Reasons that people provided positive WOM

I passed on WOM because:	Type of involvement	Mean	SD*
I felt strongly about expressing an opinion	Overall	3.93	1.07
I wanted to reward the service provider for its good service	Product	4.07	1.08
The topic was relevant to an expressed need	Other	4.07	1.06
I wanted to help them make a choice	Other	4.02	1.01
They asked for my opinion	Other	3.54	1.36
There was a lot of financial risk for the other person if they made a bad decision	Other	2.89	1.51
I wanted to help them experience good service in the future	Other	4.34	0.85
I wanted to convince them I knew something about the topic	Self	3.27	1.28
I wanted to impress them	Self	2.76	1.37
I wanted to make a contribution to the conversation	Self/other	3.16	1.23
I wanted to entertain the people with an interesting story	Self/other	2.57	1.31
I had seen a recent promotion by the service provider	Message	2.23	1.40

*Standard deviation.

Source: J.C. Sweeney, G.N. Soutar & T.W. Mazzarol (2007). The psychological motivations of WOM delivery. ANZMAC 2007 Conference, New Zealand, pp. 2923–9.

This chapter has given an outline of some of the important aspects of consumer behaviour associated with services. You should therefore be able to understand the different types of decision-making that occur with services. The behaviour of consumers in relation to services differs from their behaviour in relation to products because services are intangible, cannot usually be trialled, are hard to standardise and involve consumer cooperation for successful delivery. Therefore the recommendations of others, reputation of the service provider and nature of the service encounter are crucial factors in determining the search, choice and evaluation of a service.

The six-stage decision-making model for services consists of the pre-purchase stage (need awareness and expectations); information search; evaluation of alternatives; purchase of service; service encounter; and post-purchase evaluation.

You should be able to understand the pre-purchase stage of consumer decision-making. This consists of need awareness and the development of expectations. A consumer has a need for a service if their desired state exceeds their actual state. This triggers problem recognition. Consumer expectations determine what consumer's desire from a service, at what standard, what they will pay for that service and how much time they will devote to searching for it.

You should also have learnt how a particular service provider is chosen. Consumer choice of a provider can be based on how well the consumer expects the provider to meet choice criteria or their attitude to the provider. Marketers need to identify key choice criteria, which may differ by market segment. Purchasing services can also be risky for consumers, so they will look for ways of reducing risk by relying on the reputation of the provider and the recommendations of others.

You should understand the process of purchasing a service. Services can be paid for before or after they are consumed, and this affects the way they are evaluated. The amount paid also affects the evaluation of the service, as expectations are likely to be higher with higher prices.

The importance of the service encounter should also have been learnt. A successful service transaction depends on the actions of both consumer and provider. As it is also difficult to standardise services, there need to be strategies and procedures in place in the case of a failure of service delivery. It is also important to recognise the importance of the servicescape—the environment in which the service encounter takes place—along with any cultural and language issues.

Finally, you should have learnt about the post-purchase evaluation of services. A service transaction can be evaluated by comparing expectations with a judgment of how the service received by the consumer was performed. If expectations are not met, this can lead to dissatisfaction. If performance is equal to or above expectations, then consumers are satisfied and often engage in positive word-of-mouth recommendations to others. If service performance greatly exceeds expectations then consumers can be delighted, although the cost of continually improving service above expectations has diminishing effects on a company's profitability and share price.

Summary

Chapter 3 Customer Decision-making

Review questions

1 Given the chapter's opening statement about the five best and five worst performing services, how do you account for these differences given what you have learnt in this chapter about consumer behaviour in relation to services?

2 What are some of the different types of decision-making that occur with services? For what types is price the least important consideration?

3 What types of service decisions involve the greatest amount of search?

4 Why are consumer recommendations and the reputations of service providers important in the search for and evaluation of alternatives for services?

5 Why do services have a high level of perceived risk? What kinds of risks exist? How can these be reduced by marketers?

6 Why is the servicescape so important in the evaluation of services?

7 How can marketers meet the different expectations and search attributes of services that different groups of consumers (e.g. couples and families) who consume a service have?

8 What motivates consumers to provide word-of-mouth recommendations about services? What kind of recommendations do they provide?

9 How does the price paid for a service influence the expectations and judgment of the performance of the service?

10 How do language and culture affect the nature of the service encounter?

Further reading

Baker, S.M., Holland, J. & Kaufman-Scarborough, C. (2007). How consumers with disabilities perceive 'welcome' in retail servicescapes: A critical incident study. *Journal of Services Marketing*, 21(3), 160–73.

Boulding, W., Kalra, A. & Staelin, R. (1999). The quality double whammy. *Marketing Science*, 18(4), 463–84.

Broderick, J. (1999). Role theory and the management of service encounters. *Service Industries Journal*, 19(2), 117–31.

George Washington University, School of Public Health and Health Services, Department of Prevention and Community Health (2007). *Cases in Public Health Communication and Marketing*.

Holmqvist, J., Van Vaerenbergh, Y. & Grönroos, C. (2014). Consumer willingness to communicate in a second language: Communication in service settings. *Management Decision*, 52(5), 950–66.

McConnell, B. & Huba, J. (2003). *Creating Customer Evangelists: How Loyal Customers Become a Volunteer Sales Force*. Chicago, IL: Dearborn.

McDonald, M. & Payne, A. (2006). *Marketing Plans for Service Businesses: A Complete Guide*. Oxford, UK: Elsevier Butterworth-Heinemann.

Thomas, R.K. (2008). *Health Services Marketing: A Practitioner's Guide*. New York, NY: Springer.

Van Vaerenbergh, Y. & Holmqvist, J. (2013). Speak my language if you want my money: Service language's influence on consumer tipping behaviour. *European Journal of Marketing*, 47(8), 1276–92.

Zeithaml, V.A., Bitner, M.-J. & Gremler, D.D. (2009). *Services Marketing: Integrating Customer Focus across the Firm* (5th edn). Boston, MA: McGraw-Hill Irwin.

Weblinks

American Marketing Association. <www.marketingpower.com>
Association for Consumer Research. <www.acrwebsite.org>
Australian Association of National Advertisers. <www.aana.com.au>
Australian Marketing Institute. <www.ami.org.au>
Farmside—Connecting Rural New Zealand. <www.farmside.co.nz>
Journal of Services Research. <http://jsr.sagepub.com>
Not Good Enough.org. <www.notgoodenough.org>
Roy Morgan Research. <www.roymorgan.com.au>

Endnotes

1   Which-50 (2016). Poor customer experience costing Australian Businesses $122 B a year. 3 April.
    <https://which-50.com/poor-customer-experience-costing-australian-businesses-122b-year>.

2   J. Klien & L. Huang (2007). After all is lost: Meeting the material needs of adolescent disaster
    survivors. *Journal of Public Policy and Marketing*, 26(1), 54–9.

3   C. Rodgers (2011). Expanding text messages run hot for Wellington firm. *The Dominion Post*, 8
    August, p. 1; *The Marlborough Express* (2011); New phone service for rural customers, 15 July,
    p. 19; Farmside.co.nz (2018); Modicagroup.com (2018).

4   Based on D. Baken (2001). The quest for emerging customer needs. *Marketing Research*, 4,
    30–4.

5   A. Parasuraman, L.B. Leonard & V.A. Zeithaml (1988). SERVQUAL: A multiple-item scale for
    measuring consumer perceptions of service quality. *Journal of Retailing*, 64(Spring), 12–40.

6   K. Teas (1993). Expectations, performance and the evaluation of quality. *Journal of Marketing*,
    57(October), 18–34.

7   ibid.

8   J. Meng, J. Summey, N. Herndon & K. Kwong (2009). Some retail service quality expectations of
    Chinese shoppers. *International Journal of Marketing Research*, 51(6), 773–95.

9   M. Gabbot & G. Hogg (1994). Consumer behaviour and services: A review. *Journal of Marketing
    Management*, 10, 311–24.

10 S. Altobello Nasco & D. Hale (2009). Information search for home, medical, and financial
    services by mature consumers. *Journal of Services Marketing*, 23(4), 226–35.

11 Based on John D. Hertz. Wikipedia. <http://en.wikipedia.org/wiki/John_D._Hertz> Released
    under CC-BY-SA. <http://creativecommons.org/licenses/by-sa/3.0>.

12 M. Fishbein & I. Ajzen (1975). *Belief, Attitude, Intention, and Behavior: An Introduction to Theory and
    Research.* Reading, MA: Addison-Wesley.

13 R. King (2009). Consumer demographics and maintaining clients in your targeted asset
    category. *Journal of Financial Planning*, 22(9), 10–13.

14 D. Cox (1967). Risk taking and information handling in consumer behavior. Paper presented at
    Risk Taking and Information Handling in Consumer Behavior Conference, Boston, MA, pp. 1–20.

15 J. Jacoby & L. Kaplan (1972). The components of perceived risk. In M. Venkatesan (ed.),
    Proceedings of 3rd Annual Conference. Champaign, IL: Association for Consumer Research,
    pp. 382–93.

16 K. Murray (1991). A test of services marketing theory: Consumer information acquisition activities. *Journal of Marketing*, 55(January), 10–25.

17 J.A. Garretson, K.E. Clow & D.L. Kurtz (1996). Risk reduction strategies used by leisure travelers in the new-buy hotel selection purchase situation. *Journal of Hospitality & Leisure Marketing*, 3(3), 35–53.

18 ibid.

19 H. Estelami (2009). Cognitive drivers of suboptimal financial decisions: Implications for financial literacy campaigns. *Journal of Financial Services Marketing*, 13(4), 273–83.

20 A. Martensen, L. Grønholdt & K. Kristensen (2000). The drivers of customer satisfaction and loyalty: Cross-industry findings from Denmark. *Total Quality Management*, 11(4/5&6), 544–53.

21 M.J. Bitner (1992). Servicescapes: The impact of physical surroundings on customers and employees. *Journal of Marketing*, 56(2), 57–71.

22 ibid.

23 J. Parish, L. Berry & L. Shun Yin (2008). The effect of the servicescape on service workers. *Journal of Service Research*, 10(3), 220–38.

24 J. Verhoeven, T. Van Rompay & A. Pruyn (2009). At face value: Visual antecedents of impression formation in servicescapes. *Advances in Consumer Research: North American Conference Proceedings*, 36, pp. 233–7.

25 K. Wakefield (1994). The importance of servicescapes in leisure service settings. *Journal of Services Marketing*, 8(3), 66.

26 K. Wakefield & J. Blodgett (1996). The effect of the servicescape on customers' behavioral intentions in leisure service settings. *Journal of Services Marketing*, 10(6), 45.

27 L. Johnson, K. Mayer & E. Champaner (2004). Casino atmospherics from a customer's perspective: A re-examination. *UNLV Gaming Research & Review Journal*, 8(2), 1–10.

28 A. Reimer & R. Kuehn (2005). The impact of servicescape on quality perception. *European Journal of Marketing*, 39(7/8), 785–808.

29 I. Vilnai-Yavetz & S. Gilboa (2010). The effect of servicescape cleanliness on customer reactions. *Services Marketing Quarterly*, 31(2), 213–34.

30 P. Jones (2009). A 'sound' strategy for InterContinental hotels. *Tourism & Hospitality Research*, 3, 271–6; Y. Lin (2010). The combined effect of color and music on customer satisfaction in hotel bars. *Journal of Hospitality Marketing & Management*, 19(1), 22–37.

31 K. Nelson (2009). Enhancing the attendee's experience through creative design of the event environment: Applying Goffman's dramaturgical perspective. *Journal of Convention & Event Tourism*, 10(2), 120–33.

32 K. Wakefield (1994). The importance of servicescapes in leisure service settings. *Journal of Services Marketing*, 8(3), 66.

33 M. Rosenbaum (2005). The symbolic servicescape: Your kind is welcomed here. *Journal of Consumer Behaviour*, 4(4), 257–67.

34 M. Rosenbaum (2009). Restorative servicescapes: Restoring directed attention in third places. *Journal of Service Management*, 20(2), 173–91.

35 M. Venkatraman & T. Nelson (2008). From servicescape to consumptionscape: A photo-elicitation study of Starbucks in the New China. *Journal of International Business Studies*, 39(6), 1010–26.

36 I. Vilnai-Yavetz & S. Gilboa (2010). The effect of servicescape cleanliness on customer reactions. *Services Marketing Quarterly*, 31(2), 213–34.

37 J. Verhoeven, T. Van Rompay & A. Pruyn (2009). At face value: Visual antecedents of impression formation in servicescapes. *Advances in Consumer Research: North American Conference Proceedings*, 36, pp. 233–7.

38 C. Hopkins, S. Grove, M. Raymond & M. LaForge (2009). Designing the e-servicescape: Implications for online retailers. *Journal of Internet Commerce*, 8(1/2), 23–43.

39 Based on P. Jones (2009). A 'sound' strategy for InterContinental hotels. *Tourism & Hospitality Research*, 3, 271–6.

40 J. Holmqvist & C. Grönroos (2012). How does language matter for services? Challenges and propositions for service research. *Journal of Service Research*, 15(4), 430–42.

41 C. Lin, C. Nguyen & B. Lin (2013). Impact of cultural differences on foreign customers' perceived local services. *Journal of Services Marketing*, 27(6), 500–10.

42 C. Baumann & S. Setogawa (2016). Asian ethnicity in the West: Preference for Chinese, Indian and Korean service staff. *Asian Ethnicity*, 16(3), 380–98.

43 *Japan Times* (2015). New Harry Potter area opens at Universal Studios Japan theme park. 15 July. <www.japantimes.co.jp/news/2014/07/15/national/new-harry-potter-area-opens-universal-studios-japan-theme-park/#.VhNhD0Ypo41>.

44 N. Emmons (2001). Universal Studios Japan employs aid of focus groups for cultural ideas. *Amusement Business*, 26 March, p. 28.

45 J.R. McColl-Kennedy, S.L. Vargo, T.S. Dagger, J.C. Sweeney & Y. van Kasteren (2012). Health care customer value cocreation practice styles. *Journal of Service Research*, 15(4), 370–89.

46 See the influential article by S.L. Vargo & R.F. Lusch (2004). Evolving to a new dominant logic for marketing. *Journal of Marketing*, 68(1), 1–17.

47 A. Smith, R. Bolton & J. Wagner (1999). A model of customer satisfaction with service encounters involving failure and recovery. *Journal of Marketing Research*, 36(3), 356–72.

48 R. Oliver, R. Rust & S. Varki (1997). Customer delight: Foundations, findings and managerial insight. *Journal of Retailing*, 73(Fall), 311–36.

49 C. Fornell, D. Van Amburg, F. Morgeneson, E. Anderson, B. Bryant-Everitt & D. Johnson (2005). *The American Customer Satisfaction Index at Ten Years: A Summary of Findings: Implications for the Economy, Stock Returns and Management*. Ann Arbor, MI: National Quality Research Center, University of Michigan, p. 54.

Robo debts and Centrelink

Ensuring the sustainability of the welfare payment system is an important part of service provided by government to the public. All welfare must be needs based, and how this is achieved is very much an example of services marketing. In 2017, Australia's Centrelink debt-recovery program was based on data matching between declared income lodged with the social welfare agency and receipts from the Australian Taxation Office (ATO). People who were found to have significant higher taxable income were sent debt-recovery letters and asked to contact Centrelink via its website. Call centres, while not the agency's method of contact, soon became inundated. This was due to a high error rate of matching across the two systems of 20 per cent.[1] As there were nearly 170 000 notices of potential overpayment of welfare benefits issued since July 2016, this soon became a political issue. Clients arriving at Centrelink offices to discuss alleged overpayments were directed to a computer terminal to connect to a website. The issue gained greater national attention when a national current affairs reporter waited over two hours to deal with the agency.[2] Clients found to be owing money also received calls from debt collectors. As many of Centrelink's clients are vulnerable and aged people, the lack of service, combined with low access of its client base to the internet created an extraordinary strain on its staff, not to mention many of its clients. This was highlighted by Labor MP Stephen Jones, who used federal parliament's first sitting day in 2017 to take aim at the government's Centrelink debt-recovery system, labelling it a 'disaster'. Mr Jones told the story of Margaret, a 77-year-old pensioner from his electorate, who had received a debt notice of $467.44 as part of the automated system. 'After contacting Centrelink to correct the mistake, it [the debt] was increased to over $1300. She didn't owe the government one single cent,' he said.[3]

The example of Centrelink shows the importance of managing service encounters for organisations. Yet customer service employees, many of whom frequently work in call centres, are some of the most underpaid and undervalued workers in many companies. Poor outcomes of managing service encounters may result in death or discrimination. The damage to an organisation's public profile from service failures may be long-standing and difficult to change, and destroy people's faith in government.

Chapter 4

The Service Encounter

Steven D'Alessandro

Introduction

Service encounters have often been termed 'moments of truth' and this opening vignette shows, how even with the advent of technology and big data, how important it is to provide a service to people. This is important as not all consumers of a service will interact with the organisation, and in the case of government services, equitable and fair treatment is important. So understanding the dynamics of the service encounter is increasingly important for all types of organisations.

Learning objectives

After reading this chapter you should be able to:

↘ describe the nature and complexity of the service encounter

↘ discuss the importance of critical incidents in diagnosing service encounters

↘ show how organisations can improve services by benchmarking and blueprinting

↘ list the core and supplementary services

↘ describe the nature of the service environment

↘ explain how to involve and motivate customer service employees

↘ state the role of the customer as a co-producer

↘ describe service encounters in peer-to-peer environments

↘ state the role of the customer as a partial employee

↘ describe dysfunctional customer relationships that need to be managed.

The nature of the service encounter

The service encounter can be defined as 'the dyadic interaction between a customer and service provider'.[4] Other service marketing experts see service encounters as 'role performances',[5] or more broadly as 'a period of time during which a consumer directly interacts with a *service*'.[6]

Services are activities, processes and events in time, rather than objects. In experiencing a service encounter, a customer can be dealing with people directly, over the telephone or not at all by the use of self-service technology (covered in detail in Chapter 6). The focus here is on personal encounters and interactions between customers and employees.

Research suggests that service provider relationships can be characterised by the following factors:

→ emotional attachment to a particular provider

→ having personal conversations with the provider

→ socialising outside the service encounter.[7]

service encounter
The dyadic interaction between a customer and service provider or a period of time during which a consumer directly interacts with a service

These characteristics suggest that the degree of intimacy and formality are major characteristics of service encounters. Many service encounters are, of course, not this complex and may involve simple, straightforward transactions. Other encounters involve a high degree of trust—for example, in legal and medical services.[8] In these service encounters, trust is also 'placed' with the provider. According to Hausman, service interactions with medical physicians often involve:

→ one-on-one interactions

→ frequent encounters with the same physician

→ intimate exchanges

→ substantial variability across encounters

→ patient cooperation to achieve successful health outcomes.[9]

For business services like accountancy, the key factors in the expectation of service encounters are meeting deadlines, relating well to the client's employees, being available, and being knowledgeable about the client's firm and industry.[10] It therefore seems that consumers wish for a degree of involvement with their service provider. In higher education, it is suggested that positive service encounters are characterised by a charismatic relationship between lecturer and student; that is, a student's learning is something that needs to be inspired and directed by the lecturer.[11] These expectations of a service encounter from students are listed below in order of importance:

1 Instils a sense of purpose in the class.

2 Is an inspiration to the class.

3 Makes me proud to be associated with them.

4 Increases my confidence in doing well.

5 Motivates me to do more than I originally expected.

6 Excites us with their vision of what we can accomplish.

7 Makes me feel good to be in their class.

8 Challenges students to think more widely.

9 I trust their ability to overcome problems.

10 Ensures we all have clear learning objectives.

The important aspect here is that higher education is a service that is co-created by the interactions of students and lecturers. One of the major difficulties in examining service encounters is that the nature of the encounter may vary according to the type of customer contact involved. This is shown in Figure 4.1, which presents different physical service encounters in higher education and financial institutions. The challenge for universities and banks is to not only manage a critical number of service interactions but also have consistency across all types of service encounters. Different groups of students and customers may also base their experiences with the university or bank on a specific type of encounter—for example, online learning or internet banking—rather than on physical contact with the service provider.

Figure 4.1 The nature of service encounters in higher education and finance

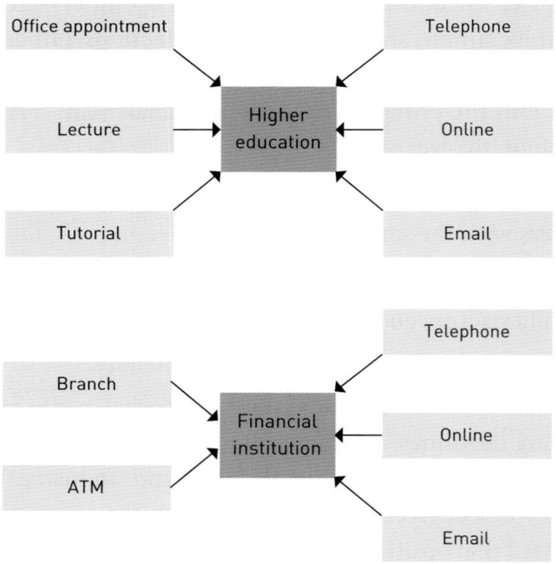

What then are the crucial elements of any service encounter? These may differ substantially, but it is possible to analyse service encounters by examining critical incidents of good and bad service as reported by customers across various types of contact; for example, both lectures and online learning, and branch and online banking.

Critical incidents and the service encounter

critical incident
A significant event that makes a positive or negative contribution to the judgment or evaluation of an organisation (e.g. a bank) or an activity (e.g. booking a hotel room online)

A critical incident is defined as a significant event that makes a positive or negative contribution to the judgment or evaluation of an organisation (e.g. Westpac Bank) or an activity by a customer[12] (e.g. booking a hotel room online). It has been found that customers base their overall satisfaction of service encounters more on negative than on positive incidents.[13] Understanding critical incidents in service encounters is important, as negative critical incidents may affect customer trust, satisfaction and future customer patronage.[14] Critical incidents in healthcare delivery have been found to include personal and organisational factors that comprise core and peripheral components of the service.[15]

As can be seen in Figure 4.2, patients were found to recall critical incidents of healthcare service from their general practitioner that were core (related directly to treatment) or peripheral (not related directly to treatment but nevertheless important to the patient). While, as expected, core critical incidents in healthcare delivery were most important in

Figure 4.2 Classification of critical incidents in healthcare

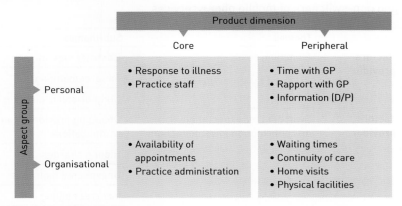

Source: M. Gabbott & G. Hogg (1996). The glory of stories: Using critical incidents to understand service evaluation in the primary healthcare context. *Journal of Marketing Management*, 12(6), 500.

predicting customer satisfaction, the peripheral services also played an important part in levels of satisfaction. Clearly, where healthcare outcomes may be similar under a public health system, the peripheral aspects of service may play a more important role.

In studies in the hotel industry in Hong Kong, China, the most common critical incidents mentioned by customers involved hotel employees responding rudely to guest requests; this is in contrast to studies conducted in Western hotels that identified service recovery as the most common critical incident.[16] It is also important to recognise which critical incidents that occur at the end of the service encounter—for example, checking out of a hotel—may be important in evaluating the outcome of a service encounter of the hotel stay.[17] Critical incidents may also be used to describe the process of changing or staying with service providers. Table 4.1 shows a summary of focus group responses collected in Australia in 2011 on types of incidents leading to changes by providers.

The respondents in this research[18] suggested that important reasons for changing mobile providers was dissatisfaction, or what is called switching for expectation disconfirmation. This dissatisfaction often resulted from poor customer service. They were able to name a number of critical incidents related to this.

> At the call centre, they don't care about my problems. At service provider Z it took 20 minutes to wait and speak to someone. And then (I) was palmed off to someone else. By the time I got to the right person, the kids needed me and I just had to hang up.
>
> Switcher, married with children >5 years old

Some participants 'battle' and 'fight', with service providers, indicating a war-like relationship. There is a strong indication of an intention or motivation to consider switching service providers due to these gaps in expectations.

> Always fighting administrative battles.
>
> Switcher, married with children >5 years old

Table 4.1 Summary of key critical incidents identified from focus group discussions of switchers and non-switchers of mobile phone services

Main categories	Themes	Sub-themes
Anchoring factors in service provider switching	Switching costs	Contract lock-in
		Time-consuming
		Comparison is complex
Repulsion factors in service provider switching	Switching for expectation disconfirmation (dissatisfaction)	Changing providers causes complications
		Hidden charges
		Unexpected high costs
		Incorrect billing
		Customer service problems
	Utility maximisation	Expensive bills
		Overcharging
		Looking for alternatives that offer better value
	Stochastic/situational factors	Bill shock
		Unresolved customer problem
		Lack of responsive service
		Poor coverage
Attraction factors of service provider switching	Loyalty/reputation/image	Trust of well-known brands
		No loyalty to a provider
		False representation of resellers
	Product attributes	Handset offers
		Data usage
		Additional benefits of inclusions, insurance, coverage, etc.
	Word-of-mouth influences	Service providers of friends
		Recommend who 'not' to go with
		Family and friends' service providers
	Media influence	Advertising
		Direct marketing
		Internet

Main categories	Themes	Sub-themes
Inertia	Habit	Staying with the devil you know
		Friends' and family's choices
		Making do with the service you have
	Knowledge and expertise	Systems and procedures
		Experience of the customer
		Price
	Passivity	Time and effort in changing providers
		Apathy in changing providers
		Lack of trust of alternatives
	Confusion	Comparison is too complex
		Can't compare offers

Source: L. Carter, D. Gray, S. D'Alessandro & L. Johnson (2015). The I love to hate them relationship with cell phone service providers: The role of customer inertia. *Services Marketing Quarterly*, 37(4), 225–40.

Although consumers buy telecommunications services for different reasons, the most basic expectation is adequate performance. If a service fails to meet the basic functionality expected, consumers may develop negative attitudes to the service provider and therefore develop intentions to switch at some point in the future:

> They just put you on a bad coverage limit! They (service providers) are just tricking us.
>
> Switcher, married with children <5 years old

The hidden charges and perceived incorrect billing experienced by customers did not meet their expectations and were of high concern.

> Just like extra charges, just silly little things that you would never know about. I was so mad about it, I even cancelled my Internet with them and changed to Y as well. So all three phones I now have are with Provider Y.
>
> Switcher, young single

This research is useful to identify not only what is going wrong with a service encounter, but how to correct it. It is also useful for competitors to examine such incidents to identify trigger points or 'moments of truth' when consumers are likely to change providers.

It is not only qualitative research such as focus groups (though the incidents can be described in detail) that can be useful here. Survey research can also be used to collect information on critical incidents that trouble consumers about service encounters and caused them to change providers. An example related to this research study is shown below:

→ poor coverage (39%)

→ poor customer service (30%)

→ they wanted a new handset (30%)

→ they used their mobile phone more than anticipated and needed a new plan (22%)

→ friends and family were on a different network (17%)

→ their mobile was being used less than anticipated (17%).[19]

As can be seen, not all critical incidents that people remember about service encounters are negative, and they may change providers for positive reasons, such as wanting a new handset. While critical incidents are one important means of examining service encounters, another important framework is the customer zone of tolerance.

The zone of tolerance in service encounters

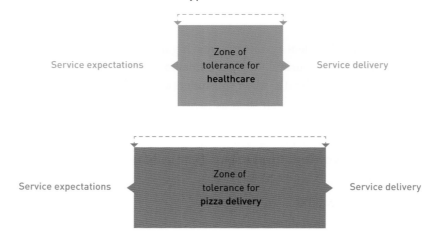

zone of tolerance (ZOT)
The range of expectations and an area of acceptable outcomes in service interactions

The zone of tolerance (ZOT) is defined as a range of expectations and an area of acceptable outcomes in service interactions.[20] An understanding of the ZOT is important, as service failures may be tolerable to the consumer if they fall within the expectations of the service provider.[21] Different types of services may have different zones of tolerance. Research on the finance industry in Singapore, for example, has shown that the reliability aspect of the ZOT is related to satisfaction and loyalty in the stockbrokerage industry, while the assurance aspect of the ZOT was important in the life insurance industry.[22]

Consumers' ZOT also appears to differ across positive and negative aspects of service. Experimental research in hospitality suggests consumers have a wider ZOT for service failures in restaurants than they do for positive experiences; that is, they are more likely to forgive poor service but not praise good service.[23] While some studies suggest that merely meeting the ZOT of consumers is enough to ensure satisfaction and perceptions of value,[24] other studies advocate the notion of exceeding the ZOT and providing delight to consumers.[25] Figure 4.3 shows the differing ZOT for two types of services: hospital services and pizza delivery. Note that for healthcare, the ZOT is much narrower than is the case for pizza delivery. This means, for example, that it is more likely for customers to be dissatisfied if they wait for healthcare services than if they wait for a pizza, as their expectations for healthcare services are higher.

Figure 4.3 Zone of tolerance for two types of services

Service expectations — Zone of tolerance for **healthcare** — Service delivery

Service expectations — Zone of tolerance for **pizza delivery** — Service delivery

The zone of tolerance in healthcare

Hospitals in New South Wales are evaluated and ranked according to a ZOT. An example is a benchmark of triage categories scored as 2 (to be seen within 10 minutes for an 'imminently life-threatening condition'), 3 (within 30 minutes for a 'potentially life-threatening condition') and 4 (within one hour for a 'potentially serious condition').

According to the Bureau of Health Information (BHI) in New South Wales, during the October to December 2016 quarter, 75.6 per cent of Emergency Department (ED) patients' treatment started within clinically recommended timeframes. Across hospitals, the percentage of patients whose treatment

started on time increased during this same quarter in 44 out of 75 hospitals. For 11 hospitals, the increase was more than 5 percentage points. Of these, for three hospitals, the increase was more than 10 percentage points. However, hospitals in Liverpool, Concord, Grafton and Kuri Kuri all saw rises in percentage of time to treat patients in ED of between 5 and 15 per cent.[26] Figure 4.4 shows this result. Note that when dealing with emergency cases, the ZOT is extremely small in terms of health outcomes. For these reasons the BHI tracks hospital service performance on these key indicators. Importantly, Figure 4.4 also shows the importance of benchmarking to

Figure 4.4 ZOT for triage services in New South Wales hospitals in October–December 2017

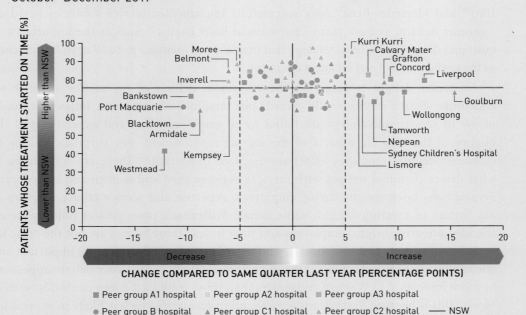

Source: Bureau of Health Information (2017). Hospital quarterly: Activity and performance in NSW hospitals. Sydney, Australia: NSW Government, p. 30. <www.bhi.nsw.gov.au/BHI_reports/hospital_quarterly/hq27>.

a state average and also to like hospitals (peer groups) so that improvements or deficiencies in health delivery can be systematically identified and best-practice cases in health delivery can be promoted throughout the system. (We discuss the importance of benchmarking later in this chapter.)

Critics of the performance of New South Wales hospitals and the funding they receive from government note that, after seeing a record 684 740 patients in that quarter, only 66 per cent of all patients in a serious emergency were treated in the recommended 10-minute timeframe.[27]

The ZOT, therefore, for public hospitals in New South Wales appears to be quite narrow when it comes to serious emergencies and the care of patients, which means there is a greater likelihood of public dissatisfaction with health than with other government services.

Customer delight

Customer delight is defined as 'a profoundly positive emotional state generally resulting from having one's expectations exceeded to a surprising degree'.[28] Customer delight has been shown in past service research to have a much greater impact than satisfaction in meeting expectations regarding loyalty, commitment and repurchase.[29] Companies such as IBM[30] and Mercedes-Benz[31] have successfully implemented service strategies based on customer delight, as have many international hotel chains.[32] Such is the importance of customer delight in business strategy that investor and manager guru Warren Buffet sees it as the cornerstone of any business operation.

Customer delight is based on the emotional drivers of joy and/or surprise we encounter when a service vastly exceeds our imagined expectations. Important causes of joy in service encounters are found to be employee effort and expertise, and the quality of the tangible aspects of the service environment. For surprises leading to customer delight, employee effort seems more important.[33] There are differences in what drives customer delight with services between men and women and age cohorts. Female baby boomers cite caring employees, expertise and service failure recovery as key factors in creating delight, while female Millennials place greater importance on friendly, attentive/helpful employees and time issues. These factors are not the same for male baby boomers and Millennials, who regard employee effort as more important and friendliness less important as drivers of customer delight.[34] Customer delight appears to be more important to Western consumers than those from East Asian countries, such as Japan. This is because East Asians were found in research to be less likely to express joy or surprise because of their more restrained culture.[35]

Could Australian banks have avoided a Royal Commission by focusing on customer service and delight?

Australian banks are some of the most profitable in the world but they have come under significant political and social pressure following a series of scandals involving staff allegedly recommending inappropriate financial services and not meeting their obligations to customers. Regulators in Australia have also become concerned that sales incentives are harming the financial industry's integrity and perhaps promoting this inappropriate behaviour. The Australian Bankers Association has also suggested that 'product sales commissions and product based payments...could lead to poor customer outcomes'.

This is a view that seems to be shared by employees in the financial sector. The Finance Sector Union of Australia (FSU) says that customer outcomes in the sector are the result of the 'conflicted remuneration' that causes 'the systematic application of remuneration and work systems that drive employees to sell and/or push products and services' to bank customers. Based on feedback from its members, the FSU says

bank staff employment is often dependent on 'their ability to gain referrals, sell the product of the week or reach a volume based target'. The FSU concludes that 'existing remuneration systems are having a detrimental effect on the lives of bank employees' and that the Australian banking industry's remuneration system is 'causing the industry harm'. The Governor of the Reserve Bank of Australia, Philip Lowe, is also concerned, saying remuneration structures within financial institutions should promote behaviour that benefits not just an institution, but its clients.

One possible solution is to change remuneration systems and bank culture to focus on customer satisfaction and delight. The irony is that such favourable service encounters will probably lead to greater cross-selling of financial services. The greater trust consumers have in Australian banks resulting from this change of service strategy could also mean that a Royal Commission into banks in Australia could have been avoided.[36]

Service failure and recovery

Most services are processes that rely on interactions with customers, so they are difficult to standardise, and it is possible that service delivery may fail. How well organisations deal with service failure and recovery is therefore an important part of managing the service encounter. Three major categories of service failures are failures in service systems, responses to implicit or explicit requests, and unprompted or unsolicited employee actions.[37] Figure 4.5 shows the various stages in service failure and recovery.[38] Service failures may not result from core service, but rather from aspects of the service process, or the service

Figure 4.5 Resolving unsatisfactory service encounters

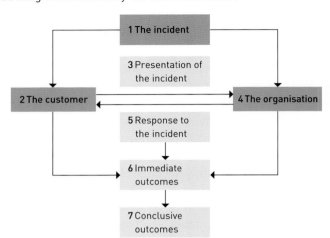

Source: D.N. Ammons & W.C. Rivenbark (2008). Factors influencing the use of performance data to improve municipal services: Evidence from the North Carolina benchmarking project. *Public Administration Review*, 68(2), 304–18.

interface, often called the *servicescape*. In one study of 1370 failures in critical incidents, 123 were identified as servicescape failures. The three primary types of servicescape failures most likely to occur, listed in order of frequency, are cleanliness issues, mechanical problems and facility design issues.[39]

There are cultural differences in the ways a service recovery can be dealt with by a provider. Research in Australia, the United States and Singapore suggests that direct compensation improved all customers' assessments of service, although it only encouraged positive word of mouth and greater purchase intention in the US sample. An apology for a service failure was found to improve satisfaction in Singapore and Australia, but not in the United States.

Experimental research, admittedly with student samples, has shown that providing a causal explanation for service failure can mitigate any ill effects.[40] The degree of magnitude of service recovery must match the seriousness of the service failure.[41] In other words, customers prefer to receive recovery resources that 'match' the type of failure they experience in 'amounts' that are commensurate with the magnitude of the failure. Research on failures in bank services has also shown that how well customer anger is placated and feelings of procedural and interactional justice are met largely determines how well a company can recover from a service malfunction.[42] It is important also to note that while retrospective excuses or reasons for failure might enhance explanations to customers for failures, even when combined with tangible compensation, these are poor substitutes for inadequate interpersonal treatment after the service failure.[43]

Customers may not switch from a service provider as the result of a service letdown. Perceived equity, trust (perceived reliability and benevolence) and relationship commitment (affective and calculative), enhance relationship maintenance and forestall customer resistance in many critical situations.[44]

It is important to remember also that not all customer complaints are service failures. Research suggests that a number of complaints made by consumers that are not due to service failures may in some cases be a misrepresentation of a service encounter.[45] These were labelled by the researchers as 'one-off complainants', 'opportunistic complainants', 'conditioned complainants' and 'professional complainants'. The main motives for articulating fraudulent complaints were found to be 'freeloading', 'fraudulent returns', 'fault transferors', 'solitary ego gains', 'peer-induced esteem seeking' and 'disruptive gains'.

Customer anger and rage

Customers who have unsatisfactory service encounters, even if the provider is not at fault, may become angry and enraged. This means that strategies and service practices need to be developed that deal with these situations. Customer anger has been found to result from three causes: broken promises, unfair treatment and expressed hostility.[46]

Customer anger has been shown to be important in predicting how dissatisfaction will lead to consumers changing service providers.[47] Other researchers suggest that anger has a less important role in consumers switching providers than does price differences or 'one-off incidents' that leave the consumer with a feeling of unease.[48] When a service transaction is seen as unjust, which can also include a service recovery, this has been shown to lead to anger, which then triggers dissatisfaction and how well the failure in service delivery can be recovered.[49] Service practices that deal with customer anger from a task-oriented perspective have been shown to be most effective, while those that aim to deal with anger stemming from personal issues are less productive.[50] Note that expression of anger as rage is more likely to occur with Western consumers than those from South-East Asian backgrounds or cultures where saving face is important.[51] In particular, respondents from China and Thailand were likely to seek revenge and express their emotions in more subtle ways.[52] It is therefore important to clearly map out service encounters with customers and have well-trained and culturally sensitive frontline staff. Many instances of customer rage and anger can simply be avoided by providing good service. Two important means of achieving this are benchmarking and blueprinting, which are discussed next.

Air Crash Investigation: Learning from deadly mistakes

Services in Action

The popular National Geographic program *Air Crash Investigation* shows a number of fatal and near-fatal aircraft accidents that have provided a basis for improved safety. This is much like service marketers learning from mistakes. An example is shown here.

Japan Airlines 123—number of deaths: 520

Cause(s)

Rupture of the air pressure bulkhead resulted in an explosive decompression when the plane was in the air, which made the aircraft uncontrollable by severing control hydraulics to the flaps and rudders, resulting in the tragedy.

Figure 4.6 A deadly outcome of a service failure

Recommendations/results

Modification to the designs of the empennage, hydraulic systems and aft pressure bulkheads. The National Transportation Safety Board made recommendations to the United States Federal Aviation Authority.[53]

The cause was at first believed to be poor maintenance of the aircraft. It was later found that only one side of the rivets on the bulkheads had been correctly affixed by Boeing staff. Nevertheless, the airline nearly went bankrupt, and several managers resigned and took responsibility for the disaster. Learning from air crashes—deadly service failures—does, however, in the long term improve service delivery.[54]

Benchmarking and blueprinting the service encounter

An important means of competitively positioning service standards for many organisations is to benchmark their service encounters. Benchmarking can be defined as making sure service performance meets defined measurable outcomes. Benchmarking can also be used to provide guidelines for quality control for each part of the service process. Often 'best practice' may be identified as the result of benchmarking services with those of successful organisations, or more formalised accreditation, where service delivery must meet defined and audited criteria, may be used. Examples of formal accreditation include the ISO certification and Standards Australia <www.sdpp.standards.org.au>, or industry-based accreditation schemes such as EQUIS (European Quality Improvement System) and AACSB (Association to Advance Collegiate Schools of Business) for higher education. Some examples of benchmarking standards are shown in Table 4.2.

Benchmarking is also a tool for developing outside-in capabilities, as it compares organisational aptitudes in relation to competitors' aptitudes. Benchmarking can identify a gap between competitors' and organisational capabilities and, hence, provide direction and targets for improvement. When combined, service blueprinting (discussed later in this chapter) and benchmarking can provide important insights into the adequacy of organisational capabilities in creating customer value.

Table 4.2 Benchmarking standards used in services industries

Standard	Use	How it is measured
ISO 9001:2008	Implemented by over 1 million organisations in 176 countries, ISO 9001:2008 provides a set of standardised requirements for a quality management system; in particular: The customer's quality requirements, and applicable regulatory requirements, while aiming to enhance customer satisfaction, and achieve continual improvement of its performance in pursuit of these objective.	The standard requires the organisation to audit its ISO 9001:2008-based quality system to verify that it is managing its processes. In addition, the organisation may invite its clients to audit the quality system. Lastly, the organisation may engage the services of an independent quality system certification body to obtain an ISO 9001:2008 certificate of conformity.
Standards Australia–AS 4083-2010 Planning for emergencies	Sets out the procedures for healthcare facilities in the planning for, and responses to, internal and external emergencies.	Specifies response colour codes for use in a specific emergency.
EQUIS (European Quality Improvement System)	Assesses universities as institutions as a whole. It assesses not just degree programs but all the activities and sub-units of the institution, including research, e-learning units, executive education provision and community outreach. Institutions must be primarily devoted to management education.	An overall report is provided to the body, which must meet the following criteria: a Industry environment b Institutional status c Governance d Mission, vision and values e Strategic positioning f Strategic direction and objectives g Strategic planning h Quality assurance i Internationalisation j Corporate connections
European Market Performance Indicator (MPI)	Incorporates the consumer perceptions of trust; offer comparability; incidence of consumer problems and complaints and the extent to which consumer expectations were met.	An overall report is provided about the conditions for each industry and market, for every member state of the European Union (EU). Results from the MPI can also be used to compare the competitive conditions across countries, and the performance of firms within industries against national and international benchmarks can be considered.
APQC Process Classification Framework (PCF)– Telecommunications	Provides guidelines and performance comparisons for implementation of business strategy in telecommunications.	Uses performance metrics for internal operations related to business strategy implementation in the telecommunications sector.
Telecommunications Benchmarking International Group	Provides benchmarking studies on various business processes in the telecommunications sector.	Benchmarking is based on site visits and survey research.

Source: A. Ceric, S. D'Alessandro, G. Soutar & L. Johnson (2016). Using blueprinting and benchmarking to identify marketing resources that help co-create customer value. *Journal of Business Research*, 69(12), 5655.

Benchmarking can also provide guidelines for quality control for each part of the service process, which in turn can be modelled in a service blueprint. Alternatively, what is in a service blueprint can be tested via benchmarking to see if it provides a competitive advantage.

Benchmarking often provides the identification of best practice (and therefore capabilities) for successful organisations, or by formalised accreditation processes, within which service delivery must meet defined and audited criteria, standards of audited service excellence. The adoption of successful benchmarking practices depends on management's willingness to compare their performance with that of other similar organisations.[55]

Research on benchmarking shows that sometimes organisations can concentrate too much on processes and procedures and not enough on meeting the expectations of customers; this is especially so in healthcare services.[56] Benchmarking can be useful as a way of building public trust about the costs of fundraising and use of donated money, particularly in the not-for-profit and charity sectors.[57] In services that can be standardised to a large extent, such as construction and supply management, benchmarking has been shown to deliver lower costs and profits.[58] Table 4.3 shows an example of benchmarking in the Australian telecommunications sector using the European Market Performance Indicator (MPI) by a provider that we will call AusBargain. These results are based on a comparison between 1050 survey respondents in Australia with respondents in the European Union (EU). As can be seen, AusBargain does better on nearly all scores of the MPI than does its competition, but it still has a considerable way to go to meet international standards of best practice.

Companies can also benchmark against their competition on measures other than those provided by external organisations. AusBargain also benchmarked itself with other telecommunications providers in Australia on satisfaction and value during

Table 4.3 Benchmarking mobile phone services in Australia with those of the EU by AusBargain

Components of the MPI	Australian industry	AusBargain	EU
Difficulty of comparability of offers (0=hard to compare)/10	5.60	5.37	6.90
Level of trust (0=no trust)/10	4.07	4.10	6.10
Live up to what you wanted (0=Did not meet expectations)/10	5.22	5.79	7.20
Problems and complaints (10=no problems/complaints)/10	7.22	7.58	8.60
The Market Performance Indicator (MPI) average of the above/10	5.53	5.71	7.20

Source: A. Ceric, S. D'Alessandro, G. Soutar & L. Johnson (2016). Using blueprinting and benchmarking to identify marketing resources that help co-create customer value. *Journal of Business Research*, 69(12), 5657.

Table 4.4 Mean quality of service and value perceptions of AusBargain compared to other Australian telecommunications providers

Components of the MPI	AusBargain	Others
Satisfaction with current provider	26.8**	18.1
Value of service provided	4.7**	3.5

(Note: ** difference significant at p<.01)

Source: A. Ceric, S., D'Alessandro, G. Soutar & L. Johnson (2016). Using blueprinting and benchmarking to identify marketing resources that help co-create customer value. *Journal of Business Research*, 69(12), 5659.

the first year of its operation (see Table 4.4). Satisfaction with its services and value provided to customers was superior to that of its competition. Note that the way this company achieved this market position was due largely to a redesign of its service, using blueprinting, which is discussed next.

Another means of improving the nature of the service encounter is blueprinting. Blueprinting can be defined as providing solutions to customer complaints by mapping out each part of the customer service process so that managers can 'identify stages in service development relative to the customer's perspective, organisational structure, and opportunities for design improvement or co-creation with the end user'.[59] The critical components of service blueprinting are shown in Figure 4.7. The four critical activities are:

blueprinting
A process of providing solutions to customer complaints by mapping out each part of the customer service process

1   *Behaviour of customers*: The behaviours surround what techniques and evaluations are presented during customers' procurement, consumption and evaluation of services. This part focuses on the steps, choices, operations and interactions of customers when they buy, consume or evaluate things.

2   *Behaviours of front-office employees*: These behaviours are parallel with behaviours of customers. The steps and processes of service delivery are what customers can see and are provided by front-office employees. These behaviours surround the interaction between customers and front-office employees.

3   *Behaviours of back-office employees*: This part operates backstage and supports front-office workers. These behaviours surround the activities that support front-office workers.

4   *Support procedures part*: This includes steps of services, and interactive behaviours of workers who are responsible for interior and support services. These parts cover all the interior services, steps and interactions of workers' support activities.

The three lines of demarcation to separate the four critical activities areas are:

1   *Line of exterior interaction*: This represents the interactions between customers and the company that provides the service.

2   *Line of visibility*: This line is the division between visible and invisible activities, which means the services in front of the line are visible to customers. The services behind the line are invisible for customers–for example, the operations and activities carried out by back-office employees.

Chapter 4 The Service Encounter

Figure 4.7 Main components of the service blueprint

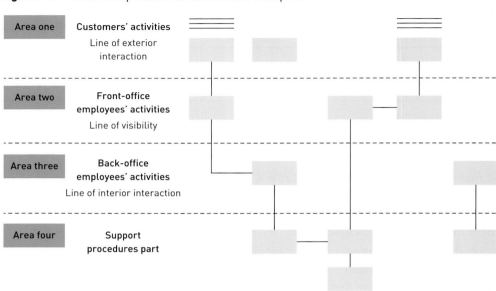

Source: M.J. Bitner, A. Ostrom & F. Morgan (2008). Service blueprinting: A practical technique for service innovation. *California Management Review*, 50(3), 66–94.

3 *Line of interior interaction*: This is the division between the workers who provide services and those who support the service providers.[60]

The main steps in blueprinting a service are:

Step 1 Identify the service process that we want to draw into the service blueprint.

Step 2 Use a flowchart to show the service process from the customers' view.

Step 3 Construct the flowchart to represent the activities of front and back offices conducted by service employees. First, draw the lines of exterior interaction and visibility, then write down the concrete process of service delivery.

Step 4 Draw the interior support activities conducted by the company and add the line of interior interaction to the service blueprint. This identifies the interior support activities, influencing customers and the front-office workers as specified by the manager.

Step 5 The service blueprint builder adds the tangible evidence seen or received from the customers through the service delivery.

An example of blueprinting is shown in Figure 4.8. As can be seen, not only processes related to customer contact are mapped, but also back-office and support services. Customer activities that relate to the co-production of the service are also mapped. AusBargain uses the service blueprint to identify relevant inside-out capabilities for creating customer value. Two critical capabilities are contract flexibility and customer service, which lead AusBargain to consider a better online activation system for prepaid SIM cards, improved call-centre support, up-to-date account information and, finally, increased and empowered

Figure 4.8 A service blueprint for changing a mobile phone provider

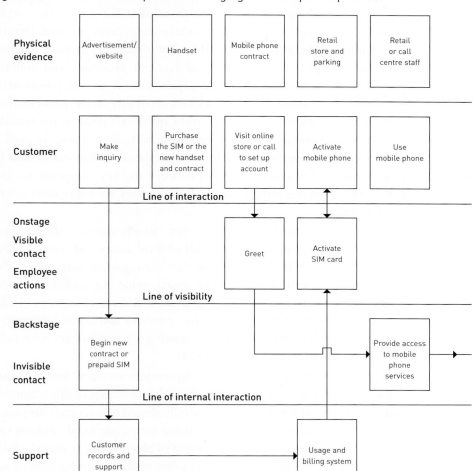

Source: A. Ceric, S. D'Alessandro, G. Soutar & L. Johnson (2016). Using blueprinting and benchmarking to identify marketing resources that help co-create customer value. *Journal of Business Research*, 69(12), 5661.

call-centre staff who can better assist consumers with difficulties. As a niche provider, AusBargain used this blueprint to improve its mobile services. The company used simple mobile phone contracts, based on SIM cards and not on more complex deals with handsets (a key capability). It also recognised the importance of coverage and formed a partnership with Australia's second-largest telecommunications company. AusBargain also provided a lower call rate and flexible contracts, where customers could choose either a pre-paid contract or a post-pay contract, and pay according to their use. Customers can change between the two types of contracts at any time using an app or the organisation's website.[61]

Service blueprinting takes employees, customers and technical logic into account, thereby integrating the service process. Employee logic clearly identifies employees' roles, responsibilities and performance, while customer logic focuses on customers' behaviour and goals. Technical logic relates to the principles that govern the service process. Understanding employees' and customers' roles enables managers to determine the activities and resources needed in each stage of the service-delivery process.[62] Service blueprinting allows the mapping of organisational internal processes and contacts with customers. As such, it focuses on inside-out capabilities. A service blueprinting map can be used to tell a story about each activity and capability in the process, their sequence, their connections with other activities and capabilities (that is, the transfer of information), as well as potential issues. More specifically, such a map is used to indicate which resources are being used in each activity, when, to what extent and for what purpose. Organisations can also distinguish between the key competencies that need to be sustained, those that need urgent action because they are being done poorly and those that are not critical.

Service blueprinting is a process design method that visually captures the complete service process, including organisational structure, all relevant actors and their activities from a customer point of view.[63] It reflects the service management assumption that organisations need to engage with customers to create value. In addition, service blueprinting identifies the resources necessary to prepare and serve customers in each stage of the service process. Service blueprinting thus provides additional information that is useful to enhance the value creation process. Knowing what customers value helps managers allocate resources to address customers' needs.[64]

Blueprinting has been found to be useful in mapping complex services[65] and providing scope for improvements in customer service.[66] One of the shortcomings of this technique, however, is that it does not provide flexibility, which ideally should be a central component in service delivery. Nevertheless, blueprinting is a useful technique for describing and diagnosing service encounters. The greatest contribution of blueprinting is that the focus of service delivery is mapped to involve not just front-office staff but also back-office and support staff.

Core and supplementary services

So far we have examined the service encounter for a service. In reality, there are many services that are consumed at a point of interaction between the provider and the customer. Take, for example, your day at a university. You not only consume the *core service* of education but also *supplementary services*, such as sports facilities, parking and ICT (e.g. checking your email and Facebook status), that are not necessarily related to your education. In this situation, the evaluation of the core service may also include an evaluation of the supplementary services. It would also be quite difficult to blueprint core and supplementary services together. They may not be consumed in a linear fashion, or they may sometimes

Where is my lecture theatre for my services marketing lecture? Elementary, my dear Watson.

IBM's cognitive computing marvel, Watson, has been taking to students at Deakin University since 2014. Watson represents a new era of cognitive computing based on its ability to interact in natural language, process vast amounts of big data to uncover new patterns and insights, and learn from each interaction.

The adviser will also assist future students and staff working with students with everything from the simplest questions to tailored personalised responses. In the coming months, Watson will consume thousands of pages of Deakin's unstructured data contained in documents, presentations, brochures and online to ensure users receive consistent, high-quality responses to the thousands of queries received across a broad range of topics such as: 'What do I need to enrol?', 'What social activities are available at Deakin?', 'Where do I find the business building?' and 'What are the computing requirements for my course?'

Over time, students who ask Watson a question can expect tailored information, personalised advice and information based on their individual profile.

Deakin University vice chancellor and president, Jane den Hollander, said students continuously told the university they want access to accurate, immediate and easily understandable information. 'Watson ticks all of these boxes,' she said.

'Watson will fundamentally change how we engage with our broad communities based here in Australia and overseas. We will be able to provide them a single destination to find the information they need, how and when they want it.

'Being the first university in the world to recruit Watson to help students navigate their way through their university experience keeps Deakin at the forefront of the digital frontier and delight our students and staff.'[67]

---

not be consumed collectively at all. Students, for example, may sometimes consume only the core service of education, without resorting to using the sports services on campus. At other times, some students may engage in social activities on campus with no regard to the core service of education. In either case they are still making an evaluation about the university as an overall service provider.

Research suggests that supplementary services, like additional retail outlets in hospitals, play a crucial role in creating a greater emotional bond, such as between the hospital, patients, outpatients and visitors.[68] Not only does the presence of more retail outlets or supplementary services make the experience of a hospital visit more pleasant, but they lead to greater word-of-mouth recommendations and referrals.

MARKETING PROFILE: RAY KROC
Marketer of McDonald's 'Speedee Service System'

Raymond Albert 'Ray' Kroc (1902–84) was a high school dropout turned American businessman who took over the small-scale McDonald's Corporation franchise in 1954 and built it into the most successful fast-food operation in the world. He was included in *Time 100: The Most Important People of the Century*, and amassed a fortune during his lifetime. Between the end of the war and the early 1950s he tried his hand at a number of trades including paper cup salesman, pianist, jazz musician, band member and radio DJ. At one time, Ray worked for room and board at one of Ray Dambaugh's restaurants in the Midwest to learn the restaurant business.

He eventually became a multi-mixer milkshake machine salesman, travelling across the country. With Prince Castle Multi-Mixer sales plummeting because of competition from lower-priced Hamilton Beach products, Ray took note of the McDonald brothers who had purchased eighty of his Multi-Mixers. Immediately after visiting the San Bernardino store, Ray became convinced that he could sell mixers to every new franchise restaurant that they opened, and so he offered his services to the McDonald brothers, who were looking for a new franchising agent. Kroc became frustrated with the brothers' desire to maintain only a small number of restaurants. In 1961, he bought the company from the brothers for $2.7 million.

Kroc maintained the assembly line 'Speedee Service System' for hamburger preparation, which was introduced by the McDonald brothers in 1948. He standardised operations, ensuring every Big Mac would taste the same whether in New York or Tokyo. He set strict rules for franchisees on how the food was to be made, portion sizes, cooking methods and times, and packaging. Kroc also rejected cost-cutting measures like using soybean filler in the hamburger patties. These strict rules also were applied to customer service standards with such mandates that money be refunded to clients whose orders were not correct or to customers who had to wait more than five minutes for their food. However, Kroc let the franchisees decide their best approach to marketing the products. For example, Willard Scott created the figure now known internationally as Ronald McDonald to improve sales in the Washington, D.C., metropolitan area.

Kroc popularised the mantra 'In business for yourself, but not by yourself'. He successfully balanced the need for central control over franchisees, ensuring that they followed a rigid, proven formula, with the need to empower restaurant owners to suggest improvements to the business model.[69]

OXFORD UNIVERSITY PRESS

The service environment

As discussed in Chapter 3, an important aspect of the service encounter is the environment or atmosphere in which the interaction between provider and customer takes place, known in services marketing as the servicescape. A *servicescape* can be defined as the effect of the physical surroundings on the quality of the service encounter.[70] See Chapter 3 for a detailed discussion of the servicescape.

MARKETING PROFILE: WALT DISNEY
The founder of servicescapes in amusement parks

After a successful career as a producer, animator and entrepreneur, Walt Disney's next great challenge was to build a theme park that would be like a land where his animations, characters and film sets came to life. His vision for Disneyland occurred when, visiting Griffith Park in Los Angeles with his daughters, he wanted to be in a clean, unspoiled park where both children and their parents could have fun. He visited the Tivoli Gardens in Copenhagen, Denmark, and was heavily influenced by its cleanliness and layout. To distance the project from the studio—which he felt might attract the criticism of shareholders—Disney formed WED Enterprises (now Walt Disney Imagineering) and used his own money to fund a group of designers and animators to work on the plans; those involved became known as 'Imagineers'. In mid-1954, Disney sent his Imagineers to every amusement park in the United States to analyse what worked and what pitfalls or problems there were in the various locations, and he incorporated their findings into his design. When Disneyland opened in July 1955, the opening ceremony was broadcast on ABC and reached 70 million viewers. The park was designed as a series of themed lands, linked by the central Main Street, USA—a replica of the main street in his hometown of Marceline. The connected themed areas were Adventureland, Frontierland, Fantasyland and Tomorrowland. The park also contained the narrow gauge Disneyland Railroad that linked the lands; around the outside of the park was a high berm to separate the park from the outside world. An editorial in *The New York Times* considered that Disney had 'tastefully combined some of the pleasant things of yesterday with fantasy and dreams of tomorrow'. Although there were early minor problems with the park, it was a success, and after a month's operation, Disneyland was receiving over 20 000 visitors a day; by the end of its first year, it had attracted 3.6 million guests. By 2014, the Disney theme parks around the world hosted approximately 134 million visitors.[71]

Language and linguistic servicescapes

The nature of services means that language, as the medium of communication, can significantly impact how the customer perceives the service provider and even the whole service encounter. It is not only the successful use of the customer's native language by the service provider that is important; service research should assess to what extent language shapes customers' experiences. Use, non-use or misuse of the customer's native language by service providers can also influence the expected cultural sensitivity of the provider towards the customer. A lack of cultural sensitivity has been shown to influence consumer satisfaction and loyalty towards the service provider.[72]

Language interactions in a service encounter can also have a symbolic nature or be used as a method of communicating information efficiently. For example, retail signage often contains little information but sends an important signal about the importance of that language and speakers of that language to the customer. This in effect creates other elements of the linguistic servicescape, like the availability of ethnic language brochures or service in the consumer's language, and can have a more informational orientation and a symbolic representation indicating that people with different language and cultural backgrounds are welcome. If language use is not well planned, immigrant consumers dominant in an ethnic language, or even international tourists, may become confused during complex service encounters and infer unintended meanings—possibly a lack of cultural understanding by the retailer or even discrimination or racism from the enterprise.[73]

Services in Action

The unexpected growth of theme parks in South Asia

There has been a recent growth in attendance at theme parks in Japan not only from locals but from international visitors as well.[74] Tourist arrivals in Japan in 2016 increased by 22 per cent to an all-time high of 24 million. These people were in a large part from mainland China who travelled to some theme parks such as Disneyland in Japan and Universal Studios' Harry Potter World. Universal Studios Japan was the fourth-most popular theme park globally in 2015, behind Magic Kingdom in Florida, Disneyland in California and Tokyo Disneyland in Japan, according to Themed Entertainment. While demand for and interest in theme parks in China and Japan have been growing, there have been significant declines in inbound tourism to theme parks in the United States. The Disneyland park in Japan is locally owned and caters for Japanese tastes and language as well as those of the Chinese visitors, making it more attractive than US theme parks. A similar success has not been repeated with Disneyland Paris, which locals have criticised as 'cultural imperialism' where the park is located in the older part of the city.[75]

OXFORD UNIVERSITY PRESS

Internal marketing orientation and service delivery

Recent research suggests that the internal marketing orientation (IMO), or the degree to which employees follow the organisation mission and strategy, is crucial for effective customer service.[76] The degree of IMO is particularly important in the not-for-profit sector, where wages are usually below those in the private sector. Also, for employees in the not-for-profit sector, customer service may be stressful or emotionally fatiguing, so there is a need for an IMO to mediate this potential impact on job performance.[77] The IMO of local managers has also been found in the government sector to be an important determinant of service quality.[78]

The customer as co-producer

For any service exchange to be successful, there must be a degree of cooperation between the provider and consumers. Consumers may, in fact, be part of the production of the service, as co-producers. The level of service between a doctor and a patient, for example, depends as much on the information provided to the doctor and the following of medical recommendations as on the expertise of the physician.[79] It is currently recognised by service researchers that any value in a service exchange is co-created by both the customer and provider.[80] Table 4.5 lists value co-creation activities that were found to occur in the treatment of chronic diseases such as cancer. As can be seen, dealing successfully with cancer requires not only medical treatment but co-creation activities from the patient and carers.

Important aspects of co-production of a service are the level of customer participation and the psychological factors at work. At a low level of customer participation the employee and company systems do most of the work. The only level of participation may be payment for a service. Examples of this are taking a train ride or attending a concert, where at a moderate level of participation, some input from the customer is required as part of the service-delivery process. Generally, customers must outline the type of service required and give some information so that the service can be provided for them; examples include tax returns and haircuts. At a high degree of participation, the level of customer interest, and information shown to the service provider is crucial; examples are medical and legal services, counselling, rehabilitation and weight-loss services. Many specialised B2B (business-to-business) services such as consulting, engineering and construction services rely on the service provider and customer working closely as partners.

Table 4.5 Customer value co-creation activities when dealing with a chronic disease such as cancer

Activity	Examples
Cooperating	– Accepting information from the service provider – Compliance with the basics of treatments
Collecting information	– Sorting and assorting information – Managing basic everyday activities
Combining complementary therapies	– Use of supplementary medicines, exercise, yoga and meditation
Co-learning	– Actively seeking and sharing information from other sources such as the internet, other doctors, books and health professionals
Changing ways of doing things	– Managing long-term adaptive changes, such as changes in financial decisions (e.g. reducing work hours)
Connecting	– Building and maintaining relationships – Keeping connected with friends and relatives
Co-production	– Assisting with the design of treatment programs
Cerebral activities engaged by the self that ultimately contribute to the co-creation of value	– Actively hoping and talking to oneself to maintain a positive attitude – Emotional labour; being guarded about fears with friends and family – Reframing and sense making – Accepting life's actual situation

Source: J.R. McColl-Kennedy, S.L. Vargo, T.S. Dagger, J.C. Sweeney & Y.V. Kasteren (2012). Health care customer value cocreation practice styles. *Journal of Service Research*, 15(4), 379.

Consumers in a peer-to-peer service environment

It is possible for service encounters to occur only between consumers. This is especially so in online and social media. Online health communities, for example, may be viewed as a service to consumers of pharmaceutical products and other health services. An online health community can be established by members, or it may be established by a corporation such as a pharmaceutical company or health insurance company. Nevertheless, many service encounters or exchanges occur in this environment without a service provider being present.

Within online communities there are a number of co-created values that seem to occur. Research on the value co-created in an online aviation community identified three general types: intellectual, social and cultural value. *Intellectual value* was the quality content and knowledge and functional information created by and available to community members. *Social value* resulted from the interactive, playful environment that is 'enthusiastic and fun', which led to the development of social ties giving members a sense of belonging. Finally, *cultural value* provides norms of behaviour that allow members to take on roles and moral responsibility and lead to feelings of pride, respect and acceptance.[81]

Research in online health forums has also shown that co-created value occurs in interactions between consumers. This was found to include emotional, esteem support, instrumental (providing practical help) and network support.[82] Well-run and moderated health forums have also been shown to enhance caregivers' relationships with medical practitioners through empowerment and knowledge of critical diseases and treatments.[83]

Customers as partial employees

Some researchers argue that consumers should be considered as partial employees because their actions are crucial to the successful outcome of a service.[84] This would seem to be the case for services that require a high degree of customer participation. This is also important since it has been suggested that around a third of all service failures are due to customer actions.[85]

Treating customers as partial employees means they may well have to be motivated and trained to use the service correctly. This entails the use of web-based information, call-centre support services and demonstrations of how to use services effectively, such as making online transactions at branch level. There may also be a need to regularly appraise customers' performance, and this would seem to be crucial in many doctor–patient relationships, where information and advice given to patients should be followed correctly.

Dysfunctional customer relationships

In some instances, relationships with customers may end up being uncooperative or even abusive. Causes of customer abuse have been found to be service failures; problems with servicescapes; and the psychological obstructionism of customers, or difficult and disruptive customers.[86] Misbehaviour by customers can affect the experience of the service of other customers; for example, bad behaviour at a sports game by obsessed fans. It is recommended that the following procedures be used to decrease the likelihood of customer abuse:

1 Have employees assume the responsibility to ensure their customers behave appropriately.
2 Have policies and procedures in place to manage customers' and guests' behaviour so as to reduce the recurrence of other-customer failure.
3 Consider communications intended to enhance attributions of globality; that is, make consumers aware of the possible causes of other-customer failure.[87]

Summary ⬊

This chapter discussed the nature of the service encounter. The service encounter is defined as a period of time during which a consumer directly interacts with a service. Service encounters may consist of core and supplementary, or additional, services.

The nature of a service encounter depends on the type of relationship, the kind of contact (direct or indirect, by email and online) and what critical incidents the consumer believes are crucial in the successful delivery of the service. Service encounters also differ according to the customer's degree of latitude or zone of tolerance. A narrow zone of tolerance, for services such as healthcare, for example, means that the consumer judges the outcome of the service harshly. It is therefore important for providers to examine what latitude they have and what they can afford when delivering services to the consumer.

When a consumer receives a service greater than what is expected then they may be delighted (surprised and joyful) about the experience. Employee factors, especially effort, have been shown to be most effective in leading to delight, although differences do occur between men and women and across cultures. Customer delight is an important factor for service marketers to consider as it has a much higher impact on loyalty and repeat custom than satisfaction.

As services are generally interactive processes involving human frailties, there is always a possibility of failure. How well service failures are dealt with by organisations has been found to influence not only satisfaction but also word-of-mouth recommendations, and future purchasing and switching behaviour.

It has been found that compensation, explanations and apologies are crucial elements in dealing successfully with a service failure, although the importance of each approach varies according to culture. The compensation and attention paid to service failure must also match the perceived importance placed on the service failure by the consumer.

Consumers who do perceive they have achieved reasonable service or who suffer a service failure may become angry and enraged. Angry customers are more likely to change providers. Dealing with service tasks that cause customer anger has been shown to be most effective, while anger resulting from personal issues is much harder to resolve. The impact of service failures and customer anger when things don't go well means that service design and the training of frontline employees is crucial.

Blueprinting and benchmarking are ways of avoiding service failures by assurance and by fault diagnosis. Blueprinting is especially successful since it not only examines customer–employee interactions but also the back-office and support services necessary for the service to be delivered.

The nature of the service environment can be determined by physical surroundings, or servicescapes. Servicescapes have been found to be important in shaping consumers' moods, emotions and evaluation of the service. Important aspects of servicescapes may include cleanliness, music, the design of physical facilities and the perceived level of crowding.

Servicescapes are particularly important in hospitality, tourism and medical services. They are also important because they can be interpreted by consumers of various ethnic subcultural and language groups as to whether or not they feel welcome at the service venue. For any service exchange to be successful, there must be a degree of cooperation between providers and consumers. This is often called value co-creation, and is mostly likely to occur in highly important legal and medical services and B2B services such as consulting. Consumers also are now increasingly creating value for services between themselves, especially in health through online health forums and social media.

Another important aspect contributing to positive service encounters is the degree of internal marketing orientation, or how we motivate employees, usually through the actions and support of company policies by employees. Successful service delivery also depends on the nature of required customer participation and the avoidance of dysfunctional customer relationships.

Review questions

1   What is a critical incident? Why is it important for service providers? List three possible critical incidents in the provision of higher education for international students.

2   What is customer delight? How can a service provider continue to delight its customers?

3   Why is benchmarking used in service delivery? What are the advantages and disadvantages of this approach?

4   What can be done when customers become angry and enraged?

5   What is the role of blueprinting in service delivery?

6   Why do consumers use online forums and social media to co-create value?

7   How does the level of customer participation influence the delivery of the service to customers?

8   What are some dysfunctional customer relationships? How can the probability of these occurring be reduced by service organisations?

Further reading

Baker, S.M., Holland, J. & Kaufman-Scarborough, C. (2007). How consumers with disabilities perceive 'welcome' in retail servicescapes: A critical incident study. *Journal of Services Marketing*, 21(3), 160–73.

Bowen, D.E. (2016). The changing role of employees in service theory and practice: An interdisciplinary view. *Human Resource Management Review*, 26(1), 4–13.

Butcher, K., Sparks, B. & O'Callaghan, F. (2003). Beyond core service. *Psychology & Marketing*, 20(3), 187–208.

Delcourt, C., Gremler, D.D., van Riel, A.C R. & van Birgelen, M.J H. (2016). Employee emotional competence: Construct conceptualization and validation of a customer-based measure. *Journal of Service Research*, 19(1), 72–87.

Dixon, M., Ponomareff, L., Turner, S. & DeLisi, R. (2017). Kick-ass customer service. *Harvard Business Review*, 95(1), 110–17.

Goold, M. & Collis, D. (2005). Benchmarking your staff. *Harvard Business Review*, 83(9), 28–30.

Guo, L., Chen, C. & Xu, H. (2016). Forging relationships to coproduce: A consumer commitment model in an extended service encounter. *Journal of Retailing & Consumer Services*, 31, 380–8.

Jayasimha, K.R. & Billore, A. (2016). I complain for your good? Re-examining consumer advocacy. *Journal of Strategic Marketing*, 24(5), 360–76.

Joosten, H., Bloemer, J. & Hillebrand, B. (2016). Is more customer control of services always better? *Journal of Service Management*, 27(2), 218–46.

Keillor, B., Hult, G., Tomas, M. & Kandemir, D. (2004). A study of the service encounter in eight countries. *Journal of International Marketing*, 12(1), 9–35.

Knowles, P., Grove, S. & Pickett, G. (1993). Mood and the service customer. *Journal of Services Marketing*, 7(4), 41.

Lunardo, R., Roux, D. & Chaney, D. (2016). The evoking power of servicescapes: Consumers' inferences of manipulative intent following service environment-driven evocations. *Journal of Business Research*, 69(12), 6097–105.

Nelson, K.B. (2009). Enhancing the attendee's experience through creative design of the event environment: Applying Goffman's dramaturgical perspective. *Journal of Convention & Event Tourism*, 10(2), 120–33.

Park, O.-J., Lehto, X. & Park, J.-K. (2008). Service failures and complaints in the family travel market: A justice dimension approach. *Journal of Services Marketing*, 22(7), 520–32.

Patterson, P. & Mattila, A. (2008). An examination of the impact of cultural orientation and familiarity in service encounter evaluations. *International Journal of Service Industry Management*, 19(5), 662–81.

Poddar, A., Ozcan, T. & Madupalli, R.K. (2015). Foreign or domestic: Who provides better customer service? *Journal of Services Marketing*, 29(2), 124–36.

Ruoh-Nan, Y. & Lotz, S. (2006). The waiting game: The role of predicted value, wait disconfirmation, and providers' actions in consumers' service evaluations. *Advances in Consumer Research*, 33(1), 412–18.

Sheng, X., Siguaw, J.A. & Simpson, P.M. (2016). Servicescape attributes and consumer well-being. *Journal of Services Marketing*, 30(7), 676–85.

Söderlund, M. & Rosengren, S. (2008). Revisiting the smiling service worker and customer satisfaction. *International Journal of Service Industry Management*, 19(5), 552–74.

Stock, R.M. (2016). Understanding the relationship between frontline employee boreout and customer orientation. *Journal of Business Research*, 69(10), 4259–68.

Tuzovic, S. & Kuppelwieser, V. (2016). Developing a framework of service convenience in health care: An exploratory study for a primary care provider. *Health Marketing Quarterly*, 33(2), 127–48.

Ustrov, Y., Valverde, M. & Ryan, G. (2016). Insights into emotional contagion and its effects at the hotel front desk. *International Journal of Contemporary Hospitality Management*, 28(10), 2285–309.

Wakefield, K.L. & Blodgett, J. (2016). Retrospective: The importance of servicescapes in leisure service settings. *Journal of Services Marketing*, 30(7), 686–91.

Wang, E., Berthon, P., Pitt, L. & McCarthy, I.P. (2016). Service, emotional labor, and mindfulness. *Business Horizons*, 59(6), 655–61.

Willis, M. & Kennedy, R. (2004). An evaluation of how student expectations are formed in a higher education context: The case of Hong Kong. *Journal of Marketing for Higher Education*, 14(1), 1–21.

Weblinks

EQUIS (European Quality Improvement System). <www.efmd.org>

European market performance indicator. <http://ec.europa.eu/consumers/consumer_evidence/consumer_scoreboards/index_en.htm>

OXFORD UNIVERSITY PRESS

QLIT (quality indicators for learning and teaching). <www.qilt.edu.au>

Standards Australia. <www.standards.org.au>

Endnotes

1 A. Fox (2017). How Centrelink has terrorised me. *The Age*, 9 February, p. 19.

2 A. Inanella, A. Valch & M. Gilbertson (2017). Leigh still holding on. *The Advertiser*, 10 February, p. 27.

3 *Illawarra Mercury* (2017). Whitlam MP Stephen Jones has used federal parliament's first sitting day for.... *State News*, 8 February, p. 9.

4 C. Surprenant & M. Solomon (1987). Predictability and personalization in the service encounter. *Journal of Marketing*, 51 (April), 73–80.

5 M.R. Solomon, C. Surprenant, J. Czepiel & E. Gutman (1985). A role theory perspective on dyadic interactions: The service encounter. *Journal of Marketing*, 49 (Winter), 99–111.

6 L. Shostack (1985). Planning the service encounter. In J.A. Czepiel, M.R. Solomon & C.F. Surprenant (eds), *The Service Encounter*. Lexington, MA: Lexington Books, pp. 243–54.

7 M. Coutler & M. Ligas (2004). A typology of customer–service provider relationships: The role of relational factors in classifying customers. *Journal of Services Marketing*, 18(6), 482–93.

8 S. Halliday, (2004). How 'placed trust' works in a service encounter. *Journal of Services Marketing*, 18(1), 45–59.

9 A. Hausman (2004). Modeling the patient–physician service encounter: Improving patient outcomes. *Journal of the Academy of Marketing Science*, 32(4), 403–17.

10 K. McNeilly & T. Barr (2006). I love my accountants—they're wonderful: Understanding customer delight in the professional services arena. *Journal of Services Marketing*, 20(3), 152–15.

11 S. Halliday, B. Davies, P. Ward & M. Lim (2008). A dramaturgical analysis of the service encounter in higher education. *Journal of Marketing Management*, 24(1/2), 47–68.

12 J. Flanagan (1954). The critical incident technique. *Psychological Bulletin*, 51(4), 327–58.

13 G. Odekerken-Schröder, M. van Birgelen, K. Lemmink, J. de Ruyter & M. Wetzels (2000). Moments of sorrow and joy. *European Journal of Marketing*, 34(1/2), 107–25.

14 J. van Doorn & P. Verhoef (2008). Critical incidents and the impact of satisfaction on customer share. *Journal of Marketing*, 72(4), 123–42.

15 M. Gabbott & G. Hogg (1996). The glory of stories: Using critical incidents to understand service evaluation in the primary healthcare context. *Journal of Marketing Management*, 12(6), 493–503.

16 E. Ching-Yick & H. Suk-Ching (2009). Service quality in the hotel industry. *Cornell Hospitality Quarterly*, 50(4), 460–74.

17 V. Dalakas (2006). The importance of a good ending in a service encounter. *Services Marketing Quarterly*, 28(1), 35–53.

18 L. Carter, D. Gray, S. D'Alessandro & L. Johnson (2015). The I love to hate them relationship with cell phone service providers: The role of customer inertia. *Services Marketing Quarterly*, 37(4), 225–40.

19 A. Ceric, S. D'Alessandro, G. Soutar & L. Johnson (2016). Using blueprinting and benchmarking to identify marketing resources that help co-create customer value. *Journal of Business Research*, 69(12), 5653–61.

20 A. Gwynne, J. Devlin & C. Ennew (2000). The zone of tolerance: Insights and influences. *Journal of Marketing Management*, 16(6), 545–64.

21 S. Michel (2004). Consequences of perceived acceptability of a bank's service failures. *Journal of Financial Services Marketing*, 8(4), 367–77.

22 S. Durvasula, A.C. Lobo, S. Lysonski & M. Subhash (2006). Finding the sweet spot: A two industry study using the zone of tolerance to identify determinant service quality attributes. *Journal of Financial Services Marketing*, 10(3), 244–59.

23 N. Zainol, A. Lockwood & E. Kutsch (2010). Relating the zone of tolerance to service failure in the hospitality industry. *Journal of Travel & Tourism Marketing*, 27(3), 324–33.

24 K. Yap & J. Sweeney (2007). Zone-of-tolerance moderates the service quality-outcome relationship. *Journal of Services Marketing*, 21(2), 137–48.

25 K. McNeilly & T. Barr (2006). I love my accountants—they're wonderful: Understanding customer delight in the professional services arena. *Journal of Services Marketing*, 20(3), 152–15.

26 Bureau of Health Information. (2017). *Hospital Quarterly: Activity and Performance in NSW Hospitals*. Sydney: NSW Government. <www.bhi.nsw.gov.au/BHI_reports/hospital_quarterly/hq27>.

27 Australian Associated Press. (2017). NSW hospital 'pressure cookers to blow'.

28 R.L. Oliver, R.T. Rust & S. Varki (1997). Customer delight: Foundations, findings, and managerial insight. *Journal of Retailing*, 73(3), 311–36.

29 D.C. Barnes, N. Ponder & K. Dugar (2011). Investigating the key routes to customer delight. *Journal of Marketing Theory & Practice*, 19(4), 359–76.

30 H. Schlossberg (1990). Satisfying customers is a minimum; you really have to 'delight' them. *Marketing News*, 24(11), 10–11.

31 D.C. Barnes, J.E. Collier, V. Howe & K. Douglas Hoffman (2016). Multiple paths to customer delight: The impact of effort, expertise and tangibles on joy and surprise. *Journal of Services Marketing*, 30(3), 277–89.

32 S. Goswami & M.K. Sarma (2011). Guest delight: Its significance in the hotel industry. *IUP Journal of Marketing Management*, 10(2), 64–84.

33 D.C. Barnes, J.E. Collier, V. Howe & K. Douglas Hoffman (2016). Multiple paths to customer delight: The impact of effort, expertise and tangibles on joy and surprise. *Journal of Services Marketing*, 30(3), 277–89.

34 M.B. Beauchamp & D.C. Barnes (2015). Delighting baby boomers and millennials: Factors that matter most. *Journal of Marketing Theory & Practice*, 23(3), 338–50.

35 A. Valenzuela, B. Mellers & J. Strebel (2008). Cross cultural differences in delight. *Advances in Consumer Research—European Conference Proceedings*, 8, 243–4.

36 Based on S. Worthington (2016). Banks can target service before sales to avoid a banking royal commission. *The Conversation*, 23 September. <www.theconversation.com/banks-can-target-service-before-sales-to-avoid-a-banking-royal-commission-65885>.

37 M. Bitner, B. Booms & M. Teterault (1990). The service encounter: Diagnosing favorable and unfavorable incidents. *Journal of Marketing*, 54(1), 71–84.

38 J. Dunning, A. O'Cass & A. Pecotich (2004). Retail sales explanations: Resolving unsatisfactory sales encounters. *European Journal of Marketing*, 38(11–12), 1541–61.

39 K.D. Hoffman, S. Kelley & B. Chung (2003). A CIT investigation of servicescape failures and associated recovery strategies. *Journal of Services Marketing*, 17(4), 322.

40 A. Mattila (2006). The power of explanations in mitigating the ill-effects of service failures. *Journal of Services Marketing*, 20(6/7), 422–8.

41 A. Smith, R. Bolton & J. Wagner (1999). A model of customer satisfaction with service encounters involving failure and recovery. *Journal of Marketing Research*, 36(3), 356–72.

42 A. Casado-Diaz, F. Mass-Ruiz & H. Kasper (2007). Explaining satisfaction in double deviation scenarios: The effects of anger and distributive justice. *International Journal of Bank Marketing*, 25(5), 292–314.

43 A.S. Mattila (2006). The power of explanations in mitigating the ill-effects of service failures. *Journal of Services Marketing*, 20(7), 422–8.

44 G. N'Goala (2007). Customer switching resistance (CSR). *International Journal of Service Industry Management*, 18(5), 510–33.

45 K. Reynolds & L. Harris (2005). When service failure is not service failure: An exploration of the forms and motives of 'illegitimate' customer complaining. *Journal of Services Marketing*, 19(5), 321–35.

46 V. Funches (2011). The consumer anger phenomena: Causes and consequences. *Journal of Services Marketing*, 25(6), 420–8.

47 R. Bougie, R. Pieters & M. Zeelenberg (2003). Angry customers don't come back, they get back: The experience and behavioral implications of anger and dissatisfaction in services. *Journal of the Academy of Marketing Science*, 31(4), 377–93.

48 C. Antón, C. Camarero & M. Carrero (2007). Analysing firms' failures as determinants of consumer switching intentions: The effect of moderating factors. *European Journal of Marketing*, 41(1/2), 135–58.

49 A. Casado-Diaz, F. Mass-Ruiz & H. Kasper (2007). Explaining satisfaction in double deviation scenarios: The effects of anger and distributive justice. *International Journal of Bank Marketing*, 25(5), 292–314.

50 M. Beverland, S. Kates, A. Lindgreen & E. Chung (2010). Exploring consumer conflict management in service encounters. *Journal of the Academy of Marketing Science*, 38(5), 617–33.

51 P.G. Patterson, M. K. Brady & J.R. McColl-Kennedy (2016). Geysers or bubbling hot springs? A cross-cultural examination of customer rage from eastern and western perspectives. *Journal of Service Research*, 19(3), 243–59.

52 ibid.

53 *National Geographic Channel. Air Crash Investigation.* <www.nationalgeographic.com.au/search/?q=japan+airlines+123>.

54 Details of this event can be viewed at <http://natgeotv.com/asia/air-crash-investigation/videos/out-of-control>.

55 D.N. Ammons & W.C. Rivenbark (2008). Factors influencing the use of performance data to improve municipal services: Evidence from the North Carolina benchmarking project. *Public Administration Review*, 68(2), 304–18.

56 G. Pinar (2005). Benchmarking in health services. *Benchmarking: An International Journal*, 12(4), 293–309.

57 T. Aldrich (2009). Benchmarking the fundraising performance of UK charities, *International Journal of Nonprofit & Voluntary Sector Marketing*, 14(4), 353–64.

58 T. Madritsch (2009). Best practice benchmarking in order to analyze operating costs in the health care sector. *Journal of Facilities Management*, 7(1), 61–7; T. Bissett & J. Buchan (2006). Global experience of benchmarking facility maintenance and turnaround contracted services. *AACE International Transactions*, 6.1–6.8.

59 M.J. Bitner, A. Ostrom & F. Morgan (2008). Service blueprinting: A practical technique for service innovation. *California Management Review*, 50(3), 66–94.

60 Open Learning Resource for Service Science. <http://wiki.service-science.ctm.nthu.edu.tw/index.php/Service_Blueprinting>.

61 A. Ceric, S. D'Alessandro, G. Soutar & L. Johnson (2016). Using blueprinting and benchmarking to identify marketing resources that help co-create customer value. *Journal of Business Research*, 69(12), 5653–61.

62 J. Kingman-Brundage, W.R. George & D.E. Bowen (1995). 'Service logic': Achieving service system integration. *International Journal of Service Industry Management*, 6(4), 20–39.

63 M.J. Bitner, A. Ostrom & F. Morgan (2008). Service blueprinting: A practical technique for service innovation. *California Management Review*, 50(3), 66–94.

64 J. Kingman-Brundage (1993). Service mapping: Gaining a concrete perspective on service system design. In E.E. Scheuing & W.F. Christopher (eds), *The service quality handbook*. New York: American Marketing Association, pp. 148–63.

65 M. Polonsky & A. Sargeant (2007). Managing the donation service experience. *Nonprofit Management & Leadership*, 17(4), 459–76.

66 A. Smith, M. Fischbacher & F. Wilson (2007). New service development: From panoramas to precision. *European Management Journal*, 25(5), 370–83.

67 Based on B. Karlovsky (2014). IBM's Watson picks up first Australian customers. *Australian Reseller News*, 8 October.

68 A. Eisingerich & L. Boehm (2009). Hospital visitors ask for more shopping outlets. *Harvard Business Review*, 87(5), 21–2.

69 Based on Wikipedia (2018). Ray Kroc. <http://en.wikipedia.org/wiki/Ray_Kroc>. This work is released under CC-BY-SA <http://creativecommons.org/licenses/by-sa/3.0>.

70 M.J. Bitner (1992). Servicescapes: The impact of physical surroundings on customers and employees. *Journal of Marketing*, 56(2), 57–71.

71 Based on Wikipedia. (2017). Walt Disney. <https://en.wikipedia.org/wiki/Walt_Disney>.

72 J. Holmqvist (2011). Consumer language preferences in service encounters: A cross-cultural perspective. *Managing Service Quality*, 21(2), 178–91. J. Bruneel, Y. van Vaerenbergh & C. Grönroos (2014). Consumers' willingness to communicate in a second language. *Management Decision*, 52(5), 950–66. P. Sharma, J.L. Tam & K. Namwoon (2009). Demystifying intercultural service encounters: Toward a comprehensive conceptual framework. *Journal of Service Research*, 12(2), 227–42.

73 E. Touchstone, S. Koslow, P. Shamdasan & S. D'Alessandro (2016). The linguistic servicescape: Speaking their language may not be enough. *Journal Business Research*, 72(3), 147–57.

74 Based on *Bangkok Post* (2017). NBC Universals buys the USJ. 17 March <www.bangkokpost.com/business/world/1207461/nbcuniversal-buys-rest-of-usj>.

75 *South China Morning Post* (2017). Theme parks: Highs and lows. 21 February.

76 V. Tortosa, M. Moliner & J. Sanchez (2009). Internal market orientation and its influence on organisational performance. *European Journal of Marketing*, 43(11/12), 1435–56.

77 C.R. Cano & D. Sams (2009). The importance of an internal marketing orientation in social services. *International Journal of Nonprofit & Voluntary Sector Marketing*, 14(3), 285–95.

78 P. Naude, J. Desai & J. Murphy (2003). Identifying the determinants of internal marketing orientation. *European Journal of Marketing*, 37(9), 1205–20.

79 J.R. McColl-Kennedy, S.L. Vargo, T.S. Dagger, J.C. Sweeney & Y. Kasteren (2012). Health care customer value cocreation practice styles. *Journal of Service Research*, 15(4), 370–89.

80 A.F. Payne, K. Storbacka & P. Frow (2008). Managing the co-creation of value. *Journal of Academy of Marketing Science*, 36(1), 83-96. S.L. Vargo, P.P. Magio & M.A. Akaka (2008). On value and value co-creation: A service systems and service logic perspective. *European Management Journal*, 26(3), 145–52.

81 M. Seraj (2012). We create, we connect, we respect, therefore we are: Intellectual, social, and cultural value in online communities. *Journal of Interactive Marketing*, 26(4), 209–22.

82 S. Stewart-Loane, C. Webster & S. D'Alessandro (2014). Identifying consumer value co-created through social support within online health communities. *Journal of Macromarketing*, 35(3), 353–67.

83 S. Stewart-Loane, C. Webster & S. D'Alessandro (2014). Empowered and knowledgeable health consumers: The impact of online support groups on the doctor–patient relationship. *Australasian Marketing Journal*, (22)3, 238–45.

84 D. Bowden (1986). Managing customers as human resources in service organisations. *Human Resource Management*, 25(3), 371–83.

85 S. Tax, M. Colgate & D. Bowden (2006). How to prevent customers from failing. *MIT Sloan Management Review*, 47(Spring), 30–8.

86 K. Reynolds & L. Harris (2009). Dysfunctional customer behaviour severity: An empirical examination. *Journal of Retailing*, 85(3), 321–33.

87 W. Huang, Y.-C. Lin & Y.-C. Wen (2010). Attributions and outcomes of customer misbehaviour. *Journal of Business & Psychology*, 25(1), 151–61.

Case

Case study A

Nomads: A new banking customer segment

Research has identified a new type of banking consumer—the Nomad. Customers who are classified as Nomads are savvy, innovative and eager to explore technology-based services. Traditional segmentation models do not apply to them, but Nomads will reward those banks that are as nimble as they are. Nomads, who represent about 30 per cent of a sample of Australian bank customers surveyed by Accenture in 2017, display conspicuously different banking characteristics from other segments.[1] Sixty per cent of Nomads would consider setting up an account with a supermarket or a retailer and, even more startlingly, even in Australia more than three-quarters (77%) would be willing to open an account with Facebook, Google or any other online financial service provider if it were on offer. Moreover, 'traditional' loyalty to a single brand is not a prominent attribute for this new segment.[2]

Nomads have a significantly greater preference for digital channels than the remaining 70 per cent of the Australian banking population, and are more demanding of convenience, insisting on being able to access services wherever they are and whenever they need them. They are more adventurous too—interested in helping to shape new products and services. But this is precisely why this group of potential customers represents one of the best opportunities banks have to grow their market share. Their propensity to explore and embrace change means they can be persuaded to join a bank that satisfies their expectations because they are currently the least well-served, satisfied and/or understood customer segment. In contrast, the other two segments identified—Hunters and Quality Seekers—are already well served by banks (see Table 1).

By considering how the services of Australian banks have evolved through simplification and digitisation, it is very likely that the existing banks will to continue to meet the needs and wants of the Hunters and Quality Seekers segments, who are more likely to remain loyal to their current primary banking institution. Banks that can recognise the needs, wants and expectations of the Nomads will have the opportunity to build a significant growth segment.

Table 1 Characteristics of other customer segments

Hunters	Quality Seekers
Prefer traditional providers	Want to remain with banks
Want banks to match tech providers' digitally driven service levels	See trust as vital
Need the human touch	Interested in innovation
Open to new services	Open to automation
	Enhanced experience

OXFORD UNIVERSITY PRESS

Contrary to popular assumptions, these digitally savvy consumers are not exclusively Millennials. In the survey, 43 per cent of Nomads fall into the 22–34 age bracket, but more are older; 37 per cent are aged between 35 and 50, and another 12 per cent are aged over 50.

Many have accumulated some wealth, which makes the Nomads a sizeable opportunity for Australian banks; their total liquid assets are estimated to be worth about A$2 trillion.[3] Nomads, as a customer segment, are difficult to retain because they prioritise convenience and immediacy before engaging in strong relationships, and they will use their digital skills to find and move to other providers if they are not satisfied. To stay relevant to Nomad customers, banks must be equally digitally savvy in understanding and serving the needs and wants of this group. Nomads are like social butterflies—they will choose banks that curate the right service options for them at a given time and, crucially, provide them with the opportunity to shape the bank's financial services.

Nomads value convenience and innovation

Australian banks are starting their transformation on a strong digital foundation. According to technology consulting firm Forrester, Australian (and New Zealand) banks are among the most digitally innovative in the world,[4] while Australian consumers are among the world's fastest adopters of mobile banking.[5] As shown in Table 2 , more than half of Nomads in the Accenture survey expected to use smartphone apps to make contactless payments and to be able to conduct transactions that way, and Australian banks already have the right platforms to serve them. More than half of the Nomads, however, expect more, with 54 per cent wanting to use personal budget-monitoring tools, and 44 per cent interested in getting face-to-face banking advice in real time via their smartphones.

Table 2   What Nomads want from a bank

Services wanted by Nomads	Percentage of Nomads
Receiving information about services exactly when they need them	52%
Receiving specific location-based offers	50%
Using mobile apps for making contactless payments	56%
Using personal monthly budget monitoring tools	54%
Peer-to-peer payment services	53%
Tools to transfer money abroad instantly and at low cost	53%
Tools providing direct access to digital money (e.g. Bitcoin)	45%

Source: *Australian Consumer Banking Survey*, Accenture, 2017.

Nomads' attachment to technology is not limited to using their devices; for example, almost 80 per cent are willing to engage with machine-generated banking advice. Although Westpac, National Australia Bank (NAB), Commonwealth Bank of Australia, ANZ and some smaller banks are in various stages of trialling 'bots' that are powered by artificial intelligence (AI), most are still at the proof-of-concept stage or positioned primarily to answer customer-service enquiries. Nomads expect digital advice that will come to resemble, in their cognitive sophistication, the advice offered by investment management firms' robo-advisers to their retail customers.[6]

Some Nomads desire services that go beyond what banks are currently willing to support. Nearly half of those in the survey (45%) would like to have tools giving them direct access to digital forms of money, such as Bitcoin. The research also shows that more than half of Nomads (53%) are interested in peer-to-peer (P2P) payment services. Although those services could exclude banks from the value chain, some Australian banks' recent investments in P2P start-ups could lead to bank-inclusive P2P services.[7]

The propensity of the Nomad segment to engage with technology may be a driver for developing a bank's capabilities. Capturing a significant share of that market segment, however, depends on the banks embracing the commercial realities of serving Nomad customers. For example, the results of the survey suggest that Nomads are highly transactional customers who want information and services in the moment—exactly when they need them and wherever they happen to be.

That service attribute is already offered to them by non-financial service providers, from retailers that provide targeted offers the second that needs arise to location-driven restaurant recommendations, and those services have created fluid expectations in Nomads that are spilling over to banking.[8] These customer expectations are more capital intensive than merely checking account balances. They may range from receiving quotes on mortgage deals while buying real estate to warnings about potential overdrafts or fraudulent activity while they are shopping. Or it may even be obtaining help while away from home. The importance of 'in the moment' means banks will discover that some realities in having Nomads as customers are severe; if Nomads cannot receive the information they need—when they need it—such as quotes that meet their price points, or a real-time service that meets their quality expectations, they will use their digital skills to quickly find another provider.

Nomads are multi-channel customers but relationship banking, however, is not high on their priority list. Only a minority (29%) say that relationship- and advice-driven services are important to them. Trying to stop Nomads exploring and switching will lead to frustrations. Instead of trying to lock them in, banks should support Nomads' transactional behaviour. Given that Nomads are willing to maintain multiple provider relationships to suit their needs, this support is likely to mean letting them transact across a wide ecosystem of partners and, paradoxically, reducing the barriers to switching. Give customers the freedom to roam; they will see a hassle-free brand they respect, recommend and engage with even if some of their needs are not met through proprietary products and services.

Most customers feel their wants and needs should be the drivers of service development and delivery, but the needs and wants of Nomads are stronger than those of other customers. Delighting Nomads means giving them seamless access to innovative new options, wherever they come from. That seamless access, however, increasingly relies on having the right ecosystem partners and integration with third-party services, and that freedom runs counter to traditional banking culture. Banks need to engage directly and continuously with Nomads in order to lead the market in specific product and service features. Fortunately, many Nomads value co-creation and want to help their banks to innovate and develop better products and services. Nearly four in 10 (38%), for example, would like their bank to create social media groups that allow them to provide input into new products and services. The major Australian banks have recognised this desire to co-create, and have set up innovation labs or hubs—National Australia

OXFORD UNIVERSITY PRESS

Bank's NAB Labs, for example—via which bank employees, customers and independent start-ups share ideas for new products and services.[9] The question that arises is how to manage the scale of the engagement with Nomads beyond a lab environment.

One area that would be responsive for customer collaboration is new forms of communication and interaction. As shown in Table 3, 39 per cent of Nomads express the desire for their banks to introduce new ways of communicating, such as via wearable devices.

Table 3   Nomads want more sophisticated digital banking services

Services wanted by Nomads	Nomads	Other consumers
I would like my bank to blend physical branches and digital services, allowing what best suits me, and which gives me a seamless experience.	54%	45%
I would like the ability to switch between online and telephone channels when I am making a purchase/ accessing a service, without it slowing down the process.	51%	34%
I would like to have instant access to face-to-face advice from my bank or insurer via my mobile device.	44%	23%
I would like my bank or insurer to introduce new ways of communicating with me, such as via wearable devices or virtual reality headsets.	39%	11%

Source: *Australian Consumer Banking Survey*, Accenture, 2017.

Given Nomads' interests in receiving computer-generated advice, AI and machine learning are also likely to be beneficial channels in bank–customer communication and collaboration. Quite simply, the results of the Accenture survey suggest that Nomads are looking for more innovation and excellence in digital banking services compared to other consumers, and while co-creation initiatives will not only help to deliver those attributes, they will also demonstrate a bank's commitment to listening and innovating. Banks will, of course, have to achieve that commitment without alienating more traditional customers—who are still in the majority—and less likely to switch to disruptive new competitors. Nomads, on the other hand, who are not having their needs and wants satisfied, will move to a bank that provides a commitment to innovation first.

Methodology

Accenture surveyed 32 715 respondents across 18 markets including Australia, Benelux, Brazil, Canada, Chile, China (Hong Kong), France, Germany, Indonesia, Ireland, Italy, Japan, Nordics (Finland, Norway, Sweden), Singapore, Spain, Thailand, the United Kingdom and the United States. Respondents were consumers of banking, insurance and investment advice services; they were required to have a bank account and an insurance policy and were asked if they used an independent financial adviser, wealth manager or asset manager (investment advisory responses totalled 9987.) Respondents covered multiple generations and income levels. The fieldwork for the survey was conducted during May and June 2016. Australian respondents numbered 2011, of which 613 (30%) were characterised as Nomads by cluster-analysis (i.e. analysis across multiple variables).

Something to think about

'Nomads', who are a customer segment with assets worth up to A$2 trillion, present a growth opportunity for Australian banks. So, should banks strive to retain their Nomads? What are the opportunities and challenges for banks in satisfying the needs, wants and expectations of a Nomad customer segment?

Endnotes

1   Accenture (2017). *Australian Consumer Banking Survey*. New growth opportunity for Australian banks. <www.accenture.com/t00010101T000000Z__w__/au-en/_acnmedia/Accenture/Conversion-Assets/DotCom/Documents/Local/au-en/PDF/1/Accenture-Australian-Banking-Global-Distribution-Marketing-Consumer-study.pdf#zoom=50>.
2   ibid.
3   Accenture analysis, based on self-reported liquid, investable assets (excluding property).
4   D. Paredes. (2016). Australia and New Zealand banks among the most digitally innovative in the world: Forrester. *CIO New Zealand*, 13 June. <www.cio.co.nz/article/601537/australian-new-zealand-banks-among-most-digitally-innovative-world-forrester>.
5   See, for example, Adobe Digital Index: State of Banking Report, 2 May 2016. <www.slideshare.net/adobe/adobe-digital-index-state-of-banking-report>.
6   J. Eyers (2016). Westpac invests in SME online loan broker Valiant Finance. *AFR*, 14 June. <www.afr.com/business/banking-and-finance/westpac-invests-in-sme-online-loan-broker-valiant-finance-20160613-gphpe4>. Cited in *Australian Consumer Banking Survey*, Accenture, 2017.
7   ibid. Cited in *Australian Consumer Banking Survey*, Accenture, 2017.
8   <https://www.fjordnet.com/conversations/liquid-expectations/>. Cited in *Australian Consumer Banking Survey*, Accenture, 2017.
9   (2016). NAB Labs prepare bank for the future. *The Weekend Australian*, 2 May.

Case study B

Tourism adds $120 billion to the Australian economy

As a service industry, international and domestic tourism added almost $120 billion to the Australian economy in 2016.[1]

International visitors

International visitors to Australia spent a record $39.1 billion in the year ending December 2016, $2.5 billion more than the previous year. The number of visitors aged more than 15 years reached 7.6 million, increasing by 766000 (11%), while nights were up 2% to 253 million (see Table 1).[2]

Chinese visitors spent $9.2 billion in 2016-17, showing growth of 7 per cent, but British holidaymaker spending dropped, as did visitor nights. The 10 major Asian markets recorded

Figure 1   Sydney Harbour

Source: Shutterstock. <www.shutterstock.com/image-photo/circular-quay-opera-house-sydney-nsw-184450940?irg-wc=1&utm_medium=Affiliate&utm_campaign=Pixabay&utm_source=44814>.

Table 1   Visitor nights and expenditure 2016–17

International visitors	Nights	Expenditure
7.6 million	253 million	$39.1 billion

double-digit percentage growth in visitor numbers last year, while 17 of the nation's key markets scored record numbers including the United States, China, Singapore and Scandinavia.[3] The Japanese market recovered on the previous year, with spending by Japanese tourists growing by 29 per cent in 2016 to $1.7 billion, the highest level in a decade. Aviation capacity between Japan and Australia—which increased by 20 per cent in 2016—together with an improving Japanese economy are the probable causes of the increase in spending by Japanese visitors.

The number of New Zealand tourists dropped 7 per cent in terms of visitor nights to 14.9 million, while British spending dropped 3 per cent to $3.7 billion and the country's visitor nights fell 10 per cent to 23.9 million. The longest-staying visitors were Taiwanese, with an average of 63 nights, while Indians averaged 60 nights. New Zealanders averaged 12 nights and were among the shortest stayers (see Figure 1).

Australia's tourism markets

Strong growth was reported from Australia's major tourism markets. Asia led the way in particular, with all top 10 Asian markets recording double digit percentage growth in visitor numbers. Overall, 17 of Australia's 20 key markets recorded increased visitor numbers during 2016 including New Zealand, the United States, Canada, China, Singapore, Hong Kong, Indonesia, Malaysia, India, Thailand, Korea, Taiwan, Germany, Scandinavia, Switzerland, France and Italy.

The top five contributors to tourism expenditure in Australia were China, the United Kingdom, the United States, New Zealand and Japan, with these countries contributing more

Figure 2 International visitors to Australia

International visitors to Australia

		Visitors	Nights	Spend
China		▲ 17% to 1.1m	▲ 16% to 45.9m	▲ 11% to $9.2bn
Britain		▲ 4% to 674,000	▼ 10% to 23.9m	▼ 3% to $3.7bn
US		▲ 16% to 668,000	▲ 10% to 14.8m	▲ 7% to $3.7bn
New Zealand		▲ 3% to 1.2m	▼ 7% to 14.9m	▲ 3% to $2.7bn
Japan		▲ 24% to 382,000	▲ 11% to 9.2m	▲ 29% to $1.7bn

Source: L. Harvey (2017). Chinese lead $39bn in tourism bonanza. *The Australian*, 15 March, p. 21.

than half (54% or $20.9 billion) of the total spend for 2016. They also accounted for just over half (53% or 4.1 million) of all international visitor arrivals. Visitors who had the highest daily spend on average were from the United States ($247), Singapore ($237) and China ($200). Those visiting for the purpose of holiday had a much higher average daily spend—China ($478), the United States ($311) and Singapore ($303).[4]

Purpose of visit

The holiday and education segments underpinned the strong growth for the year. Combined, these segments accounted for two-thirds (68%) of total trip spend by international visitors to Australia (see Table 2).[5]

Table 2 Purpose of visits

Holiday visits		
Visitors	**Nights**	**Spend**
▲ 22% to 3.8 million	▲ 11% to 84.8 million	▲ 16% to a record $16.7 billion
Education visits		
Visitors	**Nights**	**Spend**
▲ 8% to 495 000	▲ 5% to 65.5 million	▲ 13% to $9.9 billion

The key contributors to growth in holiday visitation by volume were China (up 25% or 128 000), the US (up 30% or 76 000) and Japan (up 37% or 73 000). China also made a significant contribution to growth in education (up 23% to 156 000). Travel for the purpose of visiting friends and relatives (VFR) was stable—increasing by 1 per cent to 1.9 million, while nights spent in Australia remained fixed at about 55.6 million, and spending fell by 4 per cent to $5.7 billion.[6]

Business travellers are an important market segment nationally, spending twice as much, on average, as leisure travellers. In the year ending September 2016, expenditure in Australia by business travellers reached $1.8 billion, with arrivals of 808 000 for the same period.[7]

Case Studies

Accommodation

The growth in the number of visitors arriving for a holiday was reflected in strong increases for nights staying in hotels, motels and resorts, which increased by 11 per cent to 28.8 million in total. Nights in guesthouses or bed-and-breakfasts rose by 19 per cent to 1.4 million, while the majority of nights were spent in rented houses, apartments, flats and units, which increased 2 per cent to 98.4 million nights.[8]

Visitors who stayed in backpacker-style accommodation grew by 8 per cent during the year. The total number of visitor nights spent in backpacker accommodation, however, fell by 7 per cent to 12.8 million nights on the basis of a slowdown in the European market.

There was an increase of 47 per cent in the number of visitors staying in caravan parks and travelling with a caravan, motor home or campervan, to 1.7 million nights.

Other trends

Uber was used by 14 per cent of visitors (1.1 million) during their stay, with visitors from the United Kingdom (23%), the United States (22%), other European countries (19%) and Canada (18%) most likely to use the service. Those visiting for education (34%) and employment (29%) purposes were also more likely to use an Uber service. The most common website used to book private accommodation was Airbnb, with 426 000 visitors booking through the site. Other common websites used to make bookings were Stayz (12 000), Vacation Rentals by Owner (VRBO) (12 000) and Couchsurfing (10 000).[9]

The Australian government is working to make it easier for travellers to come to Australia from key markets such as China. Together with streamlined visa arrangements, additional flights will underpin growth in the valuable Chinese tourist market already worth more than $9 billion. A new air services agreement, which is part of the China-Australia Free Trade Agreement (CHAFTA), will allow aviation connectivity between major airports in Australia and China, and facilitate international visitor movements.[10]

With the exception of the Northern Territory, all states and territories recorded growth in international visitors during 2016. New South Wales still dominates in the number of visitors with an increase of 13 per cent; Victoria and Queensland both grew by 10 per cent; while Western Australian visitor numbers grew by 12 per cent (see Table 3, on p. 148).

Domestic tourists

Holiday stays by domestic tourists in camping grounds improved by 12 per cent to 33.3 million nights in 2016, according to the federal government's National Visitor Survey, while bed-and-breakfast accommodation and guesthouses gained increases in domestic and international holiday activity with room nights increasing by nearly 30 per cent to 3.9 million. Government-run non-commercial caravan parks and camping grounds fared well, increasing by 22 per cent to 18.3 million nights.[11]

All states and territories recorded increases in overnight domestic visitors except for Tasmania, which dropped 7.1 per cent between 2015 and 2016 with a commensurate decrease

Table 3   Growth in overseas visitors and expenditure by state

State/territory	Visitor growth and spend
Australian Capital Territory	208 000 visitors +7%; who spent $452 million +15%
Tasmania	236 000 visitors +11%; who spent $378 million +8%
Northern Territory	287 000 visitors 0%; who spent $424 million -3%
South Australia	432 000 visitors +6%; who spent $971 million +8%
Western Australia	954 000 visitors +12%; who spent $2.4 billion +6%
Queensland	2.6 million visitors +10%; who spent $5.1 billion +4%
Victoria	2.7 million visitors +10%; who spent $6.9 billion +6%
New South Wales	3.9 million visitors +13%; who spent $9.5 billion +13%

Note: The total number of visitors by state is greater than total number of visitors for Australia (7.6 million) because some visitors visited multiple states.

Source: Tourism Research Australia (2016). *International Visitors in Australia*. Austrade, December.

in regional trip expenditure of 5 per cent. The highest increase was recorded in the Northern Territory with an 18 per cent increase in the number of visitors, followed by Western Australia with an increase of more than 14 per cent, and the Australian Capital Territory with a 13 per cent rise (see Figure 2).[12]

Figure 3   Total tourism expenditure, domestic and international

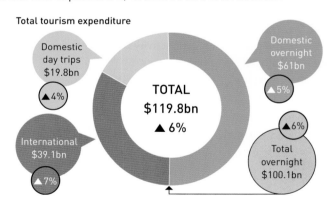

Total tourism expenditure

Domestic day trips $19.8bn ▲4%

Domestic overnight $61bn ▲5%

International $39.1bn ▲7%

Total overnight $100.1bn ▲6%

TOTAL $119.8bn ▲ 6%

Something to think about

Apart from the economic value of ancillary tourism services, such as Uber (which does not own any cars) and Airbnb (which does not own any real estate), what other value do those intangible services add to Australia's tourism industry?

OXFORD UNIVERSITY PRESS

Case Studies

Endnotes

1   L. Harvey (2017). B&B boom as tourist add $100bn to economy. *The Australian*, 29 March, p. 21. <www.theaustralian.com.au/business/business-spectator/news/bb-camping-boom-as-tourism-adds-100bn-to-economy/news-story/24da9d97affd347cc44f10ba4cd46746>.
2   L. Harvey (2017). Chinese lead $39bn in tourism bonanza. *The Australian*, 15 March, p. 21.
3   ibid.
4   Tourism Research Australia (2016). *International Visitors in Australia*. Austrade, December. <www.tra.gov.au/documents/ivs/IVS_one_pager_December2016.pdf>.
5   ibid.
6   ibid.
7   Department of Foreign Affairs and Trade (2017). Government getting down to business on corporate travel. Media release, 14 March. <http://ministers.dfat.gov.au/pitt/releases/Pages/2017/kp_mr_170314.aspx?w=yxmHAaWUZXyR1X%2BwO6Fs8A%3D%3D>.
8   Tourism Research Australia (2016). *International Visitors in Australia*. Austrade, December. <www.tra.gov.au/documents/ivs/IVS_one_pager_December2016.pdf> accessed 17 March 2017.
9   ibid.
10 Department of Foreign Affairs and Trade (2017). Government getting down to business on corporate travel. Media release, 14 March. <http://ministers.dfat.gov.au/pitt/releases/Pages/2017/kp_mr_170314.aspx?w=yxmHAaWUZXyR1X%2BwO6Fs8A%3D%3D>.
11 L. Harvey (2017). B&B boom as tourist add $100bn to economy.
12 ibid.

Part

2

Marketing Strategies for Services

Innovation in education services

Education services are a significant source of growth throughout the world, including in Australia. For instance, Coursera offers free online courses from top universities around the world.[1] In 2015 the organisation announced that it had achieved more than one million registrations as China became its second-largest market, overtaking India. Coursera was able to overcome barriers including the significant cultural differences and the Chinese government's internet firewall to achieve this result. Other organisations, including Google, Facebook and Twitter, have not being able to overcome the Chinese firewall. So how did Coursera achieve these results?

1   Coursera built local and credible Chinese partnerships that focused on translations and distribution. It partnered with Guokr, a Chinese social networking site, to localise the website and Yeeyan, a translation community, to translate its content. To facilitate distribution, it established a Coursera Zone on 163.com by partnering with NetEase and created a NetEase-hosted, Chinese-language portal to Coursera.org. It improved local performance by storing copies of its videos on NetEase servers. It partnered with Hujiang, China's largest internet learning platform, to build its own online identity and community within the Hujiang platform to access its 80 million active users. In China its major university partners offer more than 50 courses and include Fudan, Shanghai, Beijing, Xi'an, Jiaotong and Nanjing. Overall, Coursera offers more than 125 courses in Chinese (native and translations) on its platform.

2   Coursera success was facilitated through the establishment of credible connections and experience within China. For example, Coursera CEO Rick Levin, a former president of Yale University, had extensive connections within the political and university hierarchies in China (e.g. he had met two Chinese presidents, Jiang Zemin and Hu Jintao). He had an honorary appointment at Fudan University and was elected to the board of the National Committee on United States–China Relations. In addition, Yale has conducted many joint initiatives with and for Chinese universities, including helping establish international work/study programs in Beijing, and hosting a university leadership program for leaders from 14 of China's top universities.

» continued over page

Chapter 5

Developing Service Products

David Gray

» Innovation in education services continued

3   Coursera developed a deep understanding of cultural and political sensitivities among all parties (both Chinese and international educational service providers). For instance, the NetEase partnership led to a small number of Coursera's partner institutions initially leaving the arrangement. Pennsylvania State University, for example, as an equity owner in Coursera was initially concerned about political and academic freedom and wanted to proceed cautiously. Subsequently, however, Wharton Business School at the University of Pennsylvania has now established its Business Foundations specialisation in the Chinese language. Sensitivities also applied to the Chinese side, with some Chinese university leaders concerned about 'foreign ideas' being imported via MOOCs (Massive Online Open Courses) and that their cost advantage might cause the collapse of physical universities. The Ministry of Education is moving forward with MOOCs and is encouraging higher-education institutes in China to create more of them. The ministry also plans to 'set up an inspection system to supervise the teaching process and operation of the platforms, preventing harmful information from being disseminated'.

The Online Education Market

The online education market represents a considerable threat to the continuing survival of the traditional university model. Besides Coursera, there are many other well-known online providers including:

1   Udemy – <www.udemy.com>

2   SkillShare – <www.skillshare.com>

3   Simplilearn – <www.simplilearn.com>

4   QuickStart – <www.quickstart.com>

5   SkillShare – <www.skillshare.com>

6   Udacity – <www.udacity.com>

7   Khan Academy – <www.khanacademy.org>

These online learning portals seek to provide digital courses to professionals and students. They cover a broad range of topics designed by both industry experts and academics. The costs of taking these courses are usually a fraction of what it costs to take traditional university based courses. As with everything there are advantages and disadvantages with these online courses. While they are cost-effective they often do not have the same accreditation as traditional university courses. They are flexible, adaptable and agile with the ability to tap into educational development needs faster than the traditional university learning model. Within the Australian context and according to the IBISWorld Industry Report X0008, 'Online Education in Australia Report' (August 2018), the size of Australian market for 2018–19 is $5,300 million, with 1449 enterprises, 17470 employees with an average revenue per employee of $303,500. No operator in the Australian Online Education industry commands significant market share, therefore there are opportunities for a category killer to enter the market. The major players are Swinburne University of Technology with a market share of 4–5 per cent; Charles Sturt University with a market share of 3–4 per cent and Kaplan Education Pty Limited with a market share of 1–2 per cent. The demographics of the users of online education are 52 per cent aged 18–24, 37 per cent aged 24–44, 8.9 per cent aged 49 and over and 2.2 per cent aged under 17.

Introduction

It is not only educational service providers that need to consider service development and delivery. How well services are provided to the public is also a crucial part of the mission of many not-for-profit organisations and government departments. This chapter outlines some important matters all organisations need to consider to deliver effective services in the most efficient way.

Learning objectives

After reading this chapter you should be able to:

↘ explain the service offering and its components

↘ explain the different approaches to achieving a competitive advantage in the services sector

↘ understand the common strategic approaches used in services marketing

↘ understand alternative approaches to developing a new service strategy

↘ explain the different types of new services

↘ explain the development processes for new services.

The service offering

All organisations should start with their core business.[2] The starting point should always be to ask why consumers use their services in preference to the alternatives. Importantly, service organisations need to think about what is the core benefit of the service being provided. If possible, organisations should consult with their employees, suppliers and intermediaries and use external market research as to what constitutes the real customer benefit or value. Table 5.1 shows some core service benefits of organisations and the ways these are shown in the slogan or organisational mission.

As can be seen, these service organisations define how they are going to deliver their service offering. For some organisations like iiNet and Westpac there are many different types of services or packages that can be delivered, and their organisational mission or positioning statement(s) reflects how they will attend to this. In the case of Westpac, this is done by placing customers at the centre of transactions. iiNet also includes the types of services that are delivered. These are shown when users click on the link <www.iinet.net.au/customers>.

Sometimes the core benefits of service providers are not obvious to consumers or service marketers. In the case of St John's Hospital, the mission talks not about health services, but the way these are provided in different segments of the community. For Coursera, there

↘
service offering
The total service offered to the consumer. Also referred to as the *value offering*

Table 5.1 Selected core benefits in organisational missions

Organisation	Core service benefit	Organisational mission or slogan
Coursera	Flexible access to knowledge/skills from prestigious universities around the world	'We provide universal access to the world's best education'[3]
St John's Hospital	Health and healing	'Our Vision: Is to live and proclaim the healing touch of God's love where we invite people to discover the richness and fullness of their lives, give them a reason to hope and a greater sense of their own dignity.'[4]
Qantas	Air transport internationally and domestically (within Australia)	The Spirit of Australia
Westpac	Banking and financial services	We are putting customers at the centre
iiNet	Broadband services	'Who we are & what we do: iiNet is an Australian Internet Service Provider and a leading challenger in the telecommunications market. We're committed to making it simple for all Australians to get online across both our own ADSL2+ network and the exciting new NBN™ technologies. Our vision is to lead the market with services that harness the potential of the Internet and then differentiate with award-winning customer service. We employ more than 2500 enthusiastic staff across four countries—80 per cent of whom are employed to directly service nearly one million customers.'[5]

may be different reasons for people taking a course: development of specific skills, career progression and so on. The mission, therefore, reflects the organisation's wish to meet a different suite of consumer preferences. For Coursera, the mission is stated as 'We provide universal access to the world's best education'. For Qantas, an international airline, there is an emotive appeal to our heart and energy with the phrase 'Spirit of Australia', a reminder of our national heritage. However, in recent years this local appeal has been somewhat dampened as the company is increasingly forced to deal with the realities of international competition.

Service concepts: Core and supplementary elements

In addition to the core service consumers may also use related services that are linked to the core service, such as a meal on an aircraft. Consumers may use services not related to the core service benefit, or supplementary or augmented services. For instance, visitors

↘
related services
Additional services used as part of the encounter with the core service; for instance, a meal on an airline or campus food

OXFORD UNIVERSITY PRESS

to hospitals value gift shops and convenience stores within hospitals even though these stores do not necessarily contribute to the overall core benefit of health services.

Actions taken by providers may also be classified as core, augmented or supplementary services. Supplementary services could include how the service encounter is managed. This is noted in the St John's Hospital mission 'to enthusiastically go beyond what might be expected, and leaving people with, most importantly, a reason to hope and a greater sense of their own dignity'.[6] Health services delivered in this context are not only effective but show a caring attitude that gives patients a sense of hope and dignity. In other words, a related service showing how the service will be delivered is just as important to this organisation as the actual service.

The various levels of service that may be offered to the consumer are represented in Figure 5.1, which shows some core, supplementary and augmented services for a Carnival cruise ship, the *Sun Princess*.

The *Sun Princess* offers a range of services. Some are related to core services, like personal-choice dining and access to a health spa; others, such as mobile phone access and an internet café, may not be related to the core service at all, as some consumers may wish not to stay in touch with the outside world on a cruise.

It is important for service organisations like cruise liners to consider what supplementary and augmented services consumers require, as these may include additional costs. For not-for-profit and government organisations, the diagram in Figure 5.1 would have substantially fewer additional services. Likewise, for budget-based private service providers, removing

↘
augmented or supplementary services
Additional services provided that are not at all related to the core service offering; examples include gift shops and convenience stores in hospitals, and waiting rooms at car repair businesses

Figure 5.1   Core, supplementary and augmented services for a cruise liner

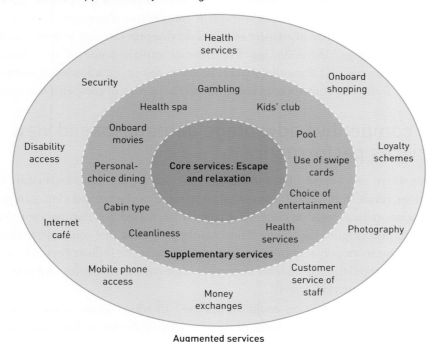

a range of supplementary and additional services may be important, as this means the organisations can charge cheaper prices. Good examples of this are budget airlines like Jetstar and Tiger Airlines in Australia, which do not provide meals or in-flight movies for consumers unless they are willing to pay extra. These airlines are simply concentrating on a core service, that of affordable air transport.

When considering a business's core offering, it is essential to ensure that the core and supplementary services are unambiguous and clearly defined. A recent example by Google shows how failure to identify the core offering could cause problems. Google had tried for many years to create its own social network, with its latest, somewhat confusing, effort called 'Spaces'. In 'Spaces the idea is that you have new ways to form group chats with your friends to discuss vacations, discuss shared interests and link each other to relevant YouTube videos and Google search results'.[7] Yet, as one commentator argued, 'its biggest problem is that nobody seems to know what the app is truly for ... Spaces can be used for practically anything, from building to-do lists to discussing *Game of Thrones* spoilers, it may as well be the Swiss-army knife of apps—a utility for all occasions and projects. It is what you make of it'. He further argued that Space's shortcoming is its lack of focus. 'Instagram and Snapchat are built around sharing user-created photos and videos. WhatsApp has become one of the world's most dominant platforms for messaging. Slack is that, but for work and business. The most successful social apps of the day are organised around a single, dedicated purpose'.[8]

Theories of competitive advantage: Services

For any service to survive over the longer term, it must have a competitive advantage. There are many theories that attempt to explain competitive advantage. There is no one single theory that explains every aspect of how a service provider can achieve a sustained competitive advantage. The following five theories explain some of the elements of competitive advantage and show that market position, resources, knowledge, competency and relational factors all contribute in some way to the pursuit of competitive advantage.

1 The competitive advantage demand-based view of services performance

The competitive advantage demand-based view contends that successful service organisations result from organisations that, compared to the competition, can produce superior value, reduce costs or enhance a competitive-based positioning view. Michael Porter, for example, argued the 'demand side' case by proposing that competitive advantage and the quest for monopoly rent over other organisations in the industry could be attained through the manipulation of market structure, segment identification and selection to create and maintain market power.[9]

Thus, a competitive position could be achieved in which 'rents' would flow to the organisation by following one or more of three generic strategies such as cost leadership, differentiation or focus. The Porter strategy of competitive positioning views the external environment as exogenous and is based on the ability of the organisation to adjust its resources to the external environment. Market success requires a portfolio of homogenous product markets with different growth rates and different market shares to achieve balance in a organisation's cash flow. In the Porter view, it is market share that is the most essential driver of profitability, and increasing market share is explained by economies of scale.

Applying the Porter view of competitive advantage to the services sector implies that for the service provider to be successful the benefits of the service must:

1 exceed the specific costs of developing the service
2 facilitate and/or enable the organisation to achieve a competitive advantage over its rivals.

2 The resource-based theory

The resource-based view arose because of increasingly turbulent and unstable market conditions contributed to by innovation and increasing competition. These trends meant that traditional theories based on the use of the 'competitive advantages' approach, in which industry and segment selection and the manipulation of market power is used to generate super-normal profit, became more difficult to implement. An alternative approach suggested focusing attention on the 'supply side' of resources and organisational capabilities/competencies as a source of sustainable competitive advantage.

The resource-based view contends that organisations should pursue an inward focus through the pursuit of their internal resources such as scarce financial, human, technological, physical and other intangibles. Under the resource-based view of the organisation, sustained competitive advantage 'derives from the resources and capabilities (both tangible and intangible) a firm control that are valuable, rare, imperfectly imitable, and not substitutable'.[10]

The resource-based approach argues that competitive advantage can be built 'through capturing entrepreneurial rents stemming from fundamental firm-level efficiency advantages'.[11] These efficiency advantages derive from investing in scarce organisation-specific resources that reduce costs, and improve product quality and/or product performance. This approach, however, does not adequately explain the organisation-wide and relational mechanisms that enable these resources and organisational capabilities/competencies to achieve these efficiency advantages.

3 The knowledge-based view and competency-based theory

The knowledge-based view is a subset of the resource-based view. It contends that marketing 'is evolving toward a new dominant logic away from the exchange of tangible goods (manufactured things) and toward the exchange of intangibles, specialized skills,

David Gray

knowledge, and processes (doing things for and with)'.[12] This new service dominant logic places emphasis on relationship interactivity, knowledge integration, customisation of service offerings and co-production where customers are involved in the creation of the offering.

Such a view focuses on the organisation making effective use of both its 'operand' and 'operant' resources to produce better value propositions than its competitors do. That is, 'operand resources' (i.e. traditional factors of production such as land, buildings, plant and equipment, raw materials and labour) are acted upon by 'operant' resources (i.e. knowledge, skills, technologies and processes).[13]

Competency-based theory extends the knowledge-based view by introducing the concept of *core competence*.[14] This theory is based on the proposition that competitive advantage arises when organisations possess certain core competencies. To be considered as a core competence it must meet three tests:

1 it must be a set of skills that enable a organisation to deliver a fundamental customer benefit
2 it must be competitively unique
3 it must be extendable.

The value of core competencies can change over time, and over long periods of time what was once a core competency may become a baseline capability. Quality, rapid time to market and quick response customer service—once genuine differentiators—are becoming routine advantages in many industries.

4 Market orientation theory

Market orientation within the context of the 'resource-based view' and 'competency-based theory' is an operant resource (i.e. competency/capability) with an external focus. 'Market orientation' acts as an enabler/facilitator of 'relational behaviour' (i.e. communication and coordination behaviour), inter-organisation relational performance and organisation competitive advantage.

Market orientation has been measured from many different angles, including from a cultural perspective,[15] a behavioural perspective,[16] a relationship perspective[17] and a system-based perspective.[18] For instance, the cultural-based approach identifies market orientation as a construct with three dimensions:

1 customer orientation (i.e. the extent to which one partner is responsive to customer needs)
2 competitor orientation (i.e. the extent to which a partner understands and responds to competitor activities)
3 inter-functional coordination (i.e. the extent to which there is inter-functional co-ordination within the partner organisation with respect to customer needs).

Within the service sector context, market orientation provides a framework in which the actors construct a common shared interpretation of the cultural context in which they operate with others. Thus, market orientation is the 'organization culture that most effectively and efficiently creates the necessary behaviours for the creation of superior value for buyers and, thus continuous superior performance for the business'.[19] It is 'a culture in which all employees are committed to the continuous creation of superior value for customers'.[20] High levels of market orientation are linked with above-average levels of financial performance and customer satisfaction in both consumer and industrial markets under most conditions.[21]

5 The theory of relational factors

This theory explains service performance through the characteristics exhibited between customers and service providers. These characteristics are particularly relevant to the business-to-business (B2B) context and include trust, cooperation, shared values, commitment and the absence of opportunistic behaviour.[22]

The relational factors model provides a good partial explanation for the relational interaction process between customer and service providers; however, it does not provide an explanation of the role and importance of the operant resources (i.e. competencies) required to develop successful inter-organisation relationships. Nor does it explain the mechanics of the relational interaction process or distinguish between the activities (i.e. flows) of interaction, such as communication behaviour and coordination behaviour, and the outcomes (i.e. stocks) of interaction, such as performance and relational capital.

Developing a service product strategy

It is more difficult to design a service product strategy than a new strategy for a tangible good, because services, unlike products, consist of processes, acts and interactions with the consumer that are difficult to standardise.[23]

Research and practice suggest many approaches that can be used to develop a service product strategy. These include first consulting with consumers, who in many cases co-produce the service value.[24] This has become possible through the use of online information, especially feedback surveys and website chat interaction, which may contain information about consumer preferences and feedback. Dell.com, for example, uses a consumer blog called Idea-storm where customers can submit ideas for improvement. The organisation also adopts the strategy of staffing for customer focus.[25] Data mining of online databases, including customer sales data, is also used by financial institutions in the redesign of their services.[26] The development of other self-service technologies also uses this approach; see Chapter 6 for further information.

Other approaches to the development of a service product strategy may involve the blueprinting of existing services. This approach helps identify problems in service delivery and provides ideas for the improvement of processes, people and systems. A simpler way to design new services may be to use traditional customer feedback surveys and observation.

David Gray

A restaurant manager may observe from the kitchen which meals are selling well and which are not, and this may be useful when considering what kind of menu choices may be appropriate in the future.

Research suggests that the direct involvement of customers in the design of new services has a positive effect on performance and loyalty. The proviso is that with highly technical complex services, consumer involvement in design does not necessarily lead to improvements in outcomes.[27] Consumers must also have better insights into their own preferences, an ability to express their preferences, and a high level of interest and knowledge about the service.

It is also important that services are developed that can be positioned competitively with a distinct unique selling proposition in the market. This can be difficult in industries where there are many similarities in core services, such as health insurance, for example.[28]

An alternative approach to the development of a service strategy is to follow that used by Kim and Mauborgne in their Blue Ocean Strategy.[29] This strategy, as shown in Figure 5.2,

Figure 5.2 Service value innovation steps

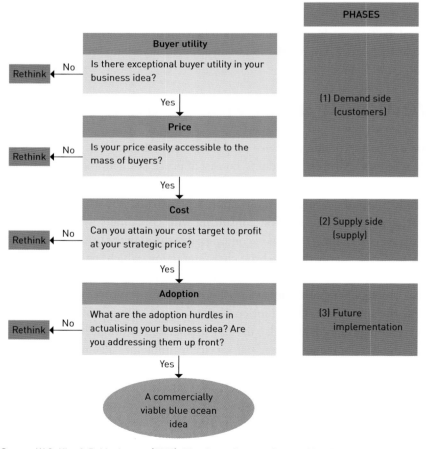

Source: W.C. Kim & R. Mauborgne (2015). *Blue Ocean Strategy*. Boston, MA: Harvard Business Review Press.

Part 2 Marketing Strategies for Services

argues that the key to making a business's competition irrelevant is to simultaneously increase buyer value and reduce costs. The authors call this process 'value innovation'. There are three process steps to their approach: demand (or revenue), profit and adoption.

Step 1: Demand (or revenue) considers buyer utility and price. This step asks whether your offer exhibits exceptional buyer utility. If not, then place the idea on hold until you either eliminate it or reach an affirmative answer. If yes, then go to step two, which focuses on setting the right strategic price—that is, can the majority of the buyers in your target market easily access (have the ability to pay) the price for your offering? If not, then they either cannot buy it or will not buy it.

Step 2: Profit assessment considers cost and profit. This step asks whether you can produce your offering at the target cost and still earn a healthy profit margin. If not, then you must ditch the idea or innovate your business model to hit the target cost. Under the Blue Ocean Strategy, it is the combination of exceptional utility, strategic pricing and target costing that allows companies to achieve value innovation—a leap in value for both buyers and companies.

Step 3: Overcome adoption hurdles. This step asks what are the adoption hurdles in commercialising your offer? Have these hurdles been addressed up front? Adoption hurdles can include potential resistance to the idea by intermediaries, partners or other stakeholders.

Different types of new services

Not all new service processes are innovations or brand-new means of delivering services. The development of new services can be minor changes such as changes in style and improvements in processes ranging through to new service offerings, market development,[30] and new service offerings for new markets. New services can consist of:

1   *Style changes*: These are minor changes to the appearance of the service to the customer and the employee who helps deliver the service. Examples include new corporate brand identity strategies, such as new corporate uniforms, refurbishment of branches, redesign of websites,[31] and minor changes in customer service strategies.[32] Note that many style changes are tangible and are likely to be noticed by consumers.[33] These changes usually involve lower costs of change and are easier to implement than other service changes.

2   *Service augmentation development*: Many service organisations may add additional related or augmented services that do not necessarily involve a redesign of the service process. A related service that has been included with many service organisations is online bookings and payments.[34] An example of the addition of an augmented service is the use of social and therapeutic horticulture and agriculture as a form of therapy in health services in the United Kingdom.[35]

3 *Service offer development*: As discussed, service offerings can be changed by altering the core values of the service. A change in the core service offering may require a brand-new service setting. Cruise liners, for example, have found that smaller ships with passenger sizes of no more than 700 provide a more intimate experience for passengers.[36] Not-for-profit organisations may also need to develop new service offerings. In health drug policy, new services have had to be developed to cope with the co-morbidity of HIV and substance abuse of youths in the United Kingdom.[37] This included the provision of better-trained outreach workers and community housing, as well as specialised healthcare centres.

4 *Process development*: This involves re-engineering the process of delivering a service to increase the quality of the service and/or reduce costs. Often this is achieved by the automation of service processes using information technology, which may transform much of the way a service is delivered (e.g. online share trading).[38] This kind of service development is often conducted when the business case for sales growth is weak. In this case, the ability to grow profits can be accomplished through improving processes. To be successful, these changes to information systems must be accompanied by staff development, internal marketing and training.[39] One important improvement in process development in new B2B markets has been the development of customer relationship business models, which aim to manage and reward high-net-worth customers.[40] Process development has also been shown to be important in logistics services—for example, in container transport where the time spent loading and unloading has been shown to be critical.[41]

5 *Market development*: This is often undertaken in parallel with other forms of development. It is concerned with improving the mix of target markets into which newly developed offers can be sold, thus enhancing the mix of customers served by the organisation.[42] Carnival Cruise Lines, as the market leader in the low-price cruise market, has positioned itself by emphasising onboard activities, targeting a relatively young market, using extensive television advertising and focusing on travel agents as its channel of distribution.[43]

Services in Action

Using speed as a competitive advantage

Entrepreneur magazine identified several service companies that use speed as a competitive advantage.[44] Speed is a competitive advantage in price-sensitive industries and where there is a consumer need for consumer gratification. It can be categorised under many different labels, including speed to market, speedy delivery and speedy service.

1 *Amazon Prime*: Focuses on order fulfilment and shipping. Customers can get guaranteed two-day shipping on all products that are Prime eligible. The benefits for Amazon are, first, that it conditions customers to prefer the two-day shipping, thus making it harder for them to switch back to the standard seven-day shipping. Second,

OXFORD UNIVERSITY PRESS

it encourages more purchases: the biggest disadvantage e-commerce has compared with brick-and-mortar retail is that consumers have to wait for products to arrive after purchasing them. By focusing on speedy delivery, Amazon has been able to mitigate this disadvantage.

2   *UberEATS:* A way of extending a well-known brand, Uber is changing the game for both businesses and consumers. Using the associated app, users simply choose one of the daily meals from selected restaurants in their area and place an order. An Uber driver then delivers food in 10 minutes or less. All payment takes place through the app, meaning there's no need to scrounge up cash for a driver tip. With meals typically ranging between $8 and $12, and a flat-fee charge for each request (not the number of meals), it's cheap, simple and extremely easy. However, such competitive advantage maybe short-lived as there is recent chatter in the media about the slowing down of the so-called 'on-demand/shut-in economy'. In this segment in the United States, for instance, there are many competitors including Caviar, Eat, Postmates, Door Dash and Grub Hub/Seamless.[45] The US on-demand laundry service world also seems overcrowded, with Laundry Locker, Instawash and Rinse all still battling it out, and competitors Washio and Prim already pushed out of the market.

There are a range of organisations that have introduced new services that have completely changed an industry sector. Customers are usually unable to conceptualise or visualise the benefits of revolutionary new services, concepts and technologies. A good example is the online auction concept. eBay was not the first of these, but it slowly became the dominant player (see Table 5.2 for further examples).

Table 5.2   A range of new services that also create new business models

Company	Industry sector	New service/new business model
eBay	Online auction	A new way of buying and selling through a community of individual users
Ryanair	Airline	A new way of consuming air travel with no-frills service and emphasis on economy
Amazon	Retailer	New way to buy goods – online retailer
iTunes	Music retailer	New way to buy and download music
Google	Internet search engine	A fast way to search for information on the internet
Uber	Ride sharing	Online taxi service offering customer convenience, driver flexibility with international scalability
Facebook	Social networking	A community of users online who can chat and share music, images and news from their own home
YouTube	Online video and film archive	A community of users sharing homemade video clips plus recorded favourite clips from movies

David Gray

Common strategic approaches in services marketing

There are a wide range of strategic approaches used in services marketing. The following section presents a brief discussion on some of the more widely used strategies, including experiences marketing; viral marketing; Blue Ocean Strategy; cause-related marketing; corporate social responsibility; ethical marketing; green marketing; guerrilla marketing; niche marketing; affinity marketing and affiliate marketing.

Experiential marketing

There are often significant segments of the population who want an engaging experience, whether that is attending a Cirque du Soleil theatre performance, visiting Disneyland in Hong Kong or taking a cruise on a Royal Caribbean line. This type of marketing is known as 'experiences marketing'. Marketers can capitalise on experiences marketing by effectively managing the environmental aspects of the relationship through customer participation and connection programs.

Most organisations can't copy the special effects of Cirque du Soleil, and customers buy the experience of visiting Disneyland in Hong Kong, possibly shopping and holidaying in Hong Kong and using it as a base for visiting the rest of China. Experiential marketing provides an inherently personal consumer engagement that sets it apart from other strategies. It is the process of personal engagement on an emotional, physical, intellectual or even spiritual level that enables the marketer to gain a competitive advantage.

For instance, the prominent booksellers Barnes & Noble envisioned shopping as far back as 1994 as entertainment in the design of its superstores—that is, upscale, sophisticated, wood-rich, library-like, people-watching, family-oriented, 'feel-good' public gathering spaces. The design objective is to keep people enjoying themselves in a superstore for two hours at a time. However, Amazon Books through its online portal eventually killed the Barnes and Noble experience by offering shopping convenience, time saving and cost advantages. These advantages overcame the experiential engagement offered by Barnes & Noble.

Other examples are Nike superstores, which have created an experience through giant screens and the opportunity to try out sporting equipment. A coffee chain like Starbucks sells coffee and complementary items like snacks and coffee mugs, but also provides a relaxing environment, with free internet access, newspapers and armchairs, so the process of buying coffee becomes a sought-after experience.

Viral marketing

The objective of viral marketing is to target an entire market by spreading a 'virus', which is otherwise known as the organisation's message. This is often undertaken via email from one user to another. This type of marketing initially came to prominence through Hotmail when that organisation added a tagline to all its existing customers' email signatures offering recipients a free Hotmail account. Within 18 months, Hotmail expanded its subscriptions base by 8.7 million users—a good result for a one sentence tagline placed at the bottom of recipients' email. Increasingly, viral marketing has become more popular, and from a financial perspective it is very cost-effective to implement as it can be tagged onto the end of existing infrastructure.

A good example of viral marketing is that employed at large gyms around Australia and internationally. A gym can send an email to its entire current client membership database that encourages existing members to recruit their family and friends to the gym and ultimately take up their own gym membership. For every email that the gym member forwards to their family and friends they receive a small gift, and for every successful recruit they receive a free month of gym membership. Quite an incentive—and now you might think back to emails you have received from your friends promoting gym membership! As with everything that becomes popular, the impact of viral marketing is being diluted and the target market is becoming immune to this type of messaging. This can be overcome by utilising messaging that captures people's attention and stands out from that of competitors.

Blue Ocean Strategy

As previously mentioned, the focus behind Blue Ocean Strategy is to create a sustainable competitive advantage through the exploitation of uncontested market space that makes the competition irrelevant and helps to sustain high performance (Figure 5.3). This is entirely different to pursuing a Red Ocean Strategy, which focuses on competing within the confines of often overcrowded existing industries.[46]

Figure 5.3   Blue Ocean Strategy

Red ocean strategy	Blue ocean strategy
Compete in existing market space.	Create uncontested market space.
Beat the competition.	Make the competition irrelevant.
Exploit existing demand.	Create and capture new demand.
Make the value/cost trade-off.	Break the value/cost trade-off.
Align the whole system of a company's activities with its strategic choice of differentiation or low cost.	Align the whole system of a company's activities in pursuit of differentiation and low cost.

Blue oceans can be created, first, by launching new industries, as eBay did with online auctions. Some other well-known examples include the Ford Model T, Apple's personal computer and Dell's made-to-order computer. Second, organisations often create blue oceans from within their core businesses. An important feature of Blue Ocean Strategy is that it rejects the notion that companies can either create greater value for customers at a higher cost (i.e. differentiation) or create reasonable value at a lower cost (cost leadership).

The creation of blue oceans demonstrates that successful companies can pursue differentiation and cost leadership simultaneously. A good example of the Blue Ocean Strategy is the success of Cirque du Soleil. Instead of following the conventional logic of beating competitors with even greater fun and thrills, it redefined the competitive landscape by offering customers 'the fun and thrill of the circus and the intellectual sophistication and artistic richness of the theatre'.[47] Specifically, 'each Cirque show has an original musical score, which drives the performance, lighting, and timing of the acts, rather than the other way around. The productions feature abstract and spiritual dance, an idea derived from theatre and ballet'.[48]

Cause-related marketing

Cause-related marketing refers to the practice of marketing that is undertaken with the aim to raise awareness and promote a specific cause. The various types of causes include, but are not limited to, education literacy, drug addiction, cancer research, homelessness, domestic violence, child abuse and alcohol abuse. In addition to raising awareness on certain issues, often the marketing drive is to raise money to contribute to the cause in some way.

This type of marketing is utilised by charities and not-for-profit organisations. It allows them to intertwine their product or service with raising awareness of a cause. The aim of cause-related marketing is to put something back into the community. Consumers and an organisation's employees generally perceive cause-related marketing favourably and consider that if consumers had a choice of two different brands, where price and quality were similar, they would purchase the brand that supported a cause. In recent years, cause-related marketing has been steadily increasing. For example, Earth Hour campaigns, which encourage consumers all around the world to turn off their lights for just one hour on a specific date, have increased in popularity over recent years. Clean Up Australia has also received tremendous support. In summary, it is clear that cause-related marketing can have a positive impact on organisations that support or are built on services' causes.

Corporate social responsibility

Corporate social responsibility (CSR) refers to the practice of an organisation going above and beyond its legal requirements to help improve the lives of a variety of stakeholders, including employees, suppliers, customers and the environment. In earlier decades CSR was viewed as a social obligation, with a strong link between CSR and the alignment of corporate actions with societal objectives and values. However, since the 1990s CSR has been perceived more for its stakeholder obligations, thus narrowing the focus from the whole of society to those aspects the organisation can influence or is influenced by. Stakeholders can be grouped into organisational, community, regulatory and media. Most recently, CSR is known as a managerial process around recognition that 'issues management' and 'environmental assessment' need to be part of management decision-making. This kind of thinking gave rise to triple-bottom-line accounting, which includes economic sustainability, social sustainability and environmental sustainability in its calculations.

On the other hand, there are critics who believe that CSR belongs to charities and that it where it should stay. The rationale used is that because it is often difficult to ascertain the return on socially responsible investment, then it must be a waste. However, on a business level companies often use CSR as a marketing tool to recruit employees, environmental programs to win large tenders and even include their CSR programs in press releases. There are certainly ways to make CSR work for an organisation.

Ethical marketing

Marketing is often the communication delivery interface between an organisation and its target market, either consumers or, in B2B marketing, other organisations. Ethical decision-making in marketing focuses on how to address the issues and associated ethical risks that arise within an organisational context. Individual ethical reasoning processes, organisational ethical culture and societal norms, social relationships, as well as compliance standards impact on the decision-making process. Ethical decision-making in marketing occurs when decisions about issues must be judged as right or wrong. Some of the ethical issues and associated risks that arise from organisational decision-making include the misuse of organisational resources, abusive behaviour, lying to customers, deceptive sales and advertising practices, channel manipulation, bribery, product issues and price fixing.[49]

In comparison, corporate social responsibility, as previously identified, is a much broader concept and includes how decisions impact on all stakeholders and society. Therefore, ethical decision-making in marketing addresses the internal managerial decisions that relate to the organisation's mission, strategy and relationships with employees, customers and suppliers. Some ethical obligations are laws of the land; however, others go above and beyond this. As such, marketing bears the responsibility of ensuring that messaging and conduct is ethical, as this communication vehicle will attract scrutiny if not undertaken correctly. This communication is not limited to customers, but also includes the messaging and conduct of an organisation towards its employees and suppliers, the government and the society in which it operates.

In terms of marketing, ethical issues relate to the four Ps, which are product, promotion, price and place (also known as distribution). Table 5.3 shows some aspects in marketing where ethical issues can arise.

Table 5.3 Ethical issues in marketing

Services	Place (Distribution)
– Planned obsolescence	– Exclusive territories
– Service quality and safety	– Distributor rights
– Service warranties	– Predatory competition
Promotion	**Price**
– Bait-and-switch advertising	– Price fixing
– Deceptive advertising	– Price discrimination
– Promotional allowances	– Price increases
– Bribery	– Deceptive pricing
	– Hidden commissions

For example, the promotion of financial advisory, loan products or investment services in many parts of the world to people who cannot afford them has become the source of considerable criticism from governments and consumer groups. Often there is a blurry line between marketing to underage drinkers and those who have just come of age and legally able to purchase alcohol. Due to public outcry, some manufacturers have banned all advertising to this segment so as not to be accused of promoting underage drinking. Another ethical marketing issue is targeting children's television programs with commercials promoting junk food. This has also come under scrutiny.

Organisations cannot afford to ignore their ethical responsibilities. Although it may mean lost revenues in certain categories, their revenues may be drastically affected when they are fined and then exposed through the media for not complying with these responsibilities. A classic example is the public scrutiny McDonald's experienced for not providing healthy meal options, not to mention the numerous lawsuits brought against them. As a result, McDonald's updated its menus to provide healthy options.

The public scrutiny afforded to large banks in Australia regarding their financial advisory practices has forced these organisations to think about their ethical standards. With the possibility of executives going to jail for unethical dealings, many organisations are now implementing ethical departments with managers responsible for various aspects of ensuring compliance with ethical standards. The Australian Banking Royal Commission in 2018 dramatically highlighted the lack of ethical practices within the financial services market. There have already been consequences, including diminished value of bank brands and shareholder value, severe penalties applied to the major banks for ethical breaches and a fall in the level of consumer trust.

Green marketing

Green marketing refers to the practice of organisations linking their products/services to environmental initiatives. It usually involves the production, promotion and reclamation of environmentally sensitive products. For the product to be considered environmentally sensitive it must contribute to the environment in some way. Interestingly, consumers have responded by purchasing these products and services even though in some cases they were more expensive and created a new market. In these instances, organisations were rewarded for their proactive environmental initiatives.

Examples of green marketing can be seen with the promotion of 100 per cent recycled toilet paper, the marketing of investment funds that only invest in environmentally friendly products, the introduction of energy-saving light bulbs and the concept of reusing bags instead of wasting plastic ones. Other growth areas for green marketing are organic food and solar power. Increasingly, consumers are opting for organic food as opposed to conventional food. Organic food uses less pesticides and manufactured chemicals, if any at all, compared with conventional food. Likewise, the increasing cost of energy is causing consumers to switch to renewable energy products such as solar.

Guerrilla marketing

Guerrilla marketing refers to an advertising strategy to promote products or services in an unconventional way with a limited budget. This involves high energy and imagination focusing on catching the attention of the consumer in a more personal and memorable way compared to conventional practices. The concept originated from Jay Conrad Levinson, with his phenomenal book *Guerrilla Marketing*, published in 1984.

An example of guerrilla marketing can be seen at large sporting events such as the tennis and football. It is very costly to advertise during these events when they are broadcast in the mainstream media and in many cases key competitors may have already secured the advertising rights, which leaves other organisations out of the picture. An alternative strategy is to hand out flyers, free drinks or wearable or visual items relating to the organisation to spectators who are just about to enter the arena. When the event is televised, the items will be seen all around the country or even the world for very little cost.

As guerrilla marketing is based on creative and innovative ideas, the main competitive advantage is that the organisation's competitors are not trying the same thing. Although they may copy the strategy in the future, the organisation will be able to reach its target market first, and because it is so innovative, it is almost certain to attract attention. Small budgets also mean that guerrilla activity must be quite targeted, and the organisation may not be able to gain exposure with as many people as a conventional campaign. Guerrilla tactics are known to offend some people if the idea is too out there, so organisations that use this strategy need to be careful of the message conveyed to the targeted audience.

Niche marketing

Niche marketing refers to marketing that targets a single segment in the market instead of the overall market. It is one of the three well-recognised competitive advantage strategies recommended by Porter.[50]

This type of marketing is a good strategy for small organisations with limited resources. It can offer high margins. The key to success with niche markets is specialisation, usually via market, customer, product or marketing mix lines. Usually this type of marketing is very profitable as generally it is considered that small groups of clients that form a niche in the market are prepared to pay a premium as their desired product is rare and not run of the mill.

Niche marketing is not only used by small and medium organisations—it is also used by large organisations. It is important to note that niche marketing is generally not a volume play in that it does not often sell a large volume of products; it sells a much smaller volume, most often at a premium. For example, a Ferrari is considered to serve a niche in the market. Consumers who purchase a Ferrari pay an absolute premium for the luxury that they desire and enjoy knowing they are driving a rare car. Instead of advertising Ferrari in mass-marketing mediums such as television or newspapers, often the company's marketing efforts utilise smaller targeted one-to-one marketing initiatives, such as exclusive dinners and luxurious events. Often, niche products overall attract a premium. It's quality not quantity! For this reason it is considered expensive to market a niche product as a lot of work goes in to making just one sale. On the flip side, the one sale has a higher average selling price than most products.

The disadvantage of niche marketing is that competitors can easily replicate niche marketing efforts and eventually steal a service provider's customers. If their service is perceived as being like the niche service, then customer defection is likely. The danger is that because the market is niche, there are not as many customers who fit the profile of your target market, and as such your small marketplace may become overcrowded and limit your sales opportunities. Innovative products and marketing can assist in overcoming this potential challenge.

Affinity marketing

Affinity marketing refers to the targeted marketing of a specific group of like-minded people sharing certain commonalities—for instance, the targeting of car clubs for Porsche or Harley-Davidson motorbike enthusiasts. These clubs have many members who own these vehicles and are equally passionate about their cars or bikes. From a marketing affinity perspective, an automotive insurance company would love the opportunity to market its insurance to these select groups of people. Its offering can be specific and allows it to tailor its message to a captive audience. Often affinity marketing achieves great results.

The advantages of affinity marketing are that the marketer can target specific individuals or organisations where there is a high propensity that they will be interested in their goods or services, should they be closely aligned with the organisation.

Marketers need to be careful to abide with privacy regulations in their respective country to ensure they handle client information in accordance with the law; for example, ensuring they have clients' permission to forward client details to third parties.

Affiliate marketing

Affiliate marketing refers to the practice of rewarding partner organisations for introducing new clients to their organisation. Its advantage is that it allows affiliates to target potential customers who ordinarily they may not have access to. Affiliate marketing has become extremely successful and is considered to be extremely cost-effective when implemented correctly. It is equivalent to paying 'finder's fees' to organisations or individuals who introduce a new prospect or client to an organisation.

Affiliate marketing can be undertaken in a variety of mediums such as email, social media (e.g. Facebook), direct mail, newsletters and advertisements, to name a few. American Express is an organisation that strongly utilises affiliate marketing. Care should be taken however, to adhere to strict privacy regulations when it comes to affiliate marketing. Unless the contact within the database has expressly provided approval that their details can be provided to a third-party organisation, it is best not to release the database. In some countries, including Australia, it is against the law to release client details without approval.

MARKETING PROFILE: MARK ZUCKERBERG
Services marketing and social networking innovator

> The thing I really care about is the mission, making the world open.
>
> Mark Elliot Zuckerberg (born 14 May 1984)

Mark Zuckerberg launched Facebook from Harvard's dormitory rooms together with his college roommates and fellow Harvard University students Eduardo Saverin, Andrew McCollum, Dustin Moskovitz and Chris Hughes. The group then introduced Facebook to other campuses. Facebook expanded rapidly, with one billion users by 2012. Zuckerberg was involved in various legal disputes that were initiated by others in the group, who claimed a share of the company based upon their involvement during the development phase of Facebook. Zuckerberg's net worth was estimated to be US$73 billion in 2018. On 24 May 2007, Zuckerberg announced Facebook Platform, a development platform for programmers to create social applications within Facebook. Within weeks, many applications had been built and some already had millions of users. It grew to more than 800 000 developers around the world building applications for Facebook Platform.

Since that time, Facebook has expanded to become the largest social media network in the world. As of the fourth quarter of 2017, Facebook (according to Statistica.com) had 2.2 billion monthly active users around the world. In Australia, there were approximately 10.6 million users in 2017. Worldwide revenue for Facebook grew from US$777 in 2009 to US$40.7 billion in 2017.[51]

David Gray

Another example of affiliate marketing is organisations that list on their website all their affiliates and allow visitors to their website to click through to special offers. Disadvantages arise when consumers are bombarded with affiliate marketing; for example, their bill arrives with multiple affiliate direct mail flyers or they are receiving affiliate marketing too frequently. When it occurs too frequently, often the recipient of the direct mail, email or social media can discard the promotional material without even looking at it.

In the Australian context, it is worth looking at some of the characteristics of social media usage. We can assess the most recent data on who uses social networking sites, the major reasons for using social networking sites, the paths taken by consumers towards purchase, the types of pre-purchase social media research and, finally, the daily usage characteristics of social media usage. The most recent Sensis (2017) report on social media usage for Australia identifies Facebook as the dominant platform, being used by at least 90 per cent of social media users across all gender, age and location segments (see Table 5.4). Twitter has increased in usage, and the visual platforms—Instagram and Snapchat—have surged ahead. Google+, Pinterest and Tumblr are steady with each again attracting about one in 10 social media users. LinkedIn seems to be dominated by males. Instagram, Snapchat, Twitter and YouTube appeal to 70 per cent or more of the under 30s. Use of Instagram and Snapchat correlates inversely with age and to a large degree that is also the case with Twitter and YouTube. LinkedIn and Google+ lack appeal to the under 30s. Females use Facebook to a greater degree than males, but all the other sites to a lesser extent.

Using the Sensis report for 2017, Table 5.5 shows that around nine in 10 users of social media see it as a way of keeping in touch with friends or family. There is increasing usage of social media for sharing photos or videos, which has risen to 57 per cent. More users are

Table 5.4   Who uses social networking sites

Social networking sites used	Male	Female	18–29	30–39	40–49	50–64	65+
Facebook	91%	97%	94%	99%	90%	94%	91%
LinkedIn	22%	14%	10%	22%	22%	25%	9%
Instagram	50%	41%	81%	56%	35%	16%	9%
Google+	11%	10%	4%	9%	15%	16%	12%
Twitter	35%	28%	70%	20%	15%	17%	13%
Snapchat	43%	36%	77%	49%	25%	10%	4%
YouTube	60%	43%	75%	45%	54%	37%	26%

Source: Sensis (2017). *Sensis Social Media Report 2017.*

Note: Google+ was shut down for consumers in April 2019.

Table 5.5   Reasons for using social media sites

Reasons for usage	2011	2012	2013	2014	2015	2016	2017
Catch up with family and friends	93%	94%	94%	95%	92%	91%	89%
Share photographs or videos	56%	51%	47%	64%	45%	36%	57%
Watch videos	NA	NA	NA	NA	NA	28%	43%
Get information on news and current events	NA	27%	29%	47%	40%	35%	37%
Play games	24%	18%	21%	26%	21%	18%	34%
Meet new friends	18%	14%	10%	20%	14%	14%	30%
Follow celebrities, bloggers or social media personalities	NA	NA	NA	NA	NA	NA	28%
Find or connect with people with the same interests	14%	13%	14%	22%	17%	16%	26%
Research products and services you might want to buy	12%	16%	20%	28%	19%	14%	16%

Sensis (2017). *Sensis Social Media Report 2017.*

turning to social media to play games (up from 24% in 2011 to 34% in 2017), to meet new friends (up from 18% in 2011 to 30% in 2017) and to find or connect with people sharing the same interests (up from 14% in 2011 to 26% in 2017). Another relatively prominent use is to follow celebrities, bloggers or social media personalities, which was mentioned by 28 per cent. Finally, there has been a gradual decline in the percentage of people using social media sites for researching products and services that they might want to buy (down from 28% in 2014 to 16% in 2017).

Table 5.6 further explores the path to purchase by showing that among the 16 per cent who use social media platforms to research products or services, the most common items they research are fashion items and electrical goods (17% each).

In addition, Table 5.7 elaborates that this research is more likely to be conducted via a mobile device rather than a computer (52% versus 35%).

Finally, Table 5.8 provides some indication as to when consumers of social networking sites are most likely to use them. This has implications for the placement of advertising. The two most popular times in 2017 were in the evening and first thing in the morning. Usage during lunchtime and work or study breaks is increasing. Usage while commuting or working occurs among almost one in five, while almost four in 10 check social media before going to bed.

Table 5.6 Consumer research and the path to purchase

What were you looking for on the last search occasion?	2014	2015	2016	2017
Clothing and fashion	29%	25%	12%	17%
Appliances or electrical equipment	15%	16%	11%	17%
Furniture and things for the home	6%	10%	6%	8%
Holiday, travel and accommodation	11%	7%	21%	10%
Entertainment	6%	4%	8%	8%

Sensis (2017). *Sensis Social Media Report 2017.*

Table 5.7 Type of pre-purchase social media research

How was that research conducted?	2011	2012	2013	2014	2015	2016	2017
Computer	79%	62%	67%	53%	43%	32%	35%
Mobile device	6%	18%	23%	40%	40%	44%	52%
Both	8%	8%	7%	7%	15%	17%	12%
Neither	8%	13%	3%	1%	3%	7%	1%

Source: Sensis (2017). *Sensis Social Media Report 2017.*

Table 5.8 When we use social networking sites

When we socially network	2012	2013	2014	2015	2016	2017
First thing in the morning	33%	37%	43%	45%	49%	57%
Commuting	16%	16%	17%	20%	18%	18%
When working	NA	12%	21%	32%	22%	21%
Breaks	25%	22%	31%	27%	33%	47%
Lunchtime	25%	22%	30%	23%	36%	47%
In the evening	63%	53%	58%	40%	63%	71%
Last thing before I go to bed	40%	42%	48%	41%	35%	39%

Source: Sensis (2017). *Sensis Social Media Report 2017.*

The evening is still the most popular time for social media usage across gender and age segments. The biggest gender differences are at lunchtime and during breaks, with males favouring those times considerably more. Those aged under 30 use social media much more than other age groups across all the times listed. For most of the options, usage declines markedly with age. The 18- to 29-year age group is most likely to access social media first thing in the morning (79%), last thing at night (65%), at work (46%) and even on the toilet (29%) compared to any other age demographic. Almost three-quarters in this age group are now also open to connecting with strangers.

OXFORD UNIVERSITY PRESS

New service development processes

In services marketing, 'nothing stays the same for ever'. For service marketers, there is now greater competition due to globalisation and deregulation, and new technologies that can provide services in different formats and, therefore, change consumer tastes and preferences. These all need to be met by the development of new services. It is best to think of such development as a new or re-engineered process, rather than as a tangible item for consumption.

The development of each type of the five new services previously outlined is best achieved in a systematic fashion. The process of developing a new service may in some ways follow that for the development of a product. There are, however, important differences in each stage of the process. This is because, unlike many products, service innovations may require partial or complete changes in systems, processes and organisational culture.

The six stages of the new development of services are:

1 idea generation
2 service concept and evaluation
3 feasibility analysis and business case analysis
4 service development and testing
5 commercialisation
6 evaluation.

Each part of the process is now discussed in greater detail.

Idea generation

Services are unique in that one type of service, for example, education, can be delivered in many ways. Organisations have developed many tools to help them generate new ideas for services. These usually include some sort of open-ended feedback from consumers or examination of best practice of service delivery by other providers. Lead end-users for many organisations are offering technical services, a crucial form of input into the development of new services.[52] Other organisations may also survey non-users to design services that match their requirements more closely. A hospital library in the United Kingdom, for example, found out from a survey of library users and non-users that non-users expected better online access and a range of specific medical texts. These non-users were also mistakenly under the impression that they were not entitled to use the service.[53] The World Wide Web has also provided a great source of information about possible improvements or the development of new services for many industries. Comments posted on social media and in online booking accommodation services such as <www.hotel.com.au> provide information from users about both positive and negative aspects of their experiences.

David Gray

From an analytical perspective, Kim and Mauborgne in their seminal development of Blue Ocean Strategy in 2005, identified six pathways towards developing unique product/service offerings to achieve competitive advantage.[54] These are:

1 *Look across alternative industries*: Famous examples are Cirque de Soleil, which refocused from being a traditional circus to a theatre production; likewise, André Rieu refocused the classical concert to a classical pop concert.

2 *Look across strategic groups within industries*: Examples are Jetstar Airlines in Australia, which operates as a low-cost alternative within Qantas Airways, and Curves fitness centres for women only.

3 *Look across the chain of buyers*: Shift the focus of the target customers towards another customer base. For example, Novo Nordisk refocused its marketing efforts from the prescribing doctor to the patient with the Insulin Delivery Pen.

4 *Look for complementary products and services*: Think about what happens before, during and after the service is used. Find out the pain points in the whole customer experience and then try to eliminate/minimise those pain points. For example, Barnes & Noble refocused its efforts from buying books to a buying experience through the inclusion of lounges, coffee bar and better-trained staff. Another example is major oil companies introducing convenience stores in service stations.

5 *Look across to other functional or emotional appeal elements of the consumer relationship*: For example, Starbucks refocused from a commodity coffee to an emotional atmosphere of coffee enjoyment; also, Viagra refocused from medical treatment to lifestyle enhancement.

6 *Look across the time dimension*: For example, Netflix took advantage of new trends by refocusing from the physical CD to on-demand movie downloads, thus providing many consumer advantages including convenience, time and cost.

Service concept and evaluation

While it is a somewhat straightforward process to develop many service ideas, these must be refined down to a select few concepts. A service concept consists of a description of the key benefits or problems solved by services for an identified market segment.

Organisations need to examine whether consumers also value a service concept with respect to other alternatives. This can be achieved by choice modelling, such as conjoint analysis.[55] In choice modelling, consumers can give marketers information on what components of service they value most and how they trade off any improvements or innovations in the price of a service. This approach is also useful in examining different service concepts that may appeal to different market segments.

The evaluation of the service concept can be facilitated through an assessment of the consumer purchasing cycle. That is, each stage of the purchasing cycle must be charted to ensure that it is able to achieve the overall goals of the service and the organisation. Netflix Inc., for instance, is an American-based international provider of on-demand

↘
service concept
The description of the key benefits or problems solved by services for an identified market segment

internet streaming video. For a small monthly fee, subscribers can download content via their smart television, PC, iPhone, iPad and other streaming devices as required. However, Netflix has run into opposition by trying to restrict its movie catalogues to specific country locations. Savvy consumers have purchased virtual private network (VPN) subscriptions to try to circumvent these restrictions.

In analysing the Netflix consumer purchase cycle, the service needs to demonstrate that it can deliver consumer utility all the way through the cycle from purchase, delivery, use, supplements, maintenance and disposal, as outlined below.

1   *Purchase*: Consumers can select movie and other downloadable content on a variety of streaming devices including television, iPhone and so on. There is no need to purchase separate devices.

2   *Delivery*: Subscription to and installation of the streaming process does not usually take more than a few minutes.

3   *Use*: The setting-up process won't be difficult. The consumer should have basic PC skills so they can follow the instructions guide to set up the streaming process.

4   *Supplements*: The consumer needs a television set and the streaming devices (e.g. video game console, iPad, etc). Usually, a family has a PC or video game console, or iPad.

5   *Maintenance*: The consumer just needs to pay the monthly fee on time.

6   *Disposal*: This is a streaming process. Thus, the consumer won't need to return the movie disc. On the other hand, the consumer won't have to purchase a DVD or go to a cinema.

Feasibility and business-case analysis

As the result of service concept and evaluation, the organisation can now consider the business case for the development of a new service. At this stage approximate demand projections, revenue and cost projections are made. For service organisations, additional costs include those associated with changing systems, processes and organisational culture. For large and established organisations, service innovations may be more difficult because employees need to be convinced of the need for the changes. It has been found, for example, that building societies are better than established banks at implementing service innovations because of employee synergy and better internal marketing.[56]

A common approach used for business analysis is to conduct a feasibility study before the service development to determine whether the organisation should spend the time and resources on the development of a new or refined service offering. A typical feasibility study approach is as follows:

1   *Service feasibility*: Is an assessment of the overall appeal of the product or service being proposed. This considers the likely forecast demand for the service and the development of a concept statement for the proposed service. The concept statement is

usually a one-page description of the proposed offering that is distributed to existing and potential stakeholders outlining the service specification. Finally, it may include a buying intentions survey to validate stakeholder feedback.

2 *Industry/target market feasibility*: Is an assessment of the overall appeal of the industry and the target market. Many approaches to the analysis are possible here, including a Boston Consulting Group (BCG)–type analysis or a Porter's five forces analysis. The critical point here is to ask the question as to whether there is sufficient short-term and long-term demand growth and profitability growth to make the development of the service offering worthwhile.

3 *Organisational feasibility*: Is conducted to determine whether a proposed service offering has the management and organisational structure, leadership, expertise and resources to successfully launch the service. Usually, it is a good idea to conduct a SWOT (strengths, weaknesses, opportunities, threats) analysis at this point.

4 *Financial feasibility*: Is conducted to determine the total start-up cash needed for the service offering and to assess the financial performance of similar offerings in the marketplace. This means developing a budget of all the anticipated capital purchases and operating expenses needed to generate the first 1 dollar in revenues. The organisation will need to assess the return on investment, break-even point and pay-back period for its invested capital. To determine the financial performance of similar offerings, there may be analysis of industry reports or the organisation may need to conduct some observational research on competitive offerings. It cannot expect senior management to invest on its service offering unless it has this information.

Adding value to services

There are many ways that organisations can add value to their services, including the following.

Value added through building brand equity

Value can be added through brand name. This is the concept of brand equity—that is, 'the added value with which a given brand endows a product'.[57] Brand equity is one of the main marketing assets.[58] In fact, as of 2010, 80 per cent of the market value of companies in the S&P 500 in the United States heavily relied on intangibles such as brand, a dramatic increase from 17 per cent in 1975.[59] Brand equity can be increased through positive brand associations, or increased brand differentiation.

Value added through complementary and support services

A business could add value through the addition of complementary services to the core service (e.g. expedited reception service at a hotel, priority check-in at an airport) and support services (additional services beyond the core and facilitating services, such as hotel restaurants, dry-cleaning services in hotel, a wide choice of in-flight entertainment on international airlines). Care should be taken to ensure these complementary services do not add cost into the basic price, particularly in price-sensitive markets.

Value added through product/service attributes

Depending on what was valued by a customer, a business could either add new components to a service, take service components away, increase their importance or reduce their importance. This can be done through a performance-importance grid and focusing on service aspects that are high on importance and low on performance. However, in taking such an approach, the business must be mindful about the cost implications of attribute changes.

Value added through customers participating in the service-delivery process

By participating in the service production process, customers contribute to the quality of services and associated outcomes. Including customers in the service-delivery process, then, can enhance their perceptions of value, presuming that the customer is a cooperative party in creating the service. Attribution theory suggests that customers are likely to view the outcomes more positively if they take a responsible role in the service process. Examples are the trend for some McDonald's restaurants to offer custom-designed menus and self-service checkouts at supermarkets.

Service development and testing

While a business can develop a prototype product for testing relatively easily, it is difficult to do so for a service. Also, there may be problems in terms of equity and ethics for many organisations if they test prototypes on existing consumers or clients without their knowledge or permission. Companies may develop a series of blueprints as to how the new service could be delivered. This might be achieved based on interactions with operations, support and marketing personnel who could identify the most economical and effective means of delivering the new service to the consumer. Companies can also start to financially model the impact of new service innovations—for example, the bundling of services in the electrical sector—to examine if they meet demand at expected cost and revenues.[60] Some large organisations may decide to release significant changes to services gradually in various locales with the aim of improving each subsequent service innovation in the next place. Examples of this include the federal government's roll-out of the national broadband system and welfare changes introduced originally to central Aboriginal communities, then extended to the Northern Territory, and then across Australia to all populations.

David Gray

Commercialisation

Commercialisation is when the service innovation goes live. It is often the time of greatest costs and risk for the organisation. The risk is that a badly received service change can impact negatively on the organisation's reputation. One of the key tasks of commercialisation is to gain acceptance of the new service and to engage the service-delivery personnel. The other is to examine all aspects of the delivery process to ensure that all facets are working well. Consumer education about the new service is also considered an important part of success.[61] To this end, many organisations may develop and encourage consumer trial and assistance by using assistants—for example, to demonstrate the use of online services on-site and provide call-centre support to help consumers understand changes.

Evaluation

The last and perhaps most important task is to evaluate the launch of the new service by examining all aspects of the service processes. As minor problems can derail a new service quickly, organisations need to provide resources and systems that enable these matters to be resolved promptly. Some online companies have a 'hot-fix' team, for example, which attends quickly to minor issues involved in the delivery of website content. Improvements to services are also a continuous process involving every aspect of the organisation. For this reason, dedication to the internal marketing efforts of the organisation is crucial.

This chapter discussed important aspects of the development and delivery of services. The first was how a service offering is constructed. This includes the development of core benefits of value, plus the addition of related and augmented services. Many service organisations now find it easier to add additional related and augmented services to the service offering rather than create a new service. We discussed the most common strategic approaches in services marketing and the different types of services that could be developed by an organisation. In addition, we reviewed the service development process including new idea generation, analysis and evaluation and commercialisation. With respect to analysis, we discussed the components of a feasibility study, the consumer purchase cycle and the different pathways towards developing a competitive new service strategy. Therefore, you should be now be able to understand the nature of the service offering and the process of developing a competitive service strategy.

Summary

Review questions

1   Explain the difference between the following terms and provide an example of each:
    a   core service offering
    b   related services
    c   augmented services.
2   Explain how value can be added to a service and give examples from
    a   a restaurant
    b   a movie theatre
    c   an ISP provider
    d   the tourism industry
    e   your university department or school.
3   Explain the different types of new services that could be developed by an organisation.
4   Explain Blue Ocean Strategy as a basis for new service development, and give examples.
5   Explain the components of a feasibility study.
6   Explain the concept of the 'six pathways' in Blue Ocean Strategy towards developing a unique service, and give examples.
7   What reasons can you think of to explain why a guest who has had a satisfactory experience with a hotel they recently stayed in may never visit the same property again?
8   What are four ways in which value can be added to a service organisation?

Further reading

Baker, T. & Collier, D.A. (2005). The economic payout model for service guarantees. *Decision Sciences*, 362, 197–220.

Cova, B. & Salle, R. (2008). Marketing solutions in accordance with the S-D logic: Co-creating value with customer network actors. *Industrial Marketing Management*, 373, 270–7.

Dasgupta, C. & Ghose, S. (1993). Positioning health services: A mapping approach. *Health Marketing Quarterly*, 11(1–12), 191–206.

de Berntani, U. (2001). Innovative versus incremental new business services: Different keys for achieving success. *Journal of Product Innovation Management*, 183, 169–87.

Garry, T. (2007). Consumer sophistication and the role of emotion on satisfaction judgments within credence services. *Journal of Consumer Behaviour*, 66, 383–97.

Kim, W.C. & Mauborgne, R. (2005). *Blue Ocean Strategy: How to Create Uncontested Market Space and Make the Competition Irrelevant* (unabridged edition). New York: Harvard Business School Press.

Johnson, M.D., Olsen, L.L. & Andreassen, T.W. (2009). Joy and disappointment in the hotel experience: Managing relationship segments. *Managing Service Quality*, 191, 4–30.

Moeller, S. (2010). Characteristics of services: A new approach uncovers their value. *Journal of Services Marketing*, 245, 359–68.

Smith, D. (2005). Business not as usual: Crisis management, service recovery and the vulnerability of organisations. *Journal of Services Marketing*, 195, 309–20.

Xue, M., Hein, G.R. & Harker, P.T. (2005). Consumer and co-producer roles in e-service: Analysing efficiency and effectiveness of e-service designs. *International Journal of Electronic Business*, 32, 174–97.

Weblinks

Carnival Australia (Australian site for Carnival Cruises). <www.carnivalaustralia.com>
Jim's Group. <www.jims.net>
iiNet. <www.iinet.net.au>
National Australia Bank. <www.nab.com.au>
Qantas. <www.qantas.com.au>
St John of God Healthcare. <www.sjog.org.au>
Virgin Australia. <www.virginaustralia.com>
Westpac. <www.westpac.com.au>

Endnotes

1 Based on D. Shah (2015). How Coursera cracked the Chinese market. *Crunch Network*, 21 August <http://techcrunch.com/2015/08/21/how-coursera-cracked-the-chinese-market>.
2 J. Anderson & J. Narus (1998). Business marketing: Understand what customers value. *Harvard Business Review*, 76(6), 53.
3 Coursera website. <www.coursera.org>.
4 St John of God Health Care website. About us. Vision, mission and values. <www.sjog.org.au>.
5 iiNet website. About us. Who we are and what we do. <www.iinet.net.au>.
6 St John of God Health Care website. <www.sjog.org.au>.
7 B. Fung (2016). Google still trying to figure out social web with confusing new app. *Sydney Morning Herald*, 17 May. <www.smh.com.au/technology/web-culture/google-still-trying-to-figure-out-social-web-with-confusing-new-app-20160516-gownno.html#ixzz48wXKZ4AF>.
8 ibid.
9 M.E. Porter (ed.) (1980 & 1998). *Competitive Strategy: Techniques for Analysing Industries and Competitors*. New York: Free Press.
10 J. Barney, M. Wright & D.J. Ketchen (2001). The resource-based view of the firm: Ten years after 1991. *Journal of Management*, 27(6), 625–41, p. 625.

11 D.J. Teece, G. Pisano & A. Shuen (1997). Dynamic capabilities and strategic management. *Strategic Management Journal*, 18(7), 509–33, p. 510.

12 S.L. Vargo & R.F. Lusch (2004). Evolving to a new dominant logic for marketing. *Journal of Marketing*, 68(1), 1–17, p. 1.

13 ibid.

14 G. Hamel & C.K. Prahalad (1994). *Competing for the Future*. Harvard Business School Press.

15 J.C. Narver & S.F. Slater (1990). The effect of a market orientation on business profitability. *Journal of Marketing*, 54(4), 20–35.

16 A.K. Kohli & B.J. Jaworski (1990). Market orientation: The construct, research propositions, and managerial implications. *Journal of Marketing*, 54(2), 1–18; A.K. Kohli & B.J. Jaworski (1993). Market orientation: Antecedents and consequences. *Journal of Marketing*, 57(3), 53–81.

17 G. Helfert, T. Ritter & A. Walter (2002). Redefining market orientation from a relationship perspective: Theoretical considerations and empirical results. *European Journal of Marketing*, 36(9/10), 1119–39.

18 J. Becker & C. Homburg (1999). Market-oriented management: A systems-based perspective. *Journal of Market Focused Management*, 4(1), 17–41.

19 J.C. Narver & S.F. Slater (1990). The effect of a market orientation on business profitability. *Journal of Marketing*, 54(4), 20–35.

20 J.C. Narver, S.F. Slater & B. Tietje (1998). Creating a market orientation. *Journal of Market Focused Management*, 2(3), 241–55, p. 242.

21 D.M. Gray (2006). *A Competency Based Theory of Business Partnering*. Sydney: University of New South Wales.

22 R.M. Morgan & S.D. Hunt (1994). The commitment-trust theory of relationship marketing. *Journal of Marketing*, 58(3), 20–39.

23 L. Shostack (1982). How to design a service. *European Journal of Marketing*, 16(1), 49.

24 L.-B. Oh & H.-H. Teo (2010). Consumer value co-creation in a hybrid commerce service-delivery system. *International Journal of Electronic Commerce*, 14(3), 35–62.

25 K. Goodrich (2007). Transforming into Dell 2.0: The customer's strategic role in design innovation. *Design Management Review*, 18(4), 65–72.

26 T. Albert, P. Goes & A. Gupta (2004). GIST: A model for the design and management of content in customer-centric websites. *MIS Quarterly*, 28(2), 161–82.

27 P. Carbonell, A. Rodríguez-Escudero & D. Pujari (2009). Customer involvement in new service development: An examination of antecedents and outcomes. *Journal of Product Innovation Management*, 26(5), 536–50.

28 C. Dasgupta & S. Ghose (1993). Positioning health services: A mapping approach. *Health Marketing Quarterly*, 11(1–2), 191–206.

29 W.C. Kim & R. Mauborgne (2015). *Blue Ocean Strategy*. Boston, MA: Harvard Business Review Press, p. 118.

30 A. Johne & C. Storey (1998). New service development: A review of the literature and annotated bibliography. *European Journal of Marketing*, 32(3/4), 184.

31 R.A. Oliva (1988). Painting with business marketers' 'web palette'. *Marketing Management*, 7(2), 50–3.

32 T. Telschow (2004). Home at the bank. *North Western Financial Review*, 189(8), 10–12.

33 M. Zolfagharian & P. Audhesh (2008). Do consumers discern innovations in service elements? *Journal of Services Marketing*, 22(5), 338–52.

34 A. Johne & C. Storey (1998). New service development: A review of the literature and annotated bibliography. *European Journal of Marketing*, 32(3/4), 184.

35 P. Custance, M. Hingley & D. Wilcox (2011). Developing a novel health and well-being service: The value of utilising the restorative benefits of nature in the UK. *Journal of Marketing Management*, 27(3/4), 386–400.

36 K. Ranson (2007). Bigger is not always better. *Travel Weekly (UK)*, 29 June, p. 23.

37 A. Stanton, M. Kennedy, R. Spingarn & M.J. Rotheram-Borus (2000). Developing services for substance-abusing HIV-positive youth with mental health disorders. *Journal of Behavioral Health Services & Research*, 27(4), 380.

38 M. Lal Bhasin (2005). E-broking as a tool for marketing financial services in the global market. *Journal of Services Research*, 5(2), 151–67.

39 L.-B. Oh & H.-H. Teo (2010). Consumer value co-creation in a hybrid commerce service-delivery system. *International Journal of Electronic Commerce*, 14(3), 35–62.

40 H. Ernst, W. Hoyer, M. Krafft & K. Krieger (2011). Customer relationship management and company performance: The mediating role of new product performance. *Journal of the Academy of Marketing Science*, 39(2), 290–306.

41 P. Tirschwell (2004). Time is money. *Journal of Commerce (15307557)*, 5(22), 6A–12A.

42 A. Johne & C. Storey (1998). New service development: A review of the literature and annotated bibliography. *European Journal of Marketing*, 32(3/4), 184.

43 S.D. Chekitan (2006). Carnival Cruise Lines: Charting a new brand course. *Cornell Hotel & Restaurant Administration Quarterly*, 47(3), 301–8.

44 Adapted from S. Edwards (2016). 3 companies using speed as a competitive advantage. *Entrepreneur*, 5 January <www.entrepreneur.com/article/253372>.

45 J. Barmann (2016). The on-demand/shut-in economy is definitely slowing down, if not dying. *sfist*, 21 March <http://sfist.com/2016/03/21/on_demand_shut-in_economy_slowing_down_not_dying.php>.

46 W.C. Kim & R. Mauborgne (2005). *Blue Ocean Strategy: How to Create Uncontested Market Space and Make the Competition Irrelevant* (unabridged edition). New York: Harvard Business School Press.

47 W.C. Kim & R. Mauborgne (2015). *Blue Ocean Strategy*. Boston, MA: Harvard Business Review Press, p. 118.

48 ibid.

49 O.C. Ferrell, V.L. Crittenden, L. Ferrell & W.F. Crittenden (2013). Theoretical development in ethical marketing decision making. *AMS Review*, 3, 51–60.

50 M.E. Porter (ed.) (1980 & 1998). *Competitive Strategy: Techniques for Analysing Industries and Competitors*. New York: Free Press.

51 Wikipedia (2016). Mark Zuckerberg. <https://en.wikipedia.org/w/index.php?title=Mark_Zuckerberg&oldid=711483898>.

52 I. Alam (2002). An exploratory investigation of user involvement in new service development. *Journal of the Academy of Marketing Science*, 30(3), 250–61.

53 M.K. Turtle (2005). A survey of users and non-users of a UK teaching hospital library and information service. *Health Information & Libraries Journal*, 22(4), 267–75.

54 W.C. Kim & R. Mauborgne (2015). *Blue Ocean Strategy*. Boston, MA: Harvard Business Review Press, p. 118.

55 R. Huertas-García & C. Consolación-Segura (2009). A framework for designing new products and services. *International Journal of Market Research*, 51(6), 819–40.

56 C. Storey & C. Easingwood (1993). The impact of the new product development project on the success of financial services. *Service Industries Journal*, 13(3), 40–54.

57 P.H. Farquhar (1990). Managing brand equity. *Journal of Advertising Research*, 30 (August–September), RC7–RC12.

58 K.L. Keller & D.R. Lehmann (2006). Brands and branding: Research findings and future priorities. *Marketing Science*, 25(6), 740–59; D.M. Hanssens, R.T. Rust & R.K. Srivastava (2009). Marketing strategy and wall street: Nailing down marketing's impact. *Journal of Marketing*, 73(November), 115–18.

59 R.N. Sinclair & K.L. Keller (2014). A case for brands as assets: Acquired and internally developed. *Journal of Brand Management*, 21(4), 286–302.

60 Z. Baida, J. Gordijn, H. Akkermans, H. Saele & A.Z. Morch (2005). Finding e-service offerings by computer-supported customer need reasoning. *International Journal of E-Business Research*, 1(3), 91–112.

61 J. Schneider & J. Hall (2011). Why most product launches fail. *Harvard Business Review*, 89(4), 21–3.

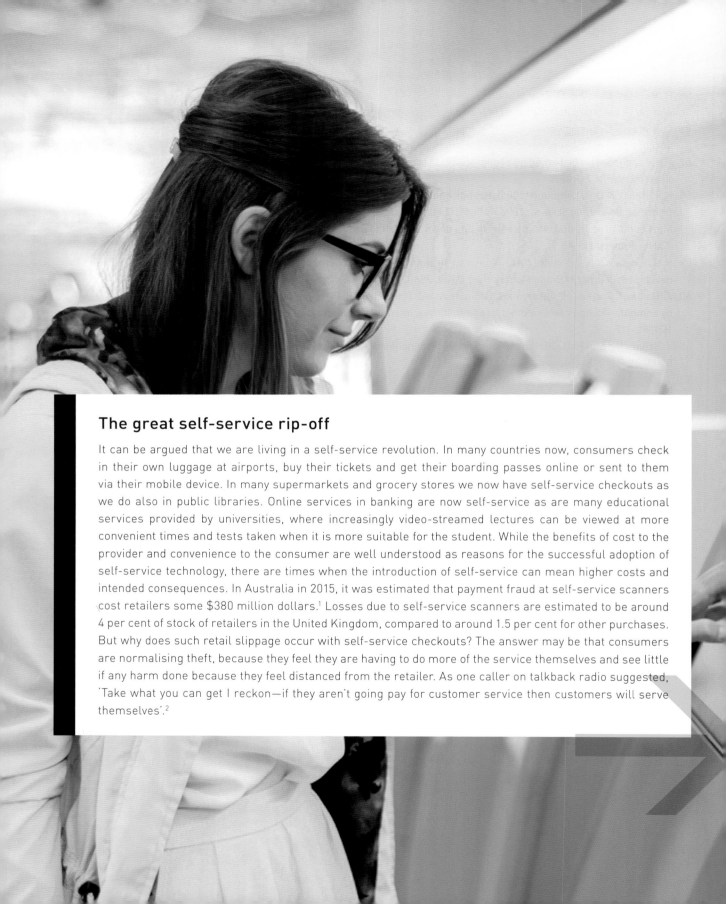

The great self-service rip-off

It can be argued that we are living in a self-service revolution. In many countries now, consumers check in their own luggage at airports, buy their tickets and get their boarding passes online or sent to them via their mobile device. In many supermarkets and grocery stores we now have self-service checkouts as we do also in public libraries. Online services in banking are now self-service as are many educational services provided by universities, where increasingly video-streamed lectures can be viewed at more convenient times and tests taken when it is more suitable for the student. While the benefits of cost to the provider and convenience to the consumer are well understood as reasons for the successful adoption of self-service technology, there are times when the introduction of self-service can mean higher costs and intended consequences. In Australia in 2015, it was estimated that payment fraud at self-service scanners cost retailers some $380 million dollars.[1] Losses due to self-service scanners are estimated to be around 4 per cent of stock of retailers in the United Kingdom, compared to around 1.5 per cent for other purchases. But why does such retail slippage occur with self-service checkouts? The answer may be that consumers are normalising theft, because they feel they are having to do more of the service themselves and see little if any harm done because they feel distanced from the retailer. As one caller on talkback radio suggested, 'Take what you can get I reckon—if they aren't going pay for customer service then customers will serve themselves'.[2]

Chapter 6

The Service-delivery Process and Self-service Technology

Steven D'Alessandro

Introduction

For many not-for-profit organisations and government departments, how well services are provided to the public is a crucial part of their mission. This chapter outlines some important matters all organisations need to consider in order to deliver effective services, whether directly or indirectly. It is even possible for organisations to manage service exchanges between other parties when they do not own or manage the core service. This is the case with Uber, which delivers ride sharing, and Airbnb, in which provides host-guest accommodation. Many service providers, however, still have to effectively manage delivering services when demand exceeds capacity, and this is when reservation and queuing systems become so important. Increasingly, to avoid customer wait times and to lower costs, many service organisations are now using self-service technology. As will be seen throughout this chapter, each approach in delivering a service is not without its advantages and disadvantages, as was shown in opening vignette about self-service checkouts.

Learning objectives

After reading this chapter you should be able to:

- ↘ discuss the role of intermediaries in the distribution of a service
- ↘ examine the sharing economy of Uber and Airbnb
- ↘ discuss how organisations deal with queues and waiting lines effectively for their customers
- ↘ understand what is meant by self-service technology and how self-service comes to be accepted by consumers
- ↘ describe other electronic distribution channels.

Distributing services through channels

Important decisions in the delivery of services are who they are being delivered to and how they may be distributed. Table 6.1 shows the various options for the delivery of services to the consumer.

Customers visit the service site

In this situation, the convenience of the location is important. Convenience may include access to parking and distance from the customer's home or work. The service site will also need to be highly visible to consumers. Traffic and pedestrian counts may be useful for this purpose. Service marketers may also consider the retail gravity model in locating their

Table 6.1 Six options for service delivery

Nature of interactions between customer and service provider	Availability of service outlets	
	Single site	Multiple sites
Customer goes to service organisation	Concert (e.g. Opera Australia) Local hairdresser	Train service (e.g. Sydney Metro) Tax preparation services (e.g. H&R Block)
Service organisation comes to the customer	Kitchen renovations Mobile pet wash	Courier services (e.g. Parcel Post) Auto club service (e.g. RACV)
Customer and service organisations transact remotely (mail and/or electronic communication)	Credit card company (e.g. Visa) Local TV station (e.g. Channel 7, Perth).	Broadcast network (e.g. Channel 9) Telephone company (e.g. Telstra)

Source: C. Lovelock. & J. Wirtz, J. (2011). *Services Marketing: People, Technology, Strategy* (7th edn). Pearson, p. 144.

stores, whereby larger shopping centres may draw in consumers from a greater distance from the centre. When customers go directly to service providers, it may be necessary to manage demand through reservation and queuing systems; this is discussed later in this chapter.

Service providers go to their customers

For other service providers, visits to the customer's place of residence or work may be unavoidable and be a central part of the value provided to consumers. Obvious examples are plumbing, electrical and handyperson services. Other call-out services that have become popular in recent times include gardening and childminding services. Generally, services provided in such a manner are expensive for the provider, given the travel, time and equipment that are involved. To deal with these issues, many companies may use intermediaries, especially franchises; for example, Jim's Mowing. The wide use of the internet and the market acceptance of smartphones now means that services can not only be delivered to the customer directly, but service exchanges can be facilitated by third parties who do not own the service but provide a means for this to occur. These companies are typically part of the 'sharing economy', which is discussed later in this chapter.

Business-to-business (B2B) services that are also provided on-site may be more specialised and may include consultancies or engineering services, or more routine services such as cleaning, security, and garden and plant maintenance. The growth of cloud computing makes it possible for many companies and providers to provide technical and consultancy services at much lower costs and on a demand basis (see also Services in Action, 'Big data services available now via cloud computing').

Jim's Group

A visit to the Jim's Group website <www.jims.net> shows a plethora of services, 26 of which can be provided to the consumer at their home or place of business. These range from gardening, property maintenance, pest control, bookkeeping and even computer services (Figure 6.1). For all of these services, the consumer simply phones one number: 131 546. Founded with just $24 capital in 1982, Jim's Group now turns over more than $300 million annually.

With about 4000 franchisees across four countries in 29 divisions, from the ubiquitous Jim's Mowing to computer services and finance, the franchise is second only to Australia Post in size.[3] Franchisees are backed by marketing support, the buying power of the company, which reduces costs, and training. The company also makes money selling franchises. Jim Pennman, the founder of Jim's Group, puts the success of his business down to the focus on customers.

'My aim is that all my customers, and especially the Franchisees who are my key customers, are not just satisfied but delighted. In other words, they must become "raving fans". It hardly needs saying that this is the goal, not the reality. I deal each day with clients and Franchisees who are not happy. Every Franchisee has my direct phone number and Email address, and any client whose complaint is not settled first time is directed to me. So I know that we have a long, long way to go'.[4]

Figure 6.1 Some of the many services provided by Jim's Group

The role of intermediaries

As can be seen with Jim's Group, many organisations find it more efficient and less resource intensive to outsource some or all of their parts of service deliveries. Hotels and cruise lines may still use travel agents because agents can specialise in finding local markets, providing information, taking orders and processing payments and ticketing. Travel agents have an incentive to provide these services because of the financial benefits of commissions, which are not available to company employees.

While there may be advantages in the use of intermediaries in terms of costs, there is still the problem of control. Organisations may wish to control how their services are provided and marketed. To do this, they may seek to administer the channel of distribution by means of contractual arrangements and/or or by franchises. Many product companies rely on intermediaries to supply services such as repair, maintenance and storage. Direct or company-owned channels do exist in services. One example is Starbucks, whose 3000 coffee shops are owned by the company in the United States. Many specialised services, such as air transport, are delivered directly.

However, where intermediaries are used in the delivery of services, there are two major types: franchises and agent/brokers.

↘
intermediary
Any person or organisation that provides services on behalf of others (e.g. agents, brokers and franchisees)

Big data services available now via cloud computing

Many specialist services can be provided by cloud computing. These can include the storage of information and hosting of online services by a contracted provider. Companies like Telstra and Microsoft now can provide big data analytic services for many retailers and clients. This saves the client time and cost in installing servers, purchasing software and training its staff in big data. Smaller companies such as Near in Australia can also provide specialist consulting services by using third-party software and cloud access to company datasets. Near used such an approach to assist McDonald's in Japan to interact with its 30 million active social media users. By tailoring individual messages and mining online and store interactions, the company was able to help McDonald's in Japan achieve a significant turnaround in sales by around 20 per cent in 2016. The important development in big data for business is that it has moved from being a technological and information-based activity to more of an overall service package for providers such as Microsoft, SAS, IBM and Telstra to provide to their clients.

Steven D'Alessandro

Franchising

↘
franchising
One of the most common methods for distributing services, usually done through contractual arrangements between the franchiser and franchisee. Common franchises in Australia include H&R Block, Mortgage Choice and Auto Masters.

Franchising is probably one of the most common types of distribution of services. According to the Franchise Council of Australia, franchises in Australia are worth some $128 billion and constitute roughly 10 per cent of the economy (see Figure 6.2). Common franchises in Australia include McDonald's, H&R Block, Red Rooster, Mortgage Choice and Auto Masters.

Franchising is used to distribute services because of the following advantages to the franchiser:

→ It provides a leveraged format for greater expansion and revenues.

→ It provides consistency of outlets.

→ Knowledge of local markets is supplied by the franchisee.

→ There is shared financial risk and more working capital for the franchiser.

Disadvantages of franchising are:

→ difficulty in maintaining and monitoring franchisees

→ highly publicised disputes between franchisees and franchisers

→ inconsistent quality

→ customer relationships controlled by the franchisee rather than the franchiser.[5]

Researchers also point to an inherent conflict in franchising—that is, the need for standardisation in order for consistent service delivery to take place versus the need for flexibility to achieve a higher adaptation to local markets and enhance franchisees' entrepreneurial attitudes.[6] Compared to wholly owned service businesses such as in the restaurant industry, franchises have been found to deliver superior financial performance.[7]

From the perspective of the franchisee, the advantages of franchises include marketing and big company support, efficient ordering systems and guidelines to a business start-up,

Figure 6.2 H&R Block is one player in the $128 billion franchising business in Australia

OXFORD UNIVERSITY PRESS

which comes almost prepacked. A main concern is the encroachment of other franchises into the local market where the franchisee operates, leading to greater competition and reducing the value of the business.

Agents and brokers

An **agent** is an intermediary who acts on behalf of a service principal and is authorised to make agreements between the principal and the customer. Agents may assist in both the selling and purchase of services. Commonly, agents assist in the selling of real estate and travel and accommodation services. Agents can also assist in evaluating land purchases for companies, and help individuals to find artworks and antiques. A **broker**, on the other hand, acts more as a facilitator of exchanges between buyers and sellers. Examples include insurance, mortgage brokers and stockbrokers (Figure 6.3).

Advantages of brokers and agents are:

→ reduced selling and distribution costs

→ possession of their special skills and knowledge

→ representation within markets

→ knowledge of local markets

→ they provide customer choice of multiple services.

Disadvantages of brokers and agents are:

→ loss of control over pricing—this is handed to the agent and the broker

→ representation of multiple service principals—they may not always act in the seller's best interest.

Overall, brokers and agents are a valuable means of distributing services because they provide a cheap means to cover a wide set of markets at little cost to the service principal,

agent
An intermediary who acts on behalf of a service principal and is authorised to make agreements between the principal and the customer

broker
Acts as a facilitator of exchanges between buyers and sellers

Figure 6.3 Many financial services, such as stocks and insurance, are delivered by brokers

Steven D'Alessandro

compared with other channels of distribution. Research also suggests that agents are useful in a market since they provide expected relevant outcomes, efficient processes, psychological security and social facilitation between buyers and sellers.[8] Agents also provide important market information to clients: for example, a country's reputation in international education.[9] Agents have been found to be useful for sellers when markets are rising or in a moderate decline. When markets are in significant decline, agents seem to add less value to service transactions.[10] Another trade-off is that there is a loss of control over prices received, and agents and brokers may also act in the interests of competitors.

The sharing economy of Uber and Airbnb

One of the more interesting developments that has been made possible by the wide adoption of smartphones among consumers is that of the sharing economy,[11] whereby providers act as brokers or facilitators of services owned by third parties with their customers.[12] A sharing economy is where resources, facilities and services are shared or rented to other parties without ownership transferring to the other party.

Since 2010, ride-share company Uber has developed markets and operated the Uber app, which allows consumers with smartphones to submit a trip request that the software program then automatically sends to the Uber driver nearest to the consumer, alerting the driver to their location. The app uses stored credit card data, so that is not necessary to transact after the ride. Prices are also set according to a demand algorithm (see also the Services in Action, 'Coming soon to a cinema near you? Ticket prices shaped by demand'). Uber drivers use their own personal cars. Drivers rate customers and customers rate drivers on the service experience, which helps build a trust and relational network similar to that of eBay.[13] In 2015 Uber was worth approximately US$62.5 billion, and in August 2016, the service was available in over 66 countries and 545 cities worldwide,[14] providing an estimated two billion riders a year.

Another innovator in the sharing economy is Airbnb, an online broker that facilitates a network for short-term rentals and homestays in residential properties. The cost of the accommodation is set by the property owner and the company receives percentage service fees from both guests and hosts in conjunction with every booking. The peer-to-peer accommodation marketplace is in many ways an example of co-created value in service exchange.[15] Importantly, both Airbnb and Uber do not own the service (car rides or accommodation), but are facilitators of exchange between owners and users of services. Like Uber, Airbnb uses an online rating system of host versus guest experiences, and hosts are not obligated to accept a guest booking. Again, this helps to build trust between hosts and guests.

Both these leaders in the new sharing economy are not without controversy. There have been concerns about the safety of guests with Airbnb and that tenants may sub-let

OXFORD UNIVERSITY PRESS

properties, potentially voiding the insurance policies of landlords. With Uber, there have concerns from lawmakers in many countries that the company is operating a taxi business (which Uber denies), is not paying its fair share of taxes, is avoiding regulation and, most importantly, is disrupting the local taxi businesses.[16] And while the sharing economy provides new opportunities for the delivery of services, many services are still delivered in traditional channels where there needs to be an efficient means of meeting demand. As services are perishable and demand can be seasonal or sometimes unpredictable, it is important to provide a just and efficient means of customers to access services in a timely manner.

Customer reservation systems, queuing and waiting lines

Perhaps one of the most annoying aspects of life is waiting in a queue, either at the end of a telephone line or in a bank. Waiting for service can be more serious if the service is an emergency service; for example, medical and ambulance services. Sometimes we can wait for services that involve inanimate objects. These include emails to be answered, appliances to be fixed, cheques to be cleared from banks and broadband connections to be installed. Customer Service Benchmarking Australia managing director Paul van Veenendaal estimates that Australians waste 20 million hours a year stuck on hold with call centres.[17]

This results from the simple fact that services, unlike products, cannot be stored for later use. While ideally no one should wait, it is not technically feasible or economically possible for this to happen. Nevertheless, there are reported differences in how well organisations are managing wait times or queues. This is shown in Table 6.2, which summarises a media report on how long customers were kept on hold by various organisations in Victoria.

As can be seen, there are sizeable differences among the major corporations' waiting times for service. In terms of banks, Westpac only placed potential customers on hold for 39 seconds, compared to 1 minute 55 seconds by the Commonwealth Bank. There are also significant differences in how well organisations place potential versus existing customers on hold. While the ANZ had a much higher on-hold time than Westpac, there is very little difference between how long existing and potential customers wait for service. Origin Energy, an electricity company, placed existing customers on hold for over half an hour (32 minutes).

The issue then for organisations is how to best manage such situations, as unattended customers may become dissatisfied. Potential customers may also seek another provider.

There are two possible solutions: ask customers to wait in line and serve them on a first-come, first-served basis; or manage the process by encouraging consumers to reserve a booking or make an appointment in advance.

Table 6.2 The length of time left on hold by selected organisations

Company	Prospective customer wait time	Existing customer wait time
Origin Energy	*6 min 25 sec	32 min 10 sec
Qantas	5 min 50 sec	5 min 50 sec
Vodaphone	3 min 47 sec, then disconnected	1 min 50 sec
Optus	2 min 47 sec	2 min 30 sec
Telstra	1 min 25 sec	2 min 2 sec
Tiger Airways	2 min 57 sec	2 min 19 sec after tech fault
Virgin Blue	2 min 27 sec	2 min 35 sec
Commonwealth Bank	1 min 55 sec	1 min 50 sec
ANZ Bank	1 min 52 sec	1 min 40 sec
NAB	50 sec	5 min 50 sec
Virgin Mobile	35 sec	40 sec
Westpac	39 sec	1 min 16 sec
AGL	30 sec	48 sec
GIO	10 sec	2 min 48 sec
AAMI	No wait	No wait

*Time taken to answer calls noon–2 pm on the same day.

Source: W. Hosking (2010). Loyalty left on hold. *Herald-Sun*, 11 October, p. 11.

Why waiting lines occur

Waiting lines occur whenever the number of inquiries or arrivals exceeds the capacity of the system to process them. In an ideal world, no one would wait for anything, but all organisations, be they profit oriented or governmental, are constrained by available resources. It is sometimes difficult to forecast the likely demand on customer services. Natural disasters, like the 2011 floods and Cyclone Yasi in Queensland, not only put strains on emergency and civil services, but also mean an increased and unexpected demand for telephone and insurance services.

Organisations may also not have the systems or resources to properly manage queues. There may be little or no incentive in organisations to reduce waiting times. This may occur because there are no competing alternatives for services and/or consumers, who may be compelled to use the service and therefore become a captive market. Government welfare agencies like Centrelink would be under less pressure to reduce waiting times than the companies listed in Table 6.2, because their clients have to deal with it as a service provider. There are also seasonal factors, such as festive holidays, school holidays and the start of the school or university year, that place greater demands on services like air transport and retailing at certain times of the year.

Managing waiting lines

Given that queues or waiting lines are a given for many customers and organisations, the issue is how best to manage waiting lines. Some suggested alternatives to the problem are to:

1   use a different queue configuration
2   tailor the queuing system to different market segments
3   manage customer behaviour and perceptions of the wait
4   install a reservations system
5   redesign the service process to reduce the time of each transaction.[18]

In this section of the text, points 1–3 are discussed in detail. Reservations are dealt with in the discussion on self-service technology and in Chapter 8, 'Managing Productive Capacity and Customer Demand', while point 5 is discussed in Chapter 4.

Different queue configurations

There are a variety of configurations of queues, each with its own set of advantages and disadvantages, which managers can use to effectively manage waiting lines. These are:

→ *Single line, sequential stages*: traditional queues that have problems of bottlenecks and difficulties dealing with unusual customer transactions (Figure 6.4). These are best used when the transaction is straightforward; for example, buying lunch at the university cafeteria.

→ *Parallel line to multiple servers*: here consumers are presented with multiple possible serving stations. This is really a collection of single-line queues. Examples include queues for bank tellers and in government offices. While capacity to process is increased, different lines may move at different speeds, and this may be quite frustrating for the consumer.

Figure 6.4   A single-line queue

Figure 6.5 A single line to multiple servers at an airport

→ *A single line to multiple servers*: sometimes called a 'snake'. This queue design aims
  to remove the problem of different lines moving at different speeds by implementing
  parallel line to multiple servers. This kind of queuing system is used in airport check-
  ins (Figure 6.5), post offices and by some retailers at checkouts, such as Target.

→ *Designated lines*: are used for specific types of customer inquiries; for example, customer
  help versus standard transactions in banks. Or they may be used for different market
  segments; for example, personal versus business accounts. Another use is to reward high-
  net-worth customers, such as business and frequent-flyer check-ins in airports.

→ *Take a number*: saves time and helps direct consumers, with the help of touch screens,
  to the appropriate service encounter. This procedure allows consumers to sit down and
  relax, reducing the stress of waiting time. It also reduces uncertainty as the numbers
  are called in sequence (Figure 6.6). Organisations that use this approach include large
  government and insurance offices.

→ *Wait list*: restaurants and sometimes travel agents have wait lists where people record
  their name and wait until a place in the queue for an available service is announced.
  There are four common means of wait listing:

  1 *Party-sized seating:* used in restaurants where the number of people is matched to
     the number on the table.

  2 *VIP seating*: people with special rights, frequent flyers and business-class passen-
     gers or celebrities in restaurants are served first.

  3 *Call-ahead seating*: allows people to hold a place on the wait list via the internet or
     telephone. Recent innovations use SMS messaging to show a person's position on a
     wait list.

  4 *Large party reservations:* services are reserved for large groups. In some instances
     the service provider may ask for a deposit; for example, a wedding or corporate
     function.

Figure 6.6 Example of a take-a-number queue system

Organisations may also use a combination of these queue designs. Selecting the appropriate design has been shown to influence customer satisfaction and perceptions of fairness. Research suggests that customers waiting in parallel lines to multiple servers reported feeling agitated and dissatisfied compared with those who waited in a single line (snake configuration) to multiple servers, even though both groups waited the same amount of time.[19] The issue of perceived fairness, of customers who wait and see others who arrived later being served before them, or watching other lines moving faster than their line, is also a real issue for the design of any queue system.

Queuing systems can be tailored to market segments

When it comes to waiting for a service, different customer groups may have different priorities. Often managers may segment their market of customers on a particular basis and design specific queue systems for each group. These may include:

→ *Urgency of the job*: Customers with urgent needs, especially in health, are often served first. In health a triage system is used to assess patients quickly when they arrive in the hospital's Accident and Emergency so as to decide which patients should be seen first. Other examples may include service organisations that specialise in 24-hour 'emergency' services; for example, 24-hour on-call plumbers and 24-hour denture repairs.

→ *Duration of the service transaction*: Banks and supermarkets may use express lanes for customers who require shorter, less-complicated tasks. Likewise, there may also be lanes for customer-service and detailed inquiries.

→ *Payment of a premium price*: Consumers who pay a premium price, for example, first-class and business passengers, may have reduced wait times and specialised queues.

→ *Importance of the customer*: A separate area or queue may be reserved for members of a special club. One example is the Qantas club, which provides refreshments and newspapers to its members so that they can wait in greater comfort.

Customer perceptions of waiting time

Customers often believe they wait longer for a service than they actually do. For example, in one study, consumers waiting for public transport believed that time passed seven times more slowly than it actually did.[20] Congested or crowded service locales increase the consumer perception of risk of not being served when waiting in queues, especially if there is uncertainty about what causes the congestion.[21] Where someone is located in a queue compared to how they are progressing in the queue has been shown to have differential effects on attitudes and behaviour. Research on call centres has shown that information about progression through a queue influences caller attitudes, while position in the queue influenced caller behaviour.[22] It is therefore important for management to provide information about a person's position in a queue and proximity to service, especially in crowded situations.

Reservation strategies should focus on yield

Many organisations often use a percentage of capacity as a measure of operational efficiency. For example, hotels may talk of 'occupancy rates', airlines of 'load factors' or professional service workers in law and accounting may discuss 'billable hours'. These figures of operational utilisation, however, do not relate to profitability or yield; that is, the average revenue expected from a unit of capacity (hotel room, airline seat, etc.). These issues force managers to consider how best to use their organisation to maximise yield by their reserving their service for customer configurations of various types. Airlines typically do not discount heavily in times of demand (e.g. school holidays), but may wish to discount when demand is low to maximise yield at a later time. Discounts may also be provided to large tour groups, since this guarantees a level of return or yield and reduces uncertainty.

Many third-party providers, such as <www.hotels.com> and <www.expedia.com>, also now assist hotels in managing and reserving capacity over the seasonal cycle of their business. Prices can be lowered to encourage advance bookings for airlines as a means of smoothing demand and last-minute bookings can then be sold at a higher price.

Create alternatives for otherwise wasted capacity

The flip side of queues and waiting lines is that organisations may still face periods of excessive capacity. Possible uses of free capacity include:

→ *Use capacity for service differentiation:* Organisations can pay greater attention to customers, through the allocation of preferential seating and upgrades in service, for example.

→ *Reward your best customers and build loyalty:* High-use consumers may be provided with the opportunity to purchase a service in future in an off-peak time. Care must be taken that future yields are not sacrificed.

→ *Customer and channel development:* This provides free or heavily discounted trials to intermediaries such as travel agents or key customer groups (events managers in hospitality).

→ *Reward employees:* Airlines, cruise lines and beach resorts often give rewards, such as heavy discounts, to their employees. These programs are normally used in off-peak seasons.

→ *Barter for free capacity:* It is possible to save costs and increase capacity by trading services with suppliers. Common examples are advertising space on airlines, airline seats and hotel rooms.

The difficulty in managing wait lines and queues has led many service organisations to consider self-service technology. Like all approaches in the delivery of services this is not without its problems, even given its advantages. The benefits of self-service technology, its costs and when consumers are more likely to use it are discussed next.

Self-service technology

What is self-service technology?

Discussion of self-service technology (SST) is not new, and it appears in business research as far back as 1961.[23] In this seminal work, William Regan discussed self-service in terms of supermarkets versus full-service, smaller grocery stores. He saw self-service techniques as helping consumers deal with changes in living patterns (buying groceries less frequently). He noted that retailers would use self-service as a means for selling mass-market products with a low margin (so cost of service is an issue) that are easily replaced and understood by the consumer. By 2010, supermarkets such as Woolworths and Coles in Australia had extended the self-service business concept to include technology such as self-scanning and the subsequent payment of items of purchase. Interestingly, Aldi, as a new supermarket

Steven D'Alessandro

entrant in Australia, has not deployed self-service checkouts and yet in 2016 had captured 10 per cent of the grocery market. Feedback from research by the company of its 399 retail outlets also showed that consumers preferred face-to-face interactions.[24]

Self-service technology (SST) can be defined as the firm–customer technological interface that encourages consumers to perform services for themselves[25] and/or automated services that can be provided such as automated teller machines, pay-at-the pump, automated hotel checkout, telephone banking and internet transactions.[26] SST is not limited solely to purchasing online or via telephone or direct mail and may include customer service that occurs after business transactions.

As can been seen, there is a wide variety of SST that can be used online and offline at the point of sale. Non-business service encounters include self-checkouts that scan books in libraries, submitting driver's licence applications online, accessing government statistics online and submitting discrimination complaints via the internet. It is necessary therefore to classify the types of SST that exist in both the business and not-for-profit sectors. Table 6.3 shows the various types of SST.

Note that not all SST is delivered online, and some, such as ATMs and vending machines, has been around for quite some time. What typifies all these types of SST is the absence of service provider personnel at the customer interface. It is suggested that the adoption of SST by many organisations is due to three factors:[27]

1   to reduce costs
2   to increase customer satisfaction and loyalty
3   to reach new customer segments.

Table 6.3   Types and examples of SST in use

Interface purpose	Telephone/ interactive voice response	Online/internet	Interactive kiosks	Video/DVDs/CDs
Customer service	Telephone banking Flight information	Package tracking Account information Online check-ins	ATMs Airline check-ins	
Transactions	Telephone banking Bill payment	Retail purchasing Financial transactions	Pay at the pump Train ticket purchases DVD and CD purchases Parking tickets	
Self-help	Information telephone lines	Information search Online and learning	Tourist information Museum information	Account preparation software DVD/TV based training

Source: Based on M.L. Meuter, A.L. Ostrom, R.I. Roundtree & M.J. Bitner (2000). Self-service technologies: Understanding customer satisfaction with technology-based service encounters. *Journal of Marketing*, 64(3), 52.

Consumers, it is argued, embrace SST when it helps them in difficult situations. This can include a parent being able to shop and bank online while their children are sleeping. SST is also likely to be used if it is better than interpersonal alternatives, such as finding government information online and after-hours online booking of hotel rooms and airline tickets. Finally, SST helps to empower consumers.[28] Consumers will dislike and avoid SST when it fails, when the SST interface is poorly designed or they make a mistake.[29] Consumers are unlikely to adopt or use SST if they cannot see the benefit to them, have low incomes, low education and low self-efficacy.[30] Situational factors are also important in the degree of acceptance and use of SST in retail. Research has shown that the acceptance of SST here depends on order size, wait-time tolerance, location convenience and employee presence.[31]

A US qualitative study of 1000 consumers of SST identified the following critical incidents that led to consumers being satisfied or dissatisfied with this type of technology. This research is summarised in Table 6.4. It would seem that the tasks here for service marketing are to show how SST can solve immediate needs, how it is better than alternatives and that it will provide the service as promised. Major issues for service providers using SST are the reliability of technology, and most crucially for marketers, the design of good service process (such as delivery and ordering in online retailing), a good interface and having a service system that helps deals with failures of SST that may be due to consumers' mistakes (e.g. providing help to reset passwords).

Table 6.4 Critical incidents that led to satisfaction/dissatisfaction with SST

Satisfying incidents	
Type	Percentage in total
1. Solved intensified need	11%
2. Better than the alternative	
2A. Easy to use	16%
2B. Avoid service personnel	3%
2C. Saved time	30%
2D. When I want	8%
2E. Where I want	5%
2F. Saved money	6%
3. Did its job	21%
Dissatisfying incidents	
4. Technology failure	43%
5. Process failure	17%
6. Poor design	
6A. Technology design problem	17%
6B. Service design problem	19%
7. Customer-driven failure	4%

Source: M.L. Meuter, A.L. Ostrom, R.I. Roundtree & M.J. Bitner. (2000). Implementing successful self-service technologies. *Academy of Management Executive*, 16(4), 96–108.

Steven D'Alessandro

Services in Action

What are the benefits versus costs of online banking?

In a 2009 study published in *Management Science*[32] tens of thousands of US bank customers over 30 months showed that, counter-intuitively, costs per financial transaction increased from US$3.62 before the adoption of online banking to US$4.27 afterwards, without any noticeable increase in customer profitability. The costs, the authors claimed, came because when customers transact online they create call-centre expenses, because they are more likely to need help from call centres. More recent research suggests that, on the other hand, customers who resided in areas of density of branches with good internet access were more likely to increase their banking activity, acquire more products and perform more transactions. It would appear then that access to bank staff paradoxically helps with the benefits of SST in banking. Both studies also suggested that the use of SST by banks is also important for another reason as it leads to greater loyalty.

How does self-service technology become accepted by the consumer?

System design consists of convenience including where and when the technology is being used, interface design and interface information.[33] Convenience is determined by ease of finding information, and depends on whether the services are provided by technology or by people.[34] Although SST-enabled services offer time and place convenience benefits, it is the time taken to complete the service process that influences the perceived value of the service outcome.[35]

There are two types of systems design that are important to consider in SST. One is where employees may be present to assist consumers in the use of SST. This commonly occurs with touch-screen airline check-ins and the self-scanning of groceries. The other is where employees are not present at the service encounter; for example, online banking. Research suggests that SST designs that provide comparative information and provide for greater customer interactivity are more likely to be accepted by consumers than static designs with less interactivity. The caveat is that the technological readiness of the consumer[36] and their familiarity with the product class will moderate any design effects.[37]

In terms of online retailing, sensory-enabled technology (SET), which can translate tactile information such the use of virtual models compared to 2D or 3D views, has been found to encourage greater satisfaction and use of SST.[38]

Readiness to adopt new technology

If the role of the consumer in the service-delivery process is unclear, overcoming consumers' learned behaviour of seeking out staff to solve their problems will be a major deterrent to using SST for the first time.[39] Consumers' readiness to accept new technology is dependent on an understanding of their role in solving their need for information; their motivation to use SST; and their ability to perform the prerequisite steps required to access and use the SST.

A readiness to adopt a new SST can be considered within the broader context of the technology acceptance model (TAM) as used in information science.[40] Under this model, constructs such as perceived ease of use and usefulness will influence a consumer's readiness to adopt technology. Table 6.5 shows the impact of the ease of use and usefulness towards the attitude of adoption of three types of SST: ATMs, phones and online banking.

As can be seen in Table 6.5, consumers adopt SST such as ATMs and phone banking for its usefulness, not for a need for information or concerns about perceived risk. Ease of use only plays a minor role in the acceptance of ATMs as an SST. For online banking, the adoption of SST is driven purely by the risk of the transaction. Consumers here may be concerned more about privacy and security risks, such as fraud, than ease of use or usefulness issues. Recent research has suggested that providing enjoyment with the use of a new SST may be as important as showing the utility or usefulness of the SST.[41] Interestingly, with the adoption of mobile self-services, enjoyment as well as ease of use and convenience seems to be an important factor for consumers.[42]

Table 6.5 Factors that affect the adoption of SST across three technologies

ATMs	
Ease of use	7%
Usefulness	36%
Need for information	n.s.
Risk	n.s.
Phone banking	
Ease of use	n.s.
Usefulness	49%
Need for information	n.s.
Risk	n.s.
Online banking	
Ease of use	n.s.
Usefulness	n.s.
Need for information	n.s.
Risk	36%

n.s.—not significant.

Source: J. Curren & M. Meuter (2005). Self-service technology adoption: Comparing three technologies. *Journal of Services Marketing*, 19(2), 103–13.

Coming soon to a cinema near you? Ticket prices shaped by demand

In March 2017, Melbourne-based start-up Choovie launched a service offering demand-based ticket pricing to filmgoers to over 100 screens across metropolitan and regional venues in Victoria, New South Wales and the Australian Capital Territory. Choovie's app will allow consumers to decide, within settings determined by the cinemas, what price they pay to see a film. For example, if you don't want to pay more than $10 to see a particular title and are prepared to compromise on where and when you see it, the app will locate a suitable session for you. This fee may fluctuate when there are discounts for concession holders or loyalty card members, or if a different type of experience is offered (such as premium pricing for Gold Class or 3D) or on predetermined days of the week (half-price Tuesdays). There may also be online booking and reservation fees. Demand pricing has been especially successful in China, where something like 70 per cent of movie tickets are sold online—the vast majority of these are via mobile devices. Dynamic ticketing platforms like Maoyan, Gewara and Wepiao in China mediate information between audiences and cinemas, and also provide opportunities for audiences to exchange information about movies with each other.[43]

Compatibility

Compatibility is a general indication of consumers' beliefs about how SST helps them to access information. Compatibility is similar to the 'technology readiness' construct proposed by Parasuraman,[44] which refers to consumers' readiness to adopt and use technology. A greater acceptance of phone banking may occur as an SST because some consumers find using phone banking more compatible than online banking because they are more used to using a telephone than a computer. Likewise, the use of technology-based self-service (TBSS), such as self-scanning of groceries, vending machines and automated check-ins at airports, may not require the consumer to radically change behaviour patterns, and they may also observe others using it and be assisted in the use of the new SST. In particular, the adoption of TBSS seems to occur differently according to the type of learning styles employed by consumers when they use such technology. These include reliance on 'regular assurance', the use of 'motivated practice' and 'cautious discovery'.[45] Research also suggests that there is a positive relationship between technological readiness, service quality and satisfaction with SST, as well as predicting future intended use of SST.[46]

Perceived risk

When consumers are apprehensive about using SST, their perception of the benefits of using SST will decrease. The likelihood of trialling SST will therefore also decrease, because

↘
technology-based self-service (TBSS)
A type of self-service technology such as self-scanning of groceries, vending machines and automated check-ins at airports

when there is a degree of perceived risk customers will resist trying to use the SST for the first time, which will further reduce their motivation to use SST.[47]

Perceived risk in using SST can be defined as the negative consequences that may occur as part of a transaction. These negative consequences can include performance/product risk,[48] financial/economic risk[49] and psychological risk.[50] In addition, perceived risk online relates to privacy and the security risk of inputting personal information.[51] Perceived risk will also limit the amount of interaction consumers have with online SST.[52]

Online service marketers can provide information or 'signals' about marketing strategies that can decrease the perceived risk of purchase or transactions.[53] This information could include offering price discounts,[54] warranties,[55] credible information about products[56] having a better web design,[57] using established brand names[58] and offering choice and convenience through multi-channel distribution, including other online and offline marketing channels.[59] These strategies have the possibility of increasing credibility and acceptance of transacting in this manner and thus minimising perceived risk, or increasing trust in the online service provider and therefore reducing the perceived risk. Finally, promotional strategies such as advertising through offline sources such as printed media and online sources such as industry e-marketplaces and commercial websites may reduce the buyer's perceived risk to purchase online or transact services online.[60]

Innovativeness

Consumer innovators are generally the early adopters of a new service,[61] which also includes SST.[62] Innovativeness is a general personality trait that has been defined as 'the degree to which an individual makes innovation decisions independently of the communicated experience of others'.[63]

Some researchers have argued that consumer novelty seeking and creativity are important antecedents to innovativeness,[64] while others[65] have suggested that innovativeness is impacted on by risk taking, openness to change and a willingness to experiment, which means that these personality factors are important antecedents to innovativeness and hence willingness to adopt new SST.

innovativeness
A general personality trait: the degree to which an individual makes innovation decisions independently of the communicated experience of others

Locus of control

Locus of control (LOC) is an important predictor of goal-oriented actions in both psychology[66] and marketing.[67] The LOC for a service refers to the customer's future-oriented beliefs about the value of the service outcome. In the case of a service,[68] the LOC may have a direct effect on consumers' adoption of SST, which in turn may influence the way that consumers accept control over the co-production of services. Consumers with an *internal* LOC are likely to adopt an active role that is based on their abilities and efforts as co-producers in the service processes.[69] Another perspective is that consumers with an internal LOC are more willing to take part in the co-production of services and, therefore, are more likely to try to adopt an SST.[70]

locus of control
The future-oriented beliefs about the value of the service outcome

In contrast, consumers with an *external* LOC are likely to believe that service outcomes are determined by the provider or by fate.[71] The expectations of these consumers are more likely to be satisfied when the provider takes control of the service and directs their interaction.[72] Consumers with external LOC are less likely to adopt SST and will not value it highly, since they will perceive the service outcomes to be the result of actions of the service provider, powerful others or chance and not themselves.[73]

The need for human interaction and personal service

Not all services can be delivered without the need for human interaction or personal service. Hotel check-ins, for example, have been found in research to be an important type of service where the need for personal interaction and service outweighs the benefits of SST.[74] Consumers who struggle with technology or are technophobic are also likely to rely on human interaction and personal service.[75] More recent research suggests that where rapport building is important in service encounters, such as in the initial hotel check-in or arriving at a doctor's surgery, then SST or technological aids in the service encounter may not be useful as they interfere with important relationship building between provider and customer.[76]

Demographics

Men and women differ in what factors influence their acceptance of SST. Males have been found to possess a greater willingness to experiment with SST while females exhibit less confidence in making new technology work and require an assurance that SST will operate reliably and accurately.[77] There are also differences in age groups. Consumers over the age of 50 were found in Australian research to be less likely to use SST in banks, and to prefer personal interaction with branch staff. It appears that within this age group there is some variation, with those who use credit cards appearing to be more accepting of SST.[78] Consumers with lower education attainment and/or with lower spending are also less likely to adopt SST.[79]

Research has also found differences between Chinese and American consumers in their readiness to adopt new technology such as SST. American consumers are more likely to adopt SST, while Chinese consumers exhibit higher levels of discomfort and insecurity about using SST. Chinese consumers were shown to have much lower levels of innovativeness and optimism in using SST than their American counterparts.[80]

Situational factors

Research suggests that situational factors such as waiting times, anxiety in crowds and time pressure will encourage consumers to have a more positive attitude of acceptance of SST.[81] Satisfaction with other channels of service delivery, for example, bank branches, as compared to online banking also affects to some extent the acceptance of SST.[82]

When is it best to use self-service technology?

It should be remembered that SST is not a panacea for service marketing. There are many instances where it may be cheaper and more effective to deliver services personally than via a technological interface. Research has shown, particularly in international markets, that there is a need for services such as installation, maintenance and customisation to be delivered by representative of the provider rather than by technological interface. For specialised services such as healthcare, advanced scientific and medical instruments, legal and architectural services, there really is no other choice than employees working closely with consumers.[83]

Costs versus benefits

It is not clear from published research whether SST saves organisations money or increases revenue for them from markets they did not have access to before. If anything, as discussed previously, SST may cost the organisation more per transaction than was the case previously. Perhaps it is best to consider how consumers see the benefits versus the costs of SST. It would appear that as long as consumers are accepting of new technology in general, SST is likely to be seen as a benefit if it does its job and is better than the alternative (e.g. standing in line at a bank). Where there are technology failures and poor processes consumers are not likely to value SST. Only a tiny fraction (4%) will blame themselves for any failure of SST. It would appear critical that organisations have systems in place that aid in co-created service recovery, such as a consumer losing their password, as this influences consumers' future beliefs about SST, in particular its value and their satisfaction with the organisation.[84] Other research also suggests that customers can become so frustrated with a SST failure that they will also need emotional as well as instrumental support.[85]

Australian Tax Office failure enters the third day

For three days in December 2016, while the main website was working intermittently, the Australian Taxation Office's (ATO) tax agent, business and Business Activity Statement portals, ATO online, the Australian Business Register, standard business reporting and superannuation online services all remained offline. The outage seemed to have been caused by faults in ATO's storage area network. The storage units owned by the ATO are capable of storing a petabyte of data, or 1000 terabytes, and the ATO's redundancy contingencies for a technology failure did not work in December due to the nature of the tech failure. The severity of the outage led tax commissioner Chris Jordan to implement an independent review into how it occurred, which is under

way by professional services firm PwC.[86] Thus government departments, like many corporations that rely on SST, also face a higher technological and in some cases a greater cyber-security risk, as was the case with the Bureau of Meteorology, which was hacked earlier in 2016.

The introduction of SST in many instances asks the consumer to be a partial employee or to forgo personal service, in return for lower costs to the provider. This may create problems of a perceived lack of fairness, if consumers are forced to use SST.[87] It may therefore be advisable in this instance to provide incentives to consumers to use SST such as assistance and discounts partially derived from the cost savings of using SST by the provider.

Service can be standardised

If the service is a standardised transaction, such as booking an airline ticket, checking a bank balance or submitting a loan request with a library, then the use of SST would seem to be well suited. Where there are many customer relationship issues that require technical assistance on-site, SST may not be suitable. Even if the service is standardised there must still be a technological interface that is suitable even for consumers with low levels of technical expertise. Recovery systems for SST failures must also be designed, including for standardised services. For TBSS, this could simply be a trigger that staff help is available when there is a failure.

Managing load factors

SST for hotels and airlines can help to manage load factors and seasonal variations of use by offering consumers incentives to book online at off-peak times, or to use a service where there is currently not a great demand (e.g. 'red-eye' special fares for airline companies). Likewise, some SSTs may have surge pricing when there is a high demand for services, as is the case with Uber.

Service is perishable

SST can help organisations manage the perishability of their services. This is because SST online can help consumers to access services at irregular times and at the last minute. TBSS can help companies provide greater customer service if standardised transactions are handled by technology. SST can also benefit organisations by reducing crowding and waiting-time effects.

Trust with the organisation

Trust with the organisation appears to be critical for the success of SST, especially with respect to online purchasing. Trust refers to 'confidence' in another party.[88] Trust in online purchasing is the promise and assurance by online sellers to deliver high-quality products or services to online buyers[89] and is the essential element in online trading.[90] Trust with the organisation online is considered vital as there is a lack of global-standard online trading regulations and therefore an increased risk of fraud.[91] Other factors influence trust between a buyer and seller, such as the reputation of the seller, the nature of the relationship and the confidence of both parties.[92]

Employee factors

Employees must be trained, be willing and have time to assist consumers with SST. The short-term implications are that there may be significant start-up costs in the development of SST. Many employees may need to be convinced of the need for SST, as much as consumers have to be. Employees also need to be valued or redeployed into more challenging and interesting roles as there is a risk that they may perceive themselves to being treated like machines.[93]

Technological advances

Technological advances such as greater broadband speeds, better touch-screen technology, smart-chip technology and smartphones all mean greater opportunities for SST in the future. The increasing use of many SST in smartphones, such as airline check-ins and online banking, means that many future SSTs will be accessed via mobile phones rather than at computer screens. The same factors as for any new technological advance will need to be considered, as already mentioned in this chapter.

Other electronic distribution channels

Besides the type of SST and TBSS discussed in this chapter, there are emerging SSTs of voice-activated telephone inquiry lines and automated telephone interviewing services, which are being used increasingly by many organisations. Combinations of SST and TBSS are also possible, with online redemption now available for cards to be used in TBSS for activities such as the purchasing of public transport tickets. It is quite possible that there will be multi-channels of SST in the future.

Services in Action

Engaging with the Australian government using SST

SST is attractive to governments because of the reduction in costs and the chance for the public to better engage with the government in a 24/7 cycle. The Australian Tax Office (ATO), for example, claimed in 2015 that the introduction of digital SST would save it around $150 million a year, through its improved online self-lodgement system, MyTax, which in 2015 had 1 million users. The problem is that such government services may be so successful that they threaten the business model of providers like H&R Block and other tax professionals who cater for the 12 million people who lodge tax returns every year.

Centrelink, the welfare agency of the Australian government, is also starting to deploy more SST, such as mobile centres with access to SST in shopping centres. A centre trialled in a shopping centre in Tasmania also aims to promote self-service options for Medicare payments. However, it seems that Australia has a long way to go to catch up with world best practice in this area. It has been suggested that government should follow three simple rules when implementing SST:

1 *Apply an agile approach to transformation*: It is not good enough for governments to say 'that is the way we have always done this'. Also governments should avoid the creation of new organisational silos between providers and technologists in self-service.

2 *New technology is not enough*: Processes need to change. In order to gain increased satisfaction from citizens, governments should examine how and why services are delivered, rather than just implementing SST.

3 *Learn from overseas*: There are great examples of the deployment of self-service in many countries. New Zealand, for example, has its own citizen identity scheme (aboutMe), which has transformed processes like updating passports, getting government contracts and paying tax.

This chapter discussed important aspects of delivery of services. The most common forms for service deliveries are franchises, agents and brokers. Franchises offer the best level of control by the service parent with the additional benefit for franchisees of marketing and infrastructure support, but they have within them a potential for conflict. Agents and brokers provide a lower-cost option, with less control, but they have a greater say in setting prices and may act in the interests of a number of clients. Related to agents and brokers providing access to services are companies that now operate in the sharing economy, like Uber and Airbnb, which facilitate peer-to-peer service transactions in a business model where neither company owns the service or uses a franchise system of delivery. These new service-delivery models are not without challenges in the areas of regulation, tax compliance and, in the case of Airbnb, guest safety.

This chapter also discussed how organisations deal with queues and waiting lines. There are a number of systems that can be used to organise service delivery, and each has its advantages and disadvantages. Consumer behaviour in queues is also important. Consumers perceive they wait longer than they actually do, have strong feelings of fairness about who is served first, and are best provided with information about the length of the queue and their position in it.

Self-service technology (SST) has also been introduced in this chapter. Factors that influence the adoption of SST by consumers include good system design, a readiness to adopt new technology, compatibility, perceived risk, innovativeness, locus of control, demographics and the situation.

Good systems design is not a given for the adoption of SST, as consumers' understanding of and comfort with new technology varies. SST is likely to be accepted if there is a readiness to adopt by the consumer; that is, SST is perceived as useful and easy to use. These perceptions vary among different types of SST. SST that is compatible with consumers' existing ways of doing things (e.g. telephone banking) is more likely to be accepted. Where the use of SST involves greater perceived risk (e.g. online purchasing), the SST is less likely to be accepted. Organisations must try to address consumer perceptions of risk, as in some cases, such as online banking, this was found to be the main determinant of its degree of use.

More innovative consumers are likely to try SST, but it appears that consumers with an internal locus of control are most likely to adopt and value SST. Older consumers are less likely to adopt SST, while men are more likely to try it than women and be more confident about it. Women on appear cautious about using SST and require greater confidence in the technology to accept SST.

The use of SST by organisations is best when the benefits to the consumer are greater than the costs, as there seems evidence that SST may actually increase transaction costs. If the service can be standardised, and is perishable, then SST may be suitable. SST may help organisations manage load, by firms providing incentives for consumers to use services in off-peak times. Trust between the organisation and consumers is crucial for the success of SST, especially for those transactions that involve purchases, as there are global concerns about fraud. Employees of the organisation also need to be trained and accept that SST is one of a number of ways of servicing customers. Technological advances, while providing the promise of new SST, must address the factors that influence the acceptance of all types of SST. The wide variety of SST means that in the future there may be multi-channels of SST, both online and TBSS.

Steven D'Alessandro

Review questions

1 What are the advantages and disadvantages of franchising?

2 What kinds of services are best distributed by brokers and agents? Why?

3 How can an organisation make waiting more pleasant for its customers?

4 Re-read the opening vignette at the start of the chapter. What factors in the chapter do you think explain why some consumers seek to not correctly pay for groceries that they self-scan? What can be done to prevent this?

5 Why are yield and the use of excess capacity important for service organisations? List some approaches that organisations use in both areas.

6 What are the main benefits that consumers derive from SST? What are the main problems they encounter with its use? How can these be addressed by a services marketer?

7 What is ease of use and usefulness in relation to SST? How do they differ across different types of SST?

8 Explain how the locus of control affects consumers' perception and use of SST.

9 What demographic factors influence the acceptance of SST? Is there anything marketers can do about it?

10 In the Services in Action feature, 'SST use in airports leads to increased "dwell time" and airports are cashing in', discuss why the use of SST in airports is so important to profits. Can such an approach be also applied to shopping malls or centres?

11 What are the main factors that organisations should consider when deciding whether to use SST? Which one is the most important?

12 In the Services in Action feature, 'Engaging with the Australian government using SST', what are the main factors discussed in this chapter that could be applied to the successful adoption of SST by government?

Further reading

Anitsal, I. & Schumann, D.W. (2007). Towards a conceptualization of customer productivity: The customer's perspective on transforming customer labor into customer outcomes using technology-based self-service options. *Journal of Marketing Theory and Practice*, 15(4), 349–63.

Bolton, R. & Saxena-Iyer, S. (2009). Interactive services: A framework, synthesis and research directions. *Journal of Interactive Marketing*, 23(1), 91–104.

Chiu, Y.-T.H. & Hofer, K.M. (2015). Service innovation and usage intention: A cross-market analysis. *Journal of Service Management*, 26(3), 516–38.

Chowdhury, I.R., Patro, S., Venugopal, P. & Israel, D. (2014). A study on consumer adoption of technology-facilitated services. *Journal of Services Marketing*, 28(6), 471–83.

Cooke, A.D.J., Harish, S., Mita, S. & Weitz, B.A. (2002). Marketing the unfamiliar: The role of context and item-specific information in electronic agent recommendations. *Journal of Marketing Research*, 39(4), 488–97.

Cova, B. & Salle, R. (2008). Marketing solutions in accordance with the S-D logic: Co-creating value with customer network actors. *Industrial Marketing Management*, 37(3), 270–7.

OXFORD UNIVERSITY PRESS

Cox, D.F. & Rich, S.U. (1964). Perceived risk and consumer decision-making: The case of the telephone shopping. *Journal of Marketing Research*, 1(4), 32–9.

Cunningham, L.F., Young, C.E. & Gerlach, J. (2009). A comparison of consumer views of traditional services and self-service technologies. *Journal of Services Marketing*, 23(1), 11–23.

Demoulin, N.T.M. & Souad, D. (2016). An integrated model of self-service technology (SST) usage in a retail context. *International Journal of Retail & Distribution Management*, 44(5), 540–59.

Ekman, P., Raggio, R.D. & Thompson, S.M. (2016). Service network value co-creation: Defining the roles of the generic actor. *Industrial Marketing Management*, 56(July), 51–62.

Evanschitzky, H., Iyer, G.R., Pillai, K.G., Kenning, P. & Schütte, R. (2015). Consumer trial, continuous use, and economic benefits of a retail service innovation: The case of the personal shopping assistant. *Journal of Product Innovation Management*, 32(3), 459–75.

Forbes, L.P. (2008). When something goes wrong and no one is around: Non-internet self-service technology failure and recovery. *Journal of Services Marketing*, 22(4/5), 316–27.

Gilchrist, F.W. (1949). Self-service retailing of meat. *Journal of Marketing*, 13(3), 295–304.

Hilton, Toni, & Hughes, Tim. (2013). Co-production and self-service: The application of service-dominant logic. *Journal of Marketing Management*, 29(7–8), 861–81.

Johnson, D.S., Bardhi, F. & Dunn, D.T. (2008). Understanding how technology paradoxes affect customer satisfaction with self-service technology: The role of performance ambiguity and trust in technology. *Psychology & Marketing*, 25(5), 416–43.

Kinard, B., Capella, M. & Kinard, J. (2009). The impact of social presence on technology based self-service use: The role of familiarity. *Services Marketing Quarterly*, 30(3), 303–14.

Makarem, S.C., Mudambi, S.M. & Podoshen, J.S. (2009). Satisfaction in technology-enabled service encounters. *Journal of Services Marketing*, 23(3), 134–44.

Mifsud, M., Cases, A.-S. & N'Goala, G. (2015). Service appropriation: How do customers make the service their own? *Journal of Service Management*, 26(5), 706–25.

Moores, T.T. (2012). Towards an integrated model of IT acceptance in healthcare. *Decision Support Systems*, 53(3), 507–16.

Ngniatedema, T., Fono, L.A. & Mbondo, G.D. (2015). A delayed product customization cost model with supplier delivery performance. *European Journal of Operational Research*, 243(1), 109–19.

Oghazi, P., Mostaghel, R., Hultman, M. & Parida, V. (2012). Antecedents of technology-based self-service acceptance: A proposed model. *Services Marketing Quarterly*, 33(3), 195–210.

Prentice, Catherine, Han, Xiao-Yun, & Li, Yao-Qi. (2016). Customer empowerment to co-create service designs and delivery: Scale development and validation. *Services Marketing Quarterly*, 37(1), 36–51.

Ramaseshan, B., Kingshott, R.P. & Stein, A. (2015). Firm self-service technology readiness. *Journal of Service Management*, 26(5), 751–76.

Reinders, M., Frambach, R. & Kleijnen, M. (2015). Mandatory use of technology-based self-service: Does expertise help or hurt? *European Journal of Marketing*, 49(1/2), 190–211.

Schuster, L., Drennan, J. & Lings, I.N. (2013). Consumer acceptance of m-wellbeing services: A social marketing perspective. *European Journal of Marketing*, 47(9), 1439–57.

Teitelman, S. (1951). Self-service meat retailing in 1950. *Journal of Marketing*, 15(3), 307–18.

Turner, T. & Shockley, J. (2014). Creating shopper value: Co-creation roles, in-store self-service technology use, and value differentiation. *Journal of Promotion Management*, 20(3), 311–27.

Tuzovic, S. & Kuppelwieser, V. (2016). Developing a framework of service convenience in health care: An exploratory study for a primary care provider. *Health Marketing Quarterly*, 33(2), 127–48.

Steven D'Alessandro

Venkatesan, R., Farris, P., Guissoni, L.A. & Neves, M.F. (2015). Consumer brand marketing through full- and self-service channels in an emerging economy. *Journal of Retailing*, 91(4), 644–59.

Westjohn, S.A., Arnold, M.J., Magnusson, P., Zdravkovic, S. & Zhou, J.X. (2009). Technology readiness and usage: A global-identity perspective. *Journal of the Academy of Marketing Science*, 37(3), 250–65.

Yaraghi, N., Ye Du, A., Sharman, R., Gopal, R.D. & Ramesh, R. (2015). Health information exchange as a multisided platform: Adoption, usage, and practice involvement in service co-production. *Information Systems Research*, 26(1), 1–18.

Weblinks

Airbnb. <www.airbnb.com.au>

Australian Taxation Office. <www.ato.gov.au>

Choovie. <www.choovie.com.au>

Jim's Group. <www.jims.net>

H&R Block. <www.hrblock.com.au>

National Australia Bank. <www.nab.com.au>

Qantas. <www.qantas.com.au>

Virgin Australia. <www.virginaustralia.com>

Uber. <www.uber.com/en-AU/drive>

Westpac. <www.westpac.com.au>

Endnotes

1 C. Low (2016). Self-service checkouts, or help yourself checkouts? *The Age*, 21 July, p. 3.

2 E. Wynne (2016). Self-service checkouts normalise, excuse supermarket stealing, research shows. *ABC News*, 21 July. <www.abc.net.au/news/2016-07-21/self-service-checkouts-normalising-theft-for-customers-research/7648910>

3 C. Sonti (2010). Jim's dimmed by franchise war. *The Age*, 25 January, p. 4.

4 J. Pennman (2017). *Every Customer a Raving Fan.* Cambridge Scholar Press, e-book. Downloaded from <www.jims.net/about-jims>.

5 A. Wilson, V. Zeithaml, M.J. Bitner & D. Gremler (2009). *Services Marketing and Integrating Customer Focus on the Firm.* London: McGraw-Hill, pp. 437–8.

6 M. Pardo-del-Val, C. Martínez-Fuentes, J.I. López-Sánchez & B. Minguela-Rata (2014). Franchising: The dilemma between standardisation and flexibility. *Service Industries Journal*, 34(9/10), 828–42.

7 M. Madanoglu, K. Lee & G.J. Castrogiovanni (2013). Does franchising pay? Evidence from the restaurant industry. *Service Industries Journal*, 33(11), 1003–25.

8 F. Larceneux, T. Lefebvre & A. Simon (2015). What added value do estate agents offer compared to FSBO transactions? Explanation from a perceived advantages model. *Journal of Housing Economics*, 29(September), 72–82.

9 S. Yousaf & N. Samreen (2016). Information agents and cultural differences as determinants of country's reputation and its subsequent effects on tourism prospects of a country in sustained crises: The case of Pakistan. *Journal of Vacation Marketing*, 22(4), 365–84.

10 J.L. Saber (2013). What have you done for me lately? Changing perceptions of residential real estate agents. *Annals of the Society for Marketing Advances Proceedings*, 2, 201–4.

11 J.W. Smith (2015). The Uber-all economy. *Marketing News*, 49(6), 26.

12 B. Libert, Y. Wind & M. Beck (2015). What Apple, Lending Club, and Airbnb know about collaborating with customers. *Harvard Business Review Digital Articles*, 2–7. <https://hbr.org/2015/07/what-apple-lending-club-and-airbnb-know-about-collaborating-with-customers>.

13 N. Ndubisi, M. Ehret & J. Wirtz (2016). Relational governance mechanisms and uncertainties in nonownership services. *Psychology & Marketing*, 33(4), 250–66.

14 E. Dupré (2016). All hail Uber. *Direct Marketing News*, 38(6), 22–5.

15 B. Libert, Y. Wind & M. Beck (2015). What Apple, Lending Club, and Airbnb know about collaborating with customers. *Harvard Business Review Digital Articles*, 2–7. <https://hbr.org/2015/07/what-apple-lending-club-and-airbnb-know-about-collaborating-with-customers>.

16 ibid.

17 K. Collier (2009). Customers unhappiest on hold. *The Courier-Mail*, 23 June.

18 C. Lovelock & J. Wirtz (2011). *Services Marketing: People, Technology, Strategy* (7th edn). Upper Saddle River, NJ: Pearson, p. 262.

19 A. Rafaeli, G. Barron & B. Laval (2002). The effects of queue structures and attitudes. *Journal of Services Research*, 5(November), 125–39.

20 J. Chernow (1981). Measuring the value of travel time savings. *Journal of Consumer Research*, 7(March), 360–71.

21 P. Kumar & K. Parthasarathy (2008). The impact of service-time uncertainty and anticipated congestion on customers' waiting-time decisions. *Journal of Service Research*, 10(3), 282–92.

22 L. Weiss, A. Rafaeli & N. Munichor (2008). Proximity to or progress toward receiving a telephone service? An experimental investigation of customer reactions to features of telephone auditory messages. *Advances in Consumer Research—North American Conference Proceedings*, 35, 791–2.

23 W.J. Regan (1961). Full cycle for self-service? *Journal of Marketing*, 25(4), 15–21.

24 S. Evans (2016). Aldi has no time for self-service checkouts after feedback review. *Sydney Morning Herald*, 10 March, p. 8.

25 P.A. Dabholkar & R.P. Bagozzi (2002). An attitudinal model of technology-based self-service: Moderating effects of consumer traits and situational factors. *Journal of the Academy of Marketing Science*, 30(3), 184–201.

26 M.L. Meuter, M.J. Bitner, A.L. Ostrom & S.W. Brown (2005). Choosing among alternative service delivery modes: An investigation of customer trial of self-service technologies. *Journal of Marketing*, 69(2), 61–83.

27 M.J. Bitner, A.L. Ostrom & M.L. Meuter (2002). Implementing successful self-service technologies. *Academy of Management Executive*, 16(4), 96–108.

28 ibid.

29 ibid.

30 E.J. Nijssen, J.J.L. Schepers & D. Belanche (2016). Why did they do it? How customers' self-service technology introduction attributions affect the customer-provider relationship. *Journal of Service Management*, 273(3), 276–98.

31 J.E. Collier, R.S. Moore, A. Horky & M.L. Moore (2015). Why the little things matter: Exploring situational influences on customers' self-service technology decisions. *Journal of Business Research*, 68(3), 703–10.

32 D. Campbell & F. Frei (2009). Cost structure, customer profitability, and retention implications of self-service distribution channels: Evidence from customer behavior in an online banking channel. *Management Science*, 56(1), 4–24.

33 D.M. Szymanski & R.T. Hise (2000). E-satisfaction: An initial examination. *Journal of Retailing*, 76(3), 309–22.

34 L.L. Berry, K. Seiders & D. Grewal (2002). Understanding service convenience. *Journal of Marketing*, 66(July), 1–17.

35 P.A. Dabholkar (2000). Technology in service delivery. Implications for self-services and service support. In T.A. Swartz & D. Iacobucci (eds), *Handbook of Services Marketing and Management*. Thousand Oaks, CA: Sage Publications, pp. 103–10.

36 S.-F. Liu, L.-S. Huang & Y.-H. Chiou (2012). An integrated attitude model of self-service technologies: Evidence from online stock trading systems brokers. *Service Industries Journal*, 32(11), 1823–35.

37 Z. Zhu, C. Nakata, K. Sivakumar & D. Grewal (2007). Self-service technology effectiveness: The role of design features and individual traits. *Journal of the Academy of Marketing Science*, 35(4), 492–506.

38 J. Kim & S. Forsythe (2008). Sensory enabling technology acceptance model SE-TAM: A multiple-group structural model comparison. *Psychology & Marketing*, 25(9), 901–22.

39 M.L. Meuter, M.J. Bitner, A.L. Ostrom & S.W. Brown (2005). Choosing among alternative service delivery modes: An investigation of customer trial of self-service technologies. *Journal of Marketing*, 69(2), 61–83.

40 W. King & J. He (2006). A meta-analysis of the technology acceptance model. *Information and Management*, 43(6), 740–55.

41 N.T.M. Demoulin & S. Djelassi (2016). An integrated model of self-service technology SST usage in a retail context. *International Journal of Retail & Distribution Management*, 44(5), 540–59; K. Cassidy, S. Baron & X. Lu (2015). How customers 'learn' to work for retailers. *Journal of Marketing Management*, 31(17–18), 1747–72.

42 K. Pousttchi & L. Goeke (2011). Determinants of customer acceptance for mobile data services: An empirical analysis with formative constructs. *International Journal of Electronic Business*, 91(2), 26–43.

43 Based on D. Verhoeven & B. Coate (2017). Coming to a cinema near you? Ticket prices shaped by demand. *The Conversation*. <https://theconversation.com/coming-soon-to-a-cinema-near-you-ticket-prices-shaped-by-demand-72260>.

44 A. Parasuraman (2000). Technology Readiness Index TRI: A multi-item scale to measure readiness to embrace new technologies. *Journal of Service Research*, 24(4), 307–20.

45 K. Cassidy, S. Baron & X. Lu (2015). How customers 'learn' to work for retailers. *Journal of Marketing Management*, 31(17–18), 1747–72.

46 C. Lin & P.-L. Hesieh (2008). The role of technology readiness in customers' perception and adoption of self-service technologies. *International Journal of Service Industry Management*, 17(5), 497–517.

47 M.L. Meuter, M.J. Bitner, A.L. Ostrom & S.W. Brown (2005). Choosing among alternative service delivery modes: An investigation of customer trial of self-service technologies. *Journal of Marketing*, 69(2), 61–83.

48 B. Doolin, S. Dillon, F. Thompson & J. Corner (2005). Perceived risk, the internet shopping experience and online purchasing behavior: A New Zealand perspective. *Journal of Global Information Management*, 13(2), 66–89.

49 D. Biswas & B. Burman (2007). The effects of product digilization and price dispersion on search intentions in offline versus online settings: The mediating effects of perceived risks. *Journal of Product and Brand Management*, 18(7), 477–86.

50 H.-Y. Ha (2002). The effects of consumer risk perception on pre-purchase information in online auctions: Brand, word-of-mouth and customized information. *Journal of Computer-Mediated Communication*, 81.

51 B. Doolin, S. Dillon, F. Thompson & J. Corner (2005). Perceived risk, the internet shopping experience and online purchasing behavior: A New Zealand perspective. *Journal of Global Information Management*, 13(2), 66–89.

52 P. Shamdasani, A. Mukherjee & N. Malhotra (2008). Antecedents and consequences of service quality in consumer evaluation of self-service internet technologies. *Service Industries Journal*, 28(1), 117–38.

53 D. Biswas & A. Biswas (2004). The diagnostic role of signals in the context of perceived risks in online shopping: Do signals matter more on the web? *Journal of Interactive Marketing*, 183(Summer), 30–44.

54 R. Gopal, S. Thompson, Y. Tung & A. Whinston (2005). Managing risks in multiple online auctions: An options approach. *Decision Sciences*, 36(3), 397–426.

55 B. Doolin, S. Dillon, F. Thompson & J. Corner (2005). Perceived risk, the internet shopping experience and online purchasing behavior: A New Zealand perspective. *Journal of Global Information Management*, 13(2), 66–89.

56 G. Pires, J. Stanton & A. Eckford (2004). Influences on the perceived risk of purchasing online. *Journal of Consumer Behavior*, 4(2), 118–32.

57 B. Yakov, V. Shankar, F. Sultan & G. Urban (2005). Are drivers and role of online trust the same for all web sites and consumers? A large scale exploratory empirical study. *Journal of Marketing*, 69(October), 133–52.

58 E. Dalgado-Ballester & M. Hernandez-Espallardo (2008). Effect of brand associations on consumer reactions to unknown online brands. *International Journal of Electronic Commerce*, 12(3), 81–113.

59 H.-J. Lee & P. Huddleston (2006). Effects of e-tailer and product type on risk handling in online shopping. *Journal of Marketing Channels*, 13(3), 5–28.

60 E. Ko & Y. Park (2002). Antecedents of internet advertising effects: Advertisement types and clothing involvement. *Irish Marketing Review*, 15(2), 51–8.

61 L. Flynn & R. Goldsmith (1993). Identifying innovators in consumer service markets. *The Service Industries Journal*, 13(3), 97–106.

62 S. Ward, B. Chitty & G. Graham (2007). Finding the tutorial I want: An examination of factors leading to the adoption of online service technology. *Proceedings of the Australian New Zealand Marketing Educators Conference*, Otago, New Zealand, pp. 2580–5. Available via CD ROM.

63 D. Midgley & G. Dowling (1993). A longitudinal study of product form innovation: The interaction between predispositions and social messages. *Journal of Consumer Research*, 19(4), 611–25.

64 E. Hirschman (1980). Innovativeness, novelty seeking and consumer creativity. *Journal of Consumer Research*, 7(3), 283–95.

65 G. Foxall (1995). Cognitive styles of consumer initiators. *Technovation*, 15(5), 269–88.

66 H. Lefcourt (ed.) (1981). *Research with Locus of Control Construct: Vol. 1: Assessment Methods*. San Diego, CA: Academic Press; H. Levenson (1973). Differentiating among internally, powerful others and internal locus of control orientations. *Developmental Psychology*, 9, 260–5; J. Rotter (1966). Generalised expectancies for internal versus internal control of reinforcement.

Psychological Monographs, 801, no. 609; J. Rotter (1975). Some problems and misconceptions related to construct of internal versus external locus of reinforcement. *Journal of Consulting and Clinical Psychology*, 43(1), 56–67; E. Skinner (1996). A guide to constructs of control. *Journal of Personality and Social Psychology*, 71(3), 549–70.

67 G. Bradley & B. Sparks (2002). Service locus of control: Its conceptualization and measurement. *Journal of Service Research*, 4(4), 312–24; M. Busseri, H. Lefcourt & R. Kerton (1998). Locus of control for consumer outcomes: Predicting consumer behavior. *Journal of Applied Social Psychology*, 28(12), 1067–87.

68 G.L. Bradley & B.A. Sparks (2002). Service locus of control: Its conceptualization and measurement. *Journal of Service Research*, 4(4), 312–24.

69 A. Ward, B. Chitty, T. Noble & L. Tiangsoongnern (2009). How locus of control influences students' e-satisfaction with self-service technology in higher education. *Proceedings of the Australian New Zealand Marketing Educators Conference*. Melbourne: ANZMAC.

70 M. Buettgen, J.H. Schumann & Z. Ates (2012). Service locus of control and customer coproduction: The role of prior service experience and organizational socialization. *Journal of Service Research*, 15(2), 166–81.

71 A. Oyedele & P.M. Simpson (2007). An empirical investigation of consumer control factors on intention to use selected self-service technologies. *International Journal of Service Industry Management*, 18(3), 287–306.

72 C. Moore & T. Wang (2007). Adult learning styles of modern Chinese educational learners: Challenging the stereotype. In *Proceedings of Conference of the Australian Association for Research in Education*, Fremantle, 26–29 November.

73 R. Beyth-Marom, K. Saporta & A. Caspi (2003). Synchronous vs asynchronous tutorials: Factors affecting student's preferences and choices. *Journal of Research on Technology in Education*, 37(3), 245–62; J. Drennan, J. Kennedy & A. Pisarski (2005). Factors affecting student attitudes towards online learning in management education. *Journal of Educational Research*, 98(6), 331–8; A. Oyedele & P.M. Simpson (2007). An empirical investigation of consumer control factors on intention to use selected self-service technologies. *International Journal of Service Industry Management*, 18(3), 287–306.

74 A.K. Panda, S.J. Dash & P.K. Rath (2011). An investigation of reasons affecting customer adoption and rejection of technology based self-service TBSS on consumer satisfaction and consumer commitment. *BVIMR Management Edge*, 4(2), 100–4.

75 A. Oyedele & P.M. Simpson (2007). An empirical investigation of consumer control factors on intention to use selected self-service technologies. *International Journal of Service Industry Management*, 18(3), 287–306. A. Beatson, L.V. Coote & J.M. Rudd (2006). Determining consumer satisfaction and commitment through self-service technology and personal service usage. *Journal of Marketing Management*, 22(7/8), 853–82.

76 M. Giebelhausen, S.G. Robinson, N.J. Sirianni & M.K. Brady (2014). Touch versus tech: When technology functions as a barrier or a benefit to service encounters. *Journal of Marketing*, 78(4), 113–24.

77 K. Elliott & M. Hall (2005). Assessing consumers' propensity to embrace self-service technologies: Are there gender differences? *Marketing Management Journal*, 15(2), 98–107.

78 J. McPhail & G. Fogarty (2004). Mature Australian consumers' adoption and consumption of self-service banking technologies. *Journal of Financial Services Marketing*, 8(4), 302–13.

79 E.J. Nijssen, J.J.L. Schepers & D. Belanche (2016). Why did they do it? How customers' self-service technology introduction attributions affect the customer-provider relationship. *Journal of Service Management*, 273(3), 276–98.

80 K. Elliott, J. Meng & M. Hall (2008). Technology readiness and the likelihood to use self-service technology: Chinese vs. American consumers. *Marketing Management Journal*, 18(2), 20–31.

81 P. Dabholkar & R. Bagozzi (2002). An attitudinal model of technology based self-service: Moderating effects of consumer traits and situational factors. *Journal of the Academy of Marketing Science*, 30(3), 184–201.

82 K. Eriksson & D. Nilsson (2006). Determinants of the continued use of self-service technology: The case of internet banking. *Technovation*, 27(May), 159–67.

83 R. Jack, S. As-Saber & R. Edwards (2009). Reassessing product inseparability and its impact on a firm's entry mode choice: Service delivery via trans-human exports. *European International Business Academy*, Valencia, Spain, 13–15 December; R. Jack, S. As-Saber, R. Edwards & P.J. Buckley (2008). The role of service embeddedness in the internationalisation process of manufacturing firms: A case study of Australian manufacturers in the UK. *International Business Review*, 17(4), 442–51.

84 B. Dong, K. Evans & S. Zou (2008). The effects of customer participation in co-created service recovery. *Journal of the Academy of Marketing Science*, 36(July), 123–37.

85 K. Gelbrich (2009). Beyond just being dissatisfied: How angry and helpless customers react to failures when using self-service technologies. *Schmalenbach Business Review*, 61(January), 40–59.

86 Y. Redrup (2017). ATO online failure enters third day. *The Financial Review*, 4 February, 2.

87 A. White, M. Breazeale & J.E. Collier (2012). The effects of perceived fairness on customer responses to retailer SST push policies. *Journal of Retailing*, 88(2), 250–61.

88 J. Sheth (1973). A model of industrial buyer behavior. *Journal of Marketing*, 37(October), 50–6; J. Sheth & M. Venkatesan (1968). Risk prediction processes in repetitive consumer behavior. *Journal of Marketing Research*, 5(August), 307–10; T. Shimp & W. Bearden (1980). Warranty and other extrinsic cue interaction effects on consumers' confidence. *Advances in Consumer Research*, 7, 308–13.

89 R. Cowcher (2001). E-trust. *The British Journal of Administrative Management*, November/December 28, 22–3.

90 M. Eastlick, S. Lotz & P. Warrington (2006). Understanding online B-C relationships: An integrated models of privacy concerns, trust and commitment. *Journal of Business Research*, 59(8), 877–86.

91 S. Wang, S. Beatty & W. Foxx (2004). Signalling trustworthiness of small online retailers. *Journal of Interactive Marketing*, 18(1), 53–69.

92 R. Morgan & S. Hunt (1994). The commitment-trust theory of relationship marketing. *Journal of Marketing*, 58(3), 20–38.

93 A. McWilliams, I. Anitsal & M.M. Anitsal (2016). Customer versus employee perceptions: A review of self-service technology options as illustrated in self-checkouts in US retail industry. *Academy of Marketing Studies Journal*, 20(1), 79–98.

Steven D'Alessandro

Congestion pricing on suburban roads

Traffic jams cost more than road users realise. The traffic jams that occur daily in cities across Australia increase the socio-economic cost of road congestion to more than $16 billion a year.[1] Almost 40 per cent of that cost—$6 billion—is paid directly by consumers who use overloaded public transport systems to go to work, school or social outings and home again. According to a report by the Bureau of Infrastructure, Transport and Regional Economics (BITRE), employers currently pay about $8 billion in congestion costs, but in 15 years the total of capital cities' congestion costs is expected to rise to $37 billion.[2]

Consumers are now spending an average of 85 minutes a day trying to move around Australia's capital cities. More people are commuting greater distances and clogged roads are costing the economy and adversely affecting the lifestyles of residents of Australia's capital cities. The congestion costs for 2015 were $16.5 billion; a 30 per cent increase on the cost of $12.8 billion in 2010. The 2015 cost consisted of $6 billion in private time, $8 billion in business time, $1.5 billion in extra vehicle operating costs and $1 billion in additional air pollution costs. About 87 per cent of travel is in private vehicles, and the distance travelled by each vehicle each year is expected to increase by 2 per cent a year to 2030 with expected delays to increase by about the same rate.[3]

Congestion pricing—which is sometimes called value pricing—is a way of using market forces to reduce the waste associated with traffic congestion. Congestion pricing works by shifting purely discretionary rush-hour highway travel to other transportation modes or to off-peak periods, taking advantage of the fact that the majority of rush-hour drivers on a typical urban highway are not commuters.

Removing as few as 5 per cent of the vehicles from a congested roadway by congestion pricing enables more motor vehicles to be driven through the same physical space. Similar variable charges have already

» continued over page

Chapter 7

Pricing Service Products

William Chitty

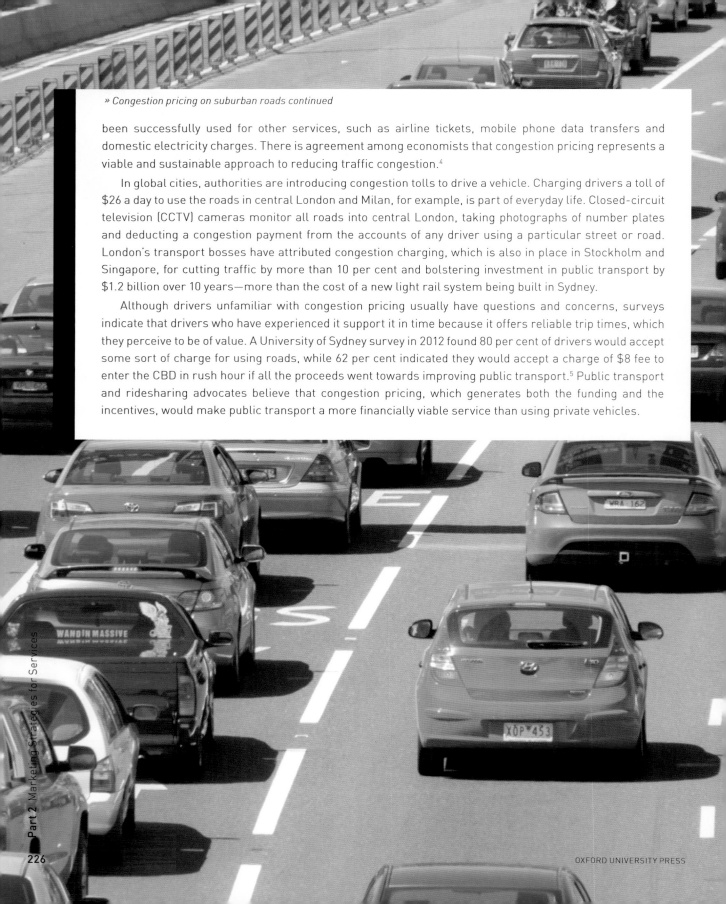

been successfully used for other services, such as airline tickets, mobile phone data transfers and domestic electricity charges. There is agreement among economists that congestion pricing represents a viable and sustainable approach to reducing traffic congestion.[4]

In global cities, authorities are introducing congestion tolls to drive a vehicle. Charging drivers a toll of $26 a day to use the roads in central London and Milan, for example, is part of everyday life. Closed-circuit television (CCTV) cameras monitor all roads into central London, taking photographs of number plates and deducting a congestion payment from the accounts of any driver using a particular street or road. London's transport bosses have attributed congestion charging, which is also in place in Stockholm and Singapore, for cutting traffic by more than 10 per cent and bolstering investment in public transport by $1.2 billion over 10 years—more than the cost of a new light rail system being built in Sydney.

Although drivers unfamiliar with congestion pricing usually have questions and concerns, surveys indicate that drivers who have experienced it support it in time because it offers reliable trip times, which they perceive to be of value. A University of Sydney survey in 2012 found 80 per cent of drivers would accept some sort of charge for using roads, while 62 per cent indicated they would accept a charge of $8 fee to enter the CBD in rush hour if all the proceeds went towards improving public transport.[5] Public transport and ridesharing advocates believe that congestion pricing, which generates both the funding and the incentives, would make public transport a more financially viable service than using private vehicles.

Introduction

Pricing a service product involves a more complex set of choices than what are at first apparent. While economic theory can be used to make sense of pricing decisions for services, most economic theories were developed for pricing tangible goods and therefore fail to capture the complexity associated with the four defining characteristics of services and the interactions that take place between customers and service organisations.

The issues that determine the optimal pricing models for services are different from those that apply to tangible goods because pricing strategies for services must account for the four inherent characteristics of a service: intangibility, inseparability, variability and perishabilty.[6]

The *intangibility* of a service product may cause consumers to use the extrinsic cues that are associated with service encounter rather than the intrinsic attributes of the service *per se*. The price of a service product may be used by consumers as an extrinsic cue to construct perceptions of the quality of that service. The distinction between intrinsic and extrinsic cues can be distinguished by using product information about the service. Intrinsic attributes are objective service features, while extrinsic attributes are part of a service's value that can be changed without basically changing the service. Because service products have few intrinsic cues, customers often use the extrinsic cues—such as the physical facilities of service organisations, the courtesy of its service providers, and the behaviour of any other consumers who may be using the service at the same time—to infer the performance quality of a service.[7]

The second characteristic of a service is the *inseparability* of the service encounter. The basis of a service encounter is that both the provider and consumer co-produce the service, which consists of *what* the service offers, together with the service interaction, which is *how* the service is delivered. For example, the professional advice of a financial adviser, which is the core service product, allows the service provider to design, deliver and determine the price of the service—to satisfy the needs of the chosen target market—at a price they are willing, and able, to pay.

The third service characteristic that affects optimal pricing strategies for services is the *variability* of a service. Variability relates to the difficulty of providing a uniform standard of service quality because, while service providers may perform the same service, not all service providers deliver a service the same way. That makes managing customer demand more reliant on price to smooth fluctuating demand.[8] The degree of variability is also a decisive factor in determining the level of service customisation, while customer involvement with a service provider often determines the length of time to deliver that service and hence its final price. Where possible, service organisations manage the variability of their service encounters by substituting technology for service providers because technology is ultimately cheaper than the labour costs of service providers.

Trading banks, for example, have widespread ATM networks to offer uniform simple banking services using technology—rather than tellers—as service providers.

The last characteristic of a service that may influence the pricing strategies is *perishability*. Services are acts, or performances, that cannot be readily stored to satisfy future customer demand, and because they are perishable, managing customer demand and yield management is more problematic than it is for tangible products.

The inputs required to produce a service product, such as the physical facilities and personnel, are a service organisation's productive capacity, but those two factors of production are not the service product. If there is no customer demand for a service, productive capacity is unused and no income is generated. If, however, customer demand is greater than the organisation's productive service capacity, many customers may have to wait longer for the service or they may have to accept a lower level of service quality, both of which will affect the relationships that customers develop with a service brand.

Some service organisations, such as car-rental companies, provide low-margin services and often minimise the service-delivery costs by using online marketing communications and offering a minimal or standardised level of customer service. Those types of service organisations do not incur customer-retention costs—for example, loyalty programs—that must be included in the pricing strategies for a service. Service businesses, like branded hotel chains that use loyalty programs, coupled with high levels of personalised customer service, must account for the costs of those customer benefits that are associated with their service product.

Price can be a strong marketing tool for a service brand because price provides a set of cognitive shortcuts to a service organisation's target market and this is important when setting the upper limits of a price.[9] Services that are priced higher than their counterparts are generally aimed at customers seeking luxury experiences and offer an experience advantage that mass-market services never achieve. The six-star accommodation offered by a Ritz-Carlton hotel or the first-class air travel provided by Singapore Airlines is a luxurious service that indicates what those relevant brands represent before prospective customers have any interactive experience with them. Customers know where those brands fit in their perceptions of value and whether the services should be included in their evoked set, primarily based on their price.

Price and brand perception together exert a stronger influence on a consumer's buying decision process than the other elements in the marketing mix for a service. Price should not be considered as an afterthought; nor should it be seen as the end result of creating a service and then adding a profit margin to its selling price. Service brands that lead with their price aim to create top-of-mind awareness by using price to indicate where those services belong according to their customers' perceptions of value, and for whom they are intended. The price may, in fact, be the most important determinant for those customers who are considering buying the value associated with that service.

Learning objectives

After reading this chapter you should be able to:

↘ explain the various factors that influence the price of services

↘ discuss the different approaches that can be used to develop pricing strategies for services

↘ explain the relationship between customer demand and the price of services

↘ discuss how various characteristics of a service influence revenue management strategies.

Factors that influence the pricing of services

Developing pricing objectives for a service product is a fundamental aspect of managing the marketing of a service. The initial stage in determining the pricing objectives for a service is to understand:

→ the financial costs of producing a service

→ customer demand for particular services

→ the non-monetary costs of marketing a service

→ the legal and ethical considerations of setting a price for a service.

The financial costs of producing a service

The first step in setting the selling price of a service is to identify—and quantify—the financial costs associated with creating and marketing that service. Those costs play a major role in setting the selling price of a service because if a service organisation charges less than what it costs to produce that service, the organisation will not be able to keep paying the production costs, and subsequently will lose money. The various costs that are incurred in producing a service are different to those that are associated with producing a tangible good.

There are two types of costs that commercial organisations incur when producing tangible goods; the first are variable costs, and the other are fixed costs. When a service organisation such as a five-star hotel produces a service product, it incurs variable costs that are also considered to be the unit costs of production, and those costs vary according to the number of service units that are demanded by customers.

↘
variable costs
Those production costs that vary in response to variations in customer demand

↘
fixed costs
Those production costs that remain fixed—at least over a short production cycle—even if there is no customer demand

Chapter 7 Pricing Service Products

The units of production vary according to the specific type of service industry and not the particular service organisation. For example, the units of customer demand for the accommodation industry—which includes hotels, resorts, B&Bs and backpacker hostels—are room nights. Service organisations generally incur fewer variable costs than a business that manufactures tangible products, and often the major variable cost in providing a service is the cost of employing extra service providers who may work part-time during busy periods of customer demand. Other variable costs incurred by a service business would be any material items that are consumed as part of providing a service product. For example, selling an extra seat at a football match incurs very little extra labour costs; in fact, the cost is close to zero. Semi-variable costs fall between fixed and variable costs and tend to rise and fall in a stepwise manner based on changes in customer demand.

> ↘
> **semi-variable costs**
> Those production costs that fall between fixed and variable costs and tend to change in response to changes in customer demand

Customer demand for services

It is desirable—although it can be somewhat difficult to achieve—that service organisations understand the responsiveness of customer demand to changes in the price of their services. In practice, it generally requires many years of sales data to accurately determine the price sensitivity of the many customer segments that constitute the market for a service. Lack of sales data for many small service organisations means that many must forgo accurate forecasts of their customer demand and rely instead on subjective estimations of their customers' price sensitivity of demand.

The price elasticity of demand is a method to measure the sensitivity of customers to changes in the price of a service. The price elasticity of demand is calculated by comparing the percentage change in quantity demanded with the percentage change in price.[10]

The formula for calculating the price elasticity of demand is:

> ↘
> **price elasticity of demand**
> A method to measure the sensitivity of customers to changes in the price of a service

$$\text{price elasticity of (E)} = \frac{\text{percentage change in quantity demanded}}{\text{percentage change in price}}$$

$$= \frac{(Q_2 - Q_1)/Q_1}{(P_2 - P_1)/P_1}$$

where Q = quantity, and P = price.

If the co-efficient of price elasticity is >1, as shown in Figure 7.1, then demand is said to be *price elastic*; that is, customer demand is highly responsive to a change in price. When demand for a service is price elastic, an organisation may gain extra revenue if it reduces the price of its service.

If the co-efficient of price elasticity of demand is <1, as shown in Figure 7.2, then demand is said to be price inelastic; that is, it is unresponsive to a change in price. When demand for a service is *price inelastic*, increasing the market price may lead to an increase in revenue for the organisation.

Figure 7.1 Elastic demand ($P_{ed} > 1$)

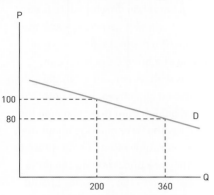

Source: Tutor 2U (2015). Explaining price elasticity of demand. <www.tutor2u.net/economics/reference/price-elasticity-of-demand>.

Figure 7.2 Inelastic demand ($P_{ed} < 1$)

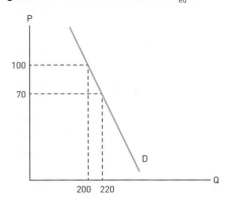

Source: Tutor 2U (2015). Explaining price elasticity of demand. <www.tutor2u.net/economics/reference/price-elasticity-of-demand>.

For example, in the first quarter 2016 when the price of oil fell below the 2015 cost per barrel, one of the major operating costs to airlines (jet fuel) was reduced, and the airlines passed this on to customers as cheaper fares. Economy return fares from Melbourne to London were advertised at A$1545, while flights to New York from Sydney were priced at A$919.[11] If demand for those cheaper flights increased as a result of the cheaper fares, that would demonstrate a situation of elastic demand, as shown in Figure 7.1. If, however, the change in fares had little or no effect on the number of flights that customers were willing to purchase, then that would indicate a case of inelastic demand, as shown in Figure 7.2.

By understanding the price elasticity of demand, service organisations can manage their customer demand by setting their prices to satisfy that demand and generate a profitable return. Price elasticity becomes more important for service organisations that offer standardised services—like hotels—because their demand is constrained by relatively fixed supply; hotels have only a fixed number of rooms. In the longer term, that fixed capacity can influence customer satisfaction because if the hotel cannot accommodate any increased demand, prospective customers are likely to become dissatisfied.

A price-value matrix for setting hotel room rates

Services in Action

Many factors influence the pricing strategies that a hotel charges for its rooms, one of which is the various rates that competitors charge for different quality rooms.

A marketing objective of a hotel is to develop pricing strategies that place its brand in an advantageous position relative to its competitors, and one way to visualise the application of that concept is

Chapter 7 Pricing Service Products

to examine the price-value matrix shown in Figure 7.3.

The position that a hotel's rooms occupy within the price-value matrix is a function of the hotel's brand proposition, its pricing objectives and the strength of its competitors. A hotel's pricing objectives should consider the following questions:

- Is the hotel aiming to maximise short-term revenues or profit?
- Is the hotel seeking higher profit margins in a luxury market that has fluctuating sales?
- Does the hotel need to differentiate its accommodation to penetrate the market?
- Is the hotel operating merely in 'survival' mode?

Figure 7.3 Price-value matrix

High price, low quality
High price, high quality
Price
Low price, low quality
Low price, high quality
Quality

Source: Economics Help. <www.economicshelp.org>.

When a hotel has developed its pricing objectives, it can plot its prices—and those of its competitors—on the price—value matrix, and at a glance the hotel can assess how well its pricing strategies align with its pricing objectives. If the hotel's rates need adjusting—either because the rates portray the wrong image about the hotel's brand relative to its competitors or because they are undermining the hotel's pricing objectives—the marketer should consider using one or more of the following pricing strategies shown in Figure 7.4 to re-position the hotel.

Price/positioning strategies

Skimming

The aim of a skimming price strategy is to position one hotel above the rest. The price should inform prospective customers about the benefits of the hotel's accommodation and that the room rates offer more value than a competitor's advertised room rates. A skimming price strategy can be lead to higher profit margins, but higher prices also imply a higher quality for many customers. It is critical, therefore, that prospective customers understand why they are being asked to pay more to stay at the hotel.

Figure 7.4 Price/positioning model

	Skim	Match	Surround	Undercut	Penetrate
Highest	$99				
Higher	$89	$89	$89		
Equal		$79		$79	
Lower			$69	$69	$69
Lowest					$59

For example, a five-star hotel that sets its room rates higher than its competitors uses marketing communications to make prospective guests—who are generally willing to pay more for spacious and luxurious rooms—aware of the benefits of staying at that particular hotel.

Matching

A price-matching strategy for a four-star hotel puts a hotel's pricing on par with its competitors, but not necessarily at the same rate for all of its rooms.

Adopting a matching pricing strategy requires a hotel to set the rates of its standard rooms at the same rate as the competition, but offer other rooms that have a distinctive benefit—such as a gym—at a slightly higher rate. A matching pricing strategy allows a hotel to stay competitive for a larger segment of customers, but does not undercut the competition.

Surrounding

A surround-pricing strategy positions the rooms of a three-star hotel as the cheapest in the market, but can offer particular rooms with better amenities at a price that is close to its competitors' 'rack rate' (i.e. the standard rate for a hotel room before any discounts or promotional

pricing have been offered). That means all rooms of similar three-star hotels can be viewed as being substitutes, which limits the range that one hotel's rooms can deviate from the industry average. A hotel's rack rate is the price that the hotel will charge a prospective guest who requests a without having a reservation. For example, when guests use an online agency to book a hotel in a capital city, they will be asked for a check-in date and check-out date so that a computer-based algorithm can the find cheapest room rates of the various hotels on its database for those dates and then display the room rates.

Some hotels have effectively made their 'online rate' their hotel rack rate, but during off-peak times the internet rate may be cheaper. For example, the guests at business hotels mainly buy rooms at the rack rate during the week, leaving the hotel with vacant rooms on weekends. Those hotels then offer cheaper rates to walk-in guests at weekends. A hotel that adopts a surround-pricing strategy does so to maximise yield by minimising the fluctuations in revenue by attracting guests who are willing to pay for a room within a price range between the rack rate and the discount rate.

Undercutting

By using an undercutting pricing strategy to offer cheaper rooms than its competitors' rates in some categories, a hotel can potentially attract more customers.

To undercut, the hotel offers a price that's comparable to its competitors and another at a lower room rate. For example,

William Chitty

Figure 7.5 Hotel A

Parking package	✓ from **USD 359**

ROOM ACCOMMODATION AND UP TO 14 DAYS FREE PARKING
- No penalty for changes/cancellations until 6.00 PM hotel time on 05/16/2018.
- No deposit required

⊕ SELECT YOUR ROOM

Figure 7.6 Hotel B

⊟ AIRPORT PARKING PACKAGE	Average nightly rate starting from **$189.00** USD

<u>Airport Parking Package - 1 King Guest Room</u>
Includes 14 nights of parking

$189.00 USD *
<u>Rate Details</u>

Book Now

consider the online offers from two hotels shown in Figures 7.5 and 7.6.

Both hotels A and B are located near a major city airport, and both have the same star ratings and amenities; but look at their airport parking packages for 14 days. Hotel A offers a room rate of $359 plus free parking for up to 14 days, while the offer from Hotel B is a room rate of $189 per night without the cost of parking. These hotels are offering similar rooms, but with different conditions. Hotel B has chosen to undercut its competitor for this package in the expectation of attracting more cost-conscious travellers to stay—especially if the guest intends to stay away for only three or four days.

Penetrating

Offering lower priced hotel rooms has benefits and disadvantages. A low-price strategy is aimed at attracting people through the door and into rooms. For new hotels without the backing of a strong brand name, a low-price strategy often seems to be the best marketing approach to encourage guests to try their accommodation. But that pricing strategy also can depress market prices, lower margins and portray a poor brand image as the business grows. Figure 7.7 shows some of the advertisements that prospective guests see when they peruse cheaper hotel options online.

Hotels that use a penetration-pricing strategy are profitable in the short term, but hotels are long-term investments that have a return on investment (ROI) that is dependent on achieving the best price for their rooms over the life of a hotel. Hotels in the major chains usually have an operating life of 10 to 12 years, after which they must undergo a multi-million hotel refurbishment.[12]

Figure 7.7 Comparative ads for hotel rooms

Non-monetary costs

When marketers consider the pricing objectives of a service, there are a range of non-monetary costs that must be included in the overall cost of acquiring that service. Non-monetary costs represent the costs that are incurred by customers in their purchase and consumption of a service. Non-monetary costs include time costs, search costs and psychological costs, which are included when customers make decisions to buy, or re-buy, a service.

Time costs

Due to their inseparability, where every service transaction requires time and effort from customers and the service providers, each service experience may require customers to spend time waiting for the actual transaction. In the case of professional services—like having a tax return completed—a customer not only pays financial costs for the service, but also the time spent waiting in reception. Because labour is the highest variable cost in any service encounter, this is where many service organisations confront the dilemma of managing time—that is, whether to spend more time personalising the service transaction and have the customers perceive the service experience as having more value; or spend less time on the service experience and create the perception that the transaction has less value.

It has been suggested there are several characteristics of time spent waiting that service marketers can manage, to change a customer's perception of the wait time and its related costs. They are:

→ Unoccupied time feels longer to customers than occupied time.

→ Pre-process waits feel longer than in-process waits.

→ Anxiety makes waits feel longer.

→ Uncertain waits feel longer than known waits.

→ Unfair waits are longer than equitable waits.

→ The more valuable the service, the longer a customer will wait.

→ Waiting alone feels as though it lasts longer than when waiting with others.[13]

Some service organisations that do not offer personal services—such as retail banks—provide an effective solution to the dilemma of spending less time with their customers by adopting self-service technology—ATMs (see also the discussion in Chapter 6). That approach removes the higher labour cost of the service transaction, and makes customers responsible for their time spent on the service delivery, and therefore the value of the service experience.

Search costs

Search costs include the effort that customers invest in deciding which service to purchase. Search costs are usually higher for services than for physical goods because the price of a service is not readily discernible until the customer begins the consumption process for the service.

Another factor that influences search costs is the fact that each service organisation typically offers only one brand, unless that organisation is acting as an agent for other firms or customers, such as real estate agents or insurance brokers. The internet has helped to reduce the search costs of some services because it allows customers to check the websites of a number of service organisations, such as travel agents and hotels.

Psychological costs

Psychological costs refer to the costs paid by customers after they evaluate what the service provided for the price they paid. If customers are disappointed in the service they have received, they are likely to experience cognitive dissonance, which is a psychological cost. Cognitive dissonance usually occurs when the separation between what customers expected and what they experienced is too far apart. For service organisations, however, there is also a cost associated with that dissonance, which is a loss of customer equity in their service brand. Many consumers who experience a less-than-satisfactory service experience can now join social networking platforms and air their negative service interaction with their friends and thousands of others. Social networking makes it important for organisations to identify and improve those service processes—and maybe their physical facilities—that cause psychological costs for customers.

For some service organisations, integrating the financial and psychological cost components to offer guarantees of money back, or discounts if service benchmarks are not met, are strategies that can reduce the psychological costs for customers purchasing their services. Some service organisations, such as gymnasiums, allow prospective customers to trial their services for a week—before committing those likely customers to three- or six-monthly contracts—to reduce any doubts that those future customers may have about joining that particular gymnasium.

Legal and ethical considerations in pricing services

Legal and regulatory environment

The commercial environment of Australia is founded on the rationale that the market will self-regulate and that prices will move in line with customer demand. That premise of self-regulation is subject to the supply of services being made available, providing there is the likelihood that a service organisation will make a profit from selling its services. The key federal legislation that influences the selling price of services includes the *Competition and Consumer Act 2010* (a subset of the *Trade Practices Act 1974*—the TPA) and the Fair Trading Acts administered by the Australian state and territory governments.

As discussed in Chapter 1, the *Competition and Consumer Act* introduced a new national consumer law regime known as Australian Consumer Law (ACL), which is enforced by an independent Commonwealth statutory authority, the Australian Competition and Consumer Commission (ACCC). The ACCC was established to promote competition and fair trade in the marketplace by enforcing 'fair and open' competition for consumers, and to protect them from unlawful pricing behaviour by business organisations. The competition provisions prohibit such activities as:

→ price fixing

→ misuse of market power

→ exclusive dealing

→ resale price maintenance

→ anti-competitive behaviour.

Through the provisions of the ACL, the ACCC has substantial power to protect consumers and prosecute those organisations that breach the provisions of the Act. For example, under new rules that took effect in September 2016, if organisations that have 50 employees or earn more than $25 million in revenue annually charge customers more than the transaction costs of accepting credit cards for purchases, they can be fined $108 000—rising to $1.1 million if the dispute proceeds to court. The new regulations were introduced to prevent organisations from charging excessive fees when customers paid using credit or debit cards.[14]

Optus to compensate customers short-changed on data, call and text inclusions

Services in Action

The Australian Competition and Consumer Commission (ACCC) has accepted a court-enforceable undertaking from Optus Mobile Pty Ltd (Optus) in relation to alleged misrepresentations Optus made about the amount and period of validity of data, calls and texts provided with certain prepaid products and services.[15] The company has admitted that its conduct was likely to have contravened sections 18 and 29(1)(g) of the Australian Consumer Law (ACL).

Optus is one of several suppliers of telephone and internet services to consumers in Australia and offers various prepaid mobile broadband devices, prepaid mobile phones and prepaid mobile plans for sale (together, the Optus Prepaid Products).

During 2013, Optus advertised various promotions that offered consumers a

William Chitty

certain amount of data, calls and/or texts valid for a specified period of time (the inclusions) from when they either activated or recharged the SIM card that was supplied with the purchase of an Optus Prepaid Product.

From 2015, Optus changed the inclusions that were provided upon activation or recharge of the SIM card supplied with the Optus Prepaid Products. These changes included reducing the inclusions and/or reducing the length of time before the inclusions would expire, and in some instances the inclusions were increased but the expiry period was reduced. Consumers who purchased one of the Optus Prepaid Products before the implementation of these changes, but activated the SIM card after the changes, received the reduced inclusions and/or shorter expiry period. Optus did not notify these consumers about the changes or advise them that they should activate their SIM card before a certain date in order to receive the full inclusions and expiry that they purchased. These consumers therefore received less inclusions and/or a shorter expiry period than they were promised.[16]

To address the ACCC's concerns, Optus provided the ACCC with a section 87B of the ACL undertaking that:

↘ For a period of three years it will not, in trade or commerce, reduce the amount of data and/or other inclusions advertised as available upon activation of a prepaid SIM card (including a prepaid SIM card bundled with another product) unless certain conditions have been met.

↘ It will contact affected consumers and provide them with a credit.

↘ In recognition of the loss to those consumers whom Optus is unable to provide redress, Optus will donate any money it is unable to refund to an appropriate organisation to be agreed with the ACCC.

↘ It will publish notices in Optus and third-party stores, and on the Optus website, informing affected consumers that they may be entitled to a credit.

↘ It will update its compliance program and an internal staff template to ensure Optus considers its obligations under the ACL before updating or implementing similar future promotions.

Ethical considerations

The primary ethical considerations associated with pricing services are price fixing, predatory pricing and price discrimination.

Price fixing is a business arrangement whereby two or more organisations decide the price they will charge for a service. It is not how the agreement to fix prices was made, or even how effective it is, but the fact that 'so-called' competitors are setting their prices collectively and not individually. Agreements made between competing organisations to fix their prices are illegal under s. 45 of the *Competition and Consumer Act*.

Predatory pricing is anti-competitive behaviour, where one organisation sets a low price for its services for the purpose of driving its competitors out of the market. That leaves the organisation with less competition, allowing it manipulate its prices and exploit consumers.

Lowering the price of a service, or underselling competitors by engaging in a 'price war', is not necessarily considered to be predatory pricing but, when those pricing strategies are used by an organisation that has substantial market power for the purpose of driving a competitor from the market, that action is considered to be the misuse of market power. Predatory pricing is unlawful under s. 46(1) of the *Competition and Consumer Act* and can only occur when the price setter has a substantial degree of market power, such as being the market leader for that service.

Price discrimination is the practice of offering similar services to different customers at different prices. In business-to-business (B2B) markets, price discrimination is considered to be anti-competitive if it is used to drive competitors from a business market. Generally, the *Competition and Consumer Act* does not prohibit an organisation from refusing to supply another organisation with a service or supplying on different terms. Price discrimination in the consumer market occurs when a similar service is offered to different markets at different prices, because that difference in price is unrelated to the cost of supplying that service. Common examples occur when discounts or concessions are given to students or pensioners for the purchase of various services; for example, public transport concessions.

Developing pricing strategies for services

Understanding the elements of pricing models

For commercial service organisations, pricing is defined as *a seller's approach to setting the purchase price of a service*. Pricing strategies are the actions that a service organisation takes to achieve its pricing—and hence marketing—objectives. A pricing strategy is implemented through a pricing model, using strategies to set a service organisation's selling price that will generate a predetermined level of profit.

⬊
pricing
The actions that a seller takes to set the purchase price of a service

In general, the term 'margin' refers to the difference between the selling price and the seller's costs for the services being sold, and is usually expressed as a percentage of selling price.

Before a service organisation sets a selling price for its services—which is the price that customers normally pay for the specific service, not the price at 'special sales' or discounted prices—service marketers must develop the pricing objectives of the specific service. Pricing objectives are usually developed on the basis of achieving one or more of the following marketing objectives:

→ to maximise unit sales and market share (defined as units sold)

→ to maximise sales revenues and market share (defined as sales revenue)

William Chitty

Chapter 7 Pricing Service Products

→ to maximise gross profits

→ to leverage sales of related products and/or services.

Sellers also use pricing strategies to pursue service positioning objectives such as:

→ communicating and reinforcing the brand's value; that is, the brand's equity

→ creating customers' perceptions of desirable quality and/or value.

To achieve these pricing objectives, service marketers must understand the relationships between price on one hand versus customer demand, sales revenues, product costs, gross profits and product positioning on the other. Figure 7.8 depicts how some of those relationships may occur for a business hotel located in a capital city.

Sales revenue, gross profits and service costs are functions of demand and unit price (room rate per night). For the hotel example shown in Figure 7.8, the maximum sales revenue occurs at a room rate of $130, which assumes 100 per cent room occupancy; optimal sales revenue occurs when rooms are sold at $156 per night; and the maximum gross profit is achieved by selling rooms at $160 per night. Pricing analyses—such as that shown in Figure 7.8—are often used when the maximum number of service units (room nights) are sold, enabling maximum sales revenue and maximum gross profits to be predicted at different price points. A 100 per cent occupancy is seldom achieved because even the

Figure 7.8   Price relationships for demand, sales revenue and profit

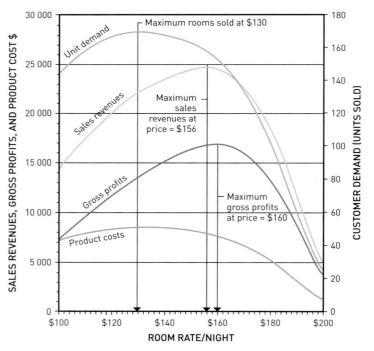

Source: M. Schmidt (2018). Pricing strategies, pricing models, demand curves. <www.business-case-analysis.com/pricing.html>.

best maintenance programs are unable to predict the likelihood of breakdowns in the air-conditioning, plumbing or electrical systems that will make a hotel's rooms uninhabitable, for example. It is therefore more realistic to assume an optimal occupancy of 90 per cent for calculating potential sales revenue.

Customer demand and pricing analysis

Figure 7.8 indicates how a service marketer's forecast of customer demand is influenced by the selling price of the service. The price/demand data, and subsequent curve (the green line), is crucial to analysing price for two reasons.

The first is that customer demand—as a function of price—is the basis of determining the other variables associated with pricing, such as sales revenue, service costs and gross profit, because they are functions of both price and demand. That means the price/demand data must be determined first.

The second reason is that customer demand is generally more difficult to estimate than price, because it depends on dynamic consumer behaviour, which is more uncertain. Almost all of the uncertainty associated with revenue, cost and gross profit estimations arise from the assumptions that underpin the price/demand forecasts.

Pricing calculations for the major elements of a pricing model are:

→ sales revenue = service demand × selling price

→ service costs = fixed costs + (unit demand × variable cost per service)

→ gross profits = sales revenue – service costs

Pricing strategies

Marketers of services implement their pricing strategies based on the following approaches:

→ To achieve specific pricing objectives, such as maximising sales or increasing market share.

→ To achieve strategic organisational objectives, such as being recognised as the low-priced market leader or to increase the brand's equity in the quality services segment.

In many instances the terms 'pricing strategies' and 'pricing models' are used interchangeably to mean the same thing. These terms, however, are not the same, and should be distinguished:

→ *Pricing strategies*, as presented below, describe how marketers can use pricing to achieve the commercial objectives of service organisations.

→ *Pricing models* should be considered as being detailed rules; that is, the actions required to implement pricing strategies.[17]

Cost-plus pricing strategies

When a cost-plus pricing strategy is chosen, service marketers set a price equal to the costs of supplying a service unit plus a percentage of the service costs; or they set a price equal to the selling price of a service unit plus a fixed percentage increment. The advantage of cost-plus pricing is that it is simple to apply and ensures that the organisation would never sell a service unit at a loss. The limitations of a cost-plus pricing strategy, however, are that it does not account for fluctuations in customer demand or competitors' prices, and importantly does not effectively communicate the brand's value to customers.[18]

Unit pricing strategies

Pricing for market penetration aims to maximise unit sales, which means setting the service unit sales price as near as possible to the peak of the customer demand curve. For example, in Figure 7.8 the peak of the demand curve for the hotel is to charge $130 per room night. For many service demand curves, however, choosing a service unit pricing strategy may mean selling at near to a loss because market penetration strategies should only be used initially at the introduction stage of a service to establish market awareness. Penetration pricing that is adopted as a means of driving competitors from the market is called predatory pricing and is unlawful under the *Competition and Consumer Act*.

The advantage of penetration pricing is that through the price/demand curve, service marketers can increase their market share and brand recognition by taking into account prevailing competitors' prices and the number of substitute services. The disadvantage of using penetration pricing is that it may build brand recognition at the expense of creating customer perceptions of the service as being a low-quality brand. Many budget airlines, known as low-cost carriers (LCC), typically offer lower fares than full-service airlines, but charge their customers for food and beverages, in-flight entertainment and non-cabin luggage to offset their low fares.[19]

Maximise sales revenues/gross profit

Setting the sales price to maximise sales revenue or gross profit requires a complete understanding of the behaviour of the price/demand curve and the relationship between price and revenue. As shown in Figure 7.8, when a revenue-maximising strategy is chosen, prices are set as close as possible to the price point under the peak of the price/revenue curve or the price/gross profit curve; those prices are $156 and $160, respectively. When the primary objective is maximising gross profit, the pricing strategy is known as *contribution margin-based pricing*.

This strategy is most beneficial for an established service organisation selling a mature service in a stable mature market. For newer businesses or for services new to the market, the sellers' long-term financial interests may be better served by other pricing strategies that will increase market share, improve brand equity or communicate service quality.

Australian trading banks, for example, benefit from adopting a maximising-sales-revenue pricing strategy.[20]

Premium pricing strategy

When adopting a premium, or prestige pricing strategy, service organisations set their prices high enough to achieve a predetermined margin over their costs, plus an additional price component. The additional price component is meant to communicate a level of service quality, brand value, prestige exclusivity or any other positive service attribute. Premium pricing is possible when brand image has become an established service attribute because premium pricing *per se* enhances customers' perceptions of the service quality. One of the disadvantages of adopting a premium pricing strategy is that it attracts competitors who may then underprice the premium-priced seller. Technology-based services, which often have a short service lifespan, can suffer from the competitive pressure of underpricing.[21]

Value-based pricing strategy

When value-based pricing is adopted, the price of a service unit is based primarily on customers' perceptions of service value. A service organisation's delivery costs play a minor role in setting the selling price because a competitor's prices will have a limited impact on customers' perceived value of the service. When the service product is something like a large, customised software program for managing customer service or a complex, customised service contract, the selling organisation will often dedicate specialised operational or marketing personnel to communicate the value to the buyer by demonstrating the product's benefits.

In most situations, when value-based pricing is chosen by a service organisation, its sales personnel may realise significant margins if they can successfully communicate the service's value to a customer. When the value-based selling price has been agreed, and the service contracted for delivery, the organisation must deliver the service at the agreed price. If an organisation underestimates the actual costs of delivering the product, the transaction will generate inadequate margins and may cause a possible loss for the business.[22]

Dynamic pricing (time-based pricing)

In some selling situations, customer demand and a willingness to pay may vary from time to time and cause service organisations to vary their prices as often as daily as they attempt to attract customers. Travellers know, for example, that hotel room rates can vary significantly on a day-to-day basis depending on the number of unsold rooms and the likely demand for each of those days.

When a hotel experiences high demand and is booked to optimal capacity, room rates will be high; for other nights when demand is low, the room rates are likely to be lower. The advantage of using dynamic pricing—where customer demand and a willingness to pay can change daily—is that it delivers higher revenue than when prices are fixed over all levels of demand. Hotel rooms and airline seats are more likely to be sold at higher prices under conditions of dynamic pricing.[23]

Other pricing strategies

The pricing strategies discussed above are often modified or combined to produce other strategies. Some of those modified strategies are:

→ *Price skimming*: is often adopted at the introduction stage of a service when the service organisation sets a high price to gain maximum profits from the early adopters or those customers who are not price sensitive. Price skimming is adopted when an organisation seeks to recover service development costs early in its life cycle, with the selling price later reduced to attract the more price-sensitive segments of the market.

→ *Price-point pricing*: is a form of psychological pricing and is the practice of setting prices just under price-point thresholds such as $20. Twenty-dollar bank notes are commonly carried by consumers and a service that is priced at $19.99 is more likely to attract a customer than a service priced at $20.89, which includes GST. Small service providers, like hairdressers, are more likely to adopt this type of pricing strategy.[24]

Customer demand and pricing a service

The practice of setting the price for a service is based on several business disciplines ranging from economic theory to consumer psychology and decision-making, and each plays a different role in the pricing processes. The economic model of supply and demand is used to determine the selling price of a service. It assumes that in a competitive market, the unit price for a particular service will fluctuate until it reaches a point where the quantity demanded (D) by consumers (at the current price) will equal the quantity supplied (S) by a service organisation (at the current price), thereby producing a state of economic equilibrium at a price (P) and quantity demanded (Q) for that service.

The four basic economic laws of supply and demand are:

1   If demand increases and supply remains unchanged, then it leads to a higher equilibrium price and higher quantity.

2   If demand decreases and supply remains unchanged, then it leads to a lower equilibrium price and lower quantity.

3   If supply increases and demand remains unchanged, then it leads to lower equilibrium price and higher quantity.

4   If supply decreases and demand remains unchanged, then it leads to higher equilibrium price and lower quantity.[25]

Equilibrium is defined as the price-quantity point where the quantity demanded is equal to the quantity supplied, and is represented by the intersection of the demand and supply curves. Market equilibrium is a situation where the price is such that the quantity that consumers wish to purchase is correctly balanced by the quantity that organisations wish to supply.

The interaction of supply and demand on pricing

Economic theory assumes that consumers are rational decision-makers. If, for example, the price of a particular service increases, and customers understand all the relevant marketing information underpinning that price increase, demand for that product can be expected to decrease. Conversely, if the price decreases, demand would be expected to increase; that is, an increase in demand will result in a downward-sloping demand curve. A demand curve shows the quantity demanded at various price levels. The price of a product (P) is determined by a balance between production at each price point (supply, S), and the desires of consumers with purchasing power at each price point (demand D). Figure 7.9 indicates that a positive shift in demand for a service product—from D1 to D2— will produce increases in both the price to P2, and the quantity sold to Q2.

If a seller reduces the price of a service, the service may become more attractive to a larger number of buyers, thereby expanding the total market for that particular type of service. The demand for a particular industry type of service, for example, motor vehicle insurance—which is not based on only one insurance company's brand—is known as the *primary demand* for that service. If all motor vehicle insurers were to set their prices high, the primary demand would be unlikely to expand, and would result in lower total revenue for all insurers in that market. Demand-oriented pricing focuses on the nature of the demand for the service being offered.

Figure 7.9   Model of supply and demand

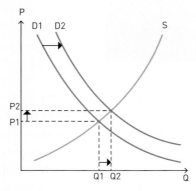

Source: Boundless Business. Pricing products. <www.boundless.com/business/textbooks/boundless-business-text-book/product-and-pricing-strategies-15/pricing-products-96/impacts-of-supply-and-demand-on-pricing-449-1939/images/price-affected-by-supply-and-demand>.

The demand curve is shaped primarily by the structure of the industry in which a service organisation competes; that is, if a service organisation operates in a market that is competitive, price may be used for strategic advantage in acquiring and maintaining market share. Conversely, if a service organisation, such as a full-service airline, operates in an environment with few competitive airlines, the range in which prices can be vary will be minimal, given that the high costs of production (labour and capital) are similar for all those competing airlines.

↘ INDUSTRY INSIGHT

What does it cost to fly an aircraft from A to B?

According to an International Air Transport Association (IATA) analysis, the costs for both international and domestic full-service flights include the costs of fuel, a food and beverage service, and airport taxes and navigation charges levied by air-traffic control. Fuel, which accounts for about 30 per cent of the flying costs, is one of an airline's largest expenses followed by labour costs for aircrew, cabin staff, ground crew and maintenance staff.

Data from the Bureau of Infrastructure, Transport and Regional Economics (BITRE), and from Qantas, indicates that a typical Qantas Airbus A380-800 flight from Sydney to Los Angeles in November 2013 cost the airline $11 414 for food and beverages, $12 625 for staff pay and $37 157 for airport taxes and navigation charges to fly the 484-seat aircraft for the 14-hour journey. An

Airbus A380-800's fuel tanks have a capacity of 320 000 litres of fuel, which at an industry price of 77c a litre costs about $246 000 to fill. Against those costs, Qantas charged its passengers an average $13 129 for one of its 14 first-class suites, $10 425 to travel in business class, $2975 in premium economy and $1599 in economy, which delivered an average of $1.215 million in revenue, based on a load factor of 78 per cent.[26]

Analysis of Virgin Australia's operating costs and data from BITRE reveal a similar pattern. In the same period, Virgin Australia's Sydney to Los Angeles flights—operated by Boeing 777-300ER aircraft—cost $9652 for food and beverages, $9653 in staff pay, $31 117 in airport taxes and navigation charges, and over $140 000 in fuel to fly the 361-seat aircraft on its 14-hour journey. To generate revenue, Virgin Australia charged $7351 for a seat in business class, $2283 for a seat in premium economy and $1479 in economy, earning about $591 000 in revenue based on a load factor of 77 per cent.[27]

On shorter and less profitable routes, costs are higher and fares are often lower. For example, on Qantas' Sydney–Hobart services, also in November 2013, the airline charged an average $246 per seat to fill 146 seats in the 168-seat plane—generating

$35916 in revenue. The airline, however, had to provide food and beverages at a cost of $3840, pay staff $10830 and pay $5976 in airport taxes and navigation charges in addition to the cost for fuel.

In February 2016, Qantas announced a significant increase in pre-tax profit to A$921 million for its operations in the first half of the 2015–16 financial year.[28] During the same period, Virgin Australia generated an underlying profit of A$81.5 million.[29] Over the 2015–16 financial year, the price of jet fuel dropped by about 50 per cent, so those results should not come as a surprise. During the preceding four years, fuel expenses were the largest single cost for airlines, but with the current low cost of fuel, the largest expense for an airline is now labour, followed by fuel.

According to analysts, the capital costs of operating an airline include the costs of purchasing or leasing aircraft plus interest repayments, including the money spent on operations. It does not provide a comprehensive account of other key costs, such as aviation fuel, which many airlines purchase in advance as a 'hedge' against future price rises. An airline's total operational costs are typically about 95 per cent of what it earns, but that analysis can only provide an operational overview because of the difficulty in obtaining accurate, but commercially sensitive, data on the costs of operating an airline.

Revenue management for service industries

The underlying concepts of revenue management

Revenue management was initially developed by the airline industry in the United States with a focus on maximising the revenue yield from using a combination of selling price and available capacity. More recently, it has also been adopted by the hospitality, tourism and events industries. Revenue management ensures the effective utilisation of an organisation's capacity because it reserves capacity for those customer segments that are willing to pay higher prices for services. It is a method of concurrently managing customer demand in response to the price sensitivity of each segment at various times of a day, a week or season, and managing the varying capacity constraints of supply.[30]

Revenue management evolved from yield management models that were tactical responses to managing revenue, rather than strategies, and had a narrow focus—for example, selling a seat on a particular flight, a ticket to a sporting event or a booking for a hotel room—and did not include any 'secondary' customer spend in other associated areas of supply, such as food and beverages, additional baggage allowance, or the opportunity costs of completing the sale (such as discounts given to customers). Revenue management is seen as a development of yield management, by having a more strategic perspective of creating value for a service organisation.[31]

Revenue management in practice

An important consideration for many service organisations is that different customer segments have different buying behaviours. Revenue management involves setting prices according to demand forecasts for those different segments. The *least* price-sensitive customers are generally the first segment to be offered allocated capacity because they will pay higher prices than the other segments, which pay progressively lower prices. The higher-paying segments often buy closer to the time of consumption, so service organisations set aside dedicated capacity for customers in those segments, instead of selling on a first-come, first-served basis. For example, business customers often book airline seats, hotel rooms and tickets to events at short notice while leisure travellers tend to book months in advance.[32]

Traditionally, before the advent of revenue management, there were two key elements that were monitored independently when managing sales: namely, the time when the service is used and the duration of the service experience. Sales revenue is made up of selling price multiplied by number of units sold. Revenue measurement is based on average spend per customer, or average price achieved, and the percentage of capacity utilised. In hotels, those elements form the average room rate (ARR) and the percentage occupancy; that is, the percentage of rooms that were used. For airlines, these elements form the revenue per available seat kilometre (RPK), which is the key measure of profitability per flight. For events such as concerts, it is the average ticket price and percentage of capacity sold, whether that is festival space, seating capacity or venue capacity, depending on the type of event. Even for these traditional mechanisms, managers usually know from past experience the price points of when to discount and when not to discount.

In some service interactions there are price points where discounting or offering lower prices are needed to encourage customer demand; that is, the number of service units sold. Depending on the type of service being offered, discounting can vary—for a beach resort it may be during the winter, for a business hotel it is the weekends, or a holiday package may be seasonal. In some market environments, such as summer holiday trade, there is a peak season, shoulder seasons either side of the peak and an 'off-season' period.

There are many definitions of revenue management, but generally they relate to selling the right product, to the right customer, at the right time, at the right price. From the examples given above, different types of customers have different buying behaviour, and in order to maximise revenue returns on any given day, service organisations need to be aware of those customers who are willing, and able, to purchase the service at a particular time. Note that a customer must have both the ability and the willingness to purchase the service at a particular time.

↘
revenue management
Generally relates to selling the right product, to the right customer, at the right time, at the right price

Revenue management goes beyond a manager's experience; it is a process of managing market demand based on sophisticated multivariate modelling of past buyer behaviour to make predictions about future demand. The system effectively 'allocates' saleable service units to specific market segments, based on predictions of their future demand, often through the use of sophisticated revenue management software.[33]

The role of service characteristics in managing revenue

Revenue management is based on the integration of information systems and pricing strategies that allocates the optimal capacity to customers at the right time. In practice, that means an organisation determines a price for its services according to a predicted demand level that appeals to price-sensitive customers who are willing to purchase during off-peak periods, while customers who are not price sensitive—and want to purchase during periods of peak demand price—can do so. There are several characteristics of service products that service organisations must consider when they incorporate revenue-management strategies into their operations, and these are discussed next.[34]

Relatively fixed operational capacity

The definition of capacity varies depending on the type of service industry. It is, however, typically based on physical attributes of the service product. For example, hotel capacity is usually measured by the number of serviceable rooms available on any given night—hence 'room/nights' is the measure of hotel capacity. In some instances, capacity is measured by time. Barristers, accountants and marketing consultants define their capacity as 'chargeable hours', while golf clubs and theatres use hours in operation to define their capacities. The key issue when measuring capacity is to define the capacity constraints that apply to various service organisations. As previously discussed, the optimal capacity of hotels is the number of serviceable rooms a hotel has available to rent out per night. Similarly, a theatre may have an installed capacity of 1200 seats, but if some rows have poor visibility of the stage, or the stage is too small for large-scale productions, those constraints limit the nominal capacity (1200 seats) of theatre to an optimal capacity of 1000 seats.

The capacity of service organisations is generally considered to be fixed over the short term, although a number of service organisations have some degree of flexibility to either reconfigure their current capacity or add additional short-term capacity. For example, an airline can reassign a larger aircraft to a particularly popular route and convention centres can reconfigure their meeting spaces. In the case of those two examples, both organisations are dependent on having 'sufficient' time—prior to consumption of their services—to implement the required changes to their delivery operations.[35]

Perishable inventory

One of the key characteristics of service organisations that use revenue management is that their capacity, whether physical or non-physical, is perishable and cannot be stored for later use. For example, a missed hairdresser's appointment, an unsold cabin on a cruise ship or an accountant's unused hour all represent forgone revenue. That is why some service organisations offer incentives, such as discounts or promotions, to fill their unused capacity.

Customer demand can be managed using a reservations system or by implementing a queuing system. Most service organisations that use revenue management use reservations or 'sales in advance' to manage their demand.

Reservations have a value because they provide a service organisation with the opportunity to sell and manage its inventory ahead of actual consumption, and the organisation often receives a payment in advance for that service. Organisations that do not accept reservations can use queues in the short term to manage their capacity. For example, popular nightclubs use queues to select which customers they will admit. The door attendant has the authority to allow only those customers who are perceived to be the 'highest value' customers to enter the club while denying access to the lower value would-be customers.[36]

High fixed costs

Together with a perishable capacity, service organisations that use revenue management tend to have high fixed costs. The pricing structures of those organisations force them to fill their capacity because any revenue they generate after meeting their variable costs can offset their high fixed costs.[37]

Time variability of demand

Customer demand consists of two basic elements—the time when the service is used and the duration of the service experience. Customer demand varies by time of year, day of the week and time of the day. For example, the demand for tour packages to skiing resorts is higher in designated 'high seasons'—the winter time at the resort—which means managers of these resorts must be able to forecast the seasonality of demand so that they can implement effective pricing and capacity decisions.

Allied with the duration of a service is the time that customers spend in contact with a service organisation. Some, like car-rental companies, have a relatively limited level of time with their customers and very low interaction with customers after they have completed the initial rental transaction. On the other hand, professional service organisations such as law firms spend a great deal of time in direct contact with their customers for the duration of the service transaction, such as the number of days that barristers spend in a courtroom.

The key factor that must be considered when delivering a service is whether service organisations charge their time *explicitly* or *implicitly*. When organisations sell time explicitly, they are able to manage their capacity more effectively because they know—with some certainty—the beginning and the duration of the service interaction. For example, the 9 a.m. Qantas flight from Perth to Melbourne is expected to depart at 9 a.m. Western Standard Time and arrive in Melbourne at 3.30 p.m. Eastern Standard Time. Service organisations that provide service experiences sell time implicitly. A theatre, for example, sells tickets to a show but does not explicitly state that a customer has exclusive use of that seat for the two-and-a-half hours that the show is on stage. The challenge for service organisations is to deliver the service that customers are expecting while controlling the time it takes to deliver that service experience.[38]

Using rate fences to manage revenue

An inherent proposition of revenue management is the customisation of price for different consumer segments. When customers are segmented by their value to a service organisation, service marketers can use different rate fences to isolate the low-value customers from their high-value counterparts. Most service organisations have multiple prices for what is essentially the same service in order to create a perception that the service is a series of different products. In that way customers from different value segments feel as though they are purchasing different products. For example, a hotel may charge three different room rates per night—$175, $200 and $250. Customers who pay the $250 rate may receive additional amenities such as breakfast, a larger room with a view and late checkout, while those customers who pay the $175 rate may have to book two weeks in advance and receive a smaller room without being offered breakfast. The conditions that separate the different price categories are known as 'rate fences'.[39]

Rate fences can be either physical or non-physical barriers. Physical fences are tangible service differences that are related to different prices, such as seat location in a theatre, the size and furnishings of a hotel room or the bundle of service amenities. Business class, for example, is better than economy-class air travel because of larger seats and superior food and beverages. Non-physical fences refer to consumption, experience or buyer characteristics, but remain the same basic service. For example, whether customers purchase a discounted ticket 35 days in advance of the flight or pay the full economy fare, there is no difference in economy class on a flight.

Examples of non-physical fences include having to book a certain length of time ahead of the service interaction, not being able to cancel or change a booking (or having to pay cancellation or change penalties), or having to stay over a weekend. Examples of some common rate fences are shown below in Table 7.1.[40]

William Chitty

Table 7.1 Major categories of rate fences

Rate fences	Examples
Physical (service related) fences	
Basic service product	Class of travel (business or economy)
	Size of rental car (6 cylinder or 4 cylinder)
	Size and amenities of hotel room (superior or deluxe)
	Seat location in a theatre or stadium
Amenities	Free breakfast at hotel; airport pick-up
	Valet parking; free golf buggy
	Extra baggage allowance
Service levels	Separate check-in counters
	Improved food and beverages
	Dedicated service phone numbers
Other service benefits	Dedicated airport lounges
Non-physical fences	
Transaction characteristics	
Time of purchase	Discounts for advance purchases
	Discounts for online purchases
Flexible usage	Penalties for cancellations
	Non-refundable reservation fees
Consumption characteristics	
Duration of service	Must stay over a Saturday night
	Must stay more than three nights
Buyer characteristics	
Frequency	Member of loyalty program
Volume of consumption	Top-tier pricing for Platinum members
	Season tickets to football matches
Group membership	Student/seniors' discounts
	Group discounts based on numbers of people

Source: S.E. Kimes & J. Wirtz (2013). Revenue management: Advanced strategies and tools to enhance firm profitability. *Foundations and Trends in Marketing*, 8(1), 17.

↘
INDUSTRY INSIGHT

How revenue management works for airlines

Organisations that typically use revenue management techniques to sell their physical space for a given length of time use a range of prices. Successful adoption of revenue management techniques is defined as maximising the revenue per available space for a given time. In the past, airlines chose not to fly with 100 per cent of their seats sold on every flight because to do so implied that passengers wanting to buy tickets close to the time of departure would be unable to obtain seats. A study by Boeing Commercial Aircraft in 1985 found that when a flight load averaged 60 per cent, 7 per cent of flights would be full and unable to accommodate any additional late-booking passengers. When an aircraft's load factor reached 70 per cent, the 'turn-away' rate increased to 21 per cent.[41]

Since 1985, the widespread adoption of revenue-management techniques that are based on computerised econometric models for analysing demand forecasts has given the airline industry the means to optimise its marginal revenue opportunities. Those variations in price/demand revenue have arisen from segmenting the willingness of airline passengers to pay different prices for a seat on a particular flight. If the market for a particular fight follows a simple linear price/demand relationship, a single fixed fare of $100 for a flight on an aircraft with 100 seats should generate $100 000 in revenue. The same price/demand relationship, however, generates $162 500 when passengers are offered multiple prices for the same flight.

By the mid-1990s, most airline pricing strategies were using computerised yield-management techniques that adopted measures of price elasticity of demand, but were focused on more detailed segmentation by implementing O&D (origin and destination) systems that used passenger data from computer booking platforms such as Amadeus and Sabre. They are basically similar to software platforms that airlines use to sell seats to passengers all over the world and are collectively known as global distribution systems (GDS). Some broad differences however do exist; Amadeus is the largest GDS but is very weak in the United

States, whereas Sabre is strong in North America, but weak elsewhere.

As an example, the activity for Australian domestic aviation in January 2016 was:

↘ 4.82 million passengers were carried on Australian passenger (RPT) flights in January 2016, an increase of 3.3 per cent compared with January 2015. Revenue passenger kilometres (RPKs) flown for the same period were 5.80 billion, an increase of 3.3 per cent compared with January 2015.

↘ Capacity, as measured by available seat kilometres (ASKs), increased by 1.6 per cent compared with January 2015 to a total of 7.54 billion.

With revenue passenger traffic increasing at a faster rate than capacity, the industry-wide load factor—ascertained by dividing RPKs by available seat kilometres (ASKs)—increased from 75.7 per cent in January 2015 to 77 per cent in January 2016.[42] The limitations on airline load factors in the linear price/demand relationship suggested by the 1985 Boeing study, no longer apply to the current revenue management techniques adopted by airlines.

Airlines, in fact, try to achieve the trade-off of marginal yields from consumers in segments that are competing for the same number of airline seats. Detailed analysis of the variables associated with price elasticity of demand using complex computations is now achieved using computational power that was unknown in the early 2000s to optimise load factors, while maximising revenue.

As shown in Figure 7.10, revenue management relies on creating adequate fences between consumers so that all passengers do not attempt to purchase a flight at the lowest price offered by the airline.

William Chitty

The demand curve shown in Figure 7.10 indicates the 'buckets' of inventory that are available for the various price categories. That allows airlines to segment consumers using the time of purchase as the determinant attribute, where those passengers who make a booking close to time of departure pay the highest-priced fares.

Figure 7.10   Different rate fences, at various stages of a demand curve, for airline seats

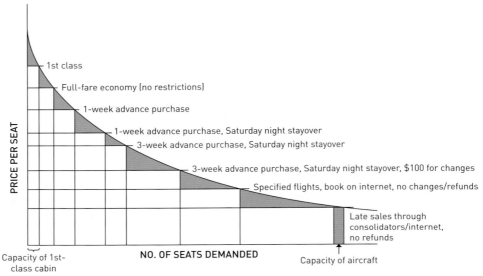

* Dark areas denote amount of consumer surplus (goal of segmented pricing is to reduce this)

Source: S.E. Kimes & J. Wirtz (2013). Revenue management: Advanced strategies and tools to enhance firm profitability. *Foundations and Trends in Marketing*, 8(1), p. 20.

Revenue management started as an inventory allocation system. The increased growth in computational power, and its concomitant decrease in costs, means that the management of price, capacity and time can now help smaller capacity-constrained service organisations make more profitable use of their resources and improve their customers' service experiences.

Summary

This chapter has discussed the various elements that are associated with developing a pricing strategy for a service. Pricing a service is about creating value for the customer and the organisation, and the types of costs that are incurred in the production of a service form the basis of the price of a service. Those costs can be broadly classified as being fixed or variable, and include the financial costs and the time taken to provide a service, as well as the social and psychological costs that are based on the emotional responses of customers. When developing pricing strategies, organisations must also consider competition and consumer legislation (specifically, the *Competition and Consumer Act 2010*) to avoid being accused of unethical behaviour by government agencies such as the ACCC.

The supply of, and demand for a service, is an economic model of determining the price for a service. A demand curve is a representation of the quantity demanded at various price levels, and the shape of a demand curve for a service is influenced largely by the structure of the service industry in which an organisation competes. A pricing strategy is derived from pricing objectives that are generally based on the central issue of what price to charge for a unit of service capacity at a particular point in time. The unit of capacity differs from one service organisation to another.

Different approaches can be used to develop pricing strategies for services and they include:

→ to achieve specific pricing objectives, such as maximising sales or increasing market share
→ to achieve strategic organisational objectives, such as being recognised as the low-priced market leader or increasing the brand's equity in the quality services segment.

Customer demand—and whether it is elastic or inelastic—influences the pricing strategies of a service. Some services are inelastic—that is, as the price of a service increases, the demand for that service does not change significantly because it is a premium service sought after by customers. Most services, however, are elastic in demand, which means that the price for those services may vary due to a number of environmental conditions in the market. Demand considerations also include the nature and times of customer demand for services. Seasonal-demand services such as flights and accommodation are examples of elastic demand in practice.

Revenue management is a strategy that helps to manage customer demand and to develop prices for different segments based on their perceptions of value. Revenue management is the integration of information systems and pricing strategies that allocates the optimal capacity to customers at the right time. There are several characteristics of a service that organisations must consider when they incorporate revenue-management strategies. The first is that the definition of capacity varies depending on the type of service industry, but it is typically based on physical attributes. The second is that capacity—whether physical or non-physical—is perishable and cannot be stored for later use, while the third is that service organisations that use revenue management tend to have high fixed costs. The fourth characteristic to consider is that customer demand consists of two basic elements: the time when the service is used and the duration of the service experience.

Various features provide practical examples of the conceptual frameworks that have been discussed.

Review questions

1 Fully explain who the likely customers would be for the following services:

    a   an undergraduate university degree

    b   a regular car service

    c   an everyday banking account.

    Which costs are the most influential for those customers when they purchase the above services?

2 Is it possible to move a service from having an elastic demand to an inelastic demand? Why, or why not?

3 Why is developing a pricing strategy for services more difficult than the pricing of goods?

4 Explain which pricing strategy (cost-based, competition-based or demand-based) is the most equitable for customers.

5 Long customer lines may be a sign that a service organisation has not effectively managed its customer demand. What pricing strategies could a service organisation adopt to keep its service affordable while minimising long queues?

6 How can an organisation charge different prices to different segments without customers feeling the organisation is engaging in unethical behaviour and disregarding the Australian Consumer Law?

7 What is the role of non-monetary costs for a service organisation? Discuss how those non-monetary costs influence a customer's perception of value.

8 What roles do pricing and revenue management play in setting the different room rates for a five-star hotel and a three-star hotel?

Further reading

Burnham, T.A., Frels, J.K. & Mahajan, V. (2003). Consumer switching costs: A typology, antecedents, and consequences. *Journal of the Academy of Marketing Science*, 31(2), 109.

Grönroos, C. (2016). *Service Management and Marketing: Managing the Service Profit Logic* (4th edn). West Sussex, UK: John Wiley & Sons Ltd.

Hoffman, K.D., Turley, L. & Kelley, S.W. (2002). Pricing retail services. *Journal of Business Research*, 55(12), 1015–23.

Monroe, K.B. (2005), *Pricing: Making Profitable Decisions* (3rd edn). Boston, MA: McGraw Hill Irwin.

Swartz, T.A. & Iacobucci, D. (eds). (2000). *Handbook of Services Marketing & Management*. Thousand Oaks, CA: Sage Publications.

Weblinks

Australasian Professional Services Marketing Association. <www.apsma.com.au>

Australia and New Zealand Marketing Academy. <https://anzmac.wildapricot.org>

Australian Competition and Consumer Commission <www.accc.gov.au>

Not Good Enough. <www.notgoodenough.org>

Robert F. Lusch discusses the past, present, and future of service dominant logic. <www.youtube.com/watch?v=BegxLWmKapU>

Endnotes

1 Bureau of Infrastructure, Transport and Regional Economics (BITRE) (2016). *Lengthy Commutes in Australia*, Report 144, Canberra, ACT.

2 M. Farr (2015). Clogged roads are expensive and is one reason why we spend an average of 85 minutes a day commuting. news.com.au, 11 November. <www.news.com.au/finance/economy/australian-economy/clogged-roads-are-expensive-and-one-%09reason-we-spend-an-average-85-minutes-a-day-commuting/news-%09story/934ad0c2fca8f15dca346fe6934401c7>.

3 ibid.

4 US Department of Transportation (2017). Congestion pricing. <http://ops.fhwa.dot.gov/publications/congestionpricing/sec2.htm>.

5 B. Brook (2015). Radical road charges urged to fight Australia's traffic troubles. news.com.au, 23 October. <www.news.com.au/finance/money/costs/radical-road-charges-urged-to-fight-australias-traffic-troubles/news-story/30749b65f56b2d39149aeca01acf45b4>.

6 P.J. Kraus (2000). Pricing the service offering. In T.A. Swartz & D. Iacobucci (eds), *Handbook of Services Marketing & Management*. Thousand Oaks, CA: Sage Publications, pp. 191–200.

7 V. Zeithaml (1988). Consumer perceptions of price, quality and value. A means-end model and synthesis of evidence. *Journal of Marketing*, 52(July), 2–22.

8 P.J. Kraus (2000). Pricing the service offering. In T.A. Swartz & D. Iacobucci (eds), *Handbook of Services Marketing & Management*. Thousand Oaks, CA: Sage Publications, p.192.

9 S. Sammartino (2016). Leading with price. *Marketing*, 6 April. <www.marketingmag.com.au/hubs-c/leading-with-price-pricing-steve-sammartino/?inf_contact_key=f53bcec86b6d6a75210e4d3eb536029f2ed74a5be994ebb04c4dc38689bdf29c>.

10 Tutor 2U (2015). Explaining price elasticity. <www.tutor2u.net/economics/reference/price-elasticity-of-demand>.

11 L. Allen (2016). Oil prices mean there's never been a better time to fly away. *The Weekend Australian*, 23–24 April, p. 10.

12 Adapted from B. Carroll (2015). Price positioning strategies. eCornell Blog, 7 March <http://blog.ecornell.com/price-positioning-strategies>.

13 R.B. Chase & R.M. Haynes (2000). Service operations management: A field guide. In T.A. Swartz & D. Iacobucci (eds), *Handbook of Services Marketing & Management*. Thousand Oaks, CA: Sage Publications, p. 466.

14 M. Roddan (2016). High card charges to attract penalties. *The Australian*, 27 May, p. 21.

15 Australian Competition and Consumer Commission (2018). Public registers: Optus Mobile Pty Ltd. <http://registers.accc.gov.au/content/index.phtml/itemId/1202416>.

16 Australian Competition and Consumer Commission (2017). Optus to compensate customers shortchanged on data, call and text inclusions. Media release, 5 June. <www.accc.gov.au/media-release/optus-to-compensate-customers-shortchanged-on-data-call-and-text-inclusions>.

17 M. Schmidt (2018). Pricing strategies, pricing models, demand curves. <www.business-case-analysis.com/pricing.html>.

18 ibid.

19 ibid.

20 ibid.

21 ibid.

22 ibid.

23 ibid.

24 ibid.

25 Boundless Business (2018). Product and pricing strategies: The meaning of prices.

26 news.com.au (2014). What it costs to put a plane in the air. 9 March.

27 ibid.

28 M. Bingemann (2016). Joyce says Virgin's move upmarket is backfiring. *The Australian*, 26 February, p. 29.

29 M. Bingemann (2016). Borghetti hits home run as Virgin profit rockets. *The Australian*, 12 February, p. 28.

30 C. Lovelock & J. Wirtz (2011). *Services Marketing: People, Technology, Strategy* (7th edn). Upper Saddle River, NJ: Pearson Education, p. 167.

31 Revenue and yield management. Goodfellow Publishers online.

32 C. Lovelock & J. Wirtz (2011). *Services Marketing: People, Technology, Strategy* (7th edn). Upper Saddle River, NJ: Pearson Education.

33 Revenue and yield management. Goodfellow Publishers online.

34 S.E. Kimes & J. Wirtz (2013). Revenue management: Advanced strategies and tools to enhance firm profitability. *Foundations and Trends in Marketing*, 8(1), 3.

35 ibid., p. 5.

36 ibid., p. 6.

37 ibid., p. 5.

38 ibid., p. 7.

39 ibid., p. 14.

40 ibid., p. 14.

41 M.W. Tretheway & T.H. Oum (1992). *Airline Economics: Foundations for Strategy and Policy*. Vancouver: Centre for Transportation Studies, University of British Columbia, p. 5.

42 Revenue and yield management. Goodfellow Publishers online.

Capacity and demand

Consider the cases of a hotel providing accommodation, a restaurant, a budget airline or public transport. All are in a similar situation with respect to capacity. They all have a fixed level of capacity at any one point in time; that is, the hotel has a fixed number of available rooms, the restaurant has a fixed number of seats, the airline has a fixed number of airline seats and public transport (say buses or trains) can carry a maximum number of passengers. However, the level of demand over time is variable. The objective in all these cases is to optimise revenue through the effective and efficient matching of supply and demand. While capacity can usually be increased over time with increased capital spending, the level of demand can vary dramatically from day to day. The cost of the infrastructure behind the service is very high. This makes increasing capacity to meet increasing or high demand difficult. Acquiring land to build new train lines or bus ways in most cities is very expensive, as is the cost of acquiring new aircraft or building a new hotel.

So, on a day-to-day basis, service and operational management must wrestle with a similar question of how to optimise the matching of demand and supply given the constraints on supply. While the approaches of each market sector vary, they use a standard range of marketing mix practices. For instance, the restaurant knows that on Monday and Tuesday demand is weakest. The solution could be to manipulate the price dimension by offering two main courses for the price of one, or to augment their product offering with a free dessert or free coffee. A hotel located in a beach resort could appeal to a different market segment by partnering with local tourist attractions to provide family packages during winter months. Airlines already have sophisticated pricing mechanisms in place to vary their prices either up or down during the day and the season and on public holidays or festivals. For instance, when demand exceeds supply, airlines can quickly increase prices to regulate that excess demand.

» continued over page

Chapter

8

Managing Productive Capacity and Customer Demand

David Gray

The consequences of not being able to manage the matching of supply and demand can be dire. Customer dissatisfaction, loss of brand reputation and increasing customer complaints are some of the typical outcomes of the inability to manage these processes. The case of public transport, however, is one of the hardest to solve because of the political fallout from any changes in the pricing mechanism and the influence of various stakeholders in the decision-making process. The most recent example of this is the development of the light rail project in the city and eastern suburbs of Sydney. The cost over-runs incurred in building the light rail, disruption to local businesses, and disruption to traffic flows have caused reputational damage to the New South Wales Government and annoyed most stakeholders over the construction phase. Combined, these elements make planning for new services and the management of existing services anything but easy. All the examples presented demonstrate why it is important for marketers to manage capacity to meet demand even at the busiest time of the day.

Introduction

Managing productive capacity is one of the more important aspects of services marketing. The goal is to match productive resources to service demand to create customer value. An organisation does not want to have too many resources sitting idle, but it also does not want consumers and staff to become stressed by poor management of the service process. Therefore, it is critical that an organisation can predict consumer demand in all aspects of service delivery at all times. However, there can be significant difficulty in predicting demand. The foundations of success in this area are to develop operational processes that support strategy implementation, value creation, capability enhancement and, ultimately, increased profitability.

Many businesses would love to be in the position where their products are in such demand that consumers are lining up to buy them. For consumers, being in a line is a two-edged sword: the advantage is that the line acts like a reminder that their decision to consume this service is the correct one; the disadvantage is that standing and waiting to give someone money is one of the more negative experiences consumers are likely to have.

For an organisation, it is also a double-edged sword: the advantage is that the marketing has worked perfectly to the point of over-demand for the product. The disadvantage is that staff are now under stress and pressure to serve customers, and resources are stretched too far and too thin. As a result, customers who have had enough of the queue leave, with a resulting decline in brand reputation.

Even on the internet, queues can occur due to bandwidth and download speeds, and if you have ever tried to buy something in high demand online, such as concert tickets, you might have experienced delays or even the website crashing. So even with the internet dominant in many aspects of service delivery, getting this aspect of services marketing correct is essential to being able to deliver a service that creates value for both the organisation and the consumer.

Learning objectives

After reading this chapter you should be able to:

↘ explain what is meant by demand, capacity and constraints

↘ describe the strategies that can be used to manage demand and capacity

↘ understand how an organisation can adapt its service capacity to match customer demand

↘ explain how the information age has helped manage capacity, demand and service recovery after service failures.

David Gray

Capacity, constraints and demand

Service capacity in a services marketing context is the extent to which a business can serve many customers before service quality standards decline due to demand exceeding supply. Service capacity only makes sense in the context of the resources needed to meet service demands. Much of the emphasis in relation to capacity management rests with both labour capacity and the service interface, often called the servicescape. The most significant types of servicescape failures are cleanliness, mechanical problems and facility design issues.[1]

The capability to produce enough of a specific product or service will depend on the ability of the organisation to effectively and efficiently combine sufficient labour, equipment, storage and transport resources to meet customer demand. For instance, the capacity requirements for a chef in the kitchen would be determined by the number of cooks, ovens and stoves, mixing equipment, pots and pans, refrigeration storage capacity, and availability of recipes. The major difference between capacity management in services compared to manufacturing is that the load on service capacity cannot be levelled by inventory buffering, because services are produced and consumed simultaneously.

Constraint management was originally developed by Eliyahu Goldratt in his 1984 book *The Goal*.[2] The theory of constraints (TOC) considers the interaction and linkages between all systems operating within the firm. These linkages and interactions form part of a chain that can be weakened or broken by resource constraints and bottlenecks. Constraints weaken the performance of the whole system to that of the weakest link. Therefore, the objective of constraint management then becomes the minimisation or elimination of the constraint(s) and the maximisation of utilisation.

Demand forecasting is the first step in developing an organisation's financial budgets. It can be difficult and frustrating, depending on the level of uncertainty surrounding the variables that influence both the internal organisational and external environments. The greater the level of uncertainty, the more difficult it is to forecast the period ahead. Demand itself can also have a wide range of meanings in business. Yet understanding demand in practice is important. Demand is simply defined as a consumer's desire for a product. It is important to understand where demand comes from and how it can be predicted. To do this, we will look at one of the first steps of the marketing process: segmentation.

Demand in services marketing

In this section, we consider the influence of the segmentation process, organisational driven demand and the associated costs, risks and benefits, and their effect on demand in services marketing.

Segmenting the market by customer size and value

The process of segmentation, targeting and positioning, as shown in Figure 8.1, is the most important one in marketing (see also Chapter 3). Without segmenting the market, an organisation has no idea who to target, and if it cannot target anyone then it cannot use the marketing mix to position its products in the mind of the consumer.

Segmentation means that an organisation can target the segments that are sizeable, profitable and likely to exist for some years. It can design and develop the value offering for the highest capacity the service can handle before quality starts to decline.[3] The firm can also slightly alter the offering so that it is attractive to each segment for a reason unique to that market. This is called the unique service proposition and allows the organisation the opportunity to build a competitive advantage (see Chapter 3) in each segment.[4] Typical value factors include cost, quality, response time, delivery reliability, convenience, style/fashion, ethical issues, technology, flexibility and personalisation.

This process also gives the organisation a good estimate of how many customers it may have and how many possible customers may demand the product. Organisations can then design their servicescape to handle lengthy periods of sustained demand at full capacity. For example, retailers will often have many checkout counters, which for most of the time will not be staffed. However, during periods of high demand when the store may operate at full capacity, such as Christmas Eve, all counters will be staffed to manage demand without compromising service standards.

To ensure that they can always meet the demands of their target markets, organisations need to continually monitor their markets for any movement in size, value and direction.[5] A good example where this has not been effectively done is in the Australian retail sector, particularly department stores. They failed to realise that much of their market had started to buy products online and were bypassing their brick-and-mortar stores. Many department stores and other retailers are now trying to catch up with their market and convince them of the value of buying products locally.

↘

unique service proposition
The one unique aspect of a service that is not replicated by other service providers. Usually it becomes the competitive advantage for a firm.

Figure 8.1 The six steps in market segmentation, targeting and positioning

Market segmentation	Market targeting	Market positioning
1. Identify segmentation variables (needs and behaviour) and divide market into segments 2. Develop profiles of resulting segments	3. Evaluate the attractiveness of each segment 4. Select the target segments to enter	5. Identify possible positioning concepts for each target segment 6. Select, develop and communicate the chosen positioning concept

Services in Action

Customer service for Millennials

Accurate and deep profiling of your market segment is critical to demand forecasting. Millennials are important because they are the largest segment and outnumber baby boomers. The question to ask is: do your customer service practices match Millennials' needs in both the business-to-customer (B2C) and business-to-business (B2B) markets?

Focus on building intuitive technology

Tech-savvy Millennials are accustomed to the use of multi-function devices including the smartphone and home internet that communicate, entertain, map and educate. They are early adopters of technology compared to previous generations. All these technologies are now easier and more intuitive to use compared to previous generations. The lessons to be learnt from Apple, Google, Facebook and other innovators are that organisations should be careful not to develop technology, systems and processes that are not customer centric, or that are cumbersome or difficult to use.

Purchasing and social networking

Millennials purchase both online and offline and are strong social networkers compared to previous generations. They use Facebook, WhatsApp, Snapchat, Twitter, blogs, YouTube and other social media sites to share their feelings, opinions and behaviours about brands and purchase decisions and other aspects of their lives through electronic alerts, brand reviews and other social media.

Opportunities for brand co-creation

Traditionally brand communication has been a one-way process: from brand to consumer. With brand communication being composed of paid (mainly past), owned (usually static websites) and earned, this is really the era of earned communication. Because of the availability of social media, Millennials have more opportunity to collaborate with brands. This means that if brands better target their messaging to be more relevant to Millennials their communications programs will be more successful. Millennials are in a position because of social media to co-create the product, the brand, with you. Firms that understand this and develop strategies to tap into the co-creation process with Millennials will have a competitive advantage by building greater levels of customer loyalty.

In Australia, however, as shown in Table 8.1, in recent years the proportion of users following businesses or brands via social media has declined. This is particularly noticeable across all age and gender categories except among those aged 30–39.

What do consumers want from businesses or brands that they follow?

Reflecting on the Australian user of social networking, as outlined in Table 8.2, shows that rising importance of discounts and give-aways are the most popular benefits people like to receive from brands that they follow. Importantly, the table also shows that 29 per cent said they were not after anything from businesses or brands on social media, which compares with 34 per cent in 2016.

Customer service and the expansion of self-service options

Millennials have adapted to customer self-service options and generally accept the way technology can reduce the need for human gatekeepers and associated waiting lines. For example, supermarkets have for some time adopted self-service checkouts and soon there will be supermarkets, department stores and the like which will be without checkouts at all. While, of course

Table 8.1 Social networking sites and brand followers

Follows a social networking group associated with a particular brand or business	2011	2012	2013	2014	2015	2016	2017
Total	20%	25%	35%	33%	32%	36%	24%
Male	15%	25%	35%	27%	31%	36%	21%
Female	23%	25%	36%	37%	34%	35%	27%
18 to 29	20%	32%	42%	43%	48%	45%	18%
30 to 39	23%	38%	31%	41%	30%	35%	41%
40 to 49	8%	17%	31%	31%	25%	39%	28%
50 to 64	22%	14%	23%	18%	33%	30%	19%
65+	7%	17%	16%	11%	6%	17%	9%

Sensis (2017). *Sensis Social Media Report 2017*.

Table 8.2 Brand follower expectations

What do consumers want from businesses or brands that they follow?	2011	2012	2013	2014	2015	2016	2017
Discounts	57%	64%	66%	62%	45%	41%	54%
Give-aways	45%	54%	56%	51%	35%	30%	48%
Product information	41%	48%	49%	49%	27%	31%	30%
Invitations to events	41%	38%	38%	34%	26%	26%	22%
Tips and advice	n/a	41%	48%	45%	24%	26%	20%
Information about the company	32%	30%	35%	37%	24%	25%	22%
Feedback forums	32%	31%	34%	34%	20%	19%	19%
Industry information	NA	30%	32%	30%	21%	22%	14%
Entertainment	NA	NA	NA	NA	NA	30%	16%
None of these	NA	NA	NA	26%	34%	34%	29%

Sensis (2017). *Sensis Social Media Report 2017*.

there is cost imperative on behalf of these stores to reduce labour costs through the introduction of self-service options, younger customers, through years of experience with online and self-service solutions, have grown used to these services.

The rise of experience marketing and its use by Millennials

Given rising incomes and educational levels among there is a segment of Millennials who can take advantage of some of the offers provided by experienced marketers. Authentic, personalised and on-demand services provide an opportunity for adventure and discovery and enlightenment. Millennials often view commerce and even obligatory business travel as opportunities for adventure rather than as a burden.

They care about your values as a company

Millennials are more likely to align their values with their purchase behaviour, firms they support and their day-to-day interactions. Whether it's the concern for the environment or focus on healthy lifestyle, political or ethical issues, more than 50 per cent are likely to trial or buy products or services from brands that support the causes they care about, according to research from Barkley, an independent advertising agency. And they're twice as likely to care about whether their food is organic than are their non-Millennial counterparts, according to Boston Consulting Group. They also care about what's genuine and authentic.[6]

Services in Action

Market segments: The fragility of NextGen

Adapted from J. Van den Bergh (2017). *The (fr)agile reality of the Next Generation. How Cool Brands Stay Hot*, **14 September.**

Born into a world where information is at their fingertips, NextGens—that is, according to Van den Bergh (2017), the generation making up Generation Z and their young Millennial counterparts—are experts at instantly notifying others and being notified of everything happening around them. With their smartphones on hand 24/7/365, they are always connected and informed, rendering other devices such as laptops unnecessary. Maintaining their online social presence—which is mainly in the form of live broadcasting, particularly via Snapchat, Instagram or Facebook—is a regular part of their daily routine, outweighing their offline identity.

The unstable environment in which NextGens are being brought up—with easy access to information such as the war on terror and extreme poverty; and being the offspring of what Van den Bergh (2017) calls the 'divorce generation'—is likely to increase the level of fragility among NextGens compared to their older Millennial counterparts, despite the technological advantages of their generation.

Even children aged seven (the youngest of the NextGens) are considered better informed than their parents when it comes to purchases. As well as becoming the main consumers of the future, they already have a great influence on household purchases, from groceries to holiday destinations. As such, they will play a large part in shaping the future of brands.[7]

Organisation-driven demand

Some organisations believe the risks to their brand through a negative consumer experience because of capacity constraints are just too high to contemplate. Other organisations do not have the resources that a major competitor might have and so may wish to create demand at a time when they can offer customers the best possible customer service. For these organisations, a good strategy is to create demand for services. They can do this by a variety of means, such as sales promotions, scheduling more staff, longer or shorter opening hours, or even by altering the value offering. A good example of this is McDonald's, the hamburger chain that no one publicly admits to going to, yet everyone knows about. Several years ago, McDonald's changed its strategy to increase demand across the entire day instead of being focused on just dinner time. It did this by offering a wider range of meals, particularly healthy ones, for each meal period of the day: breakfast, lunch and dinner. It also introduced the McCafé brand, designed to appeal to a more Gen X market. McCafés were still part of the same location, though situated on the fringe of the restaurant. Subsequently, McDonald's experienced a dramatic period of growth, even during the global financial crisis (GFC), and was better able to manage demand within the existing capacity of many of its stores.

Other organisations, such as some in the hospitality industry, offer sales promotions to encourage customers to use services at quieter times of the day. This spreads demand across a wider period of the day and reduces customer wait times.[8] Sales promotions can also increase demand for new services, something that telecommunications companies have used widely to drive consumers to adopt smartphones, by heavily subsidising handsets or spreading their cost over a long period.

Extending opening hours is another tactic that can be used to create demand. In many states in Australia there is trading seven days a week, often for up to 10 hours each day. Retailers can spread demand across the entire day, especially in the evening peak, when things can get hectic. This eases pressure on resources and encourages consumers to shop at other times of the day when the store may be quieter.[9]

The downside is that some organisations do not offer the same quality of service across the day. Customers who arrive early or late in the day may not find suitable staff working, or stock running low on items that were promoted to attract them to use the service at that time. This often happens with public transport, for example, where there can be a substantial drop in service frequency and capacity during off-peak times. Staff who work

David Gray

early or late shifts may also be less motivated than staff who work normal business hours. The ugly side of customer service may be exposed when a tired customer and a tired staff member try to resolve a service issue early or late in the day.

Any organisation that does try to create demand will need to closely examine the costs, risks and benefits of doing so. In fact, examining the costs, risks and benefits of meeting any demand is something organisations should do in all circumstances.

Costs, risks, benefits and value implications

One of the big challenges in demand and capacity management is the cost of providing a higher service capacity. Is it worth the risk? Will all stakeholders benefit? Many organisations have regretted the decision to increase capacity to serve what they think is a fast-growing market only to see that market disappear or splinter before they have had time to make their money back. But increasing capacity can work well. Shopping-centre sizes have increased, and their owners' profits have grown similarly. The growth in shopping centres has largely been driven by the entertainment now on offer in shopping malls, from movie cinemas to restaurants and bars. However, paradoxically the rapid rise in online shopping is likely to place shopping centres in a more difficult position as the types of products traditionally available in-store move online.

Marketing planning helps organisations to understand the costs, risks and benefits of any decision on managing capacity. It also gives organisations a way to model and measure service capacity in a variety of contexts before making any costly decisions.

Capacity can affect service value. Typical service value factors include cost, quality, response time, delivery reliability, convenience, style/fashion, ethical issues, technology, flexibility and personalisation. When capacity cannot meet demand, customers may choose to go elsewhere rather than wait. A capacity shortage can create waiting lines (i.e. a backlog) and therefore affect response time, dependability of delivery and flexibility.

Strategies for matching supply and demand

As summarised in Figure 8.2, the following section considers a range of strategies that organisations can use to match supply and demand.

Demand strategies

Demand-management strategies for services are different from that of manufacturing because services are produced and consumed simultaneously. In many services from

Figure 8.2 Strategies for matching supply and demand for services

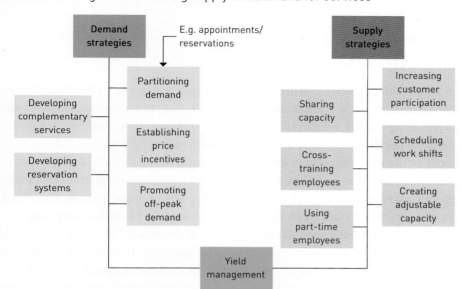

restaurants to hairdressing, education and car repairs, demand smoothing during the forecast period is important because it helps to minimise operating costs through better scheduling of resources.

Demand-management strategies are designed to smooth the load on capacity, and different strategies apply to different service segments including time, space, price and special promotions. For instance, the use of appointments could be used where time is a constraint (e.g. legal, medical and dental services). Reservations could be used to manage demand where space is a constraint (e.g. restaurants, airlines, hotels and movie theatres). Pricing can also be used to smooth demand fluctuations such as Uber's use of surge pricing during periods of peak demand. Special promotions including weekday or early-bird specials can be used where weak demand is a constraint. Likewise, early-bird specials can be used to bring forward demand. Complementary services provide another opportunity to smooth demand; for example, service variations with different price points could be used to provide greater opportunity for sales staff to redirect customers into slower moving services.

Services in capital-intensive industries with high fixed costs and low marginal costs such as movie theatres, sporting events, airline tickets, hotels, electricity and gas services use yield management to match supply and demand. Yield management maximises revenues through differential pricing, including price incentives, reservation systems and overbooking. It requires segmenting the customer base, using multiple price levels (e.g. movie theatres, sporting events, airline tickets, hotels, electricity and gas pricing). In

David Gray

electricity and gas pricing, off-peak energy consumption attracts a lower rate per kilowatt than the peak demand price.

Supply strategies

On the supply side, capacity constraints can be smoothed by increasing flexibility using casual and part-time workers and labour hire firms. These approaches can also have negative aspects regarding quality, reliability and increased transport time, but there are trade-offs in all capacity decisions. Other strategies used to smooth supply include sharing capacity (e.g. hotels at capacity referring guests to other hotels in the chain; the sharing of office space, computer facilities and admin staff between businesses); cross-training employees so they can carry out multiple functions or cross-sell multiple services (e.g. banking services and insurance)—although the cross-sell of services in the banking industry has caused considerable reputational damage because of disclosures in the Australian Royal Commission. Another supply-side strategy used to ease capacity constraints is to increase customer participation in the buying process, such as implementing self-service checkouts in supermarkets. Capacity constraints can also be eased through work-shift scheduling and the creation of adjustable capacity using alliances and partnerships.

Managing capacity: challenges and opportunities

Managing capacity in a service setting needs to present challenges and opportunities, not problems.

The challenges

Challenges in managing capacity come in many forms for organisations. They can be resource-based challenges, such as people and equipment, or they can be in the form of rapid growth in demand for services beyond what the organisation can handle. Perhaps the challenges may lie with the consumer market itself; for example, some services require the consumer to self-learn how to use technology before they can access the product. Challenges, if managed correctly, can become opportunities for the organisation, but managing them is easier said than done.

There are five main types of resource-based challenges in managing capacity for an organisation:

1 *people*—staff selection, training of staff, managing staff and staff numbers
2 *process*—do the processes in place allow for an effective service to be delivered and maintained?

3   *physical evidence*—such as equipment and the servicescape setting
4   *financial*—such as profits, financial risk and funding of services
5   *time*—time taken to produce a service.

People

People are one of the biggest challenges in managing capacity and demand. Without the right number of people to serve customers, wait times will be longer, existing staff more stressed and customers angry about having to wait to be served.[10]

However, as every organisation has its own culture, training and systems, finding the right people to serve customers is not easy. First, the right staff must be selected. In some industries, such as online call centres where staff turnover is very high, companies take anyone who meets very basic criteria. Yet in more specialised service industries, such as medicine, education and finance, staff selection can take months and is a highly competitive and expensive process.

Then there is the training of staff. This is not an easy or fast process if it is done properly. Some jobs, such as highly specialised medical occupations, can require over a decade of training. You yourself are undergoing a degree that will take several years for you to be trained to do some occupations in business that will also require you to do further training on the job. Yet training is necessary for people to be able to do their job properly and therefore help manage consumer demand.

Managing staff is also important. Imagine working in a high-customer-contact position such as in a call centre or the returns desk of a big retailer on Boxing Day. Eight hours of doing a job like these would be a challenge for most people. Yet having people to do such jobs is important for the organisations concerned. Therefore, the management of employees is crucial to ensure they not only want to stay in the job but also enjoy doing the job so that customers' expectations are exceeded.

Management also must understand that to successfully manage consumer demand and capacity it needs to have the right number of staff on at the right time. Many successful service-based organisations will have the most number of experienced staff scheduled to work at times of peak demand. It is essential with staff scheduling for organisations to look at the times of peak demand and not average demand. This will help to minimise the gaps in service delivery, ensure a more consistent service quality and reduce the time it takes to deliver a service to a consumer.[11]

If there are queues, this is usually because management has not correctly identified the periods of peak demand and does not have enough staff rostered to manage the demand. Correct staff management will also mean that an organisation can increase its consumer capacity. It may be able to spread its peak demand period across a longer period and smooth out the peaks and troughs in demand across the entire day. This will not only help with people management, but also increase the organisation's basic services and help reduce any gaps in quality.

David Gray

Having the right number of well-trained and highly motivated staff will help an organisation that wants to exceed the expectations of its consumers, not just meet them.

Process

Managing customer demand and capacity effectively also means having the right processes in place. Processes help streamline service delivery, ensure that staff have a benchmark system in place to deliver a high-quality service always, and manage critical incidents even at times of high demand on the organisation.[12]

Having the right procedures in place reduces the complexity in servicing the customer. This means that when staff serve customers they understand their role and can work as a team to provide the best possible service. For example, in most banks during peak demand times staff focus on their role in the process of serving customers.

Multi-skilled staff who are trained in multiple processes can help the organisation manage consumer demand and increase organisational capacity by being able to take on different tasks.[13] Although it can be challenging to train staff to learn different tasks, it does give the organisation that additional capacity and flexibility to handle most situations without gaps emerging in service quality, even when short-staffed.

For many organisations, the time spent on establishing and maintaining processes can seem inefficient. Yet it is these very processes that can help overcome the challenges faced by staff in managing demand and allow them to create new opportunities for the organisation.

Physical evidence

The servicescape model considers the effect of the physical non-human surroundings in which the service encounter takes place. The servicescape does not include processes (e.g. methods of payment, billing), external promotions (e.g. advertising, public relations, social media, websites) or functions of the back office, which customers do not normally visit. The challenges associated with servicescape are that many firms cannot afford to design their business to be service-friendly. And not all businesses with well-designed servicescapes serve their customers well. An effective servicescape design can facilitate throughput, capacity utilisation and the level of demand.

Not having an adequate servicescape environment can restrict the capacity of many businesses.[14] Many retailers in large shopping centres have only limited space and control over their servicescape environments, and need to use other tactics, such as hard seats, to help turn over consumers quickly without affecting the service quality.

Some servicescapes, such as many public transport locations, also have no way of managing queues and wait times for products, leaving consumers frustrated with the quality of service that they receive. This is mainly because they were never designed to be consumer-friendly or do not have the flexibility to meet changing demand, as the opening vignette of this chapter highlights.

throughput
Net sales (S) less totally variable cost (TVC), generally the cost of the raw materials (T = S − TVC). Note that T only exists when there is a sale of the product or service. Producing materials that sit in a warehouse does not form part of throughput but rather investment. This is different from the traditional definition, which usually defines 'throughput' as the rate at which products are produced, regardless of whether they are sold.

Financial

Another significant challenge faced by many organisations in managing capacity is financial constraints. But not all organisations can afford to address even one of the aforementioned points; even large organisations need to budget and plan where to spend their resources across the organisation.

Consumers are very unforgiving of negative experiences and many often wonder why a service that they think is making a huge profit for the organisation cannot be expanded and improved almost immediately. However, the profit from one service might be funding another service that yields a far lower profit.

The lack of adequate financing can also occur quickly for organisations. Rising interest rates, costs of labour and rents all hurt organisations every year, yet are also difficult to pass on to consumers without negative impacts.

Fluctuating levels of demand can also be challenging. Some services are profitable during peak periods but not at other times. While organisations can put limitations on when these services are offered, this can lead to the loss of consumers in non-peak times.

The challenge for organisations when it comes to financial resources is whether or not to offer as many services as possible at a lower quality level or to offer very few services but at a higher quality level. It's a tough challenge, but if you work in services marketing it is one you will need to answer.

Time

Time also presents a big challenge to service-based organisations. To a customer, one minute may feel like 10, 10 minutes an hour, and an hour a lifetime! In nearly all such industries, time is not just important from a consumer perspective, it is how the organisation measures its efficiency, profitability and effectiveness.[15]

Time can be an opportunity. If the organisation can reduce the time it takes to serve a customer, then it can not only deal with a situation of high demand but also increase its capacity to serve more customers. It is a challenge because there are some services, such as medical or legal, where the organisation cannot reduce the time it takes to serve a customer because to do so would place too great a risk on all involved in the transaction.

Organisations can, however, try to manage their time better. They may want to encourage customers to purchase a service at a quieter time of day, such as with a 'happy hour' type of promotion, and thereby spread their customer load across a longer period. They also may want to use more staff, as well as more-experienced staff, at times of high demand to ensure that wait times do not increase too much.

Other tactics with time might include placing more services on electronic delivery platforms such as the internet or phone. This will help customers manage their time better and allow the organisation to increase its customer capacity at the physical point of contact. The trading hours of a business can also be expanded to allow customers to access services across a longer period of the day. For example, in recent times banks have sought

David Gray

to increase their trading hours, with some banks now including weeknights and weekends in their standard hours of business.

Time is one aspect of capacity demand that can be considered both a challenge and an opportunity.

INDUSTRY INSIGHT

Amazon's approach to supply chain management

Amazon.com has focused on supply-chain management and technology innovation to improve online retailing.

Rapid growth through supply-chain strategies

Like Dell in a previous generation, Amazon's focus on the speed of delivery presents a major competitive threat to other similar retailers. Amazon's strategic approach has enabled it to achieve more than $100 billion in sales revenue and an annual average growth rate of 20 per cent.

An innovative delivery service

The Amazon Prime service was launched in 2005. Its annual membership fee, like Costco's, would alter the competitive dynamics of the industry. In return for their subscription, customers were guaranteed a two-day shipping turnaround. When its competitors started offering similar services, Amazon responded by offering its Amazon Prime Now one-hour delivery service.

Supply-chain management practices

Amazon has followed the precedent set by Dell's adventurous supply-chain strategies of the 1980s and 1990s by using its demand-configuration website to deal directly with customers. Amazon boasts strategically located warehouses, first-rate transport systems and sophisticated inventory management. Its supply chain is now more efficient than any other major company's in the world. The basis of its success is due to several factors, including:

↘ *It outsources inventory management and insources logistics:* By focusing on its infrequently purchased products, Amazon is able, through outsourcing, to quickly supply a vast array of products in a timely manner. Essentially, it follows the Pareto 80/20 model, with nearly 82 per cent of Amazon's sales comprising third-party sellers. Amazon meets its one-hour or same-day shipping promise by using its own delivery vehicles.

↘ *It offers a variety of delivery options:* Amazon has successfully segmented its delivery systems to cater for different customer time requirements including Prime customers' delivery, one-day delivery, first-class delivery and free super-saver.

↘ *It has a push—pull strategy for supply-chain success:* Amazon has strategically located its warehouses close to major population centres. For selling products in its warehouses it uses a push strategy; when selling third-party products it uses a pull strategy.

↘ *Its warehouses are classed and zoned*: Amazon maintains more than 70 fulfilment centres in the United States and employs more than 90 000 people full-time. The location, size and number of warehouses and the scale of its operations enable it to achieve fast delivery times. Its warehouses are divided into five storage areas: books and magazines, high-demand full-case products, high-demand products in smaller quantities, irregularly shaped and low-demand products, and a storage area for random products.

Amazon in Australia

Amazon Australia opened its online store on 5 December 2017. While Amazon will be a relatively small player in the Australian market for a while, this opening will increase the pressure on local retailers to lift their game. Its first offering in the Australian market was a little underwhelming with free delivery only available on certain products, and to qualify for it the minimum spend was $49. Shipping rates varied according to where products were to be shipped and how soon they were required. Since shipping speeds are the main reason for shopping online, Amazon will no doubt find ways of improving on this.

Warehouse automation and robotics

In 2015, Amazon rebranded Kiva Systems (a company it acquired in 2012) as Amazon Robotics. Amazon Robotics enables warehouse activities to be completed quickly without human involvement. As of January 2017, Amazon had more than

45 000 warehouse robots. Amazon seems to be ahead of its competitors with respect to robotics. However, the Amazon competitive advantage is likely to slow in the next few years as competitors catch up.

Minimising the supply-chain cost

Amazon has the economy of scale and the industry-leading supply-chain strategies to minimise its overall supply-cost per unit. This has presented a significant competitive barrier to its rivals, whose sales volumes are lower and who only have their own warehouses.

Drones: A look into the future

In 2013, Amazon revealed its Amazon Prime Air delivery service: a drone-based delivery system for delivering product weighing less than 2.25 kilograms in locations within 16 kilometres of Amazon's fulfilment centres in no more than 30 minutes. In November 2017, the company announced it had developed a self-destructing drone—the purpose being that it could self-destruct while in flight in case of an emergency such as potential property damage or injury to people. This initiative shows Amazon's innovative and forward-thinking capacity to maintain its industry leadership position by adapting industry practices as technology advances.

Amazon as a manufacturer

Due to its scale, Amazon can achieve low-cost production of a wide range of products such as batteries, backpacks and Bluetooth speakers. This has made Amazon financially strong and enabled the company to steal market share from other manufacturing companies. By

David Gray

combining manufacturing to support its retail operations, Amazon has an important revenue growth opportunity.

In summary

Amazon's supply-chain innovations and economies of scale have proven to be quite a challenge for its competitors. It is able to keep the pressure on its competitors by forcing its major suppliers to invest more in supply-chain automation, reducing delivery time, increasing the number of warehouses and even engaging in product manufacturing. Simultaneously, Amazon's acquisition of Whole Foods cements its move into bricks and mortar, further emphasising the convergence of traditional retail and e-commerce strategies. With impending advances in robotics, drones and other autonomous vehicles, who knows what the future holds for Amazon.[16]

The opportunities

Opportunities exist everywhere when it comes to managing capacity. Organisations can work with consumers and undertake market research to better understand the service needs of their clients. Market research need not be expensive. Even a very simple survey that produces only descriptive results will give some valuable insights and is better than no research at all.

Predictive and causal research is the best type of research to conduct to understand the needs of consumers, but not everyone can afford that cost. Survey websites such as <www.surveymonkey.com> are cheap and effective to use. The opportunities for using market research for an organisation are endless when it comes to understanding how to deal better with capacity and meet the needs of its consumers.

Electronic service-delivery methods have already changed the face of many industries. Telephone interfaces have been around for a long time now but more recently the cheapest service-delivery method, and the one that is also the cheapest to increase in periods of high demand, the internet, has become very popular for service-based firms to meet the needs of their consumers at any time of the day or night.[17]

Organisations can also view demand for one service as an opportunity to see where consumer desires are the strongest. If they can increase resources in this area, they can also increase their capacity and therefore their customer base. Managing capacity well can create the opportunity to increase the range of services on offer or add value to existing services. If one service is in high demand and capacity is tight for that service, the organisation can add value by creating a flexible service offering differing service components that can be adapted to changing demands and segments,[18] or it can create new services to meet the needs of a growing customer market.

There are many other opportunities that organisations can take advantage of by effectively managing capacity and demand. Among them are the opportunity to strengthen the brand and to build stronger relationships with consumers and so make the entire business more viable and profitable.

Demand forecasting

The following sections consider the relationship between demand forecasting and risk management, the various kinds of functional risks and the steps necessary to build an effective forecasting system.

Demand forecasting and risk management

Virtually all demand forecasts carry a certain amount of risk, and many will be wrong due to uncertainty, bias and random fluctuations. The accuracy of demand forecasting for services will depend on a wide range of factors including the type of service, the industry, the time horizon used, the experience of the forecasters and the availability of past data. The relationship between demand forecasting and risk management (see Figure 8.3) shows the interplay between marketing goals and strategies and the major variables that drive those goals and strategies.

Once the goals and strategies are defined, the targeted demand forecasts can be made. However, the achievement of those demand forecasts will be substantially influenced by the number of internal and external resources invested to achieve the targets. The investment decisions used to achieve the targeted demand levels will then be translated into management processes, which will be subject to risk multipliers including the lead time required to implement all the necessary marketing mix elements and the operational cycle of the organisation. For instance, as part of the promotional program in the case of an insurance broker, it may take a month to design a new website or develop a new social media campaign. To get a new client on board, the operational cycle could take a week to obtain all the necessary details of the insured property and to check the credit-worthiness of the new client.

Figure 8.3 Demand forecasting and risk management

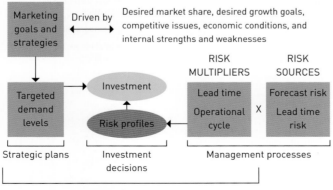

David Gray

As highlighted in Figure 8.3, the sources of risk include both lead-time risk and forecast risk. The lead-time risk relates to the amount of time it takes to mobilise all the resources necessary to implement the marketing mix program. The forecast risk relates to the accuracy of the forecast. Forecasters should be measuring both the absolute error between forecast and actual and be cognisant of forecast bias. The presence of bias in a forecast indicates a problem with the forecast model or that someone is intentionally trying to manipulate the forecast. The classic case is where a sales manager will produce a conservative sales forecast to improve the likelihood of achieving the target.

Demand forecasting and functional risks

Organisations that supply services can be subject to a multitude of functional risks, and some examples are shown in Figure 8.4. These functional risks can have a significant effect on the level of demand forecast accuracy. The extent of the risks will depend on exogenous factors including the degree of market volatility as well as internal factors such as the quality of process controls implemented throughout the organisation. For instance,

Figure 8.4   Influences on demand forecast accuracy

Sales and marketing	Sevice design	Supplier interface	Operations	Channels	Systems	Finance and admin
• Competitors' activities	• Poor design	• Supplier relations	• Poor quality	• Shortages	• Schedule vs demand	• Poor feedback
• Changes in customers' requirements	• Design interference	• Poor contracts	• Inappropriate systems/ equipment	• Poor quality	• Data accuracy	• Poor records
• Change in market needs	• Product variety	• Procurement processes	• Poor workflow	• Long lead times	• Batch sizes	• Poor costing
• Seasonality	• Lead time	• Poor logistics	• Urgent orders	• Inefficient transport	• System knowledge	• Wrong KPIs
• Ill-defined service specifications	• Service changes	• Long supply chain	• Bottlenecks	• Changes in customer demands	• Staff training	• Payment terms
• Late specifications	• Non-standard components	• Long lead times		• Poor warehouse location		• Lack of accountability
• Poor economic and market data				• Demographics		
• Poor communication				• Inadequate facilities		
• Inconsistent advertising						
• Discount structures						
• Ad-hoc promotions						

in the sales and marketing area, activities such as unexpected promotional programs by the organisation or its competitors, or the launch of unexpected new services by the organisation or its competitors, can disrupt demand forecasts.

In the finance and administration function area, for example, poor credit control could result in longer customer repayment cycles or increasing bad debts. In the operations area, poor-quality service control, bottlenecks or the facilitation of urgent orders could lead to reduced throughput and delays to order recognition. Therefore, those responsible for demand forecasting need to be cognisant of these kinds of potential risks.

Building an effective demand forecasting system

There are real benefits to be achieved in improving your organisation's demand forecasting, which will help to:

→ increase profitability

→ achieve greater customer satisfaction

→ improve communication between departments

→ make it easier to manage the operational process

→ avoid the high costs of under- or over-resource utilisation.

One of the key aspects of forecasting is to recognise that forecasting is a process that requires a methodical approach if it is going to be both effective and efficient. The following five steps are highlighted in Figure 8.5, and usually form the basis of most forecasting systems.

Step 1: Establish policies and procedures

Policies and procedures set the ground rules for demand forecasting by clearly identifying who has responsibility for forecasting, what the process will be and how all the organisational units interact with and support the process. They don't have to be complex, but they do have to be clear, logical and disseminated throughout the organisation.

Step 2: Select the forecasting tools and techniques

The forecasting tools and techniques identify which qualitative and quantitative methods are to be used. For instance, the Delphi method is a survey-based forecasting method that is sent to an expert panel where their forecasts are shared in an attempt to reach a consensus.

Typical forecasting techniques used are judgmental, time series trend analysis and causal forecasting. Judgmental forecasting can be problematic because it relies on the experience of the forecaster. For instance, there could be bias, conflict between different organisational levels (e.g. a 'don't rock the boat' mentality, domination by senior personnel,

David Gray

Figure 8.5   The five steps of the forecasting system

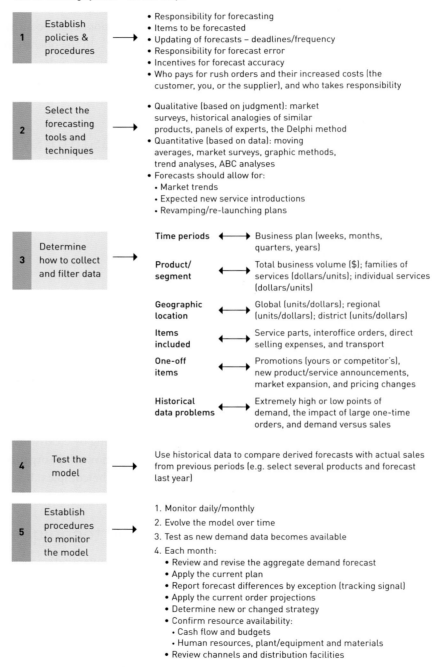

The forecasting system – the five steps

1 Establish policies & procedures
- Responsibility for forecasting
- Items to be forecasted
- Updating of forecasts – deadlines/frequency
- Responsibility for forecast error
- Incentives for forecast accuracy
- Who pays for rush orders and their increased costs (the customer, you, or the supplier), and who takes responsibility

2 Select the forecasting tools and techniques
- Qualitative (based on judgment): market surveys, historical analogies of similar products, panels of experts, the Delphi method
- Quantitative (based on data): moving averages, market surveys, graphic methods, trend analyses, ABC analyses
- Forecasts should allow for:
  - Market trends
  - Expected new service introductions
  - Revamping/re-launching plans

3 Determine how to collect and filter data

Time periods ◄──►	Business plan (weeks, months, quarters, years)
Product/ segment ◄──►	Total business volume ($); families of services (dollars/units); individual services (dollars/units)
Geographic location ◄──►	Global (units/dollars); regional (units/dollars); district (units/dollars)
Items included ◄──►	Service parts, interoffice orders, direct selling expenses, and transport
One-off items ◄──►	Promotions (yours or competitor's), new product/service announcements, market expansion, and pricing changes
Historical data problems ◄──►	Extremely high or low points of demand, the impact of large one-time orders, and demand versus sales

4 Test the model

Use historical data to compare derived forecasts with actual sales from previous periods (e.g. select several products and forecast last year)

5 Establish procedures to monitor the model

1. Monitor daily/monthly
2. Evolve the model over time
3. Test as new demand data becomes available
4. Each month:
   - Review and revise the aggregate demand forecast
   - Apply the current plan
   - Report forecast differences by exception (tracking signal)
   - Apply the current order projections
   - Determine new or changed strategy
   - Confirm resource availability:
     - Cash flow and budgets
     - Human resources, plant/equipment and materials
   - Review channels and distribution facilities

defence of previous positions or the bandwagon effect) moving towards a consensus when such is not desirable. The use of trend analysis is a well-trodden path where forecasters look for the trend, the cycle, seasonal fluctuations and random fluctuations. Causal forecasting aims to develop the best statistical relationship between a dependent variable and one or more independent variables. For instance, predicting sales (the dependent variable) may be a function of many independent variables including seasonality, location, demographic characteristics and size of order. The most common model approach used in practice is regression analysis. Common weaknesses with causal forecasting are the possibility that the relationships between the variables are not linear.

Other forecasting techniques often used are 'Pareto analysis' (the 80/20 rule) and A-B-C analysis. Pareto analysis focuses on the 'critical few', not on the 'trivial many'. In applying Pareto analysis to demand forecasting the key question is: which products/services (and which customers) generate the bulk (say 80%) of the revenue? The answer is that in most cases, approximately 20 per cent of the products and customers generate 80 per cent of the revenue.

With respect to A-B-C analysis, the A items represent the greatest volume of sales and are reviewed on a detailed basis. The B items are only reviewed when there is a significant deviation between the forecast and actual demand (i.e. exception reporting, which is a very powerful concept). The C items are only reviewed on an aggregate basis. The A-B-C categorisation of items must be reassessed on a periodic basis, as items can move from one category to another. The overall objective of this kind of forecasting analysis is to get sales forecasters to concentrate on the critical items.

Step 3: Determine how to collect and filter data

Determining how to collect and filter the data is particularly important because it will shape the organisation's ability to effectively analyse the results of trends. This requires selection of the forecasting time period, the service segments to analyse, the geographic locations to analyse, the depth of coverage for each service segment and also the interlinkage with direct costs associated with each of the demand-generation areas.

Step 4: Test the model

This is essentially a trial-and-error approach, which may require refinement throughout the demand forecasting cycle when forecasts can be compared to actual results.

Step 5: Establish procedures to monitor the model

The monitoring step represents an ongoing evolving process that covers the frequency of analysis, comparison against budgets, the development of dashboards to visually represent the analysis process and the modification of the system based on the latest inputs.

David Gray

Services in Action

Forecasting in primary healthcare: case study

What factors should you consider when trying to forecast demand and manage capacity in primary health care? Heroman, Davis and Farmer investigated demand forecasting and capacity management in a primary healthcare context in the United States. In the context of healthcare, demand forecast is defined as an estimate of the number of care events and their duration required by a given population. Heroman et al. maintain that good forecasting requires an iterative process based on accurate historical data and good judgment. This case investigated primary healthcare clinics (e.g. internal and family medicine; paediatrics) in the military sector, including current personnel, their families and retired families. The activity recorded included such things as number of visits, mammograms, immunisations and prescription renewals.

Demand forecasting

Demand forecasting is used to determine the allocation of healthcare resources and for budget development. Effectively and efficiently allocating resources is critical for planning and managing care, as well as for access and continuity of care. A clinic's patient-visit history in conjunction with a history of services patients obtained elsewhere help to determine its demand forecast. However, it is also important to plan for the possibility of increased demand (due to, for example, services that can't be counted) as capacity and access increase. More planned and available preventative services can also increase demand.

Heroman et al. used the clinic's visit history—including emergency room visits, urgent care and other primary healthcare clinics in the group—when establishing the demand forecast, but they did not include visits out of the local area. The objective is to determine and then narrow the gap between demand and capacity (e.g. by developing mitigation strategies such as outsourcing urgent cases during busy periods), which is crucial for improving access and continuity of primary healthcare. This gap can be narrowed by increasing capacity or decreasing demand, thereby minimising patient dissatisfaction and increasing overall care. Not having a gap between demand and capacity could lead to overstaffing, so good planning and the ability to adjust capacity to meet demand are important in order to achieve a workable balance.

Capacity management

In a primary healthcare context, capacity management includes the number of available appointments; the types of appointments; examination rooms; hours; access to available appointments (phone and/or online) and clinical information; the number of support staff and their duties; patient flow; and access to the primary healthcare team when a physical visit is not needed.

Demand management

Heroman et al. suggest that an alternative way of closing or narrowing the gap is to decrease demand. This could be achieved using proactive measures such as delivering coordinated care and long-term healing relationships to reduce episodic care based on illness and patient complaints. A healthcare team that focuses on prevention and education can also decrease the need for physical visits. This can then be replaced with over-the-phone advice, which can be given by healthcare staff other than the doctor.[19]

Adaptive service capacity and value co-creation

Flexibility and service adaptability are critical requirements for service organisations to more effectively match supply and demand. In this section, we discuss the role of adaptive service capacity and value co-creation.

Adaptive service capacity

Adapting service capacity to meet the needs of the target market is the most common method used by organisations in periods of high demand. Adaptive service capacity means that organisations need to have the ability to adapt to changing consumer service demands on the organisation.[20] This does not mean that the organisation must keep some capacity aside, and therefore can never run at 100 per cent capacity. What it needs is to have strategies in place to increase capacity if required, or perhaps even decrease capacity if a service starts to fall in demand to the point where it is no longer profitable.

An example of this in practice is a local public transport network. During peak hours, when there is a high demand, the network is able to run trains or buses at very frequent intervals. During the day, when demand is less, the service can still run at a profit by reducing the number of services to match the lower demand.

adaptive service capacity
An organisation's ability to adapt to changing consumer service demands

Value co-creation

Value co-creation provides a mechanism for adaptive service capacity. It allows an organisation to have more flexible capacity and to adapt more to rapid changes in demand without affecting its level of service quality.[21] Value co-creation occurs when the consumer works with the organisation to produce their own service. Using public transport again as an example, many of us will now buy tickets from an automated machine and swipe this ticket ourselves to enter and exit the service.

Value co-creation is most noticeable as an adaptive-service-capacity strategy in technology.[22] Technology allows consumers to serve themselves across a wide range of

David Gray

services, from banking to education to healthcare, and they can now serve themselves 24/7/365. Some services have now expanded from the internet to smartphones to adapt to people's increasingly busy lives, again helping to increase the capacity of the service offering while maintaining acceptable levels of service quality. From premium weather services to online entertainment, smartphones are more than capable of matching most computer-based services. The advent of computer tablets has already accelerated the mobility of service delivery and consumption.

Causes of customer experience program failure

Customer experience (CX) programs can often fail to meet their objectives, getting bogged down in simple transaction metrics.[23] Over time, data accumulates and analysis paralysis establishes itself. The business objectives that were originally set become lost in the organisation and inertia leads to, at best, an incremental approach rather than the gleaning of deep and useful customer insights that should result from these kinds of CX programs.

So, what are the characteristics of CX failure?

Most CX programs fail because of a:

1   lack of innovation focus
2   lack of metrics integration and the goals of the business
3   lack of leadership, bureaucratic reporting and process inertia.

1 Lack of innovation focus

A CX program's purpose needs to be clear. A CX program leader must be able to articulate the customer or business benefits of the program. CX programs track performance to identify performance weaknesses and to improve performance over time. So, continual improvement is a natural part of any CX program. It's about incremental continual change, which is the basis of any quality assurance program.

Effective CX programs usually analyse the drivers of performance and then measure actual performance against the business goals. However, it's the actions that result from analysis of the performance drivers that are critical. If change doesn't take place, it may be due to reporting paralysis, lack of 'think time' or lack of collaboration.

In order to avoid reporting paralysis and ensure you are strategic with your data, the *purpose* of data must be kept in mind at all times.

Effective inter-functional cooperation and coordination is required to ensure that the CX program results in real change. CX stakeholders need to actively work on making improvements that are customer focused. This can be difficult to achieve, with different departments often having competing objectives.

2 Lack of metrics integration and the goals of the business

Performance improvement can be the result of a complex interaction of variables. CX programs often use performance drivers to measure success; however, it is sometimes difficult to ascribe cause with effect because of this complex interaction between variables. Furthermore, not all aspects of the business can be controlled, which can create a level of uncertainty about the potential results of the CX program. For instance, climatic events, strikes or government intervention could interfere with the performance of a CX program. Importantly, KPIs for the program should be approved by the chief marketing officer.

Things to consider include:

↘ *Cost to acquire and serve a customer (CAC and CSC):* These costs can vary significantly between market segments. The objective here is to lower CAC and CSC without diminishing the CX.

↘ *Customer penetration and share:* Customer penetration is about having more customers than your competitors. There is market share and share of wallet. These critical measures are the ultimate measures of how consumers spend their money. Double jeopardy[24] is also an important marketing construct which asserts that, with few exceptions, brands with relatively low market share have far fewer buyers in a time period and relatively lower brand loyalty.

↘ *Customer lifetime value (CLV):* A good CX program should analyse customer lifetime value. CLV is the net current value of future customer revenues (revenues – costs incurred). CLV is important because not all customers are created equal. Once you recognise your most profitable customers using CLV, you can optimise the allocation of your resources for maximum profits. You can also customise your future marketing strategies for a specific audience.

↘ *Customer churn:* Customer churn measures the extent to which customers switch to alternative brands. A well-run CX program can help to minimise the number of customers who stop using your brand (attrition) or abandon it altogether (defection).

↘ *Net promoter score[25] (NPS):* The NPS generally uses a single customer survey question, namely: 'How likely is it that you would recommend our company/product/service to a friend or colleague?' The scale is usually from 0 to 10. 'Promoters' score 9 to 10 and are likely to buy, remain customers for longer and refer other potential customers. 'Detractors' score 0 to 6 and are less likely to recommend your product or services. 'Passives' score 7 and 8, with their behaviour falling in the middle of promoters and detractors. The NPS is calculated by deducting the percentage of detractors from the percentage of promoters. (For the purposes of calculating an NPS, passives are considered part of the total respondents, so they reduce the count towards the total number of respondents, thus decreasing the percentage of detractors and promoters and pushing the net score towards 0.) A word of caution, however: satisfied customers are not necessarily money-making customers.

3 Lack of leadership, bureaucratic reporting and process inertia

Customer needs are continually evolving, so CX programs must also evolve. An effective CX leader will revitalise CX programs regularly and avoid process inertia, but they must be given ownership of the program if they are to be successful, without any bureaucracy. A CX leader must have the expertise to run the program and the authority to access the resources for it.

David Gray

Summary ↘

In this chapter, we have described how to manage productive capacity and consumer demand. The differences, and the relationship, between demand (a consumer's demand for a product) and capacity (the maximum service production level) were explained in a services marketing context. Effectively managing each maximises the value return for both the organisation and the consumer.

For *demand*, some of the important strategies and techniques that can be used by management are segmentation, organisation-driven demand, planning the costs, risks and benefits of demand, and using marketing research methods to measure, model and predict demand.

Strategies to manage *capacity* used by organisations include resource-based (people, process and physical evidence), financial, time and opportunity strategies. These should be used as part of a coordinated strategy with managing demand to maximise returns on resources, time and investments by the organisation and the customer.

With services, not everything can be predicted, so organisations need to be able to adapt to changing demand by having the ability to also change their capacity at short notice. This can be done by using consumers to help produce their own service through value co-creation, such as with self-service technology, or through altering the marketing mix or spreading demand across different services of the organisation.

In conclusion, if an organisation can better manage demand and capacity, it will also be able to better manage relationships and value creation with all of its customers.

Review questions

1   Why is segmentation so important in services marketing?

2   If you were the marketing manager for a large hotel, would you try to create demand for your services? If so, how would you manage this demand? If not, why not?

3   Should challenges and opportunities be treated the same when it comes to managing capacity and demand?

4   Discuss the functional forecasting risks in operating a restaurant.

5   For the following types of services, rank and describe the priority you would give to people resources, process resources and physical evidence resources:

    a   doctor's surgery

    b   public transport system

    c   public library.

6   What strategies would you use to minimise the time it would take to serve a customer while at the same time maximising the value offering of the organisation? Use at least two practical examples to support your answer.

7   What are the common reasons that customer experience programs fail?

8   Adaptive service capacity is important in handling periods of high and unexpected demand from consumers—but does this mean that an organisation is never able to run at full capacity because it is keeping some capacity in reserve? Discuss.

9 Discuss the major steps required to develop a services forecasting model.

10 Discuss the potential strategies for matching demand and supply forecasts.

11 Discuss how constraint management might apply to the operations of a hotel.

Further reading

Frohlich, M.T. & Westbrook, R. (2002). Demand chain management in manufacturing services and web-based integration, drivers and performance. *Journal of Operations Management*, 20 (November), 729–45.

Grönroos, C. & Ojasalo, K. (2004). Service productivity: Towards a conceptualization of the transformation of inputs into economic results in services. *Journal of Business Research*, 57(4), 414–23.

Lovelock, C.H. (1983). Classifying services to gain strategic marketing insights. *Journal of Marketing*, 47(3), 9–20.

Lovelock, C.H. & Gummesson, E. (2004). Whither services marketing? In search of a new paradigm and fresh perspectives. *Journal of Service Research*, 7(1), 20–41.

Rust, R.T. & Chung, T.S. (2006). Marketing models of service and relationships. *Marketing Science*, 25(6), 560–80.

Trenwith, C. (2011). Businesses reeling under pressure to join daily deal craze. *WA Today*, 3 June. <www.watoday.com.au/small-business/smallbiz-marketing/businessesreeling-under-pressure-to-join-daily-deal-craze-20110602-1fi87.html#ixzz1aQYt4hsw>.

Williams, B. (2011). Oh baby, this little business is really growing. *The Age*, 10 October. <www.theage.com.au/small-business/growing/oh-baby-this-little-business-is-reallygrowing-20111010-1lgxi.html#ixzz1aQZUiUN6>.

Weblinks

Center for Excellence in Service. <www.rhsmith.umd.edu/ces>

Interview with Kmart CEO, Guy Russo, on changing demand and economic cycles. <www.youtube.com/watch?v=NtjSCgCzQZA>

Endnotes

1 K.D. Hoffman, S. Kelley & B. Chung (2003). A CIT investigation of servicescape failures and associated recovery strategies. *Journal of Services Marketing*, 17(4), 322.

2 E. Goldratt (1984). *The Goal: Excellence in Manufacturing*. Great Barrington, MA: North River Press.

3 C.H. Lovelock (1983). Classifying services to gain strategic marketing insights. *Journal of Marketing*, 47(3), 9–20.

4 S. Maklan & S. Knox (1997), Reinventing the brand: Bridging the gap between customer and brand value. *Journal of Product and Brand Management*, 6(2), 119–29.

5 A. Parasuraman (1987). Customer-oriented corporate cultures are crucial to services marketing success. *Journal of Services Marketing*, 1(1), 39–46.

6 Adapted from M. Solomon (2016). Millennial customers will dominate in 2017. Is your customer service experience ready for them? *Forbes*, 27 December. <www.forbes.com/sites/micahsolomon/2016/12/27/millennial-customers-will-dominate-2017-is-your-customer-service-experience-ready/#68ec943d44d0>.

7 Adapted from J. Van den Bergh (2017). The (fr)agile reality of the Next Generation. *How Cool Brands Stay Hot*, 14 September. <www.howcoolbrandsstayhot.com/2017/09/14/the-fragile-reality-of-the-next-generation>.

8 R. Larsson & D.E. Bowen (1989). Organization and customer: Managing design and coordination of services. *Academy of Management Review*, 14(2), 213–33.

9 C.F. Kaufman (1996). A new look at one-stop shopping: A TIMES model approach to matching store hours and shopper schedules. *Journal of Consumer Marketing*, 13(1), 4–25.

10 R. Batt (2002). Managing customer services: Human resource practices, quit rates, and sales growth. *Academy of Management Journal*, 45(3), 587–97.

11 D. Sarel & H. Marmorstein (1998). Managing the delayed service encounter: The role of employee action and customer prior experience. *Journal of Services Marketing*, 12(3), 195–208.

12 S.G. Bitran (1997). Managing the tug-of-war between supply and demand in the service industries. *European Management Journal*, 15(5), 523–36.

13 L.L. Berry, K. Seiders & D. Grewal (2002). Understanding service convenience. *Journal of Marketing*, 66(3), 1–17.

14 J. Baker & M. Cameron (1996). The effects of the service environment on affect and consumer perception of waiting time: An integrative review and research propositions. *Journal of the Academy of Marketing Science*, 24(4), 338–49.

15 G. Tom & S. Lucey (1995). Waiting time delays and customer satisfaction in supermarkets. *Journal of Services Marketing*, 9(5), 20–9.

16 Adapted from R. Leblanc (2017). How Amazon is changing supply chain management. *The Balance*, 1 December. <www.thebalance.com/how-amazon-is-changing-supply-chain-management-4155324>; and J. Ryan (2018). Amazon Australia: one month later. *The Sydney Morning Herald*, 16 January. < https://www.smh.com.au/technology/amazon-australia-one-month-later-20180116-h0iv0c.html>.

17 M.L. Meuter, A.L. Ostrom & S. Drill (2000). Self-service technologies: Understanding customer satisfaction with technology-based service encounters. *Journal of Marketing*, 64(3), 50–64.

18 P.A. Dabholkar (1996). Consumer evaluations of new technology-based self-service options: An investigation of alternative models of service quality. *International Journal of Research in Marketing*, 13(1), 29–51.

19 Based on W.M. Heroman, C.B. Davis & K.L. Farmer (2012). Demand forecasting and capacity management in primary care. *Physician Executive*, 38(1), 30–4.

20 S. Stidham (1992). Pricing and capacity decisions for a service facility: Stability and multiple local optima. *Management Science*, 38(8), 1121.

21 R.T. Rust & T.S. Chung (2006). Marketing models of service and relationships. *Marketing Science*, 25(6), 560–80.

22 E. Gummesson (2007). Exit services marketing—enter service marketing. *Journal of Customer Behaviour*, 6(2), 113–41.

OXFORD UNIVERSITY PRESS

23 Adapted from R. Smith & L. Williams (2016). The most common reasons customer experience programs fail. *Harvard Business Review*, 28 December. <https://hbr.org/2016/12/the-most-common-reasons-customer-experience-programs-fail>.

24 A.S.C. Ehrenberg, M.D. Uncles & G.G. Goodhardt (2004). Understanding brand performance measures: Using Dirichlet benchmarks. *Journal of Business Research*, 57 (12), 1307–25.

25 F. Reichheld & R. Markey (2011). *The Ultimate Question 2.0: How Net Promoter Companies Thrive in a Customer-Driven World* (rev. and expanded edn). Boston, MA: Harvard Business Review Press.

Tourism New Zealand is encouraging Aussies to take a road trip to the South Island

The latest evolution of the successful South Island Road Trip campaign 'Every day a different journey' was launched in 2015 by Tourism New Zealand with the primary target market being the eastern seaboard of Australia. The campaign highlights the diversity of the naturally hidden gems and experiences of the south island of New Zealand and encourages Australians to visit the island. The three-year partnership between Tourism New Zealand and the Regional Tourism Organisations (RTOs) will cost $3 million dollars, and offers Australians a road trip around the South Island. In addition to the direct spend, there will be a wide range of media and travel agent activity that will see the value delivered by the campaign reach as much as NZ$4–6 million.[1]

Research indicates that when Australians fly into Christchurch, they visit more regions and stay longer—both key goals of the current campaign. With that in mind, the campaign includes working with

» *continued over page*

Chapter 9

Marketing Communications for Services

William Chitty

Christchurch International Airport to encourage more direct flights to the southern city, and to promote travel throughout the South Island.

The Tourism New Zealand team, and the RTOs, have created five 'Great Journeys' of the South Island, which start at the top of the island and finish at the bottom—with everything in between. Whether Australian visitors have a long weekend to spend in New Zealand or as much as a few weeks, there will be a journey available for them. Itineraries will be available via a dedicated campaign page on <www.newzealand.com>.

The campaign will be rolled out across key media channels with a significant digital presence, as well as using social media and print. As with previous campaigns, this campaign will be completely integrated and also include a significantly weighted trade and public relations component.

According to Tourism New Zealand research, its target market in Australia is looking for a holiday destination where they can have fun, learn and experience new things, and feel relaxed, welcome, safe and comfortable. Those aged over 40 are more likely to value feeling safe and welcome, and less likely to prioritise reducing stress and escaping everyday life; those under 40 are more likely to value personal challenge and getting an adrenalin rush.

To support the digital and outdoor presence, a 12-page lift-out about the South Island was distributed to prospective visitors across Australia by News Ltd publications. In the trade market, Helloworld is the major retail partner, and will run various marketing awareness activities in metro and regional markets. All South Island regional tourism organisations are involved in the campaign, as is Air New Zealand by promoting its direct services between Sydney, Brisbane, Melbourne and Christchurch over the summer period.

Table 9.1 shows Australia visitor arrivals in New Zealand in the 12 months between January 2017 and January 2018. Over many decades, Australia has provided both volume and market value to New Zealand. Australian tourists visit New Zealand an average of four times, compared to 1–1.5 times for visitors from other countries, and together with the increased number of Australian stay days, Australians have become high-value visitors because they also spend more.

Table 9.1 Australian visitor arrivals January 2017–January 2018

	Numbers	Annual growth (%)
Year end total	1 475 472	+4.3
Year end (holiday)	592 432	+4.7
Month end total	131 072	+2.6
Month end (holiday)	60 688	+2.6
Duration of stay (days)		
Total stay days	14 329 440	
Total stay days (holiday)	6 192 912	
Average length of stay	9.7	
Average length of stay (holiday)	10.4	

Source: *Australia Market Overview*, Tourism New Zealand. <www.tourismnewzealand.com/markets-stats/markets/australia>.

Introduction

Marketing communications are the practices of selecting and coordinating all the communication elements in marketing a service organisation's brand by establishing shared meaning with the organisation's target market. They involve the planning, creation, integration and implementation of various forms of marketing communications, such as advertising, sales promotions, online marketing, personal selling, sponsorships and publicity that are delivered to a service organisation's target customers and prospects over time. Integrating these forms of marketing communications is imperative to build the brand equity of a service organisation. To understand the role that marketing communications plays in building the brand equity of a service, it is necessary to examine the two basic constructs—marketing and communication.

Marketing is the practice of creating exchanges between customers and sellers that are valued by both parties to the transaction. A service organisation's marketing strategies must achieve the three primary functions of marketing; these are:

1 identifying potential consumers' needs, wants and expectations
2 segmenting the market on the basis of its demographics, values and lifestyles and behaviour
3 satisfying the needs, wants and expectations of the target market's customers more effectively and efficiently than its competitors.

Communication is a process that facilitates the transmission of messages between a sender (usually an organisation) and a receiver (usually the target audience). The purpose of communication is to establish commonality of meaning between a sender and receiver using messages—and one or more forms of media—to impart brand knowledge that will ultimately influence the behaviour of the receivers.

Together, marketing communications are activities that create commonality of meaning about the features and benefits of a service organisation's brand and how those attributes can satisfy its target market's expectations. In other words, the target market's interpretation of the meaning of a service brand's message should be the same as that intended by the service organisation. In the absence of tangible product cues, marketing communications define the service; they build images of what the service brand stands for by differentiating that brand's salient features from competitors; they reinforce the strong, favourable and perhaps unique associations that consumers hold about the brand; and finally, marketing communications inform, persuade and remind consumers to purchase that particular service.

marketing communications
Includes all elements of a service organisation's communication mix to facilitate exchanges by establishing shared meaning between the organisation and its target market

marketing
The practice of creating exchanges between customers and sellers that are valued by both parties to the transaction

communication
A process that facilitates the transmission of messages between a sender and a receiver

Learning objectives

After reading this chapter you should be able to:

↘ explain the role of marketing communications for services
↘ discuss how marketing communications create meaning for service brands

William Chitty

↘ understand how marketing communications create meaning

↘ understand how the major elements of the marketing communications mix apply to services

↘ explain the five stages in implementing marketing communications strategies for services.

The role of marketing communications in marketing services

Marketing communications strengthen a service organisation's marketing messages, which are generally based on the perceived value of the service being offered, to communicate a strong, favourable and perhaps unique image of the service brand. The basic premise of marketing communications is therefore to communicate the benefits and attributes of the service organisation's brand by creating consumer awareness of that brand and building a positive attitude based on the value that customers associate with the service brand.

Services are similar to tangible products because they share three common characteristics that influence consumers' buying behaviour and build profitable relationships:

1   Both have a brand—related to image and often forming the basis of marketing communications.

2   Both have various attributes—perceived as being of value and which will influence brand choice.

3   Both provide benefits to consumers—in the case of a service, may be used to differentiate it from other services.

Service organisations also use marketing communications to develop and maintain favourable long-term exchange relationships with their customers because the viability of a service organisation depends on building lasting customer relationships rather than one-off exchanges. The reliance on maintaining long-term exchange relationships with customers is driven by four marketing developments:

1   customers are more knowledgeable and they demand high-quality services that are competitively priced and supported by reliable customer service

2   the cost-effectiveness of retaining existing customers rather than acquiring new customers

3   reduced dependence on mass-media marketing communications

4   increased focus on technology for more customer-focused marketing communications.

The initial stage of the marketing communications process requires a services marketer to profile prospective customer segments, and to then determine what types of marketing messages and media channels will best achieve the communication objectives of informing, persuading, reminding and encouraging action from that market segment.[2] (Chapter 2 provides examples of the various techniques that can be used to profile a prospective customer segment.)

The three basic objectives of marketing communications are to inform, persuade and remind target market consumers about the organisation and its service product(s). The *inform* function is generally used when the service is in the early stages of its product life cycle to convey information about the brand, attributes and benefits of a new service, or to explain how to use a service that has been modified by new technology, such as providing an online service centre to enable customers to access their bank accounts. The *persuade* function should convince the target market customers that a particular service is the best one to satisfy their needs, wants and expectations. The objective of *reminding* customers is to encourage them to continue buying that service and generally occurs when the service is in the mature stage of its life cycle. The role of marketing communications is to establish marketing and communication objectives and to monitor the results of marketing communications campaigns.

How service characteristics influence marketing communication strategies

In the services marketing environment, one of the key communications challenges is to manage service promises. Any difference between the promises made by marketing communications and the service that is delivered can have a significant impact on customer satisfaction. As will be discussed in Chapter 11, managing customer expectations is a precursor to generating customer satisfaction. If, for example, an airline's marketing communications show smiling cabin staff, then in most cases, when customers board an aircraft of that airline, they will expect to be greeted by smiling cabin staff. Promises made by marketing communications that raise customers' expectations to unrealistic levels will, however, invariably lead to customer dissatisfaction and discourage repeat purchase.

To achieve its objectives, marketing communication strategies must, in addition to informing, persuading and reminding customers about a service, also inform and educate customers about the roles they are expected to play in purchasing and consuming that service.

The core element of a service is an intangible act or performance that satisfies a customer's primary needs, so the first service characteristic to consider is its *intangibility*. The intangible nature of a service means that customers may find it difficult to evaluate the quality of the service, because it cannot be taken for 'a test drive' in order to determine its value. There are, however, some tangible elements of a service, such as a hotel's beds, the speed of a telecommunications company's mobile network, or in the case of Singapore Airlines in Figure 9.1, a tangible brand cue—Singapore Girl—who personifies the quality of the airline's service.[3] Those tangible elements of a service often play a major role in a service marketing communications program to persuade customers to purchase the service.

Figure 9.1   Singapore Girl personifies the quality of the airline's service

Source: *Australian Business Traveller*, 16 January 2017. <www.ausbt.com.au/singapore-airlines-two-all-new-business-class-seats-for-2017-18>.

The second characteristic of a service that influences a service organisation's marketing communications is its *inseparability*, which requires customers to be in contact in some way with a service provider, its physical facilities and the service-delivery process of the service organisation. Customers in effect co-produce the service—through the inseparable nature of the service encounter—and learn how to use the service process to maximise their satisfaction. During the service process, service organisations also have the opportunity to communicate the benefits and attributes of a service to their customers without needing to use multiple media channels. Those service benefits may be transmitted by the actions of the service personnel—who are the service providers—or by the tangible brand cues that are an inherent part of the service encounter. Both the tangible cues and service providers can be used to encourage customers to pass their comments about the service to their friends by word-of-mouth on social media. If the service is a high-involvement purchase such as childcare services, positive word-of-mouth can lessen any financial or performance risks that parents may associate with purchasing a childcare service.

Variability is the third characteristic of service that determines the marketing communications strategies that a service organisation may employ. Managing variability in a service encounter requires maintaining a consistent level of quality in that encounter. This can be difficult because both the service processes (*how* the service is produced) and the service outcome (*what* is produced) depend on the interactions between the customers and the service providers. In most cases, that means managing the 'human' element of the service encounter. One of the arguments for using technology to provide customer service—apart from offering 24/7 contact for customers—is that technology maintains a consistent level of service quality for routine service encounters, such as using an ATM for basic banking services.

The *perishability* of a service is the fourth characteristic that influences a service organisation's marketing communications. Perishability means a service cannot be stored, and so greater reliance must be placed on managing supply and demand to ensure the availability of the service. Managing the availability of a service also includes controlling its benefits, such as providing a faster service than competitors, minimising customer waiting times and using technology to offer extended hours of service. Figure 9.2 depicts the ATMs of the Commonwealth Bank in Melbourne. By having several ATMs available, it is implied that customers will not spend a great deal of time processing their financial transactions. Marketing messages should, therefore, communicate those benefits by highlighting the user-friendly aspects of the organisation's physical facilities, its service providers and/or its delivery processes.

Figure 9.2   Marketing communications should highlight the user-friendly aspects of an organisation's service processes

Source: Shutterstock.

Positioning a service brand

A positioning statement of a service suggest the benefits of what the service brand represents—when compared with its competitors—in the minds of a target market. Positioning statements, as part of marketing communications, are marketing messages that have a specific meaning that motivates consumers to develop strong, favourable and perhaps unique service associations with that particular service brand. Service quality and the price of the service are two important elements of a service positioning strategy, and it is essential that a positioning statement is communicated the same way every time the target market has contact with the service brand. The basis of effective marketing communications is to consistently deliver a solution to the target market's needs, wants and expectations across all chosen media channels.

↘
positioning statement Suggests the benefits of what the service brand represents— when compared with its competitors—in the minds of a target market

A service's brand can be positioned on the service's features or attributes, superior service quality, or perhaps a user-friendly secure website that offers secure 24/7 convenience. Positioning can also be based on a service's benefits that satisfy three consumer needs; that is, consumers' functional, symbolic and experiential needs.[4]

A service that offers solutions to consumers' *functional needs* generally communicates convenience, safety or perhaps personal well-being offered by a particular service brand. For example, Telstra is operating Australia's first integrated health system, Telehealth, that aims to provide technological solutions in telemedicine with a full range of consumer healthcare options from general practitioner (GP) care through to specialists and allied health professionals.[5]

Services that are positioned in terms of their ability to satisfy consumers' psychological needs and wants are based on appeals to *symbolic needs*, and attempt to associate using the service with an expectation of being part of a desired group. Marketers of luxury services such as exclusive holiday resorts or prestigious international events such as golf championships frequently appeal to consumers' symbolic needs to be part of a special group.

Services that satisfy *experiential needs* represent consumers' desires for some forms of sensory pleasure or variety, such as concerts and theatre performances. In some instances, services that satisfy experiential needs may be personal and individual services, like hairdressing or a body massage, that promise to make the user look elegant or feel refreshed

Services in Action

Promising the luxury of a timeless escape

The Saffire Freycinet luxury lodge, as shown in Figure 9.3, is situated at Coles Bay on the east coast of Tasmania and

Figure 9.3 Tasmania's Saffire Freycinet combines customers' desire for luxury with their environmental concerns

Source: Saffire Freycinet.

caters for guests in 20 pavilion suites that fan out from the stingray-shaped main communal Sanctuary lodge.[6]

In conjunction with Wildcare, an environmental volunteer group in Tasmania, the Menzies Institute for Medical Research and the Tasmanian Parks and Wildlife Service rangers, the Sanctuary lodge provides a rehabilitation centre for endangered Tasmanian devils. The rangers conduct information sessions for guests staying at the lodge to raise funds that are being used to develop a vaccine that will combat the contagious facial tumours that are threatening the survival of the local Tasmanian devils.[7]

at the end of the service. As service organisations develop and become more successful over time, many will adopt some form of repositioning strategy. That repositioning may occur because customer demand has changed from using simple no-frills services such as bed-and-breakfast holidays to higher-quality accommodation, or the service organisation may look to build its market share by meeting the needs, wants and expectations of profitable sub-segments in the service category.

How marketing communications create meaning

The ultimate objective of marketing communications is to encourage the target consumers to purchase the branded service—rather than a competitor's—and that means using the most effective elements of the marketing communications mix to achieve that objective. All marketing communications activities must establish commonality of meaning between the service organisation and its prospective customers. As shown in Figure 9.4, the communication process generally includes the following elements:[8]

→ The source is the organisation that is marketing its services and that organisation has thoughts and ideas about its services that it wants to share with its target market. Service organisations encode their thoughts and ideas into marketing messages that must be easily understood by the receivers; in other words, the organisation creates meaning about its services for the receivers—its target market.

→ The message is some form of expression about the sender's thoughts and ideas.

→ The channel consists of the various types of media that can transmit the marketing message to the receivers.

→ The receivers are the target market who decode and create meaning from the marketing messages that were transmitted by the service organisation.

→ Noise is an extraneous and distracting stimulus that can occur anywhere in the media channels and influences the communication process.

→ Feedback is the process that enables the service organisation—the source—to monitor how accurately the target market has interpreted the intended meaning of the message.

Establishing commonality of meaning is fundamental to the marketing communications process. Meaning can be considered to be perceptions (the consumers' thoughts) and affective reactions (their feelings) that consumers experience when exposed to a stimulus, which in the case of services marketing is a particular service brand. The concept of meaning is also fundamental to marketing communications. The nature of meaning can be more easily understood using semiotics, which, in broad terms, is an analysis by customers of the signs—such as a service organisation's logo—that are associated with an organisation's brand. Those brand associations create meaning by a constructive

William Chitty

Figure 9.4   Elements of the communication process

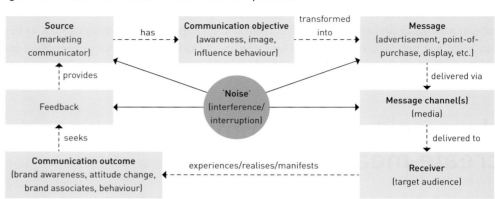

Source: W. Chitty, E. Luck, N. Barker, A-M. Sassenberg, T.A. Shimp & J.C. Andrews (2018). *Integrated Marketing Communications* (5th edn). Melbourne: Cengage Learning Australia, p. 45.

process when the values and lifestyles of the consumers for that service interact with the signs contained in the service's marketing communications. Consumers' interpretation of marketing messages assists in the transfer of meaning from a service organisation to prospective consumers. It is important to note that marketers can use a variety of different signs, ranging from verbal to non-verbal visualisations and anything that can be perceived by a consumer's senses, to create the desired meaning of their service brands; meaning in this sense is the interpretive residue in the minds of the target market after contact with a service organisation's marketing messages, not necessarily the marketers' messages *per se*. A dollar sign ($), for example, is generally understood to represent currency by most people from different backgrounds.

The meaning of a sign is contextually dependent, so that the same sign can interpreted by different consumers in different contexts to mean different things. Signs and meaning, therefore, should not be construed as being synonymous. Given the abstract characteristics of services—primarily their intangibility—the signs used in marketing messages for particular services communicate meaning that is derived from a culturally constituted environment and transfers meaning to that particular audience. So, when consumers are exposed to marketing messages, they not only draw information from an advertisement, they also assign meaning to the signs associated with communicated brand. For example, if a well-known spokesperson is chosen for a new mobile phone service campaign, will prospective customers take more notice of the information in the marketing message, and develop a more diverse meaning of the brand, as a result of interpreting the stimuli that are part of their culturally constituted environment? The most important consideration when different verbal and non-verbal signs are used to create the desired meaning for a service brand is to ensure that they both deliver a consistent meaning; this is the basis of all marketing communications. Meaning resides in the minds of consumers so it is imperative that marketers understand the psychological factors that determine how consumers derive meaning from marketing messages.

How the major elements of the marketing communications mix apply to services

The elements of the traditional marketing communications mix for services marketing are advertising, sales promotion, personal selling, sponsorship marketing, publicity, direct marketing and online elements. We will now look at each of these seven elements.

Advertising

Advertising involves either *mass* communication using newspapers, magazines, radio, television and other media such as billboards, the internet or cinema, or *direct* communication targeted at each business-to-business (B2B) customer or the ultimate consumer using social media platforms. All forms of advertising are paid for by an identified advertiser, but are considered to be non-personal because the service organisation is simultaneously communicating with multiple receivers (perhaps millions), rather than with a specific person or a small group.

As shown in Figure 9.5, total advertising spend in Australia by media platform for 2017 was $15.74 billion, and is forecast to reach $17.31 billion by 2021.[9]

Figure 9.5 Australian advertising spend 2017, and the 2021 (forecast) spend

Advertising spend: 2017–2021

2.1 per cent total market compound annual growth rate (CAGR) to reach $43.7 billion, consumer spending 2.2 per cent CAGR to reach $26.4 billion and advertising 1.9 per cent CAGR to reach $17.3 billion

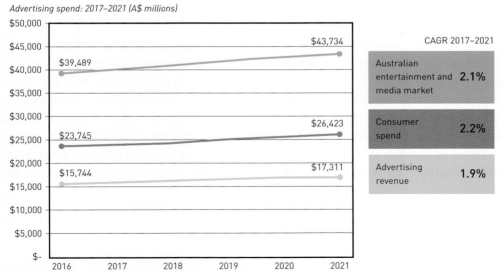

Source: PWC (2017). *Outlook: Australian Entertainment and Media 2017–2021.*

Sales promotions

Sales promotions include all marketing activities that attempt to stimulate buyer action or encourage immediate sales of a service. In comparison, the role of advertising is to accomplish other communications objectives, such as creating brand awareness and positively influencing customer attitudes. Sales promotions may be directed towards both trade intermediaries, such as wholesalers and retailers, and end-user consumers. *Trade-oriented sales promotion* includes the use of various types of allowances to encourage wholesaler and retailer responses, while *consumer-oriented sales promotion* includes using price reductions, contests/sweepstakes and celebrities to influence consumers' service-buying behaviour.

Personal selling

Personal selling is based on person-to-person communication, where the salesperson creates awareness, interest and then desire in an organisation's service to persuade prospective buyers to purchase that branded service. These selling efforts often include providing service distributors, such as real estate agents, with promotion materials and assisting their sales efforts with company advertising campaigns.

Sponsorship marketing

Sponsorship marketing is the practice of promoting the interests of a service organisation by associating the company and its brands with a specific *event*. For example, Korean Air was a major partner in sponsoring the PyeongChang 2018 Winter Olympic Games in South Korea.

Publicity

Like advertising, publicity involves non-personal communication to a mass audience. Unlike advertising, however, a service organisation does not pay for media time or space. Publicity usually takes the form of news items or a press release about the service organisation's activities or services. These news items, or comments, receive free print space or broadcast time because the media representatives consider the information relevant and newsworthy for their audiences; in that sense, the publicity is 'not paid for' by the company receiving its benefits. Press releases issued by Qantas, for example, provided newspapers, trade magazines and other news media with news items about the introduction of its new business-class seating for its A330 aircraft (Figure 9.6).[10]

Direct marketing

Direct marketing for services involves sending marketing messages directly to consumers, either via conventional postal services or online using the internet or social media channels,

OXFORD UNIVERSITY PRESS

Figure 9.6 Qantas used press releases to make customers aware of its new business-class seating

to encourage an immediate consumer response. For example, the home pages of service providers like airlines, banks and hotels are influential in encouraging consumers' buying behaviour. The integration of the various types of communication media, for example, using advertising together with direct marketing, generally yields better results for service organisations than using only one form of marketing media.

Online elements of the marketing communications mix

The online elements of the marketing communications mix are a collection of digital media channels that are activated by various digital devices. The Australian online advertising market, which consists of General Display, Search and Directories, and Classifieds, grew by $799 million to $7.6 billion—an annual growth rate of 11.7 per cent—for the financial year ending 30 June 2017 (see Figure 9.7).[11]

Category highlights

General display

In the General Display category, mobile display represented over 50 per cent of expenditure for the first time, while video advertising had rapidly increased its share, accounting for 32.9 per cent of general display advertising expenditure, compared to 24.3 per cent in 2016.[12] The auto category was once again the number one display category in 2017, and saw the largest year-on-year growth, increasing from 17 per cent of category share in 2016 to 18.5 per cent in 2017. Automotive, along with real estate and retail, account for 41.1 per cent of the General Display advertising market.

Figure 9.7 Online category expenditure of the marketing communications mix

ONLINE ADVERTISING GROWTH FY2017 BY CATEGORY

General Display	Search and Directories	Classifieds	Mobile	Video
$2.7bn	$3.5bn	$1.4bn	$2.6bn	$0.9bn
+10% on 2016	+12% on 2016	+15% on 2016	+33% on 2016	+49% on 2016
Driven by growth in mobile and video	S&D achieves double digit growth despite its significant base	Classifieds lead year on year online advertising growth	Mobile drives growth in both the Search and General Display categories	Significant year on year growth demonstrates the strength of video advertising

Source: IAB Australia (2017). Online advertising spend reaches $7.6 billion in 2017 financial year. Press release, 5 September. <www.iabaustralia.com.au/news-and-updates/iab-press-releases/item/22-iab-press-releases/2374-online-advertising-spend-reaches-7-6-billion-in-2017-financial-year#COrReG11tSbiK2wv.99>.

Classifieds

This category continues to grow faster than other categories due to the strong Australian specialised organisations that can serve wider audiences without the restrictions of physical boundaries or long distances. Classifieds grew more than general display and search and directories, up almost 15 per cent year on year.

Mobile advertising highlights

Mobile advertising expenditure now exceeds $2.6 billion, an increase of $641 million (or 32.7%) compared to 2016. Of this $2.6 billion expenditure, 46 per cent was attributed to mobile search, 54 per cent to mobile display; with 70 per cent attributed to smartphones and 30 per cent to tablets.

Video advertising highlights

Video advertising accounted for $894.4 million of expenditure, up $294.4 million (or 50%) compared to 2016.

↘
INDUSTRY INSIGHT

The online media environment in Australia

Australians and social media

Ninety-nine per cent of Australians who access social media, on average, use one of the three most popular internet-enabled devices. The penetration of smartphones rose 5 per cent to 81 per cent in 2017 to become the most commonly used device, overtaking laptops, which dropped 16 per cent (11 percentage

Table 9.2 Device ownership by gender and age

Device	Total 2016	Total 2017	Male	Female	18–29	30–39	40–49	50–64	65+
Smartphone	76%	81%	83%	80%	99%	96%	88%	75%	47%
Laptop	70%	59%	59%	59%	51%	59%	64%	66%	55%
Desktop	54%	51%	50%	52%	26%	45%	53%	67%	66%
iPad or other tablet	53%	45%	41%	48%	16%	42%	51%	64%	50%
Internet-enabled TV	29%	28%	26%	29%	20%	39%	38%	27%	16%
iPod touch or similar device	17%	14%	13%	15%	5%	16%	17%	18%	13%
A wearable device such as Apple Watch or Fitbit	6%	10%	9%	11%	4%	16%	13%	12%	6%
None of the above	1%	<1%	0%	<1%	0%	0%	0%	0%	<1%

Source: Sensis (2017). *Sensis Social Media Report 2017.*

points) to 59 per cent; there was a drop in the ownership of tablets (45%) and desktop computers (51%). Ownership of internet-enabled televisions decreased to 28 per cent and the ownership of devices—such as the iPod touch—was lower at 14 per cent. Table 9.2 indicates the diverse nature of device ownership by gender and age.[13]

Smartphone penetration continues to grow as the most likely device people use to access social media (81%) because most users prefer to access social media through an app as opposed to using a website. In the 18–29 and 30–39 age cohorts, smartphones are used for social media interaction by more than 95 per cent of people.

As shown in Table 9.3, Facebook has maintained its almost ubiquitous appeal, being accessed by 94 per cent of online users. The results of the Sensis 2017 survey also indicated that the average number of Facebook friends is 234, down from 272 in 2016, and that 50 per cent of social media users nominate Facebook

Table 9.3 Social networking sites used

Facebook	94%
YouTube	51%
Instagram	46%
Snapchat	40%
Twitter	32%
LinkedIn	18%
Tumblr	11%
Google+	10%
Pintrest	10%
Reddit	3%
Vine	1%

Source: Sensis (2017). *Sensis Social Media Report 2017.*

as their favourite site, far more than any other sites. The main attraction of using Facebook is contact with family and friends, but its user-friendliness is also a prominent appeal. The average number of times people access Facebook has dropped to 25 times a week

William Chitty

from 32 times a week in 2016, but the amount of time spent on each occasion has remained constant at 24 minutes, which is an average of almost 10 hours per week.

Seventy-nine per cent of internet users now use social networking sites, which is 10 points higher than in 2016. Frequency of use has also grown, with 59 per cent now accessing those sites daily or more, which has almost doubled since 2011 when it was 30 per cent. The proportion of internet users who check their social media sites more than five times a day has increased from 26 per cent in 2016 to 35 per cent in 2017. Usage, and frequency of using social media, declines with age, although it remains popular with the older age groups; comparing gender, and frequency, indicates that social media is used slightly more often by females than males.[14]

Almost seven in 10 users feel they have not changed the amount of time spent on social media over the past year, while 18 per cent said their usage had increased and 13 per cent said it had decreased. Seventy-one per cent are comfortable with the time they spend on social media (up from 62%) with 21 per cent feeling it is excessive (down from 31%). Eight in 10 expect to spend the same amount of time on social media in the coming year.[15]

When analysing which devices and applications are being used to access social media, smartphones are preferred to other devices for social networking, with 81 per cent of now accessing their social media accounts on a smartphone, compared with 72 per cent in 2016. The use of laptops (30%), desktops (28%) and tablets (25%) to access social media is lower than previously observed in 2106.[16]

Australian businesses and social media

The 2017 Sensis survey found that the main reason for the take-up in social media from businesses was to aid marketing and sales, with providing a means of business communication being the next biggest influence. There was a reduction in the number of businesses with a social media presence over 2016 with just under half (47%) of small and medium businesses (SMBs) having a social media presence, while 60 per cent of large businesses had a social media presence.[17]

About 10 per cent of SMBs without a social media presence intended to have one in the future, while the large businesses did not have plans to add a social media presence. The main reasons businesses are reluctant to be on social media are concerns around the investment in time, as well as not perceiving it to have any benefits for their individual business. The take-up of social media among consumers increased 10 points to 79 per cent in 2017, and they continue to be more engaged with social media than businesses. Nine in 10 small (90%), medium (87%) and large businesses (93%) using social media have a Facebook profile.

LinkedIn is used by more than one in three small (35%) and medium (41%) businesses but is mostly used by large businesses (82%). Twitter is the third-most popular platform for small businesses (24%).

In 2016, 76 per cent of large businesses were using social media platforms as a two-way communication channel but in 2017 nearly all did so (95%); that compares with 58 per cent of small firms (previously 46%) and 41 per cent of medium firms (previously 45%).

While 90 per cent of large businesses, and more than 40 per cent of SMBs, now have a strategy for growth in their social media investment, many SMBs are still finding their way:

↘ Just over one-third of the small firms (34%) and nearly half (45%) the medium firms don't know how much money they have invested in social media.

↘ A quarter (25%) of small businesses and 10 per cent of medium businesses do not have an annual budget for social media.

↘ Almost half allocate 10 per cent or less of their marketing budget to social media.

↘ Only 23 per cent of small businesses and 20 per cent of MSBs measure their ROI on social media.

Implementing marketing communications strategies

Given the recent developments in the convergence of technology and marketing, marketing communications are moving from a marketing planning paradigm to a strategic business communications process based on the general objectives of marketing communications, such as:

→ evaluating all the elements of marketing communications and associated media

→ understanding and changing customers' buying behaviour

→ building strong, favourable and lasting relationships between customers and an organisation's brand.

The specific foundations for this concluding section of the chapter are based on the five stages of implementing the marketing communications process:

1　Profile the identified target market.

2　Develop marketing communication objectives.

3　Plan the media channels needed to achieve the marketing communication objectives.

4　Influence the target market's buying behaviour.

5　Build strong, favourable and lasting customer relationships with an organisation's brand.[18]

Profile the identified target market

Implementing the marketing communications process begins with *profiling the consumer* or *prospect* segment, to determine the most appropriate messages and the type of media that will inform, persuade and/or remind these prospective consumers to respond

William Chitty

positively towards the service organisation's brand message. Profiling a target market involves collecting consumers' demographic data, determining their values and lifestyles and analysing consumers' buying behaviour to answer the following questions:

→ How much of the service (in volume/units/dollars) will the target market buy?

→ How often will they buy that service?

→ Where do they purchase that service?

Marketers use marketing communications to share ideas about a service's brand image and its attributes and benefits, with the intended audience of the marketing message; that is, the target market. When consumers in the target market receive a marketing message, they interpret it to determine what is being said, who the source of the marketing message is, and how that marketing message influences their buying decision-making processes and their subsequent buying behaviour.

↘ INDUSTRY INSIGHT

An easier way to pay for 5.5 million Australians

Following the recent partnership signed between Tyro Payments and PayPal Australia, more than 500 000 small- and medium-sized businesses now have the opportunity to accept mobile payments in-store from the 5.5 million active Australian PayPal users. The new mobile payment system—called Tyro Mobile—gives Australia's small- and medium-sized enterprises (SMEs) the capability to meet consumer demand for mobile payment facilities via the PayPal Australia consumer app.[19]

Tyro CEO Jost Stollmann said that a growing number of Australians want to pay for their purchases quickly and conveniently, and Tyro's partnership with PayPal Australia means consumers with the PayPal app can now use their smartphones to do so in a second.

He added that while research has shown 61 per cent of Australians are keen to pay in-store with their mobiles,[20] only slightly more than a third of Australian merchants (36%) accept mobile payments.[21]

The high percentage of SMEs that currently do not accept mobile payments, and the 5.5 million active Australian consumers with mobiles, means there is a potential for a significant number of those businesses to join PayPal mobile payments. This technology gives those smaller businesses the ability to compete with the big traders like Coles and McDonald's in their markets and to offer better service to a greater number of customers.

Research has found the major reasons that Australian smartphone users want to pay in-store with their mobiles for their purchases are:

↘ 'It's a convenient way to pay' (32%).

↘ 'It's a fast way to pay' (27%).

↘ 'I do not need to carry or use a physical wallet, when my details are stored' (22%)

↘ 'It's easier than paying by cash or card' (19%).[22]

When service organisations segment the potential consumers for a service using demographic variables, such as age, gender, income and occupation, and perhaps family life cycle, marketers will be able to predict, with reasonable accuracy, the size of the various market segments for their services. For example, by using demographics the major trading banks can forecast the likely number of first homebuyers who require mortgage finance, and therefore can ensure that they allocate sufficient funds to meet the likely demand of first homebuyers over the course of a planning cycle—usually a financial year.

Determining how consumers' values and lifestyle influence their responses to marketing communications is an important consideration for service organisations because demographics provide only a one-dimensional profile of a target market. By using values and lifestyle information of a consumer segment, and their demographic data, marketers can develop a dynamic profile of consumers' behaviour and forecast their demand for the organisation's services. For example, luxury cruise operators on Europe's major rivers primarily target customers who have the time to take cruising holidays and who enjoy the different types of European sightseeing excursions compared to land-based resorts (Figure 9.8). Club Med also offers holiday packages, but its services are targeted to younger consumers who do not have the time to take extended holidays and who want their entertainment in one location. Buyer behaviour is generally required to complete a profile of a market segment. Demographic variables, values and lifestyle information, and buyer behaviour typically provide marketers with sufficient information and data to define their target market.

When the usage behaviour of particular market segments is known, marketers can determine how to reach the consumers in each segment and the number of times that members of the target market will need to be exposed to the marketing message. One of the more recent changes in determining how many times consumers must be exposed to a marketing message for them to understand its meaning is recency planning. This

Figure 9.8 European river cruises promise a relaxed holiday experience

William Chitty

planning approach is based on the premise that the first exposure to a marketing message is the strongest in influencing consumers' brand choice, and that consumers' needs, wants and expectations often determine effectiveness of a marketing communications campaign.[23]

Target market responses

An important consideration of the marketing communications process for services is to maintain the image of a service organisation's brand. Because a service is intangible, the marketing message for a service must develop a strong, favourable and perhaps unique brand image in the target consumers' minds. In other words, the marketing message should create a favourable perception because once a service brand's image has been created it will persist in consumers' minds and form the basis of what they expect that brand to provide in terms of benefits and value. The marketing communications process is also influenced by the inseparable nature of a service because the service's employees, who are usually present to deliver the service, play an important role in developing the organisation's brand image. In some cases, those employees are the service product. For example, hospital patients spend most of their time in a hospital's medical environment, interacting with the nursing staff who are trained to provide a consistent level of medical service and are informal channels of marketing communication for the hospital in terms of their knowledge, behaviour and appearance.

Another aspect of the marketing communication process for a service is customers' perceptions of the risks associated with purchasing or using a new service. The purchase of a new service is usually perceived by consumers to be a more risky financial proposition than buying a tangible product because the characteristics of a service do not allow potential customers to physically examine its features and attributes. That means consumers are more likely to engage in an extended information search for credible sources of information about the service, and given the four defining characteristics of a service, will often rely on their friends' recommendations.

Hierarchy of effects

An important consideration in developing an effective marketing communications campaign is knowing how the target market will respond to a marketing message and adopt a specific behaviour; for example, purchasing the promoted service. There are a number of stages that a consumer moves through, from being unaware of the service brand through to the actual service purchase. The hierarchy of effects model, as shown in Figure 9.9, explains how consumers respond to the effects of advertising.[24] The underlying principle of the hierarchy of effects model also applies to integrated marketing communications.

Determining the persuasive power of marketing communications requires understanding how marketing messages influence the target market's attitudes and their subsequent

Figure 9.9 The hierarchy of effects model indicates how consumers respond to the effects of advertising

Source: R.J. Lavidge & G.A. Steiner (1961). A model for predictive measurements of advertising effectiveness. *Journal of Marketing*, 25(October), 61–5.

behaviour. There are three general stages in the hierarchy of effects model that are based on the tri-component model of consumer attitudes:

1 The *cognitive stage*, which indicates what the target audience knows or perceives about the particular service or its brand.

2 The *affective stage*, which indicates what the target market feels, in terms of liking or disliking the service.

3 The *conative stage*, which refers to the target markets' intended actions towards the brand; that is, to trial, to purchase, to adopt or to reject the brand.

Each of these stages forms part of marketing communications effects and they can be measured to evaluate the effectiveness of various marketing strategies. The major marketing objective, of course, is to move the target market through the response processes to ultimately purchase the service.

The hierarchy of effects model assumes that the target consumers move through a series of sequential steps from initial awareness to the actual purchase of the service. The basic premise of the hierarchy of effects model is that persuasion occurs over time.[25] Marketing messages may not lead to an immediate behavioural response or purchase, because their influence includes moving consumers through a series of steps from *liking*, *preference* and *conviction*, which must occur before the target consumers develop a *purchase intention*.

Develop marketing communications objectives

The different types of marketing communication—such as advertisements, sales promotions, personal selling, direct marketing, publicity and event sponsorships—must present the same brand message and convey that message consistently across diverse message channels or points of consumer contact. Marketing communications for a brand must, in other words, 'speak with a single voice'. Coordination of messages and media is critical to achieving a strong and unified brand image and to moving consumers to action.[26] In general, the single-voice, or synergy, principle involves selecting a specific positioning statement for a service.

Communication effects

Communication effects are the relatively enduring brand associations that consumers develop by their interactions with a service organisation's marketing communications that connect its brand to those potential consumers. There are five communication effects that are formed from consumer interactions with a service organisation's integrated marketing communication. They are:

1   category need
2   brand awareness
3   brand attitude
4   brand purchase intention
5   purchase facilitation.[27]

Figure 9.10 depicts the various elements of a communications effects pyramid, and indicates that each communications effect is transformed for a service brand in an ascending sequential order, starting with a category need. To understand communication effects, which are the basis of communication objectives, it is necessary to examine the influence that each particular effect has on the development of consumers' brand associations.

Figure 9.10   Communication effects pyramid

Source: J.R. Rossiter & L. Percy (1997). *Advertising Communications and Promotion Management* (2nd edn). Boston, MA: Irwin McGraw-Hill, p. 110.

Category need

A service category can be defined by a prospective consumer as being the basic level of a service. It is the level at which consumers can instantly name a collective group of services, such as banks, mobile phone networks or hotels, as being basic service categories. For a category need to exist, therefore, there must be some consumer interest in a service category, and potential buyers in the target market must believe that a service in that category will satisfy their perceived needs, wants and expectations.

A general category need arises when consumers are motivated to satisfy their needs, wants and expectations, and a particular service category is seen as the best means of satisfying those requirements. The satisfaction process therefore requires a connection between a service and a buyer's motivation, and that connection should be driven by the service organisation's message in its marketing communications.

There are two broad types of buyer motivations. The first is *negatively based* and includes actions that help consumers to remove a problem or perhaps avoid a problem. For example, when people have to lodge their annual tax returns, tax agents such as H&R Block, for example, promote their service on the basis of solving taxpayers' problems of knowing what items can be claimed as legitimate expense deductions.

The second type of motive is *positively based* and includes service outcomes such as sensory pleasure, intellectual stimulation and social approval. For example, when people attend concerts they experience some form of sensory pleasure from the musical event, while consumers who play computer games may experience intellectual stimulation, and after 'beating the baddies' may receive social approval from other online gamers.

When a connection between the service category and consumers' motivations is established, marketing communications can stimulate primary demand. A category need is the communication effect that influences primary demand. So, to stimulate customer demand, marketing communications must also influence brand-level effects such as brand awareness, brand attitude and brand purchase intention.

Brand awareness

Brand awareness is based on consumers' ability to identify, either by recognising or recalling, a particular service brand within a service category in sufficient detail to make a purchase decision. At the service category level, consumers will not buy unless they have a category need; at the brand level, consumers cannot buy unless they have been made aware of the service brand. Brand awareness, therefore, is a universal marketing communications objective. The distinction between brand awareness objectives—that is, between brand recognition and brand recall—is important because there are two different types of consumer purchasing decisions.

The first type of purchasing decision-making is made at the point of service category selection and that requires *brand recognition*—consumers have a category need and the service brand is recognised when consumers see it. For example, if prospective customers use an online booking agency to make a hotel reservation for an interstate holiday, the hotel that they select will probably be the hotel brand that they recognise—provided that its tariff is within their budget!

The second type of purchasing decision is made prior to the point of purchase and that requires *brand recall*, where the relevant brands in a service category can be recalled before consumers actually see them. Both brand recognition and brand recall associate the brand with a category need, and both are learned associations. Marketers cannot assume, however, that because a service brand has achieved brand recognition by potential consumers that it will have also achieved brand recall. Typically, consumers can recognise many service brands, but can only recall a few because they only tend to buy a few service brands.

Brand attitude

Brand attitude is the potential buyer's evaluation of the service brand with respect to its perceived ability to satisfy a current need. The primary purpose of marketing communication is to establish commonality of meaning between the service organisation and the target market. Unless the service is trivial, brand awareness *per se* will not be enough to drive the prospective consumer to buy the service. For a purchase to occur, potential buyers evaluate the service brand with respect to its perceived ability to satisfy their current needs, wants and expectations. That evaluation is generally based on the consumers' beliefs and knowledge about the brand's benefits, and their related emotional feelings about the brand. Like brand awareness, which must precede it, brand attitude is a prerequisite communication objective.

Brand attitude is the most complex of the communication effects and influences four aspects of consumer decision-making:

1   The first is the overall summary judgment that connects the service brand in the consumer's mind to a purchase motive. It is possible for consumers to hold several attitudes towards a service depending upon their motives for purchasing.

2   The second influence of a brand attitude consists of one or more beliefs about the specific benefits that the service offers based on consumers' emotional judgments.

3   The third influence of brand attitude on consumer decision-making is the free-standing emotional factors associated with the brand. Many marketing communications campaigns, for example, will attempt to instil a specific emotional association with the service in a customer's mind that may or may not be tied to discernible brand benefits.

4   The last influence of brand attitude is that it may cause a consumer to develop a set of choice rules such as: 'I will only consider those services within a given price range' and then, 'I will only select a service based on my predisposition towards that brand'. This choice rule of course assumes that the predisposition towards the particular service brand is favourable!

Although the brand attitude communication effect is complex because of its multiple components, achieving a service brand attitude objective is relatively straightforward:

1   Determine the target market's current attitude towards a service brand.

2   Set a realistic service brand attitude level for that target market.

3   Develop a marketing communications campaign to achieve the communication objectives for the service.

The steps involved in the marketing communication strategies to alter buyers' current attitudes towards a service brand are shown in Table 9.4.[28]

Brand purchase intention

A prospective buyer in the target market can have many favourable attitudes towards many service brands. Brand purchase intention, however, is a conscious decision to purchase one

Table 9.4 Marketing communications strategies to alter buyers' current brand attitudes

Buyers' current attitudes	Communication objectives
Brand attitude—unaware	*Create* brand attitude
Moderately favourable brand attitude	*Increase* brand attitude
Maximally favourable brand attitude	*Maintain* brand attitude
Any buyer with a favourable brand attitude	*Modify* brand attitude
Negative brand attitude	*Change* brand attitude

particular service brand or to take some type of purchase-related action, often based on such thoughts as 'I'd like to try that service' or 'I'll buy from that service'.

So depending on which stage of the consumers' decision-making process is chosen, the marketing communication message strategies that can be adopted for a service include:

→ to propose, where the message is targeted to the *initiator*

→ to recommend, where the message is targeted to the *influencer*

→ to make a selection, where the message is targeted to the *decider*

→ to buy, where the message is targeted to the *purchaser*

→ to buy more of a service, where the message is targeted to the *user*.

Purchase facilitation

Purchase facilitation is the organisation's assurance to the buyer that all the elements of the marketing mix for the service are coordinated. Quite simply, purchase facilitation ensures that the service will be sold at a price that consumers are willing and able to pay, and it will available at a location that is convenient for those consumers to access the service.

The communication effects are based on consumer associations with a service brand and are the basis of developing the communication objectives of an effective marketing communications campaign. The marketing objective of a services marketing communications campaign is to induce a behavioural change in the target market— that is, to influence the consumers' purchase decision-making processes that in turn encourages them to purchase the service and, ultimately, increase the organisation's profitability.

The media planning process

A marketing communications message will only be effective when it is placed in the media and vehicles that can best reach the chosen target audience. In addition to selecting the general media channels, such as television, radio, print, outdoor or online media, media planning also requires selecting specific vehicles within those media channels, subject to the constraints of the marketing communications budget.

media planning
Is premised on a media
scheduling plan that
includes a marketing
communications
timetable and media
vehicles that together
will help to achieve a
service organisation's
integrated marketing
communications
objectives

Media planning is the design of a strategy that quantifies how investments in advertising dollars and time will contribute to the achievement of the marketing communications objectives. The challenge in media planning is to determine how best to allocate the fixed advertising budget for a particular planning period, usually a financial year, between various promotional media, across vehicles within that media and over time. As shown in Figure 9.11, the media planning process involves coordination of four levels of strategy formulations: selecting the target market, developing marketing and communication objectives, developing message strategies and implementing media strategies. The overall marketing strategy, which consists of identifying the target market and selecting the appropriate services marketing mix, provides the impetus and direction for the choice of both communications and media strategies. As a practical example, Virgin Blue has adopted a strategy to reposition the airline as 'a new world carrier' by offering a service that allows business customers to change their flight timetable without a financial penalty.

Figure 9.11   The media planning process

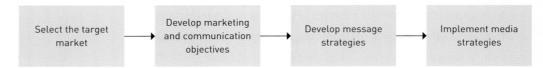

Developing media strategies consists of three interrelated activities:

1   specifying media objectives
2   selecting media categories and vehicles
3   cost considerations.

Specifying media objectives

When the market target has been selected, the next stage of the media planning process is to specify the objectives that the marketing communications schedule will accomplish during the advertising period. Media planners, when setting objectives, must consider the following issues:

→ What proportion of the target population will be reached with the marketing messages during a specified period?

→ How frequently do members of the target market need to be exposed to the marketing message during that period?

→ How much marketing communications weight is necessary to accomplish the reach and frequency objectives?

→ How should the marketing communications budget be allocated over time?

→ How close to the time of purchase should the target audience be exposed to the marketing communications message?

→ What is the most cost-effective way to accomplish the other marketing objectives?

Reach

Reach represents the percentage of the target audience that is exposed, at least once during a specified time frame, to the vehicles in which the marketing communications message is inserted; that is, the specific broadcast programs or print choices that carry the marketing messages. The timeframe used by the majority of media planners is usually a four-week period, which produces 13 four-week media planning periods during a year. Some media planners, however, may use a single week as the planning period.

Regardless of the length of the planning period, reach represents the percentage of all target customers who have an opportunity to see or hear the service organisation's message one or more times during the planning period. *Opportunity to see* (OTS) refers to all marketing media, whether visual or auditory. Advertisers can never be certain whether members of their target audiences actually see or hear an advertising message; they only know what media vehicles the target audience has been exposed to. From that vehicle exposure data, such as the television audience data collected by OzTAM, it can be inferred that people have had an opportunity to see the advertising message carried in the various media vehicles. The other terms that media planners use for describing reach are *1+* ('one-plus'), *net coverage*, *unduplicated audience* and *cumulative audience* (or 'cume').

The determinants of reach

Several factors determine the reach achieved by a service brand's media schedule during a four-week planning period. Generally, more prospective customers are reached when a media schedule uses multiple media vehicles rather than a single platform. For example, if a marketing message was aired only on national television, it would reach fewer people than if it were also published in magazines and national newspapers. In general, the more types of media vehicles that are used, the greater the chances are that a marketing message will come into contact with people possessing different media consumption habits. If a service organisation used only newspapers to promote its brand, the marketing message would only be seen by two-thirds of the adult population in Australia who regularly read a daily newspaper. Similarly, marketing messages aired only on various television programs would miss those consumers who do not watch those programs. Using integrated media therefore increases the possibility of reaching a greater proportion of the target audience.

A second factor that influences reach is the number and diversity of media vehicles used in a campaign. For example, if a service organisation like Trivago chooses to promote its hotel booking service in one or two magazines rather than a wider variety of print vehicles, fewer consumers would be reached by its marketing communications.

Third, reach can be increased by diversifying the day and night-time television-slots used to air a marketing message. For example, using commercial television during prime time and pay television during other times would reach more potential customers than by airing the marketing message only during prime time. Reach is an important consideration when developing a media schedule for a service brand. By itself, however, reach is an inadequate objective for media planning because it does not indicate how often target customers need to be exposed to the brand's marketing message for that message to accomplish its objectives. The frequency of marketing communications exposures must also therefore be considered.

Frequency

↘
frequency
The number of times, on average, within a four-week period that consumers in a target market will be exposed to a service organisation's market messages

Frequency is the number of times, on average, during the campaign period that members of the target audience will be exposed to the media vehicles that carry the marketing message for a service brand. Frequency actually represents a media schedule's average frequency, but the term *frequency* is usually adopted when referring to average frequency.

If the frequency of a particular adverting schedule is 2.2, that in effect means 90 per cent of the target audience are reached one or more times:

→ 20 per cent of the target audience are reached once

→ 40 per cent of the target are reached two times

→ 20 per cent of the target audience are reached three times

→ 10 per cent of the target audience are reached four times.

That hypothetical situation indicates that 90 per cent of a service organisation's target audience is reached by the advertising schedule, and that they are exposed an average of 2.2 times during the four-week advertising schedule for a particular television program.

Weight

↘
weight
The intensity that a communications schedule will deliver and is calculated by multiplying reach by frequency

A third important objective of media plans is to determine how much weight is required to achieve the service organisation's marketing communications objectives. Gross rating points (GRPs) represent the gross weight (or duplicated audience) and is the intensity that a service organisation's communications schedule will deliver; it is calculated by multiplying reach by frequency. Weight is also determined by allocating a fixed budget that generally aims to reach as much of the target audience as possible at the lowest costs.

In Australia, target audience rating points (TARPs) are used as an indicator of marketing communications weight. TARPs measure the audience of a specific media vehicle at a given point in time and are expressed as a percentage of the potential audience. One TARP is therefore 1 per cent of the television population of the *target audience* demographic. A time slot that attracts 10 TARPs had 10 per cent of the selected target audience tuned to the program at the time that the marketing message was aired.[29]

Effective rating points

Alternative media schedules are usually compared in terms of the number of TARPs that each generates. It is important to note that a greater number of TARPs does not necessarily indicate the superiority of one particular media schedule.

Consider, for example, two alternative media plans, X and Y, both of which require the same budget. Plan X generates 180 TARPs while Plan Y provides 160 TARPs. Which is the better plan? Plan X may achieve greater reach, but Plan Y has a higher frequency level. If the communication objective for the service brand in question requires a greater number of exposures for the marketing message to be effective—that is, *informing* the target market about the brand—then Plan Y may be superior even though it yields fewer TARPs.

So there is a need to consider media effectiveness that takes into account the number of times members of the target audience have an opportunity to see the marketing message for the particular service. The terms *effective reach* and *effective frequency* are often used interchangeably by media agencies to signify that an effective media schedule delivers a sufficient, but not excessive, number of ads to the target audience. Because the term effective reach creates less confusion when discussing the meaning and calculation of effective rating points, that term is preferred to effective frequency.

Effective reach is based on the premise that a marketing communications schedule is effective only if it does *not* reach members of the target audience too few or too many times. In other words, there is a theoretical optimum range of exposures to a marketing message, with minimum and maximum limits. But what constitutes too few or too many exposures? The only answer that can be given with certainty is, 'It depends!'

It depends, in particular, on variables such as:

→ the level of consumer awareness of the brand being promoted

→ its competitive position

→ the target audience's degree of brand loyalty

→ message creativity and novelty

→ the objectives that marketing message was intended to accomplish for the brand.

In fact, high levels of weekly exposure to a service's marketing message may be unproductive for loyal consumers because of a decreasing level of marketing communication effectiveness.[30] Specifically, services with higher market shares and greater customer loyalty typically require fewer exposures to marketing messages to achieve minimal levels of marketing communications effectiveness. Similarly, a distinctive marketing message that catches the audience's attention requires fewer exposures. Conversely, when a marketing communication objective is to move consumers to a higher level in the hierarchy of effects model, more exposures are needed to achieve that goal. For example, more exposures would be needed to convince a target audience that Bank A's customer service is superior to that offered by Banks B, C and D, rather than merely making them aware that Bank A's brand is associated with an excellent customer service.

How many exposures are needed?

The minimum and maximum numbers of effective exposures can be determined only by conducting continual research. Because this type of research is time-consuming and

William Chitty

expensive, marketers and media planners generally adopt 'a value judgment' in place of research to determine exposure effectiveness. Advertising industry practice has been heavily influenced by the three-exposure hypothesis, which is based on the minimum number of exposures needed to achieve the marketing communication objectives.

The creator of the three-exposure hypothesis was psychologist Herbert Krugman, who had an interest in how consumers learnt about products from being exposed to advertising. He argued that a consumer's initial exposure to a brand's marketing message would initiate a response of 'What is it?', while the second exposure would trigger a response of 'What of it?' The third and subsequent exposures would then become merely reminders of the information that the consumer has already learnt from the first two exposures to the marketing message.[31]

Many advertising practitioners have interpreted the three-exposure hypothesis to mean that media schedules are ineffective if they deliver average frequencies of less than three exposures to the media vehicle that carries the marketing message for a particular service brand. Although there is some intuitive appeal to the premise that average frequencies of fewer than three are insufficient, this interpretation of the three-exposure hypothesis is literal and fails to recognise that Krugman's hypothesis was based on the target market having three exposures to the marketing *message*, and not three exposures to the media *vehicle*.[32]

The difference is that vehicle exposure, which presents an *opportunity to see* (OTS) a marketing message, is not the same as *exposure* to the marketing message. In order for the target audience to understand the message, the marketing communication must develop specific links between a service and its benefits, and this requires prospective consumers to pay attention to the message to learn what benefits the brand offers, rather than merely being exposed to the particular media vehicle. Magazine readers will be exposed to some promotions in a particular issue, but there is a reasonable probability that they will not be exposed to all, or even most, of them. Similarly, a person watching a television program will probably not pay attention to all commercials aired during that program.

Therefore, the number of consumers who are actually exposed to a particular advertising message carried in a particular vehicle—which is the basis of what Krugman had in mind—is less than the number of people who are exposed to the vehicle that carries the message.[33]

It is important to note that there is not a specific number of minimum exposures—whether it is 3+, 5+ or *x*+—in other words, an optimum number for all marketing communications. What is effective, or ineffective, for one service brand may not necessarily be so for another: 'There is no magic number, no comfortable "3+" level of advertising exposures that works, even if some marketers refer to exposure rather than [the more correct term] OTS.'[34]

Influence the target market's behaviour

The final goal of marketing communications is to positively *influence the behaviour* of the target market. Marketing communications must do more than just create brand awareness or enhance consumer attitudes towards a service brand; a service organisation's communication efforts must encourage some form of behavioural response from its target market. That is, the marketing message must move the target market to action because marketing communication is *ultimately* evaluated in terms of whether it influences customer buying behaviour, which produces sales.

Prior to purchasing a new service, consumers generally need to be made aware of the service brand and its benefits, and then encouraged by persuasive marketing messages to develop a favourable attitude towards it. Marketing communications directed at accomplishing these intermediate, or pre-behavioural, goals are necessary, but a successful marketing communications program must accomplish more than encouraging consumers to like the service brand. That is why sales promotions and direct-to-consumer advertising are used extensively for services because both practices yield a more cost-effective behavioural change—for example, a trial subscription of a gymnasium—than other forms of marketing communications.

The Transport Accident Commission of Victoria

Services in Action

A challenge confronts state police departments who plan campaigns to change drivers' attitudes towards driving more safely. Although most motorists understand that speeding and drink driving are the major causes of road accidents and fatalities, they tend to think that these events only affect other drivers and not them. The goal of the latest strategy is to reduce road trauma for young drivers in their first months of solo driving and beyond, and instilling safe driving behaviours and attitudes from a young age is key to achieving this goal.

Positive role modelling by the parents of five- to 12-year-olds has the potential to have a significant influence on their child's future driving behaviour. The truth is that kids learn more from their parents' behaviour than the parents think they do.

While 18- to 25-year-olds represent around 14 per cent of all licensed drivers, they accounted for more than a quarter (28%) of all fatalities on Victoria's roads, which means that despite a large reduction in Victoria's road fatalities since 1989, 18- to 25-year-olds remain over-represented in road trauma. In their first year of driving, young Victorians are almost four times more likely to be involved in a fatal or serious injury crash than more experienced drivers.[35]

Source: Transport Accident Commission. <www.tac. vic.gov.au/road-safety/tac-campaigns/young-drivers/ strings>.

Build customer relationships

Successful marketing communications requires the organisation to build *a relationship between the brand and the customer* that becomes an enduring link.[36] Successful relationships between customers and brands develop strong, favourable and perhaps unique associations with the brand that lead to repeat purchases and generate customer loyalty towards the brand.

To understand how relationships between brands and customers are developed, marketers need to know how brand experiences build customer-based brand equity. As shown in Figure 9.12, the first stage in building brand equity occurs when consumers begin to identify the salient features of the brand.[37] Consumers then begin to understand the points of differences and points of parity that are based on the service brand's performance and its image, and evaluate the brand's credibility based on their judgments and feelings. The final stage is resonance, which is about brand relationships that, if positive, will develop into longer-term brand loyalty.

Figure 9.12 The customer-based brand equity pyramid

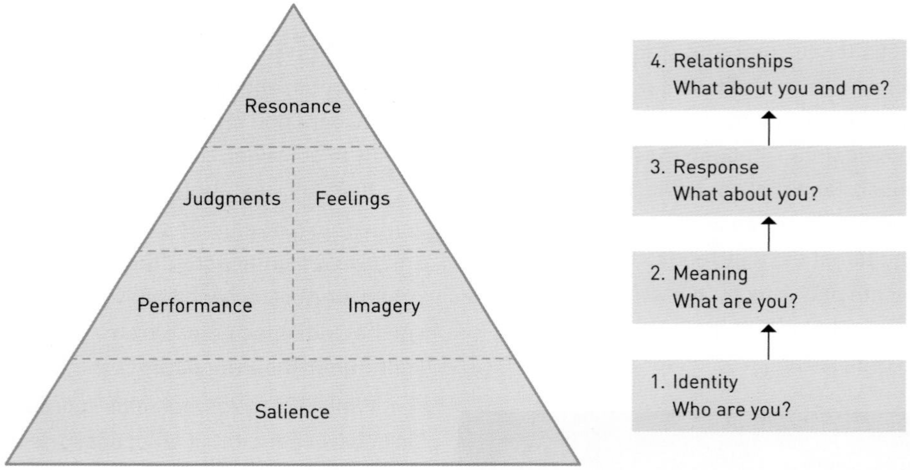

Source: K.L. Keller (2003). *Strategic Brand Management: Building, Measuring and Managing Brand Equity*. Upper Saddle River, NJ: Pearson Education, p. 76.

Resonance can improve the profitability of service organisations while at the same time allowing them to improve customer satisfaction by offering individual customised service encounters.

Marketing communication establishes a commonality of meaning between a service organisation's brand and its target market base. The concept of meaning is fundamental for effective marketing communications because marketers use brand-specific objectives to *create* meaning about a service, while the intended target market *constructs* meaning as they decode marketing messages.

This chapter has considered the fundamentals of marketing communications, which is a service organisation's coordinated efforts to promote a consistent brand message using the various elements of the marketing communications mix that 'speak with one voice'. One of several key features of marketing communications for services is the use of service providers as potential message-delivery channels. Another key feature is that the marketing communications process starts with the target customer, rather than the service organisation as the brand communicator, to determine the most appropriate and effective methods for developing persuasive communications programs. Setting marketing communications objectives depends on consumers' behaviour in their interactions with particular service categories. The hierarchy of effects model provides an explanation of consumers' responses to service advertisements and illustrates the implications of those responses for setting advertising objectives.

Selecting advertising media and vehicles is one of the most important of all integrated marketing communications decisions. Media planning must be coordinated with marketing and communications strategies. The strategic aspects of media planning for services involve four steps:

1   Selecting the target audience towards which all subsequent efforts will be directed.
2   Specifying media objectives, which are typically stated in terms of reach, frequency and weight.
3   Selecting general media categories and specific vehicles within each ad medium.
4   Selecting media based on maximising reach, frequency or TARPs. Media and vehicle selection are influenced by the target market's behaviour and communication considerations.

Media planning identifies those strategies that will reach the designated target audience and be compatible with a service organisation's marketing message.

There are several distinguishing factors that influence the marketing communications for services:

→ The service provider is often the service, and the customer is the co-producer of the service that is purchased.
→ The quality of the service may be less consistent and less recognisable than for tangible products, which can be more readily evaluated prior to purchase.
→ The reputation of the service organisation, and its brand image, are more important for services than for tangible products.
→ There is greater reliance on word-of-mouth communication among the consumers of services because they are more dependent on credible sources of marketing information.
→ For high-involvement services, such as business travel, personal relationships are more important than mainstream mass media.

Review questions

1   Why is profiling the target audience the first step in developing a media strategy?
2   Fully explain the differences between marketing and communication objectives and provide reasons as to which is more important when marketing a service.

3 Explain how the four characteristics of a consumer service influence the marketing communications for that service.

4 What role should a positioning statement play in developing a marketing communications strategy for a consumer service? Fully explain how marketing communications is used to position a consumer service.

5 Which elements of a marketing communications model can establish commonality of meaning between a service organisation and its target market?

6 Explain the advantages and limitations of using online media instead of a more traditional element of marketing communications—such as television—to market a consumer service.

7 With reference to Krugman's three-exposure hypothesis, explain the difference between, '...three exposures to a marketing message, and three exposures to a media vehicle'.

8 Using the hierarchy of effects model, explain how a target market will respond to a service organisation's marketing message.

Weblinks

The following organisations are some of the marketing and media industry associations that provide current marketing communications data and information.

Australia

ACNielsen Media Research. <www.nielsen.com/au/en.html>

AdNews. <www.adnews.com.au>

Advertising Federation of Australia Ltd. <www.afa.org.au>

Australian Bureau of Statistics. <www.abs.gov.au>

Australian Direct Marketing Association. <www.adma.com.au>

B&T. <www.bandt.com.au>

Interactive Advertising Bureau of Australia. <www.iabaustralia.com.au>

Outdoor Media Association. <www.oma.org.au>

OzTam. <www.oztam.com.au>

Roy Morgan Research. <www.roymorgan.com>

New Zealand

ACNielsen. <www.nielsen.com/nz/en.html>

Advertising Standards Authority. <www.asa.co.nz>

Commerce Commission. <www.comcom.govt.nz>

Communication Agencies Association of New Zealand (CAANZ). <www.caanz.co.nz>

Ministry of Consumer Affairs. <www.consumeraffairs.govt.nz>

Singapore

Advertising Standards Authority of Singapore. <https://asas.org.sg>

Department of Statistics. <www.singstat.gov.sg>

Media Corporation of Singapore. <www.mediacorp.com.sg>

OXFORD UNIVERSITY PRESS

Endnotes

1 Based on Tourism New Zealand (2015). Latest campaign encourages Aussies to take South Island roadie. 17 February. <www.tourismnewzealand.com/tourism-news-insights/tourism-insights/latest-campaign-encourages-aussies-to-take-south-island-roadie>.

2 S.J. Gould, A.F. Grein & D.B. Lernan (1999). The role of agency–client integration in integrated marketing communications: A complementary agency theory-interorganizational perspective. *Journal of Current Issues and Research in Advertising*, 21(Spring), 1–12.

3 D. Flynn (2017). Singapore Airlines: Two all-new business class seats for 2017–18. *Australian Business Traveller*, 16 January. <www.ausbt.com.au/singapore-airlines-two-all-new-business-class-seats-for-2017-18>.

4 C.W. Park, B.J. Jaworski & D.J. McInnes (1986). Strategic brand concept-image management. *Journal of Marketing*, 50(October), 123.

5 Telehealth website. <www.telstrahealth.com/home/solutions/telehealth.html>.

6 S. Kurosawa (2015). The devils made me do it. *The Weekend Australian*, 20–21 June, p. 4.

7 ibid.

8 W. Chitty, E. Luck, N. Barker, A.-M. Sassenberg, T.A. Shimp & J.C. Andrews (2018). *Integrated Marketing Communications* (5th edn). Melbourne: Cengage Learning Australia, p. 45.

9 NewMediaWorks (2016). PwC outlook: Adspend grows with lift in digital. 8 June. <www.newsmediaworks.com.au/pwc-outlook-adspend-grows-with-lift-in-digital>.

10 D. Flynn (2015). Qantas begins A330 business suite flights to Hong Kong. *Australian Business Traveller*, 24 March. <www.ausbt.com.au/qantas-begins-a330-business-suite-flights-to-hong-kong>.

11 IAB Australia (2017). Online advertising spend reaches $7.6 billion in 2017 financial year. Press release, 5 September. <www.iabaustralia.com.au/news-and-updates/iab-press-releases/item/22-iab-press-releases/2374-online-advertising-spend-reaches-7-6-billion-in-2017-financial-year#COrReG11tSbiK2wv.99>.

12 ibid.

13 Sensis (2017). *Sensis Social Media Report 2017*. 22 June. Melbourne: Sensis Pty Ltd, Chapter 1, p. 9. <www.sensis.com.au/socialmediareport>.

14 ibid., Chapter 1, pp. 12–13 & 17.

15 ibid., Chapter 1, p. 23.

16 ibid., Chapter 1, p. 26.

17 ibid., Chapter 2, p. 3.

18 W. Chitty, E. Luck, N. Barker, M. Valos & T. Shimp (2015). *Integrated Marketing Communications* (4th edn). Melbourne: Cengage Learning Australia, pp. 6–7.

19 Tyro (2015). An easier way to pay for 5.5 million Australians. Press release, 4 June. <http://tyro.com/press-releases/an-easier-way-to-pay-for-5-5-million-australians>.

20 Telstra (n.d.). *How Mobility is Changing the Rhythm of Australian Retail*. <www.telstra.com.au/business-enterprise/download/document/business-enterprise-teg1398_mobility_retail_white_pages_v08_hr_singles.pdf>.

21 PayPal (2015). *PayPal Money Habits Study—Global. Research Findings*. 1 September. <www.paypalobjects.com/webstatic/en_US/mktg/pages/stories/pdf/paypal_money_habits_study__media_deck_global_final.pdf>.

22 PayPal (2014). *PayPal Mobile Research 2014/2015. Global Snapshot*. <www.paypalobjects.com/ webstatic/en_US/mktg/pages/stories/pdf/paypal_mobile_global_snapshot_2015_2.pdf>.

23 T.A. Shimp (2010). *Advertising, Promotion and Other Aspects of Integrated Marketing Communications* (8th edn). Mason, OH: South Western Cengage Learning, p. 336.

24 R.J. Lavidge & G.A. Steiner (1961). A model for predictive measurements of advertising effectiveness. *Journal of Marketing*, 25(October), 61–5.

25 ibid.

26 This 'one voice' perspective is shared by several authors; see in particular D.E. Schultz, S.I. Tannebaum & R.F. Lauterborn (1993). *Integrated Marketing Communications*. Lincolnwood, IL: NTC Publishing Group, p. 46; and G. Nowak & J. Phelps (1994). Conceptualising the integrated marketing communications phenomenon: An examination of its impact on advertising practices and its implications for advertising research. *Journal of Current Issues and Research in Advertising*, 16 (Spring), 49–66.

27 J.R. Rossiter & L. Percy (1997). *Advertising Communications and Promotion Management* (2nd edn). Boston, MA: Irwin McGraw-Hill.

28 W. Chitty, E. Luck, N. Barker, M. Valos & T. Shimp (2015). *Integrated Marketing Communications* (4th edn). Melbourne: Cengage Learning Australia, p. 257.

29 ibid.

30 G.J. Tellis (1988). Advertising exposure, loyalty and brand purchase: A two stage model of choice. *Journal of Marketing Research*, 25(May), 134–44.

31 H.E. Krugman(1972). Why three exposures may be enough. *Journal of Advertising Research*, 12(6), 11–16.

32 This assertion was made by H.M. Cannon & E.A. Riordan (1994). Effective reach and frequency: Does it really make sense? *Journal of Advertising Research*, 34 (March/April), 19–28.

33 ibid., p. 21.

34 ibid., p. 24.

35 Transport Accident Commission, TAC Campaigns. <www.tac.vic.gov.au/road-safety/tac-campaigns/young-drivers/strings>.

36 S. Fournier (1988). Consumers and their brands: Developing relationship theory in consumer research. *Journal of Consumer Research*, 24(March), 343–73.

37 K.L. Keller (2003). *Strategic Brand Management: Building, Measuring and Managing Brand Equity*, Upper Saddle River, NJ: Pearson Education, p. 76.

Case

Case study C

Take a break

According to the findings of a press release from Roy Morgan Research, as shown in Figure 1, Australian employees have accrued about 16 days of annual leave per employee, with more than a third—34 per cent of the 8.5 million Australian employees—having at least four weeks of unused annual leave.[1]

Figure 1 Annual leave accrued by Australian paid workers

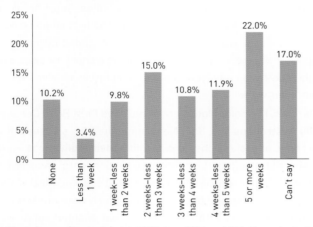

Source: Roy Morgan Single Source (Australia), July 2015–June 2016, n=4,984. Base: Australians 14+ in paid employment who are entitled to take annual leave.

In good news for tourism operators, destination marketers and hotels, just over 80 per cent of paid employees in Australia said they intended to take a holiday sometime in the coming 12 months.[2] Choice Hotels Asia-Pacific, which offers a wide range of accommodation—250 hotels in diverse locations in Australia and New Zealand—saw an opportunity in the results of the Roy Morgan research to develop an integrated marketing campaign that encourages those employees with accrued annual leave to take a short break from work and stay in a Choice Hotel. In conjunction with its agency partners Gravia Media and Akkomplice Group, Choice Hotels launched an integrated marketing campaign, which they called 'Need a Break', on 5 June 2017.

Objectives

The overall objective of the Need a Break campaign was to encourage Australian and New Zealand employees with accrued annual leave to consider taking short breaks of one to three nights away from work. The media objective was to develop a multi-channel year-long campaign to encourage employees with accrued leave to take a short break to safeguard their mental well-being and better manage their levels of stress.

Research has confirmed that 82 per cent of Australians and 83 per cent of New Zealanders feel revitalised after a short break and that short breaks renew happiness, healthiness, work motivation and a sense of connection to partners and children.[3] The message objective was to position Choice Hotels as the preferred leader in accommodation for the short-term leisure market in Australia and New Zealand by creating top-of-mind brand awareness for consumers who are considering taking a short break from work.

Strategy

A short-term getaway was selected as the basis of a strategy that focused on encouraging workers with accrued leave to take a short break from one to three nights away from home. Short-term breaks are more affordable and therefore more likely to be achieved by all employees having different incomes and demographic profiles. Short breaks are also easier to take for workers who have limited time at their disposal. The first step in formulating a strategy was to ensure that the message would resonate with its intended target audience. It would be pointless, for example, for the message to promote taking a short break as a means of relieving employee stress if the Australian and New Zealand workforces believed they were not actually feeling stressed from their work.

To that end, in March 2017 Choice Hotels commissioned First Point Consulting to conduct an online survey of 1000 Australians and 1000 New Zealanders, who earned at least $50000 and worked in a diverse range of professions, to determine their motivations—and any subsequent barriers—to taking short breaks, and to identify the respondents' associated behavioural and attitudinal assumptions.[4] The responses from the target audience were then split into three groups: Millennials, generation Xs and baby boomers, which were chosen to further refine the different stress factors associated with each group. That enabled solutions that were based on the groups' associated attitudes and behaviour to be devised that eliminated the different factors in each group, given the different profile of each group.

The results were very different from what was expected. Two-thirds of Australian (67%) and 65 per cent of New Zealanders[5] believed they were experiencing moderate to extreme levels of stress and that those levels of stress were driven by the fact that almost a quarter of people had not taken a break from work in 2016. The survey results also indicated that taking regular short breaks was the preferred primary solution to relieving stress, and was ranked above exercise, consuming alcohol, shopping, sleeping, having a bath, eating and even sex. Three-quarters of Australians felt they had a better work–life balance—with most feeling happier—after having a short break from work.

Execution

After analysing the survey results, Choice Hotels developed its integrated, multi-layered campaign. In Australia, the Need a Break campaign included the key initiatives of launching a new web page (needabreak.com), the branding and wrapping of a Jetstar airliner, a new television commercial, sponsorship on Channel Nine's *Today* breakfast television program, location-specific large-format out-of-home advertising and targeted radio advertising on the *Hamish & Andy Drive Show*, social media advertising and public relations.

The following channels included initiatives to create top-of-mind awareness and motivations to take short breaks.

Websites

The needabreak website encourages Australians and New Zealanders to take a short break with motivation and advice. The content includes destination reviews, an online planner, and a quick and easy booking facility to all the Choice properties.

Television commercial

Choice secured a daily slot on *Today*, one of Australia's top-rating breakfast programs. The creative execution depicted an office falling into chaos after a seemingly innocuous event sets off a chain reaction that ultimately ended with a flaming photocopier being thrown out of a window.

Plane wrap

As shown in Figure 2, the same creative message that was used on the website was replicated on to a branded Jetstar aircraft that regularly flew to destinations in Australia and New Zealand where Choice Hotels had accommodation.

Figure 2   The Jetstar airliner included in the needabreak.com campaign

Source: Choice Hotels Group

Out-of-home advertising

Out-of-home adverting also used the same creative scene as the television ad where an office descends into mayhem over an innocuous event. Billboards highlighting that theme were placed at targeted locations that have high volumes of pedestrian and motor vehicle traffic, including those locations where drivers could be forced to sit in their vehicles at traffic lights.

Choice Hotels secured a sponsorship in Australia with Austereo's drive time and news radio programs during the *Hamish & Andy Drive Show*, which aired to peak-hour drivers—often the time when they would most feel like taking a break.

Digital and social

While the above the elements of the campaign were targeted mainly at creating consumer awareness, the digital and social elements were aimed at driving hotel bookings. Choice Hotels invested in creating an attribution model and tracking viewers to ensure that it could measure the impact the needabreak.com was having on converted sales via the choicehotels.com.au and choicehotels.co.nz websites. Display adverting drove viewers to the needabreak.com platform, which then through their selected destination interest, retargeted them with booking offers. The key media channels were Facebook and Instagram.

Results

To the end of October 2017, the needabreak.com website has attracted 75000 visits since its launch in June 2017. Choice Hotels has largely been able to attribute the current campaign to a current year-on-year growth of more than 20 per cent in reservations thorough the Choice Hotels websites.[6]

Something to think about

The message objective of Need a Break campaign was described as: *to position Choice Hotels as the leader in the short-term leisure market in Australia and New Zealand.* Do you think the creative message execution that depicts an office falling into chaos—after a seemingly innocuous event—that ultimately ends with a flaming photocopier being thrown out of a window resonates with employees with accrued annual leave? Why, or why not?

Endnotes

1   Roy Morgan (2016). Holidays waiting to happen: Australian workers, 134 million days of annual leave, and travel plans. Press release, no. 6974, 20 September. <www.roymorgan.com/findings/6974-holidays-waiting-to-happen-australian-workers-134million-days-annual-leave-201609200934>.
2   First Point Consulting (2017). Cited in Choose a break. *Marketing*, October/November, p. 74.
3   Choice Hotels launches brand new integrated 'Need A Break' campaign via Akkomplice. 5 June 2017. <www.campaignbrief.com/2017/06/choice-hotels-launches-brand-n.html>.
4   ibid.
5   ibid.
6   First Point Consulting (2017). Cited in Choose a break. *Marketing*, October/November, p. 77.

Case study D

Trick or treat: Cyber security in Australia

Cybercrime in Australia costs consumers around $1.06 billion a year,[1] and this does not include the cost to business and government, with *Dell* reporting some 16 million types of malware programs present in its user base in 2013.[2] A worldwide report by internet security software provider *Symantec* suggests that this occurrence is likely to increase owing to factors such as attackers gaining greater sophistication over their targets and leapfrogging their defences. Cyber-crime data shows a greater focus on extortion of consumers and organisations, demonstrated in a worldwide increase of 113 per cent on ransom-ware demands, and that such attacks are now moving to mobile devices.[3]

For the digital economy in Australia and worldwide, this is an issue of grave concern, as trust and dealing with perceived risk are the major pillars supporting use in this sector.[4] To reduce the threats of cybercrime and to gain the trust of consumers, organisations have developed a range of security measures, most recently using biometric techniques.[5] However, such technological innovations are only as good as company[6] and consumer practices[7] and do not take into account malware attacks, which occur in spite of diligent user behaviour.[8] Authentication by traditional passwords suffers from several human factors: people have difficulty remembering a huge number of secure passwords. Also, often passwords are written down, reused and recycled, meaning they are easily compromised;[9] conversely, system administrators tend to see only the cryptographic strength and other risk factors and ignore the vital issue of human mnemonic frailty. If strong passwords are enforced, or frequent changes are required, users take shortcuts by writing down passwords or recycling them. But strong passwords themselves may be stolen.

Users may be induced to give passwords up to spam or phishing attacks, or their machines may get infected by malware such as keyloggers, which grabs keystrokes and leaks passwords. Biometrics can solve the first of these, but malware requires a different approach, with software agents designed to seek out and kill malware. Malware detectors, such as virus scanners, tend to look for common patterns in malware code. This works because such code usually shares a common DNA.[10] But malware is now more sophisticated, with a number of techniques to foil scanners.[11] Users are thus engaged unwillingly in an unseen protection war against malware, while engaging in risky security behaviours, exploited by others, which compromise their authentication of passwords. It is then important to develop better authentication and protection technologies with an understanding of consumer, administrative and employee security behaviour and their acceptance of new innovations in this area. Without such research and implementation of both an understanding of human behaviour and advances in technology, it is likely we will fall further behind in the arms race with cybercriminals and online malicious malcontents.

There is, therefore, a need to develop a *greater understanding of consumer security beliefs and practices* and how these can be improved by not only technological intervention but by better education and the adoption of safer practices. Only by merging both technological solutions to increase cyber security and an understanding of user behaviour can advances in cyber-security practices occur. The integration of social sciences into understanding user security behaviour and likely acceptance of new technologies in this area is as important as any technological silver bullets in this region.

Even if users are sophisticated and prudent, there is always the unseen danger of what lurks beneath the surface in software and security. Many popular programs may have deep structural flaws that make them and users vulnerable to hackers and criminals. The interconnected $79 billion Australian digital economy means that personal details are shared and processed by a number of agents, which may be benevolent in the case of Google, but may be nefarious in others. This all points to the need for research and practice in cyber security that understands user behaviour, educates people about the risks and provides better, safer solutions that are readily adopted. There is thus a need to convince as much as educate users.

Something to think about

Service-delivery strategies are important in the area of cyber security. What type of strategies do you think might be important? What type of communication strategies might be important in preventing cyber crime in Australia?

Consider the opportunities for developing new services in cyber security. What do you see as the emerging issues of managing capacity and demand in cyber security? (Hint: additional online research can help here).

Endnotes

1 Australian Cyber Security Centre (ed.) (2015). *The Australian Threat Environment*. Australian Cyber Security Centre, Canberra: Australian Government.
2 D. Ayrapetov (2013). Cybersecurity challenges in 2013. *CIO* (13284045), 8–8.
3 Symantec (2015). *Internet Security Threat Report*, vol. 20. Mountain View, CA: Symantec.
4 A. Moloney (2009). Online banking security and consumer confidence. *Credit Control*, 30(4/5), 28–9; S. Ward, K. Bridges & B. Chitty (2005). Do incentives matter? An examination of online privacy concerns and willingness to provide personal and financial information. *Journal of Marketing Communications*, 11(1), 21–40; Y. Xia, Z.U. Ahmed, M. Ghingold, G.S. Boon, G.S. Thain Su Mei & H.L. Lee (2003). Consumer preferences for commercial web site design: An Asia-Pacific perspective. *Journal of Consumer Marketing*, 20(1), 10–27.
5 J. Kessler (2006). Banks are expected to use more behavioral biometrics technology. *ABA Bank Marketing*, 38(2), 5–5; A.K. Usman & M.H. Shah (2013). Strengthening e-banking security using keystroke dynamics. *Journal of Internet Banking & Commerce*, 18(3), 1–11.
6 B.-Y. Ng, A. Kankanhalli & Y. Xu (2009). Studying users' computer security behavior: A health belief perspective. *Decision Support Systems*, 46(4), 815–25.
7 M. Whitty, J. Doodson, S. Creese & D. Hodges (2015). Individual differences in cyber security behaviors: An examination of who is sharing passwords. *CyberPsychology, Behavior & Social Networking*, 18(1), 3–7.
8 D. Dang-Pham & S. Pittayachawan (2015). Comparing intention to avoid malware across contexts in a BYOD-enabled Australian university: A protection motivation theory approach. *Computers & Security*, 48, 281–97.
9 B. Prince (2012). Yahoo confirms 400,000 passwords stolen in hack. *eWeek*, 7–7.
10 R. Islam, R. Tian, L.M. Batten & S. Versteeg (2013). Classification of malware based on integrated static and dynamic features. *Journal of Network and Computer Applications*, 36(2), 646–56; R. Islam, R. Tian, V. Moonsamy & L. Batten (2012). A comparison of the classification of disparate malware collected in different time periods. *Journal of Networks*, 7(6), 946–55.
11 B. Acoca (2008). Online identity theft. In *OECD Observer: Organisation for Economic Cooperation & Development*, 12–13. <http://oecdobserver.org/news/archivestory.php/aid/2662/Online_identity_theft.html>; M. Saleh, E.P. Ratazzi & S. Xu (2014). Instructions-based detection of sophisticated obfuscation and packing. In *Military Communications Conference (MILCOM), 2014*, IEEE: IEEE, 1–6.

Part

3

Delivering Service Value

Favourable customer experiences boost revenue

According to the results from *Insights2020—Driving Customer-Centric Growth*, a study conducted by Millward Brown Vermeer, 74 per cent of successful companies create satisfying customer experiences that are based on data-driven insights.[1] The study, completed in partnership with the Advertising Research Foundation, Esomar, LinkedIn, Kantar and Korn Ferry, focused on combining insights and analytics in planning customers' experiences.

The research underpinning *Insights2020*, which was conducted using online behaviour analysis from LinkedIn and crowd-sourcing led by Wharton, was combined with information gained from over 350 in-depth interviews with industry leaders, and over 10 000 interviews with relevant parties across 60 global markets. The study analysed and compared over-performing and underperforming companies in terms of their revenue growth, and examined the methods and practices of successful companies and how their strategies drove company growth. As shown in Table 10.1, the research revealed some clear differences between over-performing and underperforming companies.

According to Frank Van Driest, chief commercial officer of Millward Brown Vermeer and manager of the global program, the results from *Insights2020* suggest that companies that out-perform their peers on revenue growth do so by over-performing on the key drivers of customer-centricity. Van Driest defines customer-centricity as 'a strategy to deliver business value against customer needs, guided by brand purpose'. Phase two of the project, which began in early 2016, aims to build on those factors. Based on the findings, Phase two will develop frameworks and guidelines to help marketers adopt similar procedures to these over-performing organisations and enhance customer-centricity in their brands and service products.

» *continued over page*

Chapter 10

The Service Experience

William Chitty

» *Favourable customer experiences boost revenue continued*

Table 10.1   Differences between over-performing and underperforming companies

All company activities linked to brand purpose	83% of over-performers
	31% of underperformers.
Embrace customer-centricity	78% of over-performers
	12% of underperformers.
Drive consistency across all customer touch-points	62% of over-performers
	26% of underperformers.
Focus on linking disparate data sources	66% of over-performers
	33% of underperformers.
Insights and analytics function reports straight to the CEO	33% of over-performers
	12% of underperformers

Source: B. Ice (2015). Customer-centric strategy boosts revenue performance—study. *Marketing*, 6 October. <www.marketingmag.com. au/news-c/customer-centric-strategy-boosts-revenue-performance-study/?inf_contact_key=ae92d6f19b26624d5688884ddaaeec-85d199746e3c542189c07ad72bbbc343dc>.

Introduction

Regardless of the type of service being provided, managing a customer's service experience (abbreviated as CX) can be a difficult task for service marketing managers. The successful management of CX is based on understanding that customers bring preconceived expectations about the service, and what they feel they should receive in a service interaction, before they actually have contact with the service organisation. If after the service interaction, customers perceive that they have received something less than what was expected from the service, then those customers are, according to the concepts of the disconfirmation of expectations paradigm (discussed later in the chapter), likely to feel some degree of cognitive dissonance; that is, dissatisfaction with the functional and/or technical qualities of that service.

It is important to note the differences between customer service and a customer's experience. *Customer service* is an organisational function—similar to marketing and sales—that manages the interactions with customers, while *CX* for a service is a culmination of several interactive engagements and touch points between a service organisation and its customers.[2]

That succinct definition of customer experience is based on a conceptual framework that consists of the perceptions that customers hold about the value of a service organisation's brand, and the service interactions they experience in assessing the value of the brand. Those perceptions are directed primarily at the service brand to deliver value that satisfies the customer's needs and wants, and those perceptions are emotionally engaged when the customer–organisation interaction achieves the brand's implied service promise.[3]

CX is, therefore, the perception that customers have after their experiential interactions with a service organisation. It is a mix of the technical qualities (what customers received from the service) and functional qualities (how they received the service) of the organisation's service-delivery processes, and the customer's senses and emotions evoked by each interaction, compared with the expectations that they bring to a service interaction.[4]

Service encounters are a form of communication between the service organisation and a customer and can last for weeks—for example, a having a two-week holiday at a beach resort—or for a moment, like a fleeting glance at an advertisement in a magazine. The customers' experiences also include the critical aspect of blending the technical and functional qualities of the service process. That blending process, together with customer's rational sense and emotions, is a series of interactions that creates the complete CX. Customer service is, therefore, one element of a customer's experience.

> ↘
> **customer experience (CX)**
> The perception that customers have after their experiential interactions with a service organisation

Learning objectives

After reading this chapter you should be able to:

↘ describe the elements of customers' service experiences

↘ understand the importance of customers' service experiences

William Chitty

- ↘ describe strategies to develop CX for services organisations
- ↘ discuss the emotional aspects associated with customers' services experiences
- ↘ discuss the rational factors that deliver customers' services experiences
- ↘ discuss the technological factors that deliver customers' services experiences
- ↘ describe the various methods that can be used to evaluate customers' service experiences
- ↘ describe the importance of offering favourable CX.

Elements of customers' service experiences

A customer's experience is a critical characteristic of a service organisation's core service interaction, but it is not 'sold' by the organisation. Service organisations do not charge for their service interactions because these interactions are integral elements of a service product and are not easily separated from the service encounter. For example, CX can be provided on-site, such as when a bank teller assists customers in selecting the most suitable credit card for their needs, or it can be provided over the phone from a call centre, by social media via the internet or it may be offered remotely from an ATM using self-service technology.

Customer service is a term that is widely misused by many service organisations. Some service organisations claim they provide customer service as part of their service product, yet very few do so at a level that delights their customers. As discussed in Chapter 1, customer service is a collective concept that describes the task-oriented activities that involve interactions with customers—either in person or by using technology—for the purpose of delivering support for a service product. It is a marketing function that should be designed, performed and communicated with two goals in mind: customer satisfaction and operational efficiency.

Service organisations that consistently deliver a memorable CX create value for their customers and a competitive advantage for their operations. It is, however, difficult to identify and isolate the benefits of CX because they are likely to be obscured by the multi-functional layers in service-delivery processes.[5] For example, it is difficult to identify the benefits and measure the common objective that CX can generate; that is, the need to 'delight' a customer. Delight with CX is typically generated when the CX exceeds a customer's expectations, and is likely to be an emotionally based condition derived from the expectancy disconfirmation paradigm as opposed to being merely satisfying (see Chapter 11 for a discussion of the expectancy disconfirmation paradigm). As such, delight is a second-order emotion that specifically occurs from a simultaneous combination of joy and surprise, and is associated with '... exceptionally favourable service incidents that were particularly memorable to a consumer'.[6] Usually, rational delight, which is related to satisfaction, is a necessary, but not sufficient condition, to generate positive customer behaviour, such as recommending an organisation to family and friends. That suggests customer satisfaction indicates the degree of acceptance of a rational experience, but not the complete CX, which includes both the rational and emotional interactions that deliver delight.[7]

Many service products, such as flights offered by budget airlines, are perceived as being commodities that are—more often than not—purchased purely on the basis of price rather than quality. As more budget airlines enter price-sensitive markets, competition increases and those service organisations find that it becomes increasingly more difficult to identify and differentiate their services. The solution for the low-cost carriers (LCC) is to develop a competitive advantage by providing an emotionally engaging CX that will, in turn, increase profitability and shareholder value. A satisfying CX can deliver long-term economic value to a service organisation that is difficult for its competitors to replicate. It is not enough to provide a good service product at a fair price; service organisations need to understand their customers' experiences on every level—from the delivery of value to their emotional satisfaction.

Measuring CX

For most service organisations, measuring CX is one of the biggest corporate challenges they face, with many organisations measuring their CX in the wrong way. Measuring is a critical part of any effort to quantify the drivers of any progress—or decline—of CX because if the delivery of a service proceeds without any obvious problems, the service marketers may wrongly assume that their customers' perceptions of the service interaction will be positive. Customers not only inform organisations about what they are doing right (or wrong), but also create clear CX goals for the organisation. The challenge for the managers of CX programs is that they are trying to measure an intangible act.

Many service organisations attempt to measure their CX performance using variables such as sales growth and margins. Those two variables are inadequate measures of CX because their general nature makes it difficult to translate them into remedial CX actions. How well a strategy achieves its objectives depends, to a large extent, on what actions an organisation takes *after* it measures the effectiveness of its current CX performance. Service organisations should develop a CX strategy that is not only linked to improving overall CX performance, but also how well their remedial actions will achieve the following outcomes:

1 The CX results reflect the objective the organisation wanted to achieve.
2 The CX results clearly indicate those actions that produced any positive returns to the organisation.

When a CX strategy delivers a measurement of customer satisfaction or even the nebulous concept of happiness, that metric can be identified. It is important to note, however, that while a CX strategy can make customers feel both satisfied and happy, those metrics may not increase the value of the organisation's operations. Implementing a CX strategy that produces the desired outcome for both customers and the organisation will deliver a very competitive advantage.[8]

More importantly, will that experience influence the future buying decisions and behaviour of customers, and thereby affect the service organisation's future revenue? The answer is a moot point because CX is an abstract concept that requires measurement models that go beyond measuring satisfaction; it requires measuring the tangible elements of a conceptual framework.

One such measurement model is an experience map, which measures both the *importance* of the experience and a customer's *satisfaction* with that experience. An experience map, as shown in Figure 10.1, is an analysis of customers' experience over the life cycle of their relationship with a service organisation. The basis of that analysis is a comparison of the customer's expectations prior to their perceived experience of the service activity.

Figure 10.1 An experience map

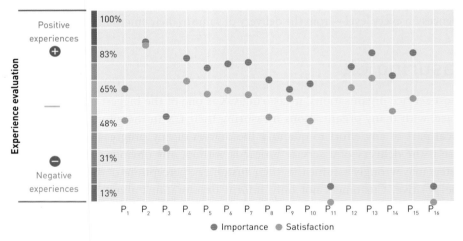

Source: The Customer Experience.es. <www.thecustomerexperience.es/en/chapters/chapter4.html>.

Not all interactions with a service organisation are important to customers, so not every interaction creates a memorable CX. To develop an experience map, therefore, marketers must do three things:[9]

1 Analyse the life cycle of the customer's relationship and map the major points of contact.

2 Design a survey to collect data about a customer's experience at each point of contact. Specifically, marketers need to determine the differences between importance and experience:

   – Importance: What are the customer's expectations of the service organisation at a specific time in the service relationship?

   – Experience: How did the service interaction with the service organisation actually turn out?

↘
importance
Relates to a customer's expectations of a service organisation at a specific time in the service relationship

↘
experience
Relates to a customer's judgment of the service interaction with the service organisation after it has been consumed

3 Develop indicators for each point of contact, and compare results for *importance* versus *satisfaction*, after each of those points of contact. Indicators should make use of a numeric scale and focus on the results that are clustered in the two areas of positive and negative experience.

Service organisations must develop CX strategies on the basis of the results suggested by an experience map.

If there is a point of contact where expectations are low and the actual experience nonetheless falls short, the issues that caused that situation must be resolved first so that a basic service experience can be delivered that matches customers' expectations. It is more important, however, to analyse those points of contact where the gaps are greatest than it is to examine the points of contact where the customers' expectations are highest. Those gaps are the 'Moments of Truth' in a service interaction, and that is where it is possible to influence a customer's perception and create an experience that they will remember.

The *2017 Australian Digital Experience Report* that was conducted by SAP Australia found that overall digital CX has improved since 2016.[10] The findings were are based on a survey of 4000 Australians who rated 14 attributes from more than 11 000 interactions. For the first time since the initial survey was conducted in 2015, banking (7%), and media and entertainment (6%) have returned positive digital CX scores.

Air travel achieved an overall score of 1, which means it has an almost even balance of delighted and dissatisfied customers. Insurance (-5%), telecommunications (-11%) and utilities (-15%) have, however, more dissatisfied customers when it comes to digital CX. The number of customers who are dissatisfied with their digital experiences has decreased from 40 per cent to 35 per cent, while the number who are delighted has increased from 26 per cent to 31 per cent. That increase in the number of satisfied customers indicates that while

some business organisations have actively improved their digital CX, there is a need for others to improve their customers' perceptions of digital experiences.[11]

Top-performing industries

For consecutive years, survey respondents indicated that among all brands Netflix offered the best digital CX, while other service brand leaders included Vodafone and Suncorp Bank. The digital CX of brands has significantly improved since the first study was conducted in 2015. The results of industry-specific digital CX gaps, as shown in Figure 10.2, suggest that among the service industries, the banking sector is improving its customer digital experience, and consequently increasing customer engagement.

Digital channels drive satisfaction

To become a digital CX leader, it is necessary for service marketers to understand the new emerging technologies, such as artificial intelligence and machine learning, to

William Chitty

Figure 10.2 Digital customer experience (CX) gaps

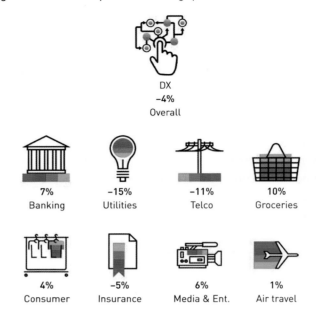

DX
−4%
Overall

7%
Banking

−15%
Utilities

−11%
Telco

10%
Groceries

4%
Consumer

−5%
Insurance

6%
Media & Ent.

1%
Air travel

Source: Adviser Voice.

facilitate the integration of those technologies and deliver personalised experiences across all channels to delight their customers.

While 33 per cent of customers are delighted with the digital experience in multi-channel environments, compared to 22 per cent in single-channel engagements, the number of unsatisfied consumers demonstrates the complexity that service organisations face in managing their CX across multiple channels. Omni-channel experiences dissatisfied 29 per cent of consumers compared to 16 per cent in single-channel experiences.

Customers have become accustomed to service interactions being provided by digital technology. Websites scored the highest satisfaction rating (41%) for digital interactions followed by email (33%) and mobile apps (25%). When compared with other customer-facing channels, such as shopfront/in-store/branch (24% satisfaction) and telephone/contact centres (20% satisfaction), interactive digital CX channels provide a better customer experience. Newer technologies such as social media (8%) and live chat (5%) offered the lowest levels of satisfaction for digital channels.

Customers in the 18-to-34 age group are more likely to use five or more channels to engage with brands (57%) compared with those aged 35 to 49 (46%) and customers aged 50-plus (30%). Similarly, younger consumers reported feeling more satisfied with their experiences in social media and live-chat channels when compared with older customers.[12] The marketing managers of the best-performing service organisations are ensuring that each customer experience is optimised, personalised and, above all, delightful at every touch point of their service experience.

Why is CX important in marketing services?

Services *per se* are intangible products and they are marketed using an expanded marketing mix of seven elements (refer to Chapter 1). Because services are intangible, the delivery process—which is an interactive transaction that delivers the service product to a customer—becomes an inherent experiential part of a service product. Customers play an expanded role in purchasing and using services as they increasingly use digital technology to interact with service brands and, as a result, increase their brand awareness. The practice of relying on either price differentiation or service attributes alone to influence customers' decision-making is being replaced by digital CX, because those experiences are perceived to be a more valued option than mass marketing communications such as advertising. An organisation's customers derive high levels of value from the positive and rewarding experiences they receive during their interactions with service brands.

A service experience that delights customers is a powerful driver of an organisation's commercial success. The underlying reasons that there has been significant improvement in CX in Australia are:

1 'Above-the-line' advertising is becoming less effective in reaching selected audiences.

2 More customers are connected via the internet and access it during almost every hour, which means they can look to others when making purchasing decisions in preference to marketing messages from an organisation.[13]

As a result, marketing strategy needs to focus more than ever on brand loyalty and customer preference and advocacy. Audiences are becoming more resistant to mass media marketing communications, which means that when they have positive experiences with an organisation—and later share their feelings online with friends and others—online technology is becoming an important marketing communication channel for service marketers.

Customers who post positive testimonials and ratings about their online service experiences are acting as advocates for a service organisation's interactive processes. CX is not solely limited to service transactions, so marketers must understand the effect that those opinions have on an organisation's image and the reputation of the service industry as a whole. For example:

→ 68 per cent of consumers go to social networking sites to read product reviews

→ 72 per cent of consumers trust online reviews as much as personal recommendations

→ 90 per cent of consumers say that positive online reviews influence their buying decisions.[14]

Personalising a customer's experience

Digital technology, artificial intelligence (AI) and customer relationship management (CRM) software are revolutionising how organisations reach and engage with customers in their target markets, and an effective CX strategy can leverage those applications. A targeted and personalised CX creates significant value for a customer, which in turn increases an organisation's profitability. In addition, external channels such as social media and mobile apps allow marketers to use technology to deliver customised CX that will further drive results.

Personalisation is a highly valued service attribute for marketers when it comes to getting CX right because it combines a thorough understanding of a customer's needs and wants with a timely and tailored delivery of relevant content. These newer media platforms enable marketers to provide personalised engagement and communication with customers, revolutionising their experience, while old mass-media options such as television, print and radio are falling behind. Apart from communicating directly with customers, personalisation also is an effective way to attract new customers because customised offers will give audiences what they want.

Why is CX important for service organisations?

There are three main reasons that CX is important to the commercial success of a service organisation:

1   Finding new prospective customers takes more time—and costs more—than simply nurturing a current customer. A CX that satisfies customers will reduce the 'loss rate'.
2   A more comprehensive CX allows for more opportunity to up-sell bundled services throughout the customer's lifetime, which increases revenue.
3   Advocacy is a profitable commodity. With every CX a customer has, the more likely it is they will develop brand loyalty and spread favourable recommendations that will have significant 'cut-through' at no cost to the organisation.

The customer journey

A customer's experiential journey includes all of the experiences they accumulate when interacting with a service brand, whether before, during or after a purchase. It includes everything from discovery to research, website browsing, shopping, customer support and warranties. The fundamental principle of CX lies in analysing a customer's journey from their perspective—not the marketer's—and developing the means to improve or even reinvent it. Service organisations that strive to competitively differentiate themselves must aim to reward customers with something they would not receive from another organisation.

So, when marketers indicate that they want to differentiate themselves from competitors using CX, what they mean is that they want to make their CX more valued than what is offered by any other organisation. To accomplish that objective, marketers must analyse every stage of the organisation's service processes—from first contact with the service brand to finishing the evaluation of the service experience—to change any customer/organisational actions that may cause customer dissatisfaction.

Developing CX strategies for service organisations

The ability to delight and engage an organisation's customers with relevant and effective experiences is the new competitive arena for which it has become especially important for the brand's marketing team to plan and develop a specific CX. Research findings indicate that a personalised CX is considered by prospective customers to be a priority for delivering a satisfactory CX, based primarily on a fast and efficient customer service process. Making that balance between CX and customer service work will ensure that an organisation—and its customers—are together working towards mutually satisfying relationships.

While the potential of an efficient and effective CX program is to produce successful results, how does a service organisation makes its CX superior? Marketers must understand their customers in terms of their demographics, characteristics and buying behaviour, which should also provide answers to what devices and portals they prefer to use. For marketers, knowing their target audience has become very important because it is almost impossible to evaluate and improve an organisation's CX if customers' feelings, when interacting with the organisation, are not understood.

When a clear picture of customer segments has been developed, there are several elements of CX that marketers will needs to review, and maybe improve. Those considerations are:

→ Is each CX unique or similar?

→ Does the service interface require a customer's permission and consent?

→ Does the interaction apply across several departmental processes?

When marketers have answers to these questions, they can integrate marketing analysis, creative development and marketing automation capabilities with customer management to develop strategic CX objectives. In the near future, there will be widespread use of mobile technology, social media, data analytics, virtual reality (VR), augmented reality (AR) and AI to encourage an organisation's prospective customers to engage with its brands by delivering differentiated and personalised experiences.[15]

Understanding how value influences CX

The basis of the service-dominant logic (S-D logic) model is premised on delivering both the core and supplementary elements of a service product that create and deliver value for customers of that service. Customer value, which is the benefit that customers receive from using a service product, was previously assumed to be delivered by service organisations. In the S-D logic model, value is seen as a dynamic, co-produced benefit that is created by the many participants in creating favourable customer service experiences. The evolution of understanding what customers value, and how it is defined, has moved through four stages in marketing services.[16]

Value in production is the first stage of understanding value, and is based on the notion that value is produced by companies and consumed by customers when they acquire a product—either an intangible service or a physical good. The production process was assumed to generate value and bind it into the completed product. According to that assumption, when consumers pay the market price to access a product's value, they subsequently consume it as part of the product. This approach to understanding value made sense when products were mass-produced commodities, but it has been made redundant as products—and services in particular—have evolved based on customisation and customer co-production.

The development of value in co-production as a concept was concomitant with the evolution of the service industries. The market at that time was also undergoing dynamic changes, with the increasing level of competition driving a constant release of new products. The second stage of understanding value is premised on the idea that while value is part of the production process that creates a product, both the organisation and the customer participate in the process of generating value.

The adoption of self-service technologies has of course hastened acceptance of 'value in co-production' by forcing customers to follow certain behaviours to have the full CX of accessing and consuming the end service product.

Value-in-use is the third stage of understanding value, and as a model, suggests that value is not part of the production process but is part of the consumption process.

Organisations can offer services that provide value, but that value has to be created by customers when they use the particular service. The value-in-use approach assumes that value exists in the experience of consumption.

Value co-creation with multiple stakeholders is a dynamic approach that assumes the rapid adoption of the internet and customer-oriented social media creates value that cannot be attributed to either production or customer consumption. In this process of value consumption, many customers contribute to the value of a service where the value is then channelled back to other firms who further enhance the service and return it to customers. This last stage of understanding value requires service organisations to be the catalysts for the dynamic cycles of value creation, and to manage the market factors that affect their CX.

value
In the service-dominant logic (S-D logic) model, value is seen as a dynamic, co-produced benefit that is created by the many participants in creating favourable customers' service experiences

value in production
Is generated by the production process and realised when consumed by customers

value in co-production
Assumes that while value is part of the production process, both the organisation and customer participate in generating value

value-in-use
Suggests that value is not part of the production process but of the consumption process

value co-creation with multiple stakeholders
Assumes that the rapid adoption of the internet and customer-oriented social media creates value that cannot be attributed to either service production or customer consumption

OXFORD UNIVERSITY PRESS

Emotional aspects of customers' experiences

Service brand managers often appear not to understand the emotional leverage that is inherent in CX, and instead focus on providing an easy or effective experience for their customers. CX plays a pivotal role in understanding customer emotions because experience generally drives emotion, which in turn triggers some form of customer reaction, such as repeat purchases. There is a strong correlation between emotion, feeling valued and repeat purchases.

The three Es of the emotional aspects a customer experience are:

→ effectiveness—how customers received value from the CX

→ ease—when customers received value without difficulty

→ emotion—why customers felt good about the CX.[17]

Emotions are difficult to define because to a large extent they are subjective, and change according to the context of a customer's interaction with a service provider. The same service interaction can create different emotions in different customers, and the same customer may express different emotions, at different times, in response to the same service interaction.[18] Affect, emotion and mood are closely related concepts that are often used interchangeably. Affect is a psychological state that is valenced either positively or negatively, and is '... the feeling side of consciousness, as opposed to thinking, which taps the cognitive domain'.[19] Emotions, however, are generally associated with a short-term event that has a specific stimulus. Emotion includes arousal, various forms of affect, and cognitive interpretations of affect that may have a single description. Emotion is therefore more cognitively involved than affect. In contrast, moods are more enduring, include more diffuse feelings that exist at a particular time and place, and are less related to specific stimuli.[20]

Emotion is also linked to a customer's satisfaction response and indirectly related to re-purchase expectations. Studies of the roles that emotion and mood play as part of the purchase and consumption of a service have found that:

→ customers with positive moods are more willing to participate in behaviour that helps a service interaction to succeed[21]

→ moods and emotions enhance and amplify experiences, making them more positive or negative[22]

→ moods and emotions affect the way that the service is used and how it will be remembered.

Service interactions have many different stimuli that can activate certain neural systems of a customer. Individually, those stimuli will not cause a customer to have feelings of emotion—that is, a perception of poor service—but cumulatively those stimuli can reach the point of 'just noticeable difference' and cause the customer to register the poor service experience for the first time.[23]

William Chitty

Consumer psychology researcher Richard Oliver found that expectations play an important role in the formation of satisfaction. As shown in Table 10.2, Oliver used the expectancy disconfirmation paradigm (see Chapter 11) to list the emotions that are likely to be linked to low, average and high levels of customer expectations.[24]

Table 10.2   Likely emotions in the disconfirmation of expectations paradigm

Levels of expectations	Disconfirmation of expectations		
	Negative	Zero	Positive
Low	Disgust, anger, withdrawal	Tolerance, resignation, despair	Hope, promise, gratitude, relief
Average	Disappointment, dismay	Contentment, no emotion, indifference	Glee, pleasure, surprise
High	Disappointment to anger, resentment, betrayal	Happiness, pleasure	Delight, elation, ecstasy

Source: R.L. Oliver (1997). *Satisfaction: A Behavioral Perspective on the Consumer*. Singapore: McGraw Hill Book Co., p. 315.

Understanding the emotional state of a service customer's pre- and post-service interaction is an important part of analysing the effectiveness of a CX. Pre-experience influences are situational factors that, while external to service interaction, are a direct result of wanting or needing to take part in that experience. The actual service experience—defined earlier in this chapter as being *the culmination of a series of service interactions*—clearly requires a service organisation to consider, if not actively control, the external factors that influence the service experience. Service organisations must consider the post-experience factors that influence what happens after the service experience, such as the delivery of ongoing supplementary after-sales services, all of which are parts of the total CX.

Rational aspects of customers' experiences

Rational elements account for about half the typical CX; the remainder are emotional. Most service organisations focus solely on the rational experience—management that concentrates on delivery times, how quickly calls are answered in a call centre, or how easy it is to purchase a service online, for example.[25] While these are important factors in a CX, they are only part of that experience. One of the problems in managing CX is that the strategy often relies on the purely rational elements. Deliberate and effective CX management has a broad and lasting effect on customer acquistion, and on customer loyalty and retention.

Customer acquisition

Service organisations spend significant amounts of money to acquire customers, only to quickly lose them; the reason for high rates of customer loss is generally because of poor CX. CX is an intangible asset that can deliver extraordinary value by ensuring that service organisations retain the customers they acquire, and thereby improve the loyalty, retention and satisfaction of those customers. To acquire customers, service organisations must inspire their emotions.

Service organisations generally use the service experience as a means to acquire customers' attention and to stimulate them—using marketing communications—to experience the benefits of their services. Customer acquisition is, however, only the beginning. After acquiring customers, organisations need to implement customer loyalty and retention strategies.

Customer loyalty and retention

Customer loyalty and retention both embody repeat behaviour, where loyalty reflects a developing relationship and retention reflects an ongoing relationship. Customer retention is an essential part of a customer relationship, and consists of both the rational and emotional elements of CX.

Customer loyalty, by definition, is not rational. In economic terms, rationality means consumers will choose a service that provides the greatest reward for the lowest cost. The benefits of a service are measured against its cost compared with other services in a consumer's set of comparable alternatives—that is, their evoked set. Yet customer loyalty means a customer is willing to forgo purchasing lower-priced identical products because of an irrational preference for a particular service brand. While service quality—the best value for the price, and convenience—are important as purely rational values, 'irrational' values like happiness, belonging and self-actualisation are equally important in service purchasing decisions.

Retaining customers is less expensive than acquiring new ones, and CX management is the most cost-effective way to develop customer satisfaction, customer retention and customer loyalty. Not only do loyal customers ensure sales, but they are also more likely to purchase supplementary, high-margin services. Loyal customers reduce costs associated with consumer education and marketing, especially when they become net promoters of a service brand. The Net Promoter Score (NPS) is a method of measuring the value of customer relationships with a service brand, while the number of net promoters of a service brand is determined by subtracting the percentage of detractors from the percentage of promoters. Detractors and promoters are the two limiting variables in the NPS.[26] The rationale of the NPS is discussed in Chapter 13.

Given today's highly competitive marketing environment, CX programs are the most effective way to differentiate a service organisation from its competitors.

↘
customer loyalty and retention
Embody repeat behaviour where customer loyalty reflects a developing relationship and customer retention reflects an ongoing relationship

Tigerair is enhancing its customers' check-in experiences

In May 2015, Tigerair Australia launched a new service innovation, known as Max Airport, to enhance its CX during check-in at an airport terminal. Max Airport is an iPad-based app that changes the way the airline's staff interact with customers at the airport. Launched at Melbourne Airport, the app provides check-in staff with technology that enables them to move from behind the desk and engage with customers anywhere within the terminal. Max Airport allows the check-in staff to print boarding passes and assist customers to change flights or purchase optional add-on items, such as additional luggage or extra-leg-room seating. Tigerair Australia is confident the app will streamline the check-in and boarding process, and improve the customer check-in experience. A new internet booking engine will also go live in the same month to make online bookings with Tigerair more convenient.[27]

Such differentiation effectively drives customer loyalty when customers are engaged on an emotional or intellectual level with a service. In terms of customer loyalty, a favourable customer experience is itself a sustainable competitive advantage.

Technological aspects of customers' experiences

While technology may have improved information and cash flow, with most transactions in Australia now paid for electronically and in an environment where many services are available 24/7, organisations need to ensure their distribution systems can handle sustained periods of maximum demand and not just average demand. One company that did not ensure its systems could cope with change was mobile telephone company Vodafone.

The Australian mobile market's third- and fourth-placed players, Vodafone Australia and Hutchison's 3, entered into a joint venture in mid-2009 to form Vodafone Hutchison Australia (VHA). VHA had 6 million customers, many of whom used smartphones. Although the smartphones were capable of managing large amounts of data, the VHA network could not deal with sustained periods of high customer demand and often dropped out without warning. That forced customers to roam on other networks—which was not a cheap option. Despite a public apology, one angry Vodafone customer was so unhappy about his experience that he set up his own website, Vodafail, to highlight his dissatisfaction with Vodafone's customer service.

In this era of social networking, technology can also play an important role in consumers seeking redress for the poor management of a service. But when it comes to technology, it is not all doom and gloom. The cheapest way for any organisation to deliver a service is via the internet. Many service organisations have embraced the internet because it allows their customers to access the innovative types of services that have been recently developed. Many organisations use the internet for self-service, allowing consumers the flexibility to search and interact with service organisations 24/7. Universities, for example, use self-service technology that allows students to manage their enrolments and study programs online. Customers can now also use many services via their smartphones. In 2010, the Linguist Society of America, which tracks the use of words in the English language, voted 'app' their word of the year. The way customers have embraced technology has helped managers spread demand for services so that most consumers are satisfied whether they use that service at 6.13 a.m. or 6.13 p.m.

Managers can use data warehouses to quickly build relationships with their customers and then manage those relationships to add value to them. A customer's details can be retrieved in seconds and displayed to the managers wherever they are in the world, which helps to enhance the distribution of a service. Regardless of the type of technology being used, people still play an important part in the management of a service interaction. In fact, many organisations call people their 'most important resource'.

Technology, especially the growth in IT and data warehouses, is increasingly being used by marketers to manage their service offerings. As technology such as smartphones is quickly accepted by Australia's population, service delivery has changed its dynamics in relation to how services are used and distributed. This has also changed how these services are managed because marketers now need to know as much about IT as they do about the marketing of services. Technology has, for example, merged the traditional four Ps concept of marketing so that it is no longer clear where a 'product' begins and its 'place' (distribution) finishes.[28] This is especially applicable to service products, such as Google Home, which are generally not functionally oriented to the four Ps framework. Google Home is a device that, when connected from Google via wi-fi to a home internet system, can control household and smart power-switches, set calendar reminders and provide weather forecasts.

Technology has provided service organisations with the means to customise service products and market them as individual offerings based on the customer's particular needs and behaviour. That has created a customer perception—which may not reflect reality— that service organisations view all their customers as individuals who are unique and valued customers.[29]

Transforming digital experiences

Whether a CX is initiated by phone, email, internet self-service, web chat, social media, chatbot or video, the latest research reveals a major shift in how people want to communicate with organisations. New technology reflects the emergence of these type-based messaging channels that are sitting alongside, rather than replacing, the traditional 'talk' channels of phone and face-to-face contact, which remain popular with consumers.

Research results suggest that organisations need to build customer experiences that satisfy traditional as well as new communication needs, but in ways that allow for interchangeable transactions where consumers can choose their preferred channel depending on where they are, what they are doing and which device they are using. The following is a list of findings from recent research:[30]

→ Digital customers want easy journeys; 56 per cent say convenience is more important than price.

→ The rapid growth of messaging provides organisations with an opportunity to build digital customer relationships; 58 per cent say they get a quicker response with chat than by emailing or phoning.

→ AI and voice-recognition technology can be used to transform efficiency; 80 per cent of customers are open to using chatbots for quick and simple queries.

→ Phone boosts digital, but service levels need improving; 81 per cent of customers say there should be a phone number on every web page or app.

→ Social media momentum continues, but needs integrating into omni-channel strategies; 38 per cent of customers say that's the best way to make contact if the issue is urgent.

→ Video continues to transform customer experience; 62 per cent of customers think they should be able to switch from chat to a voice or video call (with the same agent).

→ Safer transactions will drive revenue growth; 68 per cent of customers say they would have bought more if payments were more secure.

→ Consumers value proactive service powered by big data and AI; 78 per cent like it when organisations notice they have a problem online and contact them directly to help.

→ The challenge is delivering optimal customer journeys; 81 per cent of customers want organisations to offer different channels to meet their needs.

The convenience and control that digital channels give customers is changing their behaviour. Each channel offers different ways of interacting with an organisation's brands so it is vital to understand how and why customers are using them. Constructing customer journeys that blend both new and old channels seamlessly is becoming vital to realigning CX for digital technology.

How data analytics can improve customers' satisfaction with the service experience

CX management is important in service industries, including telecommunications, financial services and even the public sector, because service organisations are focusing on CX to help generate efficiency and new sources of revenue. CX is being driven by the expectations of customers that their experience with an organisation should be personalised and satisfactory.

1 Manage service delivery

Customer satisfaction is driven by the growing expectations being generated by service marketing communications that promise the service will be working as advertised and that is determined by how well the service process is designed and its reliability. For example, in the case of a bank, if a customer attempts to withdraw cash from an ATM, but is met with an 'Out of cash' message, that is likely to cause significant customer dissatisfaction with the particular bank.

Using Path Analysis, service organisations can predict the failure of service-delivery equipment in consumer premises before it arises and help to actively manage customer expectations. Path Analysis is also useful to predict 'path to purchase' and 'out-of-stock situations' during the customer acquisition phase and, therefore, in the example of the ATM, should not reach the stage where the machine runs 'out of cash'.

2 Tailor service development

Many organisations create service products that are 'one size fits all'; examples include mortgage financing and mobile-phone pricing plans. A customer with a phone plan that includes more data or calls than they need is likely to be overpaying the service provider and will therefore not be as satisfied with the service organisation as they could be. Analytics can help organisations understand customers' buying decisions and behaviours to tailor service products that are aligned with their needs. For example, an insurance company can use the number of kilometres a customer drives to create a car insurance product that fits the customer's needs precisely, with pricing to match. That ability can in turn be used to develop customer-retention strategies.

3 Improve customer service interactions

The quality of customer interactions often depends solely on the skills of an organisation's staff—the service providers—and the outcomes are instantaneous for every interaction. By managing customer expectations, service organisations can increase customer satisfaction. Discovery analytics performed using text analytics and sentiment analysis functions for both call-centre contacts and social media data provide new insights into customer behaviour, as well as perceptions of an organisation's performance in the market. The results can flag a customer's intention to contact the call centre well in advance of the call itself, giving organisations the opportunity to face customer problems and actively resolve them. This type of service builds ongoing customer loyalty and generates positive word of mouth.

4 Streamline channel management

Service organisations that cut channel costs by creating low-cost channels—without considering their customers' preferences—risk alienating those customers. Response rates can be low via these channels, which can include telesales and online. By contrast, organisations that use geospatial analytics to identify the frequency with which customers visit service sites can accurately tailor offers for them, and simply direct them to conveniently located service sites to bridge any online-offline gaps.[31]

Evaluating a customer's service experiences

Service providers are generally a service organisation's employees who deliver a brand's promise, which, for a service, is a satisfying CX. Brands are potent communication channels because of the messages they convey about an organisation. To create and deliver a brand's promise can only be achieved when all functional departments of a service organisation, and every operational process, are aligned with the values of the brand. That requires translating the brand's value into the brand's image, which is based on the value that is communicated to customers and then delivered as a brand promise to every branded CX that a customer has with an organisation's service providers, its service processes and, ultimately, its intangible service product.[32]

Managing CX includes having systems that can identify potential critical incidents or moments of truth, analyse trends and patterns, and have channels to communicate that CX information to the relevant functional departments of the service organisation. The CX information can then be used to train an organisation's employees to recognise those critical incidents, and subsequently be given the authority to respond to those incidents—often referred to as moments of truth[33]—because they will lead to positive organisational outcomes and desired CX. One way to identify potential moments of truth and gauge the efficacy of service recovery strategies is a research technique called *critical incident technique (CIT)*.

Critical incident technique

Critical service incidents are service experiences that are out of the ordinary—a customer complains, makes a special request, or a service employee fails to meet a customer's reasonable expectations, for example. The outcome of critical incidents—which can be

OXFORD UNIVERSITY PRESS

either positive or negative, depending on how they are managed—is, however, rarely neutral. Critical incidents are usually memorable and unusual, and tend to have a powerful effect on relationships with customers; they are the 'moments of truth' where the service provider has the opportunity to cement the customer relationship, or they can lead to customer defection. CIT is a qualitative analytical approach that can be used to identify and analyse the reasons for failures in the customer-service delivery processes. CIT is based on qualitative interview procedures to collect, analyse content and classify observations of human behaviour.[34]

The CIT procedure is a suitable analytical method to investigate customer service interactions such as events, incidents, processes or issues that are identified by respondents as being less than what they expected. The way the outcomes of those incidents are managed, and the perceived effects of the critical incidents, can be analysed by asking customers to tell a story about their service experience. When all the critical incidents have been collected, a content analysis of the stories can be carried out.[35] During an interview to collect information, respondents can be asked to recall specific CX events to enable the researcher to generate an accurate and in-depth record of those events. CIT is also useful for assessing the perceptions of customers from different cultures because it is a 'culturally neutral method' that invites consumers to share their perceptions on an issue, rather than indicating their perceptions of the researcher's questions.

The role of CIT in CX

A study of service interactions and switching behaviour illustrates the impact the CIT method has had on customer service research. An examination of 700 service interactions, from the perspective of customers, in three industries identified three types of employee behaviours—which were called *recovery, adaptability* and *spontaneity*—as the sources of satisfaction and dissatisfaction in service interactions.[36] The study was one of the first to identify *specific* employee behaviours that are associated with customer satisfaction and dissatisfaction. The investigation of service interactions also identified a fourth group of employee behaviours—*coping*—that related to managing problem customers.[37]

Basically a CIT study includes asking a customer to recall a recent interaction they experienced with a service organisation that was particularly satisfying or dissatisfying. The specific types of questions that can be asked are:

→ When did the particular incident occur?

→ What caused the incident?

→ What were the specific circumstances that led to the incident occurring?

→ Why was that incident particularly satisfying or dissatisfying?

→ How did the provider respond to the incident?

→ How did they correct it?

→ What action(s) did you take as a result of the incident?[38]

William Chitty

The analysis of CIT interviews consists of classifying these incidents into defined, mutually exclusive categories and sub-categories of increasing specificity. For example, the researcher may classify incidents into the following three categories.

1   Service-delivery system failures:
    –   unavailable service
    –   unreasonably slow service
    –   other core service failures.

2   Customer needs and requests:
    –   special customer needs
    –   customer preferences.

3   Unprompted and unsolicited actions
    –   attention paid to customer
    –   out-of-the-ordinary employee behaviour
    –   holistic evaluation
    –   behaviour under adverse conditions.

A similar classification technique should be used to group both recovery strategies and their effectiveness. As well as classifying the attitudinal and behavioural results of a customer, this identifies the ways in which the customer changed their behaviour towards or relationship with the service organisation based on the incident, such as did they:

→ purchase more or less

→ tell others about the experience (directly or via social media)

→ call for support more or less often

→ use different channels

→ change service organisations?

The end result of CIT analysis should produce a list of common moments of truth for the service organisation, showing how customers change their behaviour in either profitable or unprofitable ways as a result of this moment of truth, and an evaluation of the effectiveness of recovery strategies, giving service managers an informed perspective to train employees to recognise the moments of truth and respond in ways that will lead to positive CX.

Cause-and-effect analysis

This type of analysis can identify and explore the cause of a problem. It uses a technique that was first developed by Kaoru Ishikawa, a Japanese expert on total quality management (TQM). To begin cause-and-effect analysis requires consideration of all the likely factors that are causing the specific problem. The causes are then grouped according to their common characteristics, such as physical facilities, front-line personnel, procedures, suppliers, back-line personnel and information. This information is then drawn on a cause-and-effect diagram, popularly known as a fishbone diagram because of its shape, as shown in Figure 10.3.

OXFORD UNIVERSITY PRESS

Figure 10.3 A cause-and-effect diagram of the likely factors that can lead to delays in airline departures

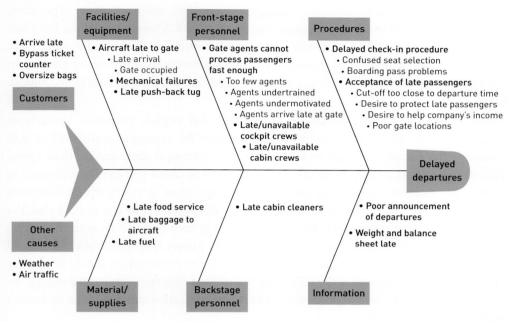

Source: C.H. Lovelock (1994). *Product Plus.* New York, NY: McGraw-Hill, p. 218.

To more easily identify probable causes for the late departures for the airline—that is, the effect—personnel have been grouped according to whether they directly interact with customers or are the maintenance personnel who have little contact with customers but may influence customers' perceptions of the airline's performance. In the manufacture of physical products, customers have little contact with the operational processes of the organisations that produce those goods. In high-contact service organisations, however, customers play a role in the production of the services, and the same holds true for customer service.

If customers do not engage in co-producing their interactive engagement with an organisation, they have little opportunity to derive any satisfaction from their customer experiences.

Blueprinting a service experience

A customer's positive service experience is a competitive advantage, but many companies overestimate the quality of their CX.

In a study by Bain and Company, although 80 per cent of companies surveyed believed they delivered superior CX, only about 8 per cent of their customers agreed.[39] That experience gap provides an opportunity for potential customer defections because managers cannot fix problems they do not identify and quantify. Even companies that attempt to be customer-centric face a dilemma. They know CX drives loyalty and share of business, but many cannot describe how they can *actually* deliver a positive customer service experience. That makes it difficult to reliably duplicate and standardise CX standards. At the front line where service providers and sales staff interact with customers, the lack of standardised, predictable CX standards is a key reason that customers become dissatisfied. Consequently, although CX has potential to create a competitive advantage, it often fails to accomplish that goal.

Blueprinting is a process-modelling approach that depicts customer interactions in chronological order, which makes it relatively easy for managers and frontline staff to manage the customer service processes. CX blueprinting is more precise than verbal explanations of how an organisation's service-delivery operates and enables managers to identify the 'moments of truth' in the customer's experience. A CX blueprint illustrates the role that customers play in an organisation's operations, and the impact that the subsequent customer interactions have on determining their satisfaction with the service experience. It is essential that a service organisation knows if its processes, people and physical facilities are providing superior CX and that the organisation is able to identify which actions in the processes are delivering the desired customer service experience. By blueprinting the customer's service experience, the organisation can delight its customers and build customer loyalty.

Developing a CX blueprint

There are three requirements to complete a customer experience service blueprint:

1   The blueprint must show the time scale for each activity because the service processes take place over time.
2   The blueprint must identify bottlenecks that will block a customer service process.
3   The blueprint must indicate how much variation from standards can be allowed without having an impact on the quality of the customer service.[40]

The key components of a CX blueprint are:

→ setting the standards for each customer interaction
→ listing the number of customer contact staff, the processes and physical equipment required to complete each customer interaction
→ detailing the main customer interactions
→ the line of visibility
→ the number of staff, processes and physical equipment required to perform the support activities.

The customer–staff interactions are the foundation for all the other components of the blueprint. Those interactions should answer the primary question: 'From the customer's point of view, when does the customer service delivery process start and stop?'

An important characteristic of a CX service blueprint is that it distinguishes between what customers experience and the activities and support processes that customers do not usually see—those areas are separated by a *line of visibility*. Some organisations that are focused on manufacturing their products often neglect the interactions between customers and their employees.

Figure 10.4 shows a CX service blueprint for staying in a hotel and ordering room service. At the top of this blueprint is the physical evidence of materials necessary for the stay, including the website, parking, key, room-service menu, the meal itself and the final invoice. It documents the steps and action taken by the guest (customer actions), by those whom the guest sees (onstage/visible employee contact) and what is done by employees who help fulfil the order but are not seen by the guest (backstage/invisible-contact employees). The blueprint also shows examples of support processes that are necessary to make the entire process run smoothly. It shows the actions of the hotel guest with staff—the moments of truth—as well as the other actions that guests engage in as part of the customer service-delivery process. By clarifying the role of employees, the operational processes and the customer interactions, customer service blueprints can facilitate the integration of the marketing, operations and human resources management within an organisation.

The example in Figure 10.4 shows only the basic steps in the CX for room service. An overview blueprint like this is a good place to start, but more complex services require more detail to fully indicate any problems in the service process where improvements could be made. For instance, assume that the hotel has received complaints from guests that room-service food is arriving cold. Clearly this is a dissatisfying customer experience, and represents additional costs for the hotel when food is sent back. By examining its room-service process, the hotel would discover where the quality gap has occurred. The simple analysis might point out that once the food is prepared in the kitchen, it is not promptly being picked up for delivery to the guest. But why is this occurring? The hotel would need to look closer at the underlying processes causing 'slow' food pick-up in the kitchen to accurately identify the real problem and find a solution.

A customer service blueprint should also identify the likely failure points so that recovery strategies can be developed to prevent or recover from system failures. Those recovery strategies should be designed to:

→ increase customer satisfaction

→ improve productivity

→ reduce the number customer service failures.[41]

Applying blueprinting in practice

The first step in applying a blueprint is to decide which of the organisation's customer service processes is to be blueprinted, and its objective. Select the service-delivery process, and the customer segment, that will be the focus of the blueprint. Different segments of customers may be treated differently, which would necessitate developing a separate

Figure 10.4 A blueprint for overnight-stay service in a hotel

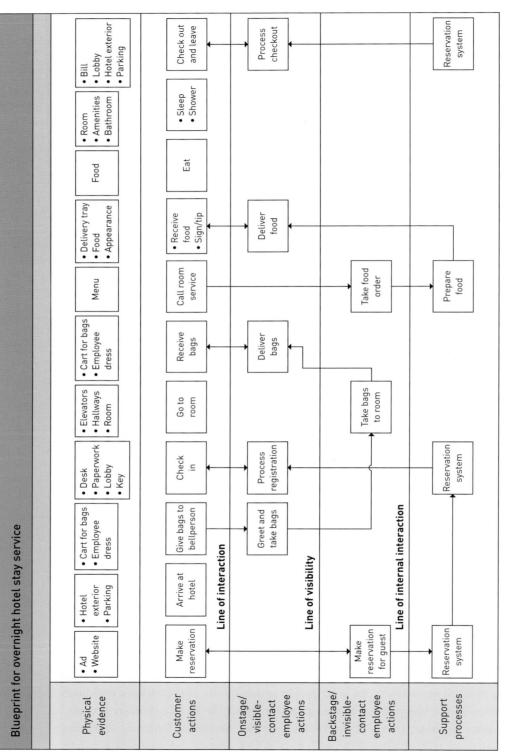

Source: M.J. Bitner, A. Ostrom & F. Morgan (2008). Service blueprinting: A practical technique for service innovation. *California Management Review*, 50(3), 66–94.

blueprint; external or internal customer segments can also be examined. Ensure each service employee understands the objectives of the blueprinting process. For a currently offered service, it may be useful to create what a 'desired' customer service process might look like. For some services, the objective may be to develop a very general concept blueprint that only highlights the key steps in the customer service process—for example, the early stages of introducing a new product or service such as Qantas offering free in-flight internet services on its domestic flights. Alternatively, the objective might be to specify specific role responsibilities for service providers, which would require a detailed blueprint of the organisation's operations.

Who should be involved in the blueprinting process?

Some thought should also be given as to which departments could be involved in the blueprinting process for a particular service. Ideally, representatives of all functional groups involved in the design, delivery and support of the associated service-delivery process should be involved. This provides the greatest opportunity to capture diverse perspectives on how a service is currently being offered by the organisation and subsequently being experienced by customers.

Modifying the blueprinting technique as appropriate

As circumstances change, it makes sense to modify the traditional blueprint. For example, when blueprinting a technology-based service, where consumers do not have any contact with frontline service staff, it may be beneficial to remove the contact employee action row and replace it with a technology row that would depict how customers interact with the organisation's technology. Some services might require both a frontline staff activity and an interaction with technology; for example, in an airline where customers check in via a self-service-technology and interact face-to-face with airline staff. Blueprints should also identify customer service bottlenecks or failure points, or situations where customers' perceptions of service quality can be enhanced; adaptability is one of the key strengths of the blueprinting technique.

Mapping the customer service process as it happens most of the time

There are always specific things that happen when providing CX. However, blueprint developers should focus on what typically occurs during the service-delivery process. When the typical service-delivery process is blueprinted, it can be compared to an ideal or competitor blueprint, depending on the organisation's objectives. The blueprint should realistically depict how the 'ideal' customer service is experienced by customers. Often just the act of creating a customer service blueprint can lead to insights that can improve the customer service-delivery processes—these insights can then be included in the blueprint.

William Chitty

Developing recommendations based on blueprinting objectives

Once the process of blueprinting the customers' interactions is substantially completed, action strategies can be developed to achieve the objectives of the blueprinting exercise. The process of blueprinting the service-delivery processes can help to identify the various roles and relational activities that occur throughout the organisation and, as such, can facilitate strategic and tactical decision-making.

Creating final blueprints for use within the organisation

Service-delivery blueprinting captures the customers' interactions in a visual and chronological sequence of events. For some organisations, developing a blueprint will produce important insights. At other times, companies want to create finished blueprints that can be shared within the organisation and used for training as well as being a resource for employees. In these circumstances, the final blueprints should be shown to participants to ensure they are correct. The accuracy of the service-delivery blueprints will be enhanced to the extent that all groups involved in the design, delivery and support of the service process participated in their development. The blueprints must also be updated over time to ensure they still accurately capture how customer service is being delivered.

Benefits of a service-delivery blueprint

Some of the benefits of a service-delivery blueprint are to:

→ reinforce a customer-centric focus among employees
→ provide a common methodology that everyone can use to improve the service delivery
→ identify service gaps that cause unfavourable CX
→ identify opportunities in the service-delivery process that will delight customers
→ clarify interdepartmental interactions with customers
→ standardise service delivery as a high-quality, repeatable process
→ identify how company resources are being used to serve customers.

Benchmarking

Another strategy that is useful in managing service interactions is benchmarking.[41] Benchmarking, as discussed in Chapter 4, is the process of using leading service organisations as a way of measuring the service. Benchmarking can be used as part of an offensive or defensive strategy. As a process, benchmarking helps managers to measure and evaluate their service products, and it can also be used to develop a new service. Managing customer contact and customer relationships is an important part of any strategy in managing the service function. Although this may seem simple to do, the nature of this aspect of service function is changing due to consumers increasingly helping organisations produce their own service and maintain their own relationship.

The basic premise of S-D logic (discussed earlier in the chapter) is that all products are services, and that the best way to deliver a service—in a way that pleases customers—is to encourage customers to co-produce their own service products. This in turn increases the value created by the co-production process as customers are more satisfied than when they are not involved in the service process. Facebook is an example of this, where consumers use nothing more than some intangible space on the internet to create social networking pages about themselves. This is an important feature for service managers because customers now have to update their details, engage with the organisation and manage their own services, and that means managing the service function takes less time and allows an organisation to focus on improving service products.

Many businesses are currently struggling to compete. Not only has technology lowered the barriers of entry into many industries, it has also given customers the power to find, research and buy almost any service, from any vendor, in any part of the world, at any time. To compete successfully in this new consumer-driven era, companies must find new ways to differentiate. A company's knowledge of and relationship with customers are what will enable it to survive in the age of the customer. The only successful strategy is to become customer-obsessed—each firm must have strategies for understanding, connecting with, serving and delighting their customers based on delivering exceptional CX.

Watermark Consulting conducted an analysis of the stock performance of CX leaders and laggards on the US stock exchange over a seven-year period, and found that CX leaders (as measured by Forrester's CX Index, of which an Australian version launched in September 2015) saw a 78 per cent return, versus the S&P (Standard and Poor's) average return of 52 per cent, and a

-3 per cent return for CX laggards. Despite the return on investment of offering great CX, a large gap still exists between executive aspirations to differentiate with exceptional CX and action. In a Forrester survey of more than 50 Australian CX professionals, 50 per cent said the objective of their company's CX strategy is to: 'differentiate our organisation from others in our industry'. Another 22 per cent said the objective of their company's CX strategy is to: 'differentiate our organisation from all other firms across any industry'.

In spite of these aspirations, Forrester's recent CX Index research covering some 58 Australian brands found that none of these brands fall into the CX 'leader' category—the category that consumers rate as delivering exceptional CX. Why is there this disconnection between aspirations and reality? CX requires sustainable discipline and investment with reliable measurement techniques and that requires companies to not only be customer-focused but also to make significant investments in establishing a business culture within an organisational and technological structure. Most

William Chitty

companies, however, do not know where to start, or how to improve their CX.

The true measures of CX need to focus on and capture customers' perceptions of an interaction with a company. While valuable as a whole, measures like overall satisfaction indicate little about the specific actions a company must take to deliver a compelling experience. Likewise, it is difficult for companies to understand whether a customer's likelihood to recommend—or disparage—them comes from their personal interactions or from what they have read on social media or stories they have heard about other people's experiences. Great customer interactions involve three core quality components: effectiveness, ease and emotion. Specifically, in any interaction with a company, customers must derive value from the interaction, they must get that value without difficulty and they should feel good during the process. While measuring customer experience quality is critical, it is also a cold, hard fact that the ideal CX cannot be just 'good' for customers—it also has to deliver revenue for the business.

The CX Index reflects this reality, providing a metric that equates to how well a company delivers CX that creates and sustains loyalty. Loyalty means different things to different organisations, so effectively measuring customer loyalty can be a challenge. A common solution is to take a streamlined approach by reducing loyalty measurement to a single metric like advocacy or retention. In many cases, however, this provides a myopic view. Rather, three types of loyalty are critical to a CX quality metric:

1 retention loyalty: the likelihood that a customer will keep its existing business with a company

2 enrichment loyalty: the likelihood that a customer will buy more from a company

3 advocacy loyalty: the likelihood that a customer will recommend a company to others.

Because the CX Index is both a measure of the quality of a company's CX and the customer's loyalty to the brand, a higher CX Index score equates to a CX that effectively helps to win and retain customers. Conversely, the lower a brand's CX Index score, the more money the brand loses from lost sales and customers. Knowing its CX score is just the first step for service marketers in understanding how customers experience the organisation's brand. CX success in the age of the customer requires customer data and company discipline. While a measurement program will determine what is working and what is not, what an organisation does with its information will determine whether its customers remain loyal or turn to another brand that makes them feel valued.[43]

Favourable customer experiences

The message for many small to medium businesses in Australia is that they cannot only compete with bigger businesses but also win, by offering favourable CX. Research indicates that it is not only the power of recommendation that results from a good experience (on average a customer will tell nine people about their positive service experience), but it also highlights the multiplier effect of poor CX.[44] Australian customers vent their frustrations at bad service to an average of 18 people. In addition, research by American Express found 72 per cent of Australians claim to have spent more with a company where they have had good CX. On average, Australians are willing to spend 12 per cent more with companies that provide a good customer experience.

In an interview with *Business Acumen Magazine*, American Express vice president for customer service Andrew Carlton said, 'Our key message is that the brand is important but service that comes with that brand is more important. We see this with many of our customers; they vote with their wallets after they receive great service.[45] Globally, American Express card members who are highly satisfied with their service interactions spend 16 percent more on their cards. It's why we are so committed to delivering our award-winning customer service.' The *American Express 2014 Global Customer Service Barometer* surveyed 10 major markets throughout the world including the United States, Canada, Mexico, Italy, the United Kingdom, India, Japan, Singapore and Hong Kong. Of the 10 nations surveyed, Australians were found most likely to use companies based on the recommendations of family and friends with 45 per cent citing this as a key influence on choosing to do business with a company. Australia was ahead of the United Kingdom and Canada (both 44%) and the United States (42%), while India (22%) and Japan (20%) were at the bottom of that table, but both were prominent in seeing a company's reputation as the most likely influence.

'Australians place a higher importance on the personal touch than other nations, with about 40 percent of respondents preferring to speak to a "real" person over the phone for difficult inquiries, and 31 percent a face to face conversation,' Carlton said. Social media is a sideline in this game, according to Carlton. 'Face-to-face, word of mouth is the preferred way to communicate views on service,' he said. 'Social media is more commonly used when people are getting frustrated.' He said even recommendations through social media were not nearly as powerful as a personal verbal recommendation. 'For a single enquiry, consumers prefer to go to the company website or get in touch by e-mail. For more complex things, they prefer to talk to somebody. The preference is the phone for most service enquiries.' Of service organisations, Carlton said, 'The majority are meeting expectations but can improve. But there is a difference between information and service… More information is available today. Most customers will go online for that. Click to chat (for service through a website) is becoming more important. In fact about 10 per cent of people have click to chat as a preference now.'

The rise of unified communications and a preference for Skype-style links were also changing things. Carlton said the increase of video chat may raise that kind of service. 'Phone at the moment is a 41 per cent preference,' he said. 'Video may soon prove to be as prevalent as instant messaging. But the key is wanting to talk to a real person. The primary reason is that customers want to talk to someone knowledgeable.' Carlton said the research outcomes 'really are a pat on the back for Australian businesses, but they also serve as a clear reminder to businesses at the busiest time of year that people have no hesitation in telling others about their service experiences, good or bad … What does good customer service really mean? About 24 per cent count that as individual recognition,' Carlton said American Express's research showed, ' … and 23 per cent is about product and service. Another 23 per cent is the value promise at the right price. Customers who believe they get good customer service are loyal and re-use—and recommend—and that means new business.'

Carlton said recommendation outcomes tended to be about who was being listened to, who was a trusted source; the channel was not nearly as important.

This chapter has discussed the elements of CX: what marketers can do to develop, maintain and implement the service function. It is important for service organisations to know what CX means to their customers. The true measure of the success of a CX program is a measure of customers' perceptions of their interactions with a service organisation. While customer satisfaction has some value as a measure of a service experience, it does not indicate any remedial action that an organisation should take to deliver an experience that is of value to a customer. All CX strategies should be developed and implemented with a view to creating value from a service encounter.

Also important in any interaction with a service organisation is that customers receive a desired form of value during the service experience and are willing to recommend the organisation to their friends. CX managers can use various approaches to develop CX strategies including critical incident technique, cause-and-effect analysis and blueprinting a service-delivery process.

Service organisations can also involve consumers in the co-production of a service as part of a broader co-creation of value of the customer experience. Service duration can be managed to ensure that demand is spread evenly across times and resources, and the complexity of the offering can also be managed to minimise the impact on resources and the overall service function.

Because it is difficult to manage predictable demand for services, there may be times when the service delivery fails, despite the best intentions of the organisation. This is when it is important for organisations to implement their service recovery strategies. If an organisation can recover from a failure and win back a customer, this is an important indicator of the service experience being provided by that organisation.

Review questions

1   Consider a service organisation that you regularly use and identify the service-delivery gaps that may exist between what customers expect to receive and what they actually receive. Briefly explain how that service organisation could close those gaps.

Would their customers' service experiences be improved if that organisation adopted a different approach to delivering their service?

2   Analyse the nature of the service-delivery processes for the following service organisations:

a   a low-cost budget airline

b   a large-scale trading bank

c   an internet provider.

Would their customers' service experiences be improved if those organisations adopted a different approach to delivering their service?

3   If you were served very quickly by a financial adviser who was employed by a bank, would you assume that the speed of delivery was a good or bad indicator of the quality of the service? Why?

4   Explain your reasons in answering the following question. Are the advertisements that say, 'Our customers come first', about the quality of CX provided by the service advertiser or is the statement merely advertising 'puffery'?

5   Under what circumstances is it acceptable for a service organisation to answer its customers' queries via the internet or using a 1300 telephone number that terminates in a call centre? Fully explain the reasons for you answer.

6   When should a service organisation analyse its customers' experiences?

7   What analytical technique would be the most suitable for a service organisation to analyse its service-delivery processes to determine what make great CX?

8   Briefly explain why managing CX is important in building the profitability of a service organisation that is a 'challenger' in the market.

Further reading

Frei, F.X. (2008). The four things a service business must get right. *Harvard Business Review*, 86(4), 70.

Grönroos, C. (1990). Relationship approach to marketing in service contexts: The marketing and organizational behavior interface. *Journal of Business Research*, 20(1), 3–11.

Grönroos, C. (2006). Adopting a service logic for marketing. *Marketing Theory*, 6(3), 317–33.

Scartz, T.A. & Iacobucci, D. (eds) (2000). *Handbook of Services Marketing and Management*. Thousand Oaks, CA: Sage Publications.

Vargo, S.L. & Lusch, R.F. (2008). Service-dominant logic: Continuing the evolution. *Journal of the Academy of Marketing Science*, 36(1), 1–10.

Vargo, S.L., Maglio, P.P. & Akaka, M.A. (2008). On value and value co-creation: A service systems and service logic perspective. *European Management Journal*, 26(3), 145–52.

Weblinks

Australian Consumer Law. <www.consumerlaw.gov.au>

Australian Customer Service Awards. <www.serviceexcellence.com.au>

Customer Service Institute of Australia. <www.csia.com.au>

Vodafail. <www.vodafail.com>

Endnotes

1   Based on B. Ice (2015). Customer-centric strategy boosts revenue performance—study. *Marketing*, 6 October. <www.marketingmag.com.au/news-c/customer-centric-strategy-boosts-revenue-performance-study/?inf_contact_key=ae92d6f19b26624d5688884ddaaeec85d199746e3c542189c07ad72bbbc343dc>.

2   B. Temkin (2009). Don't confuse customer service with customer experience. Customer Experience Matters website, 24 February. <https://experiencematters.wordpress.com/2009/02/24/dont-confuse-customer-service-with-customer-experience>.

3   H. Manning (2010). Customer experience defined. Forrester website, 23 November. <https://go.forrester.com/blogs/10-11-23-customer_experience_defined>.

4   C. Shaw & J. Ivens (2005). *Building Great Customer Experiences*. Hampshire, UK: Palgrave Macmillan, p. 6.

5   C. Shaw (2007). *The DNA of Customer Experience How Emotions Drive Value*. Hampshire, UK: Palgrave Macmillan, p. xix.

6   R.L. Oliver (1997). *Satisfaction: A Behavioral Perspective on the Consumer*. Singapore: McGraw Hill Book Co., p. 294.

7   C. Shaw (2007). *The DNA of Customer Experience How Emotions Drive Value*. Hampshire, UK: Palgrave Macmillan, p. xx.

8   C. Shaw (2017). Exposed: How to measure your customer's loyalty and CX. *Beyond Philosophy*, 24 August. <https://beyondphilosophy.com/exposed-measure-customers-loyalty-cx>.

9   ibid.

10 SAP News (2017). Australian brands close the gap between digital experience and customer expectation. 21 November. <https://news.sap.com/australia/2017/11/21/australian-brands-close-the-gap-between-digital-experience-and-customer-expectation>.

11 ibid.

12 ibid.

13 L. Tonitto (2017). Why customer experience is the future of marketing. *Marketing Voice*, 15 August.

14 ibid.

15 ibid.

16 B. Figueiredo (2015). The value revolution. *Marketing*, August/September, pp. 30–1.

17 P. Short (2015). Customer experiences failures of Australian brands. *Marketing*, 18 September.

18 A. Damasio (2011). Neural basis of emotions. *Scholarpedia*, 6(3), 1804. <www.scholarpedia.org/article/Neural_basis_of_emotions>.

19 R.L. Oliver (1997). *Satisfaction: A Behavioral Perspective on the Consumer*. Singapore: McGraw Hill Book Co., p. 294.

20 N.H. Frijda (1993). Moods, emotion episodes, and emotions. In M. Lewis & J.M. Haviland (eds), *Handbook of Emotions*. New York, NY: Guilford Press, pp. 381–403.

21 H. Gungor (2007). *Emotional Satisfaction of Customer Contacts*. Amsterdam: VossiuspersUvA—Amsterdam University Press, p. 25.

22 ibid.

23 C. Shaw (2007). *The DNA of Customer Experience How Emotions Drive Value*. Hampshire, UK: Palgrave Macmillan, p. 29.

24 R.L. Oliver (1997). *Satisfaction: A Behavioral Perspective on the Consumer*. Singapore: McGraw Hill Book Co., p. 315.

25 C. Shaw (2007). *The DNA of Customer Experience How Emotions Drive Value*. Hampshire, UK: Palgrave Macmillan, p. 123.

26 NICE Satmetrix (2017). What is net promoter? <www.netpromoter.com/know>.

27 J. Chong (2015). Tigerair Australia rolling out new mobile app for airport staff to help reduce queues. *Australian Aviation*, 6 May. <http://australianaviation.com.au/2015/05/tigerair-australia-rolling-out-new-mobile-app-at-airports-to-help-reduce-queues>.

28 R. Glazer (2000). Smart services competitive advantage through information-intensive strategies. In T.A. Swartz & D. Iacobucci (eds), *Handbook of Services Marketing & Management*. Thousand Oaks, CA: Sage Publications.

29   ibid., p. 416.

30   BT.com (2017). Digital Customer 2017 Research. Chat, tap, talk: Eight key trends to transform your digital customer experience. <www.globalservices.bt.com/anze/en/point-of-view/chat-tap-talk-transform-your-digital-customer-experience>.

31   A. Gardner (2015). 4 ways data analytics can improve customers' satisfaction and experience. *Business Chief*, 9 March. <www.businessreviewaustralia.com/technology/1572/4-Ways-Data-Analytics-Can-Improve-Customers'-Satisfaction-and-Experience>.

32   S. Smith & J. Wheeler (2002). *Managing the Customer Experience*. London: FT Prentice Hall, pp. 13–15.

33   J. Carlson (1987). *Moments of Truth*. Adelaide, SA: Griffin Paperbacks.

34   J.C. Flanagan (1954). The critical incident technique. *Psychological Bulletin*, 51(July), 327–58.

35   M.J. Bitner, B.H Booms & M.S. Tetreault (1990). The service encounter: Diagnosing favourable and unfavourable incidents. *Journal of Marketing*, 54(January), 71–84.

36   S.M. Keaveney (1995). Customer switching behaviour in service industries: An exploratory study. *Journal of Marketing*, 59(April), 71–82.

37   G.L. Shostack (1985). Designing services that deliver. *Harvard Business Review*, January–February, 133–9.

38   Kinesis CEM (2015). Critical incident technique: A tool to identify your moments of truth. 6 May.

39   S. Shankar & J. Allen (2006). Keeping up with your customers. *Insights*, Bain & Company, 3 September. <www.bain.com/insights/keeping-up-with-your-customers/>.

40   M.J. Bitner, A. Ostrom & F. Morgan (2008). Service blueprinting: A practical technique for service innovation. *California Management Review*, 50(3), 66–94.

41   ibid.

42   R.N. Bolton (1998). A dynamic model of the duration of the customer's relationship with a continuous service provider: The role of satisfaction. *Marketing Science*, 17(1), 45–65.

43   R. Strohmenger & T. McCann (2015). Analysing what makes a great customer experience. *Marketing*, 29 October. <www.marketingmag.com.au/hubs-c/analysing-makes-great-customer-experience/?inf_contact_key=6860d24039857e842eae506ccdf6f4d0014bd840c10aee8661115d0908fe82b6>.

44   M. Sullivan (2014). Great customer service is growth edge for SMEs. *Business Acumen Magazine*, 29 December. <www.businessacumen.biz/index.php/23-news/news-feature/961-great-customer-service-is-growth-edge-for-smes.html>.

45   ibid.

Eurostar: Customer satisfaction, emotion and competitiveness

On 1 September 2010, the company Eurostar International Limited (EIL) was formed to operate the Eurostar rail service. It was owned by three shareholders, French Railways (SNCF owned 55 per cent), Belgium Railways (SNCB owned 5 per cent) and London & Continental Railways (LCR owned 40 per cent). In June 2014, LCR's holdings were subsequently transferred to the UK Government Treasury.[1]

On 1 May 2015, EIL began a new direct Eurostar service to the south of France. The route, which runs from London to Lyon, Avignon and Marseille, has proven popular with passengers with more than 88 000 tickets being sold by July 2015.[2] The sale of tickets is testament to the enduring appeal of the Mediterranean and Provence regions, which offer British travellers the quintessential French holiday experience. EIL also announced that a fleet of 17 new trains—known as the e320s—with an increased seat capacity to a total of 900 passengers and capable of travelling at speeds up to 320 kph, would enter full-scale service early in 2016.[3]

Establishing an emotional bond with customers to drive loyalty

Avantage is a cultural change program that was developed after EIL research revealed that while customers thought that Eurostar staff offered a professional service, they believed the brand lacked 'emotional attachment, personality and flair'. The management of EIL felt the organisation needed to focus on building customer loyalty by establishing emotional bonds with its customers. With that caveat in mind, EIL redesigned its service processes using customers' responses with input from frontline staff, and some qualitative anthropological research. Sarah Thomas, manager of the Avantage program, said that EIL needed to create a strong bond with its customers and engage them so that Eurostar would be their first preference for travel to Europe.

» *continued over page*

Chapter 11

Customer Satisfaction and Service Quality

William Chitty

Figure 11.1   The e320 Eurostar; from London to Paris, and beyond at 320kph

Source: Siemens. <www.siemens.com/press/pool/de/pressebilder/2014/mobility/300dpi/IM2014120283MO_300dpi.jpg>.

Figure 11.2   Eurostar Business Premier (1st class)

Source: Eurostar. <http://newtrains.eurostar.com>.

Designing a service process based on customer experience

The Avantage program consists of seven steps, and includes developing the concept of service design from the customers' viewpoint. EIL used specialist anthropological researchers to create an emotional 'map' of the highs and lows of a Eurostar train journey. The researchers travelled with passengers and studied their body language to create a map that was used as the basis for a series of service design workshops. Interestingly, no EIL managers were involved—only frontline staff and customers—with the workshops generating 131 recommendations, 97 of which were implemented by the company. The anthropological research revealed that some customers became anxious during pre-boarding at Brussels, which took place in an underground area of the station.

Now, as part of the revised service process, check-in personnel actively look for signs of customer distress and provide support when necessary; that support includes allowing passengers to board earlier to ease congestion. EIL also built a special lounge in this area of the station so passengers could wait in more comfortable surroundings. The research also identified a need for passenger support in self-service ticket areas. Although this appeared counter-intuitive to staff, and some felt that providing assistance in these station areas was 'patronising' to customers, it became evident that the presence of a company representative helped answer non-ticketing customer queries, such as how to get on to a train quickly if a passenger was running late.

Measuring the return on investment of customer experience and emotion

The Avantage program is still relatively new, and EIL, like many service organisations, is examining ways to measure more complex metrics, such as customer engagement and experience. Sarah Thomas noted that EIL managers feel that measuring those satisfaction indicators is the right thing to do in facing competition from airlines; but because Eurostar is a business, they want proof that the program will be cost neutral, and deliver a positive result.

The company continues to measure satisfaction because it is a reliable indicator of operational processes. Before instigating Avantage, customer satisfaction scores were steady at about 7.5/10, but since rollout of the program, scores have increased to more than 8/10. Customers also rate Eurostar qualitatively and emotionally; with 'warm' and 'friendly' being two of the most frequent words used to describe passenger journeys. EIL has reported the highest number of passengers ever transported on Eurostar in one quarter, with more than 2.8 million customers travelling between the United Kingdom and Europe in the second quarter (Q2), 2015.

This represents a year-on-year increase of 3 per cent in passengers compared with the same period the previous year—2.7 million passengers in 2014. Sales revenues for Q2, 2015 (£232 million) increased by 1.5 per cent compared with £229 million for Q2, 2014. The number of Business Premier passengers rose by 10 per cent in Q2, 2015 compared with the Q2, 2014, with increases reported on both sides of the channel.[4]

Conclusions

EIL is typical of a number of service organisations in adopting a new approach to measuring the ROI (return on investment) for customer satisfaction. Research in measuring satisfaction suggests that:

↘ increased competition and customer feedback mean that organisations recognise that 'softer', more complex drivers will influence customer satisfaction in the future

↘ experiential and emotional elements of customer–organisation relationships are becoming more important in understanding the antecedents of satisfaction

↘ organisations value qualitative and correlational evidence

↘ organisations are increasingly willing to experiment and devolve responsibility to frontline staff

↘ organisations need to listen to customers and frontline staff about change, and implementing change.[5]

Introduction

Satisfaction is a comparative process and has been defined as being 'the psychological post-purchase evaluation that occurs as a result of an individual customer's unique and favourable service experience, including the service processes and outcomes, based on the fulfilment of her or his needs, wants and expectations'.[6]

To understand customer satisfaction requires an understanding of what it is, and how *customers* determine what service benefits and attributes contribute positively to their satisfaction. *Satisfaction* is the psychological outcome that occurs when consumers evaluate the perceived performance of the service experience based on what they expected before purchasing the service.

Consumers purchase a particular brand of service in the expectation that it will satisfy their needs and wants more effectively and efficiently than competitive services. From a customer's point of view, satisfaction is a basic requirement for achieving some form of value from a service encounter. Satisfaction, or the lack of it, is the end result of purchasing and consuming a service.

Customer satisfaction is an essential outcome for the long-term viability of a service organisation because customers who are satisfied with their service experience are more likely to repurchase that organisation's services. Even for services that have extended purchase intervals—such as a two-year contract from an internet service provider (ISP), or an annual dental check—customer satisfaction is important because online word-of-mouth can quickly lead to customers becoming dissatisfied

Service quality is a form of value that customers receive from consuming a service.[7] As a concept, value is ambiguous and subject to semantic interpretations, which makes it difficult to measure. It can be as simple as:

> Price is what you pay. Value is what you get.
>
> Warren Buffet

or it can be more inclusive, as defined by Woodruff (1997):

> A customer perceived preference for and evaluation of those products attributes, attribute performances, and consequences arising from use that facilitate (or block) achieving the customer's goals and purposes in use situations.[8]

As a concept, marketers' understanding of value has moved through four distinct stages.[9] (See also Chapter 10 for a discussion of the following points.) The first, the *traditional view of value*, is that value was created by organisations as part of the transformation of the factors of production—that is, labour and capital—into services. Customers then paid for and acquired those particular services, with the residual value being subsequently released to customers as they consumed the service product. That approach views value as being entirely created through the production stage of the service and is therefore known as 'value in production'.

The second stage, known as *value in co-production*, arose as a result of developments in the service sector of national economies. The increasing number of new competitive services made service organisations realise the need to engage their customers in the production processes so they could acquire its inherent value by consuming the service product. Airline passengers, for example, are required to follow behavioural processes—check-in either in person or online, present their luggage to be registered and loaded on to the appropriate aircraft, wait for a seat to be allocated or approved, wait in a designated area to called to board the aircraft, to be safely deposited at the expected destination. If passengers do not follow those behavioural processes, they risk not being able or allowed to board the aircraft.

Value in use was the third stage in understanding the concept of value. This approach does not include value in the production process but views value as being part of a customer's consumption process. That means service organisations can create services, but the benefits associated with those services can only be experienced by customers when they use them. The value in use locates the value of a service in its consumption and may be outside the control of the service organisation. The value of going to a football match or a concert, for example, is in experiencing the event.

The fourth and final stage, *value co-creation*, is a dynamic perspective of value for services. The rapid diffusion of the internet and social media technologies has removed the barriers that services organisations had imposed between production and consumption, and that has allowed the value associated with a service to become part of a dynamic process of value creation. For example, in the gaming industry, the interactions of multiple players at a roulette wheel contribute to the value of each game for many players because experienced players are constantly looking for new ways to engage with other players and create further social exchanges. The value co-creation stage calls for marketers to be part of the service development experience and also to act as catalysts for value creation among the multiple consumers of the service.

The first section of this chapter discusses how satisfaction relates to both the process and the outcomes of a service encounter, and the impact that each has on delivering customer satisfaction. The second section considers the differences between service quality and satisfaction and discusses the dimensions of the service quality 'gaps model'.

Learning objectives

After reading this chapter you should be able to:

↘ discuss the factors that influence the formation of customers' expectations

↘ explain how the different types of service interactions influence customers' experiences

↘ discuss the factors that influence the formation of customers' perceptions

↘ explain the differences between customers' satisfaction and loyalty

↘ discuss how service quality can be determined using the 'gaps model'.

William Chitty

Customer expectations

Expectations are predictions as to the outcome of a future service encounter, and those expectations serve as benchmarks or are adopted as standards that consumers use to evaluate the performance of the service after it has been delivered. The boundaries of service expectations range between the levels of *desired* service and *adequate* service, and are separated by a zone of tolerance.[10]

customer expectations
Predictions as to the outcome of a future service encounter

The strength of customer expectations depends on the standards that customers adopt before the service encounter. Although most customers have an idea of what to expect when they make a decision to purchase a service, the marketer of that service needs to understand what those expectations are in order to measure and manage them. The management of customers' expectations is the first step in delivering sustainable customer satisfaction.

The highest level of customers' expectations are *desired or ideal* expectations, which form the 'ideal' level of a service that they expect to receive based on what they believe can be delivered.[11] This is the level of service that customers expect to be delivered under ideal conditions. The next level are the *normative* or 'should be' expectations, which are formed after exposure to an organisation's marketing communications; they are what customers expect should be delivered by the service. The third level are customers' *experience* expectations, which are based on previous encounters with similar organisations, while the *adequate or acceptable* expectations are the lowest level of service that customers will tolerate before taking some remedial action, such as lodging a formal complaint.

In most service encounters, customers hope to receive their desired level of service performance but, recognising that this standard will not always be delivered, they will accept, however, a level of service that they consider to be adequate.[12] Adequate service represents the *minimum tolerable expectation*, the lowest level of performance that is acceptable to the customer.[13] For example, suppose you are considering a weekend getaway in the Barossa Valley. Your expectations about the type and cost of accommodation will be influenced by several factors:

→ What your friends have said about the type of accommodation that is available in the Barossa Valley; that is, whether, through positive word-of-mouth, they recommend staying at a particular establishment.

→ The effect that the marketing communications of the various businesses offering accommodation have on your decision-making as you scroll through the Barossa Valley's home page.

→ Your expectations will be influenced by your knowledge of competing wine-producing areas, and what they offer for a similar price.

→ The personal relevance that you attach to this weekend getaway will have a bearing on your expectations which, in turn, will be influenced by your degree of involvement.

OXFORD UNIVERSITY PRESS

Figure 11.3 Vineyards in the Barossa Valley of South Australia

Sources of desired service expectations

As shown in Figure 11.4, there are two major influences on a customer's desired service expectations: lasting service intensifiers and personal needs. Both determine a customer's underlying expectations about the performance of a service. Lasting service intensifiers are individual, relatively stable desired service expectations that are often derived when a customer's expectations are driven by the needs of others. Personal needs are those mental states that determine a customer's physical or psychological well-being, and can include physical, social, psychological and functional needs that have differing intensities according to the customer's reasons for using the service.

Consider the following situation. You have applied for a position with a large national marketing company, and as part of the interviewing process you are required to present some ideas as to how you would develop a marketing plan for one of the company's services. You go to your hairdresser, and explain that you need to look professional for the presentation. Your physical requirements will satisfy your functional needs, as well as satisfying your psychological need to present a professional appearance—two different expectations of the

Figure 11.4 Factors that influence a desired service

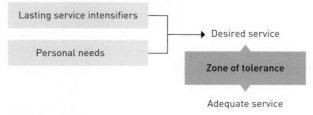

Source: V.A. Zeithaml, M.J. Bitner & D.D. Gremler (2006). *Services Marketing: Integrating Customer Focus Across the Firm* (4th edn). New York, NY: McGraw-Hill Irwin, p. 88.

desired level of service offered by the hairdresser. In those circumstances, you will have higher expectations of your hairdresser than if you were simply having a regular haircut.

The other major influence on a customer's desired level of service is their personal service philosophy; that is, their underlying attitude about the meaning of a service and the behaviour of the service provider. Many service personnel conform to standards set by the service organisation. Call-centre staff, for example, are often told that customers should not be kept waiting for longer than 15 seconds. Personal service philosophies and derived service expectations in most cases increase the level of customers' desired service.[14]

Sources of adequate service expectations

Different factors determine the level of service that customers find acceptable—that is, their expectations of adequate service. In general, these factors are short-term influences and are more likely to be specific to the situation than the factors that influence desired service. As shown in Figure 11.5, the factors that influence adequate service are temporary service intensifiers; perceived service alternatives; self-perceived service role; situational factors; and predicted service.[15]

Temporary service intensifiers are short-term, individual factors that make a customer more aware of the need for a service. In a personal situation where a service is needed urgently, such as a road accident, when an ambulance is needed to take a victim to a hospital, a customer's expectations of adequate service are heightened, especially for the required level of responsiveness that is considered acceptable in that situation.

Perceived service alternatives are the other service organisations that can provide a similar service. If customers have a choice of providers, their expectations of adequate service will be higher than if they believe it is not possible to get a better service elsewhere.

Figure 11.5   Factors that influence adequate service

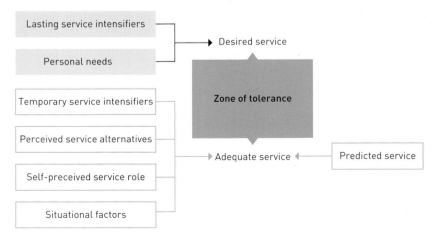

Source: V.A. Zeithaml, M.J. Bitner & D.D. Gremler (2006). *Services Marketing: Integrating Customer Focus Across the Firm* (4th edn). New York, NY: McGraw-Hill Irwin, p. 90.

For example, customers in metropolitan suburbs who are aware of alternative mobile telecommunications organisations tend to have higher expectations of adequate service and narrower zones of tolerance than their country counterparts. It is important, therefore, that service marketers know which alternative organisations customers view as offering comparable services, rather than merely knowing those organisations that customers include in their evoked sets of choice.

Customers' *self-perceived service roles* indicate the extent to which they can exert an influence on the level of service they receive. Their expectations are therefore partly shaped by how much control they believe they have in performing their own roles in service delivery.[16] Customers who are active co-producers of a service and indicate the level of performance they expect are more likely to be satisfied than those who are passive participants. Zones of tolerance are likely to expand when customers sense they are not fulfilling their roles, while those who believe they are doing their part in the service delivery have heightened expectations of adequate service and a narrower zone of tolerance.

Situational factors, which are service performance conditions that customers view as being beyond the control of the service organisation, also influence customers' perceptions of adequate service. For example, when emergencies such as winter storms disrupt public utility services, customers who understand that the source of the problem is not the fault of the service organisation are more likely to temporarily tolerate lower levels of adequate service and expand their zone of tolerance.

The *predicted service* is a level of service that customers predict they will probably receive from a service encounter. When customers predict a satisfactory service outcome, their expectations of adequate service are likely to be higher than if they predict a poor outcome. Predicted service expectations are typically an estimation of the level of satisfaction that customers would receive from a transaction-specific encounter rather than the satisfaction generated by the overall relationship they have with a service organisation. While desired and adequate service expectations are considered to be global assessments of several individual service encounters, predicted service expectations can be considered as more specific estimates of what will happen in future encounters based on the customer's previous service transactions. For example, your expectations about the time you will have to wait to see your doctor will very likely be based on the time you had to wait for your previous appointment.

Sources of both desired and predicted service expectations

When consumers buy a service they consider important, they often look for information about it from different sources. For example, they may contact several service organisations, ask their friends, search online to find the information they need to make a decision, or pay attention to any marketing communications about the particular service category. In addition to those external sources of information, consumers may also review what they

William Chitty

remember from using a similar service. The factors that influence desired and predicted service expectations are shown in Figure 11.6.

Explicit service promises are marketing communications about the service made by the service organisation to its customers. The organisation's marketing messages are considered personal when they are made by its salespeople or service personnel, or they are considered impersonal when they are delivered by mass media advertising or sales promotions. Marketing communication that promises how, what, when and where the service will be delivered influences the levels of both desired service and predicted service, and is the most effective way to manage customer expectations. On the other hand, the worst thing that service personnel can do is to encourage a prospective customer to buy the service by overpromising its benefits. That is more than likely to result in long-term customer dissatisfaction, particularly if the service is customised and not easily delivered and/or repeated. For example, some salespeople on a commission remuneration scheme may overstate the features of a new gym membership in order to encourage customers to buy a two-year plan. If the customers do not receive what was promised, in terms of benefits and/or costs, they will be far less likely to take another gym membership contract with that fitness centre.

The *implicit service promises* made for Warehouse Fitness Centre are service-related cues that lead prospective customers to infer what the service is and how it can help them. As shown in Figure 11.7, the ad for the fitness centre identifies the price of the service and the tangible benefits, such as childminding, that are associated with using that service offered by a Warehouse Fitness Centre. Customers will often have higher expectations of a service if the price is higher and the tangibles more impressive than its competitors. If, for example, you want to join a gymnasium or fitness centre and you find two gyms, each offering much

Figure 11.6   Factors that influence desired and predicted service expectations

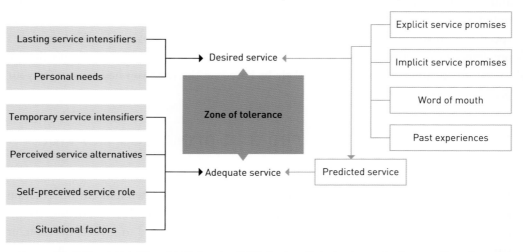

Source: V.A. Zeithaml, M.J. Bitner & D.D. Gremler (2006). *Services Marketing: Integrating Customer Focus Across the Firm* (4th edn). New York, NY: McGraw-Hill Irwin, p. 93.

Figure 11.7   Advertisement for Warehouse Fitness Centre

Source: Warehouse Fitness. <www.warehousefitness.com.au/membership-pricing>.

the same as the other but charging very different prices, which gym would you select: the one that's charging a higher price in the belief that it will provide higher-quality service and a personal trainer, or the cheaper company that does not provide training services, and hope that you can achieve your fitness goal without having hurting yourself?

Word-of-mouth communications, which are personal, or sometimes impersonal, statements made by people not linked to the service organisation that is making the promises, can influence consumers' expectations of the levels of predicted and desired service.[17] Personal word-of-mouth communication is important to customers because it seen as an unbiased source of service information that helps them to manage the risks associated with evaluating a service, both before purchase and during the service encounter. Customer reviews on an organisation's web page are a form of word-of-mouth communications.

A customer's *past experience* with using a service also influences service expectations. That past experience may, however, depend on the customer's experience with the specific service brand they are considering. For example, you may be able to evaluate your previous service experiences in using a gym, but your experience will be limited if you have only ever used one gymnasium. If you compared each gym experience with experiences you have had with other similar gyms, you then have some indication of the expected performance of a service that you believe best represents a group of similar gymnasium brands.[18]

Services marketers need to know the sources of customers' expectations and the relative importance they attach to each. The relative weight of word of mouth, explicit service promises and implicit service promises, for example, all influence the levels of desired and

William Chitty

predicted service. Some of these sources are more stable and permanent in their influence, such as lasting service intensifiers and personal needs, while others, such as perceived alternatives and situational factors, fluctuate to a greater degree over time.

Customer interactions

In everyday situations, consumers purchase a service because they expect that it will satisfy their particular needs and wants. When making a purchase decision, consumers' expectations become the motivators for initiating the purchase decision, while their perceptions of the service performance are developed as a result of interacting with the service providers—usually the staff members of the service organisation. In some cases, customers do not interact with service providers in a face-to-face role because digital technology, such as an ATM or perhaps the internet, has removed the requirement to deliver a service in a face-to-face mode.

In any service organisation, marketing is responsible for three key functions:

1 designing a service product that meets prospective target customers' needs, wants and expectations
2 communicating the service's brand, attributes and benefits to those customers
3 monitoring and controlling the service-delivery systems to ensure that the customer's needs, wants and expectations continue to be satisfied in the changing macro environment.

Marketing a physical product is predicated on communicating the tangible features and benefits of the object, while marketing a service is more reliant on the performance of the service provider. Successful management of the service tangibles, which are part of the process dimensions of a service, is paramount because customers will often use their expectations of those tangible characteristics as benchmarks to evaluate the service transaction. While there are well-developed methods for identifying the salient attributes of physical products and for testing their ability to satisfy consumers' needs and wants, the types of processes for identifying salient service attributes are constantly evolving. For example, expressions such as 'courtesy', 'an interest in customers' needs' and 'kindness' have been used to describe the personal attributes of the cabin staff of an airline. Yet, how can those service attributes be measured?

With few exceptions, a service encounter should be designed to ensure that the customers are satisfied with the service. The number of clients per hour, the waiting times and the error rates are service operational standards that are measurable. Service standards are important; but to be of value, they must be determined by the needs of the customer, not based on internal criteria generated by the company. For example, many call centres allocate a certain amount of time to attend to customers who ring in with queries about their accounts or products. It seems that when customers use call centres, they are not particular about the time it takes to resolve their queries; what they want is courteous and helpful service that is based on accurate information.

To optimise its resources, a service organisation must be able to identify those attributes that contribute most to customer satisfaction, as well as those that have the potential to create dissatisfaction. As discussed in Chapter 1, the core service is the essential set of benefits that a service organisation provides to satisfy customers' needs and remain viable. Peripheral services facilitate acceptance of the core service, and often are the expected features of a bundle of services. While they are *add-ons* or *amenities*, they are not necessary to provide the core service.

To survive, a service organisation must have basic competencies in providing both core and peripheral services because no amount of add-ons will save an organisation that is deficient in providing its core service. Peripheral services such as food and entertainment on an aircraft will, however, often influence a customer's buying decision. For example, Virgin Australia upgraded its international premium economy services with meals designed by Luke Mangan, installed seats that are 50 centimetres wide with adjustable foot and head rests, together with 97 centimetres of leg room and a 20-centimetre recline; the entertainment is now shown on 30-centimetre entertainment screens.

It is important to remember that the core and peripheral services define the lower limit of customer expectations about performance. In general, customers tend to have higher expectation levels and narrower zones of tolerance for service *reliability* than for the other service process dimensions of *tangibles*, *responsiveness*, *assurance* and *empathy*. Those service dimensions are considered in more detail later in the chapter.

The zone of tolerance

The performance of a service is considered to be variable because in many cases it differs between service organisations, between individual service providers and from one service interaction to another. Customers' service expectations have variable boundaries between a desired level of service and a level of service they consider adequate to meet their needs, wants and expectations. Customers' expectations cannot always be characterised as having a single point; rather, they are dynamic, because boundaries of expectation expand and contract according to the amount of variation in service interactions that customers will accept. Those variations in service interactions are known as a customer's *zone of tolerance* (see Figure 11.8). If service performance is perceived to be at the higher end of the zone of tolerance—close to desired service—the likelihood that customers will be satisfied with the service interaction will be greater.

The zone of tolerance can be considered to be a customer's comfort zone. When a service falls outside the boundaries of desired or adequate service, customers are likely to consider the service to be either satisfactory or unsatisfactory. For example, consider the service you receive from a bank's call centre when you have a query about a charge on your Visa card. Most customers have a range of acceptable times for this type of service encounter—probably somewhere between 4 and 5 minutes—while they listen to a recorded

William Chitty

Figure 11.8 The zone of tolerance

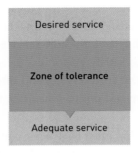

Source: V.A. Zeithaml, M.J. Bitner & D.D. Gremler (2006). *Services Marketing: Integrating Customer Focus Across the Firm* (4th edn). New York, NY: McGraw-Hill Irwin, p. 86.

message telling them not to hang-up. As their time on hold increases beyond what they consider acceptable, they begin to pay more attention to the time spent waiting and their dissatisfaction with the bank's service also increases.

Different customers possess different zones of tolerance

Customers possess different zones of tolerance. For example, if customers have limited time to participate in service interactions it will restrict the wait time they consider acceptable. This means service organisations need to be aware that some customers expect a tighter time frame from their service providers, while others, with a less restricted time frame, will have wider zones of tolerance. Delayed take-offs are a source of dissatisfaction for an airline's business customers because much of their working day relies on planned meetings and delayed take-offs disrupt their work schedules. A delayed take-off for leisure customers however is more likely to be seen as a source of annoyance rather than as a basis for serious criticism of the airline's performance.

The variation in a customer's zone of tolerance depends on a number of factors, including company-controlled matters such as price and marketing communications. When the cost of a service is higher than comparable services, customers tend to be less tolerant of any variability in the performance of the service, while promises made by an organisation in its marketing communications are expected to be fulfilled because those promises have moved the level of adequate service closer to the desired service level, thereby decreasing the customer's zone of tolerance.[19]

Customers' involvement with service attributes changes their zone of tolerance

Customers' tolerance also varies according to the importance they place on different service attributes: the more important the attribute, the narrower their zone of tolerance.

Involvement is the level of personal relevance that a customer attaches to a service attribute. In general, customers have higher levels of involvement for desired attributes, and are therefore less tolerant of unreliable service such as broken promises or basic service errors. That means that service organisations must consider which service attributes are important to their customers, because service interactions that are considered important will raise the desired and adequate service levels and reduce the customers' zone of tolerance.[20] Figure 11.9 depicts the likely difference in tolerance zones for the most important and the least important factors.[21]

Figure 11.9 Zones of tolerance for different service attributes

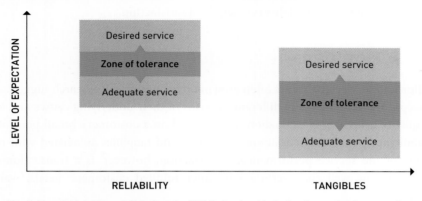

Source: V.A. Zeithaml, M.J. Bitner & D.D. Gremler (2006). *Services Marketing: Integrating Customer Focus Across the Firm* (4th edn). New York, NY: McGraw-Hill Irwin. p. 87.

The relative movements in the levels of a customer's zone of tolerance are more likely to be the result of changes in the adequate service level, which moves more readily up or down because of situational circumstances such as competition. The desired service level is an individual's assessment of the 'ideal', and tends to move incrementally upward based on customers' exposure to the promises in the service organisation's marketing communications and their accumulated experience with using the particular service.

Customer perceptions

Perception is an application of how customers develop an understanding of the sensory stimuli associated with a service. Because services have four defining characteristics, sensory perception for a service relates to how customers process the sensory stimuli of service interactions to develop opinions about how well service brands and organisations satisfy their needs, wants and expectations.

Perceptions of ambiguous service interactions can shape customers' interpretations of the outcome because they see only what they want to see. For example, how fans at a

↘
perceptions
The customer's ability to intuitively recognise objects or events that can be evaluated by 'top-down' processes using criteria such as their needs, wants and expectations

football game perceive events that occurred during the game depends on how strongly they support 'their' team, while all faults are attributed to the other side! The effect of perception has been demonstrated in many social contexts. For example, customers who are promised a positive experience by the marketing communications of a five-star hotel have been primed to expect having satisfying interactions when they interact with staff in the hotel.

Perceptions are customers' beliefs about the performance of a service encounter; they change over time, and vary from person to person, and for each encounter. Customers' perceptions of the service performance are not predetermined criteria of what service is, or even should be; customers perceive a service in terms of how a service interaction gives them some form of value and delivers a degree of satisfaction.

Satisfaction versus service quality

service quality
An overall evaluation that is based on customers' broad perceptions of the reliability, responsiveness, assurance, empathy and tangibles associated with multiple encounters of the service performance

Satisfaction and service quality are often used interchangeably, but research suggests that the two concepts are fundamentally different in terms of their underlying causes and effects.[22] Service quality is an overall evaluation that is based on a customer's broad perceptions of the reliability, responsiveness, assurance, empathy and tangibles associated with multiple encounters of the service performance.[23] Satisfaction, however, is a transaction-specific evaluation of how well each service encounter fulfilled customers' needs, wants and expectations.[24]

Transaction versus cumulative perceptions

Customers' perceptions of the performance of a service may be based on a single, transaction-specific interaction or on their overall perceptions of a service, based on several encounters with a service organisation. For example, a customer will make a judgment about a specific service encounter in a five-star hotel based on what they expected about the time it would take for their luggage to be delivered to their room after they checked in.

Customers' perceptions of a service can also be based on all their encounters with a service organisation over a series of service encounters over time. Those experiences for a hotel customer might, for example, include multiple personal encounters at the chain of hotels, using the hotel's online booking service and their experience using the hotel chain's health clubs in different locations. At a wider level, the customer may have formed perceptions of the accommodation and leisure services offered by all five-star hotels from their experiences and what they know about hotels in various regions.

Research suggests that it is important for service organisations to understand how customers' perceptions are formed, and to realise that both types of perceptions are complementary rather than competing.[25] Understanding customers' transaction-specific perceptions is crucial for diagnosing the delivery performance of a service, which can be used to make remedial changes to the delivery processes.

Customer satisfaction

There are two distinct approaches to understanding customer satisfaction. Like the rationale of transaction and cumulative perceptions, satisfaction can be considered as being a transaction-specific outcome or a cumulative construct based on repeated favourable encounters with a service organisation. Satisfactory single-service encounters are the building blocks for customers' cumulative experience evaluations, which are likely to be better predictors of the service quality of a service organisation.

In developing our definition of satisfaction, another factor that influences satisfaction includes customers' feelings that result from particular service encounters. Satisfaction research has identified the major antecedents, core mechanisms and consequences of repeated service encounters. For example, satisfaction may be viewed as being a passive response to interactions with a low-involvement service, such as withdrawing money from an ATM, which customers do regularly, but do not consider to be important. Customers' satisfaction may also be generated by feelings of pleasure; they may feel more content or happier than they expected to before using the service and may subsequently be delighted with the outcome. Although consumer satisfaction is generated at a particular point of contact, it evolves over time from the dynamic interaction of factors such as when and how often the service is consumed.[26]

The role of emotion in the satisfaction response process

Research suggests that emotions play a significant role in the satisfaction response process.[27] There are three major sources of satisfaction emotion. The first is an overall impression that the service outcome was favourable or unfavourable—that is, it was 'good for me' or it was 'bad for me'—and that produces a general effect such as happiness or sadness. The second source is specific comparisons, such as disconfirmation, inequity or regret. The third is about attributions, where consumers attribute gratitude or blame for good and bad outcomes.[28]

It could be expected, for example, that the human activities associated with delivering a service would be significant in satisfaction emotion because of the interpersonal service encounters. The net result of the human element of service delivery is a greater interplay of emotion in the generation of service satisfaction when compared to delivery of goods. That greater interpersonal influence can come into effect through the performance of a service because service encounters are more variable due to the often complex interactions service providers have with diverse customers. For example, hospital emergency services are delivered to customers in complex settings with many human interactions, which can provoke customers' claims of unfair treatment when they have to wait to be seen by a doctor. Such perceptions of 'unfair treatment' will frequently be attributed to the service provider, with a corresponding emotional response, meaning it was the service provider's fault.

Services in Action

Emotional connections and their effect on customer satisfaction

Research by the Gallup Organisation examined the nature of employee interactions with customers and found that emotions had a significantly larger effect on both parties' judgments and behaviour than rational thinking did. The Gallup research found that customers who rate themselves as being 'extremely satisfied' on surveys fall into two distinct categories: those who have a strong emotional connection to the company, and those who do not. In a multi-year study of hundreds of companies and thousands of customers and employees, Gallup found that 'emotionally satisfied' customers contribute far more to profits than 'rationally satisfied' customers do, even though the latter rate themselves as equally 'satisfied' on customer surveys.

Surprisingly, the behaviour of rationally satisfied customers looked no different from that of dissatisfied customers. In a large US bank in the study, the attrition rate of dissatisfied customers was on par with that of rationally satisfied customers, or those who described themselves as extremely satisfied but scored low on an 'emotional attachment' metric. The attrition rate of bank customers who were emotionally satisfied, however, was on average 37 per cent lower. For all types of companies in the research, Gallup found that emotionally engaged customers delivered a 23 per cent premium over the average customer in terms of profitability, revenue and relationship growth.

If service organisations are to improve, they must learn to measure and manage the quality of the employee–customer encounter. Quality improvement methodologies such as Six Sigma are extremely useful in manufacturing contexts, but they are less useful when it comes to human interactions. To address this problem, authors John Fleming, Curt Coffman and James Harter developed a quality improvement approach they refer to as 'human sigma'.[29] It weaves together a method for assessing the employee–customer encounter and a process for managing and improving it. There are several core principles for measuring and managing the employee–customer encounter. When analysing service interactions, emotion influences the judgment and behaviour of both parties. Employee–customer interactions must be measured and managed locally, because there are significant variations in service quality between the workgroup and individual levels. To improve the quality of the employee–customer interaction, organisations must conduct both transactional and transformational interventions. Employee and customer engagement are closely connected, and taken together, have a considerable effect on a service organisation's financial performance.

Satisfaction models

Satisfaction is the result of comparing customers' pre-encounter expectations of the service with their post-performance perceptions. That comparative paradigm is what distinguishes satisfaction from other states of affect, such as happiness or pleasure, which can occur without using comparative standards.[30] When pre-encounter expectations are compared to post-performance perceptions, the cognitive result is known as *expectancy disconfirmation*. Similarly, when performance is compared to needs, the result is need fulfilment, and comparisons with 'excellent' standards result in quality judgments.[31]

The disconfirmation of expectations paradigm

The traditional model that is most commonly used to determine customer satisfaction is the disconfirmation of expectations paradigm. That paradigm (see Figure 11.10) is a conceptual framework for comparative evaluation of customers' pre-encounter expectations, or other comparison standards such as their needs and wants, with their perceptions of the service performance.[32] The disconfirmation of consumer expectations can be negative, where the service performance is perceived to be less than expected; positive, where it is perceived to be better than expected; or neutral, where it is as expected. Disconfirmation is a two-sided construct, and without qualification is ambiguous as to its direction.

Generally, *positive disconfirmation* contributes to satisfaction with the service, *negative disconfirmation* contributes to dissatisfaction, and *confirmation* merely 'confirms' what the consumer expected from the performance of the service. Positive encounters have favourable implications for service organisations because, as with other satisfying experiences, customers will respond with higher levels of intention to repurchase and will

Figure 11.10 The disconfirmation of expectations paradigm

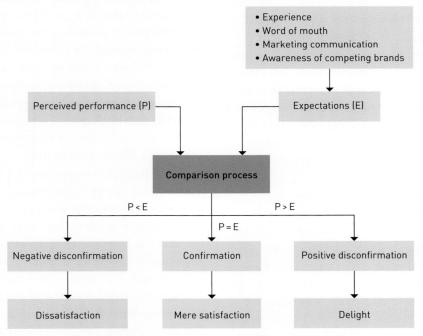

Source: P.G. Patterson (1993). Expectations and product performance as determinants of satisfaction for a high-involvement purchase. *Psychology and Marketing*, 10(5), 449–62.

William Chitty   **393**

offer more favourable recommendations to others. Research shows, however, that customers' satisfying experiences have less effect on overall satisfaction than negative incidents have on dissatisfaction.[33] One reason for this is a 'fundamental attribution error', which occurs when customers take credit for satisfying service encounters but blame others and/or other things, for a dissatisfying service.[34]

A basic equation of the determinants of customer satisfaction/dissatisfaction (CS/D) can therefore be expressed as:

$$CS/D = f(\text{Expectations, Performance and Disconfirmation})$$

where CS/D is a function of the comparison of customers' pre-encounter expectations and their post-performance perceptions of the service, and the resultant disconfirmation—which may be positive or negative.

↘ INDUSTRY INSIGHT

Navigating the challenges and opportunities in financial services

Despite the financial industry's customer-centric slogans, financial services institutions (FSIs) have historically 'under-delivered' in customer satisfaction. A review of different countries, languages, cultures, even different segments within financial services—such as banking, insurance or investments—consistently reveals the use of 'customer-centric' marketing messages. An everyday customer could therefore be forgiven for thinking that because FSIs have similar aspirations across the industry, their customer satisfaction agenda has succeeded and that 'customers are really happy'.

Evidence, however, indicates that customers' satisfaction, confidence and trust—not only of the financial system, but business as a whole—is at low levels. For example, the results of a survey of some 7800 tertiary-educated Millennials—those persons born after 1982—suggests that only half believe the world's big businesses behave ethically, and that three-quarters think that FSIs focus on their own agenda

rather than considering the impact of their actions on society (Table 11.1).

Trust is an elusive courtship

For a long time, all customers wanted from FSIs was to be able to 'trust' them; trust that their savings would be safe, that they would be given accurate information and their provider would be there when needed. However, crises of confidence continue to happen across the industry post–global financial crisis (GFC), with GFC losses exacerbated by subsequent misconduct and poor advice, further eroding trust.

While 'trust' is the major banks' biggest asset—70 per cent of customers would trust their main financial institution's mobile wallet solution versus 15 per cent for other institutions in Australia—the payments challengers are ramping up their offerings and are becoming more trusted; for example, PayPal, Visa/MasterCard, Google and Apple. Deloitte's analysts expect that the challengers' market penetration is likely to be boosted by 30 million

Table 11.1 Deloitte Millennial survey of big business

	Agree (%)	Disagree (%)
They focus on their own agenda rather than considering the wider society.	75	23
They take a strong leadership position on issues that have an effect on the wider society.	61	35
They show stronger leadership than governments on important social issues.	61	35
Their leaders are committed to helping to improve the wider society.	53	44
They behave in an ethical manner.	52	44

near-field-communication (NFC)-equipped smartphones globally that will be used at least once a month to make contactless in-store payments at retail outlets.

Customers as a source of disruption

As the phenomena of social media and the sharing economy continue, the trusted relationship with customers as it exists at present will continue to be challenged. At its simplest level, social networking and social media have transformed relationships with customers. Those customers are not merely 'consumers' of services; they are active voices in shaping the value chain at every stage. Barclays Ring MasterCard, the first credit card to put members in control, is an example of how involved the customer is becoming in defining the next product innovation, in marketing and selling the brand, and in sharing in the profitable returns that they have contributed to as a loyal customer.

But more radical than the customer's role as a competitor, business-model disruption is no longer the domain of the start-up competitor. We-commerce, the maker market, the sharing economy: all these terms represent the increasing role that customers are playing in disrupting the FSIs' value chain. The convergence of digital, data analytics and social media is liberating customers from the FSIs' guarded role as the physical safe haven of customers' financial security. At the heart of the sharing economy's success is consumers' willingness to place their trust in one another; to give and receive information that will allow them to participate in the financial market as lenders, borrowers or investors.

Brokering these relationships are the lending clubs like Zopa and Society One in the sharing economy. Moula and Prosper are creating new value propositions in the start-up community, while PayPal and Google, for instance, are building alternatives to core financial infrastructure.

Give customers what they want

Historically, FSIs focused on providing customers with the right product at the right price. Customers, however, want more; they are looking for value, but as with beauty, value is defined by the beholder. There is a view that innovators should look beyond the current value of financial services to redefine core 'meaning' for the customer. A new generation of customers are finding value in unexpected places. For example, consider Telstra and Australian Super; they both support an engaged customer community who help others to solve their technical and

William Chitty

service-delivery problems. Capabilities to allow crowd sourcing—the ability to ask questions and receive answers—have created communities of customers who appear to be gaining deep satisfaction when they are recognised for their knowledge. Customers are building their own personal brand through communities and new brand heroes are emerging. In a post-digital environment, the old customer-service propositions are not generating customer satisfaction. Customers are looking for more value from their FSIs; they are looking towards a service experience that includes personal/brand recognition. The question is, how can FSIs allow customers to 'test drive' their products to prevent disruptors becoming a major threat to their business?

The answer for FSIs is to build and deliver real-time services that add more value by making better use of their customer knowledge before someone else does. Given the challenges, Macquarie Equities Research, for instance, expects each major financial institution to add up to A$3 billion to its IT investments over the next four years.[35]

The European Customer Satisfaction Index

The European Customer Satisfaction Index (ECSI), as shown in Figure 11.11, is a conceptual framework of customer satisfaction that includes the technical and functional dimensions of a service, the image of the service organisation and customer expectations of the service.

The ECSI framework was derived from the successful application of the Swedish and US national customer satisfaction indices as a way of measuring customer satisfaction, and has been validated in diverse service industries such as telecommunications, postal services, banks, youth hostels and universities.[36] In the ESCI model, image is viewed as being a value-added antecedent of both satisfaction and customer loyalty. Customers' perceptions of value are often associated with the image of a service organisation because its service cannot be easily distinguished from other service organisations.[37] If the image of an organisation is favourable, customers will often overlook minor deficiencies in the service and remain satisfied. Conversely, an unfavourable image can increase customers' dissatisfaction. Customers' expectations develop from exposure to marketing communications, personal needs and wants, word of mouth, and their personal involvement and experience in using a service; they may change from one service encounter to another, and vary in strength for different aspects of the same service. Practice suggests that expectations are in part formed by the image created in marketing communications messages, which in turn moderate the expectations that customers have of the service organisation. Word-of-mouth evaluations reflect the value offered to service organisations based on individual experience but are, nonetheless, seen as credible sources in developing customer expectations.

The perceived technical quality of the *hardware* is the outcome of the service encounter; it is *what* is provided based on the core attributes of the service. The core attributes of a university's service, for example, are the teaching methods and course content of the various disciplines, while the peripheral services include student counselling and food services.

Figure 11.11 The European Customer Satisfaction Index model

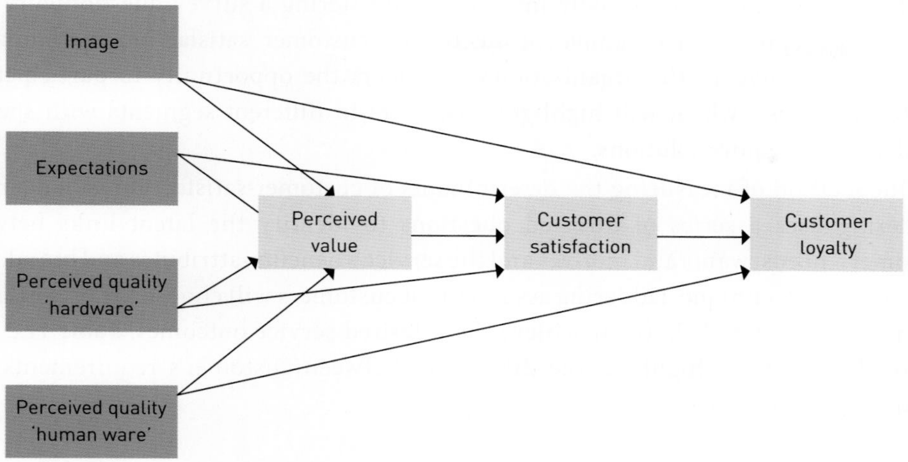

Source: K. Kristensen, A. Martensen & L. Gronholdt (2000). Customer satisfaction measurement at Post Denmark: Results of application of the European Customer Satisfaction Index methodology. *Total Quality Management*, 11(7), S1007–S1015.

The perceived functional quality of the *software*, or *human ware*, is associated with the service processes of *how* the service is delivered and is related to the personal interactions of the customers and the service providers. The customers' perceptions of those interactive service encounters play a greater role in evaluating the service outcome, and hence determining customer satisfaction, when the service is difficult to evaluate.[38] That is consistent with the view that customers tend to evaluate services that have high credence attributes on the basis of *how* the service was delivered, rather than *what* was provided, because it is difficult to separate the processes from the providers.[39]

One of the dimensions that distinguishes services is complexity, which has been likened to an inferential reasoning process in the formation of customer perceptions.[40] *Perceived value* has been broadly explained as being the perceived benefits that customers receive from the service in relation to the costs incurred in using it.[41] The perceived value of a service is based on customers' perceptions of what is received at what cost, and therefore could be judged as being low if the costs of using the service are high. Research that was conducted to determine what factors account for customer satisfaction with a backpacker hostel found that perceived value was a predictor of customer satisfaction while also having an indirect influence on customer loyalty.[42]

Measuring customer satisfaction

Successful service organisations regularly measure the strength and direction of their customers' satisfaction. Measuring customer satisfaction relies on having a service-oriented culture, which is important in competitive markets because satisfied customers

William Chitty

ensure a service organisation's continued profitability and competitive advantage. While marketing research usually involves administering a survey questionnaire to a statistically representative sample of customers, customer satisfaction measurement (CSM) should give all the organisation's customers the opportunity to participate in the CSM process, which will highlight customers in different segments with specific problems that require solutions.

One method of measuring the determinants of customer satisfaction is 'laddering'. Laddering uses a series of directed questions to identify the latent links between customers' needs, wants and motives and the service's benefits, attributes and brand. As a measurement technique, laddering assumes that customers will choose the organisation that is most likely to help them achieve their desired service outcomes. Table 11.2 uses personal banking to highlight the differences between customer's requirements and performance measures.[43]

Table 11.2 Laddering used in personal banking

Customer's requirements	Performance measures
Secure transactions	Government regulation and guarantees Access to customer's account information
Accessibility	Flexible operating hours Convenient ATM access (location and time) After-hours telephone inquiries
Advice/consultation	Sound research, relevant to customer needs Frequent updates of financial market conditions
Cost benefits	Competitive interest rates Low account-maintenance fees No minimum-balance requirements

The primary requirements of an effective CSM process differ from traditional marketing research in a number of ways:

1. The purpose of the CSM process is more than to collect data; an effective CSM process collects information about customers' behaviour and communicates the message that the organisation values the customers' opinions.
2. Acknowledging customers' participation is essential to establish their goodwill and encourage them to participate in future surveys.
3. There should be repeated measurements to ensure that the strength and direction of individuals' satisfaction can be tracked, and if satisfaction is declining, identify the reasons for the decrease.
4. The CSM process should be continual because it is more likely to reflect customers' cumulative experiences with the service organisation and highlight the customers' level of loyalty.[44]

Customer satisfaction and loyalty

Satisfaction is an important indicator of a service organisation's long-term viability because increasing levels of customer satisfaction can be linked to customer loyalty and profits.[45] As shown in the ECSI model (Figure 11.11), there is an important relationship between customer satisfaction and customer loyalty. At the opposite end of the satisfaction spectrum, researchers have also found a strong link between dissatisfaction and disloyalty, or defection. Customer loyalty can increase an organisation's profitability, but it is difficult to generalise loyalty across different market segments.[46]

There are two possible ways to conceptualise customer loyalty: to adopt either a behavioural approach that is based on repeat purchase behaviour or an attitudinal approach that reflects the affective and cognitive components inherent in customer loyalty.

Loyalty is part of an ongoing relationship with a service organisation and suggests that customers will reject other competitive services out of a belief that the chosen organisation provides a service that is clearly superior. But customer loyalty will be lost when customers reach a particular level of dissatisfaction or when they are dissatisfied with critically important service attributes.[47] Many service organisations are devoting more time and money to understanding the factors that increase satisfaction because merely satisfying customers' needs, wants and expectations will not lead to long-term loyalty. Research indicates that the emotional (affective) component of a service encounter serves as a better predictor of customer loyalty than the knowledge (cognitive) component. The findings suggest that the best predictor of overall loyalty, and the most reliable dimension of loyalty, is positive emotions.[48]

Service quality

For services high in credence dimensions, such as healthcare, financial services and education, service quality is a dominant element in customers' evaluations of a service. Researchers contend that consumers judge the quality of services by their perceptions of the technical quality, which is the outcome, what is received, the process by which that outcome was delivered and the quality of the physical surroundings where the service was delivered.[49] In the case of a legal matter, a barrister's client will judge the quality of the technical outcome, or how the court case was resolved, as well as the quality of the interactive processes. The interaction quality would include such factors as the barrister's responses in returning phone calls, empathy for the client, and courtesy and listening skills.

Similarly, airline customers will judge the airline's service on their perceptions of the flight, which is a technical outcome quality, as well as on how the airline check-in staff and cabin crew interacted with them, which is the functional interaction quality; while the cleanliness of the aircraft cabin, which is part of the physical environment of the airline, would also affect their perceptions of the airline's overall service quality.

William Chitty

All care; but, customer satisfaction?

Since the National Broadband Network (NBN), Australia's phone and internet service provider (ISP), began connecting premises to its network, customers who have problems with their internet speed (which is charged at varying prices) or even basic phone connectivity and then call the NBN often have a long wait then are told to contact their ISP. That may sound just a little like 'all care but no responsibility' to the many people who have experienced the lack of customer care from NBN staff.

An overview of broadband access in Australia that was undertaken by *Choice* magazine indicates that:

↘ 32 per cent of Australians are using ADSL2 or 2+, 14 per cent are on ADSL and 28 per cent are using the NBN to access the internet

↘ 12 per cent are on cable, 8 per cent have mobile broadband, 3 per cent have fixed wireless and 1 per cent have satellite; 2 per cent of respondents were not certain about their internet connection type

↘ people in metro areas are more likely to have ADSL2 or 2+ internet connection (36%), while those in regional and rural areas are more likely to be using the NBN (40%)

↘ 31 per cent are on an unlimited data plan, 38 per cent are on plans with data caps between 50 GB and 1000 GB, and 5 per cent are on unlimited data with some speed restrictions after a certain data limit

↘ NBN customers are more likely to be on a no-cap data plan (36%).[50]

As the NBN rollout provides access to more customers, customer complaints about landline telephones and internet services have increased by 160 per cent over the period from 2015–16 to 2016–17. The nature of the complaints lodged with the Telecommunications Industry Ombudsman (TIO) against the NBN broadband include 27 195 complaints about service delivered by the NBN network, which represents 6.7 faults per 1000 total premises activated.

The most common types of complaints made to the TIO about the broadband network were:[51]

↘ new internet connection delays: 7035
↘ unusable internet service: 4816
↘ unusable landline service: 4180
↘ new landline connection delay: 3936
↘ slow internet data speed: 3917.

The types of complaints about the services delivered by the national network are listed in the table below.

	Number	Percentage
Landline phone services	10 646	39.1
Internet services	16 549	60.9

The ombudsman said that the number of complaints may not represent a true picture of the problems because most faults were usually resolved by the ISPs before reaching the TIO. When the NBN CEO was notified about the number of complaints that reached the TIO, he said less than 15 per cent of the complaints about the NBN that were made to the ombudsman were directed to the NBN to solve which, he claimed, represented 1 per cent of the activated premises; he did, however, add that the number of complaints was being taken seriously. Satisfying customers' needs; well that depends…

The Australian Communications Consumer Action Network (ACCAN) also noted that the significant increase in the number of complaints indicated that consumer safeguards were not keeping pace with the number of connections, and that too many consumers were left with an unusable service—which was not acceptable.

The different meanings of quality

The word 'quality' means different things to people according to the context in which it is used. Garvin identified three perspectives on quality.[52]

The first perspective is a *transcendent view* of quality that is synonymous with innate excellence, a mark of uncompromising standards and high achievement that is often applied in the performing and visual arts. It suggests that consumers learn to recognise quality through their experiences gained from repeated exposure to the service.

The second perspective is a *product-based approach*, which views quality as a precise and measurable product variable that reflects any differences in quality according to the amount of some ingredient or attribute in the product. This objective view, however, fails to account for differences in the tastes, needs and preferences of individual customers or even of entire market segments.

The third approach applies *user-based definitions* to explain quality as equated with maximum satisfaction in the customer. This marketing, demand-oriented perspective recognises that different customers have different wants and needs.

Service quality cannot be measured in the same way that technical quality is measured in a manufacturing environment, because service quality is an elusive and abstract construct, in part because of the intangibility, inseparability and variable nature of service interactions with customers. While Garvin saw service quality as being synonymous with innate excellence, it has been defined as being 'the consumers' judgment about an entity's overall excellence or superiority'.[53] Most service organisations view service quality as being related to service *performance*, and therefore it is a determinant of satisfaction or dissatisfaction in the disconfirmation of expectations paradigm.

An important distinction is that satisfaction is the result of a service interaction; yet a customer must experience a service performance in order to develop a sense of satisfaction or dissatisfaction. But service quality does not depend on experience; a person may not have experienced a trip to Antarctica but can still have perceptions of the cold and isolation from friends and relatives who have been there, or from advertising and other marketing communications.

Service quality dimensions

There is a general agreement among service organisations that personal service is something that customers want, but there is no comprehensive understanding of what personal

William Chitty

service means. Also, because of the four defining characteristics of a service, it is difficult to isolate service quality as an identifiable customer benefit, and it is very difficult to develop that quality into a structured service offering. So building a model of total service quality requires an examination of consumer behaviour theories and the effects of expectations on post-consumption service evaluations.

Consumers' expectations about a service that they would use in a particular situation will determine how they evaluate the service after it has been consumed. Because services are experiential activities and rely on some form of customer interaction to be performed, individual preferences for specific services depend on the intended use of those services. The importance given to the attributes associated with those specific services also depends on their intended use. The more important the attributes, the more effort consumers will put into their evaluation of those attributes. Experience with using various services creates situational expectations that act as reference points when similar situations occur again.

Identifying gaps in service quality

The marketer's primary task in managing customer satisfaction is to balance customer expectations and their perceptions of service quality performance and to close any *customer* gaps between the two. There are, however, four potential *provider* gaps that may occur within the service organisation (Figure 11.12):

→ Provider gap 1: Not knowing what customers expect.

→ Provider gap 2: Specifying service standards that do not accurately reflect what management believes to be customers' expectations.

→ Provider gap 3: Service performance that does not match specifications.

→ Provider gap 4: Not living up to the levels of service performance that are promoted and promised by marketing communications.[54]

Improving service quality requires marketers to identify the specific causes of each gap and then to develop strategies to close them. Table 11.3 suggests a series of basic strategies to close the service quality gaps that are shown in Figure 11.12.

There are two further gaps: a *perceptions gap*, which—because customers are unable to evaluate service quality accurately—is the difference between what was actually delivered and customers' perceptions of what they received; and the *interpretation gap*, which is the difference between what the service provider's marketing communications actually promised and what the customer thought was promised.[55] The strength of the gap methodology is that it offers generic insights and solutions that can be applied across different service industries. However, it does not attempt to identify specific failures that may occur in particular service businesses. Each service organisation must develop its own customised approach to ensure that service quality is a key marketing objective.

Figure 11.12 Gaps model of service quality

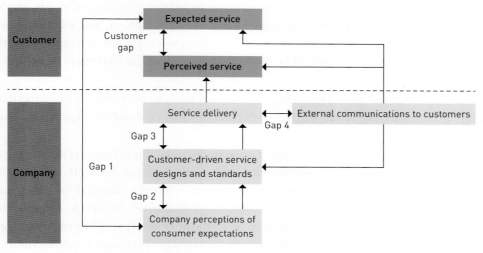

Source: V.A. Zeithaml, M.J. Bitner & D.D. Gremler (2006). *Services Marketing: Integrating Customer Focus Across the Firm* (4th edn). New York, NY: McGraw-Hill Irwin.

Table 11.3 Basic strategies for closing service quality gaps

Gap	Strategies
Gap 1: Understand what customers expect	Use marketing research, complaint analysis and focus groups to understand the reasons underlying customers' expectations as the foundation to develop remedial actions.
Gap 2: Develop the appropriate service quality standards	Deliver consistent and reliable standards for service interactions by measuring service performance; ensure service employees understand the reasons for managerial actions.
Gap 3: Manage service interactions	Match service employees to actual service-delivery positions; provide the prerequisite and ongoing training to ensure staff perform their service roles effectively.
Gap 4: Ensure that service delivery matches promises made by marketing communications	Develop market campaigns that reflect what the service organisation can provide; design marketing messages that also feature the organisation's service personnel performing their function service duties.

Source: C.H. Lovelock, P.G. Patterson & J. Wirtz (2011). *Services Marketing An Asia Pacific Perspective* (5th edn). Frenchs Forest, NSW: Pearson Australia.

Customer perceptions of service quality

Too often, improving service quality is simply advocated as a panacea to service problems without explicit reference to what is meant by service quality. For example, a technical specification of the service is frequently used as the surrogate indicator of the quality of that service, or at least as the most important feature of the perceived quality standard.

Measures such as 20 customer calls completed in an hour or 250 customers served daily are the technical outcomes of a service. To be effective in satisfying customers' needs, service quality has to be defined in the same manner as customers define it. You will have heard the term 'value-added' with respect to service quality; when you do, remember that the particular aspect of the service will be of some 'value' only if the customers perceive it to be so.

The total perceived quality level is not determined solely by the technical and functional quality dimensions, but rather by the *gap between the expected* and *the experienced levels of quality*.

Larger gaps were found to occur more often in the more important service attributes, possibly because service organisations focused more attention on easily controllable service attributes such as the tangibles associated with the physical facilities, and ignored the more 'complex' dimensions such as reliability.[56] Research suggests that customers do not perceive service quality in a unidimensional way but rather judge it based on multiple factors relevant to the service context. There are six dimensions of perceived service quality:

1 *Professionalism and skills*: Customers evaluate the service organisation's operations and its employees to determine whether it has the knowledge and skills to solve the customers' problems in a professional manner.

2 *Attitudes and behaviour*: The customers believe that the service contact personnel are genuinely interested in solving their problems.

3 *Accessibility and flexibility*: The customers feel that the service provider, the location, the operating hours and the operational structures are designed and operate to meet the needs of the customers quickly and easily.

4 *Reliability and trustworthiness*: The customers know that they can rely on the service provider, the employees and the systems to keep their commitments to meeting the needs of the customers.

5 *Recovery*: The customers know that if something goes wrong, the service provider will take immediate corrective action.

6 *Reputation and credibility*: The customers believe that the service provider's operations can be trusted to provide consistent service.

Professionalism and skills is a technical quality dimension related to the service outcome; *reputation and credibility* is related to the organisation's image and acts as a filter.

The remaining criteria—*attitudes and behaviour, accessibility and flexibility, reliability and trustworthiness*, and *recovery*—are related to the service process, and therefore represent the functional quality dimensions.

Satisfying service encounters create competitive advantages for service organisations because satisfied customers will more readily repurchase the service and become brand-loyal, while promoting more favourable word-of-mouth recommendations.

↘
technical quality
The tangible benefits that remain after the completion of the service production process. They are the outcome of the service and are commonly referred to as the *what* customers receive from a service.

↘
functional quality
The processes that dictate how the service is experienced by customers, commonly referred to as the *how* of the service experience

The dimensions of e-service quality

E-service quality is a key competitive factor for the viability of online service businesses and is defined as being a consumer's evaluation and judgment of the service quality associated with participating in online business transactions.[57] Figure 11.13 depicts the home page of Hotels.com, an e-tailer that offers a wide choice of accommodation. The absence of tangible evidence that is usually present in traditional service interactions means that consumers must depend on other cues, such as price, to determine the quality of an online interaction. To overcome that problem, researchers have endeavoured to establish the quality dimensions or elements that could more accurately define e-service quality. For example, a study by Zeithaml and colleagues[58] uncovered 11 dimensions of e-service quality: reliability, responsiveness, access, assurance/trust, security/privacy, customisation, navigation, flexibility, efficiency, site aesthetics and price knowledge.

The results of research indicate that reliability and security are the most commonly referred-to quality dimensions for e-services, followed by appearance/

Figure 11.13   Homepage for Hotels.com Australia

aesthetics, availability/access, ease of use and responsiveness, and communication. More detailed explanations of how each of these dimensions affect e-service quality follow.

↘ *Reliability:* The concept of reliability is consistent with performance and dependability, which is relevant to the website design. Reliability has two dimensions; the first is the extent to which a customer is able to use the order process on the site easily and effectively, while the second is the extent to which the company is able to fulfil its promise and obligations to customers every time a purchase is made. Reliability implies that if an online business promises to do something at a certain time, it should do it at that promised time. Reliability was also identified the most important dimension of all. In an online environment, there are many kinds of reliability such as search reliability, the reliability of payment gateway, reliable customer services, reliable delivery and reliable promises.

↘ *Security:* This dimension can be defined as being 'freedom from danger, risk or doubt during the service process'. Security is one of the main barriers to customers making online purchases and a website should indicate the extent to which it is secure; for example, its management of credit card details. This in turn will give customers peace of mind knowing that all transactions will be managed in a secure manner.

↘ *Appearance/Aesthetics:* Zhilin and colleagues[59] define this dimension

as the attractiveness of the website, which is premised on the page layout being user friendly or 'approachable' to encourage customers to continue to purchase. Its application in an online environment can be examined through graphics and images, pictures, animation, moving objects and zooming effects, all of which will make the website interesting for customers.

↘ *Availability/access:* According to research, the availability dimension concerns the ability of the website to inform customers of product availability in real time. It is also the ability to ensure that an e-commerce site continues to function as intended.

↘ *Communication:* This means receiving 'up-to-date information on orders and clear answers/instructions' from the business. Keeping customers informed is something that can be achieved by communicating with them in a language they understand, including making emails, telephone, fax and postal mail available to customers when needed. Having clear instructions, sending a follow-up confirming order, sending a welcoming letter to new customers and having customer chat rooms are also important aspects that online customers look for. In addition to text, communication also provides colour, graphics and animation and it can be used to describe service, feedback and customer reviews because the link informs and listens to customers.

- ⬂ *Ease of use/helpfulness:* This is related to an easy-to-remember URL address, well-structured and easy-to-use catalogues, concise and understandable contents, terms and conditions to help customers navigate the website. Customers expect help to be available when needed; for example, finding the right links for the products being sought, help with filling in the ordering form, guidelines, clearly defined help pages and FAQs.
- ⬂ *Responsiveness:* Responsiveness is described as offering prompt delivery and overall service, a timely response from company representatives with solutions to problems. Online customers expect the response to be quick and efficient when a problem occurs while they are online or even after receiving the ordered service product(s). A business should be able to provide appropriate and accurate information to the customer when needed. It should also be able to provide mechanisms for handling returns and have guarantees by delivering their products in the agreed period.

Summary

This chapter discusses customer satisfaction and introduces two critical concepts: customers' expectations and their perceptions of the performance of a service. Managing satisfaction is best achieved by managing the different needs, wants and expectations that customers bring to a service interaction. The types of customer expectations are defined and discussed in terms of the factors that influence each of them; namely, explicit and implicit promises, word-of-mouth communication and customers' past experiences in using the service.

Customer satisfaction is the result of customers comparing their pre-encounter expectations with post-performance perceptions, which are influenced by the benefits and attributes of the service, as well as by how it was delivered. Two customer satisfaction models, the disconfirmation of expectations paradigm and the European Customer Satisfaction Index, are discussed as possible ways of determining the degree of customer satisfaction with a service interaction.

A discussion of service quality, from the various approaches to understanding the concept of quality to the dimensions of service quality, concludes the chapter. Service quality can have different meanings depending on the context in which the service is consumed. Because service quality cannot be objectively measured in the same way as tangible goods can be, three diverse perspectives of service quality have been considered. The gap model of service quality is discussed and identifies four generic insights that can be applied to different service industries. Perceived service quality is not unidimensional, so some of the service factors that are relevant to the service context have been discussed in terms of the technical and functional quality dimensions of services.

Review questions

1. Explain the differences between the four types of customer expectations.
2. Why is the zone of tolerance bounded by desired and adequate expectations? Could it be bounded by other levels of customer expectations?
3. Explain how customers can use their perceptions to evaluate service performance.
4. Using a service organisation that you are familiar with, explain how the disconfirmation of expectations paradigm can be used to determine customer satisfaction.
5. What is the link between satisfaction and loyalty?
6. How can customers evaluate service quality?
7. Explain how the technical and functional dimensions of quality can be applied to a service.
8. Explain how the four core dimensions of e-service quality can be used to evaluate a service organisation's website.

Further reading

Burton, S., Sheather, S. & Roberts, J. (2003). Reality or perception? The effect of actual and perceived performance on satisfaction and behavioural intention. *Journal of Service Research*, 5(4), (May), 292–302.

Chenet, P., Dagger, T.S. & O'Sullivan, D. (2010). Service quality, trust, commitment and service differentiation in business relationships. *Journal of Services Marketing*, 24(5), 336–46.

Mittal, V. & Kamakura, W.A. (2001). Satisfaction, repurchase intent, and repurchase behaviour: Investigating the moderating effects of customer characteristics. *Journal of Marketing Research*, 38, 131–42.

Rust, R.T. & Oliver, R.L. (2000). Should we delight the customer? *Journal of the Academy of Marketing Science*, 28(1), 86–94.

Walker, J.L. (1995). Service encounter satisfaction conceptualized. *Journal of Services Marketing*, 9(1), 5–14.

Endnotes

1   Eurostar (2018). Behind the scenes <www.eurostar.com/uk-en/about-eurostar/company-information/behind-the-scenes>.

2   Eurostar (2015). Eurostar reports record passenger numbers in Q2 2015. Press release, 21 July.

3   ibid.

4   ibid.

5   L. Paternoster (2011). Institute of Customer Service. 4 April. <www.instituteofcustomerservice.com/1711-7132/Eurostar-customer-experience-and-emotion-and-competitiveness.html>.

6   R.L. Oliver (1997). *Satisfaction: A Behavioral Perspective on the Consumer*. Singapore: McGraw-Hill.

7   R.L. Oliver (1993). A conceptual model of service quality and service satisfaction: Compatible goals, different concepts. *Advances in Services Marketing and Management*, 2, 65–85.

8   R.B. Woodruff (1997). Customer value: The next source for competitive advantage. *Journal of the Academy of Marketing Science*, (Spring), 25(2), 139–53.

9   B. Figueiredo (2015). The value revolution. *Marketing* (August/September), 30–31.

10 V.A. Zeithaml, M.J. Bitner & D.D Gremler (2006). *Services Marketing: Integrating Customer Focus Across the Firm* (4th edn). New York, NY: McGraw-Hill Irwin.

11 ibid.

12 E.R. Cadotte, R.B. Woodruff & R.L. Jenkins (1987). Expectations and norms in models of consumer satisfaction. *Journal of Marketing Research*, 24(August), 305–14.

13 J.A. Miller (1977). Studying satisfaction, modifying models, eliciting expectations, posing problems, and making meaningful measurements. In H.K. Hunt (ed.), *Conceptualization and Measurement of Consumer Satisfaction and Dissatisfaction*. Bloomington, IN: Indiana University School of Business, pp. 72–91.

14 L.L. Berry, A. Parasuraman & V.A. Zeithaml (1993). Ten lessons for improving service quality. *Marketing Science Institute*, report no. 93–104 (May).

15 ibid.

16 ibid.

17 D.L. Davis, J.G. Guiltinan & W.H. Jones (1979). Service characteristics, consumer research and the classification of retail services. *Journal of Retailing*, 55(Fall), 3–21; W.R. George & L.L. Berry (1981). Guidelines for the advertising of services. *Business Horizons*, 24(May–June), 52–6.

18 E.R. Cadotte, R.B. Woodruff & R.L. Jenkins (1987). Expectations and norms in models of consumer satisfaction. *Journal of Marketing Research*, 24(August), 305–14.

19 A. Parasuraman, L.L. Berry & V.A. Zeithaml (1991). Understanding customers' expectations of service. *Sloan Management Review*, 32(3).

20 A. Parasuraman, V.A. Zeithaml & L.L. Berry (1994). Reassessment of expectations as a comparison standard in measuring service quality: Implications for future research, *Journal of Marketing*, 58(January), 111–24; R.L. Oliver (1994). A conceptual model; T.A. Swartz, D.E. Bowen & S.W. Brown (eds), *Advances in Services Marketing and Management Research and Practice.* Greenwich, CT: JAI Press; M.K. Brady & J.J. Cronin Jr (2001). Some new thoughts on conceptualizing perceived service quality: A hierarchical approach. *Journal of Marketing*, 65(July), 34–49.

21 A. Parasuraman, V.A. Zeithaml & L.L Berry (1988). SERVQUAL: A multiple-item scale for measuring consumer perceptions of service quality. *Journal of Retailing*, 64(Spring), 12–40.

22 V. Mittal, P. Kumar & M. Tsiros (1999). Attribute-level performance, satisfaction, and behavioral intentions over time. *Journal of Marketing*, 63(April), 88–101; L.L. Olsen & M.D. Johnson (2003). Service equity, satisfaction, and loyalty: From transaction-specific to cumulative evaluations. *Journal of Service Research*, 5(February), 184–95.

23 L.L. Olsen & M.D. Johnson (2003). Service equity, satisfaction, and loyalty: From transaction-specific to cumulative evaluations. *Journal of Service Research*, 5(February), 184–95.

24 R.L. Oliver (1997). *Satisfaction: A Behavioral Perspective on the Consumer.* Singapore: McGraw-Hill.

25 A. Parasuraman, V.A. Zeithaml & L.L Berry (1988). SERVQUAL: A multiple-item scale for measuring consumer perceptions of service quality. *Journal of Retailing*, 64(Spring), 12–40.

26 S. Fournier & D.G. Mick (1999). Rediscovering satisfaction. *Journal of Marketing*, 63(October), 5–23.

27 R.A. Westbrook & R.L. Oliver (1991). The dimensionality of consumption emotion patterns and consumer satisfaction. *Journal of Consumer Research*, 18(June), 84–91.

28 ibid.

29 J.H. Fleming, C. Coffman & J.K. Harter (2005). Manage your human sigma. *Harvard Business Review* (Jul–Aug), 83(7), 106–14.

30 R.L. Oliver (1997). *Satisfaction: A Behavioral Perspective on the Consumer.* Singapore: McGraw-Hill.

31 ibid.

32 See G.A. Churchill Jr & C. Surprenant (1982). An investigation into the determinants of customer satisfaction. *Journal of Marketing Research*, 19(November), 491–504; R.A. Spreng, S.B. MacKenzie & R.W. Olshavsky (1996). A re-examination of the determinants of customer satisfaction. *Journal of Marketing*, 60(July), 15–32.

33 E. Anderson & M.W. Sullivan (1993). The antecedents and consequences of customer satisfaction for firms. *Marketing Science*, 12(Spring), 125–43.

34 R.L. Oliver (1997). *Satisfaction: A Behavioral Perspective on the Consumer.* Singapore: McGraw-Hill.

35 Deloitte (2015). *The Deloitte Millennial Survey 2015.*

36 B. Chitty, S. Ward & C. Chua (2007). An application of the ECSI model as a predictor of satisfaction and loyalty for backpacker hostels. *Marketing Intelligence and Planning*, 25(6), 563–80.

37 C. Grönroos (2000). *Service Management and Marketing.* West Sussex, UK: John Wiley & Sons Ltd.

38 B. Chitty & G. Soutar (2004). Is the European Customer Satisfaction Index applicable to tertiary education? *Proceedings of 2004 ANZMAC Conference.* Wellington, New Zealand.

39 C. Grönroos (2000). *Service Management and Marketing.* West Sussex, UK: John Wiley & Sons Ltd.

40 R.E. Burnkrant (1978). Cue utilization in product perception. *Advances in Consumer Research*, 5, 724–9.

41 G.H.G. McDougall & T. Levesque (2000). Customer satisfaction with services: Putting value in the equation. *Journal of Services Marketing*, 14(5), 392–410.

42 B. Chitty, S. Ward & C. Chua (2007). An application of the ECSI model as a predictor of satisfaction and loyalty for backpacker hostels. *Marketing Intelligence and Planning*, 25(6), 563–80.

43 T.G. Vavra (1997). *Improving Your Measurement of Customer Satisfaction*. Milwaukee, WI: ASQC Quality Press, p. 60.

44 J.L. Heskett, W.E. Sasser & L.A. Schlesinger (1997). *The Service Profit Chain*. New York, NY: Free Press.

45 F.E. Reichheld & W.E. Sasser Jr (1990). Zero defections: Quality comes to services. *Harvard Business Review*, 68, 105–11.

46 E.W. Anderson & V. Mittal (2000). Strengthening the service-profit chain. *Journal of Service Research*, 3(November), 107–20.

47 Y.-T. Yu & A. Dean (2001). The contribution of emotional satisfaction to consumer loyalty. *International Journal of Service Industry Management*, 1(3), 234–50.

48 M.K. Brady & J.J. Cronin Jr (2001). Some new thoughts on conceptualizing perceived service quality: A hierarchical approach. *Journal of Marketing*, 65(July), 34–49.

49 A. Parasuraman, V.A. Zeithaml & L.L Berry (1988). SERVQUAL: A multiple-item scale for measuring consumer perceptions of service quality. *Journal of Retailing*, 64(Spring), 12–40.

50 R. Page (2017). Satisfaction not guaranteed. *Choice*. <www.choice.com.au/electronics-and-technology/internet/connecting-to-the-internet/articles/internet-service-provider-satisfaction-survey-2017>.

51 Telecommunications Industry Ombudsman (2017). *Telecommunications Industry Ombudsman 2016–17 Annual Report Online Edition*. <www.tio.com.au/publications/news/2017-annual-report-released>.

52 D.A. Garvin (1988). *Managing Quality*. New York, NY: Free Press.

53 V.A. Zeithaml, M.J. Bitner & D.D Gremler (2006). *Services Marketing: Integrating Customer Focus Across the Firm* (4th edn). New York, NY: McGraw-Hill Irwin.

54 C. Lovelock & J. Wirtz (2006). *Services Marketing in Asia: Managing People, Technology and Strategy* (6th edn). Singapore: Pearson Education Asia.

55 E. Bridges (1993). Service attributes: Expectations and judgements. *Psychology and Marketing*, 10(3), 185–97.

56 C. Grönroos (2000). *Service Management and Marketing*. West Sussex, UK: John Wiley & Sons Ltd.

57 Adapted from S. Pather & S. Usabuwera (2010). Implications of e-service quality dimensions for the information systems function. *Proceedings of the 43rd Hawaii International Conference on System Sciences*, Hawaii.

58 V.A. Zeithaml, A. Parasuraman & A. Malhotra, A. (2001). *A Conceptual Framework for Understanding e-Service Quality: Implications for Future Research and Managerial Practice*. Marketing Science Institute. <www.msi.org/reports/a-conceptual-framework-for-understanding-e-service-quality-implications-for>.

59 Y. Zhilin, R.T. Peterson & S. Cai (2003). Service quality dimensions of internet retailing: An exploratory analysis. *Journal of Services Marketing*, 17(7), 685–700.

United loses $250 million of its market value and shows how to make a PR crisis a total disaster!

ADAPTED FROM ARTICLES BY IVANA KOTTASOVA AND JON OSTROWER, *CNNMONEY* (LONDON), 11 APRIL 2017 [1, 2]

As reported by CNN Money in 2017 the stock price of United Airlines dropped by US$250.0 million. The reason for the drop in the share price arose from a video recorded by several passengers and uploaded to social media which showed a bloodied, screaming and bruised passenger being removed by force from an overbooked flight at Chicago O'Hare International Airport.

The social media backlash led to United CEO Oscar Munoz apologising 'for having to re-accommodate' customers. In his second statement, Munoz compounded the PR mess by describing the passenger as 'disruptive and belligerent.' However, the backlash continued, and Munoz was pressured to further apologise in his third statement by calling the incident 'truly horrific'. He pledged to 'fix what's broken so this never happens again.' 'I want you to know that we take full responsibility and we will work to make it right'; 'I promise you we will do better'.

The Department of Transportation has also said it was investigating. 'Clearly, when you watch the video, it is troubling to see how that was handled,' White House press secretary Sean Spicer said when asked about the episode at Tuesday's White House briefing. The backlash from this event was not confined to the US and was the number one trending topic on Weibo in China, attracting more than 100 million views.

Chapter

12

Complaint Handling and Service Recovery

David Gray

Introduction

Given the power of social media to very quickly either enhance or destroy a brand's reputation, today's marketplace is very different from previous decades. The United Airlines example illustrates the point of a fundamental error of judgment on the part of airline staff to rectify an overbooking issue and the unintended consequences that resulted. A YouTube video of the fracas was viewed 1.4 million times within 24 hours of the event.[3] The subsequent attempt by the CEO to address the issue was drowned out by the outcry on social media and major news outlets.

Service quality, managing customer complaints and service recovery are important aspects of services marketing. In this chapter, you will learn about how organisations define service quality, measure it, and how they can design an effective and efficient customer complaints system. Service recovery is a process that seeks to ensure that all service failures are resolved to minimise reputational damage to the organisation. In building a service recovery system in the first place, organisations need to find out what service elements are important to customers and where performance needs to be improved. For instance, the resolution of systematic on-time delivery failures requires investigation of each aspect of the process to determine the cause the service failure. It is then possible to introduce intervention actions to fix each aspect of the process that is deficient. The United Airlines example is a sharp reminder of how quickly things can turn pear-shaped in a business-to-customer (B2C) environment.

Learning objectives

After reading this chapter you should be able to:

↘ define service quality

↘ describe the major theories of service quality and illustrate the five dimensions of service quality

↘ describe the major antecedents to service provider switching

↘ discuss the methods for designing quality into a service

↘ discuss customer service standards and their relevance to service recovery

↘ discuss the concept of service recovery and its importance

↘ illustrate the major components of an effective complaint-management system.

Service quality defined

A key requirement of a services marketing strategy is to focus on service quality. If the methods used to control service quality are both effective and efficient, then service failure, subsequent customer complaints and service recovery interventions can be minimised or

↘
service failure
A breakdown in the delivery of a service. It is a failure to either meet the organisation's own internal service standards and/or to meet a customer's service quality expectations.

Part 3 Delivering Service Value

avoided. The definition of service quality can be looked at from two major perspectives (i.e. *Quality is conformance to specification* and *Quality is fitness for purpose*). These two perspectives can coexist when the specifications for service performance are based on customer expectations:

1   *Quality is conformance to specification:* This is a traditional view of the roles of quality assurance and total quality management (TQM) promoted by Edward Deming and Philip Crosby since the 1970s.[4] Examples of this approach have focused on, for instance, error-free invoicing; on-time delivery; and customer complaints acknowledged within 24 hours.

2   *Quality is fitness for purpose*: This view argues that products and services should be designed to meet customer requirements and therefore customer expectations.[5] For example, if you are an international student, a university that provides accommodation and recruits customer contact staff who understand the circumstances of international students would be a useful part of the servicescape. If you are a local student this is not going to be an issue.

Theories of service quality

Theories of service quality can assist to set a framework to minimise or avoid service failure, customer complaints and the need for the service recovery process. The two major service quality theories are the Nordic model and the SERVQUAL model.

The Nordic model identifies three components of service quality: technical, functional and reputational.[6]

1   *Technical quality* refers to 'what' is being done to meet the service provider's standard set for service quality. Did the restaurant staff properly clean the table before the next customer sat down? Were the needs of the insurance customer properly evaluated before they were signed up to the policy?

2   *Functional quality* refers to how the service provider meets the standard set for quality. Was the waiter attentive? Was the insurance representative understanding?

3   *Reputational effects* are consequences of brand image and the technical and functional provider aspects of service quality. Thus, as we have seen in the United Airlines fiasco outlined in the opening vignette, that reputation can be easily damaged through poor customer interaction. This model focuses on meeting both technical and functional customer service quality expectations.

The SERVQUAL model

The SERVQUAL model, developed by Parasuraman and colleagues,[7] focuses on service quality reliability, assurance, tangibles, empathy and responsiveness. The SERVQUAL model is measured using a 44-item questionnaire (see Services in Action) that measures

David Gray

Services in Action

The SERVQUAL Measurement Model*

DIRECTIONS: This survey deals with your opinions of ____-____-____ services. Please show the extent to which you think firms offering ____ services should possess the features described by each statement. Do this by picking one of the seven numbers next to each statement. If you strongly agree that these firms should possess a feature, circle the number 7. If you strongly disagree that these firms should possess a feature, circle 1. If your feelings are not strong, circle one of the numbers in the middle. There are no right or wrong answers—all we are interested in is a number that best shows your expectations about firms offering ____ services.

E1 They should have up-to-date equipment.

E2 Their physical facilities should be visually appealing.

E3 Their employees should be well dressed and appear neat.

E4 The appearance of the firm's physical facilities should be in keeping with the type of services provided.

E5 When these firms promise to do something by a certain time, they should do so.

E6 When customers have problems, these firms should be sympathetic and reassuring.

E7 These firms should be dependable.

E8 They should provide their services at the time they promise to do so.

E9 They should keep their records accurately.

E10 They shouldn't be expected to tell customers exactly when services will be performed. (–)

E11 It is not realistic for customers to expect prompt service from employees of these firms. (–)

E12 Their employees don't always have to be willing to help customers. (–)

E13 It is OK if they are too busy to respond to customer requests promptly. (–)

E14 Customers should be able to trust employees of these firms.

E15 Customers should be able to feel safe in their transactions with these firms' employees.

E16 Their employees should be polite.

E17 Their employees should get adequate support from these firms to do their jobs well.

E18 These firms should not be expected to give customers individual attention. (–)

E19 Employees of these firms cannot be expected to give customers personal attention. (–)

E20 It is unrealistic to expect employees to know what the needs of their customers are. (–)

E21 It is unrealistic to expect these firms to have their customers' best interests at heart. (–)

E22 They shouldn't be expected to have operating hours convenient to all their customers. (–)

DIRECTIONS: The following set of statements relate to your feelings about XYZ. For each statement, please show the extent to which you believe XYZ has the feature described by the statement. Once again, circling a 7 means that you strongly agree that XYZ has that feature, and circling a 1 means that you strongly disagree. You may circle any of the numbers in the middle that show how strong your feelings are. There are no right or wrong answers—all we are interested in is a number that best shows your perceptions about XYZ.

P1   XYZ has up-to-date equipment.

P2   XYZ's physical facilities are visually appealing.

P3   XYZ's employees are well dressed and appear neat.

P4   The appearance of the physical facilities of XYZ is in keeping with the type of services provided.

P5   When XYZ promises to do something by a certain time, it does so.

P6   When you have problems, XYZ is sympathetic and reassuring.

P7   XYZ is dependable.

P8   XYZ provides its services at the time it promises to do so.

P9   XYZ keeps its records accurately.

P10 XYZ does not tell customers exactly when services will be performed. (–)

P11 You do not receive prompt service from XYZ's employees. (–)

P12 Employees of XYZ are not always willing to help customers. (–)

P13 Employees of XYZ are too busy to respond to customer requests promptly. (–)

P14 You can trust employees of XYZ.

P15 You feel safe in your transactions with XYZ's employees.

P16 Employees of XYZ are polite.

P17 Employees get adequate support from XYZ to do their jobs well.

P18 XYZ does not give you individual attention. (–)

P19 Employees of XYZ do not give you personal attention. (–)

P20 Employees of XYZ do not know what your needs are. (–)

P21 XYZ does not have your best interests at heart. (–)

P22 XYZ does not have operating hours convenient to all their customers. (–)

* A seven-point scale ranging from 'Strongly Agree' (7) to 'Strongly Disagree' (1), with no labels for the intermediate scale points (i.e. 2 through 6), accompanied each statement. Also, the statements were in random order in the questionnaire. Where (–) is used, ratings on these statements were reverse-scored prior to data analysis.

Source: A. Parasuraman, V.A. Zeithaml & L.L. Berry (1998). SERVQUAL: A multiple-item scale for measuring consumer perceptions of service quality. *Journal of Retailing*, 64(1), Spring, 38–40.

the importance of each item relative to customers' expectations and perceptions.[8] This scale has been validated in a wide range of service encounters. Any gaps identified between expectation and perceptions can then be investigated and strategies identified and interventions implemented to close these gaps.

Reliability is demonstrated by getting 'it right the first time'; however, an efficient and effective service recovery demonstrates empathy and responsiveness. As discussed later in this chapter, reliability can be built-in or 'poka-yoked' into a service provider's operations during service preparation, encounter or resolution. While a responsive and empathetic approach can demonstrate care for others, customers who experience multiple service failures and inadequate recovery can seek revenge by actively looking for opportunities to spread bad word-of-mouth about a service.

Antecedents of service provider switching

Understanding why customers switch service providers is an important part of services marketing and an important tutor for service recovery. Being aware of the reasons customers switch service providers can help service organisations to design better complaint-handling management systems. For instance, Keaveney (1995) developed a broad model to show how gaps in customer expectations can lead to customer defection. This framework specifically identified a wide range of antecedents that can lead customers to switch service providers. The approach used by Keaveney was to identify a range of critical incidents including core service failures that led to customer dissatisfaction and then to customer switching.[9]

The following Services in Action section is adapted from Keaveney (1995). It highlights the major service failure factors that underlie the causes of customer complaints and brand switching. These include a customer's utility seeking maximisation, avoidance of inconvenience or ethical problems; involuntary switching or expectation disconfirmation.

Services in Action

Causes of customer complaints and service provider switching

Utility maximisation

Pricing and attraction by competition:

↘ *Pricing:* including high or excessive price increases, unfair or deceptive pricing practices

↘ *Attraction by competition:* even if competitors' processes were higher priced because competitors were more personable, more reliable and/or provided higher quality

Stochastic

Inconvenience, ethical problems and involuntary switching:

↘ *Inconvenience:* including provider's location, hours of operation; waiting time to get an appointment and/or waiting time for service

↘ *Ethical problems:* including behaviours that deviate widely from social norms, such as dishonest behaviour (e.g. cheated customers, stealing of personal belongings or money being charged for work not performed, or suggested unnecessary service work); intimidating behaviour; practices which are unsafe or unhealthy and conflicts of interest

↘ *Involuntary switching:* including factors beyond the control of either the service provider or the customer (e.g. the service provider had moved, the customer had moved, discontinued service)

Expectation disconfirmation

The failure of a core service, service encounter failure and unsuccessful responses to failed service:

↘ *Core service failures:* including:

a *service mistakes* or technical problems with the service, such as longitudinal problems—series of mistakes; multiple mistakes that occurred within the context of a single service encounter

b *billing errors*, such as incorrect billing, failures to correct billing in a timely manner

c *service catastrophe* causing damage to assets or causing the customer to lose time or money

↘ *Service encounter failure:* including personal interactions between customers and employees of service firms. This included situations where employees were:

a *uncaring* such as not listening, non-validation of concerns or just ignoring concerns; rushing not helpful, not friendly or not interested

b *impolite* such as being rude, condescending, impatient or ill-tempered

c *unresponsive* such as being inflexible—refusing to accommodate customer requests, uncommunicative—failed to be proactively informative, not returning phone calls or neglected to answer questions

d *unknowledgeable* where service providers were inexperienced, inept or not up-to-date, customers switched service providers.

↘ *Unsuccessful responses to failed service* consisted of:

a *reluctant responses*

b *failure to respond* such as 'too bad, you're on your own' variety, did not acknowledge the legitimacy of a complaint or ignored a customer's complaint

c *patently negative responses.*[10]

David Gray

Designing quality into a service

One way of minimising or avoiding service failure, the need for service recovery and therefore the prospect of customers switching service providers is to incorporate quality design into the service package. The three major approaches used over many decades for designing quality into a service are 'poka-yoke' (fail-safing), Taguchi methods and quality function deployment.

Service fail-safing

The SERVQUAL approach defined previously is useful for marketing analysis. However, its dimensions are limited because of their generality. They describe the service operation as a whole and do not directly relate to the activities of the server. One such approach to overcome this weakness is known as 'poka-yoke' or 'service fail-safing'.[11] This approach was recommended as a way of helping to prevent mistakes from occurring before, during or after a service encounter. The techniques used in fail-safing are inspection at every stage of the service encounter. A poka-yoke such as an inspection is a device or method used to signal that there is a service problem when it first arises. The poka-yoke reduces the feedback loop between the occurrence, detection and subsequent correction of the mistake.

Service fail-safing is a critical quality assurance approach to minimising or avoiding service provider and/or customer errors. The framework used for fail-safing is based on the classification of typical kinds of service errors. Service errors can occur at any stage or location of the service cycle with multiple forms of interaction. This means that fail-safe methods must be established for all kinds of direct interactions including mail, phone, email, SMS messaging, or online systems like e-commerce technology.

As shown in Table 12.1, service provider errors fall into three categories: tasks, treatments and tangibles. *Task errors* relate to specific service function activities such as not doing something correctly. *Treatment errors* occur in the interaction between the server and the customer, such as lack of courteous, professional behaviour. *Tangible errors* arise when there is a physical failure of the service, such as dirty waiting rooms, incorrect bills, and so on.

Because customers play an active role in the delivery of services, they also need help to avoid errors. As shown in Table 12.1, these errors fall into three categories: preparation, encounter and resolution. *Customer preparation errors* may arise due to misunderstanding, ignorance or lack of engagement in the process, both inside and outside the service facility. *Customer encounter errors* may arise due to inattention, misunderstanding or simply a memory lapse. *Customer resolution errors* may arise if customers fail to adjust their service expectations or fail to follow up on their service encounter.

To avoid the type of errors previously identified, one common technique is to design a customer service process blueprint. The blueprint identifies all steps before, during and after the service encounter and traces the flow of action and information between the server and

Table 12.1   Fail-safing errors

Server errors	Customer errors
Task	**Preparation**
Doing work incorrectly	Failure to bring necessary materials
Doing work not required	Failure to understand role in transaction
Doing work in the wrong order	Failure to engage the correct service
Doing work too slowly	
Treatment	**Encounter**
Failure to acknowledge the customer	Failure to remember steps in process
Failure to listen to the customer	Failure to follow system flow
Failure to react appropriately	Failure to specify desires sufficiently
	Failure to follow instructions
Tangible	**Resolution**
Failure to clean facilities	Failure to signal service failure
Failure to provide clean uniforms	Failure to learn from experience
Failure to control environmental factors	Failure to adjust expectations
Failure to proofread documents	Failure to execute post-encounter action

Source: R.B. Chase & D.M. Stewart (1994). Make your service fail-safe. *Sloan Management Review*, Spring, 35–44.

customers. The flow of information identifies customers' directions, service requests and the nature of their feedback. The blueprint shows a line of demarcation between front- and back-office functions as well as a line of interaction between the various actors in the service encounter. Each interaction between server and customer and/or between server and server needs to be identified. These lines of interaction are usually situations where and when errors can occur. When a service error occurs, the blueprint allows the service provider to locate its source. This can involve repeatedly crossing some lines (demarcation and interaction) several times before locating the source. Service errors most commonly occur during a one-on-one service or when a customer moves on to the next person or service stage.

After the service blueprint has been designed, the final step is to build a number of fail-safe checks to stop any mistake becoming a defect. This usually involves some kind of inspection regime including source inspection, self-inspection or sequential inspection. Alternatively, it could involve a joint inspection by the customer and the server; for example, the server could repeat the order to the customer to ensure that they have understood the order correctly.

Taguchi methods

The idea behind the Taguchi method of product design is to advocate robustness.[12] This meant that when actual performance deviated from performance to specification, corrective mechanisms would be in place to remedy those situations so that they returned to specification.

David Gray

Table 12.2 details how a motor vehicle servicing provider has implemented a quality service to ensure that the design requirements are met. When using this method, quality service is defined as 'conformance to specification'. Table 12.2 illustrates the importance of explicitly defining what it is that constitutes 'conformance to specification' in measurable terms. Effectively, whenever there is non-conformance, quality service is required to determine the corrective action to be taken.

The servicescape[13] in Table 12.2 is an example for a motor vehicle servicing operation showing that the processes to control and monitor the quality of the servicing operation are antecedents to customer and employee perceptions of the service experience.

Table 12.2   Quality service requirements for a motor vehicle servicing provider

Service package feature	Attribute or requirement	Measurement	Non-conformance corrective action
Physical resources	Building appearance	No flaking paint	Repaint
	Customer waiting areas	Clean, tidy and comfortable	Review cleaning schedule
	Equipment	No faulty equipment	Repair or replace
	Furnishing	No faulty furnishings	Repair or replace
Facilitating resources	Signage	No faulty signage	Repair or replace
	Employee uniforms	Clean and tidy	Inspect and adjust
	Customer amenities	Tea, coffee, biscuits, newspapers always available	Refill
	Toilets	Clean and tidy	Inspect and rectify
	Employee workspaces	Clean and tidy	Inspect and rectify
Explicit communication	Customer vehicle pre-check	Complete	Update
	Vehicle inspection sheets	Complete	Update
	Payment process	Complete	Update
Ambient conditions	Temperature	Within service guidelines	Monitor and adjust
	Air quality	Within service guidelines	Change filter/check
	Noise	Within service guidelines	Monitor and adjust
	Odour	Within service guidelines	Review and adjust
Implicit services	Security	All perimeter lights working	Replace defective bulbs
	Pleasant atmosphere	Telling customers 'thank you for using us'	Instruct service representative
		No customer having to wait more than five minutes for assessment of their needs	Inspect and rectify

Source: Adapted from J.A. Fitzsimmons & M.J. Fitzsimmons (2008). *Service Management* (6th edn). New York: McGraw Hill Irwin.

The impact of the servicescape on the customer will be via cognitive, emotional and physiological responses. For instance, from a cognitive perspective the dress code of the service technician and the language used on the telephone tell the customer something about the organisation and the expected outcome. From an emotional perspective, the objective of the organisation is to elicit a pleasant customer response. Finally, from a physiological perspective, customers will be affected by the ambient conditions in the service environment such as the temperature and noise. The service provider should aim to make the customer as comfortable as possible.

Quality function deployment

Quality function deployment (QFD) is a system developed in Japan to provide input into the product/service design process. It uses a matrix approach aligning each of the customers' expectations against the service elements. The QFD framework through the 'house of quality' can translate customer needs into measurable conformity specifications for product or service design and therefore maximise customer satisfaction. As a basis for preparing an organisation's marketing and customer service plan, it is essential to have an objective assessment of customer needs and how the organisation rates against the competition. There is not much point in talking about quality and service if it is not measured. Activities that don't contribute are considered wasteful. There are six major determinants of customer satisfaction. They are:

1   *quality:* completeness, accuracy, meaningfulness, reliability, accurate invoicing and paperwork
2   *timeliness:* on-time delivery, process cycle time
3   *cost/value:* actual cost (direct or indirect), value for money, fairness and equity, flexibility, commercial conditions and package
4   *dependability:* consistency, promises kept, credibility, trustworthiness
5   *cooperativeness:* responsiveness, flexibility, approachability, courtesy
6   *communication:* listening, feedback on progress/problems, awareness of needs.

Developing customer service performance standards

The development of accurate, relevant and timely customer service performance standards is an essential ingredient towards the provision of quality products and the minimisation or prevention of customer dissatisfaction. An example of a framework for developing a set of customer service performance standards is:

David Gray

1 Investigate the needs and requirements of your customers:

   a Classify customers into segments by volume, geographic location or type of business, etc; that is, into whatever the relevant classification method is for the type of business being considered.

   b Choose a method to ask for your customers' help and information through telephone interview, personal interview or email survey to identify their requirements.

   c Analyse the survey responses for general requirements.

2 Analyse the knowledge and expectations of your own employees using an inside-out approach to investigate the requirements of your organisation by asking executives from all functions of the company about their own requirements and expectations.

3 Compare expected or desired service quality standards with existing standards and past performance. This means determining what changes in each function's operations should be considered and preparing a revised budget to meet these standards.

4 Prepare the revised standards for each function. The process involves:

   a preparing written standards and performance measures (see Table 12.3)

   b circulating the standards and budgets for comment by other staff

   c scheduling a meeting(s) for discussion and review of the standards

   d making any needed corrections to the standards and budgets.

A range of examples of written standards and performance measures is provided in Table 12.3. These measures will be most effective if they are specific, measurable, relevant and work towards assisting the organisation in its business objectives.

Service recovery

Customers will complain when their dissatisfaction exceeds the complaint threshold. The complaint threshold (i.e. the sum of perceived physical, emotional and monetary costs involved in complaining) will rise as the potential for financial loss rises. Eventually it will reach a point when the benefits of complaining exceed the inertia of not complaining. This is partly dependent on who is to blame, the level of involvement and experience with the service.

Service recovery includes all the actions taken by an organisation to resolve a service failure[14] and to retain the customer's goodwill.[15] Complaints are customer-initiated expressions of dissatisfaction to the organisation;[16] they represent an opportunity for the company to remedy a problem.[17]

Services fail for many different reasons and can ultimately lead to a customer switching to another service provider.[18] To date we have discussed fail-safe servicing, Taguchi methods and quality function deployment as methods helpful in preventing service failure. However,

Table 12.3 Examples of customer service and performance standards

Examples of organisational standards affecting customer service	Examples of key performance indicators (KPIs) affecting customer service
– Existing customers shall provide at least 90% of repeat orders	– Inquiries ratio = No. of inquiries/Total orders
– At least 98% of orders will be processed within one week of order receipt	– Inquiries timeliness = Inquiries closed within time standard/Total inquiries
– At least 95% of special orders will be delivered within stated lead times	– Dollars of sales per inquiry = Sales dollars/Number of inquiries
– Emergency deliveries will be sent within 24 hours of receipt of order	– Dollar performance =Dollars delivered/ Total dollars ordered
– The ratio of complaints to total orders will be less than 0.5% of orders in any three-month period	– Order performance = No. of orders delivered/No. of orders received
– The company will receive a minimum average rating of 4 from the survey of customer demands conducted two to three times a year	– Service level = Dollars delivered on time/ Total dollars delivered
– Answers to written correspondence will be mailed within two working days	– Order timeliness = No. of orders shipped on time/No. of orders shipped
– At least 90% of customer complaints will be closed within 48 hours. The exceptions will be entries requiring documentation supplied by an outside supplier or transport company.	– Complaint ratio = No. of complaints/Total orders
– The work backlog will not exceed two days	– Complaints timeliness = Complaints closed within time standard/Total complaints
– No overtime will be required in the department	– Dollars of sales per complaint = Sales dollars/No. of complaints
– The department expenditure will not exceed budget	– Efficiency = Sales and service dollars/ Dollars (salary) to handle business
– The employee turnover shall be less than 10% per annum	– Cost per customer contact = Customer service salaries/No. of contacts
– Each salesperson will complete at least six customer contacts per day	– Correspondence timeliness = Correspondence answered within time standard/ Total inquiries
– Each telephone representative will complete between 150–200 customer contacts per week (this does not include follow-ups)	– Return ratio = Dollars of returned merchandise/Total dollars delivered
– An order entry clerk shall input an average of eight orders per hour	– Warranty ratio = Dollars credited and/or replaced/Dollars sold
– Each functional area will appear well organised, neat and tidy. All files will be removed from desks and stored at the end of each working day.	
– No papers will be left on the tops of desks at the end of each working day	

we also need to better understand the nature of complaints; that is, when customers complain, uppermost in their mind is that they are listened to and the problem is fixed. A successful resolution to a problem usually results in customer satisfaction, customer retention and word-of-mouth referrals if service providers resolve problems efficiently and effectively.[19] Customers experiencing a problem but subject to a successful service recovery are more likely to be more satisfied than customers not experiencing any problems.[20]

In a B2C context, complaints can result in many customers no longer purchasing from the business. However, if a customer has had a positive experience with the business in the past, they are less likely to react negatively to a negative experience.[21] So it's very possible for the B2C relationship to return to normal—unless the customer leaves after a complaint, or they have another negative experience shortly after the first one.

According to attribution theory, customers will react more negatively if they consider that a complaint is likely to have permanent implications. One negative experience reduces the customer's trust and also creates uncertainty in the customer's mind about whether the lower level of trust is justified. A second negative experience justifies the loss of trust, resulting in a reduction in both trust and uncertainty. As a result, the second complaint tends to be more damaging than the first one.[22]

One simple way of assessing the strength of the customer relationship is by determining how many prior purchases they have made.[23] In general, it is in the organisation's interest to offer immediate recovery to a regular customer who has made a recent complaint.

According to prospect theory, customers are more sensitive to losses than they are to gains.[24] If a customer suffers a loss (e.g. of money), the likelihood of retaining them is low. Nonetheless, the positive effect of the amount that could be gained is also limited. Accordingly, the main focus of recovery should be to exceed the customer's expectations (i.e. their threshold).

Business-to-business (B2B) organisations can also experience reputational damage. The following Services in Action feature highlights this issue and discusses some remedies.

Services in Action

Big problem for B2Bs: Resolving customer problems

In B2C, the sales process is reasonably basic because prices are usually fixed, quantities are generally low and shipping is straightforward.[25] Regulation and tax conformance is relatively simple, and products and services are relatively easy to showcase and market. On the other hand, the B2B sales context is characterised by significant price variability, higher transaction volumes, greater degrees of transaction complexity and greater product variability, thus necessitating flexible shipping and logistics solutions. Marketing is more complex, as clients need to understand how products work and interact with other systems they already have or are considering for purchase.

Given these characteristics of the B2B context, a Gallup poll in 2016 identified a range of issues that B2B customers were concerned about. Specifically, the Gallup data show that 20 per cent of B2B customers experienced a problem with their suppliers, with only 40 per cent of them believing the B2B company had resolved the problem. Additionally, only 5 per cent of those customers were 'very satisfied' with how their problem was solved.

Some key insights from the poll and recommendations to address these major B2B customer concerns are discussed below.

B2B customers' problem resolution only 60 per cent; consequence: brand damage

B2B organisations are finding that the time and energy they would like to be allocating to growth is instead being used to attend to quality and service issues, which is harming their reputation, their brand and the trust they receive. One professional services organisation that Gallup worked with had technical problems, preventing it from delivering a major report to a client. As the organisation did not notify the customer that the report would be late, the company was not invited to pitch new business.

Potential B2B customer problem-solving approaches include:

1 *Focusing on what matters the most:* B2B customers want to work with experts in their field and in dealing with customers. Having this insight and knowledge will assist organisations in determining how best to handle, resolve and prevent future problems by:
   - thoroughly understanding their customer's business and how problems affect it and its customers
   - developing service-recovery solutions customised to the customer's organisational culture
   - being aware of the customer's industry and day-to-day work environment
   - conveying creative ideas to a customer for achieving its business goals and creating positive outcomes for it and its customers.

2 *Building strong inter-company relationships by treating customers as partners:* Problems in B2B customer relationships can be the result of errors, or a product or service failure; however, they can also result from miscommunication, misunderstandings or conflicting messages between the B2B organisation and the company's buying centre.

As such it is important for B2B organisations to build strong inter-company relationships to enable timely and accurate communication. B2B companies can then use these partnerships as a basis for discussing and negotiating how to solve product, service or communication failures.

3 *Building stronger market orientation practices:* Market orientation theory[26] maintains that the behaviours required to create superior value for buyers and to ensure continual superior performance of the organisation stem from an efficient, effective organisational culture. Market orientation consists of:
   - *customer orientation*—how responsive a partner is to customer needs
   - *competitor orientation*—how well a partner understands and responds to competitor activities
   - *inter-functional coordination*—how much inter-functional coordination exists within the partner firm in relation to customer needs.

According to Gallup, few customer problems can be resolved by the account team or just one contact

David Gray

person. Instead, a collaborative effort to resolve the problem is needed across several functional teams, such as customer support, product development and technology. Additionally, the account team must present the full picture to key executives and employees in a timely manner.

In many organisations, these functional teams operate independently of each other, meaning they may have competing priorities and differing understandings of the problem and the best way to manage and resolve it. Effective and efficient problem-solving necessitates strong leadership from the account team and rewards for employees who handle problems skilfully.

4 *Increasing the involvement of senior leaders in service recovery:* Gallup argues that senior leaders can play a vital role in organising resources to design and implement service recovery. They should 'walk the walk' to inspire employees to maintain a focus on customers and to do their utmost to solve problems. In addition, it is important for senior leaders to support and empower the account team to ensure customers are engaged during the service-recovery process.

5 *Ensuring that the organisation structure is fit for purpose:* A successful service-recovery strategy begins with having the right people in place. It is the organisation's employees who are fundamentally responsible for building the customer–supplier partnership and, ultimately, for solving or handling customer problems. As such, employees must own customers' problems; have great empathy for and care about customers' feelings; and put customers' interests before their own.

6 *Ensuring employee engagement:* Gallup research indicates that engaged employees are active learners: they work on updating their knowledge of and experience with problem resolution. They will break down the barriers among teams and handle problems in ways that exceed B2B customers' expectations.

Approaches to service recovery

There are four approaches to service recovery: case-by-case, systematic response, early intervention and substitute service recovery.[27]

1 *Case-by-case* treats each customer complaint on its merits. While this approach can be effective, the time and effort involved in resolving each individual complaint can make it expensive. The other downside of this method is that the more vocal a customer is, the more likely it is that their complaint will be addressed, and this inconsistency in dealing with complaints may leave other customers feeling they have been treated unfairly.

2 *Systematic response* uses a planned and systematic response to customer complaints. It is usually based on a set of customer service standards such as described earlier in this chapter and associated responses depending on the type of service failure experienced. This is a more timely, reliable and cost-effective method than the case-by-case method; however, its success will depend on the continuing relevance of the service failure criteria.

3 *Early intervention* attempts to pre-empt service-process customer complaints. For example, where a restaurant patron is becoming impatient at the time it is taking for the food to arrive, the service person realises that this could be a problem and advises the customer that their order will arrive soon.

4 *Substitute service recovery* could sometimes be beneficial in situations where the service provider has reached its service capacity limit. For example, the reception staff at an overbooked hotel may send a customer to a rival hotel that has room for another guest.

One recent question to be considered in relation to each of the above approaches, given the increasing adoption of e-commerce and online selling, is the extent to which an online approach to service recovery should be 'mechanistic' versus 'organic'. A *mechanistic* approach establishes standard operating procedures and guidelines for employees to follow (e.g. process, behaviour and compensation guidelines), while an *organic* approach is based on motivating and supporting employees in relation to customer-oriented behaviours by providing them with a positive internal environment.[28]

The organic approach to online service recovery involves empowerment—that is, giving employees a degree of discretion when making daily service-recovery decisions— and culture—that is, the shared values and standards that show management's support for employees when implementing service-recovery procedures.[29] Both approaches can be beneficial. The mechanistic process-based approach can be useful when firms have limited budgets, because the process method is more cost-effective. The mechanistic approach, however, diminishes employee empowerment. The organic approach is the more effective approach for customer compensation because it is based on empowerment, which encourages employees to enjoy their job and to be enthusiastic about serving customers. However, managers must pick employees who are competent at compensating customers appropriately and whose judgment they trust.

Complaint-management systems

Customers complain when service provider performance is less than expected and the expectation gap exceeds their zone of tolerance—or if they feel they have been treated unfairly. (Equity theory, which explains the customer's response to being treated unfairly, will be discussed later in this chapter.) Customers also have a zone of tolerance for service and product performance. The importance of the service or the service attribute that is subject to a potential complaint will determine the extent to which a customer complains.

⬊
complaint
Expression of dissatisfaction made to or about an organisation, related to its products, services, staff or the handling of a complaint, where a response or resolution is explicitly or implicitly expected or legally required[30]

David Gray

The benefits of managing complaints

Complaints are unavoidable. The reasons for developing an effective customer complaints system are both operational and financial. As the cost of retaining existing customers is three to five times less than the cost of obtaining new customers, organisations must create appropriate service recovery mechanisms to ensure ongoing customer satisfaction.[31] To minimise the operational and financial impact of complaints, all organisations need a complaint-management system to receive, process and resolve customer complaints. When customers complain, the organisation has a chance of winning them back and retaining their future value. Additionally, complaints provide information that enables organisations to identify—and correct—the root causes of problems. In fact, having a documented complaints-handling process is strongly linked to excellent customer retention.[32] Unfortunately, it is likely that customers who don't complain have already taken their business elsewhere.

The effective and efficient management of complaints has many benefits, including a positive effect on customer retention and acting as an incentive for continual service process improvement and, ultimately, will assist in building a customer-focused organisation.

→ *Customer retention:* A customer complaint expresses dissatisfaction. How the organisation handles the complaint determines customer retention or loss. Moreover, negative word of mouth resulting from customer complaints can have a multiplier effect, encourage other customers to defect.

→ *Continual improvement:* Complaints provide useful customer feedback to the organisation on what is important to the customer and on the frequency of service failures. Complaints therefore provide an opportunity for learning and continual improvement.

→ *Building a customer-focused organisation:* The way top management treat complaints will assist in building the 'market orientation' of an organisation and send a clear signal to all staff about the importance of customer satisfaction and retention.

A successful complaints management system enables organisations to alter customer dissatisfaction and minimise the possibility of negative word-of-mouth fallout or customer defection. Negative word of mouth can have a significant negative impact on an organisation.[33] While up to two-thirds of unhappy customers do not complain to the organisation,[34] they may complain to their social networks. Unfortunately, unhappy customers are likely to tell twice as many people about their experience as are customers who have had a positive experience.[35]

However, many dissatisfied customers don't complain to the organisation. Why? Whether customers who experience a problem complain depends on a variety of factors, including the nature of the problem (minor, major, temporary, permanent), the characteristics of the customer (personality, socio-demographics, etc.) and the expected redress. That is, customers are more likely to complain if they understand the complaint process, if they believe the supplier to be responsive, and if they think the outcome will be worthwhile and the time and effort is justified.

Compared to manufacturing, the handling of complaints within the service sector is different because most customers complain directly to the contact personnel serving them and there are fewer links in the supply chain. The implication for service sector management is that all contact personnel should be trained in complaint-handling skills and not just the central customer service department (if it exists). This means that any complaint-management system in the services sector must take a whole-of-organisation approach to managing complaints, as complaints can enter an organisation from various customer touch points, such as the customer contact centre, accounts receivable, order processing, sales or logistics. Taking a whole-of-organisation approach should enable the organisation to achieve a higher level of first-time reliability, increase customer satisfaction levels and reduce the amount of rework.

The following article, following on from the chapter opening vignette, highlights the inadequate response(s) of United Airlines in relation to the service failure and recovery crisis efforts that hit the organisation in 2017.

United Airlines: What can we learn from company's 'breathtakingly bad' crisis management?

BY EMILY SAKZEWSKI, ABC NEWS

A public relations (PR) expert says United Airline's problems could have been avoided with an immediate, earnest apology. So, how did it get this bad?

Public Relations Institute of Australia president Jennifer Muir said the whole fiasco could have been avoided if United Airlines had apologised immediately.

'Once the video was live, there was only one way they could go—and that was to apologise,' Ms Muir said. Instead, Mr Munoz issued a poorly executed statement a full day after the video went viral.

'This is an upsetting event to all of us here at United. I apologize for having to re-accommodate these customers. Our team is moving with a sense of urgency to work with the authorities and conduct our own detailed review of what happened. We are also reaching out to this passenger to talk directly to him and further and resolve this situation'. Source: Twitter, Oscar Munoz, CEO United Airlines' United CEO response to United Express Flight 3411.2:27 AM—11 Apr 2017 · Houston, TX:

Ms Muir said standard practice would have been for Mr Munoz to publicly explain what reparation they would offer Mr Dao.

'His apology didn't adequately match the seriousness of what was portrayed in the video. He didn't understand how the video was being received,' she said.

In a second statement issued to staff, Mr Munoz referred to Mr Dao as 'disruptive and belligerent' and in a third statement, offered his 'deepest apologies for what happened'.

'In delicate situations of issues management, people read into every word you use and people have to be very careful about which ones they choose,' Ms Muir said.

'It seems, from the public perception, that [United were] unaware of the dangers of mistreating customers and the consequences that can have.'

Mr Munoz has since delivered his fourth statement on US television saying he felt 'ashamed' watching the video and promised the incident would 'never happen again on a United flight'.

He called the embarrassment a 'system failure' and declared United would no longer use law enforcement to remove a 'booked, paid, seated passenger' from full flights.

Critics might say a fourth apology is too little too late, but Ms Muir said this was finally an appropriate response.

'It has taken nearly four days for the United's CEO to strike the right tone of sincerity. This is a good sign that they are learning from this incident,' she said.

'Good crisis management practice should have immediately acknowledged the airlines failing and conceded that the failure was breathtakingly bad from a customer-service perspective.'

Ms Muir said that ultimately, United would have to spend millions of dollars for internal reviews and to repair the company's reputation.

'But all of this could have been avoided.

Why didn't they just apologise from the outset?

Ms Muir said large companies like United have response plans for every possible crisis scenario. She said it was possible something had gone wrong within the organisation because management had not listened to their experts and advisers.

'They've knee-jerked their response to say it's not our fault. It just comes off as arrogance.'

What's the lesson?

United Airlines has been a trending topic on social media since the video was first posted on Tuesday. But not all publicity is good.

Ms Muir said the reason it has probably held traction on social media was the social injustice of the situation—that a paying customer was removed so that airline staff could fly.

She said crisis management was a two-sided coin, with operational issues on one side and the public's perception is on the other.

'You have to look at both sides, but you can't ignore or underestimate the impact of your public reputation. That's the one you always have to deal with first.'[36]

Suggested elements of an effective apology according to AS/NZS 10002:2014

While the United Airlines context is an extreme example of service failure, the following general guidelines for handling an apology are presented in the Australian Standard: AS/NZS 10002:2014 Guidelines for complaint management in organizations:

Recognition of the harm or impact to the complainant includes the following elements:

a) *Description of the wrong*—A description of the relevant problem, act or omission to which the apology applies.

b) *Recognition of the wrong*—An explicit recognition that the action or inaction was incorrect, wrong, inappropriate, unreasonable, harmful, etc.

c) *Acknowledgement of the harm or impact to the complainant*—An acknowledgement that the affected person has suffered embarrassment, hurt, pain, damage or loss.

Responsibility of the organization: This will entail the organization making an acknowledgement or admission of its responsibility for the wrong and the harm caused. In some Australian jurisdictions a full apology (which includes an acceptance of fault or responsibility) is protected in civil litigation.

Reasons for or the cause of the problem: This will entail the organization providing the complainant with an explanation of the cause or reason(s) for the problem, or a promise to investigate the issue.

Regret for the harm suffered: Appropriately expressing regret includes the following:

a) *Making an apology*—An expression of sincere sorrow or remorse (i.e. that the action or inaction was wrong).

b) *Sincerity of communication*—The form or means of how an apology is communicated is very important as it can indicate or emphasize the level of sincerity of the apologiser.

Redress for the wrong: The provision of redress involves:

a) *Action taken or proposed*—A statement of the action taken, or specific steps proposed to address the grievance or problem, by mitigating the harm or offering restitution or compensation.

b) *Undertaking not to repeat*—An undertaking that steps will be taken to ensure that the action or inaction will not be repeated.

Release from blame: This is an optional element available to an organization when acknowledging harm suffered by a complainant. This may include a request for forgiveness.

Source: Standards Australia & Standards New Zealand (2014). AS/NZS 10002:2014 Guidelines for complaint management in organizations. SAI Global Ltd, p. 38.

The complaint-management process

There are many well-trodden paths to complaint management and the typical steps are as follows. Each step is discussed below.

1 Encourage customer communication and feedback.
2 Establish systems to minimise complaint response times.
3 Develop key complaint-management policies.
4 Document the complaint-management system.
5 Train staff in complaint management and customer interaction.
6 Conduct third-party assessment and ongoing improvement reviews.

Encourage customer communication and feedback

The first step in complaint handling is to encourage dissatisfied customers to complain; perhaps through easy-to-access website details, email or toll-free numbers. Further measures undertaken by many organisations are seeking customer feedback immediately after each transaction and using the Net Promoter Score to identify any issues (see Chapter 13). Service recovery cannot occur unless the organisation is aware of customer dissatisfaction. Dissatisfied customers who do not complain may 'vote with their feet'. The next step is to acknowledge receipt of the complaint, identify who has responsibility for handling the complaint, including their contact details and when the complaint is likely to be answered/finalised.

The relevant Australian Standard for complaint management is AS/NZS 10002:2014 Guidelines for complaint management in organizations. One key aspect of this standard is the focus on the organisational responsiveness to complaints. The Standard states:

> The organization should promptly acknowledge each complaint received. The organization should assess complaints and give appropriate priority in accordance with the urgency of the issues raised.
>
> Complainants should be advised, as soon as practicable, where the organization is unable to deal with either part or all of their complaint.
>
> The organization should deal with complaints efficiently. Where set timeframes cannot be met, internal escalation systems should be used.
>
> It is vital that the organization actively manages the expectations of complainants. This includes advising complainants about—
>
> (a) the complaint process;
>
> (b) the expected timeframes for its actions;
>
> (c) their likely involvement in the process; and
>
> (d) the possible or likely outcome of their complaint, where practicable.

Source: Standards Australia & Standards New Zealand (2014). AS/NZS 10002:2014 Guidelines for complaint management in organizations. SAI Global Ltd, p. 7.2.

Establish systems to minimise complaint response times

An important driver of satisfaction or dissatisfaction with complaint handling is the time it takes to identify, respond to and finalise a complaint. The objective of all complaint-management systems should be to minimise customer complaint response times. Several strategies can be employed to minimise response times, including:

→ establishing monitoring systems to anticipate complaints in higher risk situations such as new services and typical recurring problems

→ empowering frontline customer service staff through the delegation of sufficient autonomy to handle any unforeseen complaint situations

→ establishing procedures to deal with the routing and prioritising of complaints based on, for example, the seriousness of the problem, whether it is a key account or whether the complainants are threatening to publicise their complaint with the media or regulatory bodies.

Develop key complaint-management policies

An effective and efficient complaint-management system will contain policies covering compensation, fairness and follow-up.

Compensation

Compensation is a means of dissolving customer anger and dissatisfaction when a service has failed them.[37] In determining the level of compensation, organisations will balance the costs and benefits of the compensation against the risks of not compensating (i.e. the risk of negative word of mouth, the pursuit of legal remedies or the desire to maintain long-term customer relationships) to the organisation.

Monetary compensation (e.g. cash, discounts, free gifts or substitution) is the most common form of compensation.[38] However, monetary compensation is not always the most appropriate form of compensation: for example, when customers are treated badly and suffer some form of psychological loss.[39]

Non-monetary psychological compensation can be in the form of a replacement, an apology, an acknowledgment of causality, intervention by a supervisor, showing care or giving an explanation.[40] Psychological compensation can take the form of an apology from management addressing the fact that the service failure was responsible for the customer's psychological loss. An apology from management can even enable a customer to feel they have been treated fairly. In fact, there are certain service contexts where customers may prefer psychological compensation to receiving money.[41]

Remember, compensation should not depend on whether the complaint is justified. If the customer perceives that the seller made a mistake, they will usually want some kind of compensation, whether monetary or non-monetary. The seller can try to convince

David Gray

the buyer that the seller is not responsible for the problem experienced, but when not successful, the dissatisfaction will remain. Again, the organisation will have to balance the costs and benefits of satisfying this complaint. Compensating for an unjustified complaint may result in retaining an otherwise lost customer.

Fairness

Fairness is important because it can determine how the customer reacts after a service failure and service-recovery intervention. A customer has many choices after they experience a service failure. They could do nothing, complain to an official third party such as an ombudsman, complain to their service provider, or complain to their friends/family/other person in their personal network.

According to 'equity theory', customers who complain are seeking fairness and justice. It is common for them to compare the sacrifices they make and the benefits they do or do not experience to other customers' sacrifices and benefits. Understandably, if a customer pays the same price as other customers for a service and they receive what they perceive to be a lesser level of service than other customers they will feel the inequity. They complain because they want the service provider to fix the inequity.

A customer is likely to want one or more of the three types of justice: distributive, procedural or interactional. These three theories of justice can help to describe people's response to conflict situations.[42]

→ *Distributive justice:*
  - Represents the customer's perception of fairness in the complaint outcome, including their views of equity, equality and need.
  - Represents consistency in the service provider's recovery offer and whether this output compensates the customer for the costs they incurred from the service failure.
  - The outcomes can be compensation, re-performance or an apology. Distributive justice occurs when the customer receives the material or emotional outcome they desired after a complaint, either via an apology, a cash refund or a credit note; alternatively, the customer may demand that the service be re-performed.

→ *Procedural justice:*
  - Represents the customer's perception of the fairness of the complaints-handling process, including timeliness and process control.
  - Some processes offer quick recovery, others are delayed; in some cases complaints have to be legitimised.
  - Procedural justice is achieved when a customer evaluates as satisfactory the processes and systems encountered during the complaints-handling process. Customers are typically not prepared to complete forms, provide difficult-to-find proof of purchase or write formal complaint letters (unless these are part of the normal process) as such requirements suggest that a service provider is disorganised and unwilling to resolve the problem quickly.

→ *Interactional justice:*
  - Represents the customer's perception of fairness in the way employees treat complainants, including their empathy, politeness and effort.
  - Interactional justice is achieved when the customer deems that specific complaints-related dealings with the provider's staff have been satisfactory—including responsive and empathetic employees.

Overall it is considered that discounts lead to perceived distributive justice; a fast response suggests procedural justice; and an apology induces interactional fairness.[43]

Document the complaint-management system

The best approach would be for the organisation to follow the same process in documenting its marketing and customer service system as it has done with its quality service standards. The system documentation will consist of many different tiers of documentation, such as:

→ *the complaints service manual*, which establishes an explicit complaint-management policy. This policy would set out its commitment to the effective management of complaints

→ *complaint processes and procedures*, which support the complaints service manual. These procedures detail how complaints will be managed by the organisation, who will be involved in that process and their roles. A process is a series of interrelated or interacting actions that transform inputs into outputs. A procedure is a certain way of carrying out an activity or a process

→ *complaint work instructions*, which specify in detail the who, how, what and when complaints are to be handled

→ *complaint forms records*, which should be kept to ensure that the various complaint-management activities of the organisation produce consistent approaches and outcomes to complaint management and its consequent effect on service quality is achieved each time the activity is carried out.

An effective system to follow is the one outlined in AS/NZS 10002:2014. The Standard provides guidance for the design and implementation of an effective and efficient complaint-management system for all types of organisations.

Train staff in complaint management and customer interaction

As with senior management and middle management, organisational personnel will not be committed to the establishment of a complaint-management system unless they understand its principles. Table 12.4 lists some suggestions for staff training.

Teaching the importance of interactional and procedural aspects of fairness on customer satisfaction should be the focus of employee training programs—frontline employees must be trained to handle customers' complaints by way of an on-the-spot apology or they must offer compensation should there be a delay.

David Gray

Table 12.4 Staff training in complaint management

Relevant staff	Nature of training	Duration of training
All staff	Telephone techniques, social media responsiveness and providing customer feedback	Half-day
All staff	Dealing with difficult people	One day
All staff	Understanding the organisation's complaint-management and reporting system	Half-day
Marketing/sales staff	Professional selling skills	Three days
All staff	Delivering excellent customer service skills	One day

Where possible, frontline customer service staff should be delegated responsibility to deal on the spot with complaints, particularly for minor problems. This improves their awareness of the importance of delivering quality service. Serious complaints could be sent to a centralised processing unit for response. Another reason to centralise is if many complaints are very similar. This allows for a standardised approach resulting in economies of scale.

Conduct third-party assessment and ongoing improvement reviews

Complaint-management systems should be audited ideally by an independent third party to constructively review all aspects of the system and report any weaknesses to the organisation for improvement. In addition, there should be ongoing internal audits at least twice a year. Persons assigned to audit activities need to be adequately trained or qualified. An internal audit will be a meaningless exercise unless the auditor knows what they are doing and understands the business they are auditing. All complaint-management systems should adopt continual improvement processes and recognise that there are always opportunities for improvement.

In this chapter, we have focused on two aspects related to service satisfaction: service recovery and complaint-handling processes.

Understanding the major theories of service quality, how to measure its components and then act upon the results of these measurements benefits from having a benchmark such as SERVQUAL. In addition to using instruments such as SERVQUAL, it is critical to understand the antecedents to service provider switching so that management policies and practices can be designed to minimise the possibility of customer defection. These quality service management methods include service fail-safing, Taguchi methods and quality function deployment. Equipped with some guiding principles to tackle these issues, one can then think about developing a set of customer service key performance indicators (KPIs). Such KPIs can then be monitored and any non-conformance to them addressed during service-recovery initiatives. As such, this chapter offers a blueprint for getting your own customer complaint-management and service-recovery system going.

In this chapter, we have also looked extensively at the benefits of managing complaints and the process of how to manage them. As shown by the United Airlines vignette, word-of-mouth communication through social media makes complaint management of critical interest for the services sector. Designing an effective and efficient complaint-management approach consists of encouraging customers to communicate and provide feedback so that any corrective actions can be successfully implemented; establishing systems to minimise complaint response times; developing key complaint-management policies and documenting those policies through the complaint-management system; training staff in complaint management and customer service interaction; and conducting third-party assessment and ongoing improvement reviews. The goal of working on complaints is to create a more customer-oriented service organisation.

Review questions

1 Consider the list of the components of service quality in the SERVQUAL model presented earlier in this chapter. Discuss what these components mean in the context of a specific service environment (such as a restaurant, a bank office or an insurance company).

2 Discuss the options available to a dissatisfied hotel guest. Which of these options do you think would be most effective in resolving a consumer complaint? What factors may deter a consumer from complaining directly to an organisation?

3 What are the benefits of effective service recovery to a service organisation?

4 Visit the travel site TripAdvisor.com. Critique the site, outlining its pros and cons. Would you use this online site to complain if you had an unsatisfactory service encounter? Why or why not?

5 How would you go about recovering a customer who is angry? Justify each step.

6 Define service failure and outline the potential approaches to service recovery.

7 Discuss the benefits of implementing a complaint-management system.

8 Outline the key elements of successful service recovery.

Further reading

Knox, G. & Van Oest, R. (2014). Customer complaints and recovery effectiveness: A customer base approach. *Journal of Marketing*, 78(5), 42–57.

Parasuraman, A., Zeithaml, V.A. & Berry, L.L. (1994). Reassessment of expectations as a comparison standard in measuring service quality: Implications for future research. *Journal of Marketing*, 58(1), 111–32.

Taguchi, G. & Clausing, D. (1990). Robust quality. *Harvard Business Review*, January–February, 65–75.

Endnotes

1   I. Kottasova (2017). United loses $250 million of its market value. *CNNMoney* (London), 11 April. First published 11 April 2017: 5:44 AM ET by Ivana Kottasova @ivanakottasova <http://money.cnn.com/2017/04/11/investing/united-airlines-stock-passenger-flight-video/index.html>.

2   J. Ostrower (2017). United CEO apologizes for 'truly horrific' passenger incident. *CNNMoney* (New York), 11 April. <http://money.cnn.com/2017/04/11/news/companies/united-munoz-apology/index.html>.

3   WOW! Man violently thrown off plane because United overbooked flight. YouTube: <https://youtu.be/XHyOTEpUHIU>.

4   P.B. Crosby (1979). *Quality Is Free*. New York, NY: McGraw-Hill.

5   J.M. Juran (1964). *Managerial Breakthrough*. New York, NY: McGraw-Hill.

6   C. Grönroos (1984). A service quality model and its marketing implications. *European Journal of Marketing*, 18, 36–44; A. Parasuraman, V.A. Zeithaml & L.L. Berry (1985). A conceptual model of service quality and its implications for future research. *Journal of Marketing*, 49, Fall, 41–50; A. Parasuraman, V.A. Zeithaml & L.L. Berry (1988). SERVQUAL: A multiple-item scale for measuring consumers' perceptions of service quality. *Journal of Retailing*, 64(1), 22–37; A. Parasuraman, V.A. Zeithaml & L.L. Berry (1991). Refinement and reassessment of the SERVQUAL scale. *Journal of Retailing*, 64, 12–40; A. Parasuraman, V.A. Zeithaml & L.L. Berry (1994). Reassessment of expectations as a comparison standard in measuring service quality: Implications for future research. *Journal of Marketing*, 58(1), 111–32.

7   A. Parasuraman, V.A. Zeithaml & L.L. Berry (1985). A conceptual model of service quality and its implications for future research. *Journal of Marketing*, 49, Fall, 41–50; A. Parasuraman, V.A. Zeithaml & L.L. Berry (1988). SERVQUAL: A multiple-item scale for measuring consumers' perceptions of service quality. *Journal of Retailing*, 64(1), 22–37; A. Parasuraman, V.A. Zeithaml & L.L. Berry (1991). Refinement and reassessment of the SERVQUAL scale. *Journal of Retailing*, 64, 12–40; A. Parasuraman, V.A. Zeithaml & L.L. Berry (1994). Reassessment of expectations as a comparison standard in measuring service quality: Implications for future research. *Journal of Marketing*, 58(1), 111–32.

8   A. Parasuraman, V.A. Zeithaml & L.L. Berry (1988). SERVQUAL: A multiple-item scale for measuring consumers' perceptions of service quality. *Journal of Retailing*, 64(1), 22–37; A. Parasuraman, V.A. Zeithaml & L.L. Berry (1991). Refinement and reassessment of the SERVQUAL scale. *Journal of Retailing*, 64, 12–40.

9   S.M. Keaveney (1995). Customer switching behaviour in service industries: an exploratory study. *Journal of Marketing*, 59(April), 71–82.

10 Based on S.M. Keaveney (1995). Customer switching behaviour in service industries: An exploratory study. *Journal of Marketing*, 59, 71–82.

11 R.B. Chase & D.M. Stewart (1994). Make your service fail-safe. *Sloan Management Review*, Spring, 35–44.

12 G. Taguchi & D. Clausing (1990). Robust quality. *Harvard Business Review*, January–February, 65–75.

13 M.J. Bitner (1990). Evaluating service encounters: The effects of physical surroundings and employee responses, *Journal of Marketing*, 54(April), 69–82; M.J. Bitner (1992). Servicescapes: The impact of physical surroundings on customers and employees. *Journal of Marketing*, 56(April), 57–71.

14 F. Buttle (2011). *Customer Relationship Management: Concepts and Technologies* (2nd edn). Oxford, UK: Butterworth-Heinemann.

15 C. Grönroos (1988). Service quality: The six criteria of good perceived service quality. *Review of Business*, 9(3), 10–13.

16 E.L. Landon (1980). The direction of consumer complaint research. In J.C. Olson (ed.), *Advances in Consumer Research* (vol. 7). Ann Arbor, MI: Association for Consumer Research, pp. 335–8.

17 T.H.A. Bijmolt, P.S.H. Leeflang, F. Block, M. Eisenbeiss, B.G.S. Hardie & A. Lemmens (2010). Analytics for customer engagement. *Journal of Service Research*, 13(3), 341–56.

18 S. D'Alessandro, L. Johnson, D. Gray & L. Carter (2014). The market performance indicator: A macro understanding of service provider switching. *Journal of Services Marketing*, 29(4), 302–13.

19 S.W. Tax, A.W. Brown & M. Chandrashekaran (1998). Customer evaluations of service complaint experiences: Implications for relationship marketing. *Journal of Marketing*, 62(April), 60–76.

20 C.W. Hart, J.L. Heskett & W.E. Jr Sasser (1990). The profitable art of service recovery. *Harvard Business Review*, 68(July–August), 148–56.

21 G. Knox & R. Van Oest (2014). Customer complaints and recovery effectiveness: A customer base approach. *Journal of Marketing*, 78(5), 42–57.

22 ibid.

23 R.L. Hess, S. Ganesan & N.M. Klein (2003). Service failure and recovery: The impact of relationship factors on customer satisfaction. *Journal of the Academy of Marketing Science*, 31(2), 127–45.

24 E.W. Anderson & M.W. Sullivan (1993). The antecedents and consequences of customer satisfaction for firms. *Marketing Science*, 12(2), 125–43; R.T. Rust, T. Ambler, G.S. Carpenter, V. Kumar & R. Srivastiva (2004). Measuring marketing productivity: Current knowledge and future directions. *Journal of Marketing*, 68(October), 76–89.

25 Adapted from A. Adkins (2016). Big problems for B2B: Resolving customer problems. *Gallup Business Journal*, 22 March. <www.gallup.com/businessjournal/189986/big-problem-b2bs-resolving-customer-problems.aspx>.

26 J.C. Narver & S.F. Slater (1990). The effect of a market orientation on business profitability. *Journal of Marketing*, New York, 54(4), 20–35.

27 C.Y. Li & Y.H. Fang (2016). How online service recovery approaches bolster recovery performance? A multi-level perspective. *Service Business*, 10(1), 179–200; T.C. Johnston & M.A. Hewa (1997). Fixing service failures. *Industrial Marketing Management*, 26, 467–77.

28 G.R. Gonzalez, K.D. Hoffman, T. Ingram & R. LaForge (2010). Sales organization recovery management and relationship selling: A conceptual model and empirical test. *Journal of Personal Selling and Sales Management*, 30(3), 223–37.

29 C.Y. Li & Y.H. Fang (2016). How online service recovery approaches bolster recovery performance? A multi-level perspective. *Service Business*, 10(1), 179–200.

30 Standards Australia & Standards New Zealand (2014). AS/NZS 10002:2014 Guidelines for complaint management in organizations. SAI Global Ltd.

31 K.D. Hoffman & S.W. Kelley (2000). Perceived justice needs and recovery evaluation: A contingency approach. *European Journal of Marketing*, 34(3/4), 418–32.

32 F. Buttle & L. Ang (2006). Customer retention management processes: A quantitative study. *European Journal of Marketing*, 40(1–2), 83–99.

33 F.A. Buttle (1998). Word-of-mouth: Understanding and managing referral marketing. *Journal of Strategic Marketing*, 6, 241–54.

34 M. Richins (1983). Negative word-of-mouth by dissatisfied customers: A pilot study. *Journal of Marketing*, 68, 105–11.

35 TARP Australia. (1995). *American Express: SOCAP study of complaint handling in Australia*. Sydney, NSW: Society of Consumer Affairs Professionals in Business Australia.

36 E. Sakzewski (2017). United Airlines: What can we learn from company's 'breathtakingly bad' crisis management? *ABC News*, 13 April. <www.abc.net.au/news/2017-04-13/united-airlines-what-went-so-wrong-pr/8441796>.

37 H. Fu, D.C. Wu, S.S. Huang, H. Song & J. Gong (2015). Monetary or nonmonetary compensation for service failure? A study of customer preferences under various loci of causality. *International Journal of Hospitality Management*, 46, 55–64.

38 M. Davidow (2003). Organizational responses to customer complaints: What works and what doesn't. *Journal of Service Research*, 5(3), 225–50.

39 H. Roschk & K. Gelbrich (2014). Identifying appropriate compensation types for service failures: A meta-analytic and experimental analysis. *Journal of Service Research*, 17(2), 195–211.

40 J.R. McColl-Kennedy & B. Sparks (2003). Application of fairness theory to service failures and service recovery. *Journal of Service Research*, 5(3), 251–66.

41 J. Wirtz & A.S. Mattila (2004). Consumer responses to compensation, speed of recovery and apology after a service failure. *International Journal of Service Industry Management*, 15(2), 150–66.

42 A.K. Smith, R.N. Bolton & J. Wagner (1999). A model of customer satisfaction with service encounters involving failure and recovery. *Journal of Marketing Research*, 36(3), 356–72.

43 Based on B. Sparks & J.R. McColl-Kennedy (2001). Justice strategy options for increased customer satisfaction in a service recovery setting. *Journal of Business Research*, 54, 209–18; L. White & V. Yanamandram (2007). A model of customer retention of dissatisfied business services customers. *Managing Service Quality*, 17(3), 298–316.

Creating stronger customer engagement with services

While digital disruption is creating fundamental changes within organisations, it is also changing the way those organisations interact with their customers. Where once many companies and public-sector organisations tended to adopt a 'build it and they will come' approach to service development, they now have opportunities to create stronger customer engagement with their brands. Information technology and digital media provide powerful platforms that allow two-way communication and personalised delivery in ways that were not previously possible. Add the insights made available by analysis of customer data, and the potential to create greater customer engagement rises further.

Successful service organisations have become digitally innovative in satisfying their customers' demands. Every time customers are introduced to something new and surprising in the rapidly evolving consumer market, it influences everything that follows. It is a phenomenon that has been referred to by Mark Curtis, chief client officer and co-founder of Accenture's Fjord consultancy, as 'liquid expectations'.[1]

The organisations that have the greatest impact on their customers' engagement continually design innovative services, and communicate those innovative benefits to their customers. The disruptive nature of innovation has forced service organisations to look for solutions beyond their industry boundaries where banks, for example, no longer compare their performance against industry standards, but against other service providers such as Uber and Airbnb.[2]

In effect, Uber and Airbnb each provide a service that responds to customers instantly, which has raised customers' expectations and caused rapid operational disruption for the other service organisations that do not adopt digital technology in response to their customers' demands.

» continued over page

Chapter

13

Customer Relationship Management

William Chitty

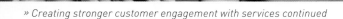

There is an urgent need for those organisations to change, but often they have rigid, silo-like structures that prevent them from launching new services to their customers on time. The challenge for large, national businesses, with multiple layers of managerial control, in being more responsive lies in knowing how, and where, to begin that transformation. The combined effect of knowing customers' needs, wants and expectations is the catalyst that drives the often disruptive transformation.

Adam Bennett, executive general manger for digital and direct banking at National Australia Bank (NAB), says different customer demographics have preferences for different communication channels, and that using digital technologies allows organisations to effectively meet those differing preferences. In the case of mortgages, Bennett said NAB customers still wanted to interact with a human provider, whether by going into a branch or contacting a call centre and having a conversation with a person. With service products—like credit cards and personal loans—however, more of NAB's customers want to interact digitally with the bank; he added it could be considered, 'a connected customer experience'. So depending on the customer, their particular demographic characteristics and choice of service product, they can use whichever channel that best satisfies their individual needs and preferences to connect with NAB.[3]

The transition to becoming a customer-responsive service organisation requires a cohesive, united strategy approach from senior management and a framework for managing the complex web of tasks associated with technological disruption. There are four areas of activity that organisations need to manage in relation to disruption, namely: organisational culture, instinct, craft and relationships.

All companies have an organisational culture that generally originates from both the current senior managers and the culture that existed in the organisation's recent past. The question is: does the prevailing culture enable the organisation to create and deliver dynamic, context-aware services? In some cases, the current organisational culture—based on executive-level behaviour—could be what is preventing the business from becoming more agile in meeting customers' needs, wants and expectations.

When considering instinct, the situation is similar to organisational culture. Instinct is the organisation's decision-making culture, and may be centralised and micro-managed, or it may be devolved and autonomous. It is the way that leaders empower staff to respond to their customers' expectations and will determine whether or not a business can keep up with its competitors.

Craft is about operational excellence: Are fundamental activities completed with care? Is attention paid to detail? In a bank, for example, are personal finance or mortgage services designed initially with customers in mind or is financial expediency the primary concern? It is the recognition of the importance of relationships—and their ongoing management—that underpins an organisation's craft. A thriving business will continually assess—and make improvements to—every service interaction with and communication to, or from, everyone with whom it has contact, regardless of whether they are a customer, an employee, a supplier or a shareholder.

It is important that businesses realise the scale of such a commitment—consider, for example, how many relationships even a small organisation must manage. The pace of change is increasing, and furthermore 'is making it difficult to know which technologies or platforms are worth prioritising and which represent a gamble'.[4] Voice-controlled software is an example of this. The first voice-controlled software was Apple's Siri, which had a reasonable level of customer acceptance, and then Alexa arrived and quickly became everybody's 'must have': the time of voice user-interface is here.

Predicting the turning point for the mainstream market acceptance of technology is difficult, but service organisations with a greater understanding of any potentially disruptive technologies that could adversely affect them in the future will be able to focus on improving their customers' experience with current services and developing digitally innovative products to satisfy their future customers' expectations.

Introduction

During the 1970s, researchers who were studying business-to-business (B2B) marketing in Europe found that suppliers who formed close working relationships with their customers tended to have customers who were more loyal to their suppliers and often gave them a greater share of their business. At the beginning of the 1990s, customer relationship management (CRM) was in its nascent stage and being indirectly linked by researchers in the United States—such as Reichheld and Sasser—to customer loyalty, and the effects that customer defections had on a service organisation's long-term profitability.[5] Although rates of defection are effective indicators of the number of customers who leave an organisation, they do not indicate the reasons for the defection. Defection analysis is, however, a guide that helps companies manage continual product improvement.

Reichheld and Sasser's early research was influential in changing how organisations manage continual improvement, but it was not widely adopted in the business environment at the time because several macro-environmental forces were working against it. Those forces included:

→ Computer-based technology and CRM practices were in the very early stages of their development; technology—such as the internet—was not widely available to the general public.

→ Technology vendors and Tier 1 consulting firms (who were the systems' integrators) overpromised the benefits of CRM and turned it into a concept that was totally reliant on technology.

→ Customers were not prepared, or perhaps were not ready, to start making the satisfaction of their individual needs, wants and expectations a condition of their continuing relationships with service organisations.[6]

Customer relationship management (CRM) systems are designed to compile information on customers' behaviour across different channels—or points of contact between customers and an organisation—which can include the company's website(s), telephone, live chat, direct mail, marketing materials and social media. CRM systems can also give customer-facing staff detailed information on customers' personal information, purchase history, buying preferences and expectations.

Service organisations that have achieved a customer-centric approach to delivering their services did not acquire their status, or reputation, overnight. The transformation to change the focus of a service organisation's CRM system must begin by adopting a customer-first approach rather continuing with a marketing approach of brand-first, which is a typical road block to implementing actionable strategies that will drive a customer-centric mindset across the organisation.

↘
customer relationship management (CRM)
A strategy to compile information on customers' behaviour across different channels—or points of contact—between the customer and the organisation

The three key strategies that services organisations need to drive their marketing strategies are:

1 *Building collaborative customer service teams:* To build customer-first strategies, senior managers need a unified view of their customers. In order to develop that view, managers must build collaborative partnerships between all associated departments, such as marketing, sales and customer service, to eliminate any communication barriers that may have isolated those teams into separate silos in the past. Creating designated customer service teams may be a fundamental cultural shift that is required across the organisation, and in some cases may require a complete rearrangement of how customers communicate and engage with the organisation.

2 *Streamlining their service-delivery processes:* As the teams become an integral part of the organisation's new customer-facing culture, the service-delivery processes may need to be restructured to enable the teams to collaborate in real time and deliver value to the organisation's customers. The change process will achieve nothing if disparate processes to distribute a service are retained, thereby preventing the team members from engaging in meaningful customer interactions.

3 *Integrating customer data and technology:* Customer data from multiple channels and touch points can overwhelm traditional internal reporting channels. The key to using the increased volume of customer data gained from delivering personalised and relevant customer experiences across digital platforms is to integrate the data using computer-based technology. A CRM process can be implemented without a technology platform, but the process will be neither efficient nor effective without software to support the process of analysing the customer data.[7]

CRM systems are most successful when all the technology platforms are integrated to deliver a satisfactory level of service quality to customers, while also assisting frontline staff to build satisfying customer relationships. Many service organisations that deliver services through face-to-face service encounters with their customers, such as banks, airlines and hotels, adopt frontline CRM systems. Those organisations use CRM systems that provide detailed customer data to enable sales staff to be more consultative and add value to their service products—be they financial loans, preferred airline seats or favourite hotel rooms.

Learning objectives

After reading this chapter you should be able to:

↘ explain the nature of customer relationship management (CRM)

↘ describe the different types of customer relationships

↘ understand the relationship between customers and information technology

↘ discuss how the characteristics of a service influence CRM

- ◲ describe the role of customer loyalty in building customer-retention strategies
- ◲ explain the concept of maximising customer value
- ◲ outline the benefits to organisations of customer relationships
- ◲ analyse customer loyalty and retention strategies
- ◲ explain how to measure the value of customer relationships using the Net Promoter Score and customer lifetime value.

The nature of customer relationships

Customer relationships with service organisations

From a services marketing perspective, relationships are the connections that customers have with a service organisation. Many people, from academic researchers to business managers, have defined customer relationships, and all provide a definition that suits their particular purpose. For the most part, service relationships involve at least one person—usually the customer—and often differentiate service organisations, especially those where face-to-face encounters create value for their customers, and determine the long-term profitability of the business. In addition to the personal interaction of a service encounter, marketing relationships are sometimes more effective in satisfying the needs and wants of both parties when they are contextually specific.[8] A broad definition of customer relationships may, therefore, be premised on the actions of the parties involved, where the actions of one will have an impact on the behaviour of the other.

The problem with defining a relationship solely on the basis of the customers' interactions lies with determining how consumers will behave when they are invited to engage in a relationship with a service organisation. The fundamental rationale of a customer relationship is having a long-term focus on the interaction between a customer and the service organisation. Many service companies profess to practising relationship marketing when, in fact, after the initial service encounter, they do not continue to interact with their customers. For example, would customers consider themselves to be in a relationship with a hotel after only one stay just because the hotel sent them an email about its special weekend room rates? While sending an email to a past customer may appear to be managing a customer relationship, it is one-way database marketing, not an interactive communication between the customer and the hotel.[9]

Types of customer relationships

While the basis of a customer relationship suggests that service organisations will accrue benefits from having a relationship with their customers, organisations that provide high-volume, low-margin services often do not want a relationship with their customers because

◲
customer relationships
Are premised on the actions of a service provider and a customer, where the actions of one will have an impact on the behaviour of the other

there are few economic benefits to be gained from each customer transaction. If buyer–seller transactions can be categorised along an exchange continuum that ranges from discrete, functional exchanges through to continual, collaborative emotional and relational encounters, it is unlikely that either party to a discrete functional exchange would be interested in forming a relationship. For example, consumers who regularly travel on the cheapest available airfares may not want to establish a relationship with a full-service airline that rarely offers special fares. For collaborative exchanges, however, such as monthly meetings with a financial adviser, there is a higher probability of establishing a provider–customer relationship because of the emotional involvement of both parties in the service transactions.

Transactional customer relationships

The basis of transactional relationships is their focus on the point of sale (POS)—the moment when a customer actually pays for the service. Traditional mass marketing creates awareness of the service brand, and perhaps positive feelings and a brand preference, and moves the service through the POS in a simple transaction. In many cases, consumers appreciate simple transactions because not all have time for two-way interactions.

As more consumers purchase products online, the ease of one-click transactions has become the preferred method of conducting service transactions. The transactional marketing process has been reduced from a several-stage encounter to a few clicks. In a mature market, where telephone services, for example, have become identifiable commodities, transactional marketing is often used to sell more to existing customers under the guise of CRM.

Behavioural customer relationships

The ideal situation for creating relationship marketing requires a level of personal commitment on the part of the salesperson, with a level of trust from the customer. Customers enter into behavioural marketing relationships in the expectation of receiving positive value from their participation in the service transaction. Behavioural relationships can provide customers with in-depth information about the service, and help them match their needs, wants and expectations with the features and attributes of the service. Such relationships also assist customers with delivery, discounts and other issues that cannot always be provided from an online transaction. Most importantly, however, is that a behavioural relationship helps customers feel confident in making their decision to purchase the service being offered—and a confident customer is more likely to repurchase the service.

Customer loyalty varies by industry and generally occurs when customers resist the influence of other brands. Research suggests that loyal customers are more profitable for a business in the long run because they are usually willing to pay more for brands of choice, and they tend to offer the most valuable kind of marketing communication: word-of-mouth endorsements. Simplifying a transaction does not mean losing customer loyalty; and making a transaction engaging does not mean losing time.[10]

Telstra's $3 billion investment in digitisation

In 2016, Telstra revealed plans to invest an additional $3 billion in network improvements, to digitise its business and improve its customers' experiences. During 2016, if a customer had a fixed-line National Broadband Network (NBN) fault, an agent in Telstra's service centre may have had to access nine systems to ascertain the cause of that fault. In 2018, the same task can be done using a single interface, and while that may not seem important, the new system has—on average—taken 6 minutes off each call made by customers to the service centre and helped to reduce the number of unnecessary field technician visits by 55 per cent. For Telstra's Chief Information Officer John Romano, that is an example of how digital technology is helping the company deliver an improved customer experience, making life easier for employees and increasing productivity. Other initiatives have included the launch a business-focused mobile app—Telstra Connect—that offers tools for enterprise customers, such as incident management,

that were previously split across 50 different portals.[11]

CEO Andy Penn said during a briefing on Telstra's full-year results in August 2017 that an incremental $3 billion expenditure would be used to fundamentally transform the service experience that Telstra delivers to its customers through investments in its networks and the digitisation of its business systems. As outlined by Penn, Telstra's digitisation program had three key pillars: delivering digital experiences to customers as well as employees, the rollout of digital platforms, and digital ways of working.

Increased reliance on cloud-based platforms and a shift to flexible programs are the two key IT-drivers of the $3 billion program that is transforming Telstra's organisational culture to deliver improved customer service delivery and bridge the divisions between the business, product and technology teams. Romano said that Telstra's operations cannot be driven solely by technology.

The organisation had to bring its technical and customer teams and the new digital platforms together to build collaborative customer-service teams that could target what Telstra's customers received, and how all participants in the service encounters interacted. What Telstra's management expected to achieve by digitising its operations was a behavioural process that would continually improve the interactions it has with its customers.[12]

Customer relationships and information technology

CRM is a combination of people, processes and information technology that is used to manage the behaviour of an organisation's customers. It is a process that focuses on customer retention and relationship development to integrate changes in information technology within an organisation.

Emerging technologies have given service organisations the means to collate and analyse customer data that can then be used to develop CRM strategies to attract, and retain, customers. Those customer relationship strategies are generally based on modelling algorithms, which are enabled by information technology (IT), to develop demand forecasts based on its customers' behaviour. Although a large part of CRM is based on IT, viewing a CRM program only as an IT solution is likely to fail, because effective implementation requires an integrated and balanced approach to technology, processes and people.[13]

It should also be noted that demand forecasts are not the same as sales forecasts for particular services. Demand forecasts are projections of the probable demand for a service by customers; sales forecasts—which are derived from the demand forecasts—are the basis of sales targets that are the possible sales that a service organisation can achieve. Sales forecasts are also subject to organisational resource constraints such as the number of trained service providers and the amount of capital available to meet costs associated with operations and customer acquisition. Service organisations usually expect CRM technology to provide benefits to their customers in terms of increasing customer satisfaction with their service products. The important elements of customers' relations with various service organisations include trust, commitment and communications, while the effectiveness of the relationships is generally measured using customer satisfaction, loyalty and/or customer retention.[14]

Information technology relies on computer-based architecture that influences three distinct aspects of CRM functionality. The first is operational functionality, which integrates front- and back-office service products and provides access to customer behavioural data and preferences. The second aspect is analytical functionality, which relies on storing reliable customer behaviour data in consolidated databases, thereby facilitating analysis of customers' future behaviour. The third aspect is collaborative functionality, where CRM creates multiple customer touch-point opportunities by developing various marketing communications channels.[15] When traditional service organisations, such as utilities (e.g. telcos) and government departments agencies (e.g. Human Services), began conducting customer transactions online, managing the allied customer-demand functions very quickly made their order-processing technology obsolete.

William Chitty

The top mobile virtual network operators in Australia

Telsyte research on mobile services in Australia revealed that amaysim, TPG and ALDImobile were the growth leaders among the mobile virtual network operators (MVNO) for the first half of 2017.[16] The analyst firm said Australian consumers are looking for lower-cost mobile plans, which led those MVNOs to register 200 000 new services in operation (SIO) collectively in the first half of the year. The mobile network resellers surpassed the individual performance of Optus, Vodafone and Telstra, while the mobile services market grew by 444 000 in the first half of 2017 to reach 33.7 million SIOs.

Price/value has overtaken network performance as the most important factor in consumers' buying behaviour when the average consumer chooses a mobile services provider, according to Telsyte. Network performance had been the foremost factor of consumers' buying behaviour when choosing a mobile service provider since 2012.

Alvin Lee, a senior analyst with Telsyte said that consumers are entering an increasingly price-competitive mobile services market in the current pre-5G period. Half of mobile users are not on contract plans, which is a steady trend according to Telsyte. Telsyte believed that recontracting of new models such as the iPhone X and Samsung Note 8 was likely to help the mobile network operators (MNOs) gain market share in the second half of 2017. Telsyte estimated up to 65 per cent of iPhone sales in the second half of 2017 would be through mobile contracts, 15 per cent up compared to previous years.

Consumers are generally receptive to new competitors with the research showing that two in five Australians would consider moving to a new TPG mobile network. Most of that growth, however, is predicated on TPG providing clear benefits such as free trial periods, unlimited data or significant bundling discounts. 'TPG mobile base has been under pressure, despite the addition of iiNet customers. While the new network is expected to have an effect, Telsyte believes it will be difficult for the carrier to reach 1 million SIOs within 2 years of launching its network', according to the research.[17]

In order to grow SIO in the coming years, carriers will need to focus on more than handsets. The growth of handsets is expected to increase only in line with population growth, while wearables, machine-to-machine and eSIM capable 2-in-1s present the best opportunities for mobile carriers in the next two to three years.

How customer relationships add value

A service encounter takes place whenever a customer interacts with a service organisation, either personally or through technology; for example, a customer makes contact with a service organisation using the internet, email or telephone, and interacts with a different provider. A service relationship, on the other hand, occurs when a customer has repeated contact with the same service organisation, while pseudo-relationships are a particular kind of encounter in which a customer interacts with a different provider each time, but within the same service organisation.

Three studies consistently showed that customers having a service relationship with a specific provider had more service interactions, and were more satisfied, than those who did not have one.[18]

It is impossible to force a person into a relationship against their will; the person will only enter into a relationship if they believe there are continued benefits to be gained from an ongoing arrangement. Digital service encounters are considered to be remote customer–company interactions via the internet or email. Customers frequently initiate the technology-based encounters because it is more convenient to make inquiries, information searches and complaints online, rather make the effort and take time to engage in face-to-face interactions.

The focus of relationships is on active customers initiating interactions and their perceptions of company responses to these interactions. An empirical study exploring the value of company responses to digital contacts indicated that many contacts are responded to promptly and satisfyingly. There were, however, significant differences in the value of the service encounter; some service encounters were perceived as un-personalised, and some were terminated without response.[19]

To understand how customer relationships influence the concept of value in a service experience, it is necessary to consider that value is directly or indirectly experienced by service customers within the contexts of their real-world experiences. Each individual service encounter that offers value to a customer and the service organisation is a building block in the systemic structure of the service organisation's relationships with its customers.

Within the bounds of service-dominant logic (S-D logic), Vargo and Lusch assert that 'value is always uniquely and phenomenologically (experientially) determined by the beneficiary',[20] with the beneficiary being both the service organisation and its customers. The benefits for the service organisation are derived from customer loyalty and retention, while the value of the service encounter, based on exchange theory, is the difference between the benefits and costs for the customer. In other words, customers must perceive themselves to be 'better off' as a result of the service experience.

William Chitty

In the context of a service encounter, customers receive value from paying the costs that they are willing and able to pay, be those costs time, effort or money. As a construct, value has three concomitant determinant attributes:

1 *Personal*—it is determined by the customers' needs, wants and expectations.

2 *Experiential*—it is experienced by the customers who are also the co-creators of the service experience.

3 *Comparative*—it is evaluated against similar previous service experiences in which customers have participated.

Research suggests that service customers make sense of experience value in an iterative way, based on their previous experiences or understanding. In addition to value being co-created through service customers' integration of the various physical resources provided by service organisations, value also emerges from service customers' integration of other cultural and social resources, including other service customers, within their experiences of previous service encounters.[21] Service customers experience value and infer credibility from other customers based on their shared experiences of value. Therefore, even though service customers experience value as individuals, they also tend to share certain types of experiences with other service customers, such as the shared experiences of attending a concert or a football match.

When a customer is confident that the perceived benefits of a service experience are greater than the perceived costs, the result will be customer value. Service relationships can add customer value in three ways:[22]

1 By establishing a CRM system that uses comprehensive customer data, service organisations can ensure that their service product satisfies individual customer's needs, wants and expectations. That may require the organisation to engage in one-to-one marketing because those customers will have individual opinions of the three attributes of value, and will also expect the organisation to minimise their perceived costs of the service experience.

2 By developing a close relationship with their customers, service organisations can create a structural bond based on trust and commitment that enables both customers and the organisations to be confident in doing business together; a 'win-win' situation that removes any concerns that customers may have about making 'the right decision'.

3 By treating customers as individuals rather than merely a statistic, service organisations can add value for the customer by enhancing the quality of the service encounter. If organisations believe their customers are important, they can no longer say, 'Your call is important to us, please do not hang up', because they will have taken the time to analyse the customer traffic to their call centre(s) and will ensure there are sufficient trained staff on duty during recognised busy periods to answer incoming calls within a set time. Those set times to answer incoming calls will be communicated to customers as part of the organisation's service-delivery promises.

The characteristics of services and customer relationships

In Chapter 1, services were defined as being *an act, a performance* or *an experience*. A service, when viewed from a service organisation's perspective, is an organisational process consisting of a series intangible activities that usually take place between customers and the physical facilities of the organisation's and/or its employees—the service providers—in systemised interactions that present some form of value to those customers.[23] Those interactions are the basis of a service experience and determine how customers perceive the quality of a service organisation. In some cases, such as internet banking, customers interact both with the physical facilities of the bank and the telecommunications supplier, but tend to only be aware of those systems when either fails to provide the promised benefits.

An important contribution to the marketing of services is the interaction that takes place between customers and a service organisation; that is, the organisation that produces the service. Without those interactions between the service producer and customers during the consumption process, effective customer relationship strategies cannot be developed, because although exchanges may have occurred at some point in the process, the successful management of the interactions leads to ongoing customer interactions.[24]

Service organisations have become more involved in the process of creating service products, such as managing the training of service providers, the delivery and maintenance of the customer service process, and the communication of service information, because these are the basic elements of producing services that assist in creating a competitive advantage. Services are *intangible* performances, which consist of a series of activities that are produced and consumed simultaneously, which is the basis of *inseparability*. Those two characteristics make it is difficult to manage customer relationships that are the foundation of long-term service exchanges and customer experiences.

Another consideration in managing a service is its characteristic of *perishability*, which makes it impossible to 'store' most services—but it is possible to store customers. For example, if a theatre is 'sold out' for a particular show, it is possible, by using a reservations system, to 'store' customers for the show at another time. Services are generally subjectively perceived by customers, who use abstract terms such as 'convenient', 'trustworthy' and 'secure' to describe service interactions. The problem, however, is how customers can give a distinctive value to 'trustworthiness'. The reason that abstractions are used to describe service exchanges is because the core benefits of service exchanges are usually *intangible*; it is the service providers (service personnel) and the physical facilities of an organisation—including the ambience of the service environment—that are the tangible elements of the service exchange, and they are therefore capable of being described in more concrete terms.

Lastly, the influence of customers, the service providers and other people in the production and delivery processes of a service often makes it difficult for a service organisation to ensure that it provides a consistent level of quality during its service interactions. In standardised service processes, the quality of the service product may not always be perceived to be the same by each customer, because the social relationships between service providers and customers are usually different. When a service is offered by technology rather than by a person—as is the case when booking a hotel room online—the 'same' service may elicit different reactions from various customers because some may have a problem understanding the specific conditions associated with booking the different room rates shown online. The inconsistency of service-delivery processes, which gives rise to the service characteristic of *variability*, creates one of the problems in the management of customer relationships.

To overcome the problem of inconsistent service delivery, service organisations can offer a customised service to meet the needs and wants of their customers. If they do customise their service, however, customers must be willing to pay the higher prices associated with providing customised services. If price, convenience and consistency of delivery are the determinant attributes in customers' evoked set in purchasing the service, then customers with those expectations are likely to be more satisfied with some degree of service standardisation at a price they are willing and able to pay. Adopting a pricing strategy based on segment and customer type is important in retaining customers in profitable relationships.

The purpose of customer relationships

The primary purpose for a service organisation in building and maintaining customer relationships is to ensure that it has groups of committed and profitable customers for its service products. In terms of service marketing, the marketing objective is to move consumers along a relationship continuum from a starting point where they are non-users or infrequent users of a service organisation's service products to the stage where they are long-term customers in a profitable exchange relationship with the organisation. From a customer's decision-making perspective, the development of satisfaction, trust and commitment demonstrates that customer's willingness to engage in an exchange relationships as a partner.[25]

From the perspective of a service organisation, as customers move up the relationship continuum from satisfaction-based interactions to commitment-based partnerships, increases in the value received and customer cooperation are both required. Both customers and service organisations benefit from customer commitment, which is the foundation of long-term service interactions.

Customer commitment to relationships

More service organisations are examining customer retention as a means of reducing 'customer churn'. In other words, if consumers are committed to a relationship with a service organisation, they are more likely to maintain their loyalty to the service brand rather than defect to the competition.

customer churn
The percentage of service customers who discontinue buying that service in a given time period. Customer churn is also known as 'customer attrition'.

Customer commitment is a more defining active aspect of customer retention in CRM because it is a means of increasing the commitment in the relationship, as well as how that relationship can be developed. Customer satisfaction, on the other hand, is a more backward-looking strategy that examines past behaviour as a way of measuring or predicting likely customer retention.[26]

There are two main types of commitment in CRM: affective commitment and calculative commitment. Affective commitment is based more on the consumer's emotions towards the relationship, which can lead to a higher level of trust and commitment to the relationship, whereas calculative commitment is based more on rational factors, such as the economic value of the relationship or lack of competitors in the market.[27] What this means in a practical context is that a service organisation should view commitment as being affective in particular aspects of customer relationships, rather than being totally linked to customer satisfaction. From a customer-retention perspective, an organisation must work towards ensuring that there is a high degree of commitment from its consumers on both the emotional and economic aspects of the relationship.

For example, in their marketing communications, service organisations must highlight the economic aspect of the relationship as well as the positive emotions a consumer may experience from entering into that relationship. Some service organisations focus on the value of their brands to provide emotional and economic value to customers, which then acts as a catalyst to build continuing customer commitment to the relationship with the company. For example, the American Express Qantas Ultimate card is a credit card that is be linked to a Qantas Frequent Flyer account that enables AMEX cardholders to earn Qantas frequent-flyer points faster than other credit cards issued by banks due to its higher earn-rate of Qantas points for each dollar spent on eligible purchases.

customer commitment
The length of time spent, level of emotion realised and net value generated by a customer and an organisation to develop in a relationship together

affective commitment
Commitment measured by the consumer's emotions towards the relationship, which can lead to a higher level of trust and commitment to the relationship

calculative commitment
Commitment measured by rational factors by both parties, such as the economic value of the relationship

The benefits of relationships to customers and organisations

When they have a choice, customers will generally remain loyal to a service organisation where they receive value greater than what they would expect to receive from a competing organisation. When organisations consistently deliver customer-perceived value, the customer has an incentive to remain in the relationship. Apart from specific inherent benefits of remaining in a relationship with a service organisation, customers also gain in other ways from remaining in long-term relationships with service organisations.

Confidence benefits

Customer confidence arises when customers develop feelings of trust or confidence in a service organisation, from knowing what to expect from that service firm. When customers can maintain a long-term relationship with a service organisation, they no longer need to be concerned about what to expect in terms of service quality because they can be confident that the service organisation will continue to satisfy their needs, wants and expectations.

Most customers would prefer not to be in constantly changing relationships with service organisations. For example, there is very little overall benefit for customers in switching mobile phone services if all telecommunications companies (telcos) offer the same basic service. To reduce the costs of customer churn, telcos sign their mobile phone customers to contracts that must be paid in full if a customer decides to move to another telco before their current contract has expired. Those contractual customer costs act as a deterrent to customers' changing their mobile phone service organisation.[28]

Social benefits

Social benefits are those that develop from having a personal relationship with a service provider from face-to-face service experiences that have developed over time; it is impossible, for example, to receive social benefits from services like ATMs that are delivered by means of impersonal technology. Personal relationships develop for B2B service transactions as well as for end-user customers. The social support benefits that often develop between service personnel—the service providers—are often the basis of a customer's loyalty to a particular service organisation, which is a risk for a service organisation when service providers leave the organisation and take customers with them.[29]

Special treatments benefits

A customer can generally call on a 'special treatment' benefit from a service organisation when that customer has been in a profitable long-term relationship with the business and may, for example, have made a late payment and had a late-payment charge waived because of their past history. Although special benefits can be critical for customer loyalty—as in the case of frequent-flyer points in the airline industry—they are often not the determinant reason for a customer to maintain a service relationship.[30]

Maximising customer value

Customer experience is often confused with service encounters and customer service and, while they are related, they are not the same thing. Customer service is only part of the customer experience equation. While customer service is a necessary component of customer experience, understanding the difference between the two concepts is critical to maximising customer lifetime value (CLV) and developing customer loyalty.

Customer service

Customer service is the delivery of a service to a customer before, during and after purchase. Present-day customers—especially those who are younger and attuned to technology—expect 24/7 customer service via online and personal channels. That expectation makes it imperative for service organisations to provide effective and efficient customer service if they want to provide a satisfying customer experience.

Customer experience

Customer experience refers to the sum of all encounters that customers have during their relationship with a service organisation. As prospective customers move through the stages of making a purchase decision and become customers, they will interact with the marketing, sales, accounts and customer-support staff of a service organisation. The key to keeping those interactions running smoothly and keeping customers satisfied is to know what customers expect from an organisation's service providers; that is, the staff. Customer sales representatives (reps), for example, should be aware of any prior communications that company staff have had with a customer. If two different sales reps call a customer on consecutive days pitching the same new service, when the customer has already had a satisfactory discussion with a customer sales rep in the previous week, the customer will quickly be aware of the organisation's poor management of its customer service functions, regardless of how positive the initial interaction with the customer sales agent was. The problem here is a lack of an overall strategic approach to managing customer encounters with the organisation.

The solution is to give the organisation's service providers up-to-date customer information by introducing a flexible and integrated CRM system that is accessible to all staff in customer-centred departments. A CRM system should record all contact with customers—whether they were physical interactions or by internet messages—and other critical customer purchase information. Individually, a service organisation's sales department may have high closure rates; its marketing team may achieve high conversion rates; and all the customers who have contact with the customer service team may have their problems resolved. That, however, does not matter if all units are contained in a silo environment that keeps them isolated from knowing how and when staff in the other departments communicated with particular customers.

In a true customer-centric service organisation, CRM will link all customer-contact departments, enabling staff to work in conjunction and provide an unparalleled customer experience. It is easier, and incurs lower costs, to retain profitable customers and provide a memorable customer experience, than trying to acquire new ones.

Australian businesses embracing emerging technologies amid accelerating pace of change

According to the results of technology research by Telsyte, Australian organisations are in the midst of a cycle of technology adoption driven by their need to create new products and services. The findings from the *Telsyte Australian Emerging Enterprise Technology Study 2017* indicate that more than half of organisations with more than 20 employees are undergoing large-scale IT transformation leading to widespread investigation, planning and rollout of various emerging technologies. Telsyte identified nine emerging technologies to better understand the rapid growth in adoption of transformative technology by Australian organisations.[31] Those emerging technologies were:

↘ Internet of Things (IoT)
↘ artificial intelligence (AI) and automation
↘ voice commands
↘ advanced networks: from fibre to 5G
↘ personal computing and collaboration
↘ high-performance computing
↘ virtual, augmented and mixed reality
↘ blockchain and crypto currencies
↘ mobile payments and near-field communication (NFC).

Enterprise IoT is quickly becoming mainstream

Most IT leaders predict there will be a five- to tenfold increase in connected devices in their organisation within five years. That surge in both end-user devices and industrial machines such as sensors and cameras is creating massive volumes of data that can be used to enhance productivity, modernise processes and help leaders make better strategic decisions.

Nearly 90 per cent of the Australian chief information officers (CIOs) who were surveyed believe that IoT will become important or critical to their organisation within five years, with almost a quarter (23 per cent) of organisations either testing, developing or in the production phase of installing IoT technology. Early adopters are showing positive return on investment (ROI) with 59 per cent claiming cost savings from using IoT technologies, and 30 per cent claiming increased customer satisfaction.

The biggest barriers are the costs of implementing IoT solutions within legacy IT infrastructures. More than two-thirds of CIOs see a positive role for IoT in their particular organisations while there is also a similar level of interest for customer service and marketing applications. While IoT gives organisations an opportunity to overhaul their systems and modernise processes, the challenge is to do this while maintaining legacy systems, said Telsyte Managing Director, Foad Fadaghi.[32] Figure 13.1 indicates the levels of IoT maturity in Australian organisations.

Artificial intelligence, machine learning and automation

There is a growing interest in using AI and automation technology in organisations as options expand for everything from physical robots to digital assistants and chatbots. Nearly two-thirds of businesses are already dabbling with machine learning to improve their operations or influence their business transactions with their customers. The

Figure 13.1 IoT maturity within Australian organisations

finance industry is at the forefront in emerging technologies, with 65 per cent of CIOs who were surveyed considering machine learning for financial modelling and fraud detection. Many organisations also believe that their customer interfaces are an important front for AI, while almost two-thirds of organisations intend to use cognitive computing in some form, including customer-service apps such as chatbots.

AI intentions are running at two speeds in the Australian market, with business managers much more positive about using automation technology than consumers. Mr Fadaghi says there is an undercurrent of fear in the average consumer about the impact of AI on jobs and future prospects for later generations in a highly automated world, while other findings in the study include:

↘ one in four IT leaders see a place for industry application of drones (or autonomous flying vehicles)

↘ more than half are exploring or already developing augmented reality applications

↘ 74 per cent indicated they had used cases for voice-recognition technology in their organisation

↘ over 60 per cent see value in smart wearable devices such as smartwatches and smart glasses in their organisation for internal operations, access control and customer-facing applications

↘ 59 per cent are investigating the potential uses or disruption from blockchain technology in their industry.[33]

Benefits to service organisations from customer relationships

The benefits to service organisations from developing a loyal customer base include external economic benefits and internal human resource–management benefits. Service organisations are leveraging CRM analytics as part of their technological initiatives to enhance their customer experience.

William Chitty

Enhancing customers' service experience

Advanced analytics is changing the way many service organisations approach their customer interactions and the processes they use to manage their customer relationships. The ability of those organisations to use their customers' behavioural data to forecast service demand also allows them to make information-based decisions about activity levels and requirements of their assets to satisfy their customers' demand for service products. Specifically, these changes are embodied in the applications of advanced analytics that are being implemented in Australian service organisations looking to disrupt their industry and gain a competitive advantage in the short term.[34]

Gaining the whole customer view

This approach allows organisations to gain a very detailed understanding of individual customers based on their transaction history, as well as being able to incorporate every piece of information from multiple sources and attribute that data to an individual customer. This allows organisations to understand their customers on a far deeper level than has been previously possible. The insurance industry is an example of how that application is being applied. Traditionally, the insurance industry has based its business decisions on actuarial data and associated risk. This experience in risk-based analysis has given many insurance companies a solid starting point for developing the pricing strategies for their services based on likelihood of an event occurring and the resulting cost to the company. What risk-based analysis has not provided is any insight into how customers will react to those pricing decisions. Building a complete picture of a customer using advanced analytics cuts across the functional silos of marketing and pricing, so insurance companies can investigate how their customers interact and respond to a price, and calculate the total value of that customer to the company.

Customer micro-targeting: acquisition and churn management

Customer acquisition and churn management is one of the most valuable applications of advanced analytics. Not only is churn management one of the key parameters used to value firms such as telcos, but most service organisations understand that customer acquisition is an expensive and time-consuming activity. Service organisations can no longer rely on their 'captive' paying customers of the past. Customers are more sophisticated and demanding than ever before, and if a service organisation is not meeting their demands and managing their service experience in a way that engages them, they will move to an organisation that can.

Customer micro-targeting: adding value

It is not surprising that customers value exceptional service, and many have come to expect it. Advanced analytics is increasingly being used to provide 'added value' to customers in a service that allows organisations to stand out from their competitors. The most interesting case of adding value comes from organisations that are using analytics to expand into new lines of business. For example, in Australia a large retailer uses its transaction data to micro-market financial services products, and at least one Australian bank plans to use its transaction data to publish targeted, non-banking, marketing information to its customers, such as real estate agents.[35]

Economic benefits

Research suggests that relationship-oriented service organisations achieve lower operating costs. Some estimates suggest that repeat purchases by loyal customers can reduce marketing expenditure by as much as 90 per cent.[36] The majority of start-up costs are based on attracting new customers, which may exceed the revenue expected to be gained from those customers in the short term, so there is a financial advantage for the organisation if it can cultivate a longer-term relationship with those customers as soon as possible.

In addition to reducing operating costs, CRM that uses cloud computing can increase employee productivity; specifically, sales teams that are remotely located from the service organisation can access the CRM system from outside the office. Cloud mobility also facilitates virtual workforces, providing a scalable solution for growing service organisations. Cloud CRM software can improve productivity through its project management features.

Customer behaviour benefits

For service organisations that conducted customer experience (CX) improvement projects during 2014, the most frequently cited reasons for doing so were those associated with collecting and analysing customer feedback and communicating actions to employees and customers (capturing the voice of the customer), followed by reconfiguring the service-delivery processes. More than one-third of participants in the Gartner Newsroom survey said their customer experience improvement projects involved significant changes to their business models. The majority of those business-model changes mentioned by the participants involved changes to the process around the production of services, including supply-chain and internal delivery processes. In one-third of cases, the business-model changes related to changes in the way customers interact with the organisation.[37]

In Australia, the NAB uses customer experience marketing techniques to:

→ deepen its understanding of customers by developing multidimensional profile/ segments

→ identify and leverage key life-stage transition points to increase service relevance and value

→ bring marketing automation and intuition together to derive better/new ways of delivering a positive brand experience.[38]

William Chitty

Loyalty and customer-retention strategies

Managing customer retention is an overarching commercial objective that focuses a service organisation's operational and marketing strategies on satisfying existing customers. The rationale of managing customer retention is to develop long-term profitable relationships with high-value customers who can contribute to the continuing growth of the organisation.

From an organisational perspective, customer retention is important for two reasons. The first is that, in many developed economies, the service sector markets are in the mature stages of their life cycle and face slowing rates of growth in potential markets. Coupled with underperforming economies, there are also fewer customers and they are spending less capita. Another consideration is that structural changes in national economies have increased competition from once–publicly owned utilities, such as telcos, which is making customer retention more challenging.

The second reason that organisations must effectively and efficiently manage their customer-retention strategies relates to increasing costs associated with marketing communications, particularly mass-marketing campaigns that use broadcast and print media channels. Allied to those costs is the need for service organisations to compete for customer attention in the cluttered media environment.

Customer-retention strategies

Most customer-retention strategies appear to be easy to implement, but it is important to understand the underlying reasons that customers switch service organisations. The areas of concern for organisations are:

→ failure of the organisation's core service

→ failure of the service provider in the customer-service interaction; that is, a failure due to a lack of care, or knowledge of the service by the service provider

→ poor service recovery; that is, a failure due to slow procedural policies

→ pricing and inconvenience.[39]

Effective strategies for managing customer retention include the following marketing management practices.

Loyalty programs

Loyalty programs offer rewards to customers who purchase frequently from an organisation. Usually rewards are designed to reward the customers who buy very frequently, in large quantities and over a long period. But the smarter programs offer programs very

loyalty program
A marketing program that rewards customers and encourages them to continue using the service; often higher rewards are offered for higher levels of customer purchase behaviour

early on in the relationship between the organisation and customer as a way of rewarding behaviour and encouraging the relationship to continue. When well designed, loyalty programs are an excellent strategy for retaining customers, regardless of the length of the relationship that members have with an organisation. A well-designed loyalty program needs to be equitable, transparent and seen as having value by both parties.

A loyalty program is a 'coalition loyalty business'—one that is the driving force behind the high level of engagement of Qantas Frequent Flyers.[40] A coalition loyalty business has business partners, such as, for Qantas, the major Australian banks and Woolworths supermarkets, which leads to a multitude effect as consumers engage in the program in multiple ways. It is often, however, the business that flows from 'coalition partners' that makes some loyalty programs viable propositions. For example, since linking with Woolworths' Everyday Rewards in 2009, the membership of Qantas Frequent Flyers has increased by more than 80 per cent. Figure 13.2 indicates the airlines with the best and worst frequent-flyer seat availability.[41]

Pricing by segment and customer type

Pricing by segment and customer type plays an important role in retaining customers. Early research by Reichheld and Sasser found that a bank in the United States could retain more customers if fees, such as the $35 charged for a dishonoured cheque, were lowered. If the bank retained just 0.2 per cent of its customers, this would offset the fee reductions.[42] On closer analysis, however, pricing by segment and customer type could have also helped to prevent customers leaving the bank, as many customers who left did so because the pricing structure for the bank's products was incorrect and did not meet their needs. For pricing to be an effective strategy in retaining customers, it needs to be fair and transparent and represent value for the product being created between both parties.

When service organisations set the price of their services, they must consider the needs, wants and expectations of the target markets in order to understand how consumers evaluate a price in terms of the type and level of service they want created for them. Many services, such as Google, Facebook and YouTube, are able to keep offering a free, basic level of services because they are clear that advertising is required to fund their website. Paid services that are successful are successful for the same reasons. It is common, for example, when travellers begin searching online for the ideal travel itinerary, for them to find that the price of a plane ticket or hotel room has changed considerably in just a few hours. Checking back on one of the many travel comparison websites a few days later will only result in more exasperation, as a hotel room price may have gone up, while the cost of the airline ticket has gone down. These service industries rely on pricing models that try to produce the greatest amount of profit from the sales of an airline ticket or a hotel room. The constantly changing selling price is by design; airlines have decades of experience in using dynamic pricing models based on supply and demand, which helps them to manage yield by balancing prices with dates, times and seat availability.

William Chitty

Figure 13.2   The airlines with the best and worst frequent-flyer seat availability

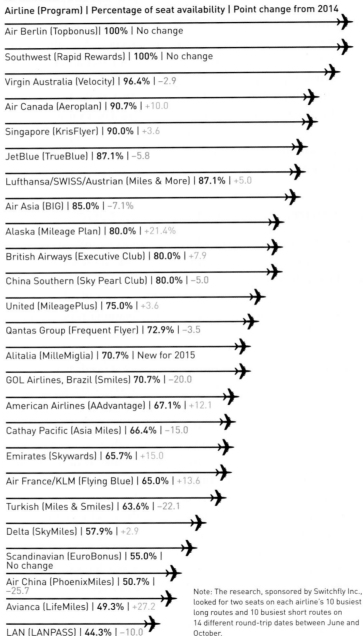

Is this seat taken?

Southwest and Air Berlin again head the list of airlines in a survey of frequent-flyer award seat availability. Below, the results of a test of 25 airlines for itineraries from June to October 2015.

Airline (Program) | Percentage of seat availability | Point change from 2014

Air Berlin (Topbonus)| **100%** | No change

Southwest (Rapid Rewards) | **100%** | No change

Virgin Australia (Velocity) | **96.4%** | −2.9

Air Canada (Aeroplan) | **90.7%** | +10.0

Singapore (KrisFlyer) | **90.0%** | +3.6

JetBlue (TrueBlue) | **87.1%** | −5.8

Lufthansa/SWISS/Austrian (Miles & More) | **87.1%** | +5.0

Air Asia (BIG) | **85.0%** | −7.1%

Alaska (Mileage Plan) | **80.0%** | +21.4%

British Airways (Executive Club) | **80.0%** | +7.9

China Southern (Sky Pearl Club) | **80.0%** | −5.0

United (MileagePlus) | **75.0%** | +3.6

Qantas Group (Frequent Flyer) | **72.9%** | −3.5

Alitalia (MilleMiglia) | **70.7%** | New for 2015

GOL Airlines, Brazil (Smiles) **70.7%** | −20.0

American Airlines (AAdvantage) | **67.1%** | +12.1

Cathay Pacific (Asia Miles) | **66.4%** | −15.0

Emirates (Skywards) | **65.7%** | +15.0

Air France/KLM (Flying Blue) | **65.0%** | +13.6

Turkish (Miles & Smiles) | **63.6%** | −22.1

Delta (SkyMiles) | **57.9%** | +2.9

Scandinavian (EuroBonus) | **55.0%** | No change

Air China (PhoenixMiles) | **50.7%** | −25.7

Avianca (LifeMiles) | **49.3%** | +27.2

LAN (LANPASS) | **44.3%** | −10.0

Note: The research, sponsored by Switchfly Inc., looked for two seats on each airline's 10 busiest long routes and 10 busiest short routes on 14 different round-trip dates between June and October.

Source: S. McCartney (2015). The best and worst airline rewards programs for 2015. *Wall Street Journal*, 14 May. <www.wsj.com/articles/the-best-and-worst-airline-rewards-programs-for-2015-1431577535>.

Airlines in particular have become adept at using virtual warehouses of data to help set their pricing at a seat level. The result is that passengers sitting in the same row on an aircraft may have paid significantly different prices for their seats. In addition to passenger supply and demand, other key variables, such as competitors' prices, seasonality and the cost of jet fuel, are all put into the complex algorithms that compute the prices of an airline ticket. This is why airlines promote their 'advance purchase' seats to encourage price-conscious passengers to fly with them.

Relationship marketing

Switching barriers are constraints in customer–organisation relationships. Berry and Parasuraman developed a conceptual framework of relationship bonds to understand the types of retention strategies that focus on developing relationship bonds with customers.[43] The framework suggests that customers fulfil the structural requirements of each successive level of bonds before they move from Level One bonds based on financial incentives to Level Two bonds that include personal communications, and finally reach Level Three bonds that build financial, social and structural relationships. Table 13.1 is a brief summary of the features of relationship marketing.

Table 13.1   The three levels of relationship marketing

Level	One	Two	Three
Types of bonds	Financial	Financial and social	Financial, social and structural
Marketing mix/ marketing orientation	Price/consumers	Personal communications/ customers	Service delivery/ clients
Service customisation	Low	Medium	Medium–High
Competitive advantage	Low	Medium	High

Source: Adapted from L.L Berry & A. Parasuraman (1991). *Marketing Services*. New York, NY: Free Press, p. 137.

Level One relationship marketing is often referred to as 'retention' marketing because at this level service organisations use price as an incentive to encourage consumers to purchase more—or more often—from the service organisation. The use of price as the primary element of the marketing mix is the easiest to copy, and price does not offer a sustainable competitive advantage for service organisations.

Level Two relationship marketing moves beyond the financial links of Level One to build social links that include pricing incentives. Level Two marketing works on personalised service delivery in the transformation of consumers to customers by staying in touch with customers to learn about their needs, wants and expectations. This level of relationship marketing is an art as much as it is a science, and can encourage a customer to remain in a relationship with a service organisation, providing, of course, that there are no price or service-delivery problems; it may also give the organisation the opportunity to respond to those problems before the customer defects.

William Chitty

Level Three relationship marketing typically builds structural bonds that cement the organisation–client service-delivery processes rather than depending on individual service-provider relationships to help clients to become more productive. Well-designed Level Three marketing strategies can make leaving a service organisation more costly for clients, because by switching to a competitor they will lose the value of business benefits they have gained; a situation in which the value of the relationship can be easily determined by the formula, 'value = get/give'. For example, the benefits of belonging to the Qantas Frequent Flyer program are based on various levels of customer activity, and accrue, depending on how often and how far passengers travel with the airline.

The highest-level relationship Qantas frequent flyers can attain—Platinum One—offers the benefits of prestige and exclusivity that Qantas says will only be available for a select group of the airline's most loyal customers; and that it is '...our way of saying "thank you" for your loyalty and in recognition of your ongoing commitment to Qantas'.[44] Those Platinum One benefits can only be retained by constant patronage in its business or first-class seats. Qantas rewards its Platinum One frequent flyers by offering a structural response—additional benefits—to compensate for the stressful reality of frequent airline travel.

Figure 13.3 Qantas Platinum One frequent flyer

Source: Qantas. <qantas.com>.

Results from research into the value of customer retention to organisations indicate that:[45]

1 It is up to seven times more costly to attract a new customer than it is to retain an existing customer.

2 A 10 per cent increase in customer-retention levels can result in a 30 per cent increase in the value of an organisation.

3 A 5 per cent increase in customer-retention rates can increase profits by anywhere from 25 to 95 per cent.

4 If online retailers retained 10 per cent of their existing customers, they could double their revenue.

It is worth remembering that the most successful of all relationship marketing strategies are built on the foundation of providing excellence in an organisation's core service—including its delivery.[46]

Measuring the value of customer relationships

Net Promoter Score

An accurate Net Promoter Score (NPS) depends on a constant flow of data from customer surveys. Frequent surveys allow organisations to monitor the NPSs for variations and to apply and test new initiatives to determine if those new approaches improve outcomes. The consistency approach to measuring variations applies to all methodologies, even to the extent of changing the wording of the questions in the customer survey. Calculating an NPS depends on the responses from short, frequent customer surveys. Organisations typically ask their customer to answer two questions:

> On a scale of zero to 10; how likely is it that you would recommend this company (or service) to a friend or colleague? [And a follow-up question then asks the reason for the allocated score.]

The answers that customers provide are classified as follows:

→ 0–6 = detractors—unhappy customers who can hurt an organisation's brand by negative word of mouth

→ 7–8 = passives—satisfied but indifferent customers who could be swayed by the competition

→ 9–10 = promoters—loyal customers who will keep buying and referring others.[47]

The NPS is simply the percentage of *promoters* minus the percentage of *detractors*; see Figure 13.4.

There are two types of NPS surveys: top-down and bottom-up. Top-down NPS surveys are based on customers' attitudes towards several organisations that are designed to indicate

Figure 13.4 Calculating a Net Promoter® Score

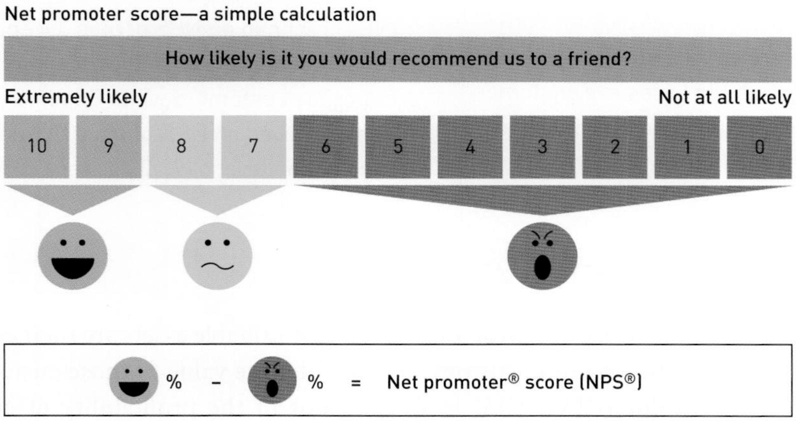

Net promoter score—a simple calculation

How likely is it you would recommend us to a friend?

Extremely likely   Not at all likely

| 10 | 9 | 8 | 7 | 6 | 5 | 4 | 3 | 2 | 1 | 0 |

☺ % − 😠 % = Net promoter® score (NPS®)

an organisation's relative performance and identify aggregate behaviour rather than individual customer insights. On the other hand, bottom-up surveys are openly sponsored by an organisation and that firm keeps track of its respondents after participating in specific transactions. For example, a bank may survey its customers after they have experienced a specific interaction at one of the bank's branch offices.[48]

More Australians consider switching banks

A customer survey of bank customers in 2017 found that Australians are not afraid to shop around for their finances, with more than one-third of those surveyed indicating they were prepared to leave their current bank. Interestingly, higher-income households were more likely to leave one of the big four banks that year. The study from COPC Inc. revealed middle-aged Australians are potentially the most dissatisfied, with 42 per cent of those aged 40–49 prepared to look outside the big four banks compared to 36 per cent of those aged under 39.[49]

The same could be said of higher-income earners, with 41 per cent of households with a combined annual income of between $100000–$150000 likely to leave their bank, compared with 33 per cent of households with a combined annual income of less than $100000. The primary reason that Australians are prepared to leave their banks is to search for better customer service. The study suggested that a bank's ability to resolve customer issues is one of the main priorities for Australians and had a strong impact on the NPS—that is, how likely a customer was to recommend a bank to others. The general sentiment revealed through the study is that smaller banks are better at resolving customer issues compared to the big four.[50]

Another study surveyed mortgage holders to ascertain their NPS, which measured the level of customer loyalty to a particular bank. Commonwealth Bank of Australia (CBA) was the best performer among the major banks with an NPS of minus 12.7, followed by Australia and New Zealand Banking Group (ANZ) with minus 13.8, Westpac with minus 20.4 and National Australia Bank (NAB) with minus 20.7.

Customer satisfaction ratings by the mortgage holders with the big four was 77.4 per cent, which was lower than the 80.7 per cent found among non-mortgage customers at the major banks.

The non-major banks scored better with NPSs as well as satisfaction levels. ING Direct had an NPS of plus 3.4 and satisfaction levels of 96.3 per cent for mortgage customers while Bendigo Bank received an NPS of plus 32.2 and a satisfaction level of 93.2 per cent.[51]

Customer lifetime value

For customer-centric service organisations, their most valuable assets are their customers. The profit generated by retaining customers is the lifetime value of those customers: the customer lifetime value (CLV). CLV is an indicator of the profitability of customers'

OXFORD UNIVERSITY PRESS

long-term relationships with an organisation's brand, which occurs when revenues from that relationship are greater than the costs of supporting the customers' service experiences. Organisations can provide better customer experiences—and thereby increase the value of their customers—by retaining existing customers rather than attempting to acquire new ones. Analysis of Australian industries, for example, indicates that customer retention is most important in situations where customers have to make regular purchase decisions, as is the case with telcos when customers have to renew annual contracts for mobile phones. It is estimated that a promoter of a branded mobile phone is worth about twice the lifetime value of a detractor, with higher retention rates accounting for almost one-third of the difference.[52] CLV has been defined by Jain and Singh as:

> The lifetime value of a customer over his/her lifetime is the net revenue obtained from that customer over the lifetime of transactions with that customer, minus the cost of attracting, selling and servicing that customer, taking into account the time value of money.[53]

To calculate CLV, service organisations can take the revenue they earn by providing their services to customers, deduct the costs of supplying and serving them, and then adjust all the monetary payments for their net present value—the time value of money, which is often based on the prime cost of capital.[54] Organisations can increase CLV by using several approaches.

The first is *personalisation*.[55] Research conduct by Econsultancy in April 2015 found that 94 per cent of business executives believe that personalisation is a critical issue for the 'current and future success' of an organisation. The research also found that for 66 per cent of client-side respondents, personalisation improved both business performance and the customer experience, and was the main driver for personalising customers' online experiences.[56]

The second approach to increase CLV is to exceed customers' *expectations*. The success of this approach is due to the fact that organisations that exceed their customers' expectations always fulfil customers' orders on time by generally exceeding their pre-set delivery dates.

The third approach that organisations can adopt to increase CLV is to reward customer loyalty. Offering loyal customers some type of reward, or exclusive content, is a very successful way of strengthening customers' brand affinity. The 'reward' can be as simple as an email thanking a customer for their order, or it may be something more elaborate such as an airline creating an airport lounge with a superior bar and dining facilities for its top-tier frequent flyers and passengers.

Research conducted into the success of loyalty programs found that most still follow the basic transactional philosophy of offering rewards simply based on the dollar volume of purchases. Few of those organisations that were investigated—about one in six—recognised and rewarded their customers for engaging and interacting with a service brand.[57] Perhaps so few organisations put time and resources into engaging and interacting with their customers because the majority believe the costs will outweigh the likely returns from their

customer lifetime value (CLV)
The value of a customer over their lifetime with the organisation. Different organisations take different approaches to measuring CLV, but most take a net value or profit perspective, deducting all the costs of dealing with the customer to arrive at a final net figure.

William Chitty

customers; this is probably true for companies that manufacture and market fast-moving consumer goods such as breakfast cereals. Service organisations can, however, make a start to encouraging their customers to engage with their service by examining the ways that customers interact with the organisation, as the first stage in managing their customers' longer-term service experiences.

While over half (51%) of organisations claim that customers' experience is driving their investments in technology, Australian service organisations that rely solely on digital means to deliver their services often forget the value of an employee's touch in delivering a service. Those organisations run the risk of falling behind their competitors who use technology to integrate their service channels and give their employees—as the service providers—the tools to personalise the service and deliver great service experiences.[58] An example of an Australian organisation that is meeting the challenge of digital transformation is the ANZ bank. While the senior ANZ management team has acknowledged technology disrupters and innovators can quickly threaten a financial institution's traditional operations, they have reiterated the overall importance of having a sound business culture to harness innovation and capture the benefits of social media to develop deeper relationships with their customers and staff. To this end, the ANZ has co-developed a business course with the Massachusetts Institute of Technology in the United States for their staff, which focuses on business leadership and the customer experience.[59]

CRM, from a services marketing perspective, is linked to customer loyalty and its ability to deliver long-term viability to a service organisation. CRM encompasses analytical practices and technology that service organisations use to understand their customers' purchasing behaviour throughout their lifetimes and to manage their interactions in the service-delivery channels. The purpose of CRM is to create profitable customer relationships based on deeper customer engagement with a service organisation. A CRM program consists of both technological systems and marketing processes to collect and collate information about customers' behaviour across different points of contact, including an organisation's internet site, telephone service, direct marketing, face-to-face communications and social media. The most important customer relationships are the commercial relationships that customers conduct with the organisation.

There are two types of customer relationships: transactional and behavioural. The basis of transactional customer relationships is their focus on the point of sale (POS); that is, the moment when a customer actually pays for the service. Traditional mass marketing creates awareness of the service brand, and positive feelings and a preference, and moves the product through the POS in a simple transaction. With more people purchasing products from their mobile phones, the ease of a one-click transaction is becoming the preferred method of purchasing.

To create the ideal situation for relationship marketing takes a level of personal commitment on the part of the salesperson and a level of trust from the customer. Customers enter into a behavioural marketing relationship in the expectation of receiving positive value from both their participation and the service product. Behavioural relationships have the potential to provide customers with in-depth information about the service, help customers to find the best fit between their needs and wants and the features and attributes of the service, and assistance with delivery, discounts and other issues that cannot always be provided in an online interaction. Most of all, however, a behavioural relationship helps customers feel confident about their purchasing decision—and a confident customer is more likely to repurchase in the future.

Customer loyalty varies by industry and generally occurs when customers resist the influence of other brands. Research suggests that loyal customers are more profitable for a business in the long run because they are usually willing to pay more for brands of choice, and they offer the most valuable kind of marketing: word-of-mouth endorsement.

The primary purpose for service organisations in building and maintaining customer relationships is to gain committed and profitable customers for their service products. In terms of service marketing, the marketing objective is to move consumers along a relationship continuum from a starting point where they are non-users or infrequent users of a service organisation's products to the stage where they are long-term customers in a profitable exchange relationship with the organisation. Where they have a choice, customers are reasonably likely to remain loyal to a service organisation when they receive value greater than what they would expect to receive from a competing organisation. When organisations consistently deliver customer-perceived value, the customer has an incentive to remain in the relationship. The benefits to service organisations from developing a loyal customer base include external economic benefits and internal human resource–management benefits.

Service organisations are leveraging CRM analytics as part of their technological initiatives to enhance their customers' experience.

Calculating a Net Promoter Score depends on the responses from short, frequent customer surveys. Organisations typically ask their customer to answer two questions: *On a scale of zero to 10; how likely is it that you would recommend this company (or service) to a friend or colleague?* And a follow-up question then asks the reason for the allocated score.

While over half (51%) of organisations claim that customers' experience is driving their investments in technology, Australian service organisations that rely solely on digital means to deliver their services often forget the value of an employee's touch in delivering a service. Those organisations run the risk of falling behind their competitors who use technology to integrate their service channels and give their employees—as the service providers, and sales reps—the tools to personalise the service and deliver service experiences that are valued.

Review questions

1   Fully explain how customer relationship marketing is different from traditional marketing. Apply those differences to a global chain of five-star hotels, such as those offered by Marriott or Accor, and Uber ride-sharing services.

2   Some direct marketing is referred to as 'junk mail' or 'spam'; how can a service organisation that has adopted the principles of CRM avoid having its marketing communications referred to as 'junk mail' or 'spam'?

3   Consider a service organisation to which you are a loyal customer, and then answer the following questions:

   a   Why do you continue to be loyal to that service organisation? What are the benefits that you value from the service organisation?

   b   What would cause you to switch to another service organisation?

4   Explain the role that service interactions play in customer relationships with service organisations.

5   How can a relationship be of value to the customers of a service organisation, and to the service organisation? Fully explain if it is possible for customers and the organisation to obtain value, at the same, from a service interaction.

6   Customer lifetime value is measured across customers' lifetimes, not particular transactions. What are the advantages and disadvantages of using this methodology for the following service providers:

   a   a specialist medical doctor

   b   an insurance agent

   c   a tax accountant

   d   a local gymnasium.

7   Customer-retention strategies are used by most commercial companies. Fully explain why you think retention strategies are used to help consumers; or, conversely, why those strategies are used to help companies increase their average revenue per customer.

8 You are considering taking a holiday. Make a list of five relevant service companies' websites; for example, a holiday resort, an airline, a tourist agency, a charter boat company specialising in snorkelling excursions, a company that offers day-long 4WD expeditions 'off the main roads'. Access the websites. List the features about each website that would encourage you to enter into a customer relationship with that company.

Further reading

Godson, M. (2009). *Relationship Marketing*. Oxford, UK: Oxford University Press.

Greenberg, P. (2010). *CRM at the Speed of Light: Social CRM Strategies, Tools, and Techniques for Engaging Your Customers*. New York. NY: McGraw-Hill.

Hsieh, T. (2010). *Delivering Happiness: A Path to Profits, Passion, and Purpose*. New York, NY: Business Plus.

Payne, A. & Frow, P. (2005). A strategic framework for customer relationship management. *Journal of Marketing*, 69(4), 167–76.

Reinartz, W., Krafft, M. et al. (2004). The customer relationship management process: Its measurement and impact on performance. *Journal of Marketing Research*, 41(3), 293–305.

Endnotes

1   A. Coleman (2017). Businesses riding the swell of customer expectations. *The Telegraph*, 12 May.

2   ibid.

3   I. Grayson (2015). Engaging with customers in a richer way. *Australian Financial Review*. 24 June. <www.afr.com/news/special-reports/digital-business/engaging-with-customers-in-a-richer-way-20150622-ghu224>.

4   A. Coleman (2017). Businesses riding the swell of customer expectations. *The Telegraph*, 12 May.

5   F. Reichheld & W.E. Sasser Jr (1990). Zero defections: Quality comes to services. *Harvard Business Review*, 68(5). (September–October), 105–11.

6   ibid.

7   sprinklr (2017). 3 transformative customer experience strategies from leading marketers. 12 July. <https://blog.sprinklr.com/customer-experience-strategies-for-customer-first-transformation>.

8   M. Godson (2009). *Relationship Marketing*. Oxford, UK: Oxford University Press, p. 38.

9   ibid.

10 J. Tysdal (2013). A study in opposites: Transactional vs relationship marketing. 19 November.

11 R. Pearce (2018). Telstra's investment in digitisation paying off, CIO says. *Computerworld*, 16 January. <www.computerworld.com.au/article/632208/telstra-investment-digitisation-paying-off-cio-says>.

12 ibid.

13 R.J. Baran, R.J. Galka & D.P. Strunk (2008). *Customer Relationship Management*. Mason, OH: Thomson South Western, pp. 113, 144.

14 J.E. Richard, P.C. Thirkell & S.L. Huff (2007). An examination of customer relationship management (CRM) technology adoption and its impact on business-to-business customer relationships. *Total Quality Management & Business Excellence*, 18(8), 927–45.

15 R.T. Rust, K. N. Lemon & D. Narayandas (2005). *Customer Equity Management*. Upper Saddle River, NJ: Pearson Prentice Hall, p. 113.

16 Article based on S. Sarraf (2017). Revealing the top mobile virtual network operators in Australia. *ARN*, 27 November. <www.arnnet.com.au/article/630453/revealing-top-mobile-virtual-network-operators-australia>.

17 ibid.

18 B.A. Gutek, A.D. Bhappu, M.A. Liao-Troth & B. Cherry (1999). Distinguishing between service relationships and encounters. *Journal of Applied Psychology*, 84(2), (April), 218–33.

19 K. Heinonen (2008). The role of digital service encounters on customers' perceptions of companies. *Journal of Electronic Commerce in Organizations*, 6(2), 1–10.

20 S. Vargo & R. Lusch (2008). Service-dominant logic: Continuing the evolution. *Journal of the Academy of Marketing Science*, 36(1), 1–10.

21 A. Helkkula, C. Kelleher & M. Pihlstrom (2012). Characterizing value as an experience: Implications for service researchers and managers. *Journal of Service Research*, 15(1), 59–75.

22 M. Godson (2009). *Relationship Marketing*. Oxford, UK: Oxford University Press, p. 41.

23 C. Grönroos (2007). *Service Management and Marketing*. West Sussex, UK: John Wiley & Sons Ltd, p. 52.

24 ibid.

25 V.A. Zeithaml, M.J. Bitner & D.D. Gremler (2006). *Services Marketing*. New York, NY: McGraw-Hill Irwin, pp. 183–3.

26 A. Gustafsson, M.D. Johnson & I. Roos (2005). The effects of customer satisfaction, relationship committed dimensions, and triggers on customer retention. *Journal of Marketing*, 69(4), 210–18.

27 ibid.

28 V.A. Zeithaml, M.J. Bitner & D.D. Gremler (2006). *Services Marketing*. New York, NY: McGraw-Hill Irwin, pp. 183–4.

29 ibid.

30 ibid.

31 Telsyte (2017). Australian businesses embracing emerging technologies amid accelerating pace of change. 25 July. <www.telsyte.com.au/announcements?month=July-2017>.

32 ibid.

33 ibid.

34 G. Seewooruttun (2015). ABC technology and games. ABC website, 4 June.

35 ibid.

36 V.A. Zeithaml, M.J. Bitner & D.D. Gremler (2006). *Services Marketing*. New York, NY: McGraw-Hill Irwin, pp. 183–4.

37 Gartner (2015). Gartner says organizations are changing their customer experience priorities. Gartner Newsroom, 9 June.

38 B. Harris (2015). NAB talks customer experience thinking. *AdTech*, 11 March.

OXFORD UNIVERSITY PRESS

39 R.N. Bolton, P.K. Kannan & M.D. Bramlett (2000). Implications of loyalty program membership and service experiences for customer retention and value. *Journal of the Academy of Marketing Science*, 28(1), 95; T. Hennig-Thurau & A. Klee (1997). The impact of customer satisfaction and relationship quality on customer retention: A critical reassessment and model development. *Psychology and Marketing*, 14(8), 737–64; P.C. Verhoef (2003). Understanding the effect of customer relationship management efforts on customer retention and customer share development. *Journal of Marketing*, 67(4), 30–45.

40 B. Gardiner (2015). Qantas: External partnerships crucial to customer loyalty growth. *CMO*, 11 March.

41 S. McCartney (2015). The best and worst airline rewards programs for 2015. *Wall Street Journal*, 14 May. <www.wsj.com/articles/the-best-and-worst-airline-rewards-programs-for-2015-1431577535>.

42 F. Reichheld & W.E. Sasser Jr (1990). Zero defections: Quality comes to services. *Harvard Business Review*, 68(5). (September–October), 105–11.

43 L.L Berry & A. Parasuraman (1991). *Marketing Services*. New York, NY: Free Press, Chapter 8.

44 Qantas (2015). New Platinum One benefits. Qantas website. <www.qantas.com.au/fflyer/dyn/flying/platinum-one-new-benefits>.

45 R.M. Brecht (2015). Five critical features that drive customer retention strategies. *DMN3*, 22 January.

46 ibid.

47 Survey Monkey, Net Promoter® Score (NPS) Survey. <www.surveymonkey.com/mp/net-promoter-score>.

48 R. Markey & F. Reichheld (2012). Net Promoter System: Creating a reliable metric. *Bain Brief*, 14 February. <www.bain.com/publications/articles/creating-a-reliable-metric-loyalty-insights.aspx>.

49 A. Banney (2017). Over 30% of Australians will leave the big four banks in 2017. *Finder*, 1 March. <www.finder.com.au/over-30-of-australians-will-leave-the-big-four-banks-in-2017>.

50 ibid.

51 M. Bolza (2017). Mortgage holders rate big four banks in the negative. *Australian Broker*, 10 March. <www.brokernews.com.au/news/breaking-news/mortgage-holders-rate-big-four-banks-in-the-negative-233856.aspx>.

52 K. Bradley & R. Hatherall (2013). The powerful economics of customer loyalty in Australia. *Bain Brief*, 29 July.

53 D. Jain & S.S. Singh (2002). Customer lifetime value research in marketing: A review and future directions. *Journal of Interactive Marketing*,16(2), 46.

54 S. MacDonald (2014). How to create a customer centric strategy for your business. *SuperOffice*, 7 April. <www.superoffice.com/blog/how-to-create-a-customer-centric-strategy-for-your-business>.

55 G. Charlton (2014). 15 ways for companies to increase customer lifetime value. *Econsultancy*, 23 April. <http://econsultancy.com/blog/64724-15-ways-for-companies-to-increase-customer-lifetime-value>.

56 ibid.

57 A. Williams (2015). Loyalty programs stuck in the past. *CMO*, 30 March. <www.cmo.com.au/article/571534/loyalty-programs-stuck-in-past>.

58 Optus (2014). The majority of Australian businesses struggle on customer experience. Media release, 18 June.

59 R. Gluyas (2015). ANZ's social makeover a key part of digital revolution. *The Australian*, 4 August, pp. 19 & 23.

Case

Case study E

Google Home: The smart-home service

In the second half of 2017, Google launched a digital service in Australia that gave local customers the opportunity to create a smart home that had a list of expected benefits ranging from connecting internet devices in their homes to asking the Google Assistant to engage with local services.[1] Google Home, as shown in Figure 1, is powered by Google's voice-controlled Google Assistant. It is a device which, when connected via wi-fi to a home internet system, can control lights, appliances and smart power switches, and answer trivia questions, set calendar reminders and provide weather forecasts.

Figure 1 Google Home connects via wi-fi to access the internet

Google Home is currently priced from around A$150 and is available from The Google Store, JB Hi-Fi, Harvey Norman, Officeworks, The Good Guys, Telstra, Optus and the Qantas Store. Google Home was launched in the United States in late 2016, and while it is the first major smart-home hub launched in Australia, it competes with the Amazon Echo smart speaker (and its Alexa voice assistant), the market leader. The Amazon Echo was released in Australia in late 2018. If prospective customers want to start building a smart-home system, Google Home is currently the more established option.

How does it work?

As shown in Figure 2, Google Home is connected by wi-fi to the internet and communicates through a Smart-Home Hub that allows customers to control lights and other appliances through spoken commands.[2]

When customers ask Google Home a question, the coloured lights on top of the speaker blink in acknowledgment, and the question is answered by a feminine voice with an Australian accent.

Figure 2 Google Home controls lights and appliances by voice commands

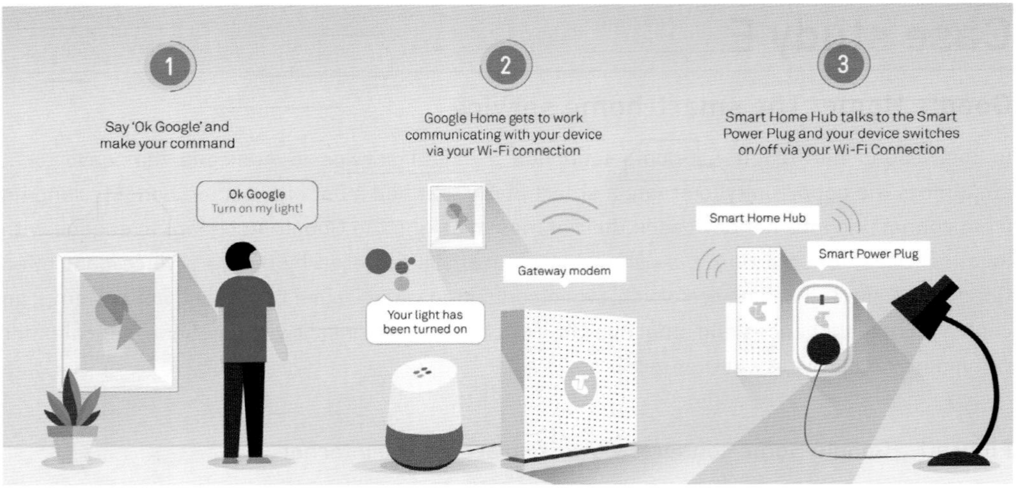

Source: Telstra. <www.telstra.com.au/content/dam/tcom/smart-home/google-home/smart-home-google-home-infographics.jpg/jcr:content/renditions/original>.

From then on, customers can ask questions and receive responses tailored to the Australian marketing environment. If they ask for the latest news, they will be given the headlines from the Australian Broadcasting Commission (ABC), localised to their suburb.

Google Assistant's language recognition has been engineered to sound natural, and provided it is woken with the key phrase 'OK, Google' or 'Hey, Google', it is ready to work. There is no need to speak like a robot or to use specific phrases in a certain order. When customers are connected to the Google Home system—which is as simple as having a Gmail address—they will be able to link their accounts and use the assistant to plan their various daily activities. After they have set their address, Google Assistant can give them the local weather forecasts and even the duration of their daily commute.

Linking their Google account gives Google Home access to customers' calendars, and they can further link their Netflix, Stan and Spotify accounts for streaming media. When customers' questions are personalised, they can ask Google: 'What's the weather like in Sydney today?' or ask it to make an entry in their diary: 'Meet Joe for coffee tomorrow at 11 a.m.'

In addition to having an Australian focus, Google Assistant will recognise different voices, download the latest trailer from YouTube to customers' smartphones, and set up language translations and sports results. Google Home is a versatile assistant; typing search queries into phones is passé; now customers can organise their lives using their voice.

Service integration

While having trivia questions answered and using voice-activated Google searches have a novelty value, a smart-home assistant like Google Home is fast becoming the central hub for all of a customer's smart devices. Google Home currently works in Australia with products from the following organisations:

- ↘ Honeywell
- ↘ Insignia Connect
- ↘ LIFX
- ↘ Nest
- ↘ Philips Hue
- ↘ Samsung
- ↘ Wink.

Because the Australian market for smart-home devices is still in the introductory stage of its life cycle, many of the global third-party brands have not yet been launched locally, and those service brands that are available locally do not necessarily offer the full range of their services. That does not, however, prevent Australian customers from accessing some very convenient services with a smart device. Google Assistant is branching out in Australia, allowing users to connect to local businesses through Google Home. If customers ask Google Home to 'talk to NAB' a National Australia Bank bot will answer their queries. Generally, customers expect very good security before they will conduct service transactions from their intelligent home speaker; being able to talk to your personal assistant to engage with local services is a start. Within a year, it is expected that Australian customers will simply talk to their Google Assistant, which uses a Google artificial intelligence and machine-learning system, to engage with a wider range of Australian services.[3]

Australians quickly accept digital devices and are seen as early adopters of new technology on a global scale, having one of the highest propensities to upgrade their smartphone per capita. While smartphones are ubiquitous, and dominate with more than 95 per cent usage for younger users, the use of other devices is more fragmented. The biggest shift is in the extent to which people are connected to each other and the degree to which they have devices that are connected to the internet (and other devices). Australians are now more connected to the internet than ever before with a significant rise in the usage of connected smart televisions, gaming consoles and set-top boxes.[4]

The Internet of Things (IoT)

IoT basically refers to devices that are connected to the internet and, often, to each other. Australians are now at a point where, as device connectivity continues to increase, their focus is not so much on the technology, but on how that technology can be made more personal and useful for them. Uppermost in the minds of customers in the IoT space is the internet-connected smart-home.

There is strong appeal for adopting smart devices and related innovation. Forty-four per cent of Australians involved in recent research found 'smart networked homes' appealing, with the greatest interest coming from males (47%), members of Generation Y (54%), and affluent customers who have a household income greater than $120 000 (55%).[5]

At a product launch in San Francisco in October 2017, Google demonstrated the versatility of Google Assistant by connecting it to a smartphone that allowed conversations to be translated into one of 40 languages via its new Pixel Buds (earbuds) in almost real time. Internationally, Google is currently rolling out Google Home devices with the ability to recognise the voice of the family member it is talking to, so that when the family member asks for the next calendar item, that person receives the correct message and not their partner's. It announced two new Google Home devices, the small Google Home Mini ($79), available in December 2017 in Australia, and the larger Google Home Max, which is expected to arrive about mid-2018.

Both those devices use machine learning to shape the music around a room and can automatically increase the volume if the ambient noise increases; for example, if an air conditioner is turned on. Similar algorithms are being built into more and more devices, which means customers will soon be able to set up sequences of events at their homes that are triggered by the time they come home or when they go to bed. If the early adopters can wait for more third-party services, Google Home will provide a very engaging customer experience.

There is a great amount of customer satisfaction to be had from using smart devices that turn on a heater before customers come home from work, or having their lights start to dim before they go to bed. There are many useful and convenient benefits that customers can expect from installing Google Home but, like any device that relies on artificial intelligence, it may take them some time before they make it their own.

Something to think about

There were 13.7 million internet subscribers in Australia at the end of June 2017, and typical home upload speeds of less than 1 Mbps (megabits per second) mean that bandwidth-thirsty smart-home devices are choking in Australian homes. What marketing advice would you offer to the organisations that are proposing to launch smart-home devices regarding internet speed in Australia?

Endnotes

1   C. Reilly (2017). The smart speaker almost perfects fitting in down under. *cnet*, 24 August. <www.cnet.com/au/products/google-home/review>.
2   Telstra. <www.telstra.com.au/content/dam/tcom/smart-home/google-home/smart-home-google-home-infographics.jpg/jcr:content/renditions/original>.
3   C. Griffith (2017). Google Home lets you access local services. *The Australian*, 10 October, p. 24. <www.theaustralian.com.au/business/technology/google-home-lets-you-access-local-services/news-story/095481af9b06dd1546cf2c36f82134df>.
4   Ernst & Young (2017). *Australia Digital: State of the Nation 2017*. <https://digitalaustralia.ey.com/Documents/Digital_Australia_2017%20edition.pdf>.
5   ibid.

Case study F

Unruly passengers

Disruptive passenger behaviour, or air rage, can be defined as aberrant, abnormal and/or abusive behaviour on the part of passengers—either in airports or onboard commercial flights.[1]

RECLINUS MAXIMUS...

Source: G. Thomas (2014). Our passengers who make your flight hell survey results. AirlineRatings.com, 15 September. <www.airlineratings.com/news/our-passengers-who-make-your-flight-hell-survey-results>.

Who is the passenger from hell? The seat recliner, the passenger who lets their children run wild in the aircraft, the chatterbox or the lurking smelly-traveller. According to the annual AirlineRatings.com survey—*Passengers Who Make Your Flight Hell*—almost 35.4 per cent of the more than 1550 respondents put the passenger who reclines their seat as their number one customer from hell. While such behaviour is usually not considered 'unruly or disruptive', the seat recliner—especially at meal times—is as anti-social as any disruptive behaviour.[2]

Statistics collected by the International Air Transport Association (IATA), together with data from various civil aviation authorities and evidence from member airlines, confirm that the number of unruly passenger incidents onboard aircraft during commercial flights has become a significant global problem. Between 2007 and 2015, IATA collected 49 084 reports from airlines concerning unruly passengers. In 2015, there was one incident in every 1205 flights, which was an increase from one incident per 1282 flights in 2014. Intoxication, from either alcohol or drugs, was identified as being the cause of unruly behaviour in 23 per cent of reported cases.[3]

There have been attempts to determine why the number of unruly incidents is increasing, including an assumption that unruly behaviour reflects the broader societal problem of anti-social behaviour where many people perceive themselves to be victims of a stressful environment; or is it, perhaps, a simple reflection of the fact that airlines are increasing the number of economy-class seats and thereby increasing passenger claustrophobia and/or stress? Reports of unruly passengers disrupting airline flights increased by almost 17 per cent globally in 2015, with incidents like verbally abusing or refusing to obey cabin crew occurring on one of every 1205 flights.

IATA has identified the key factors associated with the increased number of disrupted airline flights as being:

↘ alcohol or drug intoxication in 23 per cent of cases

↘ triggers, such as 'frustrations with the journey' including long security queues

↘ call for new laws allowing arrests where an aircraft lands, not where it is registered.

Figure 1   The growing number of incidents involving unruly passengers

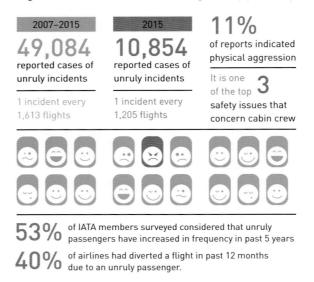

2007–2015	2015	11%
49,084	**10,854**	of reports indicated physical aggression
reported cases of unruly incidents	reported cases of unruly incidents	It is one of the top **3**
1 incident every 1,613 flights	1 incident every 1,205 flights	safety issues that concern cabin crew

53% of IATA members surveyed considered that unruly passengers have increased in frequency in past 5 years

40% of airlines had diverted a flight in past 12 months due to an unruly passenger.

Source: International Air Transport Association, June 2017.

IATA's reports of the number of unruly passengers do not include all global airlines, so the statistics are likely to significantly underestimate the true extent of the problem. Unruly passenger incidents include violence against crew and other passengers, harassment, verbal abuse, smoking, failure to follow safety instructions and other forms of anti-social behaviour.

Although those acts are committed by a very small number of passengers, their behaviour creates inconvenience, threatens the safety and security of other passengers and crew, and can lead to significant operational disruption and costs for airlines. A man whose unruly behaviour forced the pilot of a non-stop flight to New York to return to Honolulu owes Hawaiian Airlines $97 817, according to a report.[5] The man, who had been drinking before the flight, tried to order more alcohol during the flight on the plane and drank some alcohol he personally brought aboard the flight. A senior judge of the US District Court ordered the man to repay the airline the costs it incurred in turning the aircraft around, including fuel, maintenance, ground crew and costs associated with finding the passengers other flights. The sum did not include the meal vouchers worth $46 900 that Hawaiian Airlines handed out to the delayed New York–bound passengers.[6]

The Australian context

The frequency of airline travel in Australia has increased. In 2014, 33.1 million Australian passengers travelled internationally and almost double that number—60.13 million passengers—travelled domestically.[7] The majority of short-term international departures of Australian residents in 2013–14 were for holidays (60%), followed by visiting friends and relatives (23%), business (10%), and other reasons such as employment, education or attending conferences (7%); (Australian Bureau of Statistics 2014).[8]

OXFORD UNIVERSITY PRESS

Airlines are regularly called on to respond to and manage unruly passenger incidents. The term 'unruly passenger' is used in Australia to denote all passengers who, through their demeanour, behaviour or failure to comply with cabin crew directions, present a threat to the safety or security of the aircraft or those on board, but who are not engaged in an act of sabotage or terrorism. In June 2015, the Australian Institute of Criminology (AIC) held a roundtable discussion with representatives of the Australian Federal Police (AFP), regulatory and governing bodies, and five Australian airlines that provide international and/or domestic services to metropolitan, regional and remote areas. The aim of the roundtable was to examine the nature and frequency of, and responses to, unruly passenger incidents in Australia.[9]

In a situation of unruly passenger behaviour on an Australian commercial flight that was recently documented, the consequences of those actions resulted in the flight being diverted and the passengers in question were off-loaded. The captain felt these passengers may have posed a threat had the flight continued. The passengers paid a hefty penalty; they failed to reach their holiday destination and were forced to book and pay for return flights on any airline that would accept them.[10]

There are several reasons behind air rage, and subsequent unruly behaviour—including long pre-flight queues, flight delays, a lack of information, overbooking, passenger handling at airports and the non-smoking policy onboard aircraft operating commercial flights. As a result, passengers are often tired, bored, frustrated and feeling stressed. Consequently, they drink too much alcohol before boarding and follow up by consuming more alcohol during the flight. Passengers should be aware that boarding an aircraft when drunk is against the law, and may result in them being denied boarding. Drunkenness, however, is not the only form of passenger behaviour that is not tolerated on aircraft. Other types of non-acceptable behaviour include:

↘ offensive and disorderly conduct such as physical assault, verbal abuse or sexual harassment

↘ engaging in an act which interferes with the crew, or threatens the safety of the aircraft, or people on board

↘ smoking in any part of the aircraft, but particularly in the toilets

↘ disobeying instructions of the operator; whether given by signs or by the flight or cabin crew.[11]

Airlines are starting to ban passengers who have been identified as being disruptive and unruly. There has been discussion about displaying signs in airports that warn passengers of zero tolerance of unruly behaviour. Many airlines specify rules and conditions of boarding on the back of the boarding pass, while most passengers do not realise that the cabin crew has the authority to restrain drunk or violent passengers.

Civil and criminal penalties

In its *Annual Report 2016–17*, the Civil Aviation Safety Authority (CASA) of Australia reported that 71 of the 135 infringement notices were issued for passenger offences, such as smoking in an aircraft toilet, failing to comply with crew or operator instructions, or behaving in an offensive or disorderly manner.[12] Unruly passengers can be held civilly or criminally accountable for their actions through a number of avenues. The avenue through which redress is sought and the severity of the penalty depend on the actions of the passenger, including the airport of disembarkation, and the levels of safety and security risks their actions posed. At the lower end of the spectrum, an offending passenger may be met at the point of disembarkation by airline staff, and if warranted, local police may attend and the passenger may be issued a verbal or written warning.

For incidents that potentially breach civil aviation legislation, the airline can request that CASA issue the passenger with an Aviation Infringement Notice. While such requests can be made directly by the airline (which is more common in regional areas), the majority are referred to CASA by state or federal police. Incidents that could incur an infringement notice include smoking on an aircraft, failure to comply with instructions, refusing to wear a seatbelt, offensive and disorderly conduct and being intoxicated. CASA reviews all reports received and, where appropriate, issues the offending passenger with an infringement notice of up to $900. A passenger may be issued multiple infringement notices for the same incident if a number of breaches have occurred. Generally, the passenger has 28 days to pay the infringement notice. If a passenger fails to pay the infringement notice, the matter is referred to the police.[13]

Something to think about

As an airline passenger, you have heard the familiar suggestion, 'to sit back, relax, and enjoy the flight'. As Figure 1 indicates, the number of incidences of unruly behaviour by airline passengers is increasing; why do you consider that is happening? Can you suggest actions that the airlines can take—other than giving every passenger a business-class seat –to reduce the number of incidents of unruly passenger behaviour on commercial flights?

Endnotes

1   Ad Aerospace (2009). Disruptive passenger behaviour and its causes.

2   G. Thomas (2014). Our passengers who make your flight hell survey results. AirlineRatings. com, 15 September. <www.airlineratings.com/news/our-passengers-who-make-your-flight-hell-survey-results>.

3   International Air Transport Association (2017). *IATA Fact Sheet: Unruly Passengers*, June.

4   ABC News (2016). Plane rage: Airlines report 17 per cent rise in unruly passengers with alcohol and drugs a prime cause. 29 September. <www.abc.net.au/news/2016-09-29/airlines-report-17-per-cent-rise-in-unruly-passengers/7887282>.

5   T. Lapin (2017). Unruly passenger ordered to pay airline nearly $100K. *New York Post*, 30 August. <http://nypost.com/2017/08/30/unruly-passenger-ordered-to-pay-hawaiian-airlines-nearly-100k>.

6   ibid.

7   Bureau of Infrastructure, Transport and Regional Economics (2015). *Aviation: International Airline Activity 2014 Statistical Report*. <https://bitre.gov.au/publications/ongoing/international_airline_activity-annual_publications.aspx>; Bureau of Infrastructure, Transport and Regional Economics (2015). *Aviation: Domestic Aviation Activity. Annual 2014 Statistical Report*. <https://bitre.gov. au/publications/ongoing/domestic_airline_activity-annual_publications.aspx>.

8 Australian Bureau of Statistics (2014). *Overseas Arrivals and Departures, Australia, June 2014*. ABS cat. no. 3401.0. Canberra, ACT: ABS.

9 S. Goldsmid, G. Fuller, S. Coghlan & R. Brown (2016). *Responding to Unruly Airline Passengers: The Australian Context*. Canberra, ACT: Australian Institute of Criminology, April. <www.aic.gov.au/publications/current%20series/tandi/501-520/tandi510.html>.

10 Civil Aviation Safety Authority (2016). Unruly passengers. 17 February.

11 ibid.

12 Civil Aviation Safety Authority (2017). *Annual Report 2016–17*. Canberra, ACT: Australian Government, p. 7. <www.casa.gov.au/sites/g/files/net351/f/annual_report1617-intro.pdf?v=1508473336>.

13 S. Goldsmid, G. Fuller, S. Coghlan & R. Brown (2016). *Responding to Unruly Airline Passengers: The Australian Context*. Canberra, ACT: Australian Institute of Criminology, April. <www.aic.gov.au/publications/current%20series/tandi/501-520/tandi510.html>.

adaptive service capacity
An organisation's ability to adapt to changing consumer service demands

affective commitment
Commitment measured by the consumer's emotions towards the relationship, which can lead to a higher level of trust and commitment to the relationship

agent
An intermediary who acts on behalf of a service principal and is authorised to make agreements between the principal and the customer

attitude model of attributes
A model of the attitude towards an object, consisting of the sum of the strength of beliefs given evaluation of the consequences or importance of each belief

augmented or supplementary services
Additional services provided that are not at all related to the core service offering: examples include gift shops and convenience stores in hospitals, and waiting rooms at car repair businesses

B2B services
Services delivered from business to business

behavioural segmentation
The various ways that consumers buy and use service products, which are measured by answering questions such as: How much is purchased? How often is the service purchased? Where is it purchased from?

benchmarking
The process of making sure service performance meets defined measurable outcomes

blueprinting
A process of providing solutions to customer complaints by mapping out each part of the customer service process

broker
Acts as a facilitator of exchanges between buyers and sellers

calculative commitment
Commitment measured by rational factors by both parties, such as the economic value of the relationship

capacity
Can have a wide range of meanings in business. A commonly used definition of capacity refers to the ability of an organisation to produce a given level of output per unit of time; that is, being able to do produce enough of something to meet demand.

communication
A process that facilitates the transmission of messages between a sender and a receiver

competitive advantage
The part or parts of a service that an organisation can do better than all of its competitors; this may be based on a unique service proposition, but does not necessarily have to be

complaint
Expression of dissatisfaction made to or about an organisation, related to its products, services, staff or the handling of a complaint, where a response or resolution is explicitly or implicitly expected or legally required

constraint
A constraint is anything that inhibits a system's progress towards its goals

constraint management
A framework for managing the constraints of a system in a way that maximises the system's accomplishment of its goals

core service
The main service that provides customers with a solution to their needs, such as transportation or financial security

credence dimensions
The product characteristics that require consumers to trust the service provider to perform certain expected tasks or provide expected benefits

critical incident
A significant event that makes a positive or negative contribution to the judgment or evaluation of an organisation (e.g. a bank) or an activity (e.g. booking a hotel room online)

customer churn
The percentage of service customers who discontinue buying that service in a given time

490

period. Customer churn is also known as 'customer attrition'.

customer commitment
The length of time spent, level of emotion realised and net value generated by a customer and an organisation to develop in a relationship together

customer expectations
Predictions as to the outcome of a future service encounter

customer experience (CX)
The perception that customers have after their experiential interactions with a service organisation

customer lifetime value (CLV)
The value of a customer over their lifetime with the organisation. Different organisations take different approaches to measuring CLV, but most take a net value or profit perspective, deducting all the costs of dealing with the customer to arrive at a final net figure

customer loyalty and retention
Embody repeat behaviour where customer loyalty reflects a developing relationship and customer retention reflects an ongoing relationship

customer relationship management (CRM)
A strategy to compile information on customers' behaviour across different channels—or points of contact—between the customer and the organisation

customer relationships
Are premised on the actions of a service provider and a customer, where the actions of one will have an impact on the behaviour of the other

customer service
Those actions undertaken by all organisations to maximise customer satisfaction and build a customer's lifetime value to an organisation

demand
A consumer's desire for a product

demand forecasting
Gives managers the signal to order more/or less materials, labour, transport, facilities or add/reduce capacity over the forecast period

demographics
Objective variables such as age, gender, income and family structure, as distinct from values and lifestyles, used to segment consumers

determinant attributes
Service attributes that determine customers' choice between competing service organisations; those attributes that offer customers compelling reasons to purchase

equilibrium
Defined as the price-quantity point where the quantity demanded is equal to the quantity supplied, and is represented by the intersection of the demand and supply curves

experience
Relates to a customer's judgment of the service interaction with the service organisation after it has been consumed

experience dimensions
The product characteristics that can only be evaluated during and after performance of the service processes

experiential needs
Consumer needs for services that provide sensory pleasure, variety and/or cognitive stimulation

fixed costs
Those production costs that remain fixed—at least over a short production cycle—even if there is no customer demand

franchising
One of the most common methods for distributing services, usually done through contractual arrangements between the franchiser and franchisee. Common franchises in Australia include H&R Block, Mortgage Choice and Auto Masters

frequency
The number of times, on average, within a four-week period that consumers in a target market will be exposed to a service organisation's market messages

functional needs
Consumer needs that include current consumption-related problems

functional quality
The processes that dictate how the service is experienced by customers, commonly referred to as the *how* of the service experience

hierarchy of effects model
A model is predicated on the tri-component model of consumer attitudes and that marketing communication will move prospective consumers of a service from an initial stage of unawareness about a brand to a final stage of intended actions for that service brand; which may be to trial, purchase, adopt or reject the brand

importance
Relates to a customer's expectations of a service organisation at a specific time in the service relationship

innovativeness
A general personality trait: the degree to which an individual makes innovation decisions independently of the communicated experience of others

intermediary
Any person or organisation that provides services on behalf of others (e.g. agents, brokers and franchisees)

internal marketing orientation (IMO)
The degree to which employees follow the organisation mission and strategy, crucial for effective customer service

locus of control
The future-oriented beliefs about the value of the service outcome

loyalty program
A marketing program that rewards customers and encourages them to continue using the service; often higher rewards are offered for higher levels of customer purchase behaviour

market segmentation
A marketing approach for evaluating a market; it is typically based on demographics, values and lifestyles, and behavioural variables, so that service marketing strategies can effectively target one or more groups of consumers who form a market segment for a service organisation's products

marketing
The practice of creating exchanges between customers and sellers that are valued by both parties to the transaction

marketing communications
Includes all elements of a service organisation's communication mix to facilitate exchanges by establishing shared meaning between the organisation and its target market

media planning
Is premised on a media scheduling plan that includes a marketing communications timetable and media vehicles that together will help to achieve a service organisation's integrated marketing communications objectives

perceived risk
The negative consequences that may occur as part of a transaction

perceptions
The customer's ability to intuitively recognise objects or events that can be evaluated by 'top-down' processes using criteria such as their needs, wants and expectations

peripheral services
Supplementary services that facilitate the core service and are often the factors that differentiate and position the core service

positioning
The key idea that relates to a customer's unique perceptions about the brand, attributes and benefits of a service, and how these service elements are evaluated and compared with those of competing service organisations

positioning statement
Suggests the benefits of what the service brand represents—when compared with its competitors—in the minds of a target market

OXFORD UNIVERSITY PRESS

price elasticity of demand
A method to measure the sensitivity of customers to changes in the price of a service

pricing
The actions that a seller takes to set the purchase price of a service

reach
Represents the percentage of the target audience who see or hear a service organisation's marketing message one or more times during a specified timeframe—usually four weeks

related services
Additional services used as part of the encounter with the core service; for instance, a meal on an airline or campus food

revenue management
Generally relates to selling the right product, to the right customer, at the right time, at the right price

satisfaction
A transaction-specific evaluation of how well each service encounter fulfilled the customer's needs, wants and expectations

search attributes
Features or benefits of a service that influence consumer evaluation, e.g. price, location, friendliness of staff

search dimensions
The tangible attributes that allow consumers to try, taste or assess a product before purchase

self-service technology (SST)
The firm–customer technological interface that encourages consumers to perform services for themselves and/or automated services

semi-variable costs
Those production costs that fall between fixed and variable costs and tend to change in response to changes in customer demand

service (I)
An act, performance or experience that provides some form of value in the production and delivery of the service

service (II)
An economic process that provides time, place and form value in solving customers' problems

service concept
The description of the key benefits or problems solved by services for an identified market segment

service encounter
The dyadic interaction between a customer and service provider or a period of time during which a consumer directly interacts with a service

service expectations
What consumers expect from a service; can be a minimum standard or what consumers expect from an excellent service

service failure
A breakdown in the delivery of a service. It is a failure to either meet the organisation's own internal service standards and/or to meet a customer's service quality expectations.

service offering
The total service offered to the consumer. Also referred to as the *value offering*.

service quality
An overall evaluation that is based on customers' broad perceptions of the reliability, responsiveness, assurance, empathy and tangibles associated with multiple encounters of the service performance

servicescape
The effect of the physical surroundings on the quality of a service encounter

sharing economy
Where resources, facilities and services are shared or rented to other parties without ownership transferring to the other party

supply and demand
An economic model to determine the selling price of a service

symbolic needs
Consumer needs that are related to desired self-image, role position or group affiliation

Glossary

technical quality

The tangible benefits that remain after the completion of the service production process. They are the outcome of the service and are commonly referred to as the *what* customers receive from a service.

technology-based self-service (TBSS)

A type of self-service technology such as self-scanning of groceries, vending machines and automated check-ins at airports

three-exposure hypothesis

Based on the premise that there is a minimum number of exposures needed for marketing communication to be effective in achieving a service organisation's marketing communication objectives

throughput

Net sales (S) less totally variable cost (TVC), generally the cost of the raw materials (T = S − TVC). Note that T only exists when there is a sale of the product or service. Producing materials that sit in a warehouse does not form part of throughput but rather investment. This is different from the traditional definition, which usually defines 'throughput' as the rate at which products are produced, regardless of whether they are sold.

unique service proposition

The one unique aspect of a service that is not replicated by other service providers. Usually it becomes the competitive advantage for a firm.

utilisation

In the context of constraint management, is the time a resource is used and contributing to throughput divided by the time the resource was available

value

In the service-dominant logic (S-D logic) model, value is seen as a dynamic, co-produced benefit that is created by the many participants in creating favourable customers' service experiences

value co-creation with multiple stakeholders

Assumes that the rapid adoption of the internet and customer-oriented social media creates value that cannot be attributed to either service production or customer consumption

value in co-production

Assumes that while value is part of the production process, both the organisation and customer participate in generating value

value in production

Is generated by the production process and realised when consumed by customers

value-in-use

Suggests that value is not part of the production process but of the consumption process

values and lifestyles

Psychosocial personal variables, such as lifestyles, personality types and psychological traits, as distinct from demographics, that can be used to segment consumers

variable costs

Those production costs that vary in response to variations in customer demand

weight

The intensity that a communications schedule will deliver and is calculated by multiplying reach by frequency

word-of-mouth (WOM) recommendations

Positive or negative discussion with and comments to others about one's own experience with a service provider

zone of tolerance (ZOT)

The range of expectations and an area of acceptable outcomes in service interactions

OXFORD UNIVERSITY PRESS

OXFORD UNIVERSITY PRESS

OXFORD UNIVERSITY PRESS

Index

OXFORD UNIVERSITY PRESS